A Cardboard Castle?

NATIONAL SECURITY ARCHIVE
COLD WAR READERS

Series Editor
MALCOLM BYRNE

Previously published:
THE PRAGUE SPRING '68
UPRISING IN EAST GERMANY, 1953
THE 1956 HUNGARIAN REVOLUTION

A Book Prepared by the Parallel History Project
on NATO and the Warsaw Pact (PHP)
Center for Security Studies at ETH Zurich
National Security Archive, Washington
Institute for Strategy and Security Policy at
the Austrian Defense Academy, Vienna
Machiavelli Center for Cold War Studies, Florence
Norwegian Institute for Defence Studies, Oslo

A Cardboard Castle?

AN INSIDE HISTORY OF
THE WARSAW PACT, 1955–1991

Edited by
VOJTECH MASTNY
and
MALCOLM BYRNE

Editorial Assistant
MAGDALENA KLOTZBACH

CEU PRESS

Central European University Press
Budapest New York

Published in 2005 by
Central European University Press

An imprint of the
Central European University Share Company
Nádor utca 11, H-1051 Budapest, Hungary
Tel: +36-1-327-3138 or 327-3000
Fax: +36-1-327-3183
E-mail: ceupress@ceu.hu
Website: www.ceupress.com

400 West 59th Street, New York NY 10019, USA
Tel: +1-212-547-6932
Fax: +1-646-557-2416
E-mail: mgreenwald@sorosny.org

ISBN 963 7326 08 1 cloth
ISBN 963 7326 07 3 paperback
ISSN 1587-2416

Library of Congress Cataloging-in-Publication Data

A cardboard castle?: an inside history of the Warsaw Pact, 1955–1991 / edited by Vojtech
Mastny and Malcolm Byrne; editorial assistant Magdalena Klotzbach.
    p. cm. – (National Security Archive Cold War readers)
    Includes bibliographical references and index.
    ISBN 9637326081 (hardbound: alk. paper) – ISBN 9637326073 (pbk.: alk. paper)
    1. Warsaw Treaty Organization–History. 2. Warsaw Treaty Organization–History–
Sources. 3. Europe, Eastern–History, Military–20th century. 4. Europe, Eastern–History,
Military–20th century–Sources. 5. Cold War. I. Mastny, Vojtech, 1936– Byrne, Malcolm.
III. Title. IV. Series.

    UA646.8C372005
    355'.031'0947–dc22

                                                                                2005002291

Preprint by Attributum Studió, Budapest
Printed in Hungary by
Akadémiai Nyomda, Martonvásár

Table of Contents

PART FIVE – DISINTEGRATION

Preface and Acknowledgements

This volume is the first to gather in one place a comprehensive documentary record of the elusive and controversial history of the Soviet-led Cold War alliance from the inside. The product of a multi-year research effort, the book brings together formerly secret records from the archives of every member-state of the communist military grouping. Top-level communications between the alliance's leaders, verbatim transcripts of multilateral summit meetings, and lively discussions inside the various party politburos are among the many previously unavailable materials in this collection. Topics covered in depth include the evolution of the pact from stage prop to full-fledged military alliance; the surprisingly dynamic relations between Moscow and the other capitals of the "fraternal countries," particularly during times of crisis when the Kremlin was pulled in different directions by allies espousing more aggressive or cautious points of view; the upheavals in Eastern Europe in 1953, 1956, 1968 and 1980–81; and the turmoil—this time induced by the Soviet leadership itself—of the late 1980s, which led to the virtually simultaneous vanishing of the Cold War and the Eastern alliance.

The principal catalyst behind this volume is the Parallel History Project on NATO and the Warsaw Pact (PHP). An innovative, multinational research endeavor, the PHP was established in 1999 to encourage increased military transparency in the former Warsaw Pact as well as NATO countries by enlisting research institutes, military historians and archivists throughout Europe to promote the opening of historical records that would yield a broader understanding of our recent shared experience in international security. The PHP's primary institutional sponsors are the Center for Security Studies at the Swiss Federal Institute of Technology in Zurich, the National Security Archive at George Washington University in Washington, D.C., the Institute for Strategy and Security Policy at the Austrian Defense Academy in Vienna, the Machiavelli Center for Cold War Studies in Florence, and the Norwegian Institute for Defence Studies in Oslo. Readers are invited to explore the PHP website, maintained by the Swiss Center for Security Studies, at: http://www.-isn.ethz.ch/php/index.htm.

As a cooperative undertaking of more than 20 partner institutions, the PHP has collected thousands of pages of material on security-related issues of the Cold War, published a large number of online documentaries on central issues such as mutual threat perceptions and alliance management, and organized several major international conferences on war planning, intelligence, and intra-bloc tensions. Project Coordinator Vojtech Mastny has helped to spearhead these efforts, including visiting all of the relevant archives, negotiating with NATO and former Warsaw Pact officials and organizing research and collection activities. Playing a crucial role have been the dozens of scholars, archivists and former officials who make up the PHP network.

Having already established a major Internet repository of historical records, the PHP decided to produce a traditional printed volume consisting of recently released

Warsaw Pact documentation as a way to further disseminate the raw materials necessary for developing a more complete understanding of this important phenomenon of the Cold War. For reasons of maximum distribution, all of these documents have been translated into English. For reasons of space, virtually all of them have been excerpted. While the editors and Project partners believe this effort represents a significant contribution in itself, the PHP has also posted all of the original documents, in their native languages, and in full on the Project's web site, to be available to anyone who would wish to consult them in their entirety. This amounts to thousands of pages of important primary source material made accessible through the most democratic medium of information storage and retrieval ever devised. Beyond merely simplifying the task of researching these materials by collecting them in one place, this measure will guarantee the permanent availability of these records by removing them from the political or bureaucratic whims of governments that may choose to reimpose access controls at any time.

This volume appears as part of the National Security Archive Cold War Reader series under the CEU Press imprint. The Archive is the book's other main contributor, in addition to being a PHP partner. As part of its own mission to help uncover the hidden history of the Cold War and broaden public access to it, the Archive established this reader series under the umbrella of its Openness in Russia and Eastern Europe project. The series represents a culminating phase of the project which, in partnership with scholars based in Central and Eastern Europe since 1992, has helped to pry loose new historical materials and organize ground-breaking international conferences to bring the latest analysis—and further public exposure—to the ever expanding record. Previous volumes in the series cover the Soviet bloc crises that occurred in 1953 in East Germany, in 1956 in Hungary and in 1968 in Czechoslovakia, with additional titles forthcoming on the collapse of communism in Eastern Europe in 1989. The current volume is a perfect complement to those compilations since the Warsaw Pact figured in varying degrees during each of those crises but examines the history of that period through its institutional prism, which provides additional dimensions to the subject.

As with other volumes in this series, this one has several basic components. One of them is the documents. The majority of these have never been published in English before; many have not appeared even in their own language. Together they comprise a unique, multi-archival resource that affords a variety of perspectives from inside the once-closed Eastern alliance. The only notable gap is on the former Soviet side. Persisting restrictions on access to Soviet military records are an exasperating obstacle that the PHP, among others, continues to contest. Still, the relative availability of Eastern European records, while uneven, helps to compensate to a considerable degree.

To provide an analytical and interpretive framework for the materials, another main component of the book is the introductory essay by Vojtech Mastny, widely recognized as an expert in the field. The essay traces the evolution of the "Cardboard Castle" from its origins to its ignominious demise between the downfall of the communist regimes in Eastern Europe in 1989 and the disintegration of the Soviet Union at the end of 1991. The narrative is linked directly to the documentary part by providing footnote references to individual documents. The extensive footnotes provide numerous further avenues for research in virtually all the languages of the alliance. The third component are "headnotes" that introduce each document, presenting item-specific context that explains the significance or special relevance of every entry. They were prepared by Malcolm Byrne in cooperation with Vojtech Mastny. A fourth component consists of additional research aids—a chronology of relevant events, a listing of key officials, a glossary of acronyms found in the documents as well as those used to identify the archival source of each record, and a selective bibliography on the Warsaw Pact.

* * *

A great deal of effort and cooperation by a number of individuals has gone into the preparation of this volume, for which the editors are deeply grateful.

First, we would like to thank Magdalena Klotzbach of the National Security Archive who toiled on a wide range of tasks from translating Polish documents to helping research and write the chronology and glossaries, to organizing and copy-editing the text. Jason Roberts, also of the Archive, energetically pursued research assignments relating to the front matter. In another capacity, Archive Executive Director Tom Blanton, who helped forge the Archive's connection to and support for the PHP network, was the first to raise the idea of publishing this volume as part of the Cold War reader series with CEU Press.

Enthusiastic support for this project has also come from the other PHP partners and associates, particularly Andy Wenger, Chris Nünlist and Anna Locher in Zurich, Csaba Békés in Budapest, Jordan Baev in Sofia, Wanda Jarząbek in Warsaw, Sven Holtsmark in Oslo, Oldřich Tůma in Prague, Petr Luňák in Brussels, Matthias Uhl in Berlin, and Svend Aage Christensen in Copenhagen.

Additional scholars, researchers and archivists played a critical part in this process, identifying, locating and bringing to light many of the records from which this selection was made. A number of documents were originally published by the Cold War International History Project, a PHP associate and one of the leading sponsors of international Cold War research. CWIHP is directed by Christian F. Ostermann and assisted by Mircea Munteanu and Dee Beutel.

Another major group of individuals to thank are the translators. Several items were previously translated under the auspices of other programs, including CWIHP and the National Security Archive. But most of the materials were translated especially for this book. For that, the editors, knowing the demands that were placed on these talented individuals, are particularly grateful. In alphabetical order, they are: Andreas Bocz, Viorel Nicolae Buta, Jan Chowaniec, Greg Domber, Ursula Froese, Małgorzata Gnoińska, Thomas Holderegger, Anya Jouravel, Greta Keremidchieva, Magdalena Klotzbach, Mark Kramer, Marian Kratochvíl, Anna Locher, Jiří Mareš, Stan Mareš, Mircea Munteanu, Catherine Nielsen, Christian Nünlist, Vania Petkova, Sergey Radchenko, Karen Riechert, Jason Roberts, Svetlana Savranskaya, Bernd Schaefer, Douglas Selvage, Karel Sieber, Lena Sirota, Paul Spitzer, Rebekka Weinel, Vladislav Zubok.

Special gratitude to Karen Riechert and Bernd Schaefer for their extra efforts on our behalf, and to Oldřich Tůma and Jordan Baev for facilitating expeditiously the excellent work of their colleagues.

The editors, and their home institutions, wish to express their abiding gratitude to the foundations that have provided the support necessary for this book and allowed their other work to move forward. Funding for the Openness Project over the years has come primarily from the Open Society Institute, the John D. and Catherine T. MacArthur Foundation, the Carnegie Corporation of New York, the Smith Richardson Foundation and the German Marshall Fund of the United States.

Finally, we are grateful to CEU Press for its continued interest in and support for this series. Their generous underwriting of many of the translations was vital. Thanks to István Bart, Péter Inkei, Linda Kunos, Krisztina Kós, Martin Greenwald and their colleagues.

The Editors

Washington, September 29, 2004

Acronyms and Abbreviations

ABM	Anti-Ballistic Missile
BCP	Bulgarian Communist Party
BPR	Bulgarian People's Republic
CC	Central Committee
CCP	Chinese Communist Party
Cde.	Comrade
CDU	Christian Democratic Union (FRG)
CET	Central European Theater
CIA	Central Intelligence Agency
CMD	Committee of Ministers of Defense
CMEA	Council for Mutual Economic Assistance
CMFA	Committee of Ministers of Foreign Affairs
Col.	Colonel
COMECON	See CMEA
CPCC	Central Party Control Commission
CPCz	Communist Party of Czechoslovakia
CPSU	Communist Party of the Soviet Union
CSCE	Conference on Security and Cooperation in Europe
ČSR	Czechoslovak Republic (until July 11, 1960)
ČSSR	Czechoslovak Socialist Republic (after July 11, 1960)
CSU	Christian Social Union (FRG)
CzPA	Czechoslovak People's Army
DKP	[West] German Communist Party
DPRK	Democratic People's Republic of Korea
DRV	Democratic Republic of Vietnam
EEC	European Economic Community
ENDC	Eighteen-Nation Disarmament Committee
FRG	Federal Republic of Germany
GDR	German Democratic Republic
Gen.	General
GSFG	Group of Soviet Forces—Germany
HPR	Hungarian People's Republic
HVA	Main Intelligence Administration, *Hauptverwaltung Aufklärung* (GDR)
HWP	Hungarian Workers' Party
INF	Intermediate-Range Nuclear Forces
KGB	Committee for State Security (USSR), *Komitet Gosudarstvennoi Bezopasnosti*
KPD	German Communist Party, *Kommunistische Partei Deutschlands* (FRG)

MBFR	Mutual and Balanced Force Reductions
MFA	Ministry of Foreign Affairs
MGCMI	Multilateral Group on Current Mutual Information
MLF	Multilateral Force
MNO	Ministry of National Defense (Czechoslovakia) *Ministerstvo národní obrany*
MNR	Mongolian People's Republic, *Mongolskaia Narodnaia Respublika*
MoD	Ministry of Defense
NATO	North Atlantic Treaty Organization
NLF	National Liberation Front (Vietnam)
NPT	Non-Proliferation Treaty
NVA GDR	National People's Army of the GDR, *Nationale Volksarmee*
PCC	Political Consultative Committee
POW	Prisoner of War
PPA	Polish People's Army
PPR	Polish People's Republic
PPWO	Permanent Political Working Organ of the Member-States of the Warsaw Treaty
PRC	People's Republic of China
PRH	See HPR
PRL	See PPR
PUWP	Polish United Workers' Party
RCP	Romanian Communist Party
RFE	Radio Free Europe
RPR	Romanian People's Republic (until 1965)
RSR	Socialist Republic of Romania (after 1965)
RWP	Romanian Workers' Party
SALT	Strategic Arms Limitation Treaty
SCD	Special Commission on Disarmament Questions
SDI	Strategic Defense Initiative
SED	Socialist Unity Party of Germany (GDR), *Sozialistiche Einheitspartei Deutschlands*
SPD	Social Democratic Party of Germany (FRG), *Sozialdemokratische Partei Deutschlands*
SRR	Socialist Republic of Romania
U.N.	United Nations
UAF	Unified Armed Forces
USSR	Union of Soviet Socialist Republics
WP	Warsaw Pact
WTO	Warsaw Treaty Organization

ABREVIATIONS USED IN DOCUMENT
SOURCE CITATIONS

AAN	Modern Records Archives (Warsaw), *Archiwum Akt Nowych*
AMR	Romanian Military Archives (Bucharest), *Arhivele Militare Române*
AMSZ	Archive of the Ministry of Foreign Affairs (Warsaw), *Archiwum Ministerstwa Spraw Zagranicznych*
AMZV	Archive of the Ministry of Foreign Affairs (Prague), *Archiv Ministerstva zahraničních věcí*
AÚV KSČ	Archive of the CPCz CC (Prague), *Archiv Ústředního výboru Kommunistické strany Československa*
AZN	Archival access number, *Archivzugangsnummer*
BA-MA	Federal Archives of Germany, Military Branch (Freiburg i. Br.), *Bundesarchiv-Militärarchiv*
č.	Number (Czech), *číslo*
č.j.	Reference number (Czech), *číslo jednací*
CC PCR	Central Committee of the Romanian Communist Party
GŠ-OS	Operations Directorate of the General Staff (CzPA), *Generální štáb-Operační správa*
inv.	Inventory number (Czech) , *inventární číslo*
KaMO	Cabinet of the Minister of Defense (Czech), *Kabinet Ministra obrany*
kar.	Box (Czech), *karton*
KC PZPR	Central Committee of the Polish United Workers' Party, *Komitet Centralny Polskiej Zjednoczonej Partii Robotniczej*
kr.	Box (Czech), *krabice*
krab.	Box (Czech), *krabice*
KV	Czechoslovak Government Commission for Analysis of the Events of 1967–1970 (Czechoslovakia), *Komise vlády ČSFR pro analýzu událostí let 1967–1970*
MfAA	Ministry of Foreign Affairs (GDR), *Ministerium für Auswärtige Angelegenheiten*
min.	Ministry (Czech), *ministerstvo*
MNO	Ministry of National Defense (Prague), *Ministerstvo národní obrany*
NSA	National Security Archive
ő.e.	Preservation unit (Hungarian), *őrzési egység*
Op.	Inventory, Opis [Russian and Bulgarian]
OS-OL	Operations Directorate, Olomouc Collection, *Operační správa, Olomouc*
SAPMO	Foundation "Archive of the Parties and Mass Organizations of the Former GDR" in the Federal Archives (Germany), *Stiftung Archiv der Parteien und Massenorganisationen der ehemaligen DDR im Bundesarchiv*

Sb.	Collection (Czech), *sbírka*
Sekr.	Secretariat (Czech), *sekretariát*
sg.	Identification number (Czech), *signatura*
sig.	Identification number (Czech), *signatura*
SÚA	Central State Archives (Prague), *Státní ústřední archiv*
TsDA	Central State Archives (Sofia), *Tsentralen D'rzhaven Arkhiv*
ÚV KSČ	See CC CPCz
VHA	Military History Archive (Prague), became Central Military Archives (VÚA)
VKO	Military Defense Commission (of the Central Committee of the Czechoslovak Communist Party), *Vojenská komise obrany*
VS	Warsaw Treaty (Czech), *Varšavská smlouva*
VÚA	Central Military Archives (Prague), *Vojenský ústřední archiv*
ZK SED	Central Committee of the Socialist Unity Party of Germany (GDR), *Zentralkomitee der Sozialistischen Einheitspartei Deutschlands*
ZPA NL	Central Party Archive of the SED, Personal Papers (Berlin), *Zentrales Parteiarchiv, Nachlässe*

Chronology of Events

1949

April 4: The North Atlantic Treaty Organization (NATO) is established.

1950

February 14: The Soviet Union and China sign the Treaty of Friendship, Alliance, and Mutual Assistance in Moscow.

1954

October 20–23: Western foreign ministers meeting in Paris agree to end West Germany's occupation status, and invite it to become a part of NATO.

November 29: The Soviets convene a meeting in Moscow to discuss establishing an all-European security system. The Western governments decline to attend, leaving eight communist countries which would eventually form the Warsaw Treaty Organization.

1955

May 9: West Germany joins NATO.

May 14: Eight Soviet bloc states sign the Warsaw Treaty. The signatories—Albania, Czechoslovakia, Bulgaria, Hungary, East Germany, Poland, Romania, and the Soviet Union—are joined by China, North Korea and North Vietnam as observers.

May 15: The Soviet Union and the Western powers sign the Austrian State Treaty providing for Austrian neutrality.

July 18–23: The USSR, France, Great Britain and the United States hold a summit in Geneva. Soviet Premier Nikolai A. Bulganin presents the draft of an all-European security treaty.

1956

January 18: The East German army is created.

January 27–28: The first meeting of the Political Consultative Committee (PCC) takes place in Prague. The group approves a Soviet-designed Statute of the Unified Command. It decides to create a commission on foreign policy coordination as well as a Secretariat but does not implement the decision.

February 25: At the CPSU XXth Congress, Khrushchev delivers the "secret speech" in which he denounces Stalin and his crimes.

October 19: Khrushchev and several Soviet Politburo members confront the Polish leadership led Władysław Gomułka over its "national communist" course, but Soviet military intervention is averted.

October 23: Street demonstrations in Budapest lead to the outbreak of the Hungarian revolution. Reform communist leader Imre Nagy is brought in to try to stem the revolt but anti-communist sentiment is too powerful.

October 30: As popular unrest mounts in Poland and Hungary, a Soviet declaration proclaims readiness to respect the sovereignty of Warsaw Pact allies.

November 1: Premier Imre Nagy announces that Hungary will leave the Warsaw Pact and become a neutral country after learning that Soviet troops are preparing to invade the country.

November 4: Soviet forces invade Hungary to crush the growing anti-communist revolutionary uprising.

1957

January 1–5: A meeting of party and government representatives, excluding Poles, takes place in Moscow to discuss military matters—arming of the East European armies, and improvement and organization of air defenses.

October 2: In a speech to the U.N. General Assembly, Polish Foreign Minister Adam Rapacki calls for the creation of a denuclearized zone in Central Europe. The idea becomes known as the Rapacki Plan.

October 4: The Soviet Union launches Sputnik I, the first artificial satellite to orbit the earth, unofficially marking the start of the space race between the United States and Soviet Union, and fueling a parallel effort in the broader area of high technology, especially in the military sphere.

November 14–19: A Moscow meeting of communist party leaders codifies relations based on the Soviet model and experiences—strengthening the Warsaw Pact and Comecon. A declaration affirms the unity of the camp and the results of the XXth party congress of February 1956.

1958

January 6: The Soviets, after breaking up the U.N. disarmament subcommittee, announce a unilateral reduction of 300,000 troops.

January 8: The Soviets propose reducing international tensions by replacing military groupings with a collective security system, by having the West reduce military forces as Moscow had done, by creating a nuclear-free zone in the two Germanys, Poland and the ČSR, and other measures.

May 5: The Soviet Union proposes a non-aggression treaty between NATO and the Warsaw Pact.

May 24: The second PCC meeting is held in Moscow. The group approves withdrawing Soviet troops from Romania and planning for unilateral reductions of all Warsaw Pact forces, as well drafting an appeal for a non-aggression treaty between the Warsaw Pact and NATO. The group's declaration calls for an end to nuclear tests, the creation of nuclear-free zones in Europe, the solution of the German question, and a summit meeting.

November 10: In a speech delivered in Moscow (followed on November 27 by notes to the Western powers), Khrushchev sparks the second Berlin crisis by threatening to conclude a separate peace treaty with East Germany, which would terminate the Western powers' right to access to West Berlin.

1959

April 27–28: A meeting of the Warsaw Pact's ministers of foreign affairs takes place in Warsaw. It presses for an East–West summit that would result in a peace treaty with Germany and elimination of the occupation regime in West Berlin.

September 15–27: Khrushchev visits the United States. His meeting with Eisenhower encourages his belief in the possibility of achieving a solution to the Berlin question on Soviet terms.

1960

January 14: Khrushchev in speech to the Supreme Soviet announces his intention to reduce Soviet troop levels by 1.2 million.

February 4: At a PCC meeting in Moscow, Khrushchev's optimistic assessment of the likelihood of Western concessions on Germany elicits criticism from the Chinese observer of what he sees as a Soviet policy of conciliation toward the West.

May 1: U-2 pilot Francis Gary Powers is shot down over the Soviet Union. The discovery of the spy mission leads to Khrushchev's cancellation of the Paris Summit with Eisenhower set for May 15–19.

June 2: The Soviet Union makes a proposal for general and complete disarmament.

June 20–25: During a Soviet–Chinese row at the Romanian party congress, Albania sides with China.

July 25: Soviet Marshal Andrei Grechko replaces Marshal Ivan Konev as Warsaw Pact supreme commander.

September 27: At the United Nations, Romania, with Soviet support, proposes a Balkan collective security treaty, and a nuclear- and foreign base-free zone.

September 28: Bulgarian party chief Todor Zhivkov urges a reduction of forces in the Balkans to the level of border guards, and calls for the Balkans to be the first area of general and complete disarmament.

1961

March 28–29: A PCC meeting is convened in Moscow to deal with the deteriorating problem of East German refugees and SED leader Walter Ulbricht's pressure for the closing of crossings into West Berlin. It also deals with the growing crisis over the Vlorë naval base in Albania. The Committee condemns Albania for its harassment of Soviet sailors, but the subsequent worsening of the situation leads Moscow to withdraw its ships from the port.

April 19: A separate Polish Front within the Warsaw Pact established.

June 3–4: President John F. Kennedy and Khrushchev meet in Vienna. The U.S. president refuses to yield to Soviet demands on Berlin. The Soviet Union directs the Warsaw Pact to prepare for a possible military confrontation.

July 25: President Kennedy announces a troop buildup in Europe.

August 3–4: At a Warsaw Pact summit in Moscow, the Soviets agree to the closing of the borders between East and West Berlin. They also prepare for the signing of a separate peace treaty with East Germany and a possible military confrontation with the Western powers over access to West Berlin.

August 13: Construction of the Berlin Wall begins.

September 8: The Warsaw Pact's ministers of defense meet and agree to increase military preparedness and to proceed with "Buria," the first military exercise to involve all the Warsaw Pact armies as a coalition.

September 28–October 10: The "Buria" exercise takes place, the first of its kind to model a massive invasion of Western Europe.

October 17: Khrushchev at the XXIInd party congress rescinds his decision to sign a separate peace treaty with East Germany.

October 27–28: A confrontation between U.S. and Soviet tanks at the Checkpoint Charlie crossing into West Berlin takes place.

October 31: Chinese observers are excluded from Warsaw Pact meetings.

December 19: The Soviet Union and Albania sever diplomatic relations after a stormy period that included disputes with China, a covert Soviet attempt to oust Albanian leader Enver Hoxha, and the expulsion of Soviet vessels from the Vlorë naval base.

1962

March 8: The Soviets make a proposal for general and complete disarmament.

June 6–7: At a Comecon meeting in Moscow, a Soviet proposal is discussed for a division of labor within the economic grouping; it is opposed by Romania and the dispute later contributes to Bucharest's taking a dissident position within the Warsaw Pact.

June 7: A PCC meeting in Moscow publicly urges the conclusion of a peace treaty with Germany although Khrushchev has already given up on the idea.

October 14: The discovery of Soviet nuclear-capable missiles on Cuba marks the start of the Cuban missile crisis.

October 22: Marshal Grechko informs Warsaw Pact representatives about the Cuban situation and the Warsaw Pact orders an alert that lasts until November 21.

1963

February 20: The Soviets propose a NATO–Warsaw Pact nonaggression pact at the ENDC.

April 18–22: The Warsaw Pact exercise "Mazowsze" in Poland prepares for possible nuclear war with NATO that would result in the likely destruction of most Polish cities.

May 5: Khrushchev at a meeting with Castro rules out Cuban membership in the Warsaw Pact or a Soviet–Cuban military alliance.

July 5–20: Inconclusive Soviet–Chinese discussions in Moscow fail to repair the rift between the two countries.

July 15: Mongolia applies for admission to the Warsaw Pact.

July 25: The limited nuclear test-ban treaty is concluded between the United States, Soviet Union and United Kingdom.

July 26: A PCC meeting in Moscow supports the test-ban treaty, fails to consider Mongolian membership in the Warsaw Pact, and rallies the Warsaw Pact allies behind Moscow in its dispute with Beijing.

October 4: Romanian Foreign Minister Corneliu Mănescu secretly informs Secretary of State Dean Rusk that in the event of a nuclear confrontation between East and West Romania would remain neutral.

December 28: In a speech, Gomułka proposes freezing nuclear armaments in Central Europe. The proposal becomes known as the Gomułka Plan when it is formally offered on February 29, 1964.

December 31: In a message to world leaders, Khrushchev proposes an international agreement on nonuse of force in territorial and border disputes.

1964

January 2: A GDR proposal for the denuclearization of both German states preempts the Gomułka Plan.

January 8–9: Warsaw Pact consultations in Moscow about the Gomułka Plan are subsequently sidetracked by the Soviet Union.

January 10–14: At a confrontational meeting with Khrushchev, Gomułka accuses Khrushchev of pursuing Soviet interests in Germany at Poland's expense and urges reconciliation with China.

February 29: The Gomułka Plan is submitted but the USSR opposes the verification measures proposed in the plan.

April 22: Romania publicly affirms its independent course in foreign policy.

June 12: The GDR and Soviet Union sign a treaty on friendship and mutual assistance.

September 14: During a demonstration of new armaments, Khrushchev expresses doubts about their utility since war between the superpowers has been ruled out because of the danger of nuclear arms.

October 14: The Warsaw Pact plan for the Czechoslovak army's offensive into Western Europe is approved.

October 14: Khrushchev is dismissed as first secretary of the Soviet Communist Party.

October 16: China tests its first nuclear device.

October 20: East German leader Ulbricht takes the initiative in proposing a long-delayed PCC meeting.

December 10: A meeting of Warsaw Pact deputy foreign ministers is held in Warsaw to prepare for a PCC meeting. Romania urges that Albania be invited. Because of a wide range of disagreements, the meeting ends without a joint communiqué.

1965

January 19–20: At a contentious PCC Meeting in Warsaw, opposition to NATO's Multilateral Force project (MLF) and a draft of the nonproliferation treaty provoke disagreements, especially with Romania. The PCC excludes Albania from further participation, Poland proposes a European security conference, and Hungary urges creation of a committee to discuss common foreign policy, but does not succeed.

April: An abortive coup by Bulgarian generals aims at a more independent foreign policy.

December 15: Soviet and Czechoslovak officials agree to allow the future stationing of Soviet nuclear-armed missiles at three Czechoslovak sites.

1966

January 7: Brezhnev proposes to Eastern European leaders consultations about reorganizing the Warsaw Pact.

February 4–9: A special meeting of Warsaw Pact chiefs of staff in Moscow, convened to discuss the Statute of Unified Command and the creation of new military bodies, ends inconclusively.

February 10–12: A meeting of Warsaw Pact deputy foreign ministers in Berlin discusses strengthening the PCC and creating additional institutions, but ends without an agreement, mainly because of Romanian obstruction.

May 27–28: A conference of Warsaw Pact defense ministers in Moscow approves a draft Statute of Unified Command, with Romanian reservations; it is to be forwarded to the PCC and the national governments for approval but makes little progress toward creation of new military institutions.

June 6–17: A conference of Warsaw Pact foreign ministers reaches no consensus on measures for organizational improvement of the alliance.

July 4: Meeting in Bucharest, the PCC does not act on the draft Statute of Unified Command.

July 5–7: An informal meeting of Warsaw Pact party secretaries and heads of governments includes a contentious discussion over a proposed declaration on Vietnam, but its main result is to issue the "Bucharest Declaration" calling for a conference on European security. The reorganization of the Warsaw Pact is postponed.

October 21: A meeting of Warsaw Pact party chiefs with Brezhnev agrees to press the campaign against the Vietnam War and convene a conference of European communist parties on issues of security.

1967

January 31: Romania establishes diplomatic relations with West Germany without consulting East Germany.

February 8–10: A foreign ministers conference in Warsaw, convened in response to Romania's diplomatic recognition of West Germany, agrees to step up a campaign for the international recognition of East Germany and for a European security conference to isolate West Germany and promote divisions within NATO.

April 24–26: At a conference of communist parties in Karlovy Vary, without Romanian and Yugoslav representation, participants call for the dissolution of NATO and ejection of the United States from participation in the security of Europe.

June 5–11: The Six-Day War takes place in the Middle East.

July 11–12: A conference of party chiefs, including Tito but not Ceauşescu, takes place in Budapest to discuss common action with regard to the Middle East; Romania alone fails to sever diplomatic relations with Israel.

November 9: A meeting of Warsaw Pact party leaders is held concerning preparations for a conference of world communist parties in 1968.

November 16: A meeting of chiefs of general staff in Dresden urges creation of a staff of the Unified Command and a committee on technology as a first step toward reorganization of the Warsaw Pact. Romania opposes it.

December 14: NATO adopts the Harmel Report defining the organization's goals as both defense and détente.

1968

January 5: Alexander Dubček replaces Antonín Novotný as leader of the Czechoslovak communist party. The Prague Spring ensues, eventually prompting the Soviet-led invasion of August 1968.

February 26–27: Deputy foreign ministers meeting in Berlin reach no agreements because of Romanian opposition to the Soviet draft of a nonproliferation treaty.

February 29–March 1: A meeting of Warsaw Pact chiefs of staff in Prague is held to resume the project of reorganizing the alliance. The group agrees to create a Military Council despite Romanian opposition.

March 6–7: A PCC meeting held in Sofia agrees, with Romanian abstention, to create a Warsaw Pact staff and a Military Council. The Romanians present amendments to the nonproliferation treaty but no agreement on it is reached.

March 23: A Dresden meeting of Warsaw Pact leaders warns against alleged deterioration in the combat readiness of the Czechoslovak army and urges acceleration of the reform of the alliance.

June 4: A memorandum to Dubček by 30 research associates of the Military Political and Military Technical Academies outlines principles of Czechoslovakia's military doctrine. On July 2, it is published in the press.

June 18–July 2: The "Šumava" exercise of Warsaw Pact armies is carried out on Czechoslovak territory to pressure the Czechoslovak leadership into rolling back its reform program.

July 1: The Nuclear Non-Proliferation Treaty (NPT) is signed by 61 nations, including Romania.

July 9–11: A Czechoslovak army conference in Bratislava urges elaboration of a national doctrine within the Warsaw Pact framework and "internationalization" of the alliance's command.

July 14–15: The leaders of the Soviet Union, Hungary, Poland, East Germany and Bulgaria, meeting in Warsaw, warn Czechoslovakia to reverse its reformist course.

July 18: Warsaw Pact Supreme Commander Marshal Ivan Iakubovskii accuses Gen. Václav Prchlík, head of the Czechoslovak army's political administration, of revealing Warsaw Pact secrets in a conversation with journalists.

July 20: A Soviet note to the Czechoslovak government criticizes it for allegedly insufficient protection of the country's Western borders and for tolerating activities that undermine the alliance.

July 29–August 1: At a meeting with Czechoslovak leaders at Čierna nad Tisou, the Soviet leadership alleges a NATO threat to Czechoslovak borders, and claims a common Warsaw Pact responsibility for their defense.

August 3: At a high-level Soviet–Czechoslovak meeting in Bratislava, the Soviet side asserts that it is the duty of all socialist countries to uphold socialist achievements.

August 20: The invasion of Czechoslovakia by Soviet, Polish, East German, Hungarian, and Bulgarian armies begins.

September 2: Marshal Grechko, at a meeting with four other Warsaw Pact defense ministers in Legnica, Poland, discusses options for occupation forces in Czechoslovakia.

September 12–17: At a Moscow meeting, deputy chiefs of staff prepare final documents for the reorganization of the Warsaw Pact.

September 13: Albania formally withdraws from the Warsaw Pact in protest against the invasion of Czechoslovakia.

October 16: The Soviet Union and Czechoslovakia reach agreement on the stationing of Soviet troops in Czechoslovakia.

October 18: A meeting of five Warsaw Pact defense ministers in Moscow decides to withdraw non-Soviet troops from Czechoslovakia.

October 29–30: Warsaw Pact defense ministers meeting in Moscow approve agreements on new alliance structures. Romania signs on, but reserves the right to examine the provision allowing the supreme commander to deploy forces on member-states' territories in peace time.

1969

March 14–15: After an incident on March 2, armed clashes peak between Soviet and Chinese troops along disputed border on the Ussuri River.

March 17: Meeting in Budapest, the PCC strengthens the unified command and establishes a committee of defense ministers, a military council, and a committee on technology. It adopts the statute on unified command in peace time and issues an appeal for convocation of a European security conference.

May 12–16: Warsaw Pact defense ministers and chiefs of staff meet in the Polish capital to discuss mobilization readiness.

May 21–22: Deputy foreign ministers from the Warsaw Pact countries meet in Berlin to discuss a common strategy with regard to the European security conference.

June 15–17: A conference of 75 communist parties, meeting in Moscow but boycotted by China, Yugoslavia, North Korea, Vietnam, and Albania, calls for a new European security system and the simultaneous dissolution of NATO and Warsaw Pact.

July 11: A report by four Chinese marshals considers a U.S. attack against China unlikely, noting that the USSR poses a greater threat.

September 11: Kosygin and Zhou Enlai meet at the Beijing airport to try to defuse Sino-Soviet tension, but their discussion ends inconclusively.

October 6: The Polish Foreign Ministry prepares a proposal for a European collective security treaty and a draft charter for a European security organization.

October 21: Following West German elections on September 28, Willy Brandt becomes chancellor and soon initiates a new policy toward the East (*Ostpolitik*).

October 22–28: The Warsaw Pact conducts the "Oder–Neisse 69" exercise. It is the largest joint military exercise to date. The USSR, GDR, PPR, and ČSSR armies, except for strategic missile units, participate.

October 30–31: Warsaw Pact foreign ministers meet in Prague to discuss coordination of preparations for an all-European security conference. They call for bilateral and multilateral preparatory meetings, accept U.S. and Canadian participation, and draft agreements on the renunciation of force and expanded cooperation.

October 30–November 3: Meetings of deputy defense ministers take place in Prague on the subject of armed forces development in 1970.

November 17–December 22: The United States and Soviet Union hold preliminary Strategic Arms Limitation Talks (SALT) in Helsinki, Finland.

December 2–4: A meeting of Warsaw Pact heads of state takes place in Moscow to assess West Germany's new *Ostpolitik* and decide on common responses to it.

December 9–10: The first meeting of the Warsaw Pact Military Council in Moscow discusses shortening the alarm times needed to achieve combat readiness.

December 22–23: The first meeting of the Warsaw Pact committee of defense ministers takes place in Moscow. The group calls for an increase in both conventional and nuclear capabilities because of the uncertainty of détente.

1970

January 26–27: A conference of Warsaw Pact deputy foreign ministers in Sofia welcomes the Western response to the European security conference. The group anticipates holding it before mid-1970 but their discussion reveals differences in tactics among the different countries.

March 19: The first high-level meeting between West German and East German leaders, Chancellor Willy Brandt and Premier Willi Stoph, takes place in Erfurt, East Germany. The enthusiastic popular welcome given to Brandt shows the effects of *Ostpolitik*.

April 3: At a meeting with Warsaw Pact party chiefs (minus Romania) in Budapest, Brezhnev solicits their views on talks between the state secretary in West Germany's Chancellery, Egon Bahr, and Soviet Foreign Minister Andrei Gromyko before proceeding with further negotiations with Bonn.

April 5: Albania offers military assistance to Yugoslavia and Romania in case of a Soviet attack.

April 27: A meeting of the Warsaw Pact Military Council in Budapest stresses the importance of training for the forcing of nuclear mines barriers, and provides for the appointment of representatives of the supreme commander to the national commands.

May 6: New Soviet–Czechoslovak and Soviet–Hungarian treaties include obligation to assist USSR against any attack, implying one by China.

May 18–19: A Brezhnev–Ceaușescu meeting in Moscow fails to resolve policy disagreements between the two governments.

June 19–20: At a deputy foreign ministers' meeting in Budapest, Soviet representative Leonid Ilichev cautions against an East German demand for "enhancing" the GDR's international position and boosting GDR–FRG relations.

May 21–22: A meeting of the committee of defense ministers in Sofia discusses unified air defense and naval cooperation in view of NATO's alleged ability to conduct a surprise air strike without mobilization or displacement of aircraft.

June 21–22: A foreign ministers' meeting in Budapest proposes to expand the agenda of a European security conference by creating a permanent organ to deal with questions of security and cooperation. All countries would be represented in such an entity, and decide issues by consensus. The ministers oppose discussing mutual reductions of conventional forces at the conference.

August 12: The Soviet–West German treaty and declaration of intentions, signed in Moscow, rules out the use or threat of force and proclaims the inviolability of existing borders while leaving open the possibility of their peaceful change. It also opens the way to agreements on normalization of relations between West Germany and Poland as well as between the two German states.

August 20: At a PCC meeting in Moscow, Brezhnev defends the Soviet–West German treaty as a compromise favorable to the East, but Polish and Czechoslovak leaders fear an increased West German influence in their countries.

October 27: At the Military Council meeting in Varna, Soviet Marshal Iakubovskii justifies recent large-scale maneuvers by persisting international tensions, despite certain recent improvements.

December 2: A PCC meeting in Berlin welcomes the recently negotiated Polish–West German treaty providing for Bonn's effective recognition of the Oder–Neisse Line as Poland's western border. The treaty, signed on December 7, opens the door for the establishment of diplomatic relations between all Warsaw Pact countries and West Germany after the ratification of the treaties by the Bonn parliament, and calls for the continued coordination of policies on the Conference on Security and Cooperation in Europe (CSCE).

December 21–23: The committee of defense ministers' meeting in Budapest agrees on a plan for the development of armies, with an emphasis on improving communications systems.

1971

January 15: The Soviet Union makes a proposal to China on the nonuse of force, including nuclear weapons, but it is later rejected.

February 18–19: A meeting of Warsaw Pact foreign ministers in Bucharest concludes there has been a slowing down of progress toward the CSCE and calls on member-states to activate their diplomatic channels to accelerate the process.

March 2–4: Defense ministers meeting in Budapest hear Soviet Marshal Grechko say that the international situation has deteriorated and call for strengthening the alliance's offensive capacity.

March 30–April 4: At the 24th CPSU Congress, Brezhnev favors a reduction of both nuclear and conventional forces, especially in central Europe.

May 12–15: At a meeting of the Military Council in Berlin, Marshal Iakubovskii describes the situation as extremely tense and calls for the introduction of a common alert system.

August 2: At the first of his annual meetings with Warsaw Pact leaders in the Crimea, Brezhnev gives an optimistic assessment of the international situation, but Bulgarian leader Todor Zhivkov warns against a Beijing–Bucharest–Tirana–Belgrade axis threatening the alliance.

September 1: A Warsaw conference of foreign ministers approves the holding of experts' meetings on problems relating to convocation of the CSCE.

September 3: The United States, Soviet Union, Great Britain and France sign the Quadripartite Agreement securing access to West Berlin and clarifying its status in relation to West Germany.

September 13–18: An East German–Polish–Soviet command exercise, "Herbststurm 71," envisages offensive operations against Denmark in cooperation with the Warsaw Pact's Baltic navies, aimed at the destruction of reserves of NATO's Baltic Straits Command and the occupation of the Jutland Peninsula.

October 26–29: A meeting of the Military Council in Warsaw decides to hold exercises with tactical missiles involving all member-states except Romania, which criticizes the holding of too many exercises by the Pact.

November 30–December 1: A Warsaw meeting of foreign ministers appeals for accelerated preparations for a security conference, aiming to convene it in 1972.

1972

January 25–26: Addressing a PCC meeting in Prague, Brezhnev praises the results of West German *Ostpolitik*, anticipates the possibility of a largely peaceful future relationship between the two major alliances, and stresses the importance of the CSCE as the foundation for a new European security system.

February 9–10: At a defense ministers' meeting in Berlin, Warsaw Pact Chief of Staff Sergei M. Shtemenko says that despite "some détente," NATO remains a threat; the Romanians balk at the idea of joint air defense measures.

February 21–27: President Nixon makes a historic first visit to China.

February 22–24: Brezhnev, in Prague, calls for military détente through the reduction of forces and armaments in Europe, or at least a part of Europe.

April 10–12: A meeting of the Military Council takes place in Bucharest, dealing with routine matters.

May 22–26: During a state visit to the USSR, Nixon and Brezhnev sign the SALT I treaty, which limits the growth of strategic nuclear weapons, and an anti-ballistic missile (ABM) treaty limiting strategic defense systems.

May 29: The United States and Soviet Union sign an agreement on "basic principles" of peaceful coexistence and the right to "equal security."

July 31: At a meeting of Warsaw Pact leaders in the Crimea, Brezhnev stresses the need for military détente, improved relations with the United States, and the problem of growing Chinese hostility.

September 4–11: The "Shield-72" exercise starts with a Western attack through Poland in direction of Lvov, Ukraine. The plan envisions nuclear weapons being used, a counterattack by Warsaw Pact forces through West Germany, also using nuclear weapons, but at a slower rate of advance than in the plans from the 1960s.

October 17–20: At a meeting of the Military Council in Minsk, Gen. Shtemenko announces that the annual Shield exercise for 1973 has been cancelled without giving reasons.

November 15: At a Moscow meeting of deputy foreign ministers, in advance of the Helsinki preparatory talks on the CSCE, agreement is reached to resist Western attempts to go beyond the framework of these talks by raising political issues, particularly the free movement of people, ideas, and information. These issues would later be part of Basket III in the final agreement at Helsinki.

November 22: The Multilateral Preparatory Talks for the CSCE begin in Helsinki.

1973

January 15–16: A conference of Warsaw Pact foreign ministers in Moscow discusses forthcoming preparatory talks between the two alliances on mutual and balanced force reductions (MBFR).

January 31–June 23: Preparatory negotiations for the MBFR take place in Vienna.

February 6–8: At a committee of defense ministers' meeting in Warsaw, Grechko warns that the growth of détente increases the danger of Western ideological subversion.

April 16–19: The "Kraj" exercise is held, designed to practice territorial defense for Poland in case of a nuclear war; it was to be held every five years but was never repeated.

April 24: The "Convention on Legal Competences, Privileges and Immunities" for

Warsaw Pact staff and agencies is signed at the deputy foreign minister level, and published.

May 16–17: A meeting of the Military Council in Sofia discusses NATO's "Reforger-4" exercise as a demonstration of the growing U.S. ability to swiftly intervene in the European theater. Soviet Gen. Shtemenko emphasizes the need to counter NATO's increased emphasis on electronic warfare, while Marshal Iakubovskii sees the current situation as not permitting reductions in Warsaw Pact armed forces.

May 21–22: A Moscow meeting of deputy foreign ministers agrees to speed up the CSCE process now that the final stage of the preparatory conference has been reached. They further agree not to allow the inviolability of borders to be linked with other issues, to reject the demand for advance notice of troop movements, and to consider human rights issues only if this is in the interests of the socialist states.

June 8: The Helsinki preparatory meeting ends with a call for convening the CSCE. The Warsaw Pact regards the negotiations as a success.

June 12–15: A meeting of Warsaw Pact chiefs of general staff in Sofia proposes preparation of a statute on the command of unified forces in war time.

June 18–25: Brezhnev visits the United States for talks with Nixon.

June 23: A US–Soviet agreement is signed on the prevention of nuclear war.

July 3: The CSCE opens in Helsinki to discuss aspects of security, human relations, and economic and scientific affairs. Talks continue in Geneva over the next two years.

July 30–31: At a Crimea meeting of Warsaw Pact leaders, Brezhnev gives an upbeat assessment of Soviet global ascendancy in view of a perceived U.S. retreat, and a lasting, rather than temporary, American interest in détente. He is confident of the West's acceptance of the CSCE on Soviet terms, and anticipates mutual force reductions, starting in Central Europe.

October 6–22: The Yom Kippur War in the Middle East exposes Warsaw Pact deficiencies, primarily in electronic warfare and communications.

October 23–25: Representatives of Warsaw Pact ministries of foreign affairs and defense, minus Romania, meet in Moscow to prepare for the forthcoming MBFR negotiations in Vienna. The Soviet Union favors downsizing while preserving "the existing balance of power."

October 30–31: A meeting of deputy foreign ministers is held in Berlin to counter the FRG's effort to represent Berlin at the United Nations, following the admission of both German states as members of the body.

October 30–November 1: A meeting of the Military Council in Prague provides no evaluation of the development of individual Warsaw Pact armies, as called for in the 1971–1975 plan, presumably because the plan was being reviewed.

October 31: An amended version of the Polish defense doctrine is adopted by Poland's Committee for the Defense of the Homeland.

February 5–7: Warsaw Pact defense ministers meet in Bucharest where Nicolae Ceaușescu, who is opposed to a unified communications system for the alliance, criticizes the building of a regional command post in Bulgaria.

March 26–29: A session of the Military Council in Budapest draws lessons from the
Yom Kippur War, and calls for new air defense missiles and automated command systems.

March 26–April 4: The "Elektronik-74" exercise shows that GDR telecommunications capabilities are not ready for wartime conditions.

April 17–18: At a meeting of the PCC in Warsaw, East Germany criticizes Romania
for playing into NATO's hands; the PCC makes abortive preparations to celebrate the Warsaw Pact's 20th anniversary in 1975.

April 26: At a meeting of the Military Council, the USSR urges better preparation
of all Warsaw Pact territory in the event of war.

July 2–5: A meeting of Warsaw Pact chiefs of staff takes place in Prague.

December 5: At the MBFR talks, the Warsaw Pact proposes a freeze on troop levels while negotiations are in progress, but NATO is opposed since this would
block its efforts to redress force imbalances.

1975

January 7–8: At a defense ministers' meeting in Moscow, the GDR representative
explains NATO's modernization process in detail and discusses NATO's new
electronic warfare capabilities that are mainly sponsored by the FRG and United
States.

January 29–30: At a Moscow meeting of deputy foreign ministers, preparations are
made to celebrate the Warsaw Pact's 20th anniversary in the Polish capital in
May and to hold a PCC meeting in 1975, neither of which materializes.

March 18: Brezhnev at meeting with Warsaw Pact party secretaries in Moscow singles
out the conclusion of the CSCE as the common highest foreign policy priority.

March 19–20: Warsaw Pact deputy foreign ministers meet in the Polish capital to step
up coordination of policies toward the Nordic countries, considered of particular importance "to promote positive tendencies in international relations."

May 21–24: The GDR holds its first annual exercises designed to prepare both state
and society for war.

August 1: The Final Act of the CSCE is signed in Helsinki by 35 countries. They
pledge to resolve conflicts peacefully and agree to respect human rights and
basic freedoms.

October 7: A new Soviet–GDR treaty provides for mutual defense of borders in addition to guarantees provided by the Warsaw Pact.

October 28–30: A Military Council meeting in Bucharest approves the shortening of
alert times. Romania joins a common air defense plan as well a plan for joint
counterintelligence, but balks on other points such as allowing transit of Warsaw
Pact forces across the territories of member-states.

November 18–19: A committee of defense ministers' meeting in Prague calls for increased use of helicopters, automation of troop command and improvement of transportation.

1975: Soviet planning for coalition warfare reaches its peak this year; 20–40 percent of forces assigned for offensive action against NATO are East European.

1976

February 19: At the MBFR talks, the Warsaw Pact proposes proportional reductions on the assumption that a rough equilibrium exists. It also accepts the Western idea of reductions in stages, but opposes an asymmetrical approach, as favored by the West.

May 25–27: A meeting of the Military Council in Kiev hears a report on increases in NATO's capabilities.

September 9–16: "Shield-76" maneuvers in Poland, with participation of Western observers as well as defense minister Raúl Castro of Cuba.

November 25–26: PCC meeting in Bucharest submits draft of treaty for an all-European security conference against first use of nuclear weapons, decides to create a committee of foreign ministers and Unified Secretariat as PCC organs (only the former implemented), and approves creation of special forces equipped with up-to-date weapons. East Germany, Czechoslovakia, and Bulgaria urge closer coordination in view of the disruptive internal effects of Helsinki.

December 10–11: Defense ministers meet in Prague and discuss NATO's modernization of intelligence, command, and fighting capabilities which they regard as the most crucial transformation since the "equipment of NATO forces with nuclear weapons." Romania opposes the creation of a Warsaw Pact agency for the standardization of equipment.

1977

January 18: Brezhnev in a speech at Tula, south of Moscow, denies any Soviet desire for strategic superiority.

March 21–29: The "Soiuz-77" exercise is held in Hungary and ČSSR, including Soviet forces. It presumes a NATO attack involving use of Austrian territory, but presupposes that by the second day the Warsaw Pact will already begin a counteroffensive that pushes the enemy back.

May 25–26: The first meeting of the Committee of Ministers of Foreign Affairs takes place in Moscow, to prepare a common position for the upcoming CSCE Belgrade conference.

May 30–June 9: The "Zapad" exercise in the GDR, which is intended to take into account NATO's progress in combat readiness, shows that the Warsaw Pact's response is not fast enough.

September 5: Warsaw Pact Supreme Commander Marshal Viktor G. Kulikov creates new administrative bodies to enhance the organizational structure of the Warsaw Pact command.

October 20: At a meeting of the Military Council in Sofia, Romania refuses to participate in forthcoming Warsaw Pact staff training because of a lack of clarity on the principles of unified command in war time.

November 29–December 3: A meeting of defense ministers in Budapest deals with preparation of the statute for Warsaw Pact command in war time.

December 1977: The deployment of the SS-20 Soviet intermediate-range missiles in Europe begins.

1978

February 12–18: The "Druzhba" exercise takes place. It presumes a NATO attack, then a counterattack with conventional weapons escalating to use of nuclear weapons.

April 24–25: Warsaw Pact foreign ministers meet in Sofia to discuss political and military détente and disarmament measures. Romania sees détente endangered by the global competition of the superpowers over spheres of influence.

May 16–19: A meeting of the Warsaw Pact Military Council in Budapest is concerned with the rise in NATO's budgets and military issues such as the West's capability to destroy aircraft on the ground.

June 12–14: A meeting of chiefs of general staffs in Sofia discusses the development of Warsaw Pact forces in 1981–1985, and presses for finalization of a statute on command in war time over Romanian opposition.

July 10: Soviet Defense Minister Marshal Dmitrii Ustinov in Helsinki demands joint military exercises with Finland, but the Finns sidetrack the demand.

November 22–23: A PCC meeting in Moscow agrees to prepare a statute on command in war time for the November 1979 meeting of the committee of defense ministers. The group calls for the qualitative development of forces and creation of state-of-the-art special units within each national army.

December 4–7: A committee of defense ministers meeting in Berlin concludes that NATO's May 1978 program aims at the attainment of military superiority over the Warsaw Pact.

1979

May 12–19: The "Shield" exercise takes place in Hungary, with Soviet, Czechoslovak and Bulgarian participation. It includes only an offensive, not a defensive, stage.

May 14–15: A meeting of foreign ministers takes place in Budapest to prepare a common policy at the forthcoming CSCE conference in Madrid, with an emphasis on military détente. The ministers call for an agreement that would prohibit the first use of nuclear weapons.

June 15–18: U.S. President Jimmy Carter and Brezhnev meet in Vienna to sign the SALT II treaty.

October 6: Brezhnev in East Berlin announces the unilateral withdrawal of 1,000 tanks and 20,000 troops from the GDR.

November 21–27: Discussions within the Supreme Command working group in Bucharest reveal fundamental differences over the statute on wartime command between Romania and other Warsaw Pact countries.

December 3–6: A meeting of defense ministers in Warsaw discusses a Soviet draft of principles of command in war time, a proposal for creating a unified early warning system against nuclear strikes, and other issues. The Romanians advocate unilateral reductions of military budgets.

December 5–6: Warsaw Pact foreign ministers meet in Berlin to discuss the 25th anniversary of the alliance, the forthcoming CSCE conference in Madrid, and NATO's imminent "dual track" decision that would provide for preparing for the deployment of intermediate-range missiles while negotiating for their mutual abolition.

December 12: NATO adopts its dual track decision regarding the deployment of intermediate-range missiles and talks over their elimination.

December 25: The Soviet Union invades Afghanistan and installs a new government.

1980

March 18: Warsaw Pact party chiefs meeting in Moscow approve a statute on unified forces and command in war time. However, Ceauşescu demurs, leaving the document binding only for those who signed it.

April 11: Warsaw Pact governments agree on principles of military assistance to developing countries.

April 30: Warsaw Pact members, except Romania, agree on the appointment of Brezhnev as commander-in-chief of the alliance.

May 14–15: The PCC 25th anniversary meeting takes place in Warsaw. The group issues a declaration against Western armament programs. The Romanians condemn the Soviet intervention in Afghanistan and urge withdrawal of Soviet forces from the country.

May 22: At a Military Council meeting in Moscow, Marshal Kulikov praises the functioning of the system of military collaboration among Warsaw Pact armies.

July 9: In preparing for next session of the Madrid CSCE conference, Warsaw Pact deputy foreign ministers meeting in Prague agree to pursue military détente by trying to exploit Western disunity.

August 14: Workers' strikes break out at the Lenin Shipyards in Gdańsk, Poland, leading to the creation of the "Solidarity" trade union and a prolonged political crisis in Poland.

October 19–20: At a meeting of the Committee of Ministers of Foreign Affairs in Warsaw, participants agree on a strategy for the Madrid talks while keeping their agenda separate from the Polish developments.

October 22: Polish Defense Minister Gen. Wojciech Jaruzelski secretly creates a special group within the army command to prepare a proclamation of martial law.

October 27–30: The Warsaw Pact Military Council meets in Hungary

December 1: Plans for the invasion of Poland, prepared in the Soviet general staff and envisaging a supporting role for the Polish army, are handed to Polish Defense Ministry representatives in Moscow.

December 1–3: Warsaw Pact defense ministers meet in Bucharest, but do not discuss ways to resolve the Polish crisis.

December 4–5: An emergency meeting of Warsaw Pact party secretaries either reaches or confirms a decision not to intervene militarily in Poland but to allow the Polish party leadership another chance to restore full communist authority.

December 8–10: The "Soiuz-80" exercise involving Soviet, Czechoslovak, and East German troops gets underway, but does not extend into Poland.

1981

January 13: A closed meeting of the Warsaw Pact Supreme Command, chaired by Marshal Viktor Kulikov, decides that the Polish crisis must be resolved by the Polish communists themselves. Polish Defense Minister Wojciech Jaruzelski is entrusted with finding the solution.

January 19–20: A deputy foreign ministers' meeting takes place in Berlin with the participation of Mongolia and Cuba. They decide to strengthen the presence of Warsaw Pact representatives in West Berlin.

March 16: The "Soiuz-81" and "Druzhba-80" maneuvers are held on the territory of the GDR and Poland.

March 19: The Bydgoszcz crisis occurs in Poland, marking another high-tension point in the Polish crisis.

April 2: Brezhnev and Defense Minister Dmitrii Ustinov indicate at a Soviet Politburo meeting the decision to shelve plans for military intervention in Poland and to put pressure on Polish party leaders to crack down on the Solidarity opposition forces themselves.

April 21–23: At a meeting of the Warsaw Pact's Military Council in Sofia, Kulikov reports that Polish party leader Stanisław Kania and Prime Minister Jaruzelski had requested the establishment of a collective Warsaw Pact command center at Legnica.

June 13: Marshal Kulikov, on a visit to Dresden, asks East German generals to be prepared for "all eventualities" in regard to Poland.

September 4–12: The "Zapad-81" exercises take place in the Baltic and Belorussia. They are the first to practice the Operational Group Maneuver concept of deep conventional thrusts into NATO territory to destroy its military infrastructure.

October 27–30: A Warsaw Pact Military Council meeting concludes it is high time for the Polish leadership to use force against Solidarity.

December 1–2: A meeting of Warsaw Pact foreign ministers in Bucharest, convened after a one-year interval, discusses arms control issues rather than Poland.

December 1–4: During a defense ministers' meeting in Moscow, where Poland is not the main item on the agenda, Polish Defense Minister Florian Siwicki attempts vainly to obtain the Warsaw Pact's public support for the imposition of martial law.

December 10: A Soviet Politburo meeting rules out military intervention in Poland.

December 13: Jaruzelski declares martial law in Poland.

March 29: Jaruzelski, at a meeting with Honecker in Berlin, proclaims martial law a success and welcomes recent Warsaw Pact maneuvers in Poland, where the East German army was present "both politically and in combat."

Mary 17–27: The Warsaw Pact's "Dukla-82" exercise is held in Czechoslovakia in response to the U.S. strategy to win a war in Europe by conventional means only.

June 18: The Soviet exercise—"seven-hour nuclear war"—simulates an all-out first strike against the United States and Western Europe.

September 8–10: A meeting of chiefs of staffs in Minsk demonstrates the use of the first automatic field command system. The Romanians were not invited to attend.

September 24–October 1: The Warsaw Pact "Shield" exercise takes place in Bulgaria without Romanian participation.

October 21–22: The committee of foreign ministers meets in Moscow to prepare strategy for the Madrid CSCE conference in order to "save" détente.

November 10: Leonid Brezhnev dies; Iurii Andropov becomes the new general secretary of the Soviet communist party two days later.

1983

January 4–5: At a PCC meeting, recently appointed Soviet leader Iurii Andropov maintains that under the Reagan administration the threat of war has increased dramatically. Romania, Poland, and East Germany debate differing concepts of the Warsaw Pact.

January 11–13: A committee of defense ministers meeting in Prague criticizes what it perceives as NATO's striving for superiority and attempts to draw lessons from the recent Iran–Iraq and Falklands wars.

March 23: President Ronald Reagan proposes the Strategic Defense Initiative (SDI), or Star Wars.

April 6–7: Foreign ministers at their meeting in Prague agree to streamline the Warsaw Pact's consultative mechanism and urge the conclusion of a Warsaw Pact–NATO nonaggression treaty, while Romania presses for a reduction of military outlays.

April 26–28: At a meeting of the Military Council in Bucharest, Marshal Kulikov urges modernization of armaments and equipment in order to keep up with NATO, whereas Ceauşescu insists that prospective Western deployments of medium-range missiles ought to be answered not by counter-deployments but by removal of all nuclear missiles from Europe.

May 30–June 9: The joint "Soiuz-83" exercise envisages the occupation of Denmark, the FRG, the Netherlands, Belgium, and France by the 35th–40th day of the war. Kulikov stresses the need to be able to start hostilities immediately, not only after mobilization, as was the case before.

May 31: The Soviet Politburo, meeting in Moscow in anticipation of NATO's "Euromissile" deployments, stresses the need to consolidate the Warsaw Pact in view of its lack of unity and growing national divergences.

June 28: An extraordinary meeting of top Warsaw Pact leaders discusses measures in response to the likely deployment of Euromissiles; East Germany and Czechoslovakia reluctantly agree to counter-deployments of Soviet missiles on their territories.

September 1: Soviet fighters shoot down a South Korean civilian airliner, KAL 007, that mistakenly entered Soviet airspace.

October 13–14: A committee of foreign ministers meeting in Sofia warns NATO against precipitating another arms race and threatens the deployment of additional weapons systems as well as the strengthening of Warsaw Pact conventional forces. Romania opposes the idea and demands the creation of a commission of experts to deal with all arms control issues.

October 20: The committee of defense ministers holds an extraordinary meeting in Berlin to prepare for the Western governments' impending approval of the Euromissile deployment.

October 29: The Warsaw Pact Military Council meets in Lvov, Ukraine.

November 9–10: The Warsaw Pact heads of parliament issue an appeal against the deployment of Euromissiles.

November 22: Approval by West Germany's Bundestag opens the way for the deployment of Euromissiles.

December 5–7: A meeting of the committee of defense ministers in Sofia takes note of the Soviet withdrawal from the Geneva arms control talks but takes no other measures in response to the Euromissile deployments.

1984

February 9: Iurii Andropov dies; two days later Konstantin U. Chernenko assumes the post of Soviet party general secretary.

April 19–20: During a meeting in Budapest, Warsaw Pact foreign ministers, with the exception of Romania, endorse the Soviet position that a return to conditions that held prior to the deployment of Euromissiles is a precondition for resumption of negotiations on intermediate-range missiles.

April 24–27: At a meeting of the Warsaw Pact Military Council in Prague, the Czechoslovak government for the first time requests training for defense, in addition to offensive warfare.

September 5–14: The "Shield-84" exercise prepares for both defensive and offensive operations.

December 3–4: A meeting of the committee of foreign ministers in Berlin prepares material for a Warsaw Pact summit.

December 3–5: At a defense ministers' meeting in Budapest, Marshal Sergei F. Akhromeev urges "permanently increased combat readiness" in response to the results of NATO's 1979 long-term development program.

March 11: Following the death of Chernenko, Mikhail Gorbachev is appointed general secretary of the Soviet communist party.

April 26: As the Warsaw Pact's 30th anniversary approaches, the alliance is extended for another 20 years.

May 20–23: The Warsaw Pact Military Council meets in Budapest.

May 22: A conference celebrating the 30th anniversary of the Warsaw Pact is held in Moscow.

October 22–23: At a PCC meeting in Sofia, Gorbachev justifies the Soviet Union's return to the Geneva arms control talks. East Germany and Czechoslovakia propose the creation of a chemical-weapons-free zone in Europe.

November 18–21: The first summit between Reagan and Gorbachev takes place in Geneva. They agree to accelerate arms reduction talks.

November 21: At a meeting of Warsaw Pact leaders in Prague, Gorbachev reports about the Geneva summit.

December 2–5: At a defense ministers' meeting in Berlin, Marshal Kulikov and Gen. Anatolii Gribkov express bleak views about NATO intentions, arguing that NATO's operational training is increasingly being shaped by an offensive U.S. military doctrine aimed at launching a surprise attack.

1986

January 15: Gorbachev outlines a plan for nuclear disarmament by the year 2000.

January 28–29: A deputy foreign ministers' meeting is held in Berlin. The delegates stress the need for mutual consultations about questions concerning developing countries.

February 25: Addressing the XXVIIth Soviet party congress, Gorbachev calls for Warsaw Pact unity but says that "unity has nothing in common with conformity." He says that security cannot depend on defense or deterrence but must be found by political means.

March 7: At a conference of deputy foreign ministers in Budapest, the Soviets inform the delegates on the progress of negotiations in Geneva.

March 19–20: A Warsaw Pact committee of foreign ministers meeting in Warsaw supports as its main goal the general abolition of weapons of mass destruction, and provides for participation of Warsaw Pact member-states in international arms control negotiations

April 23–25: A Warsaw Pact Military Council session in Warsaw, held after the U.S. air strike against Libya, calls for measures to overcome the increase in NATO's defensive and offensive capabilities.

April 26: The Chernobyl nuclear disaster occurs, demonstrating to Warsaw Pact leaders the potential effects of nuclear war.

June 10–11: Meeting in Budapest, the PCC appeals for reductions of conventional forces by 25 percent. Gorbachev urges more emphasis on political and economic collaboration within the alliance.

September 8–12: The "Druzhba-86" exercise envisages an attack by Western conventional forces, under the guise of exercises, which would likewise be repelled by conventional means.

September 11–12: A Bucharest meeting of Warsaw Pact experts discusses a Romanian proposal for a unilateral freeze and reduction of armed forces and defense expenditures.

October 14–15: At a foreign ministers' meeting in Bucharest, Soviet Foreign Minister Eduard Shevardnadze reports on the recent Gorbachev–Reagan summit in Reykjavik.

November 11–20: A meeting of the Warsaw Pact's leading general staff officers takes place in Bratislava.

November 12–14: At the Warsaw Pact Military Council, Kulikov warns of an increased danger of war because of NATO's growing potential, especially after the installation of Euromissiles.

December 1–3: At a Warsaw Pact committee of ministers of defense meeting in Warsaw, Soviet Defense Minister Sokolov dwells on the continuing danger of unpredictable U.S. actions that may lead to war.

1987

February: "Group 23," comprising the NATO and Warsaw Pact states, begins informal consultations in Vienna that eventually lead to the 1990 signing of the Conventional Forces in Europe (CFE) Treaty.

March 24–25: A meeting of foreign ministers in Moscow supports the Soviet effort to remove intermediate-range nuclear forces and seeks common positions on the CSCE negotiations in Vienna.

May 28–29: At a PCC meeting in Berlin, the Warsaw Pact officially abandons its offensive strategy in favor of a strictly defensive one.

July 3: A meeting of the main political administrations of the Warsaw Pact countries in Moscow reaches agreement to create a coordinating political organ of the Supreme Command and an information office for the unified forces.

July: The so-called Jaruzelski Plan for "Nuclear and Conventional Arms Disengagement in Central Europe" is promulgated.

August 5: Warsaw Pact chiefs of staff meeting in Moscow agree to, but are skeptical of, forthcoming negotiations with NATO on cuts in conventional forces.

September 6–14: The "Soiuz-87" exercise features strategic defense for the first time, and provides for a gradual transition from a peace to a wartime footing.

October 14: A meeting of Warsaw Pact chiefs of staff in Moscow deals with military doctrine.

November 24–26: Defense ministers meeting in Bucharest discusses new troop postures in view of the adoption of a defensive doctrine and the outcome of the Stockholm conference on confidence-building measures.

December 8–10: At the Washington summit, Reagan and Gorbachev sign the Intermediate-Range Nuclear Forces Treaty (INF).

February 8: Gorbachev announces that a withdrawal of Soviet forces from Afghanistan will take place within a year.

February 23: At a foreign ministers' meeting in Prague, Shevardnadze informs the delegates about a recent visit by Secretary of State George Shultz, and notes a wide convergence of views between the United States and the USSR.

March 29–30: At a conference of Warsaw Pact foreign ministers in Sofia, Shevardnadze is optimistic about the positive effects of the reduction of conventional forces while East German Foreign Minister Oskar Fischer is concerned about being on the losing side. Shevardnadze proposes the creation of inter-parliamentary organizations within the Warsaw Pact countries.

May 13: At a foreign ministers' meeting in Berlin, Shevardnadze notes a "visible weakening of anti-Soviet tendencies of U.S. policy," and thanks the Warsaw Pact partners for helping the USSR to gain U.S. confidence.

May 17: A meeting in Moscow, hosted jointly by the Soviet General Staff and Foreign Ministry, discusses the preparation of data exchanges between NATO and the Warsaw Pact.

July 4: Romania offers a proposal for the reorganization and "democratization" of Warsaw Pact organs.

July 5–8: At a meeting of the committee of defense ministers in Moscow concerning perspectives on the development of NATO and the Warsaw Pact up to 2000, Gorbachev notes the Warsaw Pact's new dynamism, and observes that all its member-states have become "independently active."

July 15–16: The PCC meets in Warsaw to prepare for negotiations on reducing conventional weapons and on confidence-building measures within the framework of the Vienna CSCE talks. The Romanians stress the negative tendencies of recent developments, while others welcome a reduction of tensions.

October 3–5: The Warsaw Pact Military Council, meeting in Budapest, decides that combat training must reflect the new defensive doctrine.

October 17–18: An extraordinary meeting of defense ministers in Prague, concerning problems resulting from the disclosure of data about troop strength and armaments, rejects a Romanian proposal for reform of the alliance.

October 28–29: Warsaw Pact foreign ministers meet in Budapest to implement the results of negotiations on conventional arms reductions and confidence-building measures. The group notes that the transition from confrontation to détente is a "determining trend," but different countries disagree over the desirability of compromises at the CSCE in Vienna, particularly on human rights.

November 17: A Honecker–Ceauşescu meeting in Berlin marks a rapprochement between the Warsaw Pact's most conservative regimes.

November 25: The GDR's National Defense Council seeks a review of the 1957 agreement on the stationing of Soviet troops.

December 7: In a landmark speech to the United Nations, Gorbachev announces drastic unilateral Soviet force reductions in Eastern Europe, and formally renounces the "Brezhnev doctrine."

December 8–9: A meeting of Warsaw Pact foreign and defense ministries' experts in Moscow opposes the Romanian proposal for reorganization of the alliance.

December 13–15: The Warsaw Pact Special Disarmament Commission in Bucharest supports the lowest possible level of troops and armaments that is needed for defense and a restructuring of forces such that neither side would have the benefits of surprise and an offensive capability.

December 17: A committee of defense ministers meeting in Sofia decides to publish figures on manpower and armaments, and discusses the specifics of defensive restructuring.

1989

February 14–15: The second meeting of Warsaw Pact foreign and defense ministries' experts in Bucharest opposes the Romanian idea of creating a PCC separate from the Warsaw Pact and replacement of the CMD by a military committee. The group further sees the need for a permanent political working body, a stronger role for the general secretary, and creation of a multilateral information group.

February 28: A meeting of the special Warsaw Pact commission on disarmament in Bucharest discusses Soviet draft documents for Vienna on the reduction of conventional forces (in which asymmetries and inequalities between the two alliances are to be abolished during the first stage).

March 27–31: A Moscow meeting of Warsaw Pact intelligence representatives concludes that the alliance's new defensive doctrine requires intensified counter-intelligence collaboration against subversion.

March 29: The third meeting of Warsaw Pact foreign and defense ministries' experts in Prague makes no progress on reform of the alliance because of obstruction by Romania, and considers the creation of a special Warsaw Pact commission on human rights.

April 10: A "closed circle" meeting of foreign ministers, at Niederschönhausen near Berlin, is established to encourage informal discussion among the principals.

April 11–12: At their meeting in Berlin, Warsaw Pact foreign ministers reveal a deepening cleavage between conservative member-states and those, such as Poland and Hungary, that are intent on accommodating Western principles.

April 28: Warsaw Pact chiefs of staff meet in Moscow to prepare for the Vienna talks on conventional force reductions.

May 16–18: A meeting of the Comecon Council in Moscow favors a reorganization that would make the council resemble more closely the European Community.

May 22–24: A Military Council meeting takes place in Berlin.

May 23: The "Vltava" maneuvers practice defensive operations.

June 4: In Poland's first largely free elections, the anti-communist opposition wins a landslide victory.

June 13–14: At the fourth meeting of defense and foreign ministry experts, convened to discuss reorganization of the Warsaw Pact, Hungary opposes expanding the PCC agenda to include political and economic cooperation and internal developments, and proposes suspension of the Military Council.

June 14: The Bulgarians offer a proposal for reform of the Warsaw Pact.

July 7–8: A PCC meeting in Bucharest approves the Soviet concept of military reductions and defensive restructuring, but supreme commander Petr Lushev fears the "destruction of the present structure of the Unified Armed Forces." Gorbachev favors a transformation into a primarily political alliance amid deepening disagreement among the partners about the extent of desirable change.

August 19: Romania demands collective Warsaw Pact action against "counter-revolution" in Poland.

September 8: Hungary presents the proposal for creating unilaterally a "security, confidence-building, and a cooperation zone" along the borders with Yugoslavia and Austria.

October 3–5: At a Military Council session in Warsaw, Jaruzelski warns that although no NATO aggression is to be expected in the near future, the Warsaw Pact must be prepared for the possibility that the situation could change quickly.

October 26–27: A foreign ministers' meeting in Warsaw is unable to agree on a common position to be taken at the CSCE negotiations in Vienna.

October 30–November 2: A meeting of Warsaw Pact chiefs of staff in Sofia discusses the development of Warsaw Pact forces up to 2000.

November 2–3: A meeting of chiefs of staff and foreign ministry representatives in Sofia discusses the latest results of the Vienna talks, and prepares further reductions of forces.

November 9: The Berlin Wall falls.

November 27–29: A committee of defense ministers' meeting in Budapest welcomes the reduction of international tensions but calls for more effort to make it irreversible.

December 1–3: U.S. President George Bush and Gorbachev meet near Malta. Gorbachev indicates his intention to remodel the Warsaw Pact along NATO lines in order to make it an instrument of political dialogue.

December 25: After the bloody overthrow of Romania's leadership, Nicolae and Elena Ceauşescu are executed.

December 29: Václav Havel is elected president by Czechoslovakia's parliament under the impact of a popular upheaval that forced the communist regime from power.

1990

January 29: A Warsaw Pact meeting at the Soviet General Staff discusses new proposals for the Vienna talks. The Soviets envisage keeping 275,000 troops in Central Europe, including the GDR and Poland.

February 11–13: A meeting of Warsaw Pact and NATO foreign ministers takes place in Ottawa to discuss arms control and President Bush's Open Skies plan.

February 26: Agreement is reached on the withdrawal of Soviet troops from Czechoslovakia.

February 26: A new Polish defense doctrine assumes that future wars will be a clash between coalitions, and provides for remaining in the Warsaw Pact until a new European security system has been established.

February 27–28: A meeting of the group of experts on Warsaw Pact reorganization in Budapest favors creation of an office of general secretary with headquarters in Warsaw; only Czechoslovakia dissents.

March 17: A Warsaw Pact foreign ministers' meeting in Prague agrees on the right of Germans to reunification but not on the future political and military status of Germany. The group calls for the transformation but not termination of the alliance, which it sees as a component, together with NATO, of the European security system.

March 25: Free elections take place in Hungary.

April 9: A Havel–Jaruzelski–Szűrös meeting in Bratislava fails to agree on a common strategy regarding the future of the Warsaw Pact.

June 6–7: A PCC meeting in Moscow rejects the "ideological enemy image" and fails to agree on reform of the alliance amid growing doubts about its feasibility.

June 14–15: At a committee of defense ministers' meeting at Strausberg, an East German proposal to abolish all Warsaw Pact military structures fails because of Soviet opposition, but no agreement on the manner of their preservation is reached.

July 6: NATO heads of state sign the London Declaration stating that the Warsaw Pact is no longer an enemy.

July 18: Hungarian Prime Minister József Antall visits NATO Headquarters.

September 12: West German Chancellor Helmut Kohl and Gorbachev sign an agreement that restricts the extension of NATO into former East Germany as long as Soviet troops remain present on its territory.

September 25: The GDR formally withdraws from the Warsaw Pact.

September 30: Warsaw Pact foreign ministers meet in Vienna at Czechoslovak initiative to discuss troop and armament quotas under the CFE agreement.

November 18–21: Thirty-four members of the CSCE meet in Paris. NATO and the Warsaw Pact sign the CFE Treaty, followed by the Charter of Paris for a New Europe, formally recognizing the end of the Cold War.

1991

January 21: In response to Soviet repression in the Baltic republics, a Budapest meeting of Polish, Czechoslovak and Hungarian foreign ministers sets mid-March as the deadline for dissolution of the Warsaw Pact's military structures.

February 25: A meeting of Warsaw Pact foreign and defense ministers in Budapest agrees to end the military functions of the alliance by March 31.

July 1: The political remnants of the Warsaw Pact are dissolved at a meeting in Prague.

The Warsaw Pact as History

By Vojtech Mastny

When the Warsaw Pact was founded in 1955 as a counterpart of NATO, Western officials disparaged it as a "cardboard castle."*[1] Fifteen years later, they had come to respect it as a military machine capable of overrunning most of Europe and perhaps defeating the West. Yet in another fifteen years, the machine fell apart and disappeared—with a whimper rather than a bang. Such a story is worth pondering not only for its drama but also for its value as a cautionary tale.

The history of the Warsaw Pact, recounted and documented in this book, bears on some of the key questions of the Cold War. Why did the war remain cold? Was the Soviet threat real or imaginary? What was the nature of the threat perceived by the West—and of the one perceived by the other side? How did military power influence the balance between East and West? Did nuclear weapons deter war? Or was it the conventional forces that made a difference? Considering the enemy's intentions, did deterrence work—or was it irrelevant? How did the Cold War experience change the thinking about security as well as its substance, and with what consequences?

This book is the first to document and explain the history of the Warsaw Pact from the archives of its member-states other than the former Soviet Union. The all but complete lack of access into the Soviet military archives from the period limits the scope of the documentation but not necessarily our ability to better understand the alliance's history. Copies of many of the Soviet records that are still being kept out of sight in Moscow can be found in the more readily accessible Eastern European archives, thus making it possible to draw a coherent and comprehensive, even if not complete, picture.

The picture is very different from that which prevailed at the time the Warsaw Pact was widely regarded in the West as an effective, even legitimate, counterpart of NATO. This was the time when "bean counting" of troops, missiles, tanks, artillery pieces, and combat aircraft reigned supreme amid inconclusive speculation about how Moscow's Eastern European allies would actually behave if push came to shove. The inside evidence we have today shows that the "bean countings," though not necessarily wrong, were of secondary importance in the Warsaw Pact's assessments of itself as well as of its adversary and were in any case largely irrelevant in determining its real strength.

---

*Note: The footnote citations of numbered documents refer to the documents printed in this book.

[1] Quoted in Robert Spencer, "Alliance Perceptions of the Soviet Threat, 1950–1988," in *The Changing Western Analysis of the Soviet Threat,* ed. Carl-Christoph Schweitzer (London: Pinter, 1990), pp. 9–48, at p. 19.

Outside observers rightly considered "alliance management" an important secondary function of the Warsaw Pact. Impressed by its façade, however, they overestimated Soviet ability to successfully manage the allies, as well as the Kremlin's readiness to impose its will upon them. The inside evidence shows abundantly that genuine discussion and discord, though tame and subdued by NATO standards, were much more common than met the eye as well as more disruptive. This was because the exacting standards of obedience and conformity required under the Soviet system were ultimately unattainable in real life.

Whatever generalizations can be made about the Warsaw Pact, few apply to it at all times. Outsiders often erred in viewing the alliance as static rather than evolving, resistant to change rather than vulnerable to internal and external influences, subject to the will of its managers rather than moving by its own momentum. The essay that follows shows how much the Warsaw Pact changed over time, often unexpectedly and not infrequently against Soviet wishes, with its purpose not always clear even in the minds of its leaders. Indeed, uncertainty about its mission was the communist alliance's inauspicious birthmark from the very time it came into the world under unusual circumstances in 1955.

1. THE ORIGINS (1955–1956)

It has been said that "alliances which fail to increase [their] partners' security levels almost never form."[2] The Warsaw Pact at its inception was such an alliance. When established in 1955, it was superimposed on the network of bilateral treaties of mutual assistance that had linked the Soviet Union and its dependent states in Eastern Europe with one another since the end of World War II. The supplementary alliance was not formed in response to the creation of NATO, which had already been in existence for six years. Nor was it the result of any increased military threat perceived by the Soviet Union or of growing East–West political tensions. On the contrary, in 1955 Soviet leader Nikita S. Khrushchev had concluded that the threat of war had diminished, and proceeded to promote what became known as the "first détente." He initiated—unilaterally—the first substantial cuts of Soviet conventional forces since the onset of the Cold War.[3]

Far from presaging the Warsaw Pact's later function as the Soviet Union's instrument for waging war in Europe, the proclamation of the alliance in the Polish capital on May 14, 1955, was a primarily political expedient that arose from the particular international situation at the time. At issue was reversing NATO's incipient ascendancy, buoyed by the addition of West Germany to its membership—a turn of events the Soviet Union had strenuously, but unsuccessfully, tried to avert by diplo-

---

[2] Michael F. Altfeld, "The Decision to Ally: A Theory and Test," *Western Political Quarterly* 37 (1984): 523–44, at p. 538.

[3] For details about the origins of the Warsaw Pact, see Vojtech Mastny, "The Soviet Union and the Origins of the Warsaw Pact in 1955," in *Mechanisms of Power in the Soviet Union*, ed. Niels Erik Rosenfeldt, Bent Jensen and Erik Kulavig (New York: St. Martin's Press, 2000), pp. 241–66.

matic and other means.[4] These included the threat to conclude a military alliance with its Eastern European dependents, the preparations for which were being improvised as the ratification process required for West Germany's admission into NATO proceeded toward a conclusion. Once the process was completed in early May despite the Soviets' best efforts to derail it, Moscow had little choice but to make good on its word.

Contrary to Soviet public statements, West Germany's entry into NATO did not change the existing military balance in Europe; the planned formation of twelve West German combat divisions was still far away in the future. What did change was the trend in what the Marxist leaders in the Kremlin, accustomed to thinking in the longer term, called the "correlation of forces"—a construct that properly took into account other attributes of power in addition to strictly military ones. The primacy of political considerations in their assessment was implicit in their entrusting the planning for the new alliance to the Soviet foreign ministry rather than the general staff. At issue in the challenge they perceived was the prospect of West Germany using its growing political and economic potential to accelerate Europe's consolidation under U.S. leadership—a prospect all the more distressing after the Soviet Union had overestimated the depth of the crisis NATO had gone through the year before and misjudged its irreversibility.

The military content of the alliance concluded by the Soviet Union, Poland, East Germany, Czechoslovakia, Hungary, Romania, Bulgaria, and Albania in Warsaw, with high-ranking Chinese, North Korean, and North Vietnamese representatives in attendance as interested observers, was rudimentary. The document on the establishment of a unified command, not published in its entirety, specified the size of the forces each of the signatories pledged to contribute, except for East Germany, whose contribution was left to be decided later. Not until a late stage in the planning had defense minister Marshal Georgii K. Zhukov been brought in, almost as an afterthought, and instructed by Khrushchev to draft a document on command structure. Its particulars were to be clarified at a separate meeting in Warsaw with Eastern European military representatives. Nothing was clarified, however, since Zhukov, according to the Polish liaison officer who was present, whittled down the particulars to an all but meaningless one-page document.[5]

The timing of the signing ceremony was significant. Established the day before the conclusion of the State Treaty providing for Austrian neutrality—the most tangible result of détente thus far—the Warsaw Pact preventively tied Soviet dependencies closer to Moscow. It implicitly served them notice that the enviable status

[4] The thesis that the Soviet Union may have actually welcomed West Germany's integration into NATO because of the safeguards US control of the alliance provided against resurgence of German militarism, as argued in Marc Trachtenberg, *A Constructed Peace: The Making of the European Settlement, 1945–1963* (Princeton: Princeton University Press, 1999), pp. 140–200, defies any available evidence of Soviet origin.

[5] For the text of the Warsaw Treaty, see Document No. 1; for its background, resolution by Soviet party central committee, April 1, 1955, 06/14/54/4/39, AVPRF. On Zhukov, Tadeusz Pióro, *Armia ze skazą: W Wojsku Polskim 1945–1968 (Wspomnienia i refleksje)* [The Defective Army: In the Polish Army, 1945–1968 (Memories and Reflections)] (Warsaw: Czytelnik, 1994), pp. 210–13. A copy of the text provided by Zhukov is in Gen. Pióro's possession.

about to be granted Austria was not for them. This particular purpose, however, was secondary to that of giving the West an incentive to start negotiating about the creation of a new European security system that would supersede the two military groupings. Accordingly, the text of the Warsaw Treaty followed closely the model of NATO's founding charter—the Washington Treaty of April 4, 1949.

The similarities between the two documents included the signatories' professed intent to refrain from the use or threat of force, the almost identical description of the consultations they pledged to mutually enter into in case of an enemy attack, their explicit—if qualified—promise to assist each other against such an attack by "all the means deemed necessary," and the compatibility of the commitments they were assuming with their existing ones. Less crucial, but still important, affinities between the two treaties consisted in their invoking the principles of the U.N. Charter, their twenty-year validity, and their allowing for accession by additional countries—formally easier in the Warsaw Pact than in NATO.[6]

The dissimilarities mattered less in practice but were more revealing of the Warsaw Pact's main intent. Unlike NATO's inspiring affirmation to uphold its members' common democratic values and institutions, its counterpart merely proclaimed platitudes about the promotion of peace and friendship, besides advancement of economic and cultural relations. More to the point was its founding document's call for the establishment of a collective security system in Europe, reduction of armaments, and ban on weapons of mass destruction—all leitmotifs of Soviet diplomacy at the time. Officially billed as a "Conference of European Countries for the Preservation of Peace and Security in Europe," the Warsaw Pact's inaugural session did not mean—as Soviet premier Nikolai A. Bulganin specifically pointed out—the end of the campaign for an all-European security treaty. Indeed, it marked an intensification of the campaign, leading to the formal Soviet presentation of the draft of such a treaty at the four-power summit in Geneva in July 1955.[7]

The proposed "General European Treaty on Collective Security in Europe," several provisions of which were identical with those of the Warsaw Pact or elaborated on it, spelled out explicitly what its creation aimed at implicitly, namely, parallel dissolution of both alliances. Their dismantling would have entailed the demise of the well-established NATO along with an alliance that only existed on paper, while Moscow's network of its bilateral security treaties would remain intact. This is what NATO officials meant by referring to the Warsaw Pact as a "cardboard castle, ... carefully erected over what most observers considered an already perfectly adequate blockhouse ... no doubt intended to be advertised as being capable of being dismantled, piece by piece, in return for corresponding segments of NATO." The outcome would have left the Soviet Union the dominant power in Europe and the arbiter of its security.[8]

---

[6] For the text of the Washington Treaty, see *NATO: Basic Documents* (Brussels: NATO Information Service, Brussels, 1989), pp. 10–13.

[7] "General European Treaty on Collective Security in Europe," July 20, 1955, *FRUS*, 1955–1957, vol. 5, pp. 516–19.

[8] See note no. 1.

It is hardly surprising that the West declined to entertain such a bad deal; what is surprising that the authors of the proposal apparently assumed that it might. Khrushchev acted as if he believed his capitalist adversaries could somehow be maneuvered into a situation from which they would see no way out but to acquiesce, regardless of their better judgment, in the "collective" security arrangement he wanted. A true believer in the irresistible advance of "socialism" and the Soviet system's ability to outperform its capitalist rival in a peaceful competition, he was confident that he could afford to reduce Soviet dependence on military power and rely instead on the system's other assets. It was an innovative and coherent, if flawed, strategy.

"After we created the Warsaw Pact," Khrushchev later reminisced, "I felt the time had come to think about a reduction of our armed forces." A "change of the international situation following the Geneva conference" justified the first round of his successive cuts of Soviet conventional forces. He directed the East Europeans to follow suit by reducing the size of their contingents assigned to the Warsaw Pact and announced the reduction of the Soviet Union's own forces by 640,000 men before the end of the year. [9]

As long as Khrushchev remained convinced that he could trade away the empty shell of the Warsaw Pact for the living body of NATO, there was little urgency in filling the shell with military substance. It took three months before the secret Statute of the Unified Command, which gave vaguely defined but potentially vast powers to its Soviet supreme commander, was sent from Moscow to the Eastern European party chiefs for their information.[10] Issued without even a pretense of consultation, the document became the object of much resentment among the allies. For the time being, however, it made little difference in practice. The Unified Command remained secondary to the system of Soviet "advisers," which survived from the Stalin era as the main instrument of Moscow's control over Eastern European armies. Additionally, Soviet officers were sometimes installed outright in key positions—none more conspicuous than Poland's defense minister Marshal Konstanty Rokossovski, masquerading as a Pole.

At the Moscow gathering of party chiefs in January 1956, the Warsaw Pact's future mission was addressed only indirectly, rather than directly. From the record of the meeting, it is clear that the Soviet leaders themselves had difficulty providing an answer. There was a power struggle going on in the Kremlin between foreign minister Viacheslav M. Molotov, who was the master of ceremonies, and Khrushchev. Molotov recited what he described as the latest successes of Soviet foreign policy— the normalization of relations with Yugoslavia, the Austrian state treaty, the establishment of diplomatic relations with West Germany, the opening to the Third World— all of which were actually Khrushchev's accomplishments he had opposed and tried

---

[9] *Khrushchev Remembers: The Last Testament* (Boston: Little, Brown, 1974), p. 220. Khrushchev to Bierut, August 12, 1955, KC PZPR 2661/3, AAN. *Izvestiia*, August 13, 1955. On the rationale of the troop cuts, Matthew Evangelista, *"Why Keep Such an Army?" Khrushchev's Troop Reductions*, Cold War International History Project, Working Paper no. 19 (Washington: Woodrow Wilson International Center for Scholars, 1997).

[10] Document No. 2.

to block. Much like Stalin, whose main foreign policy aide he used to be, Molotov harped on supposedly undiminished threat of war, and exalted the importance of the Warsaw Pact for thwarting the machinations of Western militarists.[11]

Khrushchev, who would soon ease Molotov out of office, saw the situation differently. He played down the threat Molotov was playing up, warned against succumbing to a war scare, whose cultivation he attributed to the West, and dwelt mainly on economic matters. He urged better coordination of industrial production, linking it with reduced output of military items, and distressed Eastern European representatives by describing as redundant some of the military aircraft that were being manufactured in their countries.

The most consequential result of the meeting was its giving approval to the arming of East Germany—a decision Moscow had long been reluctant to make because of the general Soviet mistrust of Germans and particular disdain for East German communists. Once West Germany had been admitted into NATO, however, the Soviet Union could not afford to give an impression that it trusted "its" Germans less than the Western Allies trusted "theirs." The Warsaw Pact provided the framework for the creation, control, and possible utilization of East Germany's armed forces that, in a manner analogous to West Germany's Bundeswehr, became incorporated into the alliance in their entirety. This differed from all other member-states, which officially only placed specified units under the unified command. In another slight to the East Germans, their general staff had to be called "main staff," lest connection be made with the epitome of Prussian militarism.[12]

Membership in the Warsaw Pact nevertheless provided the pariah East German regime a unique opportunity to impress its indispensability on its Soviet patrons, earn respect to enhance its international status, and achieve significant bargaining influence, if not bargaining power.[13] As a result, none of the alliance's other members, including the Soviet Union, would have more of vested interest in its consolidation and preservation than East Germany—its politically weakest but most ambitious constituent.

The first meeting three weeks later of the Warsaw Pact's Political Consultative Committee (PCC)—formally its supreme policy-making body analogous to NATO's North Atlantic Council—was mainly intended for show. Besides rubberstamping the decision to rearm East Germany, it indulged in public speeches for propaganda purposes. Its decision to create a unified secretariat and a standing commission on foreign affairs, which would prepare recommendations for the PCC, was not implemented. Neither was the PCC's proclaimed intention to meet at least twice a year. Most importantly, the Warsaw Pact failed to create a military structure anywhere

[11] Records from the meeting, Büro Ulbricht, J IV 2/202/193, SAPMO.

[12] Law on the establishment of the National People's Army, January 18, 1956, *Gesetzblatt der Deutschen Demokratischen Republik,* 1956, part 1, p. 81. Also at http://www.documentarchiv.-de/ddr/1956/nationale-volksarmee_ges.html.

[13] The distinction made by Hope M. Harrison in her "The Bargaining Power of Weaker Allies in Bipolarity and Crisis: The Dynamics of Soviet–East German Relations, 1953–1961," unpublished Ph.D. dissertation, Columbia University, 1993, p. 13.

comparable to NATO's. For the time being, it remained the "cardboard castle"—a façade for Khrushchev's maneuvering to best the capitalist enemy without resorting to military means.[14]

2. ALLIANCE ON HOLD (1956–1958)

Propelled by Khrushchev's efforts to demilitarize the Cold War, détente climaxed in 1956. As he stepped up his political offensive, his building down of conventional forces proceeded apace, generating "nervousness and uncertainty" among the Soviet military who saw the cuts as a "terrible blow to our defense capacity."[15] Khrushchev, however, was not worried. This is how he explained his unorthodox strategy to a closed session of the Polish party Central Committee:

> We have to smartly … move toward disarmament. But, we should never cross the line, which would endanger the survival of our conquests. We have to do every-thing to strengthen defense, to strengthen the army. Without these things, nobody will talk to us. They [Western enemies] are not hiding the fact that they have the hydrogen bomb, nuclear arms, and jet-propulsion technology. They know that we have all these things, and therefore they have to talk to us…; but [do] not be afraid…, this is a game …We must work … to reduce the troops and increase defense.[16]

When Eastern European leaders complained about economic hardship resulting from cuts in military production, Khrushchev defended his policy by arguing that "It is quite natural, for now it is peace time, and understandably, military industry can-not work at full capacity."[17]

In June 1956, Khrushchev hosted Yugoslav chief Josif Broz-Tito in Moscow, who suggested that the Warsaw Pact should be disbanded. Khrushchev did not act on the suggestion, but later that year revolutionary upheavals in Poland and Hungary raised the possibility of the alliance breaking up because of desertion by its members. When Poland began to take a new course under a nationalist communist leadership, Molotov and other Soviet politburo members became alarmed that the country was going to leave the Warsaw Pact and the whole "socialist bloc."[18] The new Polish party secre-tary, Władysław Gomułka, managed to reassure them that he would not allow this to happen, but they remained on edge. As revolution was brewing in Hungary, they tried to calm the situation by proclaiming Moscow's readiness to treat its Eastern European dependencies more respectfully than in the past.[19]

---

[14] Records of the PCC meeting on the PHP website, http://www.isn.ethz.ch/php/documents/collection_3/PCC_meetings/coll_3_PCC_1956.htm.

[15] Gen. Ivan Tretiak, quoted in Matthew Evangelista, *"Why Keep Such an Army?,"* pp. 10–11.

[16] Excerpt from speech by Khrushchev at closed session of the Polish party central committee, March 20, 1956, *Cold War International History Project Bulletin* 10 (1998): 31.

[17] Record of Moscow meeting of Warsaw Pact leaders, June 22–23, 1956, 64/230, TsDA.

[18] Referred to in the record of Gomułka–Zhou Enlai conversations, January 11–12, 1957, in Krzysztof Persak, "Polsko-čínské rozhovory v lednu 1957" [The Polish–Chinese Conversations in January 1957], *Soudobé dějiny* [Prague] 4, no. 2 (1997): 337–66, at p. 347.

[19] V.K.Volkov, *Узловые проблемы новейшей истории стран Центральной и Юго-Вос-точной Европы* [Key Problems in the Recent History of the Countries of Central and South-eastern Europe] (Moscow: Indrik, 2000), pp. 170–71.

The landmark Soviet declaration on "relations among socialist countries" of October 30 had important implications for the Warsaw Pact. It announced Moscow's intention to recall its unwanted military advisers from Eastern Europe and start discussions about ending the similarly unwelcome presence of Soviet troops in Poland, Hungary, and Romania. The document further stated that any deployment of troops from one country of the alliance to another should only take place by agreement among all of their governments and with the explicit consent of the government affected. The inclusion of the statement suggested that the Kremlin at that time was still hoping to resolve the mounting Hungarian crisis by political means rather than the use of force.[20]

The Soviet military intervention in Hungary that followed a few days later has been widely but erroneously regarded as having been triggered by the decision of the Budapest government to leave the Warsaw Pact. In reality, the Kremlin had already reversed itself—in the morning of October 31 when it decided to dispatch troops into Hungary—before reformist premier Imre Nagy later in the day told a mass rally in Budapest that his government had begun to negotiate about terminating the country's obligations under the Warsaw Treaty, which in fact it had not done. The declaration by the Nagy government on the following day that announced Hungary's withdrawal from the alliance and asked for recognition of its neutrality under United Nations' auspices was by then a desperate and unsuccessful attempt to stay the Soviet invasion already in progress.[21]

The October 30 declaration was not without potentially disruptive effects on the Romanian and Polish membership in the Warsaw Pact as well. The day after it was issued, which was the day the Soviet party presidium authorized the invasion, the Bucharest politburo decided to demand the withdrawal of Soviet forces and advisers from Romania—as party chief Gheorghe Gheorghiu-Dej, impressed by Moscow's willingness to withdraw them from Austria the year before, had already unsuccessfully attempted to do in August 1955. With Soviet troops pouring into Romania on their way to Hungary, however, the time was not propitious, and Romanians chose not to raise the issue.[22]

The Poles were not similarly inhibited. Even while Hungary was being forcibly reintegrated into the alliance, the Polish general staff established a special commission to seek a radical reform of the Warsaw Pact and renegotiation of Poland's sta-

---

[20] The English text of the declaration is in Csaba Békés, Malcolm Byrne and János M. Rainer, *The 1956 Hungarian Revolution: A History in Documents* (Budapest: Central European University Press, 2002), pp. 300–302.

[21] Document no. 3. Soviet troops already present in Hungary began to move on November 1, and a massive invasion of additional forces through Romania began on November 4. "Как решались 'вопросы Венгрии': Рабочие записи Президиума ЦК КПСС, июль-ноябрь 1956 г." [How the "Hungarian Problems" Were Solved: The Working Minutes of the Presidium of the CPSU Central Committee, July–November 1956], *Istoricheskii Arkhiv*, 1996, nos. 2–3.

[22] Summary of meeting of Romanian politburo, October 31, 1956, file 359/1956, pp. 1–2, Political Bureau Records Group. Archives of the Central Committee of the Romanian Workers' Party, ANR. On the 1955 attempt, undertaken through politburo member Emil Bodnăraş, see Dennis Deletant, *Communist Terror in Romania: Gheorghiu-Dej and the Police State, 1948–1965* (London: Hurst, 1999), pp. 273–74.

tus in it. Deputy chief of staff Gen. Jan Drzewiecki wrote a biting commentary on the controversial Statute of the Unified Command and a devastating legal analysis of the bilateral agreements through which Moscow controlled the long-term development of Poland's armed forces. He found the agreements without legal basis and not really bilateral because they obligated one side only.[23]

In a memorandum urging reform of the Warsaw Pact, Drzewiecki did not question its merit, which he saw in its protecting Poland against the supposed German threat, but rather its provisions. Besides taking exception to the supranational status of the supreme commander and his staff that gave them prerogatives incompatible with Poland's independence and sovereignty, the document lambasted the member-states' "purely formal" representation on the unified command, the arbitrary assignment of their respective military contributions, and the lack of clarity about the conditions under which an ally's forces may be deployed on another's territory—an issue rendered topical by the Hungarian developments.[24]

The Poles separated their radical critique of the Warsaw Pact from their demand for regulation of the Soviet military presence in their country, necessary to maintain Moscow's lines of communication with Soviet forces in East Germany. Invoking an analogy to foreign military personnel stationed in different NATO countries and alluding to the manner in which the U.S. military presence could be made tolerable to such countries as the Philippines, Libya, and Ethiopia, the demand was fortunate in its timing. Faced with worldwide indignation at the bloody suppression of the Hungarian revolution, the Soviet Union granted Poland a status-of-forces agreement more favorable than it accorded any other country. The agreement recognized the host nation's jurisdiction with regard to violations of Polish law by Soviet soldiers and provided for giving the Warsaw government advance notice of any movement of Soviet troops on Polish territory. While the former provision would henceforth often be only honored in its breech, the latter would be generally observed.[25]

Still, for much of 1957, the Poles remained black sheep in the alliance. Khrushchev did not include their representatives among the top party leaders he invited to Moscow in early January to discuss the Hungarian situation and military matters, particularly the sensitive issue of development of Eastern European armed forces.

[23] Document No. 4. "Analiza strony prawnej dokumentu p.t. 'Protokol soveshchaniia po planu razvitiia Vooruzhennykh Sil Polskoi Narodnoi Respubliki na 1955–65 gg.' oraz następnych protokołów wnoszących do niego zmiany" [Analysis of the Legal Aspects of the Document Entitled "Protocol on the Consultation about the Plan for the Development of the Armed Forces of the Polish People's Republic in 1955–65" and Its Subsequent Amendments], November 3, 1956, microfilm (o) 96/6398, reel W-15, Library of Congress, Washington [LC].

[24] Documents Nos. 5 and 6. Cf. "Wykaz zagadnień wojskowych wymagających omówienia i uregulowania na nowych zasadach" [An Outline of Military Problems Requiring Discussion and Regulation according to New Principles], by Drzewiecki, November 8, 1956, KC PZPR 2661/137-38, AAN.

[25] Commentary by Drzewiecki, undated (November–December 1956), KC PZPR 2661/124, AAN. Soviet–Polish status-of-forces agreement, December 17, 1956, Jagdish P. Jain, *Documentary Study of the Warsaw Pact* (Bombay: Asia Publishing House, 1973), pp. 220–225. Memorandum for Polish party presidium on negotiations concerning stationing of Soviet forces, March 8, 1958, KC PZPR 2631, pp. 340–342, AAN.

And when Polish defense minister Marian Spychalski came to the Soviet capital with the Drzewiecki memorandum to discuss reform of the alliance he got nowhere. Marshal Ivan S. Konev, the supreme commander, was incensed at the suggestion that his post should be filled by rotation. "What do you imagine?" he exploded, "That we would make some kind of NATO here?" In trying to reassert control over the Polish military, Moscow preferred bypassing the Warsaw Pact, relying instead on the country's counterintelligence services, still headed by a Soviet officer, and on party channels. As late as August, Khrushchev nevertheless complained to Gomułka that most Polish leaders were hostile to the Soviet Union.[26]

The situation was not so simple. Not only had the Polish communists learned the lesson of Hungary—that leaving the alliance was unacceptable—but they also never forgot how much, despite the current popularity of the Gomułka regime, they depended on Soviet backing to keep themselves in power over their notoriously anti-Soviet subjects. They had wanted to reform the Warsaw Pact with rather than against Moscow, and having failed, strove for their country's recognition as a privileged Soviet ally. By posing as defenders of national interests they could hope to earn popular legitimacy.[27]

This was the kind of reasoning that inspired Gen. Zygmunt Duszyński's project for a separate "front" within the Warsaw Pact under Polish command, as well as the better known plan by foreign minister Adam Rapacki for the creation of a nuclear-free zone in Central Europe. Designed to include, besides Poland, the two German states and Czechoslovakia, the Rapacki Plan, if implemented, would have made Poland and the other countries wards of an international agreement underwritten not only by the Soviet Union but also by the Western powers, thus breaking Poland's exclusive dependence on Moscow for security and loosening its subordination.[28]

The Soviet Union showed little enthusiasm. Although the Rapacki plan was con-

[26] Iordan Baev, "Изграждане на военната структура на организацията на Варшавския договор, 1955–1969 г." [The Building of the Military Structure of the Warsaw Pact Organization], *Voennoistoricheski sbornik* [Sofia] 66, no. 5 (1997): 56–77, at p. 62. Pióro, *Armia ze skazą*, pp. 280–82. Andrzej Albert, *Najnowsza Historia Polski, 1918–1980* [Contemporary History of Poland] (London: Puls, 1991), pp. 805–806. Andrzej Werblan, "Nieznana rozmowa Władysława Gomułki z Nikitą S. Chruszczowem," [An Unknown Conversation between Władysław Gomułka and Nikita S. Khrushchev], *Dziś* [Warsaw], 1993, no. 5, p. 81.

[27] Marcin Zaremba, *Komunizm, legitymizacja, nacjonalizm: Nacjonalistyczna legitymizacja władzy komunistycznej w Polsce* [Communism, Legitimation, and Nationalism: The Nationalistic Legitimation of the Communist Regime in Poland] (Warsaw: Trio, 2001).

[28] Paweł Piotrowski, "Front Polski—próba wyjaśnienia zagadnienia" [An Attempt to Clarify the Issue], in *Wrocławskie Studia z Historii Najnowszej* [Wrocław Studies in Contemporary History], ed. Wojciech Wrzesiński, vol. 6 (Wrocław 1998), pp. 221–233. Piotr Wandycz, "Adam Rapacki and the Search for European Security," in *The Diplomats, 1939–1979*, ed. Gordon A. Craig and Francis L. Loewenheim (Princeton: Princeton University Press, 1994), pp. 289–317. Teresa Łós-Nowak, "Geneza planu Rapackiego utworzenia strefy bezatomowej w Europie Środkowej: źrodła motywacyjne, podstawowe założenia i cele" [The Genesis of Rapacki's Plan of Nuclear-Free Zone in Central Europe: Motives, Principles, and Goals], in idem, ed., *Plan Rapackiego a Bezpieczeństwo Europejskie* [The Rapacki Plan and European Security] (Wrocław: Wydawnictwo Uniwersytetu Wrocławskiego, 1991), pp. 17–35

sistent with its own earlier proposal, the Kremlin did not officially endorse the plan until it became certain that the West would reject it. In his further quest for demilitarization of the Cold War, Khrushchev nevertheless proved ready to risk loosening the Warsaw Pact when he agreed to withdraw Soviet troops from Romania, thus reversing the position he had taken earlier. He apparently did so in order to gratify Tito by making them leave the country neighboring on Yugoslavia, for he gave the first indication of his intention at an August 1957 meeting at Snagov, near Bucharest, where he was courting Tito's friendship. Khrushchev hardly realized that he was depriving himself and his successors of an instrument that could be used to discipline the Romanians, with potentially far-reaching consequences for the integrity of the alliance.[29]

The October 1957 launching of *Sputnik*, the first artificial satellite to orbit the Earth, boosted Soviet prestige and Khrushchev's self-confidence enormously. This had important implications for East–West relations but not for the Warsaw Pact. Its importance as an instrument of alliance management did not increase, because Khrushchev preferred using the Comecon for that purpose, the Soviet bloc's organization for economic development, and his priority was the strengthening of economic rather than military ties within the bloc. It was within the Comecon, rather than within the Warsaw Pact, that multilateral agreements first began to replace the bilateral arrangements that Moscow had traditionally been using to manage relations with its dependent states.

The November summit of world communist leaders in Moscow endorsed Khrushchev's view that "socialism" could prevail over "capitalism" by nonmilitary means. By rejecting the Chinese view that violence was needed, the conference set the terms of the emerging Sino-Soviet rift that would increasingly influence relations within the Warsaw Pact as well. The conference heard Mao Zedong's strategic advice, which in effect wrote off Eastern Europe as expendable. If the Soviet Union were attacked from the west, he recommended, its army should retreat behind the Urals and wait there for about three years, by which time the Chinese would come to the rescue and push the enemy back. "If worst came to worst and half of mankind died," the Chairman added cheerfully, "the other half would remain, while imperialism would be razed to the ground and the world would become socialist."[30]

Although appalled, Khrushchev himself was not above rattling nuclear weapons at the enemy, but sharing them with friends was another matter. In a conversation with the American media magnate, Randolph Hearst, he hinted broadly that the Soviet Union would equip its Eastern European allies with nuclear weapons if the United States were to share them with its NATO allies. Rapacki, in promoting his plan for a nuclear-free zone during a speech in Warsaw, echoed the hint, and the Polish politburo prepared to send specialists to the Soviet Union in the production of missiles. No evidence has been found, however, that Moscow—in contrast to Wa-

[29] Sergiu Verona, *Soviet Troops in Romania, 1944–1958* (Durham: Duke University Press, 1992), pp. 124–127.

[30] Michael Schoenhals, "Document: Mao Zedong: Speeches at the 1957 'Moscow Conference'," *Journal of Communist Studies* 2, no. 2 (1986):121–122.

shington— ever trusted the allies enough to consider putting the doomsday weapons in their hands.[31]

At the end of 1957, Khrushchev resumed his campaign for the simultaneous dissolution of the Warsaw Pact and NATO. Early the next year, the Soviet Union pulled out of the U.N. disarmament subcommittee, disparaging further negotiations proposed by NATO as "sterile." While pressing for a Soviet–American summit, it resurrected the idea of collective security for Europe. On May 15, 1958, Khrushchev summoned at short notice a meeting of the Political Consultative Committee, which had been in recess for more than two years, asking foreign and defense ministers to come as well. A Comecon meeting on economic questions was to take place immediately beforehand. Not since the Warsaw Pact's foundation two years ago had there been such an outburst of Soviet activity.[32]

There was no military urgency for calling the committee into session nor was there a political crisis. On the contrary, ever since the triumphant flight of *Sputnik* the "correlation of forces" had been moving the Soviet way; tangible results, however, were still wanting. For Khrushchev, the urgency was in taking advantage of the favorable international situation by testing whether the West would now be more amenable to his proposals on European security than it had been before.

The proposals were much the same, but new incentives were added. Besides making public a draft of the NATO–Warsaw Pact non-aggression treaty, the PCC approved additional troop cuts. It announced the withdrawal of Soviet forces from Romania, thus giving an example for the United States to emulate in Western Europe. It called for an East–West summit to negotiate on a whole array of contentious issues—the cessation of nuclear tests, the creation of nuclear-free zones in Europe, the German question. Indeed, so vast was the proposed agenda that it invited doubts about whether it could have possibly been meant seriously.[33]

As in 1955, Khrushchev still seems to have believed he could compel the West to negotiate on his terms. The PCC authorized Romania, Poland and Czechoslovakia besides the Soviet Union itself, to conclude non-aggression treaties with NATO on behalf of the of the alliance. When none ensued, Khrushchev three months later followed up with even more improbable proposals: for a treaty of friendship and cooperation between Europe as a whole and the United States, for a radical reduction of all foreign forces in Germany, for an air inspection zone in Central Europe. All of these overtures predictably failed.[34]

[31] Khrushchev–Hearst conversation, November 22, 1957, as reported by the TASS press agency. Speech by Rapacki, December 13, 1957, *Europa-Archiv* 13 (1958): 10485 sq. Minutes of Polish politburo session, March 15, 1958, Antoni Dudek, Aleksander Kochański, and Krzysztof Persak, eds., *Centrum władzy: Protokoły posiedzeń kierownictwa PZPR, wybór z lat 1949–1970* [The Center of Power: Selected Minutes of Sessions of the Polish United Workers' Party Leadership from 1949–1970] (Warsaw: Institute of Political Studies, 2000), pp. 287–91, at pp. 290–91.

[32] "Soviet Reaction to the NATO Heads of Government Conference," January 7, 1958, CM (58) 2, NATO Archives. Khrushchev to Gomułka, May 15, 1958, KC PZPR, XIA/102, AAN.

[33] Document No. 8. Records of the May 24, 1958, PCC meeting on the PHP website, http://www.isn.ethz.ch/php/documents/collection_3/PCC_meetings/coll_3_PCC_1958.htm.

[34] Czechoslovak report on the PCC meeting, June 7, 1958, AÚV KSČ, 02/2/180/244, SÚA, also at http://www.isn.ethz.ch/php/documents/collection_3/PCC_docs/1958/Information580607.pdf.

Neither did the Comecon meeting that preceded the PCC session go well. It was there that Moscow's row with Romania started over Khrushchev's plan for a "division of labor" that would reserve industrial activities to the Soviet bloc's more advanced countries while limiting the others to less rewarding agricultural production and supplying of raw materials. Gheorghiu-Dej's defense of Romania's right to industrialize was a precedent heralding its successful defiance of Moscow in the future.[35]

The initiation by Khrushchev of the Berlin crisis in November 1958 took place against this background of his recently frustrated aspirations. It had been encouraged by two developments outside Europe that let him believe the West was susceptible to pressure as he was himself increasingly susceptible to pressure by the Chinese. The first was the military coup in Iraq in July, where Khrushchev convinced himself the West had abstained from intervening because of his threatening military maneuvers against Turkey. The second development was the shelling a month later of the offshore islands of Quemoy and Matsu by the Chinese, who thereby threatened conflict with the United States, aggravated their relations with Moscow, and challenged Khrushchev to dare the enemy.[36]

The effect in Europe was a reversal of Soviet strategy from inducements to threats. For all intents and purposes, this marked the end of Khrushchev's pursuit of a collective security system that would entail the dissolution of both military groupings—a scheme in which the initial creation and subsequent maintenance of the Warsaw Pact played crucial roles. Ironically, the crisis would not make the alliance redundant but rather change its original purpose in ways Khrushchev neither anticipated nor desired.

3. THE IMPACT OF THE BERLIN CRISIS (1958–1962)

The Warsaw Pact played no substantive part in the launching of the Berlin crisis. In secretly explaining his scheme to eject the Western powers from the divided city, the only utility Khrushchev ascribed to the alliance was to serve as a pretext for keeping Soviet forces in the GDR after his planned renunciation of the World War II agreements on Germany would have removed the legal basis for foreign military presence in the country. On the day he issued the ultimatum, several of the Soviet allies in their capacity as Warsaw Pact members were participating in the opening in Geneva of negotiations with their NATO counterparts about the prevention of

[35] Minutes of Comecon meeting, May 20–23, 1958, J IV 2/202-196/2 Bd 3, SAPMO. John Montias, "Background and Origin of the Rumanian Dispute with Comecon," *Soviet Studies* 16, no. 2 (October 1964): 125–151.

[36] On Soviet–Romanian–Bulgarian maneuvers during the Iraq crisis, Jordan Baev, "The Communist Balkans against NATO in the Eastern Mediterranean Area, 1949–1969," paper presented at the conference, "The Cold War in the Mediterranean," Cortona, October 5–6, 2001. See also Sergei N. Khrushchev, *Nikita Khrushchev and the Creation of a Superpower* (University Park: Pennsylvania State University Press, 2000), pp. 283–93. On the Quemoy–Matsu crisis, see Vladislav Zubok and Constantine Pleshakov, *Inside the Kremlin's Cold War: From Stalin to Khrushchev* (Cambridge: Harvard University Press, 1996), pp. 220–29.

a surprise attack. Those negotiations quickly fell victim to rising East–West tensions.[37]

As the confrontation over Berlin unfolded, without progress toward a resolution, Khrushchev kept alive the idea of a NATO–Warsaw Pact non-aggression treaty, raising the proposal time and again as the prospects for attaining his goals in Germany kept fluctuating. The prospects looked the best after the September 1959 Camp David meeting with President Dwight D. Eisenhower that made Khrushchev to believe that substantial Western concessions were forthcoming. In anticipation of those concessions, he in early 1960 went the farthest ever in his reductions of Soviet conventional forces, which he memorably justified to the party presidium by arguing that having a big army "does not make sense" since no "country or group of countries in Europe would dare to attack us" anyway. He was confidently looking forward to the resolution of the German question on his terms at another summit meeting with Eisenhower.[38]

The upbeat tone of Khrushchev's keynote speech at the February 1960 meeting of the PCC reflected that hopeful outlook. He said that the need for disarmament was now widely accepted and that recent international developments were conducive to it. He particularly welcomed the establishment of the United Nations' ten-nation disarmament committee, singling out for special praise the parity of representation accorded there to the Warsaw Pact and NATO. In addition to the latest troop cuts, Khrushchev raised the possibility of withdrawing Soviet forces from Hungary and Poland. He went so far as to recommend replacing his country's huge standing army by territorial militia—a horrifying prospect for the Soviet generals that would have also spelled the end of any military purpose of the Warsaw Pact.[39]

The PCC meeting ended on a sour note when Chinese observer Kang Sheng, acting on Mao Zedong's special instructions, challenged Khrushchev's rosy view of the international situation and the propriety of his policies. Kang alleged an undiminished threat of U.S. "imperialism" and, in view of the communist world's rising power, the need to confront it by force rather than conciliation. His speech and its publication in Beijing over Soviet protests marked further deterioration of Sino-Soviet relations after Khrushchev's fruitless efforts to keep China within the Soviet fold. These had reportedly included an attempt the preceding June to lure it into the Warsaw

[37] Record of Khrushchev–Gomułka conversation, November 10, 1958, KC PZPR 2631, pp. 449–462, at p. 453, AAN. Jeremi Suri, "America's Search for a Technological Solution to the Arms Race: The Surprise Attack Conference of 1958 and a Challenge for 'Eisenhower Revisionists'," *Diplomatic History* 21 (1977): 417–51.

[38] Draft of non-aggression treaty prepared by Warsaw Pact conference of foreign ministers, May 27–28, 1959, DY/30, 3392, SAPMO. Oleg Grinevskij, *Tauwetter: Entspannung, Krisen und neue Eiszeit* (Berlin: Siedler, 1996), pp. 273–74. Memorandum by Khrushchev to party presidium, December 8, 1959, *Cold War International History Project Bulletin* 8–9 (1996–97): 418–20, at p. 418. Vladislav M. Zubok, "Khrushchev's 1960 Troop Cut: New Russian Evidence," ibid., pp. 416–18.

[39] Report on the PCC meeting by Anton Iugov to Bulgarian party presidium, February 11, 1960, F.1-B, Op. 5, A.E. 415, l. 3-17, TsDA. Czechoslovak report on the meeting, February 20, 1960, AÚV KSČ 02/2 249/332, SÚA. Also on PHP website, http://www.isn.ethz.ch/php/documents/collection_3/PCC_meetings/coll_3_PCC_1960.htm.

Pact at his meeting with defense minister Marshal Peng Dehuai, who had managed to sidetrack it before falling out of Mao's favor, ironically, on suspicion of collusion with Moscow.[40]

Khrushchev's optimism began to falter once he realized that he had misjudged U.S. readiness to yield on Berlin, and eventually gave way to anger, prompting him to scuttle the May 1960 Paris summit with Eisenhower after an American U-2 spy plane had been shot down over Soviet territory. As the Berlin confrontation started escalating, the consequences for the Warsaw Pact were profound, if largely unintended, having been brought about less by design than by the dynamics of a confrontation spinning out of control. They entailed transformation of the alliance from the primarily political tool used by Khrushchev as an accessory to his unorthodox diplomacy into a potential military instrument for use in a conflict with NATO, as well as a more effective mechanism for managing the allies—a task more topical now that the risk of the conflict increased.

Even before Khrushchev's gratuitous provocation of the Berlin crisis, the Soviet general staff had begun to harness Eastern European armies for war, yet without substantial changes in the essentially defensive strategy inherited from the Stalin era. Occasional exercises held under the auspices of the Warsaw Pact in the presence of its supreme commander, Konev, were still organized on a bilateral rather than multilateral basis. Czechoslovakia was the bellwether of strategic changes because of its particular position as a country that bordered directly on NATO territory yet had no Soviet forces stationed on its soil.[41]

As late as April 1960, Soviet officials still "unequivocally emphasized" that "in view of the political situation"—presumably one conducive to a satisfactory Berlin settlement—the Czechoslovak army was not to be equipped with ground-to-ground but only ground-to-air missiles, meaning defensive rather than offensive arms. Six months later, however, the decision was reversed, with an amendment to its long-term procurement program providing for the reception of a variety of hardware for mainly offensive use, notably tactical missiles capable of carrying Soviet nuclear warheads. The Berlin crisis had begun escalating precisely during those six months.[42]

The Soviet military chafed under Khrushchev's pressure for troop reductions. His relationship with Konev—a World War II veteran notorious for his profligate use of

---

[40] Speech by Kang Sheng, February 4, 1960, KC PZPR, 2662/421-34, AAN. Also at http://-www.isn.ethz.ch/php/documents/collection_11/docs/speech_040260.pdf. The Peng Dehuai episode in Lorenz M. Lüthi, "The Sino-Soviet Split," unpublished Ph.D. dissertation, Yale University, 2003, p. 130, citing Liu Xiao, *Chushi Sulian banian* [Eight Years as Ambassador to the Soviet Union] (Beijing: Dangshi ziliao chubanshe, 1998), pp. 109–111.

[41] Documents Nos. 7, 15. and 21.

[42] "Zpráva o návrhu změn v plánu výstavby ČSLA na léta 1961–1965" [Report on the Proposed Changes in the Development Plan of the Czechoslovak People's Army for 1961–1965], November 19, 1960, VS, OS (OL), krab. 7, č.j. 39030/19, VÚA. "Průběh informace náčelníka generálního štábu o důsledcích konsultace" [Information by the Chief of General Staff on the Consequences of the Consultation], October 15, 1960, GŠ-OS, 1960, 0039030/22, VÚA. The nuclear warheads remained stored on Soviet territory but could be brought into Czechoslovakia and fitted on the missiles there within 48 hours.

troops in combat —was particularly bad. In July 1960, Khrushchev replaced him by Marshal Andrei A. Grechko as the Warsaw Pact's supreme commander. He expected Grechko, respected as a professional as well as a disciplinarian, to remain loyal— wrongly, as it would turn out four years later when Grechko would join the conspiracy against Khrushchev. For the time being, however, the generals were kept in line—more than what could be said about the Eastern European allies.[43]

Albania—the most remote of the allied states because of its lack of a common border with any of the others—began to defy Moscow in 1960 for reasons that remain obscure. Soviet overtures toward Yugoslavia, a neighbor with a recent history of designs on Albanian independence, undoubtedly played a role, as did Soviet arrogance in dealing with a country Stalin used to cite as an epitome of insignificance. In any case, Albanians took to harassing Soviet military personnel at the Vlorë naval base—the Warsaw Pact's strategic outpost in the Mediterranean. Khrushchev plotted without success to topple the Albanian leader, Enver Hoxha, who then retaliated by insulting him at Moscow conference of communist parties in November, accusing him of an unwillingness to consult and other improprieties. The Warsaw Pact had not yet been built, and it had already started to crumble.[44]

The March 1961 session of the PCC was, in contrast to the preceding one, an emergency meeting. Hoxha's defense minister, Beqir Balluku, had responded insolently to Grechko's protest against Albanian abuses of Soviet sailors. Khrushchev complained that the Vlorë base was no longer operational, thus damaging the Warsaw Pact's military capability. Although the committee dutifully condemned Albania's behavior the situation subsequently got worse rather than better, leaving the Soviet Union no choice but to withdraw most of its ships from the base while the Albanians snatched some of the submarines. "I trusted them," Khrushchev later fumed. "Who would have thought that after all that they got from us they would spit in our face! Only pirates act like that. Evidently they have it in their blood, after their ancestors."[45]

Khrushchev accused Hoxha of risking to embroil the Warsaw Pact in a war by having raised a false alarm about NATO's imminent attack on Albania. It was Khrushchev himself, however, who was ready to risk war over Berlin as he prepared to escalate his threats during his forthcoming first meeting with President John F. Kennedy in Vienna. Before his departure from Moscow, Khrushchev admitted to the party presidium that although "there is a risk ... the risk that we are taking is justified; if we look at it in terms of a percentage, there is more than a 95 percent probability that there will be no war." This meant he was ready to tolerate a five percent likelihood of it, with the possibility of nuclear escalation. After reiterating the estimate

[43] I.S. Glebov, "Интриги в генеральном штабе" [Intrigues in the General Staff] *Voenno-istoricheskii zhurnal* 1993, no. 11: 37–43, at p. 42

[44] Document No. 13a.

[45] Documents 13b-f. Summary of Khrushchev–Novotný conversation, March 30, 1961, AÚV KSČ, Novotný collection, vol. 31, SÚA. Records of the March 28–29, 1961, PCC meeting on PHP website, http://www.isn.ethz.ch/php/documents/collection_3/PCC_meetings/oll_3_PCC_1961.htm.

at a meeting with the Czechoslovak leaders on his way to Vienna, he hardly made it sound more comforting by adding that "with the Americans, one has to be tough and rely on power, which we have."[46]

The Warsaw Pact took the possibility of war seriously. Already two months before, the PCC had approved a secret resolution providing for a large-scale restructuring and modernization of the alliance's armed forces over the next five years. As immediate measures, it decided to shorten the alert times, create stockpiles of supplies and ammunition, review the organization, size, and equipment of troops, and revise the rules of engagement in the air and at sea. To tighten central control, the unified command would appoint its permanent representatives in each of the member countries, in addition to technical specialists assigned there temporarily at the request of their governments. At the May meeting of the party presidium, Khrushchev also announced his decision "to deliver artillery weapons and basic weapons [to Soviet forces in Germany], and afterwards to bring in troops so that we will have strong positions there." He gave his generals the "deadline of half a year to do it," and "if additional mobilization is necessary," he added casually, "it can be carried out without declaring it."[47]

While the Warsaw Pact allies supported the Soviet plan to conclude a separate peace treaty with East Germany despite the attendant risks, they had different stakes in its accomplishment. Most of them were lukewarm about backing the East Germans, who were the main driving force behind the scheme to capture control of West Berlin. Czechoslovakia was reluctant to underwrite the growing economic cost of the venture. Poland hoped to resume the initiative for a European security treaty that Khrushchev had originally favored but now abandoned. The Romanians dwelt on the need for consultation—as the Albanians had done to no effect.[48]

The June 1961 Vienna summit, where Kennedy stumbled but in the end refused to be intimidated, raised the specter of war more alarmingly than Khrushchev had bargained for. This marked the bankruptcy of his attempted "demilitarization" of the Cold War that has been at the birth of the Warsaw Pact six years before and gave a major impetus to its militarization. It was through its Unified Command that the East European armies were put into combat readiness in preparation for a con-

[46] Minutes of Soviet party presidium meeting, May 26, 1961, *Презндум ЦК КПСС 1954–1964* [Presidium of the CC CPSU, 1954–1964], vol. 1: *Черновые протокольные записи заседаний, Стенограммы* [Draft Minutes and Stenographic Records of Meetings], ed. Aleksandr A. Fursenko (Moscow: Rosspen, 2004), pp. 500–507, at p. 503. English translation at http://millercenter.virginia.edu/pubs/kremlin/kremlin_steno.pdf. Record of Khrushchev's meeting with Czechoslovak party leaders, June 1, 1961, "'Ленин тоже рисковал': Накануне встречи Хрущева и Кеннеди в Вене в июне 1961 г." ["Lenin Also Took Risks": On the Eve of the Khrushchev–Kennedy Meeting in Vienna in June 1961], *Istochnik*, 1998, no. 3: 85–97, at pp. 89–90. English translation at http://www.isn.ethz.ch/php/documents/collection_8/docs/KhrSmolenice_610601.htm.

[47] Document No. 14. Minutes of Soviet party presidium meeting, May 26, 1961, Fursenko, *Президиум ЦК КПСС 1954–1964*, p. 505.

[48] Record of Ulbricht–Novotný meeting, May 23, 1961, ZK SED, J IV 2/202-360 Bd. 1, SAPMO. Minutes of briefing for Bulgarian diplomats, June 5, 1961, F. 1-B, Op. 33, A.E. 662, l. 1, pp. 20 and 29, TsDA, Sofia.

flict likely to result from the conclusion of a separate East German peace treaty Khrushchev remained committed to sign.[49]

The change of Soviet strategy from defensive to offensive under the impact of the Berlin crisis is reflected in several documents in this volume. It was more likely cumulative than sudden, and was completed by 1961. A secret document prepared five years later in the Czechoslovak defense ministry described retrospectively what happened: "The former strategic concept that gave our armed forces the task to 'firmly cover the state border [and] not allow penetration of our territory by enemy forces ...' was changed ... and the Czechoslovak People's Army was assigned an active task."[50] The Warsaw Pact's offensive posture remained in effect for the next twenty-six years.

The mass exodus of East German population through West Berlin's open borders, precipitated by the crisis, highlighted the precarious condition of the communist state. Not without reason, its regime felt acutely threatened by West Germany's rising power and influence in NATO, which it perceived as a military threat. It regarded a secret document obtained by its spies from the files of the Bonn government in 1955 as an authentic and credible blueprint for a takeover of East Germany after a popular revolt in the country would have opened the door to Western forces to march in.[51]

It was paradoxically because of its very weakness that the Warsaw Pact's feeblest member, by drumming up the threat, was able to exert disproportionate pressure on the Soviet Union. Although Walter Ulbricht, the East German leader, could never impose his priorities on Khrushchev, the prospect of East Germany's collapsing was enough to compel the Soviet leader to heed them. This was the rationale behind the building of the Berlin Wall that Ulbricht had been pressing for—not as a substitute of the peace treaty but as its supplement.[52]

In letting the East Germans erect the Wall, which violated the Allied agreements on Berlin, Moscow tried to spread the political risk by presenting it as a Warsaw Pact action, necessitated by the common need for protection against alleged subversive activities emanating from the western part of the city. A special meeting of the alliance's party secretaries only authorized the construction a few days in advance. It is uncertain whether Khrushchev at this time regarded the Wall as a preliminary to the signing of the separate peace treaty—as he led the East Germans to believe

---

[49] Document no. 17. Georgii M. Kornienko, "Упущенная возможность: Встреча Н.С. Хрущева и Дж. Кеннеди в Вене в 1961 г." [A Missed Oppoprtunity: The 1961 Khrushchev–Kennedy Meeting in Vienna], *Novaia i noveishaia istoriia* 1992, no. 2: 97–106. "Umierać za Berlin? Rozmowa z gen. dywizji w stanie spoczynku Brunonem Marchewką, w 1961 r. szefem sztabu Śląskiego Okręgu Wojskowego (ŚOW)" [Dying for Berlin? An Interview with Ret. Gen. Bruno Marchewka, in 1961 the Chief of Staff of the Silesian Military District], *Sztandar Młodych* [Warsaw], 12 August 1991.

[50] Document No. 35.

[51] Document No. 11.

[52] Of the two thorough analyses of the available evidence, Hope M. Harrison, *Driving the Soviets up the Wall: Soviet–East German Relations, 1953–1961* (Princeton: Princeton University Press, 2003) goes farther in interpreting the client-patron relationship as the "tail wagging the dog" than does Michael Lemke, *Die Berlinkrise 1958 bis 1963: Interessen und Handlungsspielräume der SED im Ost-West-Konflikt* (Berlin: Akademie, 1995).

—or whether he had come to regard the blocking of the escape routes to the West as a satisfactory solution of the Berlin problem without a treaty. Most probably he remained undecided, for the Warsaw Pact preparations for a possible military showdown continued unabated.

After the closure of crossings into West Berlin on August 12 and the subsequent building of the Wall had elicited from the Western powers no adverse reaction other than verbal protests, the alliance's defense ministers on September 8 held their first meeting as a group. Besides taking measures to increase defense preparedness and accelerate the modernization of armaments, they approved a major military exercise that would start on September 28 under the code name of "Buria" (Storm), with all their armies performing for the first time as parts of a coalition.[53]

The scenario of the exercise was revealing. Using as its starting point the conclusion of the putative East German peace treaty on October 1, it was suggestive of a timetable of the confrontation Moscow had been preparing for. To outside observers, who could merely see well-publicized alert drills and road marches, it may have appeared as little more than "a hastily organized show of physical force [intended to] imprint [the] image of resolve on NATO." There was more going on, however, at the headquarters of the Soviet forces in Germany at Wünsdorf, on the outskirts of Berlin, where the war game was conducted on maps. To the amazement of some of the Eastern European officers present, the theme was the conquest of Western Europe by the coalition forces in a broad sweep, although it was not made clear whether they would stop in Paris or march all the way to the Pyrenees. There was also some confusion when Marshal Ivan I. Iakubovskii, the director the exercise, identified Luxembourg as the capital of Belgium.[54]

Although the Berlin crisis eventually passed without provoking an armed confrontation—since Khrushchev decided not to sign the East German treaty after all—the plan for an offensive into Western Europe remained its lasting legacy, to be refined and further elaborated. The Warsaw Pact's military functions expanded while its political significance diminished. Apart from the shift from defense to offense, joint maneuvers continued to be held with growing frequency to train the armies for coalition warfare even after the Berlin alert had been called off. The streamlining of their political indoctrination, the establishment of a joint air defense system, and the organization of civil defense along the Soviet model all served to put the alliance more readily at Moscow's disposal.

Meanwhile the Warsaw Pact's geographical reach had diminished because of the exclusion of Albania from its councils in December 1961. The Soviet Union also

[53] The Soviet party central committee approved the closing off of West Berlin on July 1, 1961. Aleksandr A. Fursenko, "Как бюла построена берлинская стена" [How the Berlin Wall Was Built], *Istoricheskie zapiski*, 2001, no. 4: 73–90, at p. 73. But East German documents suggest that Khrushchev must have made the decision much earlier. See Matthias Uhl and Armin Wagner, *Ulbricht, Chruschtschow und die Mauer: Eine Dokumentation* (Munich: Oldenbourg, 2003). Cf. "Как принималось решение о возведении Берлинской стены" [How the Decision on Building the Berlin Wall Was Made], *Novaia i noveishaia istoriia*, 1999, no. 2. Documents Nos. 18 and 19.

[54] Documents Nos. 20a and b. The quote is from Jeffrey Simon, *Warsaw Pact Forces: Problems of Command and Control* (Boulder: Westview Press, 1985), p. 19.

excluded from them the potentially disruptive Chinese observers through a procedural maneuver. It set highest-level representation as a condition of participation in PCC sessions—a requirement humiliating to Mao Zedong and in any case difficult for him to meet because of the distance involved. Protesting indignantly, China had little choice but to terminate its observer role. So did North Vietnam and North Korea without rancor, whereas Mongolia's top leader Yumjaagiyn Tsedenbal, looking to the Warsaw Pact for support against Beijing's designs on his country's territory, found the distance no problem, and continued to attend PCC meetings all the more diligently.[55]

A major gathering of the Comecon in Moscow in June 1962, where Khrushchev again vainly tried to push for a "division of labor," was followed by a more perfunctory session of the PCC. It amounted to little more than issuing repetitive public declarations calling for a NATO–Warsaw Pact non-aggression treaty and a solution to the German question. Khrushchev did not reveal to the allies the more important project that he had already set in motion, with potentially ominous implications for their security—the surreptitious deployment in Cuba of nuclear missiles aimed at the United States.[56]

The Warsaw Pact did not figure at all in the adventure. As the Cuban missiles crisis unfolded, following the discovery of the missiles, Romanian minister of defense Leontin Sălăjan later remembered that "Marshal Grechko ordered increasing the combat readiness of our army, while party and state leaders were not informed and did not give their agreement." Only *post factum*, once the scare was over, did Khrushchev see it fit to inform the stunned Eastern European leaders at a special briefing that the outbreak of a nuclear war had been but "a few minutes away." The brush with a disaster in Cuba highlighted the nuclear weapons' growing, yet elusive, role in the relations not only between the two hostile alliances but also within each one of them.[57]

4. "NUCLEAR ROMANTICISM" (1962–1965)

While Khrushchev was trying to exact concessions from the West by nuclear bluff, the Warsaw Pact was increasingly preparing for nuclear combat. As long as Stalin's defensive strategy, with its reliance on conventional forces, remained in effect,

[55] CPSU central committee to the Chinese communist party central committee, September 15, 1961, KC PZPR, XIA/103, pp. 490–493, AAN. Chinese party central committee to East German and other central committees, November 20, 1961, DY 30/3386, SAPMO. Ho Chi Minh to Ulbricht, December 3, 1961, DY 30/3386, SAPMO. Tsedenbal to Gomułka, April 12, 1962, KC PZPR, XIA/103, pp. 503–504, AAN. Also on PHP website, "China and the Warsaw Pact under Mao and Khrushchev," http://www.isn.ethz.ch/php/collections/coll_11.htm.

[56] For records of the June 7, 1962, PCC meeting, see PHP website, http://www.isn.ethz.ch/php/documents/collection_3/PCC_meetings/coll_3_PCC_1962.htm.

[57] Sălăjan to Ceauşescu, May 9, 1966, V2, file 4/34, pp. 124–125, Romanian Military Archives. Also in *Romania and the Warsaw Pact, 1955–1989*, ed. Mircea Munteanu, vol. 1 (Washington: Cold War International History Project, 2002), pp. 273–81, at p. 280. Report by Novotný to Czechoslovak party central committee, November 2, 1962, AÚV KSČ 01/98/85, SÚA.

little effort had been spent on preparing Eastern European armies to fight under nuclear conditions. Once nuclear bombs became more readily available, however, Soviet planners began to design exercises on the assumption that they could and should be used in offensive operations. They presumed that the advancing forces would be able to blast their way quickly through Western Europe while dozens of the bombs would be detonating all around, and even benefit from the devastation.[58]

Such was the "nuclear romanticism" of the period, as Soviet general Valentin V. Larionov quaintly dubbed it in retrospect. "It was like in the fairytale," Polish Gen. Tadeusz Pióro recalled about the exercises that he used to attend. "At the time of the battle, clouds burst, and the downpour made the enemy troops soaking wet while our own became pleasantly refreshed." Absurd though they were, the scenarios were nevertheless meant seriously. There cannot be a doubt that the plans that had been drawn were intended to be put into effect if war came, whatever the chances that they could actually be successfully implemented.[59]

The shift to offensive strategy required closer integration of the Eastern European armies into Soviet planning. Already the first of the joint exercises that served this purpose, "Buria," indicated what was in store for them if war were to come. The term doubled as the code name for a massive nuclear strike to be delivered against NATO, ostensibly to pre-empt the enemy's attempt to deliver it first. Just how sincerely the Warsaw Pact planners believed that NATO would be the first to strike, and if so, how certain they were that pre-emption would work, were tantalizing questions for Western strategists. The inside evidence we have now provides a better insight into the Soviet thinking that inspired the planning though hardly conclusive answers to the questions—if there ever were such answers.[60]

According to Gen. Anatolii I. Gribkov, who had been in charge of shipping the missiles to Cuba before he became the Warsaw Pact's chief of staff, the Cuban experience resulted in a shift in Soviet planning from the increasingly improbable strategic nuclear exchange between the superpowers to the more easily imaginable war in Europe—in which the Warsaw Pact would be prominently involved. The official Soviet line was that such a war would be started by NATO and would inevitably become nuclear; more importantly, the initial NATO aggression was also the standard assumption in all Warsaw Pact exercises. The definition of that aggression, however, was fuzzy. In trying to justify pre-emption, Konev offered the spurious argument that since NATO had been conducting its exercises on the wrong assumption that the Warsaw Pact was planning to attack it, the Warsaw Pact must exercise on the supposedly right assumption that NATO was the one planning to attack.[61]

---

[58] Document No. 16.

[59] Larionov quoted in William E. Odom, *The Collapse of the Soviet Military* (New Haven: Yale University Press, 1998), p. 70. Pióro, *Armia ze skazą*, p. 191.

[60] Document No. 12.

[61] Statement by Gribkov, March 25, 1995, *Global Competition and the Deterioration of U.S.–Soviet Relations, 1977–80: The Carter–Brezhnev Project: A Conference of U.S. and Russian Policymakers and Scholars Held at the Harbor Beach Resort, Fort Lauderdale, Florida, March 23–26, 1995* (Providence: Watson Institute for International Studies, Brown University, 1995), p. 186. Document No. 9.

The rationalization of this view was ideological. According to the Marxist–Leninist doctrine, whatever defensive plans the West may have had, "objectively" they were irrelevant since a capitalist alliance was aggressive by nature, regardless of any "subjective" disposition of those in charge. For the same ideological reasons, the plans of the communist alliance, whatever the individual disposition of their authors and despite their supposedly defensive intent, exuded a militancy and even exhilaration about war that were rarely to be found on the Western side. A confidential study, prepared in 1964 by the chief of the Soviet military intelligence, Gen. Petr I. Ivashutin, for Marshal Matvei V. Zakharov, the head of the General Staff Academy, is a case in point.[62]

Ivashutin described war as a welcome opportunity rather than a deplorable necessity. He contended that, thanks to the availability of nuclear weapons, "complete annihilation of the imperialist coalition within a short time" is no longer "pure adventurism" but "an entirely realistic task." There will always be "enough time to launch the required massive number of combat-ready missiles before the first detonations of enemy nuclear missiles on the territory of the socialist countries" would take place. And even though a few might get through, most of them supposedly would not, for the Soviet Union had—in his view if not in reality—solved the problem of how to destroy ballistic missiles in flight. In any case, whatever the damage either side would suffer, the "imperialistic camp is more sensitive to strikes against [nonmilitary] targets than is the socialist community."[63]

In the prospective European conflagration, Moscow's allies were assigned different tasks. The 1964 war plan of the Warsaw Pact's "Czechoslovak Front" is the only such plan of either alliance that has come to light so far. According to the plan, the Czechoslovak army, was supposed to be capable of sweeping through southern Germany, and reach Lyon, in the heart of France, on the ninth day of hostilities. It had already prepared leaflets to drop that encouraged NATO soldiers to surrender and orders that admonished the populace to welcome the "liberators."[64]

The East German army, never to be relied upon in engaging West Germany's *Bundeswehr*, was mainly to serve as an auxiliary to the advancing Soviet troops, leaving more critical missions to the other armies. Polish plans envisaged landings in Denmark by crack paratroopers and amphibious units as well as offensive operations against West Germany. In one of the exercises, for example, the city of Hannover would surrender to the Polish army, whose political commissars would then join with "progressive" local forces, including the Social Democrats, in setting up a local government. The Poles were expected to roll alongside their Soviet brothers-in-

---

[62] P.H. Vigor, *The Soviet View of War, Peace and Neutrality* (London: Routledge & Kegan Paul, 1975). "Материал по развитии военного искусства в условиях ведения ракетно-ядерной войны по современных представлениях" [Material Concerning Contemporary Views of the Application of Military Art in the Conduct of Nuclear War], Ivashutin to Zakharov, August 28, 1964, pp. 396–395, copy of excerpts from the original at the Central Archives of the Ministry of Defense of Russia, in the Volkogonov collection, container no. 30, Manuscript Division, Library of Congress; also at http://www.isn.ethz.ch/php/documents/collection_1/docs/ivashutin-I.pdf.

[63] Quotes from the Ivashutin study on pp. 338–40, 345, 358, 370, 373–74.

[64] Documents Nos. 27, and 26

arms into the Low Countries, crushing the Dutch and Belgian armies and not stopping until they reached the English Channel.[65]

On the southern flank, the Hungarian army's task was to take part in an operation during which Munich, Verona, and Vicenza would all be incinerated by nuclear bombing, as would Vienna, the capital of neutral Austria. The plans took the violation of Austrian neutrality for granted—presumably first by NATO "under the cover of the Austrian armed forces," and afterward by invading Hungarian and Czechoslovak troops as well. But at least one field manual anticipated their unprovoked passage through "neighboring territory," in order to bypass NATO's nuclear minefields in West Germany. In the Balkans, Bulgaria was to be engaged against Turkey and Greece. Operations against Yugoslavia, jointly with Romania and Hungary, were contingent on Belgrade's conduct. The nonaligned communist Yugoslavia was a country with a respectable army and an advanced territorial defense system, which made it something of a wild card in the strategic calculations of both alliances.[66]

The war described in Warsaw Pact documents was to be initiated by the West in a singularly foolhardy way. Contrary to military common sense, NATO would presumably decide to attack despite its own estimate that it was inferior in both manpower and firepower by the ratio of 3:2. Moreover, the preparations for its "surprise" attack would be so poorly concealed as to give the enemy ample warning, thus allowing the Warsaw Pact forces to meet the attack fully combat ready. In a 1965 Czechoslovak war game that enacted what would presumably happen, the commanders, "having declared alarm, were able to lead the bulk of their forces away from the impact of the enemy nuclear strike, took advantage of the favorable situation, and transitioned into an offensive operation following the previously prepared plan."[67]

In reality, if war were to come the Soviet allies would have to bear the brunt of it. The Warsaw Pact exercises admitted that NATO's nuclear bombs would be falling on their territories but were typically silent about any bombing of Soviet territory, presuming that the putative enemy attack would be turned into a rout long before it reached Soviet borders. This may have been Moscow's wishful thinking. In the meantime, to be sure, Eastern Europe would be thoroughly devastated although estimating the extent of its devastation was a matter of pure guesswork—as was the case with comparable Western estimates as well. According to the irreverent Gen. Pióro, "army chemists, posing as nuclear experts while possessing but preschool knowledge

    [65] Paweł Piotrowski, "Desant na Danię" [The Landing Operation in Denmark], *Wprost* [Warsaw], June 25, 2002; English translation, in "A Landing Operation in Denmark," http://www.isn.ethz.ch/php/documents/collection_12/texts/piotrowski.htm. Documents Nos. 22, 23, 73.

    [66] "Vojensko-politická charakteristika a stav operačně-taktické přípravy armád NATO" [Military and Political Characteristics and the Operational and Tactical Condition of NATO Armies], 1963, MNO VŽV kr. 192, 17/1/1, VÚA. "Jaderné miny americké armády, jejich zjišťování a zneškodňování" [US Army Nuclear Mines: Their Detection and Deactivation], February 15, 1967, p. 52, Vševojsk-2–5, VÚA. Document No. 31.

    [67] "Úvodní přednáška řídícího cvičení VESNA" [An Introductory Lecture by the Director of the "Vesna" Exercise], September 6, 1965, and "Výsledky schválení zámyslu VESNA" [The Results of the Approval of the "Vesna" Exercise Scenario], MNO, GŠ-OS 1967, HSPV; sg. 4/4-21/106 and 29, č.j. 0017600/29/19, VÚA.

of the subject" concluded that the damage would be tolerable. Not only would the troops keep heroically fighting on to win but also ordinary citizens would stoically go about their daily business to support the front.[68]

Czechoslovak damage assessments expected that some factories would be destroyed completely or substantially yet industrial production would continue. Hungarian estimates painted a more realistic picture, showing that "with the exception of Budapest, Ózd, and Salgótarján, all significant industrial cities have been destroyed or seriously damaged. About 1 million people have died and 1 million have been injured." The Hungarians were rare in admitting that the enemy's goal to paralyze the economy, cut off supplies to the army, and demoralize the population would have in fact been "largely accomplished." In 1966, one of their studies made it clear that there was no defense against a surprise nuclear attack.[69]

The Warsaw Pact's operational plans originated in the Soviet general staff. Most of the surviving Eastern European officers in a position to know have been evasive about how much they were involved in their elaboration and intended execution. Polish general Tadeusz Tuczapski has been exceptional in describing candidly the peremptory and casual manner in which the Soviet superiors ensured their Eastern European subordinates' complicity in what amounted to a planned mass sacrifice of their troops as cannon fodder. Concern about this dismal prospect was a smoldering issue behind the Warsaw Pact's façade of solidarity, particularly in the aftermath of the Cuban missile crisis that dramatized the perils of not only Moscow's nuclear adventurism but also of the irresponsibility of some of its clients.[70]

Cuban leader Fidel Castro tried to persuade Khrushchev to use strategic nuclear weapons against the United States if American troops invaded the island. Having failed to obtain such a commitment, he then tried to lay hands on the Soviet tactical nuclear missiles that that had been deployed in Cuba unbeknownst to Washington, but did not succeed either. After he had to acquiesce in their withdrawal, Castro during his visit to the Soviet Union in May 1963 made a bid for his country's admission to the Warsaw Pact, which would have entangled its members in any military conflict between Havana and Washington. Khrushchev astutely turned him down with the explanation that entry into the alliance would allow the Americans to claim that Cuba was a Soviet satellite and harm rather than help its security.[71]

Two months later, however, Khrushchev took the opposite view on Mongolia's application to join the Warsaw Pact, which raised the prospect of extending its protection to a prospective battlefield with China. In the interim, the Sino-Soviet split had reached the point of no return during inconclusive talks between the two par-

[68] Pióro, *Armia ze skazą* p. 191. Document No. 22a.

[69] "Předběžné vyhodnocení atomových úderů..." [A Prelimnary Evaluation of the Effects of Atomic Strikes...], MNO 1963, GŠ/VD, sg. 5/2/6, VÚA. Report by the head of the materiel and technology division of the Hungarian Ministry of Defense, June 6, 1963, Records of the Hungarian People's Army Headquarters First Group Directorate, 1964, Box 9 Unit 3, pp. 1–9, War History Archive, Budapest; also at http://www.isn.ethz.ch/php/documents/collection_4/docs/11_060663_-T.htm. Document No. 38.

[70] Document No. 22 b.

[71] Aleksandr Fursenko and Timothy Naftali, *"One Hell of a Gamble": Khrushchev, Castro, and Kennedy, 1958–1964* (New York: Norton, 1997), pp. 331–334.

ties in Moscow in July. Even while the talks were still in progress Khrushchev supported the application, but both Romania and Poland took exception, although it is not clear to what extent they communicated their objections to Moscow.[72]

A more important reason why Khrushchev subsequently reversed himself and let the Mongolian application lapse was the wrong signal that the Warsaw Pact's expansion would have sent the Western powers at a time he was bent on rapprochement with them. Once his relations with China proved beyond repair, he proceeded toward signing the limited nuclear test ban treaty with the United States and Great Britain—an act decried by Beijing as a sellout and impediment to its own nuclear ambitions. The East Europeans gave full support to the treaty, which put constraints, however limited, on the runaway growth of the superpowers' nuclear arsenals. But the next agreement that was being negotiated between Moscow and Washington—the nonproliferation treaty aimed at preventing the spread of the doomsday weapons to additional countries— became contentious within the alliance.[73]

At issue was not only the acquisition of the bomb by China, which could hardly be prevented, but also the sharing of U.S. nuclear weapons by the NATO allies, particularly Germany, under the Multilateral Force (MLF) project that became highly controversial among them, and thus easier to influence. In opposing the Soviet draft of the nonproliferation treaty, Romania supported Chinese criticism of the superpowers' reluctance to divest themselves of their nuclear arsenals. It was trying to project itself internationally outside of the Warsaw Pact by cultivating relations with both Beijing and Washington. In October 1963, foreign minister Corneliu Mănescu informed Secretary of State Dean Rusk in deepest secrecy that in the event of a nuclear confrontation between the superpowers Romania would remain neutral—a stunning act of disloyalty to the Soviet alliance without parallel in anything that ever happened in NATO.[74]

Nor was the Soviet Union a paragon of loyalty to its allies. In another remarkable disclosure hidden from the public eye at the time, two days before Mănescu 's meeting with Rusk, Moscow revealed to the Polish and East German leaders its intention to acquiesce in the MLF by accepting Washington's assurances that any nuclear weapons in West German hands would remain firmly under U.S. control. This apparent bid for American support against China's looming nuclear threat appalled both Gomułka and Ulbricht, for whom the greater worry was the perceived West German threat. Gomułka took it upon himself to lecture Khrushchev about the need for reconciliation with Beijing.[75]

---

[72] Documents Nos. 24 and 25. Minutes of meeting of Romanian politburo, July 18, 1963, CC PCR, Cancelarie, 39/1963, f. 122–28, National Archives of Romania, Bucharest, also at http://www.-isn.ethz.ch/php/documents/collection_11/docs/180763.pdf.

[73] Report by Kádár to Hungarian politburo, July 31, 1963, MOL-M-KS-288.f.5/309.őe, Hungarian National Archives, Budapest, also at http://www.isn.ethz.ch/php/documents/collection_3/-PCC_docs/1963/1963_2.pdf.

[74] Raymond L. Garthoff, "When and Why Romania Distanced Itself from the Warsaw Pact," *Cold War International History Project Bulletin* 5 (1995): 111.

[75] Douglas Selvage, *The Warsaw Pact and Nuclear Nonproliferation, 1963–1965*, Cold War International History Project working paper no. 32 (Washington: Woodrow Wilson International Center for Scholars, 2001), pp. 20–35.

In view of Khrushchev's tendency toward a rapprochement with West Germany, his overthrow in October 1964 by an intraparty conspiracy understandably gratified the two leaders of the Warsaw Pact's strategically crucial "northern tier." The Soviet military, notably the alliance's supreme commander and Khrushchev's former protégé, Grechko, had supported, though not initiated, the plot against him, which was mainly motivated by other than military reasons. The Warsaw Pact was not high on the minds of the new Kremlin leaders as they tried to consolidate their power. It was left to Ulbricht to take the next step by calling for a session of the PCC—the first time such a call came from anywhere else but Moscow.[76]

Raising alarm at the MLF, Ulbricht wanted the allies to counter it by coordinated diplomatic action to sway individual NATO states against the project. East Germany attempted to shape the agenda of the forthcoming meeting by supplying drafts of the nonproliferation treaty and a joint declaration against the nuclear arming of West Germany. Leonid I. Brezhnev, Khrushchev's successor as Soviet party general secretary, endorsed Ulbricht's initiative in hopes of rallying the alliance behind the new Soviet leadership. Already the preparations for the meeting, however, revealed an unprecedented amount of disagreement about perceptions, priorities, and policies.[77]

Ulbricht tried to pre-empt the "Gomułka Plan"—a variation on the Rapacki Plan prepared by the Polish leader under his own name, which proposed freezing the superpowers' nuclear arsenals in both German states. Regarding the proposal as not conducive to advancing East Germany's paramount goal—international recognition—Ulbricht pressed instead for a ban on nuclear weapons that the two German states would together underwrite as equals—an idea Gomułka derided as unrealistic. Other allies cared less about German sharing of nuclear weapons than about good relations with the Bonn government. With an eye on lucrative West German trade, Hungary's János Kádár counseled against pressing too hard on the MLF. So did Romania's Gheorghiu-Dej, arguing plausibly, if disingenuously, that taking a common stand against it would only have the effect of prompting NATO to close its ranks.[78]

When the PCC finally gathered in late January 1965 for its most contentious meeting to date, the first since Khrushchev's ouster, the MLF was all but dead, yet the discord it helped stir over related issues persisted. Faulting the East German nonproliferation draft as unacceptable to China, the Romanians hinted they would not sign it unless Beijing had been consulted. Kádár proposed to do so by restoring the presence of Chinese observers at the alliance's meetings. In vain did Brezhnev

---

[76] Ulbricht to Brezhnev, October 20, 1964, DY 30/3387, SAPMO.

[77] Draft PCC declaration, end October 1964, MfAA A-9673, PAAA. Brezhnev to Ulbricht, November 4, 1964, DY 30/3387, SAPMO. Draft nonproliferation agreement, November 6, 1964, DY 30/3387, SAPMO.

[78] Gheorghiu-Dej to Ulbricht, November 18, 1964, DY 30/3387, SAPMO. "Stellungnahme des Politbüros des ZK der SED zur Notwendigkeit einer baldigen Einberufung des Politischen Beratenden Ausschusses des Warschauer Vertrages," November 24, 1964, DY 30/3387, SAPMO. Minutes of meeting of deputy ministers of foreign affairs, December 10, 1964, MfAA A-9673, PAAA. Selvage, *The Warsaw Pact and Nuclear Nonproliferation*, pp. 158–159.

enjoin the Romanians not to disrupt unity. Unable to agree on the draft, the committee merely issued a tepid statement against proliferation.[79]

Consultation was the keyword. Gomułka retrospectively condemned Khrushchev's habit of not consulting. Ulbricht proposed that the foreign ministers regularly consult about policy—as their Western counterparts had been doing. Kádár pointed out that not only NATO but also Asian and African ministers mutually consulted at the U.N., but the Soviet Union and its allies did not. Brezhnev agreed that "we need to give an expression to our unity and striving for more concerted work." He lent support to the Hungarian proposal for a Warsaw Pact council or committee to coordinate foreign policy—a proposal Kádár had made to Khrushchev without results.[80]

The Romanians retorted that they were "for consultation but against the creation of any organs." They took exception to Moscow's practice of submitting drafts at short notice, expecting quick approval. Gheorghiu-Dej then criticized as misguided Brezhnev's proposed strategy of responding to NATO's armament plans by adopting military countermeasures rather than by seeking détente. Romania appropriated to itself Khrushchev's idea of a simultaneous dissolution of both military blocs and made it into a staple of its policy. Before the PCC disbanded, the Soviet Union felt compelled to convene a caucus of its faithful to discuss common strategy without the Romanians—no good omen for the unity Brezhnev professed to be striving for.

The conference also had to deal with an incendiary 21-page message from the government on Tirana, which urged the PCC to condemn Moscow for its hostility against Albania. The message spelled out extravagant conditions the Albanians wanted to be met before they would agree to resume participation in the alliance. They included not only restitution of all the damage the Soviet Union had purportedly inflicted upon them but also abrogation of the 1963 nuclear test ban treaty and, for good measure, the provision of all of the Warsaw Pact member-states with nuclear weapons. In response, the committee made Albania's temporary exclusion final.[81]

The quarrelsome gathering set the tone for years to come. The Romanian dissidence came into the open, and became well-known, but the more subtly independent ways of other countries remained largely out of sight. While the Romanians strove for maximum freedom of action by reducing Soviet role in a weaker Warsaw Pact, the Polish communists sought more influence in shaping Soviet policy through a stronger alliance. Their assertion, with Moscow, of larger common interests against the special interests of East Germany contrasted with Romania's advocacy, against

[79] Romanian records of PCC meetings on January 19–20, 1965, dated January 26, 1965, CC PCR, Secția Relații Externe, 15/1965, f. 5–91 and f. 112–27, and of drafting committee meeting on January 19, 1965, 16/1965, f. 217–36, ANIC, part also at http://www.isn.ethz.ch/php/documents/collection_3/PCC_docs/1965/1965_10.pdf. Communiqué, January 20, 1965, Jain, *Documentary Study of the Warsaw Pact*, pp. 405–409.

[80] Document No. 30. Complete record at http://www.isn.ethz.ch/php/documents/collection_3/PCC_docs/1965/1965_9.pdf.

[81] Document No. 29. Resolution on non-participation of Albania in the Warsaw Pact, January 19, 1965, 32, A.E. 7, p. 86, Archives of the Ministry of Foreign Affairs, Sofia., also at http://www.isn.ethz.ch/php/documents/collection_3/PCC_docs/1965/1965_0119.pdf.

Moscow, of separate national interests. The challenge for the Kremlin consisted in so reforming the alliance that dissent could be contained and, as in NATO, made a proof of strength rather than a source of weakness.

5. THE ALLIANCE IN CRISIS (1965–68)

The Warsaw Pact's crisis coincided with NATO's most severe crisis. Not only did the MLF fail but the Western alliance also became mired in disputes about its basic strategy. In view of growing Soviet ability to deliver nuclear bombs on the American homeland, doubts spread about the firmness of Washington's commitment to Europe's defense. The U.S.-promoted concept of flexible response, to replace that of massive retaliation, was intended to reassure Europeans by widening the range of fighting options and lifting the threshold between conventional and nuclear war. To its European critics, however, whose greater concern was the threshold between war and peace, the new strategy was not reassuring because it increased the likelihood of their countries becoming a battlefield precisely at a time when the prospects of détente appeared to be brightening.

Soviet strategists, too, were interested in expanding their fighting options, and the development of the Warsaw Pact's military structures since the 1961 climax of the Berlin crisis provided them with a framework for doing so even while NATO's adoption of flexible response remained undecided. In Brezhnev, unlike Khrushchev a champion and favorite of the military, Soviet generals found a leader more responsive to their aspirations than his predecessor had been. At the same time, in proceeding with the transformation of the alliance from mainly a tool of diplomacy and bloc management into a more effective military instrument, the Kremlin felt compelled to respect and conciliate the allies more than it had been accustomed before.

After preliminary consultations with the allies, Moscow launched in January 1966 a project for reform of the Warsaw Pact from above. Addressing a chronic sore issue, it proposed to clarify the powers of the supreme commander and his staff in peace time while leaving their extent in war time to be clarified later. It called for the establishment of a military council as the PCC's subsidiary for defense planning as well as a committee on technology to supervise research and development. The former would allow for a smoother management of the member-states' armed forces than had been the case thus far by means of the widely resented arbitrary directives from Moscow. The latter would facilitate modernization and standardization of equipment.

There were limits to the proposed reform. The thrust of the innovations was toward creating additional institutions without altering substantially the operation of the existing ones. In Soviet view, expressed at a meeting of the chiefs of staff in Moscow convened to acquaint them with the intended changes, "well-established practices"— those criticized by Poland's reform-minded generals in 1956 and now increasingly irritating to other allies as well—were to be kept. Not only the Romanians but also the Hungarians and the Czechoslovaks disagreed, demanding changes that would ensure effective participation in the command system by all the members of the alliance.[82]

A comparison of the proposed institutions with their NATO counterparts shows the limits of Soviet tolerance. As in NATO, the prospective military council was to be an extended arm of the alliance's supreme political body. But there was a difference in kind: the North Atlantic Council served as the core consultative and decision-making body involving actively all the nations whereas the Soviet-run PCC amounted, in Rapacki's apt description, to "sporadic summit meetings, usually ill-prepared and given to adopting rather spectacular resolutions." There was another telling distinction between NATO's collegial Military *Committee* and the *council* envisaged by Moscow. The NATO committee made policy decisions on behalf of the member-states through their chiefs of staff, whereas the Warsaw Pact variant was merely to complement the Soviet-controlled supreme command—itself a tool of the Moscow general staff—with the defense ministers performing but advisory roles, thus creating an appearance of participation without substance.[83]

When Grechko first submitted the draft statutes of the Warsaw Pact's proposed new military institutions to the chiefs of staff, he expected expeditious approval. At the Berlin conference of deputy foreign ministers that immediately followed, Soviet representative Leonid F. Ilichev then presented analogous statutes for the PCC, as well the for prospective committee of foreign ministers and a permanent secretariat. Intended to coordinate foreign policy, the former would approximate one of the main functions of the North Atlantic Council, whereas the latter was to fill another important void that distinguished the Soviet alliance from its Western rival.[84]

Far from sailing through as easily as Moscow had anticipated, the proposals became stalled when both meetings ended without agreement on a single point, even on whether to have further discussion. The attempt to tighten the alliance prompted the Romanians to question its fundamental principles, particularly the subordination of the national armed forces to the will and whim of the Soviet supreme commander. None of the other allies dared or desired to go that far. They did not want, nor could they hope, to make the Warsaw Pact into another NATO. They nevertheless tried to remake it in ways that would allow them to put limits on Moscow's crude and intrusive domination, much as NATO's junior partners did on the subtler and less pervasive primacy of Washington.

The Czechoslovaks wanted the military council to function as a subcommittee of the PCC, to ensure common strategy and planning—much as NATO's Military Committee did while allowing for input by its members. Without illusions that this could work, the Romanians instead sought a committee that, by giving each of its members the right of veto, would be able to block the Soviet supreme commander. Finding no support for the idea at the deputy foreign ministers meeting, Romania's representative Mircea Malița stalled, pleading lack of a mandate to negotiate. His

---

[82] Report on the February 4–9, 1966, meeting of chiefs of staff in Moscow, undated [February 1966], GŠ-OS 1966, 0039042/24, p. 2, VÚA; texts of Soviet proposals, VA-01/40404, pp. 127–141, BA-MA, and ZPA J IV 2/202-259 Bd 11, SAPMO. Documents Nos. 32 and 33 a-b.

[83] Document No. 34a.

[84] Document No. 37.

Polish colleague, Marian Naszkowski, was right to infer that Bucharest sought to avoid additional ties with the Warsaw Pact, loosen the existing ones, and finally "paralyze the alliance and transform its organs into noncommittal discussion clubs."[85]

The Poles took the lead in opposing Romanian obstructionism while trying to bolster the alliance by introducing some of the key features of NATO. Rapacki favored the creation of a genuine policymaking body analogous to the North Atlantic Council, while limiting the PCC to the consultative role implied in its name. The latter would thus assume the function of the council of foreign ministers that Moscow desired as well. Rapacki welcomed the Soviet proposal for a permanent secretariat, but wanted it to be substantive, "set up at a proper level and with proper composition"— meaning genuinely representative and capable of preparing the agenda for the Council; in short, much like the NATO secretariat. He thought it should be headed by a political personality of high standing. Unlike the supreme commander, that person need not necessarily be a Soviet citizen but should be someone "disconnected from state functions in his own country." This would have left room for respected politicians from the smaller countries—like Rapacki himself, or like most of the NATO general secretaries. In order to "emphasize the political vitality of the Warsaw Pact," Rapacki concluded, "the new measures ... should be made public"—not the preferred Soviet way.[86]

The Polish ministry of defense expounded its ideas in a separate memorandum on military matters. Without casting doubt on the need for the alliance and Moscow's leading role in it, the memorandum called for changes in the structure and operation of the supreme command that were likely to be acceptable to the Soviet Union. Similarly, it agreed that "the position of the general staff of the Unified Armed Forces as a command organ in war time is still a matter too premature to be considered." The document supported the Soviet concept of a military council, but proposed to supplement it with an advisory committee of defense ministers, reminiscent of NATO's Defense Planning Committee, that would formalize the practice of their periodic meetings. Poland also sought more input into the development of its armed forces while specifically excluding the Soviet-owned nuclear weapons from purview by the alliance's members, provided a way could be found to "define the obligatory scope and method for the use of the strategic attack forces in the common defense of the Treaty members."[87]

The oblique reference was to the hot issue of control over nuclear weapons. During the discussion of Soviet reform proposals, Romanian chief of staff Gen. Ion Gheorghe recalled how Moscow, during the Cuban missile crisis, had placed the Warsaw Pact members in "a situation that would lead them to a state of war, without their own parties and governments as the supreme organs of state power being able to make the appropriate decisions about it." The Soviet Union never revealed its contingency plans to its allies, some of whom, however, did not seem to mind the "umbrella" that nuclear

---

[85] "Vojenská poradní rada" [The Military Advisory Council], undated [February 1966], GŠ-OS 1966, 0039042/64, VÚA. Naszkowski to Rapacki, February 17, 1966, KC PZPR 2948, pp. 58–69, at p. 68, AAN.

[86] Document No. 34 a.

[87] Document No. 34 b.

weapons provided to them. An agreement concluded in December 1965 envisaged installation of Soviet nuclear-armed missiles at three sites in Czechoslovakia, thus altering the practice of keeping the ordnance outside the country, to be transferred and fitted onto the missiles only in an emergency. Moscow had signed a similar agreement with Hungary before and would sign one with Poland later. Their implementation, however, was shrouded in such secrecy that even after forty years generals in a position to know would contradict each other in their testimonies about whether any Soviet nuclear weapons had ever been in their countries at all.[88]

Instead of demanding access to nuclear weapons—something that Moscow was certain to rule out anyway—the Poles sought changes in the international environment that would reduce the likelihood of the weapons being used in the first place and make Soviet military supremacy less onerous as well. This was the gist of Rapacki's diplomacy, congenial to West Europeans' uneasiness about U.S. military supremacy regardless of their loyalty to NATO—as exemplified by NATO's former secretary general and current foreign minister of Belgium, Paul-Henri Spaak. Rapacki went to Brussels to solicit Spaak's support for his proposal to the U.N. to convene a European security conference, with both Soviet and U.S. participation, that would ban further deployment of nuclear weapons on the Continent. Poland became an ardent promoter of such a conference.[89]

With decisive help from the Poles, Moscow made progress toward reforming the Warsaw Pact the way it wanted. The Poles supported the Soviet plans for a secretariat and foreign ministers' committee, where policies could at least be discussed if not decided, and offered only such amendments to the statute of unified command that were known to be in line with Soviet thinking. Nor did the Czechoslovaks demand substantive changes in the command's functioning, as they had originally intended. For its part, the Soviet Union accepted Polish amendments that would leave the national armed forces under the control of their governments as long as there was no war, have the supreme commander issue what was to be formally called recommendations rather than directives, and give the allies a say in building their armed forces as well as determining the amount of their financial contribution to the alliance. All this, to be sure, was a far cry from the way NATO accommodated its members, but otherwise a significant step toward mollifying the grievances of Soviet dependents.[90]

In May 1966, the Warsaw Pact defense ministers agreed on the final texts of the

[88] Document No. 36. Jindřich Madry, "Sovětské zájmy v pojetí obrany Československa (1965–1970)" [Soviet Interests in the Concept of Czechoslovakia's Defense] *Historie a vojenství,* 1992, no. 5: 126–140, at pp. 131–132. Interviews with Czechoslovak generals František Šádek, Ján Franko, Jaroslav Vinkler, Vladimír Picek, Mojmír Zachariáš, and Anton Slimák on the PHP website, www.isn.ethz.ch/php.

[89] It has been suggested that the Soviet Union and some of its allies were seriously considering a NATO-style "dual key" arrangement for the control of nuclear weapons. Mark Kramer, "The 'Lessons' of the Cuban Missile Crisis for Warsaw Pact Nuclear Operations," *Cold War International History Project Bulletin* 5 (1995): 59, 110–115, 160, at pp. 112–114. Douglas E. Selvage, "Poland, the German Democratic Republic and the German Question, 1955–1967," unpublished Ph.D. diss., Yale University, 1998, pp. 157–159, 172. Nuclear weapons were eventually deployed on Soviet bases in Poland, reportedly without the consent of its government. Pióro, *Armia ze skazą,* pp. 279–280.

[90] Memorandum by Naszkowski, May 31, 1966, KC PZPR 2948, pp. 54–57, AAN.

statutes for the unified command and committee on technology, and forwarded them to the PCC for approval. The approval, however, hinged on the reservations Romania attached to the first of the documents. Moreover, Bucharest leaked rumors that it was opposed to any reform of the alliance and publicized the desirability of its abolition together with NATO, the dismantling of all foreign bases in Europe, and the withdrawal of foreign troops from all parts of the Continent. Despite the much greater threat such demands posed to the integrity of the Warsaw Pact they did to that of NATO, Moscow treated the Romanian behavior with a forbearance indicative of how much its ability to enforce discipline in its house had declined since Stalin's and Khrushchev's times.[91]

Rather than press harder at this juncture for the Warsaw Pact's institutionalization, the Soviet Union tried to keep its unity on more urgent issues—relations with West Germany, the dispute with China, the Vietnam War. These dominated the agenda of the June 1966 conference of foreign ministers as well as the meeting of the party chiefs in Bucharest the following month, where acrimonious exchanges erupted between the new Romanian leader, Nicolae Ceaușescu, and Soviet loyalists. Poland, together with East Germany, took the lead in defending the alliance against Romanian subversion while Moscow tried to mediate to prevent a break. "One must be patient with comrade Ceaușescu," Brezhnev explained to Ulbricht. "He is still young and inexperienced."[92]

At the Bucharest meeting, the Soviet Union struck an informal deal by shelving reform of the Warsaw Pact in return for Romanian support for a conference on European security—the idea Poland had been promoting now adapted to Soviet purposes. Rather than to mitigate rivalry between the superpowers through rapprochement between their junior partners, as Rapacki would have wanted, Moscow used the proposal to pursue its traditional goal of driving wedges between West Europeans and the United States, which—unlike in the Polish version—was not even to be invited to the conference. After the "Bucharest declaration," which conformed to the Soviet position, received unanimous support from the alliance, Brezhnev could congratulate himself that, "with less lecturing and shouting about friendship," relations within it had turned better just at a time when the opposite was happening on the NATO side.[93]

After France served notice of its intent to leave NATO's integrated command, President Charles de Gaulle signaled to the Kremlin his readiness to negotiate about European security without the Americans. During his visit to Moscow, he expatiated on his desire for the withdrawal of U.S. troops from Europe and recognition of its post-World War II boundaries "in the broadest sense of the word." Brezhnev was

---

[91] Document No. 39. "Osoboe mnenie" [Dissenting View], May 28, 1966, VA-01/40390, p. 20, BA-MA. Fritz Ermarth, *Internationalism, Security, and Legitimacy: The Challenge to Soviet Interests in East Europe, 1964–1968* (Santa Monica: RAND, 1969), p. 36.

[92] Documents Nos. 40 and 41. Record of Brezhnev–Ulbricht conversation, October 9, 1966, ZPA J IV 2/202/344 Bd 10, SAPMO.

[93] "Declaration on the Strengthening of Peace and Security in Europe," July 8, 1966, http://www.isn.ethz.ch/php/documents/collection_3/PCC_docs/1966/1966_10.pdf. Brezhnev quote, record of Brezhnev–Ulbricht conversation, October 9, 1966, ZPA J IV 2/202/344 Bd 10, SAPMO.

understandably gratified, although he remained wary of de Gaulle's intentions. He had reason to be concerned about the bad example France's behavior in NATO might give to Romania and perhaps other Warsaw Pact members.[94]

France's departure from NATO's integrated command proved not nearly as damaging to it as had been expected. French absence from the alliance's highest councils allowed it to lay to rest its most divisive disputes and proceed toward the adoption of the flexible response strategy. Moscow considered the strategy more effective than that of massive retaliation, as well as more dangerous because of its allowing the enemy to better fight a "limited" war—with or without nuclear weapons. NATO's annual "Fallex" exercise in 1966 impressed Warsaw Pact analysts, but it was the Middle Eastern "Six-Day" War in the following year that jolted them.[95]

The war had disturbing military and political implications for the Soviet alliance. Having been precipitated by the Egyptians misled by misinformation supplied by the Soviet military, it highlighted the perils of miscalculation. It provoked Israeli preemption—something that could be disastrous on the European battlefield because of the likely use of nuclear weapons there. In the eyes of Warsaw Pact observers, Israel's swift defeat of its enemies was indicative of what NATO might be capable of in Europe. And a review of the Eastern European armies' preparedness for a similar kind of warfare as in the Middle East proved far from reassuring.[96]

Moscow used the alliance's framework to coordinate the political response to the war, particularly the suspension of diplomatic relations with Israel. East Germany took the lead in trying to persuade the Romanians to follow the example of the other members in breaking off the relations, but did not succeed. Instead, "Everything indicates that they [the Romanians] intend to finally break relations with our camp," Brezhnev told the July meeting of the party chiefs, to which Ceaușescu did not come, and expected Romania's announcement of its withdrawal from the Warsaw Pact at any time[97]

Moscow did better coordinating with Yugoslavia. In June, Tito attended a meeting

[94] Statement by Brezhnev at PCC meeting, July 7, 1966, KC PZPR, 2663, p. 310, also at http://www.isn.ethz.ch/php/documents/collection_3/PCC_docs/1966/1966_4.pdf. Keith A. Dunn, *Soviet Perceptions of NATO* (Carlisle Barracks: U.S. Army War College, 1978), pp. 7–8; Mikhail Narinski, "Les soviétiques et la decision française," in *France et l'OTAN, 1949–1996*, ed. Maurice Vaïsse, Pierre Mélandri, and Frédéric Bozo (Brussels: Complexe, 1996), pp. 503–516.

[95] Documents Nos. 28 and 43.

[96] Aleksandr Shumilin, "За кулисами «шестидевной войны»" [Behind the Scenes of the Six-Day War], *Novoe vremia* 1992, no. 37: 22–24. On the question of whether the war was preemptive, Janice Gross Stein, "The Arab–Israeli War of 1967: Inadvertent War through Miscalculated Escalation," in *Avoiding War: Problems of Crisis Management,* ed. Alexander L. George (Boulder: Westview Press, 1991), pp. 126–59, at pp. 142–143, and Dan Reiter, "Exploding the Powder Keg Myth: Preemptive Wars Almost Never Happen," *International Security* 20, no. 2 (1995): 5–34, at pp. 16–19. Report by Kessler to National Defense Council, September 1, 1967, DW1/39486, 11–32, BA-MA, Document No. 44.

[97] Ulbricht to Gomułka, June 14, 1967, KC PZPR, XIA/104, pp. 37–39, AAN. Minutes of meeting of party chiefs in Budapest, July 11–12, 1967, in *The Soviet Bloc and the Aftermath of the June 1967 War: Selected Documents from East-Central European Archives*, ed. James G. Hershberg for the conference "The United States, the Middle East, and the 1967 Arab–Israeli War," Department of State, Washington, January 12–13, 2004, pp. 12–52, at p. 52. Also at http://wwics.si.edu/-index.cfm?topic_id=1409&fuseaction=library.document&id=102097.

with top Warsaw Pact leaders for the first time. He railed against the United States, accusing it of plotting with Israel to "liquidate the revolutionary process in the world," and urged to hold consultations more frequently, particularly in view of what he claimed were Italy's military preparations against Yugoslavia. After a second summit with Tito a month later, the Bulgarian politburo approved holding joint maneuvers with the Yugoslav army. But Belgrade's incongruous rapprochement with the Warsaw Pact led nowhere, and would soon fall victim to the Soviet intervention in Czechoslovakia.[98]

The communist alliance found it more difficult to weather its crisis than did its Western rival. The stalled reform project was an indication of how much less capable than NATO the Warsaw Pact was of generating consensus despite disagreements among its members. The Sino-Soviet rift added fuel to the disagreements, leading to disputes that could only be overcome by hammering out common positions at meetings without the Romanians.[99] As the decade was nearing its end, the opening prospect of détente was calling for a review of the principles on which each of the alliances was built. By the end of 1967, NATO had largely overcome its crisis by adopting the landmark Harmel report, which set for the alliance the twin goals of defense and détente while ensuring its members input in matters of vital concern, including especially nuclear planning. In contrast, the Warsaw Pact's climactic crisis over Czechoslovakia was just beginning.

6. THE CZECHOSLOVAK CRISIS AND RENEWAL OF THE WARSAW PACT (1968–1969)

If NATO consolidated itself by accommodating the interests of its members with those of the dominant superpower, the Warsaw Pact faced its crisis because of its inability to do so. Such an accommodation was not *a priori* impossible. After all, Eastern Europe's ruling regimes had been sharing both an ideological affinity with Moscow and dependence on Soviet support to maintain themselves in power. By the end of the nineteen-sixties, however, these two preconditions had begun to change as the hold of ideology on policy loosened while some of the regimes proved capable of improving their standing with their peoples and earning a measure of legitimacy. The 1968 Czechoslovak crisis brought these changes into focus by offering the unprecedented sight of a communist party gaining popular support as it started to democratize itself.

Although the crisis unfolded for domestic reasons and was political rather than military in nature, it affected both the integrity of the Warsaw Pact and its relations with NATO. As it mounted, the Soviet Union felt compelled to consider intervening in order to prevent the transformation of the country's political system from

---

[98] Report by Novotný on June 9, 1967, meeting of party chiefs in Moscow, in *Vojenské otázky československé reformy, 1967–1970: Vojenská varianta řešení čs. krize (1967–1968)* [Military Issues in the Czechoslovak Reform, 1967–1970: The Military Option in the Solution of the Czechoslovak Crisis], ed. Antonín Benčík, Jaromír Navrátil, and Jan Paulík (Brno: Doplněk, 1996), pp. 329–334, at p.331. Record of Bulgarian politburo meeting, July 26, 1967, 64/365, TsDA.

[99] Document No. 42.

one-party rule to limited pluralism. Moscow rightly estimated that NATO did not intend to take advantage of the Czechoslovak developments by acting to alter the military balance in Europe in its favor. Instead, the problem was that any advance of Soviet forces into the strategically crucial territory where they had thus far not had a military presence would inevitably entail a shift of that balance in their favor, which could elicit an unpredictable response by NATO.

The Warsaw Pact member-states had different stakes in the success of the Czechoslovak reform movement under the new Prague leadership of Alexander Dubček. The reactionary regimes in neighboring East Germany and Poland were most concerned about a spillover effect that could undermine their power. Ulbricht and Gomułka, joined by the like-minded Bulgarian chief, Todor Zhivkov, therefore took the lead in urging the hesitant Kremlin leaders to clamp down on the Czechoslovaks, if necessary by force. The trio were also most receptive to the renewed Soviet campaign to reform and tighten the Warsaw Pact that was being pursued by its new supreme commander, Marshal Iakubovskii, during his tour of Eastern European capitals in the spring of 1968. Conversely, the relatively liberal Kádár as well as the nationalistic Ceaușescu tried to both deflect the use of force and delay reorganization of the alliance—the former by procrastinating, the latter by outright opposition. The Romanians also intensified their efforts to derail negotiations for the nuclear nonproliferation treaty, but did not succeed.[100]

Dubček supported without reservations the Soviet proposals for reforming the Warsaw Pact. He did not do so to placate Moscow to avert its intervention—which he did not believe was coming—but because he and most of his fellow reformers believed that a strong Warsaw Pact was good for Czechoslovakia. They never indicated an intention to leave the alliance, as the Hungarians had done in 1956, or pressed for its radical reform, as the Polish generals had tried to do in that same year. Instead, they hoped to convince Moscow that the Warsaw Pact's gradual transformation into a voluntary association of partners was in the Soviet Union's own best interest as well as in Europe's. In this, they differed from the East Germans, who ominously emphasized the duty of the alliance's members to ensure each other's loyalty.[101]

It was along these lines that the chief of the Czechoslovak general staff, Gen. Otakar Rytíř, confided to his associates his misgivings about Soviet security policy and the need to recognize his country's "equal status" in the alliance. The faculty of Czechoslovakia's two main military academies elaborated their innovative views on security in a memorandum for Dubček, which soon became public knowledge. They called for clarification of the Warsaw Pact's military doctrine—known to the Soviet Union though not shared with its allies—and for the elaboration of a separate but compatible Czechoslovak doctrine. They criticized the theory and practice of deterrence as possibly beneficial to the superpowers but detrimental to everyone else. Ahead of their time, they posited a notion of security that would surpass its narrowly military dimensions.[102]

[100] Documents Nos. 45, 46, 48, 49.
[101] Documents Nos. 51, 52, 55 a-b.
[102] Documents Nos. 47 and 50.

Although the Czechoslovak critics couched their arguments in Marxist terms, the spontaneous origin of their statement and its publicity incensed Moscow. Iakubovskii took to task Gen. Václav Prchlík—the head of the Czechoslovak army's political administration, which was in charge of indoctrination of the troops. Prchlík was singled out because of his loose talk about the Warsaw Pact's shortcomings at a meeting with journalists. The supreme commander accused him of compromising alliance secrets by having criticized the controversial 1955 statute of the unified command. Other Soviet spokesmen raised alarm that the Czechoslovak army was falling apart because of the growing influence of reformers in its officer corps. In fact, the signs of Soviet displeasure had the effect of encouraging the conservative elements in it.[103]

Before deciding to intervene, Moscow used the framework of the Warsaw Pact to stage joint maneuvers in Czechoslovakia in an unsuccessful attempt to prod the Prague leadership to reverse its drift to pluralism. The maneuvers, codenamed "Šumava," revealed the depth of tensions within the alliance as even generals from countries earmarked to take part in the eventual invasion, particularly Poland and Hungary, took exception to the arrogance of the Soviet commanders. Designed to provide a pretext for intervention by demonstrating the alleged decline in the combat readiness of the Czechoslovak army, the exercise cast doubt on the reliability of other Warsaw Pact armies if their readiness were ever tested in a conflict with NATO.[104]

As Moscow drew closer to the decision to intervene, it began to charge publicly that NATO was plotting to bring Czechoslovakia to the Western fold. This was an invention, although later on East German analysts tried to interpret NATO's "Fallex" exercise as showing that such an intent existed, thus retrospectively justifying the Warsaw Pact's move against Czechoslovakia. Prior to the invasion, however, Soviet intelligence reported accurately that Western leaders hoped to save Czechoslovak reform by abstaining from any military preparations that might give the Kremlin a pretext to move in.

Neither was the Soviet Union ready to risk a clash with NATO. The Moscow high command did not rule out the possibility of NATO's entering Czechoslovakia in order to counter the Soviet forces approaching its own lines. In that case, defense minister Grechko told his subordinates, "We would have to act in accordance with the situation." A Russian officer who was with the troops preparing to invade later recalled having been instructed that "if you encounter any NATO forces, you are to stop immediately and hold fire until otherwise commanded."[105]

The July 15 warning by the "Warsaw Five"—Poland, East Germany, Hungary, and Bulgaria, besides the Soviet Union itself—which urged the Prague government to mend its ways before it might be too late, showed by how much the number of

---

[103] Benčík, *Vojenské otázky*, pp. 233–237, 241–243. Antonín Benčík, *Operace "Dunaj": Vojáci a Pražské jaro 1968: Studie a dokumenty* [Operation "Danube": The Military and the 1968 Prague Spring: Studies and Documents] (Prague: Ústav pro soudobé dějiny AV ČR, 1994), pp. 64–65.

[104] Documents Nos. 53 a-c and 56.

[105] S.M. Zolotov, "Шли на помощь друзьям" [They Went to Help Friends], *Voennoistoricheskii zhurnal* 1994, no. 4: 14–23, at p. 18. Viktor Suvorov, *Освободитель* [The Liberator] (St. Petersburg: Konets veka, 1993), pp. 175–176.

Soviet loyalists had shrunk. The invasion of Czechoslovakia on August 20 was a Warsaw Pact operation only in name, with the participating Soviet forces vastly outnumbering all the others. East German involvement in the operation was limited at the last moment to logistic support rather than providing combat troops that might make the Czechs draw awkward comparisons with the invasion of their country by the Nazi army thirty years before. Romania had not been asked to join, and was caught by surprise, as was NATO. Albania, which had already been excluded from the Pact's high-level meetings, announced its withdrawal from the alliance altogether.[106]

The intervention, though ultimately successful, exposed Moscow's weaknesses. Although the Soviet army prided itself at carrying out its assignment efficiently— whereas the Kremlin politicians botched their plan to put into power a puppet government—the operation was far from flawless. Despite the lack of organized opposition and only sporadic passive resistance, the invading forces confronted bottlenecks, got lost, and ran out of supplies—deficiencies that could be fatal if they had to fight a real enemy. To be sure, NATO's failure to anticipate the advance toward its defense perimeter did not augur well for its ability to hold out if it had been the target. By highlighting the complexity and unpredictability of warfare on the European "central front," the Czechoslovak invasion was a sobering experience for both alliances.[107]

NATO's initial fears that the balance had shifted decisively in the Warsaw Pact's favor were not substantiated. Although Soviet military leaders welcomed the opportunity to deploy their forces in Czechoslovakia, as they had long been striving for, and used it to finally deploy their nuclear missiles there, these accomplishments were largely offset by the loss of the Czechoslovak army as an effective fighting force. Even after its recovery, that army never resumed the key strategic role it had played before 1968.[108]

The political consequences of the intervention were more visible than the military ones although they were not as simple as they seemed. Moscow was not emboldened, as many people believed, to discipline its allies nor did these become more submissive, with the notable exception of the regime established eventually in Prague. The Polish and East German leaders, after all, had been those who wanted to discipline Czechoslovakia even more that the Kremlin did. Nor did the proclamation in the aftermath of the invasion of the so-called Brezhnev doctrine—which claimed Moscow's right to intervene whenever, in its own opinion, "socialism" in any country of its "commonwealth" might be in danger—proclaim anything new. It merely

---

[106] Documents Nos. 54, 58, and 59. Rüdiger Wenzke, *Die NVA und der Prager Frühling 1968: Die Rolle Ulbrichts und der DDR-Streitkräfte bei der Niederschlagung der tschechoslowakischen Reformbewegung* (Berlin: Links, 1995), pp. 151–59. Albania's withdrawal became effective on September 13, 1968. Chargé d'affaires in Tirana to Polish foreign ministry, September 15, 1968, D I sg-0-2101-2-67-68, AMSZ.

[107] Leo Heiman, "Soviet Invasion Weakness," *Military Review*, August 1969: 38–45. Vojtech Mastny, "Was 1968 a Strategic Watershed in the Cold War?" *Diplomatic History* 29, no. 1 (2005): 149–77.

[108] Documents Nos. 57 and 60.

verbalized what had always been taken for granted. More importantly, this was the last time the doctrine was actually applied in practice.[109]

Recurrent rumors that Romania was next on the Soviet invasion list proved groundless. In view of the high political cost for the Kremlin of taking on yet another country, Ceaușescu and his entourage never seemed to set much store by the reports. They adroitly avoided giving Moscow provocation and finally acquiesced in the reorganization of the Warsaw Pact that Moscow desired, although they did not cease to obstruct its functioning. They appeared confident that the Soviets, busy with more important matters, would continue to tolerate their antics—a basically, though not entirely, correct calculation.

The Soviet ability to finally push through the reform of the Warsaw Pact was not in any direct sense the result of the suppression of the Czechoslovak heresy either. The reform had been underway before and was adopted at a time when the country's "normalization"—return to hard-line communist rule—still remained to be accomplished. More pertinent to the outcome was the coincidence of the March 1969 PCC meeting, which approved the transformation of the alliance, with the escalation of the Sino-Soviet rift.

The meeting took place under the shadow of the military confrontation between the Soviet Union and China along their disputed common border—the closest the two countries ever came to war. The Romanians showed no sympathy for Moscow's predicament, refusing even to discuss the subject on procedural grounds. They also succeeded in blocking some of the aggressively anti-Western language that was originally included in the committee's resolutions intended to be made public.[110]

Rather than to confront Romania, the Soviet Union preferred to isolate it, and minimize its subversive influence by not submitting to vote decisions that required unanimity. The alliance's new institutions were so designed as to give its loyal members a greater share in its operation as well as a greater say in discussing, even though not ultimately deciding, what the Warsaw Pact did. That prerogative belonged strictly to Moscow. By giving trustworthy allies a stake in the organization's smooth functioning, the new arrangements were calculated to provide an enhanced sense of participation without endangering Soviet control. This was the main effect of the Czechoslovak experience.

The documents adopted in Budapest satisfied the Polish goal of strengthening the PCC and streamlining its procedures. Clarifying the previously nebulous division of power between the supreme commander and the national governments, the revised

---

[109] Document No. 61. On the Brezhnev doctrine, Robin Alison Remington, ed., *Winter in Prague: Documents on Czechoslovak Communism in Crisis* (Cambridge: MIT Press, 1969), pp. 412–416, and Matthew Ouimet, *The Rise and Fall of the Brezhnev Doctrine in Soviet Foreign Policy* (Chapel Hill: University of North Carolina Press, 2003).

[110] Document No. 64. Archival evidence on the Budapest meeting offers no support to the supposition that the Soviet Union asked the East Europeans to dispatch at least token forces to the Far East as a sign of solidarity. See Raymond L. Garthoff, *Détente and Confrontation: American–Soviet Relations from Nixon to Reagan* (Washington: Brookings Institution, 1994), p. 233.

statute of the unified command left the armed forces of the member-states under their national command in peace time—as the Romanians wanted—but ensured Soviet supervision through the PCC. The establishment of the Military Council, Committee of Ministers of Defense, and Committee on Technology added three new entities that finally gave the Warsaw Pact the joint military institutions it had been lacking before.[111]

The Council resembled NATO's Military Committee in representing the nations through their chiefs of staff, but differed from it by including the supreme commander as guarantor of Moscow's grip and guidance. Additionally, the Warsaw Pact's Soviet chief of staff, with much expanded personnel at his disposal, provided the council's executive mechanism while the committee on technology served as its agency in charge of research and development. The establishment of the committee of defense ministers, which regularized their previous ad hoc gatherings, introduced an advisory body on defense policy that would meet every year. The plans for the creation of the controversial committee of foreign ministers, intended to coordinate overall policy, were shelved, as were those for a permanent secretariat.

The Budapest meeting completed the Warsaw Pact's transition from Khrushchev's "cardboard castle" to a military organization in its own right that could pose as a counterpart of NATO, and in fact became increasingly recognized as such in the West. Learning from the enemy, the communist alliance introduced some of the successful features of its rival. The two military groupings nevertheless remained different in very important ways. Apart from the fundamental difference between an alliance of democracies and that of dictatorships, the Warsaw Pact never acquired the crucial operational significance for the Soviet Union that NATO always had for the United States in the event of a European war. It remained a mere extended arm of the Soviet general staff.[112]

Ironically, however, precisely at a moment when the Warsaw Pact became a more effective military instrument, its potential military utility diminished while its political significance increased because of the advent of East–West détente. In the changing international situation, Moscow found it in its interest to consult with its allies on diplomatic matters, which began to overshadow military matters. The appeal for a European security conference was a better harbinger of the future than were any of the military institutions created at the Budapest meeting.[113]

---

[111] Documents 62 a-b. Christian Nünlist, "Cold War Generals: The Warsaw Pact Committee of Defense Ministers, 1969–90," http://www.isn.ethz.ch/php/documents/collection_3/CMD_texts/introduction.htm.

[112] Vojtech Mastny, "Learning from the Enemy: NATO as a Model for the Warsaw Pact," in *A History of NATO—The First Fifty Years,* ed. Gustav Schmidt, vol. 2 (New York: Palgrave, 2001), pp. 157–77, at pp. 163–170.

[113] Document No. 63. On the extent of Soviet consultation with Warsaw Pact allies, see Csaba Békés, "Why Was There No 'Second Cold War' in Europe? Hungary and the Soviet Invasion of Afghanistan in 1979: Documents from the Hungarian Archives," *Cold War International History Project Bulletin* 14/15 (2004): 204–205.

7. THE CHALLENGE OF DÉTENTE (1969–1975)

Rather than a result of a bold decision, détente was on both sides an incremental process of overcoming suspicions and doubts. Its implications for the Warsaw Pact were not immediately clear. For the remainder of 1969, a higher priority than putting the alliance's new military bodies into action was utilizing its structures to launch what later became known as the Conference on Security and Cooperation in Europe (CSCE), or the "Helsinki process." Discussions of how to obtain Western agreement to this project revealed substantive differences about the meaning and purpose of détente not only between Moscow and its allies, but also among the allies themselves as well as between the Kremlin and the Soviet military.

Compared with Molotov's and Khrushchev's schemes for a European "collective" security system, Soviet aims at the proposed conference were limited. Initially, they entailed nothing more than Western recognition of the territorial, and implicitly also political, status quo in Europe as it had emerged from World War II, and a pledge not to use force to alter it. The importance Moscow attributed to such merely verbal pledges was suggestive of its persisting sense of insecurity in the aftermath of a crisis that had threatened the integrity of communist rule in its part of Europe as well as of a desire to avoid having to resort to force again to avert such a threat. The Soviet Union began to act on the novel and potentially far-reaching "assumption that the geopolitical status quo in Eastern Europe was only secure if ratified (and thus legitimized) by an international society whose membership extended well beyond the Warsaw Treaty Organization."[114]

Several of the Warsaw Pact members had their own ideas about how the CSCE project could best serve their interests. The Romanians welcomed a conference which, by treating all participating states as sovereign equals, would give them an opportunity to advance their long-standing goal of minimizing Soviet interference in their policies. They therefore opposed the idea of elaborating common policy as a group, an approach favored by Moscow and the other allies. Some of them saw the CSCE as an opportunity to provide their input into common policy and, aware of how badly the Soviet Union wanted the conference to take place, use the Warsaw Pact as a vehicle to promote their particular interests. The prospect seemed all the more promising since the Kremlin had not adopted a rigid position. It was initially undecided about such crucial details as whether the United States and Canada should be invited to the conference and whether any permanent all-European security institutions should emerge from it.

The East Germans tried to sway the rest of the allies to support their own foremost priority—the GDR's full international recognition, which they insisted should be made a precondition for the conference. The Poles took the initiative to prepare an ambitious draft of a European security treaty that would have mandated mutual consultations in case of a crisis and envisaged regional disarmament talks including all countries concerned. East German critics of the draft were right that the compuls-

---

[114] Daniel C. Thomas, *The Helsinki Effect: International Norms, Human Rights, and the Demise of Communism* (Princeton: Princeton University Press, 2001), p. 264.

ory consultations would give the West an entrée into the Warsaw Pact's internal discussions and that bringing additional countries into disarmament negotiations would constrain Moscow more than Washington. Faced with such awkward proposals, the Soviet Union solicited Hungarian support in fending off what its deputy foreign minister, Vladimir S. Semenov, described as "extreme Polish, Romanian, and East German demands." Such demands, he noted referring to the CSCE, might lead to "effectively strangling the baby in the cradle."[115]

The Hungarians were supportive, but advanced other ideas, which, if implemented, would have made the Warsaw Pact obsolete more quickly than they would NATO. This would have been the likely result of the launching of the security institutions they proposed, including a permanent European security council as a political body, and of the introduction of a system of follow-up conferences serving to implement the general security agreement once it has been reached. Uncomfortable about such consequences, the Soviet Union delayed discussion about the Hungarian proposals, persuaded the Poles to hold off their security project, and restrained the East Germans' clamor for international recognition.

Uneasiness among Soviet military about the budding détente became evident once the Warsaw Pact's new institutions began to function at the end of 1969. By that time the threat of war, which was their ultimate raison d'être, was receding faster than at any time since the start of the Cold War. At the inaugural meeting of the committee of defense ministers in December 1969, Grechko, by then minister of defense, referred to the international situation as "complex" [*slozhnaia*]—a term communists often used for "baffling." He contended that thanks to Soviet military superiority there was no immediate danger of war but offered no assurances for the future.[116]

As détente began to bloom, eliciting self-congratulatory pronouncements by Soviet leaders, Grechko grew more alarmed than reassured. In March 1971, the month Gromyko at the Soviet party congress waxed enthusiastic that "today, there is no question of any importance which can be decided without the Soviet Union or in opposition to it," the marshal gave the Warsaw Pact defense ministers quite a different estimate. He insisted that "the international situation had deteriorated. It has hardly been more serious, tense, and turbulent than it is now."[117]

Grechko's gloomy view was at odds with the Warsaw Pact's assessments of NATO, which reached an all-time low at that time. In the first half of the nineteen-seventies, they dwelt on such enemy weaknesses as NATO's weak flanks compared with the center, the vulnerability of its supply lines, its lack of strategic depth, inadequate command and control systems, budgetary strains, the chronic U.S.–European disagreements. Yet none of this was sufficient to have the Soviet bloc scale down its own military posture or slow down the unrelenting build-up of its armaments.[118]

[115] Documents Nos. 67, 68 a-b, and 69.

[116] Document No. 70.

[117] Gromyko quoted in Garthoff, *Détente and Confrontation*, p. 66. Report on meeting of Warsaw Pact Committee of Ministers of Defense, March 2–3, 1971, DVW 1/71027, BA-MA, also at http://www.isn.ethz.ch/php/documents/collection_3/CMD_docs/03-104-I.pdf.

[118] Evaluations of the "Wintex-71" and "Wintex-73" exercises in reports, respectively, by Keßler and Streletz to National Defense Council, February 17, 1971, and May 17, 1973, DVW1/39497 and DVW1/39500, BA-MA.

Normalization of relations with West Germany, the Warsaw Pact's supposed worst enemy, was a special challenge. After the Social Democratic government of Chancellor Willy Brandt launched its new *Ostpolitik* in the fall of 1969, Brezhnev found it necessary to summon the alliances political leaders for consultations before proceeding to negotiate the August 1970 treaty whereby the Soviet Union accepted the Bonn government as a legitimate international partner rather than an outlaw regime. Even so, East Germany, Poland, and Czechoslovakia were nervous.[119]

The Soviet willingness to dispense with the bugaboo of German militarism, which had served as the Warsaw Pact's important glue, meant not only that Moscow was no longer obsessive about German military threat but also that it had become more confident in its ability to hold the alliance together by other means. Treating its members more like partners in coordinating policy bore fruit as Eastern Europe's communist regimes acquired an incentive to harmonize their interests with a more accommodating Soviet Union. And within the Warsaw Pact, a body of high-ranking officers was gradually being formed who shared common education at Soviet military academies and felt genuine loyalty to the alliance. On the lower level, to be sure, mistrust persisted, often reflecting nationalist prejudices, nowhere more blatantly than between the East Germans and the Poles.[120]

Romania remained an exception, resisting participation in joint maneuvers and repeatedly challenging Soviet authority. Brezhnev resented Ceaușescu's insolence but tolerated it as a nuisance rather than a threat since the Romanian dissidence was effectively contained. It was not so much Bucharest's deteriorating relations with the West as its intimacy with the Chinese that worried the Kremlin. After military maps had accidentally been found in the suitcase of a high Romanian official traveling to Beijing via Moscow, thus raising suspicions of betraying Warsaw Pact secrets to China, the incident was used to justify the exclusion of Romania from joint operational planning.[121]

The planning of an offensive thrust into Western Europe continued regardless of détente, thus substantiating NATO's concern about persisting Soviet military threat. The likelihood of its materializing nevertheless diminished because Brezhnev's political investment in détente. In his keynote speech to a closed session of the PCC in January 1972, Brezhnev outlined his vision of the Warsaw Pact's future in political rather than military terms. He anticipated its gradual rapprochement with NATO, once an agreement has been reached about the inviolability of borders, nonuse of force or the threat of force, and noninterference in each other's internal affairs. He foresaw regular political consultations, as well as special consultations at times of crisis, the establishment of a common European political organ in the form of a consult-

---

[119] Document no. 71.

[120] Document no. 65.

[121] Documents nos. 72 and 77. The luggage incident was related by Soviet representative Oleg B. Rachmanin at a meeting of representatives of the international departments of party central committees of Warsaw Pact countries in Budapest on March 26, 1974. Polish memorandum, March 28, 1974, KC PZPR, XIA/587, AAN.

ative committee or secretariat, and eventual agreement on political cooperation. He implored his audience that we need "peace, peace, and again peace." [122]

Brezhnev saw the way toward the attainment of his vision leading through the European security conference, which he singled out as the Warsaw Pact's priority after what he considered a successful settlement of the German question. He wanted the conference to meet before the end of 1972 although it took another three years before it did and the Helsinki Final Act was signed on August 1, 1975. He celebrated its conclusion as the dawn of the new European security system that the Soviet Union had been yearning to create and dominate for so long. By that time, however, cracks had already begun to appear in Brezhnev's rosy picture of the future, though not because of anything that had happened in Europe. It was China that emerged in the Soviet eyes as a major threat, not only because of its rapprochement with the United States but also because of its potentially disruptive influence on the Warsaw Pact.[123]

The April 1974 meeting of the PCC was largely about China. Accusing Beijing of collusion with NATO, Moscow tried to push through a strongly worded anti-Chinese resolution, but failed because of Romanian veto. In an angry exchange with Ceauşescu, East Germany's new leader Erich Honecker charged that the Romanians were playing "objectively" into NATO's hands. Other allies supported reluctantly Moscow's rigid stand on China. Concerned not so much about the Chinese military threat as about what the unraveling of the unity of international communism might portend for their own power, the Eastern European regimes never saw eye to eye with the Soviet Union on how to deal with Beijing. With the unraveling in plain view, Polish party chief Edward Gierek's call for a celebration of the Warsaw Pact's twentieth anniversary at a special session in 1975 sounded hollow. The session never took place.[124]

The future of the alliance depended not on the supposed Chinese threat but on the course of East–West relations. The CSCE was the bellwether—Brezhnev's pet project, which European NATO members, together with some of the neutrals and nonaligned, succeeded in steering in directions different from those he had anticipated. This applied not only to its revolutionary human rights provisions, which Moscow had reluctantly endorsed in false hopes that they would remain on paper, but also to the potential of the "Helsinki process" to redefine the meaning of European security

[122] Document no. 66. Speech by Brezhnev, January 26, 1972, ZPA, DY/30/526, SAPMO.

[123] Document no. 74.

[124] Memorandum by Harry G. Barnes on conversation with Emil Bodnăraş, May 17, 1974, in Munteanu, *Romania and the Warsaw Pact*, vol. 2, pp. 163–72. Reference to Honecker's remark in Klaus Wiegrefe, "Honecker und Brežnev auf der Krim: Eine Aufzeichnung über das Treffen vom 19. August 1976," *Vierteljahrshefte für Zeitgeschichte* 41, no. 4 (1993): 589–619, at p. 606. "Zur Haltung der Sozialistischen Republik Rumänien," 4 April 1974, DY/30, J IV 2/202, SAPMO, also at http://www.isn.ethz.ch/php/documents/collection_3/PCC_docs/1974/1974_1_I.pdf. "Zur rumänischen Haltung zum Maoismus," 1974, ibid., also at http://www.isn.ethz.ch/php/documents/collection_china/74_undated_2.pdf. Speech by Gierek, April 18, 1974, KC PZPR, XIA/586, AAN, also at http://www.isn.ethz.ch/php/documents/collection_3/PCC_docs/1974/1974_6.pdf. Document No. 76.

by de-emphasizing its military dimensions. The Warsaw Pact's military ascendancy was therefore deceptive of its obsolescence, which was merely delayed by the decline and fall of détente in the second half of the nineteen-seventies.[125]

8. PREPARING FOR WAR (1975–80)

The late nineteen-seventies and early eighties were dangerous in different ways than the Stalin or Khrushchev years had been. Not only did the Warsaw Pact become an effective military machine, which it had not been before, but it also intensified its preparations for war. Less dependent on nuclear weapons, with their unpredictable and potentially catastrophic effects, its war plans were now more "realistic" than they used to be. Moreover, the political impediments to their implementation diminished as the Kremlin leadership, and thus also its control over the military, weakened under the ailing Brezhnev. If war did not come, this was not for any lack of preparations for it—preparations that could have gotten out of hand with unforeseen and undesired consequences.

The crisis of détente may be traced to the 1973 Yom Kippur War in the Middle East and the tense standoff it caused between the superpowers. The war had a European dimension in a confrontation between the Soviet and U.S. navies in NATO's back yard—the Mediterranean—from which Moscow emerged politically victorious. While NATO was split on assisting the United States' support for Israel, the Warsaw Pact maintained its unity. The Soviet Union proved capable of delivering supplies to its Arab clients through the air space of neutral Yugoslavia and even NATO member Turkey.[126]

On the ground, however, the Middle Eastern war had disturbing implications for the Warsaw Pact, whose analysts again drew conclusions from Israel's performance, as they had done after the 1967 war. Although they found the Arabs' Soviet tanks superior to the Israelis' American ones, the advantage was largely offset by the more advanced Western communications equipment and means of electronic warfare. The West's advances in high technology and NATO's organizational improvements led in the second half of the decade to a telling reversal of Warsaw Pact assessments of the adversary. Instead of dwelling on NATO's weaknesses, the assessments now grudgingly acknowledged its growing strength.[127]

Nevertheless, the military trends mattered less than the unexpected consequences of the Helsinki Final Act, whose seemingly paper provisions on human rights assumed political substance once they were effectively invoked by dissidents within the Soviet bloc. The significance of this turn of events, relevant to the internal rather than exter-

---

[125] Document no. 75. Vojtech Mastny, *Helsinki, Human Rights, and European Security: Analysis and Documentation* (Durham: Duke University Press, 1986), pp. 1–36.

[126] Lyle J. Goldstein and Yuri M. Zhukov, "A Tale of Two Fleets: A Russian Perspective on the 1973 Naval Standoff in the Mediterranean," *Naval War College Review* 57, no. 2 (Spring 2004): 27–63.

[127] "Stručný rozbor bojové činnosti na Středním východě v říjnu 1973" [A Brief Analysis of the Combat Operations in the Middle East in October 1973] VS, OS-SD, box 16, č.j. 39051/5, VÚA.

nal security of the Warsaw Pact countries, dominated the discussion at the 1976 PCC meeting. While still professing satisfaction with the CSCE, Brezhnev bemoaned the outbreak of a "sharp ideological struggle concerning the substance and perspectives of the process of international détente." He seemed at a loss trying to comprehend why détente was in trouble after he had become convinced of its irreversibility.[128]

Dismissing any effect on détente of the Soviet exploitation of anti-Western "national liberation" movements in the Third World, Brezhnev attributed its reversal to machinations by American hardliners, whose influence he had previously believed was declining. He blamed them for artificially instigating "the stir about the so-called humanitarian contacts" in order to sabotage détente, and called for common action to save it. The long-postponed establishment of the Committee of Ministers of Foreign Affairs was the result. Supplemented by frequent working sessions of deputy foreign ministers, the meetings of the committee quickly acquired key significance in the formulation of the Warsaw Pact's common policy.[129]

The alliance's initial reaction to rising East–West tension was thus political rather than military. The PCC called for "military détente," particularly the "no-first-use" pledge that would oblige both NATO and the Warsaw Pact not to be the first to fire nuclear weapons, and sent the draft of an agreement to that effect to all CSCE members. Calculated to undermine the credibility of the U.S. nuclear guarantee that was the cornerstone of NATO, this was an ostensibly military but in fact a political proposition. Whatever the doubtful value of such a pledge in an emergency, short of it the agreement would have had the immediate effect of "de-coupling" America from Europe while leaving Moscow's ties with its allies unaffected—the reason why the proposal was ignored and détente kept deteriorating.[130]

The reversal of détente saved the Warsaw Pact's military managers from the peril of obsolescence. The secret report by supreme commander Iakubovskii to the 1976 PCC meeting, read in his absence by Gribkov, differed in both spirit and intent from Brezhnev's keynote speech as well as the declarations the committee issued for public consumption. The report foresaw the attainment of "strategic nuclear parity" by 1979. This was not the parity, however, that most Western experts assumed had already been achieved by the early nineteen-seventies but a parity yet to be achieved by redressing what Moscow saw as an imbalance in Western favor implicit in NATO's challenge to Soviet strategic superiority. The message was that the Soviet Union was in the danger of losing the gains it had made.[131]

[128] Document no. 78. Speech by Brezhnev at meeting of the Political Consultative Committee, November 25–26, 1976, KC PZPR, XIA/588, AAN, also at http://www.isn.ethz.ch/php/documents/collection_3/PCC_docs/1976/1976_8_I.pdf.

[129] Anna Locher, "Shaping the Policies of the Alliance: The Committee of Ministers of Foreign Affairs of the Warsaw Pact, 1976–1990," http://www.isn.ethz.ch/php/documents/collection_3/-CMFA_texts/CMFA_intro.htm.

[130] Draft treaty, November 26, 1976, 80-1-109, OSA, also at http://www.isn.ethz.ch/php/documents/collection_3/PCC_docs/1976/1976_14_I.pdf.

[131] Summary of report by Iakubovskii, November 25, 1976, VS, OS (OL) krab. 8, č.j. 36033/4, VÚA, also at http://www.isn.ethz.ch/php/documents/collection_3/PCC_docs/1976/1976_14_I.pdf. Statement by Gribkov, March 25, 1995, *Global Competition and the Deterioration of U.S.–Soviet Relations*, p. 182–83.

Once détente faltered, its condition increasingly came to be measured not so much by the progression of the CSCE and other developments of nonmilitary nature favorable to the West as by the more ambivalent changes in the military balance between the two alliances. The balance baffled not only Soviet generals but also the American critics of détente, who became alarmed at the supposed "clear and present" danger of Soviet military supremacy. The contradictory assessments by each side of where the balance was really tilting cast doubt on the value of "bean counting" troops and weapons while underlining the greater importance of perceptions and plans.[132]

It was less the piling up of military hardware than the planning to make war in Europe more feasible and imaginable that posed a clear and present danger. Both sides had been moving away from the senseless nuclear scenario, though the Warsaw Pact more reluctantly than NATO. To fudge the awkward question of who would fire first, Soviet theoreticians invented the fiction of "converging strike" (*vstrechnyi udar, Begegnungsschlag*), which presumed the release of nuclear weapons by the opposing forces at exactly the same time. The emphasis, however, was on developing more credible scenarios for conventional war that could delay, perhaps indefinitely, resort to nuclear arms. Ideally, the war would be won by defeating NATO before American reinforcements could reach Europe. At issue was "the seizure of strategic and tactical initiative by the forces of the states of the Warsaw Treaty and the subsequent transition into the decisive strategic offensive with the transfer of operations into enemy territory."[133]

As early as 1975, when détente was still flourishing, East Germany began annual exercises to prepare the state and society for war. They bore such colorful designations as "Milestone," "Mastery," and "Mosaic Stone." Although the numerous war games conducted each year presumed, as before, hostilities initiated by NATO, rehearsing the defensive part to stop the putative aggressor became increasingly perfunctory. All planning rested on the artificial assumption that the enemy would foolishly start war without having the numerical superiority that the military common sense dictated was indispensable for successful attack, thus making the success of the Warsaw Pact's well-rehearsed "counter-attack" a foregone conclusion.[134]

The Warsaw Pact planners were well aware from reports by their intelligence that NATO's plans for war were defensive. Yet they became nervous when, thanks to

---

[132] On Western misperceptions of the competition, Dana H. Allin, *Cold War Illusions: America, Europe and Soviet Power, 1969–1989* (New York: St. Martin's Press, 1998).

[133] "Материалы разбора оперативно-стратегического командно-штабного учения 'Запад-77'" [Analytical Materials on the Strategic Operational Staff Command Exercise "Zapad-77"], May 30–June 9, 1977, VS, OS-OL, 1977, krab., 29-999-155, č.j. 22013/23, pp. 9–10, VÚA, pp. 30–32. Cf. Beatrice Heuser, "Warsaw Pact Military Doctrines in the 1970s and 1980s: Findings in the East German Archives," *Comparative Strategy* 12, No. 4 (1993): 437–57, at pp. 439–40. Document no. 81. "The Preparation and Conduct of Operations by the Unified Coalition Grouping in the Western Theater of Operations," July 22, 1981, GŠ-OS, 1981, 002/05, VÚA. John A. Battilega, "Soviet Views of Nuclear Warfare: The Post-Cold War Interviews," in *Getting MAD: Nuclear Mutual Assured Destruction, Its Origins and Practice*, ed. Henry D. Sokolski (Carlisle, PA: US Army Strategic Studies Institute, 2004), pp. 151–74, at pp. 161–63.

[134] Otto Wenzel, *Kriegsbereit: Der Nationale Verteidigungsrat der DDR, 1960 bis 1989* (Cologne: Wissenschaft und Politik, 1995), pp. 173–77. Document no. 79.

Western technological and organizational accomplishments, those plans began to include such innovative features as deep strikes against the second echelon of the advancing enemy forces, reflecting confidence that the advance could be stopped, without or without the use of nuclear weapons. The Warsaw Pact's internal assessments after the mid-nineteen-seventies contrasted with the previous dismissive estimates of NATO's capacity even to defend itself, much less attack with any chance of success. Indicative of a new respect for the alliance's prowess was the apparently genuinely held suspicion that the huge NATO maneuvers conducted annually in West Germany could be a ruse for a surprise attack, the "nearly even" balance of forces notwithstanding.[135]

Sober assessments of NATO's capabilities, based on all but complete access to its secrets by proficient East German spies, acknowledged that its forces were getting better and better. In the Warsaw Pact's command post exercises that rehearsed offensives into Western Europe, the expected rates of daily advance and the depth of penetration were now diminishing; gone was the vision of rolling to the English Channel in six days or to Lyon in nine. East Germany's Admiral Theodor Hoffmann has recalled that in the nineteen-sixties he thought his navy's brand new warships were better than NATO's, but a decade later he was no longer sure they could be a match even to the Danish navy, which had meanwhile been equipped with the latest Western technology. Now the Warsaw Pact alert times were getting shorter and NATO's more leisurely.[136]

In 1977, the Soviet Union began to train on Western Europe its SS-20 intermediate-range nuclear missiles, of which NATO had no equivalent. Poland's Gen. Wojciech Jaruzelski retrospectively described the deployment as a "desperate attempt to somehow compensate for the West's ever more obvious superiority in advanced technology." In December 1978, Gen. Petr I. Ivashutin, the chief of Soviet military intelligence—who a decade earlier had seemed supremely confident of his country's invincibility in a nuclear war—warned the Warsaw Pact's defense ministers that NATO's "technological surprise moment" might be coming. "As a result of its development and deployment of new weapons systems," he concluded, the West "could decisively influence the course and outcome of a European war."[137]

[135] "Die wichtigsten Entwicklungsrichtungen und Zustand der NATO-Streitkräfte in der Westlichen Richtung," December 10–11, 1976, AZN 32863, BA-MA, also at http://www.isn.ethz.ch/php/documents/collection_3/CMD_docs/09-088-I.pdf. "Материалы разбора оперативно-стратегического командно-штабного учения 'Запад-77'" [Analytical Materials on the Strategic Operational Staff Command Exercise "Zapad-77"], May 30–June 9,1977, VS, OS-OL, 1977, krab., 29-999-155, č.j. 22013/23, pp. 9–10, VÚA.

[136] Document no. 80. Interview with Adm. Theodor Hoffmann, Berlin, October 24, 2002. "Direktive zur operativen und Gefechtsausbildung der Vereinten Streitkräfte der Teilnehmerstaaten des Warschauer Vertrages für 1976," October 28, 1975, VA-01/35940, BA-MA. Drew Middleton, "Haig Lifts Estimate of NATO Alert Time," *New York Times*, September 15, 1977. The time was extended from 8 to 15 days.

[137] Wojciech Jaruzelski, *Mein Leben für Polen: Erinnerungen* (Munich: Piper, 1993), p. 201. "Stand und Entwicklungsperspektiven der NATO-Streitkräfte," December 4–7, 1978, pp., 60–83, at p. 82. AZN 32865, BA-MA, also at http://www.isn.ethz.ch/php/documents/collection_3/-CMD_docs/11-060-I.pdf.

Gribkov recalls that once Moscow saw all Western European targets of any value covered with Soviet nuclear-tipped missiles, "then the question had come up: what to do next?" According to former East German colonel Joachim Schunke, whose job was monitoring and analyzing NATO's innovations, the Soviet general staff never drew radical conclusions from the unfavorable turn of the technological battle—nor could it easily afford to, given the Soviet economy's systemic weaknesses. Instead, it chose to strive for incremental organizational improvements while maintaining disproportionately high combat and mobilization readiness. This hardly justified the complacency that permeated the report about the condition of the alliance prepared in January 1978 by Iakubovskii's successor as supreme commander, Marshal Viktor G. Kulikov.[138]

The November 1978 PCC meeting linked the decline of détente with the rise of NATO. It called for increased defense expenditures to meet what Brezhnev described as the "sacred task" of not allowing the West to disrupt the supposed military equilibrium. On the premise that the equilibrium was in danger, the committee decided that the Warsaw Pact's war-fighting capability must increase. The ways of doing so included a substantial boost in military expenditures and the creation of special forces equipped with up-to-date technology that would strike deep into Western Europe ahead of the advancing main armies.[139]

Romania demurred. Protesting a violation of the terms of the alliance, it refused to endorse the call for increased defense expenditures and modernization of armaments. Instead, it launched a public campaign for across-the-board cuts in defense budgets and the eventual abolition of both NATO and the Warsaw Pact. It publicized the disputes that had been taking place behind closed doors and, in trying to further distance itself from the Soviet alliance, consulted separately with Yugoslavia. At the Romanian politburo session that followed the PCC meeting, Ceaușescu aide Manea Mănescu denounced its resolution as "an emanation of Soviet militarist circles, which are pursuing a policy of excessive armament by replacing current weapons, involving the Warsaw Treaty states in a dangerous arms race and having them bear the cost of this adventurous way of acting."[140]

As one of his top priorities, Kulikov pushed for supplementing the 1969 statute on command structure in peace time with a statute to be used in war time, a project stalled since 1973. Moscow argued that a strategy aimed at the total defeat of the enemy in a total war required putting all of the alliance's resources at the disposal of the supreme commander and following strictly his orders. Designed to give him wide discretion in deploying the allies' armed forces as he saw fit, the proposed statute evoked little enthusiasm even among Moscow's most loyal followers. Going into too much detail about how the forces would be used in war seemed to make the dismal

---

[138] Statement by Gribkov, March 25, 1995, *Global Competition and the Deterioration of U.S.–Soviet Relations*, p. 183. Joachim Schunke, "Zur Bedrohungsanalyse der militärischen Führung der DDR," in *Landesverteidigung und/oder Militarisierung der Gesellschaft der DDR?*, ed. Günther Glaser and Werner Knoll (Berlin: Trafo, 1995), pp. 34–48, at pp. 47–48. Document no. 82.

[139] Document no. 84.

[140] Document no. 85. Memorandum of Frelek–Rusakov conversation, December 11, 1978, KC PZPR, XIB/127, AAN.

prospect that much more likely. The Poles reportedly submitted as many as 60 amendments, most of which were incorporated.[141]

The Romanians predictably took the lead in throwing wrenches into the works. Only in November 1979 did a special working group approve the controversial text of the statute, despite their resistance. The next March, the submission of the document for signature by the party chiefs without a discussion at their meeting in Moscow prompted Ceauşescu to storm out of town in anger. "So much for 'equality' and 'democracy' in deciding questions on which victory and defeat in war could hinge," Gribkov later commented with retrospective candor. The statute was signed in deep secrecy, and although formally valid, it remained not binding for Romania.[142]

Intended to strengthen the alliance, the manner of the statute's adoption thus revealed its weaknesses. It left unanswered the fundamental question of how much authority the supreme commander would be able to exercise in relation to the chief the Soviet general staff. The two incumbents were not on the best of terms at the time. In another sign of incipient decay, the elevation in April 1980 of the moribund but still vain Brezhnev to the honorary position of the Warsaw Pact's commander-in-chief, likewise not ratified by Romania, was greeted by other Eastern European leaders, some of whom had been eyeing a joint appointment as his peers, "with sarcastic smiles."[143]

The December 1979 Soviet invasion of Afghanistan, which dealt a *coup de grâce* to superpower détente, highlighted the pitfalls of excessive military power in search for a purpose. A frivolous decision imposed upon Brezhnev by a small coterie within the politburo, it elicited some doubts among the top Soviet military but did not make them averse to the opportunity of testing the surfeit of their manpower and equipment in a real war. This was worrisome, yet within the Warsaw Pact Ceauşescu alone dared to criticize the adventure. Others deplored his seeking "confrontation with the foreign policy line of the USSR and other Warsaw Treaty nations."[144]

Afghanistan cast a deep shadow over the CSCE follow-up meeting in Madrid, which opened in September 1980. In preparing for difficult discussions, Moscow still tried to rally its allies in pursuit of the elusive "military détente." But the discussions, which would eventually last as long as three years, concerned more and more the Soviet bloc's internal affairs, subsumed under the broad heading of "human rights," thus signaling the expansion of the meaning of security. That same year, the unexp-

[141] Document no. 83. Interviews with generals Skalski and Jasiński, in "Warsaw Pact Generals in Polish Uniforms: Oral History Interviews," http://www.isn.ethz.ch/php/documents/collection_9/docs/6Skalski.pdf, pp. 23–34, and http://www.isn.ethz.ch/php/documents/collection_9/-docs/3Jasinski.pdf, p. 6.

[142] Kulikov to Hoffmann, November 27, 1979, AZN 32866 II, BA-MA. Document no. 86. Anatoli Gribkow, *Der Warschauer Pakt: Geschichte und Hintergründe des östlichen Militärbündnisses* (Berlin: Edition q, 1995), pp. 46–47, at p. 47. On the consequences of the statute, Ryszard J. Kukliński, "Wojna z narodem widziana od środka" [The War against the Nation As Seen from the Center], *Kultura* [Paris] 475, no. 4 (April 1987): 3–57, at pp. 53–57.

[143] Resolution on the appointment of commander-in-chief, April 30, 1980, AZN 32854, p. 132, BA-MA. Gribkow, *Der Warschauer Pakt*, pp. 52–53, at p. 53.

[144] Document no. 87. Report for the Czechoslovak party presidium on the PCC meeting, May 27, 1980, AÚV KSČ, 02/8349/24, SÚA.

ected popular upheaval in Poland challenged the communist states to reassess the safeguards of their security. It heralded primacy of the internal over the external safeguards in ways that raised further questions about the Warsaw Pact's continued relevance in a changing world.[145]

9. THE NONINVASION OF POLAND AND ITS CONSEQUENCES (1980–1985)

Within the context of the Warsaw Pact, the most striking feature of the 1980–81 Polish crisis was the Soviet abstention from military intervention, despite the threat that the paralysis of the country's communist regime posed to the integrity of the alliance. This distinguished the situation from all the other crises that had challenged Moscow's domination of the strategically crucial region—a distinction all the more important since Poland was its linchpin, and not only for geographic reasons. Poland was the Warsaw Pact's largest, most populous, as well as most anti-Soviet nation, with an army second in size only to the Soviet one and more respected than any other in the region.

Once the crisis broke out in the summer of 1980, with a mass movement spearheaded by the "Solidarity" labor union contesting the communist party's monopoly of power, Moscow's instinctive first reaction was to prepare a military crackdown on the 1968 Czechoslovak model. The scenario called for staging Warsaw Pact maneuvers jointly with Poland's neighbors that could be used to prod the country's tottering party leadership into suppressing the opposition. If the current leaders proved unwilling or unable to act, the Soviet-led forces would then assume responsibility for the suppression and install a puppet government. The plan, which envisaged holding maneuvers on Polish territory while the Polish army would largely stay in the barracks, was ready to be implemented by the beginning of December. Indicative of the Soviet military stake in a swift restoration of order was the leading role of Marshal Nikolai V. Ogarkov, the chief of the general staff, in the preliminaries for the operation.[146]

There were similarities with the 1968 Czechoslovak situation, but more important were the differences. Similar was the consistency with which the two neighboring regimes, in this instance East Germany's and Czechoslovakia's, advocated an intervention. The Honecker regime was especially willing to take part in an action that would have the effect of deciding in its favor the East German–Polish competition for the status of Moscow's preferred ally. The rulers of other Warsaw Pact countries, though appalled by the sight of crumbling communist power in Poland, hoped against hope that its party leadership would manage to regain control without necessitating the use of outside force.[147]

---

[145] Document no. 88.

[146] Mark Kramer, "'In Case Military Assistance Is Provided to Poland': Soviet Preparations for Military Contingencies, August 1980," *Cold War International History Project Bulletin* 11 (1998): 102–109. Kukliński to CIA, beginning December 1980, ibid., pp. 53–54. Document no. 89.

[147] Honecker to Brezhnev, November 26, 1980, *Cold War International History Project Bulletin* 6 (1995): 124. Mark Kramer, "Poland, 1980–81: Soviet Policy during the Polish Crisis," ibid., pp. 1, 116–26, at p. 121.

The scant probability of such an outcome, rooted in the specifics of the Polish situation, was the main difference from the 1968 Czechoslovak crisis. Not only was there the obvious difference in size, of both the territory and the population, but—unlike in Czechoslovakia before—the communist party was collapsing whereas the Polish military held firm. The army had a reputation as a patriotic force even among noncommunist Poles but the reputation was ill deserved. Since the very onset of the crisis, the army's top generals had been secretly plotting a forcible suppression of the Solidarity movement—the movement that had become the authentic representative of the nation. They had not been doing so on Soviet orders but on their own initiative, driven by their conviction that wiping out the opposition they despised was both in their own interests and in the interests of communist Poland, of which they regarded themselves as guardians. Their goal, to be sure, coincided with the Soviet goal.

The emergency meeting of party secretaries in Moscow on December 4–5, 1980, was convened while Soviet-led intervention forces stood ready to move at a moment's notice, but failed to give them the final green light. It is uncertain whether this was because Polish party secretary Stanisław Kania managed to persuade Brezhnev that the Polish party was capable to keep its house in order—as Gomułka had done in 1956 when confronting Khrushchev—or whether Brezhnev had already called off the military action beforehand. Whatever the reasons for the Soviet change of mind, Brezhnev's reply to Kania, the way Kania paraphrased it, conveyed a plausible rationale for Moscow's alternative policy: "OK, we will not go in, but if complications occur we will. But without you, we won't go."[148]

In view of the persisting uncertainty about whether the embattled Polish communists could possibly deliver what Brezhnev wanted, the option of a Warsaw Pact intervention was not abandoned but merely modified. As the situation got worse rather than better, with power slipping out of the party's hands at an alarming speed, Kulikov was looking for a suitable ally from among Polish hardliners in the increasingly likely case that Moscow would decide to intervene after all. The new plan still called for maneuvers with foreign troops on Polish territory, but differed from the old plan by presuming active participation by the Polish military in a joint effort to shore up the communist regime.

When Kulikov came to Poland in January 1981 to obtain Kania's consent to the maneuvers, in which East German troops were to take a prominent part, he found the party secretary evasive. The Poles were ready to hold command post exercises but not an exercise that would bring large numbers of foreign, especially East German, troops into the country. Kulikov placed his hopes in defense minister Jaruzelski, whose record of devotion to the Warsaw Pact was without blemish. Soviet intelligence officials sent to Poland to assess the attitude of the military were satisfied that the country's

---

[148] Minutes of meeting of leading representatives of Warsaw Pact countries, December 5, 1980, *Cold War International History Project Bulletin* 11 (1998): 110–20. Kania in *Wejdą nie wejdą: Polska 1980–1982: wewnętrzny kryzys, międzynarodowe uwarunkowania: Konferencja w Jachrance, listopad 1997* [They Will Move in and They Will Not: Poland 1980–1982: Internal Crisis, International Implications: The November 1997 Jachranka Conference] (London: Aneks, 1999), pp. 165–66.

officer corps—though not necessarily the troops—could be counted upon. This was no small tribute to Moscow's alliance management since 1969.[149]

The maneuvers were indeed held in March, but their intended political effect was thwarted by the uproar created by the incident in Bydgoszcz, where police thugs had beaten up Solidarity supporters. The resulting groundswell of popular emotion put the party into a defeatist mood, and even the generals began losing heart. At the beginning of April, the Soviet politburo decided to shelve the Warsaw Pact intervention and keep it merely as a "fallback option." Instead, it adopted the policy of pressuring the Polish party and military leaders to restore order themselves, particularly by proclaiming martial law, as Jaruzelski and his team had already been preparing for several months.[150]

In the scheme to force the Polish communists to do Soviet bidding on their own responsibility, the Warsaw Pact command structure was assigned a crucial role. Attesting to the political rather than military nature of the strategy, the alliance's supreme commander, Kulikov, rather than the chief of the Soviet general staff, Ogarkov, assumed primary operational control. In turning the screws on Jaruzelski, he was assisted by Gribkov, who had now moved with his personnel out of Legnica, the main Soviet base in Poland previously intended as the headquarters for the now discarded military action. Another important figure was the Warsaw Pact's chief liaison in Poland, Afanasii F. Shcheglov, regarded by Poles as "one of the most despicable specimens of Russian chauvinism."[151]

The initial results of the campaign were disappointing for Moscow. The highest-ranking Polish communists were rapidly losing faith that anything could be done to save their regime. Faced with ever more insistent Soviet demands for declaring martial law and cracking down on Solidarity, Kania instead maneuvered for a compromise with it while Jaruzelski, dejected, tried to procrastinate. It was symptomatic of their desperation that they tried to prod Kulikov to set up a Warsaw Pact command center at Legnica after all. They argued that this would help them intimidate the populace if it could become known that Soviet, East German, and Czechoslovak troops were already present on Polish territory. But, as ideology secretary Mikhail A. Suslov lamented at a Soviet politburo meeting, "It is impossible to have much faith in what they promise they'll do." Brezhnev thus accurately summed up the Soviet predicament: "We cannot rely on the present [Polish] leadership but see presently no real possibility to replace it."[152]

[149] Document no. 90 a. "Col. Ryszard Kukliński's Interview, Washington, October 28, 1997," documents of the Jachranka conference, NSA. Kukliński, "Wojna z narodem," p. 31.

[150] On the "Soiuz" and "Druzhba" maneuvers, materials for the March 13, 1981, session of National Defense Council, DVW1/39524, pp. 32–33, 62–67, 82–84, BA-MA. Minutes of Soviet politburo session, April 2, 1981, *Soviet Deliberations during the Polish Crisis, 1980–1981*, ed. Mark Kramer, Cold War International History Project special working paper no. 1 (Washington: Woodrow Wilson International Center for Scholars, 1999), pp. 92–102, also annotations on pp. 95–97.

[151] Gribkov in *Wejdą nie wejdą*, pp. 174–75. On Shcheglov, Kukliński, "Wojna z narodem," p. 31.

[152] Document no. 90 b. Minutes of Soviet politburo session, April 30, 1981, Kramer, *Soviet Deliberations during the Polish Crisis*, pp. 115–18, at p. 117. Minutes of Brezhnev–Honecker–Husák meeting, May 16, 1981, *Cold War International History Project Bulletin* 11 (1998): 125–31, at p. 131. Quote retranslated from the original.

Polish colonel Ryszard Kukliński, who took part in the planning for martial law while working secretly for U.S. intelligence, later testified that Kulikov "took upon himself the main burden of immediate contacts and conversations with the Polish party and political leadership." This included conspiring with hardliners within that leadership and among the military to replace both Kania and Jaruzelski, as well as with East German generals to prepare for "all eventualities." He told them that Poland's departure from the Warsaw Pact could not be tolerated for strategic military reasons. Jaruzelski later recalled Kulikov having supposedly told him that the Soviet Union would not allow a situation develop in Poland that would threaten the Warsaw Pact, vowing that his "hand would not shake" to prevent this from happening.[153]

In hindsight, however, Kulikov would assert that from the military point of view Solidarity's coming into power would have made no difference. In his retrospective view, even Poland's departure from the alliance would have been a mere inconvenience rather than a serious blow to Soviet military plans. In a war with NATO, he maintained, Moscow would have had enough advance warning to secure the passage of its troops through Poland without difficulty. In 1981, Kulikov may not have thought that way—the record shows him as an ardent advocate of military intervention—but his politburo superiors did. Even as the crisis deepened, they stood firm in their decision that "our troops will not be sent to Poland." Even if "social democrats" were to "come into power instead of the communists," Suslov summed up the consensus in the Kremlin, "we will work with the social democrats. But we will not introduce troops under any circumstances."[154]

Such a position made good sense both politically and militarily. Having learned what they believed were the lessons of Hungary in 1956, Solidarity leaders went out of their way to avoid giving the impression that they would want to take the country out of the Warsaw Pact or demand the withdrawal of the Soviet troops stationed in Poland to safeguard Moscow's lines of communication with East Germany. Nor was there any strong popular sentiment against keeping military ties with the Soviet Union, as most Poles, whatever their other disagreements, shared a visceral fear of a German threat, against which they welcomed Soviet protection.

The Warsaw Pact meetings during the crisis were notable for an all but complete absence of the Polish issue from their agendas. On December 1–2, 1981, by which time Jaruzelski had almost completed his preparations for the proclamation of martial law, the alliance's committee of foreign ministers met in Bucharest after a year's interval to discuss arms control but not the Polish situation. The committee of defense ministers, sitting in Moscow, addressed it only as a third topic; once the issue was introduced, however, problems arose. Jaruzelski's right-hand man, Gen. Florian Siwicki, asked the committee to declare publicly its advance backing for the introduction of martial law. He wanted the declaration to specify that the measure

---

153 Kukliński, "Wojna z narodem," p. 40. Document no. 91. Jaruzelski cited in John Darnton, "Jaruzelski Is Now Sorry He Ordered Martial Law," *New York Times,* March 4, 1993.

154 Interview with Kulikov, Piotr Jendroszczyk, "Układ" [The Pact], *Rzeczpospolita* [Warsaw], November 7, 1997. Minutes of Soviet politburo session, October 29, 1981, Kramer, *Soviet Deliberations during the Polish Crisis,* pp. 148–56, at p. 152. Suslov cited by Gribkov, *Global Competition and the Deterioration of U.S. Soviet Relations,* p. 244.

was required by Poland's obligations under the Warsaw Pact, thus deflecting from the Polish generals the responsibility for the action they were about to take. He had brought along a draft by Jaruzelski, proclaiming the necessity of "suitable steps aimed at ensuring common security in socialist Europe" because of subversive activities allegedly spreading in the country.[155]

The draft provoked a spirited discussion. In a sharp exchange with Ogarkov, who compared the situation in Poland with that in Hungary in 1956, Hungarian defense minister Lajos Czinege found his remark that the Hungarians "possibly forgot about 1956" insulting, and refused to sign the declaration unless there were unanimous support for it. This was something his Romanian colleague, Constantin Olteanu, ensured would not be available, so the declaration did not pass. Kulikov chimed in to tell the Romanians that now was the time they should at least sign the statute on command in war time rejected by Ceaușescu the year before. The East Germans used the commotion to renew their demand for calling their "Main" Staff "general. Neither succeeded.[156]

Nor was Jaruzelski granted his wish for a Soviet military guarantee should his attempted coup d'état run into trouble. His request for the guarantee, the evidence of which only came to light sixteen years later, dispels the myth that the proclamation of martial law on December 13 was intended to avert the "greater evil" of imminent Soviet invasion. In fact, the general went ahead despite Moscow's refusal to promise military assistance. No such assistance was needed, however. Having caught the opposition by surprise, the Polish military carried out their coup with impressive precision. None of the troops, many of them Solidarity supporters, refused to obey orders.[157]

Although the restoration of communist order in Poland appeared to be the Warsaw Pact's success, this was in important ways not the case. The alliance's role during the crisis as well as the impact of the crisis on its integrity had been ambivalent. Much like in Czechoslovakia before, the East–West military balance was not at stake from the Soviet point of view. If, as originally envisaged, Warsaw Pact troops had moved into Poland in 1980 in an attempt to secure there in power a regime to Soviet liking, the cohesion of the alliance might have been tested. But the test never came, and when the final crackdown took place a year later, no such troops were involved. Leaving the solution of the Polish problem to the Poles was not a divisive issue within the alliance; even the Romanians supported Jaruzelski's action. Only his request to accord his coup political and moral legitimacy in advance had created dissension, but this did not materially affect the course of events.

[155] Czechoslovak report on conference of foreign ministers, December 7, 1981, 016.976/81, AMZV, also at http://www.isn.ethz.ch/php/documents/collection_3/CMFA_docs/CMFA_1981/-1981_2.pdf. Document no. 93.

[156] Minutes of Romanian politburo meeting, December 13, 1981, CC RCP Chancellery, File No. 101/1981, pp. 2–15, ANIC, also at http://www.isn.ethz.ch/php/documents/collection_14/1213-1981.htm. Additional documents on the defense ministers' meeting at http://www.isn.ethz.ch/php/-documents/collection_3/CMD_meetings/meeting14.htm.

[157] Document no. 94. Cf. Andrzej Paczkowski, *Droga do "mniejszego zła": Strategia i taktyka obozu władzy, lipiec 1980-styczeń 1982* [The Road to the "Lesser Evil": The Strategy and Tactics of the Ruling Establishment, July 1980–January 1982] (Cracow: Wydawnictwo literackie, 2002).

If the Warsaw Pact thus emerged relatively unscathed from the Polish drama, the same cannot be said about the Soviet Union. While the Kremlin rejoiced in the defeat of the pesky Polish opposition, it was a sobering thought for Soviet leaders that they had to rely for that accomplishment on a tormented individual whom they did not effectively control. Jaruzelski and his team had demonstrated devotion to the Soviet alliance, but their success in crushing the domestic enemy was no guarantee of their future performance. Moscow awaited with trepidation the outcome of the novel experiment in a military dictatorship intended to salvage a bankrupt communist party—an experiment alien to both Russian and Soviet political cultures, which discouraged independent political role by the military. Although Jaruzelski proved adept and his opponents inept as politicians at the moment of the coup, in the long run their respective political skills remained to be seen, and in the end the qualities would prove reversed.

Much though the communist alliance continued to impress outsiders by its apparent vigor and real arrogance, the appearances were deceptive. In the purely military sense, at issue was no longer matching its Western rival in building useless nuclear weapons but rather keeping up with the West's rising preponderance in technologically advanced conventional armaments—a battle the Soviet system was not equipped to win. After Poland, the Warsaw Pact's self-confidence was not the same as before. Although its managers went on, as usual, with aggressive military exercises, the implementation of their plans became ever more problematic. A 1982 exercise rehearsed ominously a war started by a Chinese rather than a NATO attack, in which not only Romania but also Poland would stay neutral.[158]

The meetings of the alliance's committees during the last two years of Brezhnev's incapacitating illness reflected an almost desperate Soviet effort to salvage what remained of détente. Moscow rehashed such stale ideas as a non-aggression treaty with NATO or the pledge against the first use of nuclear weapons. As the leadership was losing its grip, there was a growing divergence between advocates of an accelerated military buildup, exemplified by defense minister Dmitrii F. Ustinov, and those, like Gromyko, who understood better that the buildup was irrelevant, if not counterproductive, in waging political competition with NATO.[159] In the struggle for Western hearts and minds against the deployment of "Euromissiles," which were to be installed unless the SS-20s would be removed, the Soviet Union counted on the influence to be exerted on NATO governments by its junior allies bilaterally—another example of how Moscow became dependent on them. Predictably, Romania took the lead in opposing the threat of deploying additional Soviet missiles in Eastern Europe as bad tactics, urging instead inducement by good example, such as unilateral reduction of defense budgets and conventional forces. When the PCC met in January 1983—for the first time since Brezhnev's death two months earlier—Ceauşescu demanded that his and other Warsaw Pact countries be given a say in the

---

[158] "Die Anstrengungen der NATO zur Erringung der militärtechnischen Überlegenheit bei den Streitkräften allgemeiner Bestimmung," prepared for the November 11, 1985, session of the East German National Defense Council, DVW 1/39532, pp. 61–69, BA-MA. Documents nos. 107, 110, and 95

[159] Documents nos. 92 and 102.

nuclear arms negotiations the Soviet Union was conducting with the United States in Geneva.[160]

The coming into power of the Reagan administration and NATO's subsequent armament program created a greater scare in Moscow than in Eastern European capitals. Soviet representatives at Warsaw Pact meetings therefore tried all the harder to impress upon their participants how serious the situation supposedly was. In September 1982, Ogarkov tried to convince a gathering of chiefs of staff that "the material preparations for war, as shown also by the current maneuvers of NATO, are no game, but are dead serious." He contended that the unpredictability of the adversary had brought about a situation analogous to that which had preceded the outbreak of World War II. Indeed, in his view, the United States had "in effect already declared war on us, the Soviet Union, and some other states of the Warsaw Treaty," meaning especially Jaruzelski's Poland.[161]

In a somber keynote speech to the PCC in January 1983, Brezhnev's successor, Iurii V. Andropov, warned that the threat of war had increased dramatically. Having been a leading member of the coterie responsible for the disastrous decision to invade Afghanistan, the former KGB chief was also the instigator of the worldwide watch by his intelligence agents, initiated in 1980, to detect any signs of Western preparations for a surprise nuclear attack. The main Warsaw Pact exercise, "Soiuz-83," now presumed that NATO had become so strong that it could strike in Central Europe in several directions with little advance notice—a remarkable reversal of what used to be NATO's nightmare about the Soviet Union in the early years of the Cold War. And Warsaw Pact exercises in the nineteen-eighties increasingly indicated that it would be difficult to defeat the enemy without using nuclear weapons.[162]

The June 1983 Warsaw Pact summit, convened in anticipation of the final approval of the Euromissile deployments by the West German parliament, ended with a reluctant agreement by East Germany and Czechoslovakia to the counter-deployment of Soviet missiles on their territories. Romania continued to oppose the idea, fueling discord at a confrontational meeting of foreign ministers four months later. And once the deployments and counter-deployments had started in 1984, resentment of what was happening brought about an unprecedented rapprochement between East Germany and Hungary—the Warsaw Pact's most and least orthodox regimes. The realignment brought into focus the old issue of national *vs.* common interests.[163]

East Germany's official press reprinted, with implied approval, the writings by the Hungarian party theoretician, Mátyás Szűrös, which advanced the heretical notion

---

[160] Report on the PCC meeting, January 1983, DC/20/I/3/1908 , SAPMO, also at http://www.-isn.ethz.ch/php/documents/collection_3/PCC_docs/1983/1983_4.pdf. Speech by Ceauşescu, January 4, 1983, DC/20/I/3/1908, SAPMO, also at http://www.isn.ethz.ch/php/documents/collection_-3/PCC_docs/1983/1983_8_I.pdf.

[161] Documents nos. 96 and 103.

[162] Documents nos. 98, 99, and 120. On the nuclear attack alert, codenamed RYAN, see Benjamin B. Fischer, *A Cold War Conundrum: The 1983 Soviet War Scare* (Washington, DC: Central Intelligence Agency, 1997), also at http://www.cia.gov/csi/monograph/coldwar/source.htm.

[163] Documents nos. 100 and 101. Michael Ploetz, "NATO and the Warsaw Treaty Organization at the Time of the Euromissile Crisis, 1975 to 1985," in *A History of NATO: The First Fifty Years*, ed. Gustav Schmidt, vol. 2 (Basingstoke: Palgrave, 2001), pp. 208–21.

that the pursuit of national interests is both justified and compatible with the common ones. Hungary's particular interest was in promoting regional cooperation with small Western European countries across ideological and alliance boundaries. East Germany's interest was served by pursuing what Honecker believed was its not only economically but also politically profitable special relationship with West Germany. He claimed "special responsibility" of both German states for ensuring that war would never again emanate from German soil and insisted on their common effort at "damage limitation," meaning the damage caused by the presence on that soil of not only the American but also the Soviet missiles.[164]

As the decrepit Konstantin U. Chernenko ascended to supreme power in the Kremlin after Andropov, Honecker's hubris reached unprecedented heights. He wanted the Soviet ambassador to East Berlin, Petr A. Abrasimov, to be replaced because he found it "impossible to conduct a political dialog" with him. He seemed genuinely convinced that he could wrap some of the most important West German politicians around his fingers. When Honecker came to Moscow he lectured Chernenko about how to handle relations with Bonn and unceremoniously told off Ustinov after the latter had suggested that the East German approach might be too soft.[165]

East German arrogance was becoming a problem. It brought two junior Warsaw Pact members closest to a military confrontation after the GDR had arbitrarily extended its territorial waters, blocking egress for Polish shipping from the Oder River estuary at Świnoujście. The dispute was resolved by a compromise more advantageous to East Berlin than to Warsaw, suggestive of Jaruzelski's weak hand in dealing with Honecker. Soviet passivity in the matter reflected a growing incidence within the alliance of developments outside Moscow's control, although none yet indicated that this could threaten the integrity of the Warsaw Pact, much less its existence.[166]

10. THE GORBACHEV REFORMS (1985–1989)

Honecker welcomed Mikhail S. Gorbachev's coming into power in 1985 as heralding an era in which national interests would be harmonized with common interests and East Germany would finally be recognized as Moscow's privileged partner. The month after his appointment as Soviet party general secretary, Gorbachev in April presided over the alliance's 30th anniversary session, during which the validity of its founding charter was extended for another 20 years despite Romanian opposition. The prevailing opinion at the time was that his foremost priority was strengthening

---

[164] Minutes of Honecker–Grósz meeting, September 8, 1984, ZK SED, J IV/931, SAPMO. Vojtech Mastny, ed., *Soviet/East European Survey, 1983–1984: Selected Research and Analysis from Radio Free Europe/Radio Liberty* (Durham: Duke University Press, 1985), pp. 227–57.

[165] Memorandum of Honecker–Andropov conversation on May 4, 1983, dated May 7, 1983, J IV/827, SAPMO. On Honecker's assessment of West German politicians, record of Honecker–Hu Yaobang meeting, October 22, 1986, in *Die DDR und China, 1949 bis 1990: Politik—Wirtschaft—Kultur: Eine Quellensammlung*, ed. Werner Meissner and Anja Feege (Berlin: Akademie, 1995), pp. 369–73. Document no. 104.

[166] On the East German–Polish dispute, Kessler to Axen, July 2, 1987, and summary of Kessler–Siwicki conversation, August 12, 1987, VA-01/32676, BA-MA, and record of Honecker–Jaruzelski meeting, September 16, 1987, ZK SED, J IV/893; DY 3/2479, SAPMO.

the Warsaw Pact and that he was better equipped than his predecessors to do so. This was Gorbachev's own opinion as well. The subsequent developments to the contrary resulted from unexpected and unintended workings of his often improvised and incoherent policies, which would eventually prove fatal for the alliance he wanted to uphold, though otherwise immensely beneficial for its enemies and the world at large.[167]

In determining the course of the Cold War in its final years, the military balance did not play as important a role as contemporaries tended to believe. Nor did the Warsaw Pact serve as the engine, or even catalyst, of change; instead, its internal developments merely reflected, or at most facilitated, changes that were taking place outside its structures, in response to the larger political dynamics of the Soviet bloc. Soon after Gorbachev took power, he reportedly declared to the Eastern European leaders that they were now on their own. Nothing suggests, however, that this seemingly momentous renunciation of the "Brezhnev doctrine"—if it indeed took place—had any practical effect. Polish foreign minister Marian Orzechowski later described the discarding of the doctrine as a matter of policies rather than declarations.[168]

The policies that were beginning to take shape, though not their consequences, appeared clearer at the PCC session in Sofia in October 1985. Gorbachev defended there his decision to resume the Geneva arms control talks even though none of the conditions the Soviet Union had solemnly declared must be met before it would return to the negotiating table had in fact been met by the United States. Putting the blame for the unsatisfactory progress of the talks on Washington, he rationalized his reversal as a brilliant move that caught the adversary by surprise and left the initiative in Soviet hands.[169]

Gorbachev told the Warsaw Pact leaders that the East could banish the threat of war by achieving a "breakthrough" in relations with the West that would revive détente. In March 1986, his foreign minister, Eduard Shevardnadze, explained to his Eastern European colleagues that the ultimate goal was the abolition of weapons of mass destruction. Acknowledging the allies' vital stake in the outcome of the arms control talks between the superpowers, he promised to keep them not only informed but also involved through special committees and working groups created for that purpose. He kept his promise, thus allowing them for the first time a say in nuclear questions.[170]

With regard to security matters, the East European regimes of both conservative and reformist variety initially welcomed the new wind that was blowing from Moscow. Even the Romanians became more cooperative than usual, now that Gorbachev was

---

[167] Document no. 106. On the renewal of the Warsaw Pact, John Erickson, "Warsaw Pact: From Here to Eternity?" *Current History*, November 1985: 357–60, 387.

[168] The source for Gorbachev's alleged statement is his aide Anatolii S. Cherniaev in an interview on February 25, 1993. Raymond L. Garthoff, *The Great Transition: American–Soviet Relations and the End of the Cold War* (Washington: Brookings Institution, 1994), pp. 571–72. Orzechowski in *Polska 1986–1989: Koniec Systemu* (Poland 1986–198: The End of the System), ed. Andrzej Paczkowski, vol. 2 (Warsaw: Trio, 2002), p. 304.

[169] Speech by Gorbachev, October 22, 1985, DC20/I/3/2232, SAPMO, also at http://www.isn.ethz.ch/php/documents/collection_3/PCC_docs/1985/1985_12_I.pdf.

[170] Document no. 111.

adopting some of the ideas they had previously advanced in vain—allied input into disarmament negotiations, cuts in defense budgets, radical reductions of conventional forces, abolition of nuclear armaments. But while Bucharest supported Moscow's disarmament initiatives it insisted they should go farther. In an example of unprecedented cooperation with Bulgaria, traditionally the region's most staunchly pro-Soviet state, which did not go so far as supporting unilateral cuts of troops and armaments, Romania proposed the creation of a zone free of chemical weapons in the Balkans.[171]

None other than Honecker—the stalwart of conservative orthodoxy—became the foremost champion of Moscow's radical innovations in security policy, with the conservative regimes in Prague and Warsaw coming next. East Germany joined with Czechoslovakia in proposing a chemical-weapons-free zone in Central Europe and, together with West Germany's Social Democratic Party, prepared a proposal for a zone free of tactical nuclear weapons as well. Alluding to West German receptiveness toward such proposals, Gorbachev complimented Honecker that "this has been thanks to you, Erich." He exalted the Soviet–East German relationship as the Warsaw Pact's "cement" (*zementierender Teil*).[172]

It made sense for Honecker to advocate a reduction of the military components of the East–West confrontation in Central Europe. East German spies provided him with reassuring information about Western assessments of the balance of forces and its likely development. Thus, for example, an advanced draft of secret West German "Defense Policy Guidelines," which the spies had managed to snatch, assumed that European stability would be maintained thanks to the Soviet system's basic continuity in the foreseeable future, that the superpowers' offensive arsenals would ensure the preservation of strategic balance between them, and that the balance would not be swayed in NATO's favor by the development of high-technology conventional weapons. Although all these assumptions were false, the knowledge that the enemy believed them to be true seemed to make a relaxation of the Warsaw Pact's military posture that much more affordable.[173]

This was not the view, however, of Soviet participants in the meetings of the alliance's military bodies—the committee of defense ministers and military council—who kept beating the alarmist drum. Kulikov charged that the U.S. AirLand Battle strategy, which NATO endorsed by adopting the "Follow-On Forces Attack" (FOFA) concept, implied a readiness to start hostilities at any time, "practically to the total

---

[171] Documents nos. 118, 113, 116.

[172] Document no. 114. Records of Honecker–Gorbachev conversations, October 2, 1986, and April 20, 1986, in *Honecker–Gorbatschow: Vieraugengespräche*, ed. Daniel Küchenmeister and Gerd-Rüdiger Stephan (Berlin: Dietz, 1993), pp. 113–35, 78–105.

[173] Document no. 109. "Verteidigungspolitische Richtlinien," dated April 1987, AZN 32651, 78–86, BA-MA. On assessments of NATO by East German intelligence, an account by one of its former officers, Heinz Busch, "Die NATO in der Sicht der Auswertung der HV A," in *Das Gesicht dem Westen zu...: DDR-Spionage gegen die Bundesrepublik Deutschland*, ed. Georg Herbstritt and Helmut Müller-Enbergs (Bremen: Temmen, 2003), pp. 239–47. For an evaluation, see Bernd Schaefer, *The Warsaw Pact's Intelligence on NATO: East German Military Espionage against the West*, IFS Info No. 2/2002 (Oslo: Institute for Defence Studies, 2002), also at www.isn.ethz.ch/php/-documents/collection_17/texts/schaefer.pdf.

depth of the buildup of our armed forces in the western and southwestern theaters of war"—as NATO had believed the Soviet army to be capable of in the nineteen-fifties. The threat perceptions had gone full circle.[174]

The insistence that NATO's surprise attack was a real possibility, which appears frequently in Warsaw Pact internal documents until well into the late nineteen-eighties, may be explained by the deep impression the AirLand Battle and FOFA concepts made on Soviet strategists.[175] The novel idea of stopping advancing Warsaw Pact forces by striking against their second echelons presupposed thorough reconnaissance of the extended battlefield as well as lethal targeting, both of which the West, though not the East, had by then become capable of because of its technological advances. From the Soviet point of view, NATO's capability to detect in advance any offensive preparations by the enemy, combined with the capability to disrupt them before they could become dangerous, was bound to increase Western temptation to pre-empt by delivering a disabling strike, conventional or nuclear. And the temptation would be the greater the more the preparations would be perfected. The ingenuity of AirLand Battle was thus in turning the Soviets' offensive strategy against them.

Counting how many more tanks, guns, anti-tank weapons, and ships NATO was adding to those it already had, Kulikov lamented that not only West Germany but also Great Britain, Italy, and Turkey were becoming more aggressive. To counter that, Soviet generals dwelt on the need to enhance even more the Warsaw Pact's aggressive posture that had been the primary reason for NATO's buildup in the first place. In the opinion of Gorbachev's aide Anatolii S. Cherniaev, it was because of their insistence on ever higher defense spending that they, rather than NATO, were the "real danger."[176]

Gorbachev expounded his new thinking at the February 1986 Soviet party congress where he proclaimed that "the task of ensuring security increasingly is a political task, and can only be resolved by political means." He called for the unity of the alliance but, insisting that "unity has nothing to do with conformity," acknowledged its members' right to shape its future. "It is not at all necessary that all initiatives originate with the Soviet Union." There was fresh air in Gorbachev's admission that security cannot be absolute but only mutual as well as in his refusal to make it dependent on deterrence. He aptly noted that security "cannot be built forever on a fear of retribution." The congress gave its blessing to the doctrine of "reasonable defensive sufficiency." A brainchild of left-wing critics of NATO, the idea had always been more pertinent to the Warsaw Pact's offensive strategy and propensity for excess in troops and armaments. Marshal Sergei F. Akhromeev, the chief of

---

[174] Documents nos. 105, 108. Report by Kulikov to the December 2–5, 1985, meeting of the committee of defense ministers, DVW 1/71044, BA-MA, also at http://www.isn.ethz.ch/php/documents/collection_3/CMD_docs/18-044-I.pdf.

[175] Document No. 138. Cf. Andrei A. Kokoshin, "'План Роджерса': Алтернативные концепции обороны и безопасность в Европе" [The Rogers Plan: The Alternative Concepts of Defense and European Security], *SshA—Ekonomika, Politika, Ideologia* 9 (1985): 3–14

[176] Documents no. 108, 119. Cherniaev cited in Odom, *The Collapse of the Soviet Military*, p. 95.

the general staff, justified the new doctrine as necessary on both political and economic grounds.[177]

An accident added pressure for change. The June 1986 PCC meeting took place in the aftermath of the Chernobyl nuclear disaster that gave a foretaste of what a nuclear war in Europe would be like. Gorbachev felt compelled to report in detail about the effects of the accident, encouraging skepticism about the Warsaw Pact's war plans. "No one should have the idea that in a nuclear war one could enjoy a cup of coffee in Paris five or six days later," commented Jaruzelski, urging that the alliance's exercises be revised. The committee issued an appeal for a 25 percent across-the-board reduction of forces on both sides.[178]

Gorbachev did not consider himself to be on the defensive. On the contrary, in reporting to the allies about the Geneva arms control talks, he depicted the Western side as being on the run. He told Honecker that the United States needed the arms race because it could not function without feeding its military machine, and could therefore be defeated by being forced into the disarmament process. In trying to draw it into the process, Gorbachev rationalized the concessions the Soviet Union had been making as if they were part of a winning strategy of offering what the adversary could not afford to refuse. This was not, however, how the other side saw it. An American official who had been present at the Gorbachev–Reagan summit in Reykjavik in October 1986 thus described what happened there: "We came with nothing to offer and had offered nothing. [We] sat there while they unwrapped their gifts."[179]

In May 1987, the PCC at its meeting in Berlin officially discarded the Warsaw Pact's quarter-century-old offensive strategy. Not only was the alliance's new military doctrine, which enshrined the principles of "defensive sufficiency" and "non-offensive defense" made public but also a serious effort was made to implement it. Again, none of the Eastern European regimes objected—although the Romanians vainly tried to promote the adoption of separate national doctrines rather than a common one. Only the military grumbled about a strategic change that meant dismantling the alliance's established offensive structure without replacing it with a ready-made new one. They tried to preserve as many offensive elements as possible in a defensive guise, but eventually went along.[180]

[177] The first and second Gorbachev quotes in Garthoff, *The Great Transition,* pp. 528 and 572, the third in East-German record of meeting of party secretaries, June 10–11, 1986, DY/30/2353, pp. 2–45, at p. 12, SAPMO. Document no. 127. Cf. R. Hyland Phillips, and Jeffrey I. Sands, "Reasonable Sufficiency and Soviet Conventional Defense," *International Security* 13, no. 2 (Fall 1988): 164–78.

[178] Document no. 115. Appeal for reductions of conventional forces, June 11, 1986, VA-01/40372, 176–78, BA-MA.

[179] Record of Gorbachev–Honecker conversation, April 20, 1986, in Küchenmeister and Stephan, *Honecker–Gorbatschow,* pp.78–105, at p. 83. Speech by Gorbachev at meeting of party secretaries, June 10–11, 1986, DY/30/2353, pp. 46–73, SAPMO. Kenneth Adelman quoted in Frances Fitzgerald, *Way Out There in the Blue: Reagan, Star Wars and the End of the Cold War* (New York: Simon & Schuster, 2000), p. 360.

[180] Documents nos. 122, 123 a-e, 124, and 132. Statement by Iazov for meeting of committee of defense ministers and transcript of his informal remarks, November 24–25, 1987, VS OS-OL, krab. 60. č.j. 38505/39, VÚA.

The acquiescence of the Soviet high command in this revolutionary change had been preconditioned by the traditional dependence of Russia's military on its autocratic rulers. The interpenetration of the party and army institutions in the Soviet system further ensured the party's primacy and inhibited independent action by the generals. What clinched the issue, however, was the acute embarrassment the Soviet military suffered at the critical moment. While the PCC was in session, West German pacifist Matthias Rust landed his light aircraft next to the Red Square in the heart of Moscow, making a ridicule of the country's elaborate air defenses. The incident, which infuriated Gorbachev and horrified the Eastern European leaders, made the military more pliable than they might otherwise have been, and helped Gorbachev fire defense minister Sergei L. Sokolov.[181]

The change from the offensive to defensive doctrine required not only drawing up new operational plans, which were never completed, but also unaccustomed cooperation with the enemy. This involved both the Geneva negotiations between the superpowers on dismantling the intermediate-range nuclear forces (INF), whose significance was largely symbolic, and the talks between the two alliances about the reduction of their conventional forces, a measure that went to the very heart of the balance of power in Europe. The function of the Soviet army as an instrument of last resort to maintain Moscow's predominance in the Eastern part of the Continent became problematic once the protracted and sterile "mutual and balanced force reduction" (MBFR) talks were merged in 1987 into the more productive CSCE framework as negotiations on "conventional forces in Europe" (CFE), and began to produce results.

In response to Gorbachev's pursuit of greater openness (*glasnost*), Gribkov proposed the creation of a Warsaw Pact information office—something NATO had always had to explain itself to its publics. Now the managers of the Soviet alliance, too, realized that it was in their interests to justify the organization to its constituents while convincing its enemies of its peaceful intentions. A revision of the controversial statute on command in war time was part of the effort, but did not get very far. Another Soviet proposal envisaged the establishment of a Warsaw Pact parliamentary organization, analogous to NATO's North Atlantic Assembly. Unprecedented contacts between the two alliances included an exchange of visits by parliamentarians.[182]

More importantly, building mutual trust required the exchange of accurate data about the respective numbers of troops and armaments—an undertaking difficult to reconcile with the time-honored Soviet habit of distortion and dissimulation, often

---

[181] As the Soviet military became more interested in the acquisition of advanced conventional weapons than in nuclear weapons, they were also more willing to countenance changes in military posture that would make more resources available for the costly development of conventional armaments. Stephen Meyer, "The Sources and Prospects of Gorbachev's New Political Thinking on Security," *International Security* 13, no. 2 (1988): 124–63.

[182] Documents nos. 126, 129, and 131. For the original statute, see document no. 86. On the parliament issue, speeches by Shevardnadze, March 19, 1988, DC-20 I/3-2640, pp. 64–81, SAPMO, also at http://www.isn.ethz.ch/php/documents/collection_3/CMFA_docs/CMFA_1988_I/Speech-Shevardnadze_0388.pdf., and by Gorbachev, July 15, 1988, DC20/I/3/2687, SAPMO, also at http://www.isn.ethz.ch/php/documents/collection_3/PCC_docs/1988/1988_8_I.pdf.

for its own sake rather than for a particular purpose. Revealing the true figures was a blow to the principle of secrecy that had been one of the pillars of the Soviet system, and was bound to reverberate beyond its military structures. Gorbachev welcomed these changes as supposedly proving the strength of the system and facilitating the construction of the new "European house," in which he imagined both the Warsaw Pact and NATO would be able to live in a harmonious and mutually complementary coexistence. It was castle in the sky.[183]

At the March 1988 conference of foreign ministers, Shevardnadze's optimism about the beneficial political effects of cutting both alliances' conventional forces contrasted with his East German colleague Oskar Fischer's worries that the East was on the losing side in the battle about human rights. Neither East Germany nor its fellow Warsaw Pact regimes, however, regarded the forthcoming reduction of Soviet military strength as potentially destabilizing. Honecker took in stride the successive withdrawals of Soviet troops and tanks from his country, using the opportunity to claim more control over those that remained. He raised the question of a revision of the 1957 status-of-forces agreement that would give East Germany jurisdiction over the frequently misbehaving Soviet soldiery. Both East Germany and Czechoslovakia had nothing but praise for the U.S.–Soviet treaty on dismantling intermediate-range nuclear forces (INF), and cooperated readily in getting their territories rid of Soviet missiles.[184]

At the July 1988 meeting of the Warsaw Pact defense ministers, Gorbachev praised the alliance's "new dynamism," as its member-states were getting more "independently active." His sensational renunciation at the United Nations on December 7 of the Brezhnev doctrine—which for all intents and purposes the Kremlin had already abandoned when it ruled out intervening militarily in Poland in 1981—went even farther than contemporaries tended to believe. It signaled indifference to whatever would happen in Eastern Europe. In contrast to his crusade for reform in the Soviet Union, Gorbachev neither discouraged nor encouraged reform in the region, thus leaving both conservative and reform-minded regimes there, as well as their peoples, truly to their own devices.[185]

In contrast to Gorbachev's opportunistic indifference to the fate of Eastern Europe, his approach to disarmament was principled to the point of dogmatism. He was admirable, as Reagan was, in his sincere belief in a nuclear-free world—a mirage that made it difficult for the two leaders to reach an agreement on more practical matters at their Reykjavik meeting. Afterward, Gorbachev rallied the Warsaw Pact allies

---

[183] Documents nos. 125, 130, 135–36. Marie-Pierre Rey, "'Europe Is Our Common Home': A Study of Gorbachev's Diplomatic Concept," *Cold War History* 4, no. 2 (January 2004): 33–65.

[184] Documents nos. 128 and 139..Record of East German National Defense Council meeting, November 25, 1988, and draft of new status-of-forces agreement, VA-01/39592, BA-MA. Streletz to Smetkov, March 17, 1989, DVW1/44535, BA-MA. East German–Czechoslovak–Soviet agreement on implementation of INF treaty, June 1, 1988, MR c-20 I/3-2674, SAPMO.

[185] Document no. 134. Gorbachev's U,N, speech in *Vital Speeches of the Day* 55, no. 9 (February 1, 1989). Vojtech Mastny, "Did Gorbachev Liberate Eastern Europe?" in *The Last Decade of the Cold War: From Conflict Escalation to Conflict Transformation*, ed. Olav Njølstad (London: Cass, 2004), pp. 402–23.

to increase pressure on the United States to achieve radical disarmament. Their attention, however, was increasingly distracted by the CSCE, where they were under growing pressure to live up to their commitments on human rights. This became by then the most tangible threat to their security—internal rather than external.[186]

In his United Nations speech, Gorbachev announced deep unilateral cuts of Soviet conventional forces. He underlined the seriousness of his intentions by his wholesale dismissal of some of the most hawkish Soviet generals, including the Warsaw Pact's top brass Kulikov and Gribkov, replacing them by less known figures, who were more willing to cooperate—at least for the time being—in dismantling the Warsaw Pact's offensive military posture. The May 1989 "Vltava" exercise in Czechoslovakia showed that the new defensive strategy was being translated into practice, as well as the considerable problems this entailed.[187]

Gorbachev was unprepared for the consequences of the drastic changes he was presiding over. At the secret politburo meeting that followed his announcement of unilateral disarmament measures, he admitted to his colleagues that he had no "longer-term plan of practical measures to implement the … concept" he had announced, but he played down its absence as unimportant. What really mattered, in his view, was that the prospective force reductions "pulled the rug [out] from under the feet of those who have been prattling … that new political thinking is just about words." He claimed that the prospect of a withdrawal of Soviet military might from Eastern Europe was filling U.S. reactionaries with "concern, anxiety, and even fear" that Moscow was going to "seize the initiative and lead the entire world." Proclaiming the Soviet system's intrinsic superiority in terms reminiscent of Khrushchev's, Gorbachev did not see himself as making concessions from weakness but rather gains from a position of strength. No one in the audience contradicted him.[188]

Foreign minister Shevardnadze was the only person in the politburo to at least voice concern that time was running out for clarifying what the new defensive posture meant with regard to Eastern Europe; he feared that "we will be caught … on every … detail." At issue was the availability of force to prop up, if necessary, the Soviet Union's Eastern European empire—the "glacis" created by Stalin after World War II as an indispensable safeguard of Soviet security as he understood it. The ensuing discussion was notable for its emptiness, consisting of little more than evasive platitudes. And Gorbachev's closing description of the session as "really grand-scale policy-making" was suggestive of the terminal decay of the ruling class of a superpower that, while still bristling with troops and weapons, had already lost the will to rule.[189]

Some of Moscow's best policy analysts understood better than the men in charge what was happening with their country's vital security zone. One of their memoranda for the top leadership concluded that communism in Eastern Europe was finished

---

[186] Documents nos. 117 and 121.

[187] Documents nos. 140, 142–43.

[188] Minutes of Soviet party politburo meeting, December 27–28, 1988, *Cold War International History Project Bulletin* 12–13 (2001): 24–29, at p. 24. Cf. Celeste A. Wallander, "Western Policy and the Demise of the Soviet Union," *Journal of Cold War Studies* 5, no. 4 (Fall 2003): 137–77, at pp.161–62.

[189] Minutes of the Soviet party politburo meeting, December 27–28, 1988, *Cold War International History Project Bulletin* 12–13 (2001): 24–29, at pp. 26–29.

but Soviet predominance in the region could be preserved by its "Finlandization." This meant allowing the emergence of noncommunist states in the region whose deference to Moscow would follow the Finnish model but, unlike in the case of Finland, would be ensured through their membership in the Warsaw Pact. Whether or not the recommendation was ever considered or even read by policymakers, no attempt was made to put it into effect.[190]

In using the Warsaw Pact structures to help implement radical arms control measures, the Gorbachev leadership was trying to forge new relations with the countries of Western rather than Eastern Europe. As Moscow's interest in its empire was vanishing, it was the region's embattled conservative regimes that took it upon themselves to attempt a transformation of the Warsaw Pact into a vehicle for their political survival—an ironic final twist in the tortuous development of an alliance that had already witnessed so many redefinitions of its raison d'être.

11. DISINTEGRATION (1989–1991)

The rapprochement between East Germany and Romania—respectively the Warsaw Pact's foremost defender and its main detractor—was a sign of changing times. When Honecker and Ceaușescu met in Berlin in November 1988, congratulating each other on their countries' accomplishments, they were of one mind in perceiving a major threat in the concessions on human rights that their other allies were preparing to make at the CSCE follow-up conference in Vienna. They differed, however, in their views of how the Warsaw Pact could best preserve its integrity and, more importantly, the integrity of their regimes.[191]

Honecker saw in the enhancement of political, rather than military, functions of the alliance—which Gorbachev also favored—a sufficient guarantee that it could be steered to serve East Germany's main interests. For Ceaușescu, a structural reorganization and "democratization" were needed if the Warsaw Pact were to be made useful to him. The gist of the Romanian reform proposal, submitted in July 1988, was separation of its political and military functions. The political consultative committee was to be upgraded to supervise not only political but also economic cooperation. It could then become a watchdog against the spread of any potentially infectious deviation from the established standards of orthodoxy. Also, membership was to be made open to additional "socialist" countries—in effect North Korea, Cuba, Vietnam, perhaps China, besides former member Albania, all of which could be expected to side with the conservative regimes against the reforming ones.[192]

The Romanian project further envisaged the creation of a military committee consisting of the ministers of defense, with a rotating presidency and the power to appoint the supreme commander, for no more than a two-year term. The chief of staff, who would serve for a longer period, could be a Soviet officer but his appointment would

[190] Memorandum to Alexander Iakovlev from the Bogomolov Commission, February 1989, ibid., pp. 52–61.
[191] Record of Honecker–Ceaușescu meeting, November 17, 1988, ZK SED, IV/939, SAPMO. Document no. 141.
[192] Document no. 133 a.

be subject to unanimous approval by all members. Romania's goal remained loosening Moscow's grip on the alliance—a goal added urgency by Gorbachev's turn to reformism. The separation of the Warsaw Pact's military purposes from its political functioning was to make it more resistant to the disruptive strategic restructuring the Kremlin had set in motion. Moscow did not reject the proposal, but submitted it for discussion. A committee of experts from foreign and defense ministries was created to consider reform. It held its first meeting in December 1988.[193]

The committee met four times without making progress. The East Germans had misgivings about the Romanian proposal in its present form and Hungary objected to any role of the expanded PCC in internal matters, but no one offered other proposals until Bulgaria did in June 1989. After consultations with Moscow, it submitted an alternative plan to the radical reorganization the Romanians wanted. Instead of separating the Warsaw Pact's political and military functions, while upgrading the former and downgrading the latter, the Bulgarians sought to strengthen the alliance overall and further develop its institutions. They called for the establishment of a permanent secretariat and other improvements along the NATO model, which Moscow had been vainly trying to achieve for years.[194]

Attesting to how much the times had changed, both reform proposals stressed the need for close political consultation to address security challenges other than military. Such were the challenges emanating from the Vienna CSCE meetings, which demanded concessions on human rights that the communist regimes could not afford without endangering their identity and possibly survival. In calling the Warsaw Pact to the rescue, there was a subtle but significant difference between the Bulgarian approach, which counted on Soviet cooperation, and the Romanian one that preferred doing without it.

As communist power began to unravel in Poland while Hungary seemed ready to follow suit, none other than Ceaușescu adopted the former Soviet script by urging "collective action" by the alliance to prevent "counter-revolution" from triumphing in Poland. It was an ironic though not anomalous about-face by the Warsaw Pact's once vociferous, but always spurious, champion of independence. The establishment in Poland of a coalition government no longer controlled by communists was the farthest the Warsaw Pact came to being "Finlandized." The new government reaffirmed the country's loyalty to the alliance, guaranteed by keeping the portfolio of defense minister as well as the presidency in the hands of Jaruzelski.[195]

---

[193] Document no. 133 b. Czechoslovak report on Moscow meeting of experts, December 8–9, 1988, KaMO, 1989, č.j. 60174, and Chairman's statement, VS, OS, č.j. 38567/65, VÚA.

[194] Czechoslovak report on Warsaw meeting of experts, June 13–14, 1989, VS, OS-OL, 38567/105, VÚA. Documents nos. 137, 144–45.

[195] Reference to Ceaușescu's appeal, dated August 19, 1989, in the summary of statement by Stoian to Czechoslovak ambassador to Bucharest, August 20, 1989, Paczkowski, *Polska 1986–1989*, vol. 3, pp. 320–21. Cf. Mark Kramer, "The Collapse of East European Communism and the Repercussions within the Soviet Union (Part 1)," *Journal of Cold War Studies* 5, no. 4 (Fall 2003): 178–256, at p.198. Statement by Mazowiecki to the Sejm, August 27, 1989, in *From Stalinism to Pluralism: A Documentary History of Eastern Europe since 1945*, ed. Gale Stokes (New York: Oxford University Press, 1991), pp. 240–42.

The July 1989 meeting of the PCC took place in the midst of these startling developments. Bulgaria's Todor Zhivkov implored Gorbachev to include on the agenda both a reaffirmation by all member-states of their "internationalist duties" and their pledge to keep their political systems inviolate. But Gorbachev reiterated his belief that this was everybody's own business, and acted accordingly. The gathering struck East Germany's defense minister Heinz Kessler as "frighteningly different" from previous PCC meetings, something of an "assembly of ghosts."[196]

Gone was Honecker's confidence in socialism's irresistible advance: "If we look at international affairs as they are now," he ruefully admitted, "we cannot speak of any fundamental change for the better." He deplored retreat before the West's "human rights demagogy" and, in a reversal of his earlier enthusiasm for disarmament, warned against taking "soft positions" at the talks on conventional forces in Vienna. Gorbachev conceded that their prospective reductions would complicate matters for the Warsaw Pact, and invited discussion about how to deal with this "serious" question. He emphasized that an impression of "socialism" being in full retreat must be avoided, but did not suggest how.[197]

After Jaruzelski expressed cautious optimism about the future of the alliance, Gorbachev warned that its streamlining and democratization were hampered by the "novelty and complexity" of the task. Indeed, the project for its revitalization was stalled. Ceaușescu reverted to his vintage call for its dissolution together with NATO. Hungary suggested that the Warsaw Pact should adopt the principles of the CSCE, such as sovereign equality, and began to distance itself from the alliance.[198]

At this eleventh hour, the communist notables proved unable to agree on the desirability—or necessity—of reforming their countries' crumbling political systems. The Hungarian proposal to apply Western standards on human rights, now endorsed by the Soviet Union, spelled the end of those systems as they had been constituted. East German, Czechoslovak, Romanian, and Bulgarian officials called for a united front against the spread of pernicious Western ideas. In the end, however, the "ghosts" dispersed without having taken any common action other than to reaffirm their intention to implement the new military doctrine. In October, the foreign ministers met to wrestle with the outstanding problems, but by then the important developments were taking place in the streets.[199]

As internal threats to Eastern Europe's status quo escalated while the Warsaw Pact remained unreformed, much depended on whether the armies that were its creatures would or could be used as the means of last resort to keep the discredited regimes in power. Although Gorbachev ruled out this option, his determination not to interfere in their affairs left open the possibility that they would use force themselves, once their moment of truth came. This happened after the fall of the Berlin Wall on November 9. Rumors spread that the army might be used against protesters

[196] Memorandum of Zhivkov–Gorbachev conversation, June 23, 1989, 1b/35/133–89, TsDA, also at http://www.isn.ethz.ch/php/collections/coll_2_ doc_II.htm. Document no. 146 g.

[197] Documents nos. 146 a-b.

[198] Documents nos. 146 c-e.

[199] Documents nos. 146 f and 147 a-d.

in East Germany as well as Czechoslovakia. The East German army was the one that had consistently been rated in the West as the most competent and reliable.[200]

Whatever the rumors, in neither country had the option even reached the planning stage before the regimes collapsed by their own weight. Those in East Berlin and Prague had already become effectively paralyzed and, for structural if not any other reasons, the generals were not in a position to act on their own. In Poland, where they had acted act on their own eight years earlier and may have been tempted to do so again, it was too late. The Hungarian communists wisely decided to cede power while in Bulgaria the army supported tacitly a palace coup that deposed Zhivkov.[201]

The only country whose regime attempted to save itself by using force was Ceauşescu 's Romania—whose army was not a creature of the Warsaw Pact—and the attempt failed. Before it did, the dictator had leveled at the Soviet chargé d'affaires the bizarre accusation that anti-government riots in Timişoara had been instigated "within the framework of the Warsaw Treaty Organization." No less bizarre was Washington's apparent hint to Moscow that precisely such an intervention might be needed to help prevent Ceauşescu from crushing the opposition. Soviet deputy foreign minister, Ivan P. Aboimov, claims that he rejected the idea with the sarcastic comment that "the American side may consider that the 'Brezhnev doctrine' is now theirs as our gift."[202]

In view of the irresistible spontaneity of the popular movements that brought down communism in Eastern Europe, the subsequent disintegration of the Warsaw Pact may retrospectively be easily explained as inevitable. What cannot be so easily explained is why so few contemporaries considered such an outcome possible or even desirable—not only the Soviet leaders but also their opponents within Eastern Europe's new noncommunist governments, as well as nearly all of their Western counterparts, including NATO officials. They all had their reasons for wanting or expecting the Warsaw Pact to stay, reasons which were only gradually exposed as fallacious.

Once the magnitude of the collapse in Eastern Europe became obvious, Gorbachev acquired new interest in the Warsaw Pact as a mechanism that could possibly hold together the remnants of Soviet power in the region or at least block the absorption of East Germany by West Germany and the integration of a united Germany into NATO. A month after the Berlin Wall went down, he declared that "we will see to it that no harm comes to the GDR. It is our strategic ally and a member of the Warsaw Treaty." East Germany's new defense minister, Adm. Theodor

---

[200] Document no. 112.

[201] Hans-Hermann Hertle, "The Fall of the Wall: The Unintended Self-Dissolution of East Germany's Ruling Regime," *Cold War International History Project Bulletin* 12–13 (2001): 131–64. András Bozóki, ed., *The Roundtable Talks of 1989: The Genesis of Hungarian Democracy* (Budapest: Central European University Press, 2002). Jordan Baev, "1989: Bulgarian Transition to Pluralist Democracy," *Cold War International History Project Bulletin* 12–13 (2001): 165–80.

[202] Document no. 149. Record by Aboimov of conversation with U.S. ambassador Jack F. Matlock, Jr., on December 24, 1989, dated 25 December 1989, *Cold War International History Project Bulletin* 10 (1998): 190–91.

Hoffmann, seconded him by stating publicly that "as long as the two military blocs exist and their balance of forces represents one of the most important factors of European security, we will need to maintain the NVA [East Germany's "National People's Army"] as part of the Warsaw Pact at such a strength ... which satisfies the principles of balance and mutuality." Behind closed doors, however, he informed his fellow defense ministers that the East German army had deteriorated so badly that it was no longer certain whether it could meet its obligations toward the alliance.[203]

Most Western governments, sympathetic to Gorbachev's predicament, underestimating the momentum of change that swept through Eastern Europe, and leery about German reunification, did not press for a radical transformation, much less dissolution, of the familiar Eastern alliance. West German Chancellor Helmut Kohl was an exception in not only anticipating that unification would become inevitable in the near future but also acting shrewdly on this prospect by negotiating with Gorbachev a deal, which amounted to a thinly disguised Soviet surrender. The final agreement on German unification, concluded in September 1990, provided for the withdrawal of Soviet army from the territory that had been the crown jewel of its victory in World War II. In return, the Bonn government agreed to subsidize the retreat of Soviet forces from East Germany and promised not to allow NATO deployments there. Moscow acknowledged the right of united Germany to belong to NATO without restrictions and left the interpretation of the term "deployments" up to German discretion. Whether or not the Western alliance would eventually expand eastward, however, depended ultimately on the maintenance of the existing balance of power, which was rapidly falling apart.[204]

The main reason why the West wanted to keep the Warsaw Pact afloat, at least temporarily, was its utility in the negotiations about reductions of troops and armaments that were crucial to the balance and had been proceeding within the framework of the two alliances. This was perhaps the most constructive function the Warsaw Pact ever performed. Much of Europe's remarkably stable "security architecture" that would ultimately emerge from the Cold War was built upon the restraints agreed to in 1990 as a result of those negotiations. The pillars of the new security system were the elaborate and precise treaty on conventional forces along with the document on confidence-building measures, signed at the CSCE's summit in Paris on November. Their importance overshadows the grandiloquent "Charter of Paris for

[203] Speech by Gorbachev to Soviet party central committee, December 9, 1989, *Europe Transformed: Documents on the End of the Cold War*, ed. Lawrence Freedman (New York: St. Martin's Press, 1990), p. 385. Quote by Hoffmann from his interview in *Neues Deutschland*, December 28, 1989, cited in Dale R. Herspring, *Requiem for an Army: The Demise of the East German Military* (Lanham: Rowman & Littlefield, 1998), p. 91. Document no. 148. Theodor Hoffmann, *Das letzte Kommando* (Berlin: Mittler, 1993), p. 122.

[204] "The Treaty on the Final Settlement with Respect to Germany," September 12, 1990, in Stephen F. Szabo, *The Diplomacy of German Unification* (New York: St. Martin's Press, 1992), pp. 131–34. See also Robert L. Hutchings, *American Diplomacy and the End of the Cold War: An Insider's Account of U.S. Policy in Europe, 1989–1992* (Washington: Woodrow Wilson Center Press, 1997), pp. 138–39.

a New Europe," whose adoption marked the formal end of the Cold War. It did not yet mark the end of the Warsaw Pact, whose fate depended upon its members.[205]

None of the alliance's signatory states was in a hurry to quit, albeit for different reasons. For those countries that had Soviet troops on their soil, the higher priority was getting them out. Czechoslovakia and Hungary acted most quickly, and successfully. The withdrawal of Soviet troops from East Germany followed German reunification. The Polish government, ironically, was the most reluctant to let them go and most hesitant to leave the Warsaw Pact. This was in part because the Poles' early victory over communism entailed a compromise that left communists in several key positions, notably Jaruzelski as president and his close associate Siwicki as defense minister. Poland's new defense doctrine from February 1990, which still assumed that the future war would be a clash between two coalitions, attested to the residual influence of the old Warsaw Pact hands.[206]

Not only the communist generals but also some of their leading democratic opponents, particularly Premier Tadeusz Mazowiecki and foreign minister Krzysztof Skubiszewski, initially assumed that staying in the alliance was in Poland's best interests. Concerned about the likely consequences of Germany's reunification, they believed that both NATO and the Warsaw Pact were indispensable for European stability and should remain in place until superseded by an all-European security system. The Polish government missed an early chance to get rid of Soviet troops because of the mistaken assumption that their presence might be needed as leverage to obtain united Germany's recognition of Poland's disputed western border. In the event, the Germans granted it without ado, but it later took months of arduous negotiations to get the Soviet army out.[207]

The crypto-communist successors of Ceaușescu in Romania and of Zhivkov in Bulgaria took no clear position on the future of the alliance. It was left to East Germany, Hungary, and Czechoslovakia to take the lead in deciding this issue. Before East Germany expired, its pacifist new minister of "disarmament and defense," Rev. Rainer Eppelmann, still dreamed about a "third way" between capitalism and communism, mused that "socialism was no dead dogma," and considered NATO a threat to peace. His idea of transforming the Warsaw Pact from a "military–political to a political–military organization" and other such nebulous propositions were swept away

---

[205] Document no. 151. *Treaty on Conventional Armed Forces in Europe, Paris, November 19, 1990* (Washington: US Information Agency, 1990). Richard A. Falkenrath, *The Origins and Consequences of the CFE Treaty* (Cambridge: MIT Press, 1995). The Charter of Paris at http://www.osce.org/docs/english/1990-1999/summits/paris90e.htm.

[206] Jindřich Pecka, *Odsun sovětských vojsk z Československa, 1989–1991* [The Withdrawal of Soviet Forces from Czechoslovakia, 1989–1991] (Prague: Ústav pro soudobé dějiny AV ČR, 1996). Document no. 154. "Doktryna Obronna Rzeczypospolitej Polskiej" [The Defense Doctrine of the Republic of Poland], *Monitor Polski*, February 21, 1990. Cf. Stanisław Koziej, *Wizja polskiej doktryny obronnej u progu XXI wieku* [The Vision of a Polish Defense Doctrine on the Threshold of the 21st Century] (Warsaw: Akademia Sztabu Generalnego, 1990).

[207] Documents nos. 147 c and 150.

once East Germany, on September 25, 1990, formally left the alliance, thus setting an example for others to follow.[208]

Hungary had gone the farthest in having restricted its ties with the Warsaw Pact even before communism fell; afterward, however, there was no agreement in Budapest about what to do next. Among the wide range of far-flung ideas, notable were two proposals by leading reform-minded communists—that by party chairman Rezső Nyers to reduce the alliance to the PCC and ex-foreign minister Gyula Horn's suggestion that Hungary should enter the political, but not military, structures of NATO, which created an uproar at the time. Horn's successor Géza Jeszenszky let it be known that Hungary's aspiration was neutrality and that his country would remain in the Warsaw Pact "as long as necessary, but not one day longer." When the PCC was convened in Moscow in June 1990 for what turned out to be its swan-song meeting, the Hungarian delegation made it clear that it desired the alliance to be dissolved, although it did not yet act on the desire.[209]

The person who did more than any other to help expedite the Warsaw Pact's demise was Czechoslovak president Václav Havel. This could have hardly been predicted in early 1990, when the former dissident and playwright held simplistic ideas about the dissolution of both Cold War alliances and their substitution by a "broader European organization." On his first visit to the United States in February, he shocked Washington officials by suggesting that all foreign troops should leave Europe. By the time Havel attended the June PCC meeting, however, he had matured enough to take the lead in the contentious drafting of its final communiqué. The consensus among the participants was still that the alliance should reform rather than dissolve itself and serve as a vehicle for political rather than military cooperation, but their confidence in the feasibility of such a transformation was rapidly evaporating. Gorbachev's plea that the Warsaw Pact should stay because not only the Soviet Union but also supposedly the United States wanted it to stay did not impress them.[210]

The PCC's final declaration stated that the "ideological enemy images have been overcome through mutual efforts of East and West," allowing the two terms to regain their "purely geographical significance." NATO responded by declaring that it no longer regarded the Warsaw Pact an enemy, and proposed a non-aggression treaty—the perennial Soviet specialty. The mutual renunciation of hostility gave the Eastern alliance a lease on life. In less than half a year, however, that lease was cut short by

---

[208] Document no. 152. Memorandum by Eppelmann for conversation with Stoltenberg, April 27, 1990, DVW1/44501, BA-MA. Minutes of Eppelmann–Siwicki and Eppelmann–Jaruzelski conversations, May 22, 1990, DVW1/44501, BA-MA.

[209] Alfred Reisch, "The Hungarian Dilemma: After the Warsaw Pact, Neutrality or NATO?" *Report on Eastern Europe*, April 13, 1990, pp. 16–22. Document no. 153 a.

[210] On January 30, 1990, Havel confirmed the existing operational plan of the Czechoslovak Army with the handwritten addition, "in case of NATO attacking the Warsaw Pact." Miroslav Vacek, *Proč bych měl mlčet* [Why Should I Keep Silent?] (Prague: Nadas, 1991), pp. 49–50, 64–65. Jan Obrman, "Foreign Policy: Sources, Concepts, Problems," *Report on Eastern Europe*, September 14, 1990, pp. 6–16. Document no. 153 a. Speech by Gorbachev, June 7, 1990, DC20/I/3/3000, SAPMO, also at http://www.isn.ethz.ch/php/documents/collection_3/PCC_docs/1990/1990_1_I.pdf.

the indignation provoked, especially among its Central European members, by the bloody Soviet suppression of the nationalist opposition in Latvia and Lithuania in January 1991. In forging a common response, Czechoslovakia played a crucial role in persuading Hungary and Poland to use the outrage, which Gorbachev had sanctioned, for demanding the alliance's dissolution. On February 12, the presidents of the three countries met in the Hungarian town of Visegrád, and formed a grouping of their own. In trying to pre-empt the formation of a hostile bloc within the Warsaw Pact, Gorbachev played the last card by proposing termination of its military, though not yet political functions.[211]

The February 25, 1991, Budapest meeting of foreign and defense ministers that ended the military functions of the Warsaw Pact marked its clinical death. Its physical death would be certified four months later by the formal termination of its no-longer-existing political functions at another meeting in Prague. The ministers, however, provided for the corpse's afterlife by concluding an agreement which stipulated that none of the alliance's records may be given to third parties or disseminated without consent by the Unified Command and the defense ministers of all the member-states. The Unified Command, however, disappeared along with the military functions and some of the states, particularly the Soviet Union and Czechoslovakia, subsequently disappeared, too. As a result, access to the documents was left in limbo.[212]

Most of Eastern Europe's post-communist governments subsequently ignored the agreement, thus making it possible for historians to study the Warsaw Pact from its own records and produce a documentary volume such as this one. But one country, besides Russia, remained an exception. Polish authorities invoked repeatedly the 1991 agreement to bar access to their military files related to the Warsaw Pact. Successive Polish governments regardless of their political complexion reaffirmed the ban, leaving historians, journalists, and the general public, both inside and outside the country, to wonder why.

In response to a journalist's question in 2003, one of Poland's former defense ministers recalled the time when "we were facing the difficult question of the withdrawal of the Soviet forces from Poland." So, keeping the documents out of sight was, in the opinion of another minister, "a price worth paying for the smooth dissolution of the Warsaw Pact." "Of course," he added, "certain people linked to the old order don't like the release of certain documents. But it is also an open question whether publicity about Poland as an active participant in the Warsaw Pact's aggressive plans would bring much benefit at the present time." In these subtle and not so subtle ways, the journalist aptly observed, "The Warsaw Pact Lives."[213]

---

[211] Document no. 153 b. NATO's London Declaration, July 6, 1990, at http://www.nato.int/-docu/basictxt/b900706a.htm. Douglas L. Clarke, "Central Europe: Military Cooperation in the Triangle," *RFE/RL Research Report*, January 10, 1992, pp. 42–45.

[212] Document no. 155. Agreement on termination of the Warsaw Pact, July 1, 1991, in Anatolii I. Gribkov, *Судьба Варшавского Договора: Воспоминания, документы, факты* [The Fate of the Warsaw Treaty: Recollections, Documents, Facts] (Moscow: Russkaia kniga, 1998), pp. 201–202.

[213] Quotes by Janusz Onyszkiewicz and Bronisław Komorowski, in Piotr Śmiłowicz, "Układ Warszawski wiecznie żywy" [The Warsaw Pact Lives], *Rzeczpospolita* [Warsaw], July 25, 2003. English translation at http://www.isn.ethz.ch/php/news/MediaDesk/Rzeczpospolita_030725_-engl.htm.

CONCLUSION

The more the Warsaw Pact recedes into history, the more it may seem in retrospect a "cardboard castle" that was bound to eventually fall down. Clearly, that was not the case. At its height, the alliance was a formidable military machine, which could have inflicted tremendous devastation on Europe if it had been set in motion. It had plans to do so and its Soviet commanders were both capable and willing to act on them without qualms. If the circumstances that would have prompted them to action never arose, this was by no means predetermined. Indeed, accidents and miscalculations that could have precipitated a catastrophe are much easier to imagine than the improbable way in which the armed standoff actually ended.

The inside story of the alliance shows an essentially cautious Soviet political leadership, but also one repeatedly prone to miscalculation. The Soviet military, on the contrary, were anything but cautious in their planning, and although they were under the control of the party, that control kept weakening with the passage of time. Nor was Moscow's authority over its client regimes as effective as it appeared on the surface; the East European regimes, however, tended to exert a restraining influence, for it was primarily on their territories that a war would have been fought. None of them was so reckless as, for example, Fidel Castro when he pressed Khrushchev to risk nuclear war at the height of the Cuban missile crisis. The regimes in Eastern Europe, if not necessarily their peoples, generally welcomed the Warsaw Pact as protection of last resort. Romania, of course, was a notable exception.

The documentary evidence leaves no doubt that the Soviet Union and its dependents felt genuinely threatened by the West. That the threat was more general than specific did not make their fears any less real. They felt endangered by the dynamism of the West's free societies, the strength of its economic system, its technological superiority, as well as its larger population—all factors that would have been decisive in a war of attrition. Marxist–Leninist doctrine provided a ready-made framework for the conceptualization of this kind of threat and justification for a military response to it.

The notion that the West would be the first to attack—the common denominator of all Warsaw Pact plans and exercises—followed logically from the dogma that capitalism was inherently aggressive. This view was internalized rather than merely paraded for propaganda purposes. Hence the offensive plans of the communist alliance, drawn up in anticipation of a hypothetical attack, were not abandoned until the ideological glue that held it together began to crack.

The history of the Warsaw Pact does not tell the whole story of the military rivalry during the Cold War; in particular, it does not tell much about the nuclear competition between the superpowers. But there was always an air of unreality about that competition whereas in Europe, where war was a vivid memory, its prospect appeared all too real. In Warsaw Pact documents, a war in Europe was considered separable from the increasingly improbable global nuclear confrontation. There is little in the documents about the role of nuclear deterrence that figured so prominently in Western, especially American, strategic thinking and planning. This suggests that the deterrence was not so much effective as irrelevant in terms of its impact on the enemy.

With the benefit of hindsight, it may be comforting to attribute NATO's longevity to its virtues as a voluntary alliance built on mutual respect and the Warsaw Pact's demise to its opposite vices. Yet the communist alliance lasted as long as 36 years— no mean accomplishment. Rather than its authoritarian character, its main weakness was a lack of clarity about its purpose. Unlike NATO, it was not originally created to counter a perceived military threat, and once it became a military instrument, its utility was never tested by fire. There was always an uncertainty about how its non-Soviet components would perform if such a test came to pass—a much greater uncertainty than NATO faced with its constituents.

If the military utility of the Warsaw Pact was thus doubtful, so was its political value. The Warsaw Pact never succeeded in its original goal of getting rid of NATO and its performance as a handmaiden of Soviet diplomacy fell short of expectations as well. In the end, the alliance failed to save the regimes it was supposed to protect. Unnecessary as a military alliance and ultimately ineffective as a political alliance, it is perhaps not surprising that in the end the Warsaw Pact just melted away.

The story is a cautionary tale in one important respect. The collapse of the Warsaw Pact without firing a shot against its main enemy is a reminder of how quickly an impressive military machine can fall to pieces once the necessary will and money are no more. This applies in general but to modern military establishments in particular because of their dependence on complex and expensive technology. Their vulnerability is especially high in democratic countries, where the material support depends on the commitment of fickle electorates and the comings and goings of their temporary representatives. These should be sobering thoughts for anyone inclined to believe that any power, including a superpower, can permanently secure its interests in the world by relying on something as fragile, paradoxically, as military force.

The Formative Years

Document No. 1: The Warsaw Treaty, May 14, 1955

The following document, signed in Warsaw, formally established the Warsaw Treaty Organization. Drafted by the Soviets without consultation with their allies and accepted without meaningful discussion, the treaty was drawn up as a counterpart to NATO's Washington treaty of 1949. The two documents bear many formal similarities: calling on the signatories to refrain from the threat or use of force, to consult and to render any assistance deemed necessary in case of enemy attack. There were also important dissimilarities. Mainly, whereas the NATO charter emphasized a commitment to common values as an expression of a more egalitarian partnership, the Warsaw Treaty was more vague, referring primarily to general principles of peace and friendship while making sure not to override existing bilateral treaties between Moscow and its allies, which were the real basis for addressing Soviet security concerns in Europe.

The Contracting Parties,
- reaffirming their desire for the establishment of a system of European collective security based on the participation of all European states irrespective their social and political systems, which would make it possible to unite their efforts in safeguarding the peace of Europe;
- mindful, at the same time, of the situation created in Europe by the ratification of the Paris agreements, which envisage the formation of a new military alignment in the shape of "Western European Union," with the participation of a remilitarized Western Germany and the integration of the latter in the North-Atlantic bloc, which increased the danger of another war and constitutes a threat to the national security of the peaceable states;
- being persuaded that in these circumstances the peaceable European states must take the necessary measures to safeguard their security and in the interests of preserving peace in Europe;
- guided by the objects and principles of the Charter of the United Nations Organization;
- being desirous of further promoting and developing friendship, cooperation and mutual assistance in accordance with the principles of respect for the independence and sovereignty of states and of noninterference in their internal affairs,
- have decided to conclude the present Treaty of Friendship, Cooperation and Mutual Assistance and have for that purpose appointed as their plenipotentiaries:
- who, having presented their full powers, found in good and due form, have agreed as follows:

Article 1

The Contracting Parties undertake, in accordance with the Charter of the United Nations Organization, to refrain in their international relations from the threat or use of force, and to settle their international disputes peacefully and in such manner as will not jeopardize international peace and security.

Article 2

The Contracting Parties declare their readiness to participate in a spirit of sincere cooperation in all international actions designed to safeguard international peace and security, and will fully devote their energies to the attainment of this end.

The Contracting Parties will furthermore strive for the adoption, in agreement with other states which may desire to cooperate in this, of effective measures for universal reduction of armaments and prohibition of atomic, hydrogen and other weapons of mass destruction.

Article 3

The Contracting Parties shall consult with one another on all important international issues affecting their common interests, guided by the desire to strengthen international peace and security.

They shall immediately consult with one another whenever, in the opinion of any one of them, a threat of armed attack on one or more of the Parties to the Treaty has arisen, in order to ensure joint defense and the maintenance of peace and security.

Article 4

In the event of armed attack in Europe on one or more of the Parties to the Treaty by any state or group of states, each of the Parties to the Treaty, in the exercise of its right to individual or collective self-defense in accordance with Article 51 of the Charter of the United Nations Organization, shall immediately, either individually or in agreement with other Parties to the Treaty, come to the assistance of the state or states attacked with all such means as it deems necessary, including armed force. The Parties to the Treaty shall immediately consult concerning the necessary measures to be taken by them jointly in order to restore and maintain international peace and security.

Measures taken on the basis of this Article shall be reported to the Security Council in conformity with the provisions of the Charter of the United Nations Organization. These measures shall be discontinued immediately the Security Council adopts the necessary measures to restore and maintain international peace and security.

Article 5

The Contracting Parties have agreed to establish a Unified Command of the armed forces that by agreement among the Parties shall be assigned to the Command, which shall function on the basis of jointly established principles. They shall likewise adopt other agreed measures necessary to strengthen their defensive power, in order to protect the peaceful labors of their peoples, guarantee the inviolability of their frontiers and territories, and provide defense against possible aggression.

Article 6

For the purpose of the consultations among the Parties envisaged in the present Treaty, and also for the purpose of examining questions which may arise in the operation of the Treaty, a Political Consultative Committee shall be set up, in which each of the Parties to the Treaty shall be represented by a member of its Government or by another specifically appointed representative.

The Committee may set up such auxiliary bodies as may prove necessary.

Article 7

The Contracting Parties undertake not to participate in any coalitions or alliances and not to conclude any agreements whose objects conflict with the objects of the present Treaty.

The Contracting Parties declare that their commitments under existing international treaties do not conflict with the provisions of the present Treaty.

Article 8

The Contracting Parties declare that they will act in a spirit of friendship and cooperation with a view to further developing and fostering economic and cultural intercourse with one another, each adhering to the principle of respect for the independence and sovereignty of the others and non-interference in their internal affairs.

Article 9

The present Treaty is open to the accession of other states, irrespective of their social and political systems, which express their readiness by participation in the present Treaty to assist in uniting the efforts of the peaceable states in safeguarding the peace and security of the peoples. Such accession shall enter into force with the agreement of the Parties to the Treaty after the declaration of accession has been deposited with the Government of the Polish People's Republic.

Article 10

The present Treaty is subject to ratification, and the instruments of ratification shall be deposited with the Government of the Polish People's Republic.

The Treaty shall enter into force on the day the last instrument of ratification has been deposited. The Government of the Polish People's Republic shall notify the other Parties to the Treaty as each instrument of ratification is deposited.

Article 11

The present Treaty shall remain in force for twenty years. For such Contracting Parties as do not at least one year before the expiration of this period present to the Government of the Polish People's Republic a statement of denunciation of the Treaty, it shall remain in force for the next ten years.

Should a system of collective security be established in Europe, and a General European Treaty of Collective Security concluded for this purpose, for which the Contracting Parties will unswervingly strive, the present Treaty shall cease to be operative from the day the General European Treaty enters into force.

Done in Warsaw on May 14, 1955, in one copy each in the Russian, Polish, Czech and German languages, all texts being equally authentic. Certified copies of the present Treaty shall be sent by the Government of the Polish People's Republic to all the Parties to the Treaty.

In witness whereof the plenipotentiaries have signed the present Treaty and affixed their seals.

[*Source:* American Foreign Policy 1950–1955: Basic Documents, vol. 1. (*Washington, DC: Government Printing Office, 1957), pp. 1239–1242.*]

Document No. 2: Statute of the Warsaw Treaty Unified Command, September 7, 1955

The Statute of the Unified Command governed the structure and division of authority within the Warsaw Treaty Organization. Like the treaty itself, it was supplied by the Soviets and imposed on their allies. Unlike the treaty, it was kept secret throughout the Cold War, although it was occasionally referred to in public, for example in 1956 and in 1968 when the Poles and Czechoslovaks, respectively, criticized it for assigning all prerogatives to the Soviet Union and all obligations to the East European signatories. In fact, the provisions of the statute were left deliberately vague so that the Soviet Union could interpret them to its advantage. Later, in 1969, the document was revised and the language made more precise. This version of the statute came from the Polish archives.

Draft
TOP SECRET

General Provisions of the Warsaw Treaty
Armed Forces Unified Command

PART I

The Supreme Commander of the Armed Forces

The Supreme Commander chairs the unified armed forces of the members of the Warsaw Treaty on friendship, cooperation and mutual aid, adopted on May 14, 1955.
The responsibilities of the Supreme Commander are:
a) to carry out resolutions of the Political Consultative Committee, which deal directly with the unified armed forces;
b) to supervise and direct operational and combat preparation of the unified armed forces and to organize unified exercises of troops, fleets and staff under the command of the Unified Armed Forces;
c) to have a comprehensive knowledge of the state of troops and fleets under the command of the Unified Armed Forces, and to take all necessary measures in cooperation with the governments and ministers of defense of the respective countries in order to ensure the permanent combat readiness of the forces;
d) to work out and present to the Political Consultative Committee constructive proposals on the further improvement of the qualitative and quantitative state of the available staff.

The Chief of Staff has the right:
- to evaluate the fighting trim, strategic and fighting readiness of the Unified Armed Forces and to give orders and recommendations based on the results of the evaluations;
- to address the Political Consultative Committee and the governments of the Warsaw Treaty states with any questions regarding his activities;
- to call periodically, depending on need, meetings with his deputies representing their governments within the Armed Forces, in order to discuss and solve the occurring problems.

PART II

The Deputies of the Supreme Commander
of the Armed Forces

The Deputies to the Supreme Commander carry full responsibility:
a) for combat and mobilization readiness, as well as operational, combat, and political preparation of the troops under the command of the Unified Armed Forces;
b) for staffing of troops and fleets under the supervision of the Unified Armed Forces; for the available personnel; for supplying armaments, technical equipment and other military items, in accordance with accepted systems of armaments; as well as for the accommodation arrangements and service of troops.

The Deputies to the Supreme Commander are obliged to report systematically on the state of the military and mobilizing readiness as well as the state of the political, strategic and combat instruction of troops and fleets at the disposition of the Unified Command.

PART III

The Staff of the Unified Armed Forces

1. The Chief of Staff supervises the activities of the Staff subordinated to the Supreme Commander of the Unified Armed Forces.

2. The composition of the Staff of the Unified Armed Forces consists of:
a) permanent representatives of the General Staff from the Warsaw Treaty states;
b) special bodies responsible for strategic, tactical and organizational issues;
c) inspectors of the armed services.

3. The responsibilities of the Staff of the Unified Armed Forces:
a) to posses comprehensive knowledge of the state and conditions within the troops and fleets, to take necessary measures in cooperation with the General Staff of the Warsaw Treaty states to ensure permanent combat readiness of the Armed Forces;

b) to work out proposals for measures for the further qualitative and quantitative improvement of the Unified Armed Forces;

c) to reach conclusions on the system of armaments, and the armaments and military-technical property needs of the troops under the command of the Unified Armed Forces.

4. The Chief of Staff has the right:

– to discuss the range of his activities with the deputies of the supreme commander and with the Chiefs of the General Army Staff of the Warsaw Treaty countries;

– to determine information about the state and conditions of troops and fleets under the command of the Unified Armed Forces.

PART IV

The relationships between the Staff of the Unified Armed Forces and the General Staffs of the Warsaw Treaty states

1. The activities of the Staff of the Unified Armed Forces must be carried out in cooperation with General Army Staff of the member-states.

2. The General Army Staff of the member-states are obliged:

a) to systematically inform the Staff of the Unified Armed Forces about the combat and quantitative composition of troops, and about their mobilizing and fighting readiness; about the condition of armaments and military technology; about the operational, combat and political training of troops and fleets under the command of the Unified Armed Forces, in accordance with procedures established by the Staff;

b) to coordinate with the Staff of the Unified Armed Forces the deployment of troops, fleets and staff under the Unified Command.

PART V

Communications

The Supreme Commander and the Chief of Staff utilize the diplomatic pouch and other means of communication provided by the member-states for their communications with the deputies to the supreme commander and the chiefs of the General Staff of the Warsaw Treaty states.

[*Source:* "Polozhenie ob obedinennom komandovanii vooruzhenykh sil-gosudarstv-uchastnikov dogovora Varshavskogo soveshchaniia," *undated [September 7, 1955], KC PZPR 2661/16–19, Archiwum Akt Nowych, Warsaw. Translated by Lena Sirota for the Cold War International History Project.*]

Document No. 3: Imre Nagy's Telegram to Diplomatic Missions in Budapest Declaring Hungary's Neutrality, November 1, 1956

This document reflects the first instance of a Warsaw Treaty member declaring its intention to withdraw from the alliance. This took place during the course of the 1956 Hungarian revolution, after an initial intervention by Soviet forces. Imre Nagy, the Hungarian communist leader, attempted to declare his country's neutrality and have it recognized by the United Nations in hopes that this would deter the Soviets from mounting a second invasion of the country. For many years, it was widely believed that the Soviet move came in response to the neutrality declaration; however, recent archival evidence shows that Moscow had already decided to intervene before the declaration was issued.[1] Given the rudimentary nature of the alliance in the military sense, the main question for Moscow concerning Hungary's possible withdrawal was a political one, and included the desire to prevent other member-states from considering a similar move.

The prime minister of the Hungarian People's Republic, in his role as acting foreign minister, informs your excellency of the following:

The Government of the Hungarian People's Republic has received trustworthy reports of the entrance of new Soviet military units into Hungary. The President of the Council of Ministers, as acting Foreign Minister, summoned Mr. Andropov, the Soviet Union's special and plenipotentiary ambassador to Hungary, and most firmly objected to the entrance of new military units into Hungary. He demanded the immediate and fast withdrawal of the Soviet units. He announced to the Soviet ambassador that the Hungarian government was withdrawing from the Warsaw Pact, simultaneously declaring Hungary's neutrality, and that it was turning to the United Nations and asking the four Great Powers to help protect its neutrality.

The Soviet Ambassador acknowledged the objection and announcement of the president of the Council of Ministers and acting foreign minister, and promised to ask his government for a reply without delay.

Your Excellency, please accept with this my most sincere respects.

[*Source: Hungarian People's Republic,* The Counterrevolutionary Conspiracy of Imre Nagy and his Accomplices *(Budapest: Information Bureau of the Council of Ministers, [1958]). Also published in József Kiss, Zoltán Ripp and István Vida, ed., "Források a Nagy Imre-kormány külpolitikájának történetéhez," Társadalmi Szemle 48, no. 5 (1993): p. 86. Translated by David Evans.*]

---

[1] For further documents and analysis, see the relevant volume in this CEU Press series, Csaba Békés, Malcolm Byrne and János Rainer, eds., *The 1956 Hungarian Revolution: A History in Documents*, (Budapest: CEU Press, 2002).

Document No. 4: Gen. Jan Drzewiecki's Critique of the Statute of the Unified Command, November 3, 1956

*One of the more sensational documents to come to light after the Cold War, this cri-
tique of the Statute of the Unified Command shows how far the Poles, in this instance,
were willing and able to go to question the very foundations of the Warsaw Treaty just
over a year after it was established. In the fall of 1956, Jan Drzewiecki was in charge
of operational planning for the Polish army when a committee was formed in the Defense
Ministry concerned with the reform of military relations between Poland and the Soviet
Union. This was a controversial issue because the defense minister, Konstanty Rokossowski, was a Soviet citizen. Drzewiecki was asked to prepare a memo analyzing the
statute. Objecting to the arbitrary powers allotted to the Soviets, he argues that the rights
and prerogatives of the Soviet-dominated command are incompatible with the sovereignty of independent states, which were members of the Warsaw Treaty. He also extends
his criticism to other, previous agreements imposed by the Soviet Union, which were
not subject to ratification by the Polish parliament or even made available for the information of the Foreign Ministry.*

REMARKS AND PROPOSALS REGARDING THE DOCUMENT:

"Statute of the Unified Command of the Armed Forces
of Member-States of the Warsaw Treaty"

I. GENERAL REMARKS

The document in its present form grants the Supreme Commander of the Unified
Armed Forces certain rights and obligations, which contradict the idea of the independence and sovereignty of member-states of the Warsaw Treaty.

Particularly:
a) the document does not specifically determine the manner of subordination and
responsibilities of the Supreme Commander; moreover, his subordination to
the Political Consultative Committee is described very loosely;
b) from the above one can infer the supranational character of the Supreme
Commander and his staff, which may also be concluded from their rights and
responsibilities;
c) the competences of the Supreme Commander regarding combat training are
contradictory to [the idea of] maintaining the national character of the army,
and are the basis for introducing in all armies compulsory regulations governing the routine and order of military life;

d) the Supreme Commander has the right to issue post-inspection instructions;

e) the Staff of the Unified Armed Forces does not constitute an international institution in the full sense of the term; furthermore, the responsibilities and rights of certain army representatives of this staff are imprecise. As demonstrated by previous practice, the function of these representatives is clearly of a representative and formal character;

f) relations between the Staff of the Unified Armed Forces and the General Staffs of the respective armies are regulated too categorically, and are based partially on subordination of the latter;

g) the composition of forces designated by the PPR for the Unified Armed Forces is defined extensively yet not quite precisely, which allows for various interpretations. From the point of view of our interests as well as the possibility of realizing these plans, the number of designated forces is too high.

Despite the reduction in the size of the Polish Army by five divisions, the number of divisions designated for the Unified Forces has decreased by only one.

II. PROPOSED CHANGES TO THE DOCUMENT

1. In the introduction to chapter I, one should specifically define subordination of the Supreme Commander, as well as his responsibility to deliver reports concerning his work to an international institution.

2. With regard to the responsibilities and the rights of the Supreme Commander, [the terms] of his direction and control of operational-tactical training should remain unchanged; however, the expression "combat training" should be omitted because this term involves matters of order and routine in military life, which should be regulated in accordance with the national characteristics and traditions of each army.

3. In point (b), chapter I, remove the word "comprehensively" (to know the state of forces...); whereas in the rights of the Supreme Commander, exclude his right to issue post-inspection instructions.

4. The definition of the composition of the Staff of the Unified Forces [...] should be changed. The Staff should comprise officers and generals from all armies of member-states of the Treaty. The number of officers designated for the Staff by different states, as well as appointments to the main positions in the Staff, ought to be approved by a higher international political institution.

5. In subpoint (a), point 3, chapter III, remove the word "comprehensively", while in subpoint (w) [...] of the same chapter, the word "conclusions" should be changed to "recommendations".

6. In point 4, chapter III, it should be established that the Chief of Staff of the Unified Armed Forces defines the method of providing information in agreement with interested General Staffs.

7. In chapter VI, point 2 should be changed with the aim of decreasing the amount of data transferred by the General Staffs to the Staff of the Unified Forces (for example, the matter of deployment of forces, etc.), and should be formulated in a less categorical way.

8. From the point of view of our realistic possibilities (considering a planned decrease of forces, possible operational assignments and the need to secure the country by air and sea), the PPR may designate the following forces for the Unified Armed Forces:
  – one general army composed of 6–7 divisions;
  – one air force composed of 5 divisions [...]
Prepared by Drzewiecki on November 3, 1956, based on the Commission's conclusions.

[*Source: Microfilm (o) 96/6598, reel W-15, Library of Congress, Washington D.C. Translated by Magdalena Klotzbach for the National Security Archive.*]

Document No. 5: Polish Memorandum on Reform of the Warsaw Pact, January 10, 1957

This memorandum, also prepared by Polish Gen. Drzewiecki, deals with the question of reform of the Warsaw Treaty Organization. Prepared for Polish leader Władysław Gomułka for discussion with the Soviets, the memo does not question the need or the merits of the alliance—a highly sensitive topic in view of the Hungarian and Polish crises of 1956—but it does point out deficiencies within the organization. These include the obligations imposed on the East European members and the burden of high military spending which undercut the policy of raising living standards in the region. Of course, the attempt at reform was unsuccessful. As indicated elsewhere, the Soviet supreme commander angrily dismissed the objections, saying: "What do you imagine, that we would make some kind of NATO here?"[2]

MEMORANDUM

"The Warsaw Treaty and the Development of the Armed Forces of the People's Republic of Poland"

The Warsaw Treaty, adopted in May 1955 (especially its military provisions), as well as different bilateral agreements signed by the representatives of the USSR and People's Republic of Poland prior to the Warsaw Treaty and ratified after the adoption of the Treaty, require a thorough analysis and revision. This mostly concerns Polish obligations regarding organizational, quantitative and technical supplies of the Armed Forces, the production of military equipment, and the strategic positioning of the country.

The need to revise earlier agreements is caused by the political and economic conditions of our country.

The earlier agreements and the ensuing obligations do not correspond to the policy of independence and sovereignty of our country enunciated by the party and the government of the People's Republic of Poland.

Despite the constant changes in the obligations acquired by Poland on the basis of the bilateral agreements, their implementation would not be feasible without considerable financial expenditures assigned to the Armed Forces and military industry. Such a policy would be inconsistent with the course of the party and the government aimed at the constant improvement of living standards of the Polish people.

Taking into consideration the above-mentioned situation, the General Staff of

---

[2] See footnote 26 in the Introduction to this volume.

the Polish Armed Forces has analyzed the obligations and provisions deriving from bilateral agreements with the Soviet Union as well as the Warsaw Treaty and our obligations deriving from them. Our proposals are listed below:

Military obligations originating from the Warsaw Treaty

The present balance of power in the world, our strategic position as well as our ideological ties with the socialist camp prove the importance of the Warsaw Treaty and of the unification of the military efforts of the member-states for the further protection of our common interests.

Nevertheless, we believe that the military protocols originating from the Treaty require radical revision.

1. The organizational concept of the Unified Command of the Armed Forces foresees the allocation of part of the member-states' armies under a Unified Command.

The above-mentioned concept is similar to the structural concept of NATO. Some parts of the armies of the United States, Great Britain, France and other countries are placed under the Unified Command.

Nevertheless, the structural position of the NATO countries is somewhat different from the position of the Warsaw Treaty states. The only exclusion to the rule is the Soviet Union.

The strategic interest of the major participants of NATO is applied to the numerous theaters of war operations; therefore the specific theater of war would require only a portion of the armed forces of the respective countries, with the remainder of the forces allocated to different pacts—the Baghdad Pact, for instance.

The conditions under which the Warsaw Treaty was created are completely different. Our interest is in the European War Theater, which involves all the participants of the Treaty, excluding the Soviet Union (the interests of the latter only partly lie in Europe). Therefore, we believe that the total complement of our armed forces should participate in our common defense initiative in Europe.

The above-mentioned facts illustrate the superficiality of partitioning armed forces by the participants in the Warsaw Treaty; namely, the structure in which one part of the armed forces is under the Unified Command and the other part is under the command of the national armed forces. In the current situation, Poland cannot allot one part of its armed forces under the Unified Command due to the unrealistically large number of divisions required (see part II of the memorandum). Despite the recent reduction in the Polish armed forces by five divisions, the number of required divisions for the Unified Command was only reduced by one.

2. The organizational structure of the Unified Command of the armed forces is based on a single authority. The collective decision-making process bears only a formal character (it is not mentioned in a treaty). The process of the supreme commander's subordination to the international political body is not clear.

The above-mentioned determines the supranational character of the supreme commander and his staff, which does not correspond to the idea of independence and sovereignty of the Warsaw Treaty participating states. The supranational positioning of the supreme commander and of his staff is illustrated in "Statute" in the chapters dealing with the rights and responsibilities of the supreme commander and his staff.

The authority of the supreme commander on questions of leadership in combat and strategic training is incompatible with the national character of the armies of the corresponding states. This imposes the introduction of common rules and regulations determining the order and conditions of military life (for example, the Garrison Duty Regulations, Drill Regulations, Disciplinary regulations, etc.)

The supreme commander has widespread rights in the sphere of control. The volume of reporting information required from the General Staff is tremendous. The Staff of the Unified Armed Forces is not an international body in the full sense. The rights and responsibilities of the representatives of the corresponding armies are not stated clearly. Existing practice demonstrates the formal character of their functions.

Relations between the Staff of the Unified Command and the General Staff are based on the complete subordination of the latter to the former.

3. Current events prove continuously the unilateral character of the obligations acquired by the People's Republic of Poland. No international agreement dealt with the legal status of troops located on or passing through the territory of a Warsaw Treaty state.

The above-listed questions should be regulated in the spirit of the Declaration of the Soviet Government issued on October 30, 1956.[3]

4. In order to correct the above-mentioned organizational and structural concepts, we suggest the following changes to the military articles of the Warsaw Treaty.

    a) The Warsaw Treaty states are interested in using all their armed Forces for defense purposes; the Soviet Union would agree with other member-states on the quantity of Soviet troops to be allotted to the Warsaw Treaty common actions in Europe;

    b) The involvement of troops of any of the Warsaw Treaty states in military operations would require prior approval by the appropriate body in its home country according to the Constitution;

    c) In peace time the armed forces of each of the countries are subordinated to their national command.

    d) We recognize the need for close cooperation between all Warsaw Pact countries in the following areas:

        – in strategic plans and tactical issues;

        – in logistics prior to tactical moves;

        – in standardization of major weapons types;

        – in regulations of military production and deliveries in times of war and peace;

        – in joint strategic training on the territory of one of the countries.

---

[3] The Soviets broadcast the text of this major declaration proclaiming more equal relations and respect for sovereign rights of socialist states on October 30, 1956, and published it in *Pravda* the following day, in the midst of the Hungarian revolution. The egalitarian principles espoused in the declaration did not prevent the Kremlin, on November 1, from ordering a massive invasion to crush the Hungarian revolt. For the full text, see Csaba Békés, Malcolm Byrne and János Rainer, *The 1956 Hungarian Revolution*, Document No. 50.

e) We recognize the need to create a "Military Consultative Committee" for the implementation of the above-mentioned proposals. The Military Consultative Committee would consist of the ministers of national defense and the chairmen of the General Staff of the Warsaw Pact countries.

The chairman of the Committee would be one of the members of the Committee elected once a year.

f) The working body of the Military Consultative Committee would be the Permanent Staff Committee. It would consist of the officers and generals of the Warsaw Treaty states. The Supreme International Political Body would stipulate the number of officers allotted to the Permanent Staff Committee by each country.

g) The Supreme International Political Body would determine the location of the Military Consultative Committee.

h) All proposals concerning the issues listed in part (b) must be approved by the Supreme Political Body. They become compulsory for all Warsaw Treaty states, if approved.

i) The Permanent Staff Committee can present its recommendations regarding the issues in part (d) to the General Staff.

The implementation of these recommendations depends on the decisions of responsible parties in the national governments of Warsaw Treaty states.

In case of war, the International Political Body can appoint the Supreme Command of the Unified Armed Forces.

The Staff of the Supreme Command will consist of officers and generals of the respective states, and their appointments will be confirmed by the Supreme International Political Body.

[...]

[*Source:* "Memorandum w sprawie Układu Warszawskiego oraz planu rozwoju Sił Zbrojnych PRL" *and Russian translation entitled,* "Memorandum o Varshavskom Dogovore i plane razvitiia Vooruzhennykh Sil PNR," *microfilm (o) 96/6398, reel W-25, Library of Congress, Washington DC. Translated by Lena Sirota for the Cold War International History Project.*]

Document No. 6: Gen. Drzewiecki's Interview regarding Memorandum on Reform of the Warsaw Pact, May 8, 1997

This interview with Gen. Jan Drzewiecki, the author of Documents Nos. 4 and 5, is of interest because he is able to explain the origins and significance of those documents after the end of the Cold War. Despite his later modesty, his efforts to press for greater Polish independent action within the Warsaw Treaty were, in the setting of 1956, quite daring. It is interesting to note that in 1956 the Polish military was in the forefront of challenging the Soviets whereas in 1980–81, at the time of the Solidarity crisis, it was a reactionary force, having by that time acquired a vested interest in the alliance as it was then constituted.

Gen. Drzewiecki: One should be aware of the situation in which the memorandum came into being. Of course, there were no miracles. I was not the exclusive author; I put it down on paper. It was the result of the thoughts of many colleagues—officers, generals—with whom I cooperated at the time. The document could only have come into being against the backdrop of the changes of the time, adopted after October [1956].[4] It could be that we were naive. We believed that that Plenum really initiated some period of change in the history of People's Poland. The results were unpleasant [although] the document is relatively cautious. It is true that it contains theses, which sound—sounded at that time—let's say, revolutionary. But certain postulates were considered cautious because the Hungarians were planning to leave the Warsaw Pact. And how did things end up for them? We were also aware of this at the time. Someone could link it with the developments that occurred after '89. The authors and I personally at the time did not go so far in our views. It also had reform of the system as its goal, but within limits, in the framework, in which we found ourselves earlier. That is, all the theses, although they had many reforms as a goal, did not come out against the basic strategic assumption—that is, against the participation of the armed forces in the Warsaw Pact.

[Party general secretary Władysław] Gomułka took the memorandum with him when he went to Moscow for the first time after October '56, a sort of triumphant journey. At the railway stations the train was stopped, crowds of people came; they raised the banner cry to Gomułka that he should not yield in Moscow. And when he returned, similar demonstrations took place. He took the document to Moscow and left it there. And for the longest time there was no response. After that, some cosmetic changes ensued. Basic changes occurred, however, only after the reorganization of the Polish armed forces. That is, then we finally gave up on a corps structure. The armies had a divisional structure; the operational and strategic tasks of the Polish armed forces were brought up to date.

---

[4] The coming into power of the "national communist" regime of Władysław Gomułka.

These activities were of a formal character. The Committee of Ministers of Defense was established as the organ deciding not only about political cooperation; it also had the adjective "consultative." Formally, the powers of the representatives of the individual countries were increased in the Unified Staff. The number of advisers was decreased. The basic character of the command of the Unified Armed Forces was not changed. For a certain period it was even the so-called Eleventh Administration of the General Staff of the Soviet Army. The representatives [of other countries] did not generally have access to it. The rooms in which they were located had cars [assigned to them], but they could not interfere in many things. And already with regard to operations, it was completely ruled out.

[*Source: "Warsaw Pact Generals in Polish Uniforms: Oral History Interviews," PHP website,* http://www.isn.ethz.ch/php/documents/collection_9/texts/Stalin_Legacy.htm. *Translated by Douglas Selvage.*]

Document No. 7: Soviet Directives to the Czechoslovak Army on Operational and Combat Preparations, September 25, 1957

This Soviet directive to the Czechoslovak army enumerates general operational principles that are to form the basis for training in 1958. It is one of the few descriptions of how the Soviets prepared themselves and their allies for a war in which nuclear weapons would be used. Unlike later documents that are available, this one does not reflect offensive intentions or strategy, but emphasizes a basically defensive orientation in trying to adapt to war conditions after the onset of nuclear strikes by the enemy. At this time, the management of East European forces was still taking place on a bilateral basis, not yet utilizing the Warsaw Treaty Organization as a framework.

TOP SECRET [crossed out] Copy No. 1

Operational Training Tasks for the 1958 Training Year

The basis for operational training of generals, senior officers and staffs in the new training year is to be the study of army offensive and defensive operations with the use of modern means of waging warfare in conditions of the early stage of war.

With that, attention should be paid to the following:

- mastering broad maneuvering actions, skilful use of forward groups for deep outflanking, surrounding and breaking through to the rear of the main forces of the enemy in order to crush them decisively;
- learning to move forces quickly out from under an enemy atomic strike and concentrating them in other most important directions;
- improving the actions of forces and staffs during a night-time offensive, of breaking through the enemy defense and crossing water obstacles right away [*s khodu*];
- learning to organize skillfully the order of actions of forces during the day and night in order to provide them with the necessary rest period;
- creating an insurmountable, deeply echeloned defense, rooting out [the practice of] organizing it schematically and [with a] linear arrangement of battle zones and positions; [...]
- improving the work of intelligence of all kinds. Finding and studying methods of collecting intelligence on enemy atomic weapons, unpiloted devices and radar systems. Learning to determine, in a timely manner, enemy force groupings and weapons, targets of strikes on the battle field and in the enemy's rear against all types of weapons, and particularly for atomic weapons.

Appendix No. 1

Battle Readiness Tasks for Forces for the 1958 Training Year

1. The main aim of the 1958 training year is to ensure the further improvement of continuous battle readiness and fighting capacity of army units and divisions for conducting military operations under conditions of the application of modern means of waging warfare. [...]

2. To learn to use atomic weapons, air force and artillery effectively in order to destroy the main army groupings of the enemy, his atomic offensive facilities, air force and radar systems.

3. To study and inculcate the best means of protection against atomic and chemical weapons. To practice extensively changing the regions where forces are deployed, and the basing of aircraft and ships. To master the technique of quickly eliminating the consequences of enemy atomic and chemical strikes and of recovering and sustaining the battle readiness of forces. [...]

On the preparation of ground troops

In terms of preparation of forces, principal attention is to be paid to the conduct of swift, surprise offensives, to the implementation of deep break-throughs into the battle order of the enemy, to the skillful use of breaches and spaces, and to the conduct of bold outflanking and surrounding maneuvers with the aim of decisively crushing the enemy.

To teach troops to prepare military operations covertly, to construct orders of battle with skill and avoiding conventional patterns [*ne shablonno*], to exploit skillfully and quickly the results of atomic strikes, and to implement unceasingly the combination of fire and movement.

To master the sequencing of units and their components in conducting non-stop offensive operations day and night.

To teach troops how to act aggressively in operations without redeployment, particularly in meeting engagements, to seize the initiative, and to deploy quickly in order to deliver a strike at the flank or rear of the enemy.

To master the technique of rapid and organized movement across water obstacles and marshy areas. To teach troops to capture the opposite bank straight off, using rapid actions by advance squads and tactical airborne troops for this purpose.

To master the technique of creating a firm, deeply echeloned and stable counter-atomic defense, with an extensive network of trenches, passages and dugouts.

To learn an effective system of firing, especially anti-tank [fire] in combination with remote-controlled explosive barriers. To teach the troops insistently to manifest firmness and stubbornness in defending borders and battle zones, and teach them to conduct forceful counter-attacks during the day and night.

[Source: MNO/SM 1957, box 16, sig. 4/1-5, VÚA. Translated by Sergey Radchenko for the National Security Archive.]

Document No. 8: Draft of a Warsaw Pact–NATO Nonaggression Treaty, May 24, 1958

During the early years of the Warsaw Treaty Organization, Soviet Premier Nikita Khrushchev presented various proposals for the simultaneous dissolution of the Warsaw Treaty and NATO, indicating that the original purpose of proclaiming the Eastern alliance was to eliminate, or at least weaken, its Western counterpart. Khrushchev's proposals were calculated to soften Western public opinion and to pressure politicians to be more amenable to Soviet arguments. Generally, Warsaw Treaty meetings, in this case a meeting of the Political Consultative Committee (PCC), were used as a platform for launching these initiatives. Khrushchev was at a minimum hoping to prod the West to begin negotiations. A major question for the West was whether he was serious. Certainly, his interest in initiating talks was genuine but his ultimate purpose and what exactly he was willing to concede are still matters of debate. A "true believer" in the advantages of socialism, Khrushchev undoubtedly felt that the important thing was to begin the process of talks, at which point opportunities would arise for the Soviet Union to gain an edge over its adversaries.

The contracting parties, states, parties to the Warsaw Treaty of Friendship, Cooperation and Mutual Assistance of May 14, 1955 on the one hand and states, parties to the North Atlantic Pact of April 4, 1949 on the other hand, being desirous of putting into effect in international relations the purposes and principles of the Charter the United Nations; attaching great importance to the necessity of maintaining and developing peaceful relations and cooperation between states on the basis of equality, non-interference in internal affairs, nonaggression, mutual respect for territorial integrity and state sovereignty; inspired by the desire to promote the relaxation of international tension and the creation of an atmosphere of universal confidence in relations between states; considering that in view of the existence in Europe of two opposing alignments of states it will be of great importance for invigorating the international situation, terminating the arms race and removing the threat of a new war if the members of these alignments undertake mutual obligations not to resort to the use or threat of force in international relations; have decided to conclude the present pact of nonaggression and have authorized it to be signed:

For the states, parties to the Warsaw Treaty by the Union of Soviet Socialist Republics, the Polish People's Republic, the Czechoslovak Republic and the Romanian People's Republic:

For the states, parties to the North Atlantic Pact by...

Article 1

Noting that the use or threat of force in international relations is prohibited by international law and in particular by the Charter of the United Nations, the states, parties to the Warsaw Treaty and the states, parties to the North Atlantic Pact solemnly undertake to strictly observe this prohibition and not to resort to the use or threat of force against one another jointly or separately.

Article 2

All disputes that may arise between one or more parties to the Warsaw Treaty, on the one hand, and one or more parties to the North Atlantic Pact, on the other hand, shall be resolved by peaceful means only, on the basis of the invariable observance of the principle of non-interference in the internal affairs of states, in the spirit of mutual understanding and through negotiations between the parties concerned, or by using other means of peaceful settlement of international disputes as provided for by the United Nations Charter.

Article 3

Should a situation arise which might endanger the preservation of peace or security in Europe, the states, parties to the present pact shall consult together with a view of taking and implementing such joint measures as, in conformity with the United Nations Charter, may be deemed appropriate for a peaceful settlement.

Article 4

The present act has been concluded for a period of 25 years.

The pact shall come into force on the day of its signing by duly authorized representatives of the states, parties to the Warsaw Treaty of Friendship, Cooperation and Mutual Assistance of May 14, 1955, and the states, parties to the North Atlantic Pact of April 4, 1949.

In the event of the North Atlantic Pact of April 4, 1949, and the Warsaw Treaty of May 14, 1955, being terminated, the present pact will become invalid.

Article 5

The present pact, of which the Russian, English and French texts are authentic, shall be deposited for safe-keeping with the secretary-general of the United Nations. Duly certified copies thereof shall be transmitted by the secretary-general of the United Nations to the governments of states, parties to the present pact.

In faith whereof the undersigned plenipotentiaries have signed the present pact and affixed thereto their seals.

Done in the city of ..., 1958.

[*Source: Jagdish P. Jain,* Documentary Study of the Warsaw Pact *(London: Asia Publishing House, 1973) pp. 309–311.*]

Document No. 9: Marshal Ivan Konev Analysis of a Czechoslovak Army Operational Exercise, March 31–April 7, 1959

This speech by Warsaw Pact Supreme Commander Ivan S. Konev analyzes a bilateral exercise with the Czechoslovak army. It is included here because it provides insights into how Soviet military leaders viewed—and rationalized—NATO's plans. Konev asserts that NATO exercises are based on a false scenario—an attack from the East requiring defensive operations. He rejects the implication that the East would be the aggressor, and declares that any war would actually begin with an attack from the West. This line of argument illustrates the kind of approach the Soviet military used to try to reconcile its conception of an aggressive West with evidence that NATO's plans were actually defensive.

Comrades!

[...]

The scope of the operational game covered the central part of the Western military theater including as important an operational direction as Prague–Saarland.

The terrain of this region is well known to all of you.

We know from intelligence information that during many exercises involving the U.S. Army and NATO's unified forces, in order to study the early period of the war, they stage a situation where the "East" attacks and NATO's armies hold them back, and as reinforcements arrive they launch an all-out counter-attack. Such a situation applied, for instance, in the NATO command-staff exercises in March 1957, under the code name "Black Lion", in 1958 "Blue Lion," etc.

Our exercise was conducted under conditions, which accurately reflect the truly aggressive plans of the probable enemy. As you know, the war was started by the "Western" side, which began it with a sudden air raid and the subsequent advance of land forces.

To conduct this military game the following start position was created:

[...]

In connection with the deterioration of political conditions, the "West" began covert preparations for war.

[...]

The "East," having established that the "West" was preparing for war, brought their military forces to combat readiness in order to counteract a possible enemy attack and took measures to strengthen the defense of the state borders.

In case the "West" started a war, the "East" planned to deliver an immediate counter-strike in order to destroy the enemy's main forces in a battle near the border before the arrival of his strategic reinforcements. The counter-strike, according to the Unified Command plan, was delivered by long-range and battlefront air forces and missiles using the full force of nuclear weapons against administrative and political as well as industrial centers, airbases, missile launch pads, nuclear weapons depots, command points and forces in order to defeat the aggressor, and paralyze his state [administration] and military command.

With this, the quantity and power of the "East's" nuclear ammunition were not inferior to the "West's" devices.

The "East" had 16 divisions in this exercise, of which eight divisions were in the front echelon, two divisions were in the country's rear and yet another six divisions were mobilized. On the 5th–6th day of war, the Unified Armed Forces entered Czechoslovak territory for joint actions with the Czechoslovak People's Army.

[…]

The "East" had the following goals: to bring the forces up to battle readiness; upon the initiation of military hostilities, not to allow the enemy's invasion of the territory of the Czechoslovak Republic; to resolutely destroy him [the enemy] in a battle near the border and advance in the general direction of Nuremberg.

The unified forces of the Western front were on the right flank; on the left the forces of the Hungarian People's Army. Austria remained neutral.

Under the staged conditions, the general balance of forces in the Prague direction at the start of hostilities was equal in terms of the number of divisions and artillery, the "East" had 1.6 times more tanks and 1.3 times more aviation than the "West".

However, the "Western" side, as the attacking one, had the advantage in deployment and, besides, it hoped that by delivering sudden massive strikes with nuclear weapons against the "East's" air forces, unmanned airborne devices and land forces it could gain an advantage in the air and sharply change the correlation of forces in its favor.

[…]

The "Eastern" command generally correctly appraised the grouping, probable intentions and possible timing of the "West's" attack, and took all necessary measures to bring their forces up to battle readiness.

To implement the received directive, the commander of the "East" decided [...] to cover the state border with a part of the forces of the 1st and the 4th armies [...]

Therefore, protection of almost the entire Western state border was delegated to the 1st Army, thinly spread across a wide front; the 4th A[rmy] was deployed in a secondary direction and did not have an active task. An unclear demarcation line between the armies limited the maneuverability of forces and the capabilities of the 1st and 4th A[rmies] in the threatened direction, and created overlaps.

The main shortcoming of this decision is that it was oriented mainly towards defense and did not correspond to the main goal set by the "East" in the directive, which prescribed a resolute counter-attack. The armies were mainly entrusted with defensive goals; in case the enemy penetrated their defenses, the plan was to deliver a counter-strike in order to restore the *status quo ante* on the border line. The task of developing the counter-strike into a counter-attack and attack by the "East" was not considered.

One should understand, comrades, that defense is not an end but a means, by which we must seize the initiative from the enemy's hands. In the early period of the war we, probably, will conduct a temporary defense of those portions of the front where the enemy gets ahead of us in the deployment of forces, or in the directions where, for one reason or another, attack will prove impossible or inexpedient. The main aim of the defensive actions will be not to allow the enemy's incursion in a given direction, deal him maximum losses, and provide for the deployment of one's own forces, as necessary for the attack. As you see, the defense itself must be built on the idea of a subsequent attack, and one should always remember this. [...]

The greatest shortcoming in the "East's" decision to conduct a counter-strike was that it was based on a defensive concept. The armies did not aim at a resolute counter-attack to destroy the enemy. [...][5]

[*Source: VS, OS (OL), krab. 1, č.j. 12426 VÚA. Translated by Sergey Radchenko.*]

---

[5] Emphasis in the original.

Document No. 10: Conclusions from the Operational Exercise of the Czechoslovak Army, March 31–April 7, 1959

Command post exercises have always been an important part of military preparedness training. These drills were carried out on maps, mostly by officers, with the basic purpose of preparing the command structure for actual war. Maneuvers involving large numbers of troops were a different undertaking with their own specific objectives, for example training soldiers for combat conditions and gauging their performance, as well as impressing the putative enemy. While obviously important from a military point of view, these maneuvers are not as useful as command post exercises for understanding actual leadership plans and intentions.

This particular command exercise, run by Soviet Marshal Ivan S. Konev (see Document No. 9), is typical for this early period before the change to an offensive orientation later during the Berlin crisis. Some of the basic concepts of Warsaw Pact exercises are here—a surprise attack by NATO is assumed, and the goal is stated as preventing enemy entry into one's own territory as well as achieving air superiority. Although these operations are conceived as including other Warsaw Pact armies, those forces would not reach Czechoslovakia for 5–6 days, meaning the latter's army would have to fight alone for a significant period of time.

Conclusions from the Operational Exercise

The command post operational exercise was carried out at the Ministry of Defense from March 31–April 4, under the command of Unified Armed Forces Marshal of the USSR [Ivan S.] Konev and his staff. [...]

The following conclusions resulted from the exercise, and Marshal of the USSR Konev made the following analysis:

[...] The time difference between the commencement of the enemy's attack and the execution of a retaliatory strike must be as short as possible. The retaliatory strike shall be executed as soon as the commencement of the enemy's attack shall be made known.

The struggle for air superiority shall be carried out from the very first moments after the beginning of the war. Its major aim should be the annihilation of the enemy's air forces and stocks of nuclear weapons, disruption of fuel supplies, and disorganization of operations in rear areas. Thus, advantageous conditions for the activities of armed forces on land, in the air and on the sea shall be guaranteed.

In the struggle for air supremacy, an active part shall be played by air defense troops, the tactical air force, the navy, airborne units, special forces and partisans, in addition to long-range air forces and missiles of all kinds.

In the coming war, the struggle for air supremacy shall be of strategic significance. Concentrated effort must be exerted by all Warsaw Treaty armed forces.

The retaliatory strike shall be carried out and directed according to the Unified Armed Forces plan.

During the exercise, the Czechoslovak Army was reinforced by the commencement of war operations by air force units and missile regiments. Combat activities were also supported by a certain quantity of nuclear weapons.

The deployment of Unified Armed Forces attached to joint combat activities with the Czechoslovak Army can be expected according to terms stipulated by Unified Command plans. During this exercise, they arrived on Day 5–6. [...]

Transition from counterstrike to attack

The organization of an attack after a successful counterstrike is very complex. It possesses numerous peculiarities since, along with the preparation of an attack operation, combat with an enemy who is attacking and has not yet been halted must be continued.

Under conditions of early war time, the transition to an attack cannot be delayed until all enemy attack capabilities have been exhausted. As soon as the striking formations take advantageous starting positions and are ready to attack, the attack should be kicked off bravely, thus relocating combat activities to enemy territory.

With ample forces and other means, several strikes can be delivered in order to annihilate the enemy's main forces, one part after the other.

The main attack should be led against the weakest and most threatening of the enemy's points, thus allowing penetration in depth while utilizing the movement of armored units.

The formation of assault units for initiating an attack under conditions of an enemy invasion of our territory is a complicated matter. It will usually take place during operations by enemy air and missile forces, with the possibility of an armored enemy breakthrough into the depth of our territory. That calls for secure coverage of the armed forces against air strikes, plus a firm grip on lines providing for the deployment of strike units.

Troops assigned for the transition to attack must not be prematurely committed to defensive action. [...]

[*Source: VKO ÚV KSČ, krab. 1, inv. č. 2, VÚA. Translated by Marian Kratochvíl.*

Document No. 11: East German Description of a West German Plan for the Occupation of the GDR, July 29, 1959

This very interesting document, found in the East German archives, quotes verbatim from a supposed West German record describing the occupation of the GDR in case of war. According to the memoirs of East German spy chief Markus Wolf, East German intelligence obtained it as early as 1955.[6] In 1959, during the first year of the Berlin crisis, the document was published to show the aggressive intentions of the FRG, but it was widely regarded in the West as a forgery and a propaganda move. The trouble with this interpretation is that the East Germans, as seen from their internal documents, regarded the document as authentic, even though experts at the military archives in Freiburg continue to believe it was a fabrication. Another interesting detail is that the West Germans did not publicly respond when the document was first publicized. One possible explanation is that the West German paper was a draft or was prepared for background purposes somewhere in the Defense Ministry, and may never have become an official document. The important point is that the East German regime, whether or not it had justification, was genuinely worried about what might happen in the event of a military confrontation in Central Europe. In particular, it feared that, unlike the experience of Hungary in 1956, the West would intervene if a similar uprising happened in the GDR, as indicated in this document. Clearly, East Germany's fragility and its leaders' concerns on that score were extremely important factors in determining Soviet bloc policy at the time of the Berlin crisis. The building of the Wall was suggestive of this sense of insecurity.

I.

1. The main goal of the German militarists and imperialists is the forcible seizure of the German Democratic Republic and the extension of NATO's sphere of influence as far as the Oder–Neisse border. [This is] the first step toward achievement of their revanchist demands—the restoration of the "Greater German Reich" and the "New European order"—under the hegemony of German imperialism, which poses at the same time an acute threat to the Soviet Union and all the socialist countries.

The aggressive goals of the occupation of the GDR are especially evident in the DECO II and Outline plans as well as the forced establishment of an aggressive army and its arming with nuclear weapons by 1961.

The Outline plan entails the strategic political conception of "limited war." The DECO II plan is a concrete elaboration of the planned military measures against the GDR.

---

[6] Markus Wolf, *Spionagechef im geheimen Krieg: Erinnerungen* (Munich: Econ, 1997), p. 118.

The Outline plan is envisaged in three stages:

- first, psychological warfare aimed at softening the GDR and preparing the West German population for aggression,
- second, provocation of counterrevolutionary actions in the GDR with the goal of unleashing a civil war,
- third, aggression against the GDR as a precondition for the realization of aggressive plans against the socialist countries.

These stages are not to be seen as rigid; they can be entirely or partly connected with other objectives or can overlap.

"Operation DECO II" envisages "a swift coordination of ground, air, and naval forces, propaganda units, and undercover military units, which are to be infiltrated into East Berlin and other strategically important locations in the Soviet occupation zone before the onset of military operations." The forces infiltrated by the enemy are to swiftly occupy political, governmental, economic, municipal, communications and transportation centers, and use radio and press media to appeal to the population of the GDR for support of their measures. Members of the Armed Forces of the GDR are to be requested "to abstain from any resistance, lay down arms, and stay in their locations until the arrival of the armed forces of the Federal Republic."

It follows that an aggression by West German militarism and its crushing will thus differ substantially from the beginning and course of both previous World Wars. The hostilities on German territory will take the form of a civil war, especially during the initial period of the war and will substantially influence the activities of the troops.

In order to prevent surprise by the enemy, an intensified intelligence effort and closer cooperation by all intelligence agencies of the GDR are necessary. The training programs of the National People's Army are accordingly to be altered so that the struggle for the liquidation of counterrevolutionary actions—in addition to the main assignment—could be taken into account more than has been the case so far. This requires close collaboration with other armed organs of the GDR and a clear division of labor among them.

2. An aggression against the GDR must be considered from different points of view: it will bear, especially during the initial period, strong features of a civil war. Depending on the political situation, it can also be the case that the National People's Army, together with other armed organs of the GDR, may have to fight the aggressor alone for a brief period.

The troops and other units of the National People's Army would have to secure the transition to combat readiness, concentration of forces, and action against enemy paratroopers and special forces dressed as civilians as well as against counterrevolutionary gangs. In the process, under no circumstances could they allow themselves to be distracted from their primary task of securing national borders and leading counter-attacks. To this end, the system of alarm readiness must be refined. The destruction of the previously mentioned enemy forces in our interior is basically the main task of the regular police, transportation police, and workers' militia. This situation requires the armed forces of the Interior Ministry to eliminate every counterrevolutionary action in the GDR within 24 hours.

Leading the troops would place greater demands on commanders and staffs. The situation would become extraordinarily complicated. It would not be easy to recognize friend from foe in every situation. We would have to take into account interruptions in communications. It could be temporarily necessary in some locations to have individual units of the National People's Army provide support for other armed forces. This will encourage especially independent action and judgments on the part of the commanders of these units.

Should the enemy turn to open aggression against the GDR by using the forces of the Bundeswehr,[7] we would have to expect heavy nuclear attacks throughout the territory of the GDR, mainly against military targets. The units of the National People's Army would have to carry out the first direct counter-attacks without fully-staffed units, along with the units from the Group of Soviet Forces in the GDR. The military operations in particular directions would have to be conducted on the move. In such a situation, the arrival of the second echelon and reserves is often not to be expected. As a result, gaps would not be created between the units in battle. This will make their coordination more difficult. In some places, the situation might develop such that ground troop units might have to fight without direct support from airborne troops.

Since we would have to reckon with heavy losses and severe damage in the beginning phase, it would definitely get to the point where we would have to call up and introduce reserve troops as quickly as possible. A precondition for this would be a carefully prepared, well thought-out and tested mobilization system.

Similarly, creating and introducing the reserve troops would take place under the most difficult conditions (active enemy air attacks, destroyed transport lines, battles with paratroopers and enemy sabotage groups). The continued working capacity of factories and supply lines as well as transport would have to be maintained at the same time.

As soon as the allied fraternal armies have intervened, it will be necessary immediately to coordinate with them and act in accordance with the overall strategic plan of the Unified Supreme Command. [...]

[*"Erhöhung der Gefechtsbereitschaft der Nationalen Volksarmee,"* July 29, 1959, *prepared for the Security Commission of the Central Committee of the Socialist Unity Party, session of August 3, 1959, DVW 1/39568, Bundesarchiv-Militärarchiv, Freiburg. Translated by Vojtech Mastny and Paul Spitzer.*]

---

[7] West Germany's regular army.

Document No. 12: Warsaw Pact Views of NATO's Plans and Capabilities, April 28, 1960

This Czechoslovak General Staff description shows what information the Soviets and their allies had about NATO's views of war and how they interpreted them. NATO's strategy is accurately described as including the option of a surprise attack, but what is left out is the fact that the West contemplated this action only in response to an imminent Soviet offensive. Considerable detail is provided about NATO's preparedness to launch massive nuclear strikes against Warsaw Treaty air defenses and command centers, in order to prevent Soviet bloc forces from advancing beyond the Vistula and Danube rivers and Carpathian mountains. NATO's aim is described as being to knock out the peripheral countries of the Warsaw Pact (those lying between the Soviet Union and NATO), to occupy these countries and to fight the Soviet Union on its own territory. The materials also assume that Western nuclear bombers and missiles would reach Czechoslovakia within 20–25 minutes, and would be able to cover the entire country. However, the document ends on the reassuring note that complete surprise is unlikely to be achieved (see also Document No. 15).

It is difficult to tell from this document to what extent it was based on publicly available materials as distinguished from intelligence. It is known that NATO was first hoping to stop the Soviets at the Rhine and later do its best to hold them as close to West Germany's eastern border as possible, but there is no indication from available evidence that NATO had any hopes to advance as deep as this description shows—to occupy all of Eastern Europe and fight on Soviet territory. This document thus appears to contradict everything that is known about NATO's capabilities and how the alliance perceived itself. It is possible either that the Soviets, ever impressed by Western technological prowess, saw NATO as more capable than it actually was, or conceivably that the Soviet military was attempting to alarm the East Europeans by exaggerating the West's intentions.

---

1. [...] *Opinions regarding the conduct of war in its early stages*

Insofar as its preparations for a new war of aggression are concerned, the general approach of the West is based on assumptions that the future "major" war will be a global conflict, waged by coalitions of states, affecting all aspects of the lives of nations both on the frontline and in the rear, and taking place in every war theater of the world.

[...] It is expected that the achievement of operational and strategic surprise and the massive use of weapons of mass destruction, which should swing the balance in favor of the attacker even when the ratio of forces does not play into the attacker's hands at the outbreak of hostilities, will play a key role in bringing the war to an early end.

Basically, these requirements are also reflected in the West's concept of how the war will be initiated.

Preparations for mounting the aggression are being carried out in a planned fashion, under the guise and pretext of day-to-day activities, the purpose being to allow the opponent to grow accustomed to an escalation of activities and to blunt his concentration. Thus, readiness for war should be achieved in stages, through step-by-step incremental changes, so as not to draw attention, and the long-term implementation of extraordinary measures that are expected to give the impression of normalcy by being regularly repeated.

Thus, we have been witnessing combat alerts, air intrusion warnings, sorties with nuclear or hydrogen bombs on board, etc. with increasing frequency. The combat alerts invariably involve large-scale troop movements, and develop into tactical exercises and maneuvers on an ever increasing scale. They usually stop at the border of the Warsaw Treaty, in major operational assembly areas. [...]

All the measures referred to above are implemented step-by-step and in such a manner as to appear "defensive," not just in the eyes of the general public but also to members of the Western armed forces.

The examples outlined above indicate that the concept of initiating war is, beyond any doubt, based on surprise, which is expected to play the most important role in the early stage of the war, and thus also in its further course.

[...] The most opportune moment for launching this kind of a surprise attack is believed to be [at the discovery of] any deficiency or lag in the combat and political preparedness of Warsaw Treaty states, any neglected combat readiness issue, or any situation in which the Warsaw Treaty states do not have enough information on Western activities.

[...] According to Western military theoreticians, the onset and early stages of the war (up to 30 days) will be crucial; they are expected to involve massive use of nuclear weapons, whether the enemy uses them or not.

[...] Insofar as the Central European theater of operations is concerned, the key planning document is the "Planned Use of Nuclear Weapons by NATO,"[8] which is based on instructions of the NATO Council and NATO Military Committee. According to a statement by General [Lauris] Norstad, the planning is so detailed that every combat pilot knows exactly what targets he is expected to attack at the outbreak of hostilities.

The planned use of nuclear weapons reflects the overall concept of a surprise attack in the Central European theater of operations, and should meet the following objectives:

A massive strike using weapons of mass destruction and covering the entire depth of the war theater is expected to paralyze the opponent's air defense system, destroy as much of the opponent's strike capabilities (particularly guided missiles, rockets of all types, air forces, depots of weapons of mass destruction) as possible, and disrupt transportation and troop supply.

The destruction of major centers of command and control, arms industry and transport.

Prevention of the deployment of main forces of the Soviet Army on the Western front by efficient interdiction of the area of operations, covering an annular ring

---

[8] As given in the original.

roughly between the Vistula—Carpathians line and the Oder—Central Slovakia—Danube line.

Strikes against permanent garrisons, military installations, air bases and command and control facilities are expected to break up ground and air forces of border Warsaw Treaty states. They should also prevent the mobilization and operational deployment of troops, render the war industry non-functional and prevent the countries concerned from supplying themselves using their own resources.

Once the favorable situation described above is established, fast-paced operations involving tactical and operational airdrops and airlifts and continuous use of weapons of mass destruction should result in acquiring control of the territories of the German Democratic Republic, the Czechoslovak Socialist Republic, Poland and Hungary, and bring war operations to Soviet territory.

Poised against the Czechoslovak Socialist Republic in the Central European theater of operations are the main air forces with about 1,800 combat aircraft, including more than 600 supersonic aircraft.

Assuming that tactical bomber aircraft carrying atomic bombs use air bases on both sides of the Rhine, they can reach the Czechoslovak border within 25 minutes from take-off; if redeployed to new airfields east of the Rhine, the time is reduced to 20 minutes. Under normal weather conditions, they can conduct strikes against targets all over Czechoslovak territory.

TM-61 (TM-71) guided missiles launched from their current peacetime positions can hit targets on Czechoslovak territory as far as the Ostrava—Nové Zámky line, and reach the Czechoslovak border within 25 minutes from launch. If redeployed closer to the Czechoslovak border, to their assumed wartime positions, which are 100 to 150 kilometers from the Czechoslovak border, they will be able to reach the Czechoslovak border within 10 minutes from launch and hit targets all over Czechoslovak territory.

[…] The role and position of the Czechoslovak Socialist Republic in the early phase of the war make the function of our territory significantly different from that of other member-states of the Warsaw Treaty, e.g. Poland and the European part of the Soviet Union, which are some 300 to 800 kilometers from the dividing line in Europe.

[…] The stationing of the armed forces of the Federal Republic of Germany, as well as of occupational forces from the United States, United Kingdom, France and Belgium on German territory is consistent with the mounting of a surprise attack.

[…] However, we anticipate that all efforts by the imperialists to conceal their preparations notwithstanding, an attack cannot be mounted with complete surprise, since international political developments, indications of military preparations and the latest reconnaissance and surveillance assets make it possible to identify and evaluate an impending threat soon enough.

[*Source: VKO 1960, inv. č. 60/kr 15, VÚA. Translated by Jiří Mareš.*]

Document No. 13: The Soviet–Albanian Dispute,
March 22–June 3, 1961

The following materials help to understand the background of the dispute between the USSR and Albania. The clash arose in 1960 from incidents that took place at the Vlorë naval base in the Adriatic, the Warsaw Pact's only such base in the Mediterranean basin. It is not entirely clear who started the quarrel but it was more likely the style than the substance of the Soviets' overbearing behavior—mirrored in the Albanian defense minister's almost insolent tone in his letter to Soviet Marshal Grechko—that provoked Tirana to seize several Soviet vessels, including submarines. No doubt the Albanians believed they could take advantage of the fact that they were out of easy reach because of their remote geographical position.

Not surprisingly, the PCC ruled in Moscow's favor, in part out of a concern that Tirana's behavior, which included leveling accusations of a plot against it by Greece and the United States, could lead to a provocation that might drag the Warsaw Pact into an unwanted conflict with NATO. But the Soviets did not get full satisfaction. The crisis escalated in April 1961 when Soviet Premier Aleksei Kosygin notified Albanian leader Enver Hoxha of Moscow's decision to withdraw all its ships. Albanian forces blocked the base, deployed artillery and even boarded a submarine that was under Soviet command. Eventually, some ships were allowed to leave, but the Albanians kept four submarines and about a dozen smaller craft as well as a considerable amount of arms and equipment. The two countries ultimately severed diplomatic ties over a variety of issues, and Albania, despite its insistence that it was a loyal member of the alliance, was removed from participation in Warsaw Pact councils in December 1961. After the invasion of Czechoslovakia in 1968, the Albanians withdrew from the alliance altogether.

---

a) Albanian Memorandum on Incidents at the Vlorë Naval Base,
   March 22, 1961

1. On February 24, 1961, Mehmet Shehu, the chairman of the Council of Ministers of the People's Republic of Albania, at the earlier request of P. N. Pospelov, the head of the delegation of the Communist Party of the Soviet Union to the fourth congress of the Albanian Party of Labor, received the representative of the Unified Command of the Warsaw Pact, Col. Gen. A.M. Andreev. At this meeting, Col. Gen. Andreev raised a series of questions concerning the status of relations between Albanian and Soviet personnel at the naval base on Vlorë Bay which, to quote him, had become a hindrance to the battle-readiness of that base.

Related to this, on February 28, 1961, the representative of the Unified Command sent a letter to the chairman of the Council of Ministers of the People's Republic of Albania, in which he forwarded information about "an abnormal situation" between the Albanian and Soviet personnel on that base.

The chairman of the Council of Ministers gave great attention to the claims made orally or in the information of February 28. It is appropriate to mention in this regard that the Albanian government—which to a great degree values the significance of the naval base on the Vlorë Bay for the general defense of the Warsaw Pact member countries as well as that of the entire Socialist bloc—has always paid careful attention to and taken very seriously everything that relates to this base. [...]

Regarding the concerns raised on January 23, 1961, at Sazan Island fleet headquarters and garrison, the commander of the Albanian Navy, Rear Adm. Hito Chako had, on the previous day, personally informed his adviser, Captain 1st Class P. P. Kulik, and had explained the focus of his concern, and of the time when it would be announced. It should be noted that, at the Sazan Island garrison, after the concerns were made public and when the entire island reverberated, at the time when all the Soviet ship instructors were already at their posts, only the squadron adviser for defense of the waterways, Captain 1st Class A. A. Zavgorodnyi, did not show up at his post, which is totally inappropriate behavior, contradicting vigilance and military discipline, together representing an unacceptable lack of respect for the command of the Albanian Navy.

It is true that on January 23 and February 19, 1961, foreign ships were noticed in the Strait of Otranto, but this does not support the claim that Soviet advisors and instructors were not advised about that fact. [...]

Concerning this matter, it is necessary to note that, regarding such movement of foreign ships carrying out NATO maneuvers, before October 1960 the Albanian Navy Command was informed on a regular basis from Sevastopol via headquarters of the Soviet submarine squadron at the Vlorë base as well as through other means which the Command had at its disposal. However, beginning with the time in question, such data from the Soviets were stopped. [...]

As concerns the Vlorë naval base and its battle-readiness, such a question was raised by the representative of the Unified Command during his meeting with the chairman of the Council of Ministers of the People's Republic of Albania on February 24, 1961, and, as it happens, was mentioned in the information of February 28, 1961. The Albanian government totally agrees with the opinion of the representative of the Unified Command concerning the seriousness of the situation relating to battle-readiness at the Vlorë base; the Soviet government has called attention to this and other cases. The Albanian government considers that the situation created at the Vlorë base, which is the only military base of the Socialist bloc on the Mediterranean, deserves all the attention of the Soviet government and the Warsaw Pact Unified command. [...]

It is a fact that, beginning with the second half of last year, the Soviets, despite current agreements, suspended technical assistance to Albanian ship crews representing the People's Republic of Albania, as well as the delivery of equipment, all types of technical materiel, and fuel, as covered by mutually-agreed upon plans. [...]

With the position they took beginning September of last year up to today regarding the supply system in question for the Vlorë naval base, not only did the Soviets limit the range of cooperation between the Albanian staff and the Soviet advisors and instructors, but they also created a serious situation as regards the combat readiness of the base, the result being an entirely unsatisfactory atmosphere among the entire personnel of the base. [...]

[*Source: XIA/102, 151–74, Archiwum Akt Nowych, Warsaw.*]

b) Letter by Albanian Minister of Defense Beqir Balluku
   to Marshal Grechko, March 28, 1961

Comrade Marshal,

I received your letter yesterday, March 27, 1961, at 11:00, in response to my letter of February 25, 1961.

I consider it necessary, above all, to note with regret that your letter does not respond to those important fundamental questions which were presented in my letter of February 25, 1961.

Instead, it contains a series of unsubstantiated facts and unacceptable threats which I, as one who upholds the honor of my people, the Albanian Party of Labor, and the People's Republic of Albania as well as the eternal friendship between the Albanians and Soviets and the lofty interests of the Warsaw Pact Organization and the entire Socialist bloc, find entirely unacceptable. [...]

I disagree entirely with your incorrect understanding about the announcement of the plot which was organized by Yugoslavia and Greece with the cooperation of the U.S. Sixth fleet against the People's Republic of Albania and which was recently discovered by Albanian government security services. I would like to stress that no one has the right to question the announcement by the Central Committee of our Party pertaining to this issue made at the fourth congress of the Albanian Party of Labor. As we had already informed you through your Liaison in Albania, when it comes to this plot, the Albanian government would use all the necessary facts, but it did not consider it necessary to request assistance from the Unified Command of the Warsaw Pact, since it caught the entire enemy group in time and had convinced that the mounting danger had thus been averted.

Concerning the questions you raised in your letter about the Vlorë naval base, I consider it appropriate to note that the cases you mentioned such as the unacceptable relationship toward Soviet military personnel on the part of the responsible Albanian individuals are untrue. [...]

In your letter, comrade Marshal, you write that if the Albanian government is interested in continuing to keep Soviet submarines and other warships at that base, it would follow that they should complete the staffing of all the warships and squadrons so that they are serviced only by Soviet staff, otherwise you will raise the question before the Soviet government and the Political Consultative Committee about having all Soviet military ships, personnel, and specialists removed from Albania.

In conjunction with the aforementioned, I consider it necessary to announce the following:

Firstly, the Vlorë naval base, as the only military base in the Socialist bloc located on the Mediterranean Sea and being of great significance for both Albanian defense and the entire Socialist bloc, was created at the initiative of the Central Committee of the Albanian Party of Labor. [...]

Secondly, your demand to complete the staffing of warships at the naval base with only Soviet personnel, along with the threat to pull out—that is, close the Vlorë base—not only clearly contradict existing agreements but would also be an unacceptable encroachment on the sovereignty of the People's Republic of Albania and a direct contravention of Marxist principles of relations between the governments of the Socialist bloc and the Warsaw Pact. [...]

Since I consider the threats mentioned in your letter unacceptable, I consider it appropriate to note once again, comrade Marshal, that that kind of action on your part is exceptionally dangerous for the Warsaw Pact countries and the entire Socialist bloc. It would be better if you did not take this dangerous and rather irresponsible path as it is entirely inappropriate considering the high level of authority entrusted to you by the governments of all the Warsaw Pact participating countries. [...]

> Respectfully Yours,
> Minister of the People's Defense
> People's Republic of Albania
> Col. Gen. Beqir Balluku

[*Source: XIA/102, 241–44, Archiwum Akt Nowych, Warsaw.*]

c) Resolution by the Political Consultative Committee,
   March 29, 1961

The Political Consultative Committee, having reviewed the letters which were exchanged on March 27 and 28 of this year between the Unified Command of the Warsaw Pact Military Forces and the Minister of the People's Defense of the People's Republic of Albania on the situation at the Vlorë Naval Base in Albania, and taking into account the opinions expressed at the session of the Committee in conjunction with the question of Albania fulfilling its responsibilities stemming from positions held by the Warsaw Pact, regretfully notes that Albania has recently taken some steps which do not correspond to the principles and positions of the Warsaw Pact. Albania has created an abnormal situation at the Vlorë Naval Base which is unacceptable to the member-states of the Warsaw Pact and which seriously reduces the combat readiness of that base.

Participants of the Session noted that at the Fourth Session of the Albanian Party of Labor Comrade Enver Hoxha made an announcement about a supposed attack on Albania on the part of Yugoslavia, Greece and the Sixth Fleet of the United States of America. Despite the fact that such an event has exceptionally important political and military significance for all the Warsaw Pact countries, none of these countries or the Unified Command was informed of it by Albania, and they still have yet to receive any information on this matter. Such actions by the People's Republic of Albania do not comply with Articles 3 and 5 of the Warsaw Pact.

The Political Consultative Committee expects the government of the People's Republic of Albania to immediately present the Unified Command of the Warsaw Pact Military Forces with the facts and the reasons which formed the basis for the announcement by the representatives of the party and of the government of the People's Republic of Albania concerning an attack on Albania. [...]

[*Source: ZK SED, DY 30/3386, SAPMO.*]

d) Reply by Albanian Premier Mehmet Shehu to the Political Consultative Committee, April 5, 1961

The government of the People's Republic of Albania regretfully notes that the session of the Political Consultative Committee, based on one-sided and incorrect information and despite an agenda which had been accepted earlier by all the participants, has given its primary attention to false accusations aimed at the People's Republic of Albania with the intended goal of condemning and punishing the People's Republic of Albania at that same session. [...]

The Albanian government expresses its surprise at the fact that the decision of the Political Consultative Committee of the Warsaw Pact against the People's Republic of Albania included an accusation of contravening Articles 3 and 5 of the Warsaw Pact. This unfounded accusation is based on a perversion of the truth and on the fabricated assertion that comrade Enver Hoxha is supposed to have made an announcement at the Fourth Session of the Albanian Party of Labor about an attack on Albania by Yugoslavia, Greece, and the Sixth Fleet of the United States of America that had "taken place." [...] At the fourth congress of the Albanian Party of Labor, comrade Enver Hoxha announced that "Yugoslavia and Greece, in cooperation with several traitors of Albania inside the country who fled to Yugoslavia after coordinating their actions with the U.S. Sixth Fleet in the Mediterranean, organized an attack on Albania several months ago, with the goal of destroying the People's Republic of Albania. Their criminal plot was a complete failure."

The truth was that internal enemies of Albania *organized* an attack on Albania, but, in fact they were not able to *carry out* this organized attack, since the agents' network of plotters in Albania was completely destroyed. [...]

We consider incorrect the suggestion of several delegations at the last session of the Political Consultative Committee of the Warsaw Pact to send a commission of Warsaw Pact member-states to Albania to assess the accuracy of the facts about a plot. This is unprecedented in the relationships of sovereign governments, and speaks to a deep lack of trust in our government and our party and represents unacceptable interference in our internal affairs. [...]

As concerns the decision of the session of the Political Consultative Committee about the Vlorë naval base, the government of the People's Republic of Albania considers it incorrect. It was a decision made based on one-sided and mistaken information, based on malevolent fabrications, not taking into account at all the reality at the Vlorë naval base as set forth in the memorandum from the Chairman of the Council of Ministers of the People's Republic of Albania to the Supreme Commander of the Unified Armed Forces of the Warsaw Pact attached to the People's Army of the People's Republic of Albania on March 22, 1961. [...]

If the Soviet government does not agree to observe existing agreements about the Vlorë naval base and decides to remove its military forces from that base in accordance with the above-mentioned decision of the Political Consultative Committee, the government of the People's Republic of Albania—although it opposes such a decision—will not interfere and will be prepared to render assistance to the Soviet Union in evacuating its naval forces from the Vlorë naval base. There is no doubt that the Soviet government, acting in this fashion, would be taking on a great responsibility toward the Albanian people as well as toward the Socialist bloc, since, with the closing of the Vlorë naval base, the People's Republic of Albania will be exposed to the U.S. Sixth Fleet on the Mediterranean, and the Warsaw Pact will lack such powerful weaponry on the Mediterranean as the Vlorë naval base represents.

The government of the People's Republic of Albania expresses its great surprise and immeasurable distress at the fact that at the session of the Political Consultative Committee of the Warsaw Pact, Albania was threatened with no longer receiving economic assistance or assistance in outfitting its army, which makes up part of the staff of the Warsaw Pact forces. [...] If economic assistance to Albania were suspended, it would hold up the construction of Socialism in Albania. If assistance in outfitting the army were suspended, that would lead to a lower level of combat readiness of the Albanian army, which makes up part of the staff of Warsaw Pact forces. [...]

The government of the People's Republic of Albania hopes that the governments of the Warsaw Pact member-states will review and amend their relationship to the People's Republic of Albania in a positive manner.

> Chairman of the Council of Ministers
> People's Republic of Albania
> (Mehmet Shehu)

[*Source: XIA/102, 297—305, Archiwum Akt Nowych, Warsaw.*]

e) Soviet Memorandum on the Vlorë Incidents,
   May 1961

Recently the Albanian Command has intensified the battle-readiness of all the forces and resources of its naval fleet and coastal artillery in the area around Vlorë Bay. It has denied leave to its staff and distributed weapons to its officers. In the area of Sazan Island a fleet has been established consisting of warships and torpedo boats outfitted with torpedoes and ready to head out to sea. A round-the-clock naval patrol has been set up at the entrance to Vlorë Bay. [...]

Practically speaking, the Albanian Command has suspended administration of the submarine squadron, forbidding boats to leave their floating moorings and limiting movements of the Soviet troops on shore. [...]

Serious concern was created by the event which occurred on April 29 of this year on submarine S-360. [...]

At 14:30 an Albanian team of about 50 people suddenly arrived on the boat in question, headed by Lieutenant B. Gerbi, the former assistant commander of the Albanian team, who, after pushing away the watch guard, Soviet petty officer Trofimenko, led the Albanian team on board. Fifteen minutes later, Albanian Lieutenant Captain Chukai arrived on board. He also disregarded Trofimenko's warning, pushed him away and went onto the vessel. [...]

Rear Adm. Chako, justifying the actions of the Albanian command, announced that they had been called up based on the fact that, according to his data, Soviet military ships were supposed to have left immediately on May 1 or 2. Under such circumstances, Chako said, should the Soviet ships try to leave, the Albanian command would not allow it. [...]

Our position on the question of the circumstances which took place at the Vlorë naval base was laid out in detail in a letter from the First Representative of the Chairman of the Council of Ministers of the USSR, Comrade A[leksei] N. Kosygin, to the Council of Ministers of the People's Republic of Albania on April 26 of this year. In that letter, the Soviet government announced that it was obliged to recall all its submarines, surface ships, auxiliary resources, and other vessels transferred at one time or another in Albania to organize a naval base at Vlorë. On this subject, we took into consideration the announcement by the Albanian government in its letter of April 5 that it was prepared to create the necessary conditions and to render assistance to the Soviet Union in evacuating Soviet naval forces from the base. [...]

[*Source: XIA/102, 336-39, Archiwum Akt Nowych, Warsaw.*]

f) Soviet note to the Albanian government,
   June 3, 1961

It is with deep regret that the Soviet government must take note of the fact that the government of the People's Republic of Albania has not supported attempts by participants of the session of the Political Consultative Committee to eliminate abnormalities in relations between Albania and the Soviet Union, as well as between Albania and the remaining member-states of the Warsaw Pact, which have arisen recently because of the Albanians. [...]

The Soviet government, in its attempts to quickly resolve the problems connected to the situation at the Vlorë naval base, accepted the suggestion of the Albanian government to have a meeting in Tirana of authorized representatives of both governments to discuss the afore-mentioned question, and it has named its delegation for this purpose. [...] Taking into account the wishes of the Albanian delegation, the Soviet delegation arrived in Tirana on May 18, in order to hold talks before May 20 regarding the procedures for removing Soviet naval forces and technical assistance from Vlorë. [...]

The delegation was prepared to begin talks on the morning of May 19. However, the leader of the Albanian delegation, Deputy Minister for Foreign Affairs of the People's Republic of Albania, comrade Khalim Buda, instead of opening the session (and not even having informed the staff of the Albanian delegation), made an announcement in which he accused the Soviet government of deliberate detention and persecution in the Soviet Union of Albanian naval personnel studying at Soviet naval educational institutions. In doing so, the head of the Albanian delegation launched into crude and insulting attacks on the Soviet government. [...]

It was pointed out to the Albanians that this claim was absurd and provocative, insofar as no one had ever hindered Albanian naval personnel from leaving the Soviet Union. Despite this, the leader of the Albanian delegation, even on the very day when the first group of Albanian sailors arrived in the People's Republic of Albania on specially chosen Soviet airplanes in accordance with the time-table agreed to by the Albanian ambassador in Moscow, continued to make announcements as if their embassy had not had the possibility to meet with the Albanian naval personnel and that the latter were in solitary confinement. It is assumed that all this was malicious fiction from start to finish. [...]

The Albanian government continues to conduct matters such that the conditions on the base continue to deteriorate further and relations between our countries become exacerbated. Witness the fact that up to the present time, only part of the Soviet naval forces and technical assistants have left Vlorë, while four Soviet submarines, the floating base "Nemchinov," 10 small surface boats, 22 auxiliary vessels and a significant amount of weapons, technical equipment, materiel and other property have been seized by the Albanians. [...]

In conjunction with the seizure of the above-mentioned items, the government of the Soviet Union announces a decisive protest against these illegal actions of the Albanian government and demands the return of all Soviet military ships, weapons, technical equipment and property which belong to the Soviet people. [...]

Taking this into consideration, the Soviet government has given notice to the Ministry of Defense of the USSR to recall all Soviet naval personnel currently located on ships, and other items seized by the Albanian authorities.

[*Source: XIA/102, 341–49, Archiwum Akt Nowych, Warsaw. All documents translated by Paul Spitzer for the National Security Archive.*]

Document No. 14: Secret PCC Resolution on Restructuring and Modernization of Warsaw Pact Forces, March 29, 1961

This PCC resolution, which came from the same meeting at which the Albanian crisis was discussed, reveals some of the effects of the Berlin crisis. The two emergencies happened at the same time but there was no causal connection. The resolution calls for restructuring and modernizing Warsaw Pact forces over the next five years, 1961–1965. It also recommends, among other steps, improving the ability of member-states to mobilize their economies for military production in time of war. The purpose of the resolution appears to be to prepare Warsaw Pact members, as the Berlin crisis continued to deteriorate, for the possibility of an armed conflict.

[…]

Having heard and discussed the question of specialization of military production in the Warsaw Pact states, and of the mutual supply of military equipment, the Political Consultative Committee notes that in the period since the May [1958] meeting of representatives of communist and workers' parties of socialist countries, some work has been done to develop specialization and cooperation in the production of military equipment, as a result of which serial production of certain types of classic military equipment has been organized in some countries.

However, up till now some countries have been producing the same types of military equipment in small quantities, and this does not facilitate lowering the material costs of producing it.

There are cases of violations of contractual obligations concerning the mutual supply of military equipment between countries, and this effectively hinders specialization and cooperation in the production of military equipment.

Taking into consideration the necessity of further developing specialization and cooperation in Warsaw Pact military production as a rational method, which creates opportunities for increasing output of military equipment using existing capacities, the Political Consultative Committee resolves:

- To approve, as a basis, draft proposals on the volume of production and mutual supply of military equipment for the period 1962–1965. [The drafts would be] prepared with consideration for the requirements stated by the Unified Command and examined during the Comecon[9] session on the defense industry, on March 17, 1961, in Moscow, with the participation of representatives of the State Planning Committees and General Staffs of the member-states of the Warsaw Treaty.
- To instruct the State Planning Committees and Ministries of Defense of the Warsaw Pact states, with the participation of the Unified Command of the

---

[9] Officially, the Council on Mutual Economic Assistance (CMEA).

Armed Forces, to determine, within a two-month period [and] on the basis of draft proposals, the volume of production and mutual supplies, for [inclusion in] a report to the relevant governments. The exact quantity of mutual supplies of military equipment in 1962 and the following years has been agreed to by the member-states of the Warsaw Pact through bilateral negotiations, taking into consideration changes in the organization of armies and the introduction of new types of military equipment there.

– When organizing the production of military equipment in 1962–1965, to take into account the need for further development of production of scarce parts and materials (vacuum and semiconductor devices, heat-resistant alloys, reinforced steel and others) in the member-states of the Warsaw Pact.

– In order to implement these tasks, to expedite and rationalize existing production capacity and resources more rationally and, if need be, to assure that the countries' economic plans have the minimum required funds to expand the existing capacity of the defense industry or to assimilate civilian enterprises.

The Political Consultative Committee believes that one of the most important tasks in strengthening the defense capabilities of the Warsaw Pact states is to improve the mobilization readiness of the countries' economies and especially to create mobilization capacities for the production of military equipment in time of war. The Political Consultative Committee instructs the Unified Command of the Warsaw Pact states' armies, and the Comecon Commission on the Defense Industry, together with the Ministries of Defense and State Planning Committees, to strengthen work to streamline the economic mobilization plans of the Warsaw Pact member-states, especially by identifying through the mobilization plans "bottlenecks" that could slow down mobilization schedules, and by taking measures to get rid of bottlenecks during peace-time.

[*Source: ZK SED, DY 30/3386, SAPMO. Translated by Sergey Radchenko.*]

Document No. 15: Czechoslovakia's Strategic Position in a European War, April 1961

This lecture is intended to acquaint officers of the Czechoslovak General Staff with the Soviet view of what the next European war might look like. In this scenario, Czechoslovakia is especially important because of its location. Exposed geographically, it would have to fight alone, at least at the beginning, because its allies would be able to arrive only after several days. Interestingly, the Soviets expect the Czechoslovaks to be able to handle matters on their own to a considerable extent. There is nothing in the document about any pursuit of the enemy further west.

Task and position of Czechoslovakia in the early stages of war

[...]

When estimating the direction of individual operations, the main one to be taken by the enemy's eastbound aggression will be Berlin–Warsaw. Our geographic position covers a very important auxiliary direction for an eastbound strike—from Nuremberg to Prague and Ostrava, the importance of which is that it makes it possible to strike at the flank and rear of the main operational concentration defending the Berlin–Warsaw direction.

The traditional notion of Czechoslovakia as the heart of Europe is generally still valid from the viewpoint of operations. If the enemy conquers our territory, he can penetrate the Łódź–Ostrava area rather swiftly. Then he could strike at the flank and rear of the Berlin-Warsaw concentration, plus he would gain a valuable platform for the eastbound strike. The Pilsen–Ostrava route is rather short and therefore advantageous. Disregarding Austrian neutrality already in the initial phase by advancing in the Hollabrunn–Ostrava direction is even more advantageous for penetrating into the Łódź–Ostrava area. A strike in this direction would split Czechoslovak strategic forces and create conditions for the liquidation of our Prague concentration.

This means that we are firmly established in the strategic echelon. Our geographic position, plus the way in which we shall carry out the task of fighting off the aggressor would be decisive in creating conditions for other Warsaw Treaty states, including the USSR, to ward off aggression against them.

When comparing our geographic position from the viewpoint of other states, we may see then that Poland lies some 300–800 km from the aggressor's starting area, with Hungary, Romania and Bulgaria lying still farther away. The latter two are, moreover, protected by sea, and are closer in terms of time to [receiving] Soviet army assistance.

On the other hand, even with strenuous transfers, allied forces may appear on our territory only after several days.

This makes it clear that while most of the Warsaw Treaty states would be subject to missile strikes of a strategic and major operational character, the Czechoslovak and GDR territories would be under assault by tactical missiles and by troops and air forces of all kinds.

This is the complexity of our situation, combined also with the pressure of time. From the viewpoint of time, the possibilities for surprise strikes are disadvantageous for us. For the enemy's tactical air force and guided missiles, these amount to 15 minutes for the Czech lands, and up to 60 minutes for Slovakia.

The front line enemy's units can reach our borders within two-to-six hours.

[...]

[Source: MNO/NGŠ, 1961, kar. 312, sig. 4-1/6, č.j. 0016196, VÚA. Translated by Marian Kratochvíl.]

Document No. 16: Speech by Marshal Malinovskii Describing the Need for Warsaw Pact Offensive Operations, May 1961

Soviet Defense Minister Rodion Ia. Malinovskii delivered this speech on the occasion of the evaluation of a joint Soviet-East German command post exercise. Presented at a time of growing crisis several weeks before construction of the Berlin Wall, the speech shows the developing transition from a defensive to an offensive Warsaw Pact military strategy. Malinovskii tells the participants in the exercise that it is now important to deploy ground forces capable of destroying, by rapid action, and by employing nuclear arms "very sparingly," any enemy nuclear weapons before they can be used. But at the same time, Warsaw Pact forces should be prepared for "a rapid shift of focus deep behind enemy lines" that would result in the destruction of enemy capabilities in a short period of time. Previous exercises had ended with the repulsion of the enemy without making clear where that would take place; this one specifies defeating him on his own territory largely with the use of tanks. Malinovskii implies an advance at least into West Germany, if not farther, but this is still a step removed from the concept of a deep thrust into Western Europe, which became the standard strategy by 1961 and remained so through 1987, when Mikhail Gorbachev explicitly adopted a defensive approach.

As a result of the existence of long-range missiles with nuclear warheads, the options have increased for launching strikes deep behind enemy lines. [...]

Under modern conditions the main task of destroying the enemy is realized through nuclear strikes. And the army's ground forces will be in charge of aiming for the complete destruction of enemy forces.

During the first operations in the initial phase of war, the army ground forces mainly have to exploit in their area of attack the results of strategic nuclear strikes. Only very sparingly should they use their own nuclear weapons, instead keeping the bulk of them for battle behind the enemy lines. The transition to attack must be contingent on the level of radiation resulting from nuclear missile strikes with strategic weapons.

Calculations have shown that the time needed to lower the level of radiation can be measured in hours and days. Thus there is little likelihood that our own troops will enter the contaminated zone before five or six hours.

There is only one way of avoiding this, namely to cross the contaminated area speedily with tank units and heavy armored personnel carriers protecting the crews from radiation, with helicopters, and, if possible, to bypass the areas with the highest levels of radiation by using ordinary motor vehicles and other means of transportation.

Attack must be pursued without interruption by using primarily conventional weapons, tanks and the air force. The troops have to proceed purposefully.

Our modern tank divisions are the most important assault force of the Fronts[10]. They have enormous striking power, high mobility and are least vulnerable to the enemies' weapons of mass destruction. Their actions right at the beginning of the war should guarantee a rapid shift of focus deep behind enemy lines, the destruction of the enemy's operational and strategic reserves, the destruction of its nuclear weapons and the prevention of mobilization efforts, and the disruption of the command structure and efforts in the hinterland.

Like pointed arrows, tank detachments must deeply penetrate the enemy's operational lineup, tear up its strategic front line, split its efforts, and deprive it of further options for organized resistance.

The armored as well as general army units are thus both able to break the resistance of a large enemy group, to launch a determined attack, rapidly shift the main focus of operations from one direction to the other, and independently solve larger operational tasks.

Recently we commissioned the army to solve tasks within a range of 150 to 200 kilometers behind enemy lines and with a speed of attack between 40 and 50 kilometers per day. Now we have the capability to plan an by general army units up to a range of 400 kilometers, and [to plan an attack] by tanks deep behind enemy lines with an average speed of 100 kilometers per day.

[*Source: BAMA, DVW-1/5203, Bl. 7. Translated by Karen Riechert.*]

[10] "Front" is a term of Soviet origin describing the organization of forces within a theater of operations.

Document No. 17: Czechoslovak Politburo Resolution on Mobilization Readiness with Respect to the Berlin Question, July 25, 1961

This resolution of the Czechoslovak party Presidium reflects a decision to increase defense readiness in view of the possible consequences of the signing of a separate peace treaty with East Germany. Coincidentally, the resolution comes on the same day as President John F. Kennedy's important speech announcing a troop buildup in Europe. Clearly, the Czechoslovak decision was not in response to the American move but it shows that even before the United States raised the ante the Soviets had already been preparing the Warsaw Pact for the possibility of a military confrontation arising from the expected sharpening of the crisis. This meant that Khrushchev was pushing the separate peace treaty with East Germany even though he knew he was taking a military risk. The Czechoslovak decision, coordinated with Moscow, was analogous to those reached by the Poles, East Germans and possibly Hungarians—to make arrangements for housing troops, commandeering vehicles, dispersing aircraft, and preparing for the defense of borders with the FRG. That all this was to be done by October 1 indicates that Khrushchev must have been planning to make a decision on the peace treaty, or on the building of the Berlin Wall, or both, by that date.

[...]

1. Measures to increase the readiness of the Czechoslovak Socialist Republic in connection with the solution of the German and Berlin questions. Cde. B[ohumír] Lomský, Cde. O[takar] Šimůnek, Cde. L[ubomír] Štrougal

Resolution:
The Politburo of the Communist Party of Czechoslovakia Central Committee:

I. acknowledges the report on measures that will have to be implemented in order to increase the Czechoslovak Socialist Republic's readiness in connection with the solution of the German and Berlin question, and on the potential consequences which implementation of the measures referred to above may have;

II. instructs:

a) *Defense Commissions of Provincial Committees of the Communist Party of Czechoslovakia:*

1. to provide quarters for troops pursuant to Act No. 40/1961 of the Collection of Laws on defense of the Czechoslovak Socialist Republic, in accordance with requirements of Cde. B. Lomský; [...]

b) *Cde. B. Lomský:*

1. to take efficient measures to increase the combat and mobilization readiness of the army;
2. to complete the construction of buildings housing command posts of Air Defense divisions, including all equipment (transmission and reception centers, cable circuits etc.), so that that they can be used for command purposes as of September 1, 1961;
3. to build taxiways and dispersed signs at designated airfields, to reinforce the runway of the Příbram Airfield, and to take measures allowing jet fuel to be stored on the surface
4. to build, in conjunction with Cde. L. Štrougal and in accordance with requirements related to the protection of our border with the Federal Republic of Germany, the most essential defense facilities in the foreground of and along the first line of defense by October 1, 1961, and to complete construction of the same by October 30, 1961;
5. to ask the Soviet Minister of Defense, Marshal of the Soviet Union Cde. Malinovskii, for assistance consisting of a rapid delivery of spare parts—in particular those of which there is a shortage (T-54 MBT)—from stocks of the Soviet Army; [...]

c) *Cde. J[osef] Plojhar:*

1. to check the possibility of increasing the production of drugs, vaccines, serums and blood expanders in 1961 on the basis of the requirement presented by Cde. B. Lomský; in financial terms, the increase should represent approx. CZK [Czechoslovak crowns] 170 million; at the same time, to check the preparedness of the transfusion service to step up blood donations to the maximum limit as of October 1, 1961; a report on the above issues shall be submitted to Cdes. B. Lomský and O. Šimůnek by August 15, 1961;
2. to make sure that temporary medical evacuation centers in the provinces of West Bohemia and South Bohemia, as well as medical aid stations along motorways are ready to start operation as of October 1, 1961;
3. to update, by October 1, 1961, medical evacuation plans of the Civil Defense's Medical Service in order to reflect measures for improvised casualty collection points, which should be able to process the wounded in numbers envisaged in relevant target analyses;
4. to speed up the construction of medical facilities in accordance with and pursuant to the Resolution of the Communist Party of Czechoslovakia Central Committee's Military Defense Commission of February 2, 1961, so that such facilities can commence operation in the beginning of the fourth quarter of 1961, if needed. [...]

d) *Cde. L. Štrougal:*

1. to take, by September 1, 1961, provisional measures to improve protection and air-tightness of Building K-111, to provide the building with essential equipment and food supplies, and to select people to operate the building;
2. to issue, by July 31, 1961, instructions to ministers, heads of central authorities and chairmen of Provincial National Committees (Chairman of the National Committee of the Capital City of Prague) outlining measures to be taken to ensure the combat readiness and preparedness of their respective organizations;
3. to check, by October 1, 1961, the readiness state of the measures referred to above, and to test the readiness of Civil Defense staffs and units and their ability to act in practice (by provincial and nationwide Civil Defense system exercises), especially in target cities;
4. to prepare, by October 1, 1961, the establishment of main command centers, wartime facilities and accommodation quarters for the national Civil Defense staff, as well as Civil Defense staffs of provinces and provincial capitals, including communications, and, in line with the above measures, to instruct relevant ministries to establish command posts for Civil Defense services and to bring them to a state of readiness;
5. to put in place, by October 1, 1961, measures allowing for the complete evacuation of the eleven target cities; to this end, evacuation plans should be modified, evacuation authorities prepared, and the classification level of internal evacuation plans downgraded from "M" [mobilization] to "Top Secret;"
6. to establish, by October 1, 1961, Civil Defense staffs in places where they have not yet been established, and to prepare measures ensuring that telephones in offices of National Committees in every municipality or village are permanently manned;
7. to complete and bring to a state of readiness Civil Defense facilities and buildings with a fitted or supplied NBC [Nuclear/Biological/Chemical] filtering unit in all designated towns and facilities; the Civil Defense buildings and activated shelters [should] be left to their peacetime use pending a further decision;
8. to complete, by October 1, 1961, emergency assistance plans for the population, and to supplement early warning plans with measures ensuring the announcement of a radiation alert;
9. to put in place, by October 1, 1961, measures allowing the general public to be familiarized with their duties and conduct in emergencies;
10. to put in place, by October 1, 1961, and acting in conjunction with Cdes. B. Lomský and J[án] Hečko, measures allowing seconded SVAZARM aircraft to conduct airborne radioactive ground contamination monitoring, including training of and material provisions for their crews;
11. to ensure that gas masks and mouth-screens are issued to ministries and National Committees, which will in turn take preparatory measures for their distribution free-of-charge to people, Civil Defense services and units, and persons safeguarding activities of armed corps; the protective aids listed above should be issued to the public pending and subject to a special decision;

e) *Cde. B[runo] Köhler:*

The commission established pursuant to Resolution of the Communist Party of Czechoslovakia Central Committee's Military Defense Commission of February 2, 1961, which approved essential principles of managing the country in an armed readiness situation, will evaluate the fulfillment of Item II of the present resolution, and resolve the issue of concealment and dispersion of central party and state authorities. [...]

f) *Cdes. F[rantišek] Vlasák, M[iroslav] Šmok, Jozef Púčik, František] Kahuda, O[ldřich] Černík, [Josef] Krosnář, B[ožena] Machačová-Dostálová, J[osef] Reitmajer, Jindřich Uher, O[ldřich] Beran, Karel Poláček, Josef Plojhar and Vratislav Krutina:*

1. to take, by October 1, 1961, measures ensuring combat readiness of staffs of Civil Defense services and units falling into their respective purviews, in accordance with instructions from Cde. L. Štrougal;
2. to prepare, by October 1, 1961, Civil Defense staffs of ministries for organized movements to designated places;
3. to prepare, by October 1, 1961, and acting in conjunction with Defense Commissions of territorial party authorities, measures for the evacuation of factory employees from the eleven target cities;
4. to prepare, by October 1, 1961, and in accordance with instructions of Cde. L. Štrougal, measures allowing Civil Defense materiel needed for primary rescue and disaster-relief operations in and around the nuclear epicenter, which is presently stored in the target cities, to be removed from warehouses and deployed as needed;
5. to ensure, in cooperation with Cde. O. Šimůnek, that their subordinate organizations and industrial enterprises prepare plans for transition from a peacetime to a wartime economy by September 30, 1961.

[*Source: VKO 1961, box 16, inv. č. 61, č.j. 8496, VÚA. Translated by Jiří Mareš.*]

Document No. 18: Joint Declaration of the Warsaw Treaty States on the Berlin Wall, August 13, 1961

The construction of the Berlin Wall was one of the most dramatic acts of the Cold War. At its core, the decision to build it was taken out of desperation as the only feasible way to stem the flow of refugees from East Germany to the West, over 2 million of whom had already fled. Of course, that is not how the declaration below presents things. Rather, it accuses the West of behaving with such aggressive intent against the interests of the socialist camp, and East Germany in particular, that "protective measures" were urgently needed. With astonishing understatement, the declaration acknowledges that the new structure "will bring about some inconvenience for the population." In fact, Khrushchev agreed to the building of the Wall only under pressure from Ulbricht and later spoke as if he deplored "this hateful thing."[11] In any case, despite his risk-taking, Khrushchev's hesitation was out of concern not to provoke the West into a conflict.

For several years already, the member-states of the Warsaw Treaty have attempted to bring about a peace treaty with Germany. These states are of the opinion that this problem is ripe for decision and can tolerate no further delay. As is known, the Soviet Government, with the approval and full support of all Warsaw Treaty states, has proposed to all countries, which participated in the war against Hitler Germany that a peace treaty be signed with both German states that could include the peaceful solution of the West Berlin problem by converting West Berlin into a demilitarized Free City. This proposal takes into consideration the real situation that has developed in Germany and Europe during the post-war period. It is not directed against the interests of any side, but its only purpose is to eliminate the vestiges of the Second World War—and to strengthen world peace.

Until now, the governments of the Western powers have not shown their readiness to reach a solution to this problem through negotiations. Moreover, the Western powers have answered these peaceful proposals of the socialist countries with intensified war preparations, with a campaign of war hysteria and with threats of military force. Official representatives of several NATO countries have announced an increase in their armed forces and plans for partial mobilization. In some NATO countries, plans have in fact been published for the invasion of GDR territory.

Aggressive forces are using the absence of a peace treaty to force the militarization of West Germany and to strengthen the Bundeswehr at a more rapid rate, equipping it with the most modern weapons. West German revanchists are openly

[11] In a conversation with a West German ambassador, as quoted in Hope M. Harrison, *Driving the Soviets Up the Wall: Soviet-East German Relations, 1953-1961*, (Princeton: Princeton University Press, 2003), p. 186.

demanding that they be supplied with nuclear and atomic weapons. The governments of the Western powers, which support the rearmament of West Germany in every way are thereby guilty of breaking the most important international agreements, which provide for the elimination of German militarism and the prevention of its rebirth in any form.

The Western powers have not only ignored the need to normalize the situation in West Berlin but continue to strengthen it as a center of diversion against the GDR and other socialist countries. There is no place on earth where so many foreign espionage and diversionist centers are concentrated and where they can operate so unrestrictedly as in West Berlin. These centers send agents into the GDR to commit various diversionary acts, recruit spies and incite hostile elements to organize acts of sabotage against the GDR, and to spread unrest.

The ruling circles of the Federal Republic and the espionage agencies of the NATO countries make use of the present transport situation on the West Berlin border to undermine the economy of the German Democratic Republic. By means of deception, corruption and extortion, government organs and armament trusts in the Federal Republic have caused a certain unstable part of the GDR population to go to West Germany. These victims are forced into the West German armed forces, they are recruited for the espionage organs of various countries and are then returned to the GDR to commit acts of espionage and sabotage. Indeed a special fund has been set up in order to carry out these diversionist activities against the German Democratic Republic and other socialist countries. West German Chancellor Adenauer recently called on the NATO governments to increase this fund.

It is characteristic that the diversionist activities originating in West Berlin have increased in the recent past, after the Soviet Union, the German Democratic Republic and the other socialist countries had made proposals for an immediate peace settlement with Germany. These diversionist activities not only harm the German Democratic Republic but also infringe on the interests of other socialist countries. In view of the aggressive aims of the reactionary forces of the Federal Republic and their NATO allies, the Warsaw Treaty states are obliged to take appropriate measures to guarantee their security and especially the security of the German Democratic Republic, which is vital to the interests of the German people themselves.

The governments of the Warsaw Treaty states turn to the People's Chamber and the government of the GDR and to all workers of the German Democratic Republic with the proposal that such measures be taken as will insure that the diversionist activities against the socialist countries are stopped, and that around the entire area of West Berlin including its border with democratic Berlin reliable guards and effective controls are established. Of course, these measures will not affect the prevailing regulations for controlling traffic and lines of communications between West Berlin and West Germany.

The governments of the Warsaw Treaty states understand, of course, that such protective measures along the West Berlin borders will bring about some inconvenience for the population but in view of the present situation, the responsibility for these measures lies solely with the Western powers and above all with the government of the Federal Republic. The fact that the West Berlin borders have remained open in the past was based on the hope that the Western powers would not misuse the good will of the government of the GDR. They have, however, disregarded the interests of the German people and the population of Berlin by using the open West Berlin border for their malicious diversionist activity. The present abnormal situation must be ended by a strengthened guard and control along the West Berlin border.

At the same time the governments of the Warsaw Treaty states consider it necessary that these measures be removed as soon as a peace settlement with Germany is reached and, on that basis, the solution to current problems is found.

[*Source:* Documents on International Affairs, 1961, *ed. D.C. Watt, John Major, Richard Gott, George Schopflin (London/New York: Oxford University Press, 1965), pp. 343–345.*]

Document No. 19: Resolution by the Czechoslovak Party Military Defense Commission on the Introduction of Emergency Measures, September 14, 1961

This document is another resolution by the Czechoslovak party Central Committee. Unlike the document from July 25 (See Document No. 17), this one was prepared after the construction of the Berlin Wall. By now it was clear that there would be no immediate strong reaction forthcoming from the West, but it was still an open question whether Khrushchev would follow up with a separate peace treaty with East Germany, which would surely spark an even more serious crisis. This resolution relates to the implementation of emergency measures intended to deal with the possible consequences therefrom. There is still debate as to when Khrushchev gave up on the conclusion of the treaty, but it appears that at this point the Czechoslovaks were still being told to plan on that eventuality, as were the East Germans.

Agenda: Approval of measures increasing combat readiness, ordered by the Supreme Commander of the Unified Armed Forces of the member-states of the Warsaw Treaty on September 8, 1961

Attending members of the Czechoslovak Communist Party Central Committee's Military Defense Commission: Antonín Novotný, Viliam Široký, Jiří Hendrych, Lubomír Štrougal, Otakar Šimůnek, Bohumír Lomský

Resolution: The Czechoslovak Communist Party Central Committee's Military Defense Commission
  acknowledges the report submitted by National Defense Minister Bohumír Lomský;
  agrees with the implementation of tasks recommended in the report;
  instructs
Comrade Novotný, First Secretary of the Central Committee of the Czechoslovak Communist Party and President of the Republic
  – to inform Provincial Party Secretaries about an exercise conducted under the leadership of the Supreme Commander of the Unified Armed Forces, Comrade Marshal Grechko, and on measures related thereto (as per the draft letter enclosed herewith);
Comrade Lomský, Minister of National Defense
  – to issue, by September 20, 1961, an order instituting measures to ensure permanent combat readiness of the Czechoslovak People's Army, and to increase alertness and vigilance;
  – to arrange an inspection/check of Facilities "K-116" and "S" by set dates;

- to implement measures to ensure full preparedness of the Czechoslovak People's Army for the exercise conducted under the leadership of the Supreme Commander of the Unified Armed Forces;
- to take other measures within the Czechoslovak People's Army to ensure the fulfillment of other tasks related to increased combat readiness.

Comrade Vlasák, Minister of Transportation and Communications, in conjunction with the Minister of National Defense

- to organize, by September 20, 1961, military communication directorates to check and verify, by October 15, 1961, the condition of communications equipment in storage at the Directorate of Material Reserves, and to make provisions for bypasses in accordance with requirements put forward by the Ministry of National Defense and the Ministry of Transportation and Communications when designing the communication network;
- to train, by September 30, 1961, communication operators falling under the Ministry of Transportation and Communications in order to speed up the process of handover of lines and communication assets to meet needs of the Ministry of National Defense and the Unified Command;
- to improve, by December 31, 1961, the survivability of major communication nodes of the Ministry of Transportation and Communications to the maximum extent possible;
- to transfer, by October 31, 1961, and under the 1958 agreement between the Ministry of Transportation and Communication and the Ministry of National Defense, aircraft, pilots and necessary materiel in accordance with Comrade Lomský's requirements, to meet needs of the Czechoslovak armed forces.

Comrade Šimůnek, Deputy Prime Minister and Chairman of the State Planning Commission, acting in conjunction with the Minister of National Defense

- to check and, where applicable, to complete, by December 1, 1961, modifications of existing storage depots for special ammunition and special propellants supplied in 1961 and 1962;
- to make arrangements regarding the storage and allocation of supplies for the Soviet Army, and to find a manner of compensation therefore, as per and in line with the Resolution of the Czechoslovak Communist Party Central Committee's Military Defense Commission, dated September 2, 1961;

Comrade Hečko, Chairman of Svazarm[12]

- to transfer, by October 31, 1961, and under the 1960 agreement between the Ministry of National Defense and the Central Committee of Svazarm, aircraft, pilots and necessary materiel in accordance with Comrade Lomský's requirements, to meet the needs of the Czechoslovak armed forces.

[*Source: 17/4, VKO, VÚA. Translated by Jiří Mareš.*]

---

[12] Union for cooperation with the Army.

Document No. 20: The "Buria" Exercise Preparing for an Advance into Western Europe, September 28–October 10, 1963

"Buria" was the first major exercise conducted by the Warsaw Pact as a coalition. It was widely publicized at the time. Contemporary observers interpreted this as a message that the alliance was prepared for any potential Western military response to the signing of a separate peace treaty with East Germany. There are other records that relate to this point, but one interesting aspect of this first document, a secret speech by East German Defense Minister Heinz Hoffmann, is that it gives the starting point of the exercise as October 1, which points to the possibility that the Soviets had plans to conclude the treaty on that date, and that the exercise may have been intended not for publicity but in fact to prepare in earnest for a possible Western military response. According to the Hoffmann speech, the exercise began with a Western attempt to forcibly reopen access to West Berlin, which was being blocked by the Wall. Hostilities were foreseen, and the use of nuclear weapons forecast by October 6, the sixth day of the maneuver, although it is unclear who would use them first. "Buria" ends with a Warsaw Pact offensive and the occupation of Paris by October 16.

The second document is an excerpt from a memoir by the Polish liaison with the Warsaw Pact command, Tadeusz Pióro, who published his recollections in the 1990s, after the end of the Cold War. He refers to the maneuver as part of the command post exercise taking place at Soviet military headquarters on the outskirts of Berlin, and describes how the advance into Western Europe was played out on maps. According to him, Warsaw Pact forces were not supposed to stop at Paris but take all of France and end only at the Pyrenees. So it is not fully clear from these two accounts what the real scenario was, but certainly outlandish ideas were being entertained here.

---

a) Speech by East German Defense Minister Heinz Hoffmann

We have to consider this exercise as the first step in an entire system of defense measures, to be undertaken in order to secure militarily the German Peace Treaty during the months of October and November. [...]

The simulated situation implied that a peace treaty with the GDR had been concluded. Starting at midnight, October 4, the "Western" powers could establish contact with their garrison in West Berlin only with permission from the government of the GDR. Therefore the border checkpoints had been closed, and the use of flight corridors by aircraft of the "Western" powers had been prohibited.

In this situation, the "West" tried forcibly to establish a link to West Berlin. In trying to enforce this link to West Berlin, they started to break through along the highway with troops of up to one division on October 5 at 3:00 p.m. They gradually expanded the area of incursion and tried to advance to West Berlin first by transport, then combat aircraft.

These attempts were foiled by joint efforts of the armies of the member-states of the Warsaw Treaty.

After the "West" had been compelled to realize that a forced breakthrough to West Berlin was not to be achieved, they unleashed the war on October 6 at noon by launching a nuclear attack.

By using all means of intelligence, the "East" discovered the approach of large groups of strategic and tactical air forces from the airfields of Europe and the United States. It answered at 12:05 p.m. with the first massive nuclear strike. Thus heavy battles ensued along the entire front line from the Baltic Sea to the northern border of Austria.

Because of the first strike delivered by the "East," the "West" did not succeed in changing the balance of forces to its advantage.

In the course of the hostilities, the "East" seized the initiative in the most important directions, and at the end of the second day (October 7) reached a depth of 80 to 160 kilometers in the direction of the Ruhr, Frankfurt, and Munich.

[...]

Due to the new situation, the "West" launched attacks against the flanks of the 1st Central Front aiming to interrupt the attack of the "East's" first strategic echelon in order to gain extra time for the concentration of additional forces.

In the morning of the second day, the "East" had the troops from the Polish coastal front join the battle in the direction of Hamburg to further advance the attack. On the third day, the troops of the western front were led towards the Ruhr area, and the troops of the second central front towards Stuttgart.

Introducing these troops into combat further turned the balance of forces in favor of the "East" and destroyed the resistance of the "West." At the end of the third day of hostilities, the "Eastern" troops reached the Danish border, the Weser river, the Ruhr area, occupied a bridgehead on the west side of the Rhine river in the area of Mainz and Worms, and occupied Nuremberg and Munich. [...]

Quickly the "East" advanced the attack further, and in the evening of the fifth day of combat the tanks of the first central front, consisting of two tank divisions, headed towards the Rhine river in the area between Bonn and Mannheim (170 kilometers) and reached an area 140 kilometers west of the Rhine.

Troops of the coastal front and the western front entered the North of the Jutland Peninsula and reached the Dutch and Belgian borders. At the same time, troops of the second central front and of the Southwest front reached the Neckar river, the upper reaches of the river Danube, and occupied Stuttgart. [...]

After regrouping in the Rhine area, it was the "West's" intention to organize a strong defense in order to lead a counterattack after adding additional forces. In this situation, the fronts of the "East" were supposed to continue fighting in order to reach the river Seine, the Canal of Burgundy, Châlon-sur-Saône, and Morez.

By decision of the supreme commander of all fronts, with this situation the exercise ended. [...]

[*Source: VA-01, 6103, BA-MA. Translated by Karen Riechert.*]

b) Recollections of Polish *Gen. Tadeusz Pióro*

[...]

In the first part [ten days] of September, a meeting of defense ministers of the Warsaw Treaty was held in Warsaw during which a decision to "strengthen the military's readiness for attack" was made, and shortly after that the commanders of the Silesian and Pomeranian Districts with their chiefs-of-staff were suddenly called to Warsaw. We were notified to go to Zossen-Wünsdorf [13] for a war game in which we would act as army commanders and chiefs-of-staff. Departure from Warsaw [was to be] in a few days.

We could take with us, besides personal effects, only writing tools; no maps, notebooks, not even paper—we were supposed to receive all of that at our destination. And that was it; no additional explanations. As it turned out, no one could provide these explanations, including [Defense Minister Marian] Spychalski, since the Soviet General Staff, acting under the heading of the Warsaw Pact, had deliberately limited itself to informing us about who should take part in the game and what we were *not* allowed to take along. As for the rest—the subject of the exercise, its organization, and our assignment in the exercise—we were supposed to find out about that in Wünsdorf. The special level of secrecy of the undertaking was due to the exercise being conducted in accordance with the operational plans of the member-states of the Treaty in case of war.

[...]

At our destination were General [Aleksei] Antonov, as head of the staff directing the exercise, and a group of Russian generals and officers from various forces. The Germans were also there with their minister [Heinz Hoffmann] (but not as hosts), and soon the Czechs flew in—both teams with personnel similar to ours. The next day we were given plans for a huge offensive, extending from the border on the Elbe River to the Atlantic. The central front of the Warsaw Treaty reached the Baltic with its right wing, and Switzerland and the Pyrenees with its left wing, albeit with the exclusion of Spain, which at the time was not a member of the North Atlantic Treaty. So we were supposed to simulate the annexation of almost all of Western Europe. Also envisaged in the plan of the offensive was a complete takeover of the Baltic Sea covered by air landing in Norway, but without [considering] England, which—no-one knows why—remained outside of the zone of operations.

That day we got to know the working regulations. The level of secrecy was as follows: using personal notebooks, making any kind of marginal notes, and using the services of a typist or draftsman were prohibited. We were to prepare all documentation on our own, by hand, in "centrally" distributed notebooks and on the maps, which every day after work, mostly during late night hours, we returned in special folders sealed in wax to an office operating 24 hours a day. [...]

After three industrious days which extended into the evenings, after we had drawn preliminary decisions on the maps and written resolutions for the operation, all part-

---

[13] On the outskirts of Berlin, where the headquarters of the Group of Soviet Forces in Germany were located.

icipants in the game were gathered in a huge room where reporting on the offensive plan took place. There, the cards were already laid out: gigantic maps of Central and Western Europe with the Baltic and North Seas hung on supports, which almost reached the ceiling. The position of our and NATO forces, and enormous red arrows cutting through the "Blues"[14] from the Elbe line through West Germany and France, reaching the waters of the Atlantic (our troops were marked in red and black and our enemy's in blue and brown) were drawn on these maps. There, [in a huge room] I could also see all the participants in the game.

Marshal Rodion Malinovskii, the defense minister of the USSR, together with a group of leading commanders of Soviet ground, air, and naval forces, and a group of lecturers from Moscow's General Staff Academy led the exercise. He was sitting in the first row, filling with his bulky body an armchair that was too tight for him. Next to Malinovskii, long like a stick, was Marshal Andrei Grechko; as Supreme Commander of the Warsaw Treaty in the game he performed the role assigned to him—he commanded all forces participating in the offensive. The defense ministers of the Warsaw Treaty states also all sat in the first row, with Bulgarian, Romanian and Hungarian [ministers] as observers. Near the leadership, Marshal Vasilii Chuikov occupied his place—the famous defender of Stalingrad. With a group of several hundred people he was directing the defense of the "Blues" that was a lost cause to start with. It was obvious from the beginning that he did not care, since he had to be defeated.

The room was mainly occupied by Soviet officers, and between them were Wehrmacht[15] uniforms, which GDR officers had been wearing since the war. They made quite an incredible impression. An overwhelming majority of the officers from all national teams had the rank of generals, which is to say, they were the flower of the Warsaw Pact knighthood. When I looked at this gathering, a thought quite common in similar situations went through my head: what would happen if a bomb smashed into the middle of the room? And I answered myself: nothing would happen; all these generals and colonels with their shining insignia would be replaced by somewhat better or somewhat worse officers, and the war would continue, probably without any major changes.

As to the tables and maps with the plans for the invasion of Europe—the main role was performed by the Soviet forces—a group of 400,000 comprised of six army groups and two air forces, among them two tank armies which were supposed to enter a breach made by the first two deployments to ensure success. Along the main directions of attack, the arrows pointed at the Jutland Peninsula, the Essen industrial area, Luxembourg, and Lyon—borders which our forces were supposed to reach during the first phase of the offensive. On the right flank was Gen. [Zygmunt] Duszyński's Front, with arrows cutting through Hamburg up to the northern boundaries of Denmark, and with a branch of one arrow pointing at the island of Bornholm on which an air and seaborne landing was planned, despite the fact that Poland—as I mentioned—did not possess either aircraft for carrying paratroopers or landing ships.

---

[14] Code name for NATO forces.
[15] The Nazi German army.

On the left flank, two Czechoslovak armies called the Army Group of the ČSSR (aside from Poland no Warsaw Treaty state had a "Front" organization) were advancing toward Munich and further toward Bordeaux. Two German armies did not participate in the first echelon; just in case, they were kept as reserves for the Supreme Commander with an undefined assignment. The Romanians, Bulgarians and Hungarians did not participate in the game because their forces were components of the southern sector of the Warsaw Treaty, for which the expected zone of operations was the Balkans and Appenine Peninsula.

In fact, the Polish armies were not included in the initial formation either. In Moscow, where the exercise had been prepared, they had been assigned to the second echelon, and some Soviet Front which was most likely included in the operational plans of the Soviet General Staff was put at the front lines. Only after his arrival in Wünsdorf, after maps were presented to him, did Spychalski, at Duszyński's urging, decide to ask for a more appropriate position and find out from Malinovskii why Polish forces were not visible on the map. "Oh, it's just a trifle, simply an oversight," answered Malinovskii. "We will fix it right away." And sure enough, on tables displayed later, the two Polish armies could be seen in areas where they were expected to be in case of war with NATO. But we felt clearly what the "mishap" meant; they do not trust us in Moscow, and like the Germans we were kept in reserve. Perhaps not without reason.

Reporting on the operational plan began. First was Army General Pavel Batov—small and inconspicuous, he performed the role of Chief-of-Staff of the Unified Command (he was soon to replace Antonov, who was very sick from diabetes and died in June 1962). After him came Col. Gen. Ivan Iakubovskii, "*général-en-chef*" of the most powerful group of Soviet forces (in the GDR), with the looks of a know-it-all. A distinctive episode stuck in my memory: Iakubovskii, while reporting something about Luxembourg, could not find the [Grand] Duchy on the map. At that point, Malinovskii asked him: "And what is Luxembourg?" "Maybe the capital of Belgium," replied Iakubovskii, which caused a general commotion in the room, but did not hinder Iakubovskii's further career; a few years later he assumed the position of Supreme Commander of the Warsaw Treaty (after Grechko), and became a marshal. After him [Iakubovskii], other commanders of Soviet armies and commanders of allied forces presented their decisions. After each comment from Malinovskii, correcting certain details of their plans, they all "stood at attention" and emphatically replied: "Of course, comrade Marshal!"—agreeing without a word to change what together with their staffs they had been sweating on for days and nights. Only Duszyński was stubborn, defending a decision worked out by our group and not snapping to attention, which actually did not serve him best in the future.

In this strange game, during which a World War III was played out on maps, we noticed that an enormous number of nuclear weapons had already been used in the first day of the operation. Almost every larger town in West Germany was circled on the tables, marked as a nuclear target for long-range air force. As I remember, a one-megaton hydrogen bomb was planned for Hamburg, which was a yield 50 times of that dropped on Hiroshima. Just a day after the drop, one of the Soviet motorized armies was to enter the city, showing an unbelievable lack of imagination and knowledge on the part of military planners. In addition, behind the front line, nuclear missiles were to hit the fighting forces of the "Blues" to clear the path for the armored divisions supposed to be storming ahead. These were preceded by chemical units, whose task was decontaminating the terrain, but the absurdity of this assignment was obvious since the forces were to enter that region just a few hours after the explosion, regardless of the consequences.

[...]

After two weeks of arduous labor, once the enemy sued for peace, the end of the game was declared. After a day-long break, Marshal Malinovskii went over the exercise, and afterward there was a dinner for 200 people—one of those depressing banquets during which even unlimited quantities of alcohol could not rid it of the monotony of the toasts raised: for the victors, for the defeated (that is, Marshal Chuikov), for the director of the exercise, for the brave commanders, for friendship among nations, and of course—for peace.

[...]

[*Source: Tadeusz Pióro,* Armia ze skazą: W Wojsku Polskim 1945–1968 (Wspomnienia i Refleksje) *[The Defective Army: In the Polish Army, 1945–1968 (Memories and Reflections)] (Warsaw: Czytelnik, 1994), pp. 341–348. Translated by Magdalena Klotzbach for the National Security Archive.*]

Document No. 21: Organizational Principles of the Czechoslovak Army, November 22, 1962

This set of organizational principles for the Czechoslovak army is included because it shows clearly how the emphasis of Warsaw Pact strategy had shifted to offense. (See Document No. 7 by comparison.) Offensive combat is seen as the main form of combat, and the Czechoslovaks continue to be expected to fight independently for at least 10-12 days before Soviet reinforcements would appear. The new stress on offense was one of the important consequences of the Berlin crisis.

Organizational Principles of the Czechoslovak Army
[...]
a) [...] Offensive warfare is the essential and principal form of combat and the only means to achieve victory over the enemy. This is reflected in the first principle of the development of the Czechoslovak People's Army: to build an army which, in addition to being able to handle other types of warfare, possesses primarily offensive capabilities.
b) The role and position of the Czechoslovak People's Army in the defense system of the Warsaw Treaty, as well as the specific mission the Czechoslovak People's Army has been entrusted with by the Supreme Command of the Unified Armed Forces, are reflected in the second principle: our army must be structured and built to be able to mount an independent front-sized operation.[16] Taking into account the first principle, it follows that the Czechoslovak People's Army must, first and foremost, be capable of mounting and conducting an offensive front-sized operation. In the event of a surprise attack, our army would be required to conduct initial operations on its own for 10 to 12 days, until the next operational echelon arrives and is deployed. [...]
From a strategic viewpoint, it is necessary to possess such peacetime armed forces as would be able to acquire the strategic initiative early in the war, and thus ensure achievement of the immediate strategic objective.
Of the total number of armed forces needed and able to achieve strategic objectives, the following elements are maintained in continuous combat readiness:
– strategic forces and assets in a structure needed to achieve war objectives;
– an air defense system; and
– certain other parts of the Czechoslovak armed forces.
Some armies and divisions from the ground and air forces, which are earmarked for conducting opening operations and stationed close to the border, must be main-

---

[16] "Front" is a term of Soviet origin describing the organization of forces within a theater of operations.

tained in a structure that will ensure the fulfillment of vital tasks in the initial phase of the war. The other part of these forces must provide for rapid mobilization, so that it can be deployed in opening operations during the initial phase.

[...]

The term "first strategic echelon" as used herein denotes the main group of armed forces of a country (or a coalition of countries) comprising missile units, aviation, air defense forces and assets, peacetime ground troops and also troops mobilized throughout the territory of the country/coalition. [This main group] is earmarked for conducting operations in the early stage of the war, in the course of which immediate military-political objectives, i.e. destruction of a substantial part of the opponent's armed forces, elimination of a number of members of the enemy coalition from the war, and a serious disruption of the military-economic potential of the enemy coalition, should be achieved.

The order of battle of the first strategic echelon is based on the current concept of the initial stage of the war, the substance of which is active combat, aimed at achieving the immediate strategic objective, namely, crushing the core of the main strategic echelons of the opponent's armed forces and getting hold of major economic centers and areas, as well as areas where enemy forces assemble and deploy.

The first strategic echelon can be segmented into two or more operational echelons.

The first operational echelon is the main core of the first strategic echelon, its mission being to repel a surprise attack by the enemy and conduct initial operations. As a rule, it maintains full combat readiness even in peace time.

The other operational echelons consist of troops that are allocated more time to mobilize, assemble and deploy in relevant war theaters.

The general principles outlined above determine the position of the Czechoslovak Army in the framework of the first strategic echelon of the Unified Armed Forces in the European theater. Because of the possibility of an unexpected attack by NATO armed forces along the line of contact, all units of the Czechoslovak People's Army must be viewed strictly as part of the first operational echelon.

[...]

As part of the first operational echelon of the Unified Armed Forces, troops and units of the Czechoslovak People's Army also act as a covering force, their mission being to provide cover not just for the territory of the Czechoslovak Socialist Republic, but also for the territory of the entire Warsaw Treaty, together with other allied armies.

In the present situation, the notion of a covering force is different from what it used to be in the past. Earlier requirements demanded that the border be covered in a more or less passive manner, but today's requirements are much more comprehensive. The covering force must operate within a strategic framework in which the most important role (apart from missile and air force units) belongs to the first operational echelon. It is a part of the first operational echelon that is assigned the role of the covering force. As in the past, the main task of the covering force is to ensure the deployment of main forces in accordance with the plan of initial operations.

138

However, the covering force is no longer passive, as before. Its main task, i.e. ensuring the deployment of main forces, is best accomplished by securing a line of deployment in the depth of enemy territory. This is why the covering force is expected to fulfill its task through active operations along principal strategic and operational directions.

In order to eliminate the adverse consequences of a lower level of combat readiness in peace time, a plan of step-by-step covert reinforcements is in place, which could be put into effect to increase the numbers of troops at the front to a level consistent with a high level of combat readiness, if there is an increased risk of a war breaking out or of a surprise attack. However, the measures outlined above can be effective only if taken in a timely fashion, i.e. if we do not allow ourselves to be surprised by the enemy.

[Source: GŠ-OS, 1962, 0010081, VÚA. Translated by Jiří Mareš.]

Document No. 22: The "Mazowsze" Exercise for Nuclear War and Interview with Gen. Tuczapski on Soviet Bloc Planning of Exercises, *circa* April 23, 1963

One of the changes in Warsaw Pact strategy after the Berlin crisis was to account for the possible heavy use of nuclear armaments. The first document here describes a Polish military exercise from April 18–22, 1963, which was designed to prepare for a war involving the detonation of huge numbers of such weapons. The exercise takes for granted that practically every major Polish city would be hit, causing massive casualties, yet presumes that fighting would continue and that enemy forces would actually be repelled. In retaliation against NATO's initiation of hostilities, including its first-use of nuclear weapons, the Warsaw Pact conducts a total of 61 nuclear counterstrikes against Western Europe and the United States resulting in 33 million dead in the U.S. after two days, but only 1.3 million dead in Poland. In the concluding evaluation, the defense minister repeats the unfounded Soviet claim that the USSR possessed missiles that could strike any target on earth.

In the second document below, Gen. Tadeusz Tuczapski, who was in charge of Poland's homeland defense in the early 1960s, offers a very different viewpoint in this interview conducted by Polish military historians in the 1990s.[17] Charged with ensuring the continued functioning of society, the economy, and government administration, Tuczapski was in a position to know what was feasible or not under wartime conditions. He claimed always to have been skeptical of the viability of some of the plans from the 1960s that presumed the normal functioning of government and society after a major nuclear attack. His description of how the Soviet military drew up operational plans and merely summoned generals from Poland—as they did from other countries—to sign off on the finished product raises questions for historians about the behavior and motivations of East European military and political leaders in submitting to Moscow. Were they willing accomplices of the Kremlin, and if so, was it for ideological or opportunistic reasons? Or were they protecting their countries' interests under difficult circumstances? Tuczapski implies that Poland's political leadership did not know the details of the plans, nor did it care.

---

[17] Gen. Tuczapski was among several Polish generals to be interviewed, and distinguished himself by being one of the most forthcoming and candid. For transcripts of interviews with East European former military commanders, see http://www.isn.ethz.ch/php/collections/coll_9.htm. The interviews gave the generals an opportunity to justify their record for posterity.

a) The "Mazowsze" Exercise

Situation No. 1, 05:00, 4/20 (Outline 3)

At 03:00, 4/20, the "Western" forces carried out a massive nuclear strike against the territories of the Warsaw Treaty states by using missiles, aircraft, and submarines. Following the nuclear strikes, the enemy launched offensive operations by airborne and naval forces in the western theater of operations. The airborne troops of the enemy achieved the greatest success in the operational area of Army Group "Center." The forces of Army Group "North," attacking in the operational area of the Coastal Front of the "Eastern," forces, on whose left flank Polish divisions waged stubborn resistance, did not achieve notable success.

In response to the aggression, at 03:00, 4/20, the "Eastern" forces carried out a massive retaliatory strike in accordance with the general plan of the Supreme Command of the Unified Armed Forces of the Warsaw Treaty. During the strike, directed against the European NATO countries located in the western theater of operations as well as against the territory of the United States, 276 nuclear missiles of over 188 megatons magnitude were launched, of which 190 of 8,290 kilotons magnitude were directed against the FRG, Denmark, the Netherlands, and Great Britain, and 86 of 180 megatons magnitude against the United States.

At the same time, the "Eastern" side introduced additional forces into the zone of combat. The second echelon of Soviet forces was moved into the territory of Poland. By 05:00, 4/20, the first echelon of Soviet forces had been regrouped to the western bank of the Oder river.

The overall situation in the country was as follows.

During the massive nuclear strike, despite intensive air defense that made the enemy lose 90 aircraft and about 40 missiles, the enemy succeeded in carrying out 55 nuclear strikes of 2,150 kilotons magnitude on the territory of Poland. As a result of the strikes, the air defense forces lost three battalions of missile artillery, 9 batteries of anti-aircraft barrel artillery, and 3 radio location posts. In addition, 42 aircraft were destroyed and many airfields were damaged in the course of the air war. Despite these losses, the country's air defense system remained operational.

The enemy nuclear strikes took place mainly around Szczecin, Gdańsk and Warsaw and in three main areas: the Polish-Soviet border, where 8 ground explosions of 500 kilotons magnitude were directed against transshipment points, and along the Vistula and Oder rivers, where 47 midair explosions of 1,650 kilotons magnitude were directed against communications, industrial, and military targets.

The ground and low midair explosions released by the enemy caused radioactive contamination over about 70 percent of the nation's territory, mainly the northwestern and eastern parts of Poland. The damage exceeded the acceptable norms on about 50 percent of the territory [...]

At the same time, the "Western" side landed 28 commando teams, totaling more than 270 persons, for special operations.

The massive nuclear strike caused considerable losses in the country, both among the population and in the economy. About half a million civilians were killed, and more than a million were wounded or incapacitated. Losses of medical equipment and personnel amounted to 3 percent of the total medical and paramedical personnel, 6 percent of emergency squads, and about 15 percent of the supply of medicines and 15 percent of hospital beds.

As far as means of communication were concerned, destroyed were over 7,000 railroad cars, 130 locomotives, 10 railroad bridges and 15 highway bridges; 11 railroad and 5 highway bridges were damaged. Along the transit routes crossing the Vistula, 7 out of the 11 existing bridges were totally or partially destroyed; for the Oder, the figures were 5 out of 9. These losses resulted in about 50 percent reduction in the railroad transportation capacity and about 30 percent reduction in automotive transportation.

Among industrial objects, 4 power stations were totally destroyed and 18 were seriously damaged, causing the loss of about 30 percent of power supply. Such major industrial centers as Warsaw, Poznań, Gdynia, Gdańsk, Szczecin, Stalowa Wola, and others were deprived of electricity.

Totally or partially destroyed were 80 heavy industry plants and 24 chemical plants, which, in view of the transportation bottlenecks and shortages of raw materials and power supply, caused a considerable production slowdown, estimated at 40-50 percent of the national plan requirements. [...]

In the given situation, the main tasks of territorial defense consisted in the stabilization of losses, resumption of normal functioning of the administration and economy, protection of the population and material goods, and restoration of the communications system, especially along the border transit routes across the Vistula and the Oder. [...]

The main enemy commando groups were liquidated by regular forces in the areas where they had landed, and scattered groups in the neighboring areas were liquidated by forces of territorial defense. In addition, the forces of territorial defense were active in liquidating the effects of the nuclear strikes.

Situation No. 2 (Outline 4), 22:00, 4/21

On 4/20, the "Western" forces continued offensive operations, as a result of which by 22:00, 4/20, they broke deep into the territory of the GDR in the area of Wismar. At the same time, forces of Army Group Center broke through in the direction of Northausen and Erfurt to a depth of 60 km and in the direction of Pilsen and Prague to a depth of 90 km.

In support of their ground operations, the "Western" forces on 4/20 carried out 12 nuclear strikes of 280 kilotons magnitude against the ground forces of the "Eastern" side.

On 4/21 the advance by Army Group North, whose first echelons had suffered 30 percent casualties, was stopped, and in some sectors the units of this group were forced to retreat to the territory of the FRG.

The forces of Army Group Center continued to meet with success, deepening their thrust into the territory of Czechoslovakia as far as 200 km. Because of the losses they had suffered, however, the rate of their advance began to diminish. [...]

In order to achieve its goals, the "Western" side accelerated the regrouping of troops from the European NATO countries in the direction of the front and landed fresh troops in the remaining ports as well as on the coasts of the FRG and northern France. At the same time, in the area of operations of Army Group North the

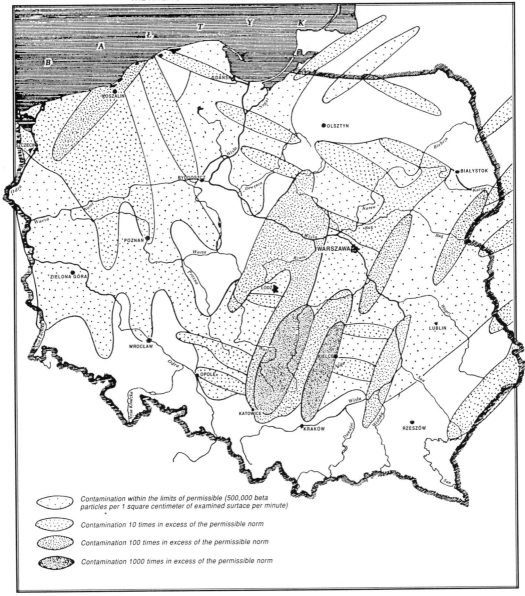

Contamination within the limits of permissible (500,000 beta particles per 1 square centimeter of examined surface per minute)

Contamination 10 times in excess of the permissible norm

Contamination 100 times in excess of the permissible norm

Contamination 1000 times in excess of the permissible norm

enemy was able to intensify air operations from the North Sea against the forces of the Coastal Front and the Baltic Fleet of the "Eastern" side. In the area of operations of Army Group Center, at 19:30, 4/21, the "Western" side landed forces by air on the scale of about a division in the area of Zawiercie and Wadowice with the goal of isolating Silesia from the east.

At the same time, the mobilization of reserves was proceeding in the [western] European NATO countries while Greece and Turkey declared general mobilization.

In the course of 4/20, "Eastern" forces conducted active defensive operations with the goal of stopping the "Western" advance and launching a counter-offensive. For this purpose, second echelon forces of the Fronts were dispatched to the battlefield.

After fresh forces arrived, the Coastal and Central Fronts, early on 4/21, went onto the offensive, as a result of which a breakthrough of 40 km into the depth of the FRG was achieved in the direction of Schwerin and Hamburg. The tactical aircraft of these fronts were moved to reserve airfields on the territory of the GDR.

The forces of the Northern Front continued intense combat with the attacking enemy forces. The arrival of the second echelon was delayed because of additional nuclear strikes by the "Western" side against mountain passages and passes.

"Eastern" submarine groups, operating in the Atlantic and North Sea, sank many transport vessels both in convoys coming from the United States and along the British coast.

On 4/20 and 4/21, the "Eastern" side carried out 61 nuclear missile strikes of 2,640 kilotons magnitude against the countries located in the western theater of operations and the United States. They were mainly directed against troops, missile, air, and naval bases, and communications centers. These strikes significantly reduced the "Western" capacity to influence developments on the ["Eastern"] domestic front.

The situation in the country was as follows. The "Western" side carried out an additional 36 nuclear strikes of 1,030 kilotons magnitude against Polish territory. They were mainly directed against communications and the air defense system.

These strikes resulted in the radioactive contamination of further portions of the country, during which a different wind direction than the one prevailing at the time of the enemy's first massive nuclear strike resulted in a different impact by the radioactive substances. This brought about an increase of radioactivity in some of the areas of previous contamination, and contamination of new areas. By the evening of 4/21, about 80 percent of Poland was contaminated, of which about 32 percent fell within acceptable limits and 48 percent was 100-to-1,000 times above acceptable limits [...] Contamination affected an area inhabited by about 20 million people.

The enemy landed 21 additional commando teams to conduct special operations.

The enemy operations inflicted additional losses on the country, including an estimated 470,000 persons killed and over a million wounded and incapacitated. Considerable losses were suffered by the medical personnel and health services; another 100,000 hospital beds were destroyed.

Of the total of 407 industrial plants, 130 were destroyed, 32 completely. Seven power stations were destroyed and 1,650 km of high-voltage power lines, as well as 59 transformers and sub-stations, were damaged. Many areas of the country were deprived of electricity; the losses resulted in a 50 percent decrease in power supply. As a result of these losses, disruption of the transport system and electric supply, as well as economic chaos, industrial production became severely restricted by the end of 4/21, up to an estimated 70 percent.

Because of the radioactive contamination of most of the country and destruction of a considerable portion of its stockpiled food, a very difficult situation developed in providing the population with food and water. [...]

Air defense forces continued to fight "Western" aviation. Engineer units were sent to build pontoon bridges across the Vistula and the Oder; by the end of 4/21, four Vistula bridges had been built. Civil defense units, security forces and other militarized units were used to eliminate the consequences of the nuclear strikes in the most affected areas. [...]

Situation No. 3 (Outline 5), 20:00, 4/22

On 4/22, paralyzed by the impact of the nuclear weapons used against them by the "Eastern" side, the "Western" forces were compelled to retreat. During the day, they carried out an additional 18 nuclear strikes of 600 kilotons magnitude against Polish territory, including 10 strikes against the Silesian industrial region with the goal of reducing the economic potential of the "Eastern" side.

In the central and northern areas, the "Western" offensive was crushed. Following the unsuccessful attempt at taking control of Silesia by airborne troops and unsuccessful operations by ground forces in the area of the Moravian Gate, the forces of Army Group Center tried to organize defensive positions to resist an "Eastern" offensive.

On 4/22, the "Eastern" side carried out additional nuclear strikes against the forces and territories of NATO states. Besides retaliatory strikes, 389 strikes of about 22 megatons magnitude were carried out against the FRG, France, Great Britain, and the United States from 20 to 22 April. As a result of these strikes, the "Western" side was seriously weakened and lost the strategic initiative. The main naval bases and ports, air and missile bases, as well as the most important industrial regions of the European NATO countries, particularly the FRG, France, and Great Britain, were destroyed, as a result of which industrial production capacity fell to a minimum and the transportation and telecommunications systems were disrupted. Panic gripped the civilian population, especially in the areas hit by nuclear strikes. Ever more often the opinion was expressed that the continuation of hostilities was pointless.

The "Eastern" nuclear missile strikes created chaos in the economy and daily life of the United States. The United States became isolated from the European theater of war and was denied the possibility of providing economic and military support to the NATO bloc in Europe.

The nuclear strikes by the "Eastern" side tilted the correlation of forces in its favor, thus creating conditions for the total defeat of the enemy in the western theater of operations and the elimination of the main European NATO countries from the war.

As a result of the enemy nuclear strikes, additional losses occurred in Poland, including population losses of 380,000 killed and 890,000 wounded and incapacitated. Total population losses during the entire period of the war amounted to 1.3 million killed and 3 million wounded and incapacitated. By comparison, the United States suffered an estimated 33 million in population losses.

During the elimination of the effects of nuclear strikes, by 20:00 on 4/22, 60 percent of the affected population were transported and evacuated from Warsaw, and about 30 percent from Olsztyn, Gdańsk, Kielce, and the Koszalin area. About 10 percent of the damaged telecommunications system was restored, on transit routes detours of destroyed communications centers were laid out, and some of the least damaged railroad bridges were repaired, so that train traffic could be resumed.

In this situation, the Committee of National Defense, provincial defense committees and military districts were directing the liquidation of the after-effects of the strikes by weapons of mass destruction, especially in Silesia, paying particular attention to assistance to the affected population, restoration of the telecommunications system, maintenance of the necessary production capacity in the key branches of industry, and mopping up of the airborne groups landed by the enemy.

Following reports to the Committee of National Defense by the heads of the sections, military districts, and provincial defense committees, the exercise was concluded at 20:00, 4/22.

[*Source:* "Doświadczenia i wnioski z ćwiczenia 'Mazowsze'," *pp. 22–35, KC PZPR 5008, Archiwum Akt Nowych, Warsaw. Translated by Vojtech Mastny.*]

b) Interview with Gen. Tadeusz Tuczapski

Gen. Tuczapski: We were invited at the beginning of the sixties (1962 or 1963, I do not remember) to Moscow. I was then chief of the Operational Administration. We were invited to Moscow, the commander of the Navy and the Air Force commander were also requested to come. I took with me Gen. Szyszka and Colonel Barański. There were also a couple of officers from the Navy, including the chief of the operational division of the Navy; and Gen. Kamiński came. We sat before the maps. A general came, who was chief of the Main Operational Administration; it was not yet [Anatolii I.] Gribkov, but it was some very intelligent one (I do not remember his name).

We then sat down […] with Gen. Szyszka because [Gen. Jerzy] Bordziłewski said, "You take care of it." We read something, took the map, and we started to draw. With Colonel Barański, because he drew well. Later, we made the plan of operation for the front on the map, in its legend, in which we included everything that should be in the legend, and what could not be was thrown into the map. We said that we were ready. They then called up Marshal [Rodion] Malinovskii, and he set the hour for a meeting. We arrived with Gen. Bordziłewski, laid out the map, and reported how we would carry out the assignment, and that was it. He asked, "Have you coordinated all your needs with the General Staff?" And with that, it ended.

Q: The maps remained in Moscow?

Gen. Tuczapski: One map remained with them, the second map we brought back here. Later, on the basis of the map (there was in the Ministry of Defense a special area to which no one had access), the commanders of the Army came and worked out all those scenarios—concretely, specifically for every division. And that's how the concrete operational plan arose. […]

Q: But after you worked out that plan, you took it afterwards to Moscow? Were they not at all interested in it in general? They just left it up to you?

Gen. Tuczapski: They left it up to us. It was our business, we were carrying it out. Still, they of course were up to date since they knew what sort of plan it was, they knew later what our orders were—especially for armaments—for armaments, and they compared certain things: "That is fine; if it suffices, if it doesn't suffice, do this too, take this too, etc."

146

Q: Was this operational plan presented to the first secretary [of the Polish communist party, Władysław Gomułka], and did he voice his opinions, or someone from the government, the premier [Józef Cyrankiewicz]?

Gen. Tuczapski: I did not report on it either to the premier or to the first secretary. Certainly, the minister of national defense composed some memorandum. Still, I do not know. [...]

Q: That is a very interesting assignment, the creation of the operational plan for our front. To what extent did you have an orientation with regard to operations in the whole military theater?

Gen. Tuczapski: If it has to do with operational planning strictly speaking—what is designated the operational plan—I did not have that sort of thing. Nevertheless, I did orient myself because exercises were constantly being conducted in the theater of military operations. When my neighbor was the Minsk [forces of the Belorussian Military District], I knew what the Minsk was doing, since after all there was normal cooperation with them.

At the same time, [...] how the operational and strategic plans were supposed to look, and the development of operations in the western theater of military operations—one could only deduce it on the basis of the exercises that were being conducted. If an exercise was being conducted in the western theater and the southern theater of military operations, and all the individual national commands were being assembled, then it could be that it wasn't exactly the same—instead of the neighbor to the left, instead of Minsk, it could be the Baltic Front, or some other one. But the assignments were similar because, in the end, Western Europe looks the way it is: Denmark, Belgium, France, West Germany, and so forth [...]

But one could devise in what way to use those dozen or so parachute divisions that the Soviets had. How the initial Soviet attack would go, if there would be one, or a retaliatory Soviet attack—that was not being worked out, although one time there was a story of that sort. Please remember that the plan for atomic or nuclear attack depended on the time. In '60 it looked one way, and in '80, another. The arrangement of armies changed, the factories changed, the importance of those factories, the airfields, and so forth. But that also was not the most important. The most important thing was how the Fronts were supposed to operate, one alongside the other. It was understood that there was the Polish, three Soviet, and later, the Czech, the Bulgarian, and so forth. And the activity in the Western theater evolved, and you would not imagine anything else.

Q: General, how did you assess our direction of operational-strategic interests? [...] Was it a difficult direction?

Gen. Tuczapski: [...] All of this depended on knowledge of whom we would have had before us. If it was in the northern direction, then most likely we would have come upon the Danes, part of some West German army, and the Belgians. How would that have looked? [...]

We went, we viewed the region of the theater of military operations, we conducted reconnaissance, we sent a group of officers from the Navy. We had to assume a serious attitude regarding that, it was a task.

You know, the matter could have been put this way: You put yourselves there, and we will play the madman. That was unthinkable. After all, we had behind us the powerful Soviet Army; they would have blown us in half, if you'll pardon the expression, and that would have been it. [...] Unfortunately, we were in the Pact, since it could not have been otherwise, and we had to put a good face on it, no matter whether someone thought that it was good or bad. Quite simply, we had to carry out the assignments. [...]

I think that ours was the easiest—speaking here between us. Ours was the easiest from the point of view of the opponent. After all, the Danish Army, the Belgian Army—let's not exaggerate. At the same time, the difficulty was that it had to be linked to a certain sea operation, a commando operation. [...]

Q: General, you are an interesting case. Up to now, we have had to do with generals who, if it came to a question regarding the operational plan, they never wanted to talk.

[*Source: KC PZPR, 5008, Archiwum Akt Nowych. Translated by Douglas Selvage for the PHP.*]

Document No. 23: Polish Command Post Exercise Rehearsing Advance to Northern Germany, Low Countries, and Denmark, June 14, 1963

This is a particularly good example of a command staff exercise report because it shows in some detail how the Warsaw Pact imagined the advance of its forces into Germany and the Low Countries. One feature of special interest is that the document reveals a presumption that before the onset of war the Warsaw Pact would match the secret preparations being made by NATO—a highly dubious proposition. As early as the second or third day following a NATO attack, according to the exercise, its forces were supposed to be in a position to reverse the tide.

This is one of a relatively few Polish documents illustrative of the Warsaw Pact's actual planning. Even today, Polish authorities continue to deny access to most records from the Operations Department, and have in fact confirmed Cold War-era classification levels, despite scholars' efforts to gain their release. The reason materials on command post exercises are available is that they were kept under another department—the Department of Combat Training—not of Operations.

TRAINING INSPECTORATE

Attachment part I
for a unilateral command post exercise using maps on the subject: "Planning and Rehearsing a Combined Landing Operation Within the Framework of an Offensive Operation of the Maritime Front in the Beginning Phase of the War."

[...]

II. Details of the exercise

1. The Unified Command of the Armed Forces of the Warsaw Pact states, anticipating the possibility of "Westerners" instigating aggression, in accordance with a specific, previously established variant of the operational plan, intends:
   - with a massive retaliatory strike executed directly following the initiation of aggression by the "Westerners," to defeat the main attacking forces as well as to destroy the main facilities of strategic and operational significance;
   - with forces located on the territory of the GDR to prevent and break down the attack of ground forces of the enemy, securing the deployment and introduction of the main forces into action;
   - on the second or third day of war to engage the main ground forces in offensive actions: – the Maritime Front in the direction of: Neubrandenburg, Osnabrück, Brussels as well as the Jutland Peninsula;

- the Central Front in the direction of: south Berlin, Kassel, Leuven in order to provide suitable conditions for moving offensive operations to the territory of France;
- immediately after the commencement of war activities to take over the Danish straits, securing the possibility for unimpeded operations and deployment of the Unified Baltic Fleet to the North Sea.

2. In accordance with the accepted variant of retaliatory activities of the Unified Command of the Armed Forces of the Warsaw Pact states, the Commander of the Maritime Front intends:
- on the night of June 17 to transfer a part of the first-echelon tactical units across the Oder River into the territory of the GDR, and the remaining ones to secondary regions of risk, securing them from massive strikes by the "Westerners" and creating better conditions for the deployment and transfer of the main forces to offensive operations;
- to engage the main forces of the first echelon in a steady offensive on the second day of war in the following directions:
  - Wittstock, Nienburg, Enschede, Brussels;
  - Schwerin, Neumünster, Flensburg, Ålborg;
  having in the first echelon the 4th and 7th Army and in the second drop the 8th Army in order to break down the left wing of the operational group of the Northern Army Group and the unified German-Danish forces on the Jutland Peninsula. Together with the Soviet air-landing unit and the Unified Baltic Fleet to take over the Danish islands, to provide suitable conditions for advancement into the North Sea through the Danish straits and Kiel Canal, and the development of offensive operations on French territory.

Near-term assignment—in three days of operations, to break down the forces of the left wing first echelon of the Northern Army Group; to move operations to the territory of the FRG; to take over the Kiel Canal and secure its facilities from destruction; and to advance to the outskirts of: Sønderborg, Tønder, the coastal island of Halligen, Wesermünde, Wildeshausen, and Bielefeld. Together with airborne units of the USSR and the Unified Baltic Fleet, not to allow the "Western" naval forces to operate in the Baltic Sea, as well as to provide suitable conditions for the deployment and operations of the Unified Baltic Fleet in the North Sea. On the second day of operations, to deploy air and seaborne landing units in the region of the Kiel Canal [...] with the aim of taking over canal locks, facilities and transfers, and to hold them for the advancement of ground forces on the third day of operation.

Further assignment—to break down the advancing operational reserves of the Northern Army Group, to take over nuclear depots, naval, air force, and supply bases of the northwestern part of the FRG, Denmark, the Netherlands, and Belgium; together with airborne units of the USSR and the Unified Baltic Fleet, to take over the Jutland Peninsula and Danish islands as well as the West and East Frisian Islands, the northwestern coast of the Netherlands and Belgium up to Ostend, Roubaix, Charleroi, and Liège; and provide suitable conditions for the transfer of operations onto French territory and operations of the North Baltic Fleet in the North Sea. [...]

3. On the right [flank]—the Unified Baltic Fleet is engaged in fighting the forces of the Danish Straits Fleet in order to prevent them from advancing into the Baltic Sea. In cooperation with the Maritime Front [the Unified Baltic Fleet] takes over the Danish straits and the entrance to the Kiel Canal, secures the deployment and operations of the seaborne landing unit of the USSR and the 32nd Airborne Division. Forces of the seaborne and airborne landing units of the USSR take over the Zeeland Island and the capital of Denmark—Copenhagen.

[…]

[*Source: 18/91/15, Główny Inspektorat Szkolenia Bojowego, Archiwum Instytucji Centralnych MON, Modlin. Translated by Magdalena Klotzbach for the National Security Archive.*]

Document No. 24: Mongolian Request for Admission to the Warsaw Pact, July 15, 1963

By the early 1960s, the Sino-Soviet rift had taken on military implications. Because of its geographical location, Mongolia became a potential battleground between the two powers, the Soviet Union and China. Although Mongolian leader Tsedenbal, no friend of the Chinese, may have taken the initiative in applying for membership in the Warsaw Pact by writing this letter to Polish Premier Józef Cyrankiewicz, the history of his country's relationship with the Soviet Union—outsiders sometimes derisively called Mongolia the 16th republic of the USSR—makes it seem unlikely that he would have done so without at least strong support from Khrushchev. In that case, by raising the prospect of extending the validity of the Warsaw Pact beyond Europe to Asia, Khrushchev may be seen as issuing a warning to the Chinese in the context of their increasingly bitter rivalry.

[...]

Dear Comrade Chairman,

With the authorization of the Presidium of the Supreme National Council of the Mongolian People's Republic [MNR], I have the honor to address to you, as Head of State of the Polish People's Republic, the custodian of the Treaty of Friendship, Cooperation and Mutual Assistance between the European socialist states of May 14, 1955, the following:

In the interests of further strengthening the MNR's cooperation along all lines with the member-states of the Council for Mutual Economic Assistance, the government of the Mongolian People's Republic,

- attaching great importance to the Warsaw Treaty Organization, which in fact stands guard for the achievements of all the socialist states;
- completely approving of the goal of the Treaty—to secure the peace and security of nations;
- taking into consideration the development of events in numerous parts of the globe, in particular the Far East, where the American imperialists are undertaking measures to equip Japan with new weapons of mass destruction; [and]
- realizing in this regard the need to strengthen the defensive capabilities of the MNR;
- hereby announces its desire to accede to the Warsaw Treaty of Friendship, Cooperation and Mutual Assistance of May 14, 1955, in accordance with Paragraph 9 of the said treaty.

By joining the Warsaw Treaty Organization, which bears a defensive character and has been called upon to serve the important interests of safeguarding collective security in accordance with the Charter of the United Nations Organization, the Mongolian People's Republic, along with the fraternal socialist member-states of the

Warsaw Treaty Organization, will strictly fulfill all the responsibilities arising from the said treaty.

The Government of the MNR asks the Government of the Polish People's Republic to request the consent of the Governments of the Warsaw Treaty Organization to the Mongolian People's Republic's accession to the Treaty.

The Government of the MNR expresses its thanks in advance to the Government of the PRL for rendering assistance in bringing its application to the attention of the other participant-states of the Warsaw Treaty Organization.

With deep respect,
Yu. Tsedenbal
Chairman of the Council of Ministers
of the Mongolian People's Republic

[*Source: KC PZPR, XIA/103, k. 525–26, Archiwum Akt Nowych. Translated by Douglas Selvage.*]

Document No. 25: Polish Foreign Ministry Memorandum regarding Possible Mongolian Accession to the Warsaw Treaty, July 20, 1963

The idea of admitting Mongolia to the Warsaw Pact, presumably backed by Moscow, met opposition from other alliance members. In this memorandum for the Polish Politburo, Foreign Minister Adam Rapacki argues that membership should be limited to Europe, and that adding Mongolia would be an unnecessarily provocative move. The Romanians were also unhappy with the idea. It is not clear whether the Soviets knew of these views or whether the dissent influenced Moscow's thinking. In any case, when the PCC discussed the subject a week after this memorandum was prepared, the Soviet representative no longer supported Mongolia's application, claiming that to do so would have sent the wrong signal to the West at a time of rapprochement resulting from the conclusion of the Limited Nuclear Test Ban Treaty.

Other than the letters of Cde. Tsedenbal and Cde. Khrushchev, the Ministry of Foreign Affairs does not possess any information further clarifying the arguments to be made at the current stage of this measure.

In this situation, it is difficult to accept as politically warranted the proposal regarding the Mongolian People's Republic's accession to the Warsaw Treaty.

The military significance of such a decision for the security of Mongolia and the interests of the Warsaw Pact seem to be practically indiscernible. The political consequences for the short and the long term are dubious and risky.

1. From the point of view of the interests of the socialist camp:

a) The acceptance of Mongolia into the Warsaw Pact at this time will of course be discerned both in the socialist states of Asia and in the West as a step whose thrust is directed against the PRC [People's Republic of China]. In a situation in which the PRC, continuing its policy of deepening divisions, is making attempts to push the responsibility onto the USSR and the other states supporting its stance, an initiative with regard to Mongolia might in a certain sense play into the hands of the PRC and be used to blame our side for carrying the dispute into the area of military alliances and moving along the path of dividing the [socialist] camp along military lines. Imperialist propaganda on the other hand will try to exploit this fact with the goal of bringing into further relief the divergence within the [socialist] camp and questioning the superiority of socialism over capitalism by telling the masses all the more that such is the peaceful substance and internationalist policy of the socialist states.

b) Cde. Tsedenbal's letter underlines the point of the imperialist threat to Mongolia. Even if we could count on the fact that the Chinese comrades would accept this assertion with good will, it would also become a real basis for harmful inter-pretations: "The Warsaw Pact represents for Mongolia an additional security guarantee in the event of imperialist aggression, but at the same time it [the Warsaw Pact] is not giving such an additional guarantee to Vietnam, Korea, and the PRC, which are even more directly exposed to the danger of American/Japanese aggression."

c) The Warsaw Pact is a pact of the European socialist states directed against imperialist activities in Europe [...] and providing for an automatic military reaction by the participants in the event of aggression in Europe (art. 4). These provisions of the Treaty would have to be changed. The very political scope and character of the Treaty would have to be changed. Such a basic change of the Warsaw Pact would have an unmistakable and serious meaning, because it would lead to an actual transformation of the alliance into a general security pact for the socialist camp with the participation of all the states of the camp. Against the backdrop of the particular policy of the PRC, such a solution is unrealistic. If it is, such a change in the character of the Treaty would be more likely to weaken the anti-imperialist activity of the Treaty in Europe than to strengthen it in Asia.

d) It can be counted on that the problem of Albania in the Warsaw Pact will be brought to a sharp climax. The acceptance of a new member and a change in the contents of the Treaty requires the unanimous acceptance of the partici-pants. A change in the Treaty would require the acceptance of a relevant Proto-col, which would have to be ratified by every signatory to the Treaty in order to come into force. Albania, which has in fact disassociated itself from the Treaty, remains nominally a member of it. Its opposition would thus have a legal basis.

e) The possibility of a negative stance on the part of Romania regarding Mongolia's accession should also seriously be counted on, and a discussion on this issue might further inflame existing differences.

f) In terms of the international effects of Mongolia's accession to the Warsaw Pact, it should also be taken into consideration that Mongolia has established a [certain] position for itself among the Afro-Asiatic states (it participates in the Afro-Asiatic group at the U.N.). It should be considered whether Mongolia, by participating in a military pact, would not diminish the political credibility that it possesses in this group and its possibilities [for influence], which well serve the [socialist] camp as a whole.

2. From the viewpoint of Mongolia's interests:

Mongolia's security is guaranteed by an alliance with the Soviet Union from 1946. It would thus be an abstraction to conceive of a situation in which—in the case of aggression against Mongolia—the other socialist states would remain disengaged. If, on the other hand, certain technical-military interests on the part of the Warsaw Pact are established with regard to the territory of Mongolia, or if [there is] a desire on the part of Mongolia to exercise influence over the activities of the Pact, an agreement of a secret nature—based on the principle of consultation between the Warsaw Pact and Mongolia—could be supported.

It could also be that the main motivation behind the Mongolian comrades' proposal is their assessment of their internal situation. We do not know of such an assessment, and we do not have any information that would permit us to form our own opinion on the subject. Such an assessment could be found out in direct talks. The issue is fundamental and will of course be discussed in Moscow with the Mongolian comrades.

In any event, from this point of view, the risk arising from an eventual further sharpening of the conflict in the socialist camp should also be taken into consideration. The accession of Mongolia to the Warsaw Pact might very well represent a stepping stone for various moves by the PRC with regard to Mongolia—moves that would not have a military character and would have practically no significance in terms of Mongolia's membership in the Warsaw Pact. If there are internal difficulties, other methods for granting and demonstrating assistance and support for Mongolia should be weighed.

For example, all the CMEA's planned economic assistance to date for Mongolia and [other] possible assistance that could still be initiated could be harnessed in a special action program for the sake of Mongolia's development as the economically least developed country within the CMEA. This would also have a broader political sense for the world.

[...]

[*Source: KC PZPR, XIA/103, k. 527–30, Archiwum Akt Nowych. Translated by Douglas Selvage.*]

Document No. 26: Czechoslovak Drafts of Orders and Appeals to be Issued in Occupied Western European Territories, June 29, 1964

Part of the planning for war entailed what to do after the immediate fighting had sub-sided. These annexes to Czechoslovak planning materials include drafts of orders and public appeals that would be issued in parts of Western Europe after their occupation by Warsaw Pact forces. For example, the order of the commander of victorious forces in Germany called for treating citizens and prisoners humanely. Leaflets in the form of safe-conduct passes were to be dropped over NATO-held territories to encourage enemy sold-iers to desert. A specific appeal to French soldiers, included here, provides an example.

a) Order of the Commander of the Western Front

Political Directorate of the Western Front Special Propaganda Department
July 2, 1964

Re: Draft of Order of the Commander of the Western Front
On Soldiers' Conduct towards Population of the Liberated Territories
and on Principles of Treatment of POWs
Order of the Commander of the Western Front

Every Czechoslovak soldier must be aware of the fact that he is a soldier of a socialist army, which wages a just war for the defense of his socialist country. Our aim is not to subdue other nations, to seed fear and panic among the population, but to annihilate imperialism and to bring real freedom to the nations, which imperial-ism has brought into this hopeless war against us.

I order (therefore) all members of the Czechoslovak People's Army fighting on enemy territory:

To maintain the basic principles of socialist humanism, as well as the interna-tionally valid practices stipulated by the Geneva Convention, to maintain humani-tarian treatment of those who do not take a direct part in combat actions and of those who lay down their arms or have been neutralized in the fight by illness or injuries, as well as to comply with the demands of human dignity.

1. To maintain extraordinary vigilance and alertness, to intervene severely against those soldiers who would trespass it. To impede the activities of revanchist[18] elem-

---

[18] A derogatory communist term, imputing West German intent to regain by force the territo-ries lost in Eastern Europe after World War II, much as the French, who had originally coined the term, had intended to regain the territories of Alsace and Loraine, which they had lost to Ger-many in the war of 1870–71.

ents and their attempts to destroy objects of military significance and to wage espionage activities. Not to accept anything from the population, in particular food, drink, etc. To detain, disarm and hand over to the nearest commander anybody who has been caught committing hostile acts. To intervene immediately and in a radical way against elements caught conducting hostile acts who do not cease their resistance.

To treat citizens who do not directly participate in hostile actions in the spirit of the basic principles of human morality, disregarding their statehood, political convictions and property. Commanding officers shall take measures to avoid incorrect emotional and other reactions towards their subordinates. They will intervene as severely as possible against those who have denigrated the personal dignity of people, who willfully steal or damage their property or threaten the health and life of the people.

Every soldier taking enemy soldiers captive must be aware of the fact that fears have been raised over how they would be treated. Every Czechoslovak People's Army soldier crushes, by means of his humane attitude towards captured soldiers, the enemy's official propaganda. On the other hand, every soldier must be well aware of the fact that fear of captivity may lead captured soldiers to desperate and sophisticated flight attempts. Particular vigilance must be therefore be devoted to captives detained against their will.

In many cases, members of enemy armed forces who fall into captivity produce a surrender pass issued previously. [...] The pass is valid for individuals as well as for entire groups. The soldier who places these enemy forces in captivity must not confiscate this pass. He shall disarm them and hand them over to the nearest command point.

Enemy armed forces who have laid down their arms or were captured as a result of illness or injury, etc. shall be treated according to the Geneva Convention on Treatment of Prisoners of War of August 12, 1949, that is:

"Every soldier who detains and makes captive members of enemy armed forces must treat them humanely, protect them against insults and acts of violence, and hand them over to a higher institution. He shall remove their weapons at the same time, and secure documents of a military nature. Other means of personal protection, such as gas mask, helmet, etc., means of clothing and nourishment, as well as personal items must be left in their possession. The commanding bodies shall establish their identity, provide for eventual medical assistance and, together with a brief description of the conditions of their detainment, provide for their transfer to designated locations as soon as possible."

According to international conventions, members of organized volunteer resistance units who carry their weapons openly and fight against us lawfully must also be treated as prisoners of war once they have been rendered harmless, as must be detained citizens who in the course of our penetration into the rear areas of enemy territory took up arms voluntarily and are fighting with us openly. The advantages of POW status shall not be extended to terrorist guerrillas or a hostile population who, despite appeals of our bodies, secretly hide and bear arms, while fighting us unlawfully, deceitfully attacking and murdering our soldiers.

b) Safe Conduct (Surrender) Pass for NATO soldiers
   (English Version)

[...]
The NATO soldier who carries this *laissez-passer* is using it as a sign of his genuine wish to give himself up. He is to be disarmed, to be well looked after, to receive food and medical attention as required and to be removed from the danger zone as soon as possible. This holds good for a group of soldiers as well.

[...]

c) Appeal to French Soldiers

French Soldier!
Liberated France, the France of tomorrow shall need you. Your family shall need you to take care of them, your children shall need you to bring them up, your parents shall need you to provide for their comfortable old age. Your country shall need you to give her the strength of your hands, your mind, to make her recover her grandeur and happiness. Do you want to sacrifice your life, which is so badly needed, to the war for German interests?
French soldier!
Give up fighting, save yourself for France.

Whom Shall Your Death Help?

This war, into which Americans and Germans have drawn your country, is not your war. It is the war of North American monopolies, which attempt to subdue the whole world under them. But what can the war bring you?

[*Source: 1964, kr. 101, 17/1/1,3, VÚA. Translated by Marian J. Kratochvíl.*]

Document No. 27: Warsaw Pact War Plan for the Czechoslovak Front, October 14, 1964

This now-famous document is the only actual war plan of either alliance that has thus far surfaced in the public domain. Others have either not been declassified or have been destroyed. This is a fully developed scheme as opposed to the imaginary scenario of an exercise. It is not an overarching plan for the entire Warsaw Pact alliance, but one designed for the Czechoslovak front, describing the Czechoslovak army's role within the general operations of Soviet and other Warsaw Pact armies in case of a European war. It shows the considerable degree to which the Soviets had to rely on the Czechoslovaks because of the location of their country and the absence of permanently stationed Soviet troops on their territory.[19]

There has been some debate about the document's authenticity. Why was it preserved? If it was preserved, was it really a war plan? Certainly, the document describes what should be done in case of war. It also has high-level confirmation: it is signed by the Czechoslovak defense minister and chief of general staff and was intended for the Czechoslovak president as supreme commander. The language was Russian, which indicates that it was approved by the Soviets and had most probably been prepared by them to start with. Also the fact that it was handwritten and not typed shows that care was taken to guard its dissemination. Critics who do not believe it is authentic say that the document is too sketchy, and does not provide enough precise instructions for each unit. The counter-argument is that it may be characterized as a summary of the most important features of the overall plan for the information of Czechoslovak leader Antonín Novotný.

There appears to be no doubt about the intention to put this plan into effect if the right circumstances were to occur. Certainly, there is nothing in the document to indicate there were reservations about local unwillingness to do so. At the same time, major questions arise about the Warsaw Pact's ability to carry out the plan because of the extraordinarily swift advance through West Germany and into France it provides for. It anticipates that in just nine days the advancing forces would reach as far as Lyon, in central France. Moreover, the plan presumes that in the course of hostilities several dozen nuclear weapons would be exploded by both sides, yet the operating assumption was that this would not prevent the onward movement of Warsaw Pact forces—clearly a highly unrealistic view. Apparently this was not regarded as improbable at the time, or else no one was allowed to ask whether it was feasible or not.

---

[19] Readers should refer to the discussion about this document on the PHP website at http://www.isn.ethz.ch/php/collections/coll_1.htm.

"Approved" Supreme Commander
of the Armed Forces of the ČSSR
Antonín Novotný
1964

Plan of Actions of the Czechoslovak People's Army for War Time
Map 1:500,000, published 1963

1. Conclusions from the assessment of the enemy. The enemy could use up to 12 general military units in the Central European military theater for advancing in the area of the Czechoslovak Front from D1 to D 7-8.
   - The 2nd Army Corps of the FRG including: the 4th and 10th mechanized divisions, 12th tank division, 1st airborne division and 1st mountain division,
   - The 7th U.S. Army Corps including: the 24th mechanized division and 4th armored division;
   - The 1st Army of France including: 3rd mechanized division, the 1st and 7th tank divisions, and up to two newly deployed units, including 6 tactical missile launchers, up to 130 theater launchers and artillery, and up to 2800 tanks.

Operations of the ground troops could be supported by part of the 40th Air Force, with up to 900 aircraft, including 250 bombers and up to 40 airborne missile launchers.

Judging by the composition of the group of NATO forces and our assessment of the exercises undertaken by the NATO command, one could anticipate the design of the enemy's actions with the following goals.

To disorganize the leadership of the state and to undermine mobilization of the armed forces by surprise nuclear strikes against the main political and economic centers of the country.

To critically change the correlation of forces in its own favor by strikes against the troops, airfields and communication centers.

To destroy the border troops of the Czechoslovak People's Army in border battles, and to destroy the main group of our forces in the Western and Central Czech Lands by building upon the initial attack.

To disrupt the arrival of strategic reserves in the regions of Krkonoše, Jeseníky, and Moravská Brána by nuclear strikes against targets deep in our territory and by sending airborne assault troops; to create conditions for the successful attainment of the goals of the operation.

Judging by the enemy's approximate operational design, the combat actions of both sides in the initial period of the war will have the character of forward contact battles.

The enemy's operational group in the southern part of the FRG will force the NATO command to gradually engage a number of their units in the battle, which will create an opportunity for the Czechoslovak Front to defeat NATO forces unit by unit. At the same time, that would require building a powerful first echelon in the operational structure of the Front; and to achieve success it would require building up reserves that would be capable of mobilizing very quickly and moving into the area of military action in a very short time.

2. Upon receiving special instructions from the supreme commander of the Unified Armed Forces, the Czechoslovak People's Army will deploy to the Czechoslovak Front with the following tasks:

To be ready to start advancing toward Nuremberg, Stuttgart and Munich with a part of the forces immediately after the nuclear strike. The nuclear strike against enemy troops should be targeted to a depth up to the line of Würzburg, Erlangen, Regensburg, Landshut.

The immediate task is to defeat the main forces of the Central Group of the German Army in the southern part of the FRG in cooperation with the [Soviet] 8th Guards Army of the 1st Western Front; by the end of the first day—reach the line of Bayreuth, Regensburg, Passau; and by the end of the second day—move to the line of Höchstadt, Schwabach, Ingolstadt, Mühldorf, and by the fourth day of the attack—reach the line of Mosbach, Nürtingen, Memmingen, Kaufbeuren.

In the future, building on the advance in the direction of Strasbourg, Epinal, Dijon, to finalize the enemy's defeat on the territory of the FRG, to force a crossing of the Rhine river, and on the seventh or eighth day of the operation to take hold of the line of Langres, Besançon.

Afterward, develop the advance toward Lyon.

To have the following units in the combat disposition of the Czechoslovak Front:
- the 1st and 4th Armies, 10th Air Force, 331st front missile brigade, 11th, 21st and 31st mobile missile support base in a state of combat alert.
- the reserve center of the Army, the 3rd, 18th, 26th, and 32nd mechanized rifle divisions, the 14th and 17th tank divisions, 22nd airborne brigade, 205th anti-tank brigade, 303rd air defense division, and 201st and 202nd air defense squadrons with a mobilization timetable from M1 to M3.
- the formations, units and facilities of the support and service system.

The 57th Air Force, arriving on D1 from the Carpathian military district before the fifth or sixth day of the operation, will be operationally subordinated to the Czechoslovak Front. If Austria keeps its neutrality on the third day of the war, one mechanized rifle division of the Southern Group of Forces will arrive in the area of České Budějovice and join the Czechoslovak Front. The following forces will remain at the disposal of the Ministry of National Defense: the 7th air defense army, 24th mechanized rifle division and 16th tank division with [mobilization] readiness M20, reconnaissance units, and also units and facilities of the support and service system. Under favorable conditions two missile brigades and one mobile missile support base will arrive some time in advance on the territory of the ČSSR from the Carpathian military district:
- 35th missile brigade—past Český Brod, past Říčany, Zásmuky,
- 36th missile brigade—past Pacov, past Pelhřimov, past Humpolec,
- 3486th mobile missile support base—in the woods 5 kilometers to the East of Světlá.

Upon the sounding of a combat alarm, formations and units of the Czechoslovak People's Army, on permanent alert, should leave their permanent location in no more than 30 minutes, move to designated areas within 3 hours, and deploy there ready to carry out their combat tasks. Formations, units and headquarters that do not have

162

set mobilization dates, leave their locations of permanent deployment and take up the identified areas of concentration in the period of time and in the order determined by the plan for mobilization and deployment. The following disposition of forces is possible in the area of operations of the Czechoslovak Front for the entire depth of the operation:

- in divisions—1.1 to 1.0
- in tanks and mobile artillery launchers—1.0 to 1.0
- in artillery and mine-launchers—1.0 to 1.0
- in military aircraft—1.1 to 1.0, all in favor of the Czechoslovak Front.

In the first massive nuclear strike by the troops of the Missile Forces of the Czechoslovak Front, the front aviation and long-range aviation added to the front must destroy the main group of forces of the first operations echelon of the 7th U.S. Army, its means of nuclear attack, and the centers of air command and control.

During the development of the operation, the troops of the Missile Forces and air force must destroy the approaching deep operational reserves, the newly discovered means of nuclear attack, and the enemy air force.

Altogether the operation will require the use of 131 nuclear missiles and nuclear bombs; specifically 96 missiles and 35 nuclear bombs. The first nuclear strike will use 41 missiles and nuclear bombs. The immediate task will require using 29 missiles and nuclear bombs. The subsequent task could use 49 missiles and nuclear bombs. Twelve missiles and nuclear bombs should remain in reserve for the Front.

Building on the results of the first nuclear strike, the troops of the Front, in coordination with units of the 1st Western Front, must destroy the main group of forces of the 7th U.S. Army and the 1st French Army in cooperation with airborne assault troops, force the Neckar and Rhine rivers in movement, and defeat the enemy's advancing deep strategic reserves in advancing battle, and by D7-8 take control of the areas of Langres, Besançon, and Epinal.

Upon completion of the tasks of the operation, the troops must be ready to develop further advances in the direction of Lyon.

The main strike should be concentrated in the direction of Nuremberg, Stuttgart, Strasbourg, Epinal, Dijon; part of the forces should be used in the direction of Straubing and Munich.

The operational structure of the troops of the Czechoslovak Front is to be in one echelon with two tank and five mechanized rifle divisions for the reserves as they arrive and are deployed. The first echelon shall consist of the 1st and 4th armies and the 331st front missile brigade.

The reserve of the front includes: Headquarters of the 2nd Army (reserve), mechanized rifle division of the Southern Group of Forces by D3, 14th tank division by D3, 17th tank division by D4, 3rd mechanized rifle division by D3, 26th mechanized rifle division by D4, 18th mechanized rifle division by D5, and 32nd mechanized rifle division by D6.

Special reserves include: 22nd airborne brigade by D2, 103rd chemical warfare battalion by D2, 6th engineering brigade by D3, and 205th antitank artillery by D4.

3. On the right—the 8th Guards Army of the 1st Western Front advances in the direction of Suhl, Bad Kissingen, and Worms and with part of its forces to Bamberg.

The separation line with the Army is the ČSSR-GDR border as far as Aš, then Bayreuth, Mosbach, and Sarrebourg, Chaumont (all points exclusively for the Czechoslovak Front).

The meeting point with the 8th Guards Army should be supported by the forces and means of the Czechoslovak Front.

On the left—the Southern Group of Forces and the Hungarian People's Army will cover the state borders of Hungary.

The dividing line with them: the state border of the ČSSR with the Hungarian People's Republic, and then the northern borders of Austria, Switzerland, and Italy.

4. The 1st Army (19th and 20th mechanized rifle divisions, 1st and 13th tank divisions, 311th artillery missile brigade) with the 312th heavy artillery brigade, the 33rd antitank artillery brigade without the 7th antitank artillery regiment, the 2nd bridge-building brigade without the 71st bridge-building battalion, and the 351st and 352nd engineering battalions of the 52nd engineering brigade.

The immediate task is to defeat the enemy's group of the 2nd Army Corps of the FRG and the 7th U.S. Army in interaction with the 8th Guards Army of the 1st Western Front, and to develop the advance in the direction of Neustadt, Nuremberg, Ansbach, and with a part of the forces in interaction with units of the 8th Guards Army in the direction of Bamberg, by D1 to take control of the line of Bayreuth, Amberg, Schmidmühlen; and by the end of D2 to arrive at the line of Höchstadt, Schwabach, Heiden.

The further task is to advance in the direction of Ansbach, Crailsheim, Stuttgart; to defeat the advancing operational reserves of the enemy, and by the end of D4 take control of the line past Mosbach, Bietigheim, Nürtingen.

Subsequently to be ready to develop the advance in the direction of Stuttgart, Strasbourg, Epinal.

The dividing line on the left is Poběžovice, Schwandorf, Weissenburg, Heidenheim, Reutlingen (all the points except Heidenheim are inclusive for the 1st Army).

Headquarters—in the forest 1 kilometer south of Stříbro.

The axis of the movement is Stříbro, Grafenwöhr, Ansbach, Schwäbisch Hall.

5. The 4th Army (2nd and 15th mechanized rifle divisions, 4th and 9th tank divisions, 321st artillery missile brigade) with the 7th antitank artillery brigade and 33rd antitank artillery brigade, 71st bridge-building battalion of the 2nd bridge-building brigade, 92nd bridge-building battalion and 353rd engineering battalion.

The immediate task is to defeat the enemy group of the 2nd Army Corps of the FRG in cooperation with the troops of the 1st Army and to develop the advance in the direction of Regensburg, Ingolstadt, Donauwörth, and with a part of the forces in the direction of Straubing, Munich; and by the end of D1 to take control of the line of Schmidmühlen, Regensburg, Passau; by the end of D2—Eichstätt, Moosburg, Mühldorf.

The subsequent task is to advance in the direction of Donauwörth, Ulm, to defeat the advancing formations of the 1st French Army and by the end of D4 to take control of the line Metzingen, Memmingen, Kaufbeuren.

Subsequently to be ready to develop the advance in the direction of Ulm, Mulhouse, Besançon. Headquarters—6 kilometers northwest of Strakonice.

The axis of movement is Strakonice, Klatovy, Falkenstein, Kelheim, Rennertshofen, Burgau.

6. The Missile Forces of the Front must destroy the group of forces of the 7th U.S. Army, a part of the forces of the 2nd Army Corps of the FRG, and part of the enemy's air defense forces in the first nuclear strike.

Subsequently, the main efforts should be concentrated on defeating the advancing operational and strategic reserves and also the enemy's newly discovered means of nuclear attack.

In order to fulfill the tasks set for the front, the following ammunition shall be used:
- for the immediate task—44 operational-tactical and tactical missiles with nuclear warheads;
- for the subsequent task—42 operational-tactical and tactical missiles with nuclear warheads;
- for unexpected tasks—10 operational-tactical and tactical missiles with nuclear warheads shall be left in the Front's reserve.

The commander of Missile Forces shall receive special assembly brigades with special ammunition, which shall be transferred to the Czechoslovak Front in the following areas: 2 kilometers to the East of Jablonec, and 3 kilometers to the East of Michalovce.

The use of special ammunition[20]—only with permission of the supreme commander of the Unified Armed Forces.

7. Aviation. The 10th Air Force—the 1st fighter division, 2nd and 34th fighter-bomber division, 25th bomber squadron, 46th air transport division, 47th air reconnaissance squadron and 45th air reconnaissance squadron for target guidance.

Combat tasks:

With the first nuclear strike, to destroy part of the forces of the 2nd Army Corps of the FRG, two command and targeting centers, and part of the enemy's air defense forces.

Upon the beginning of combat actions, to suppress part of the enemy's air defense forces in the following regions: Roding, Kirchroth, Hohenfels, Amberg, Pfreimd, Nagel, and Erbendorf.

To uncover and destroy the operational and tactical means of nuclear attack, and air command and control forces in the following regions: Weiden, Nabburg, Amberg, Grafenwöhr, Hohenfels, Regensburg, and Erlangen.

During the operation to give intensive support to the combat actions of thetroops at the front: on D1—6 group sorties of fighter bombers, from D2 to D5—8 group

---

[20] Nuclear weapons.

group sorties of fighter bombers and bombers daily, and from D6 to D8—6 group sorties of fighter bombers and bombers daily. The main effort should be concentrated on supporting the troops of the 1st Army.

In cooperation with forces and means of air defense of the country, fronts and neighbors—to cover the main group of forces of the Front against enemy air strikes.

To ensure the landing of reconnaissance troops and general airborne forces on D1 and D2 to the rear of the enemy.

To ensure airborne landing of the 22nd airborne brigade on D4 in the area north of Stuttgart, or on D5 in the area of Rastatt, or on D6 in the area to the east of Mulhouse.

To carry out air reconnaissance concentrating the main effort in the direction of Nuremberg, Stuttgart, and Strasbourg with the goal of locating the means of nuclear attack, and in order to determine in time the beginning of operations and the direction of the enemy's advancing operational reserves.

In order to fulfill the tasks set for the front, it will be necessary to use the following weapons:

- for the immediate task—10 nuclear bombs;
- for subsequent tasks—7 nuclear bombs;
- for resolving unexpectedly arising tasks—2 nuclear bombs shall be left in the Front's reserve.

The 57th Air Force, consisting of the 131st fighter division, 289th fighter-bomber squadron, 230th and 733rd bomber squadron and 48th air reconnaissance squadron, arriving by D1 from the Carpathian military district, is to remain under operational subordination to the Czechoslovak Front until the fifth to sixth day for 5 army sorties.

The Army has determined the limit of: combat sets of air bombs—3, combat sets of air-to-air missiles—2, combat sets of aviation cartridges—2, and fuel—3 rounds of army refueling.

Combat tasks:

- in cooperation with the 10th Air Force, to find and destroy the enemy's means of nuclear attack, its aviation and command and control centers with a concentration of the main efforts in the direction of Nuremberg, Strasbourg;
- to support combat actions of troops at the Front when they force the Naab, Neckar and Rhine rivers, and when they counter an attack by the enemy;
- to support combat actions by the 22nd airborne brigade in its landing areas;
- to protect the troops at the front from enemy air strikes;
- to carry out air reconnaissance with concentration of the main effort on discovering the enemy's means of nuclear attack and deep operational and strategic reserves.

The 184th heavy bomber squadron of long-range aviation should use nuclear bombs in the first nuclear strike against the headquarters of the 2nd Army Corps of the FRG, the 7th U.S. Army, 2nd/40 Corporal artillery battalion, 2nd/82 Corporal artillery battalion, 5th/73 Sergeant artillery battalion, and the main group of forces of the 4th mechanized division and 12th tank division of the 2nd Army Corps of the FRG. Total use of nuclear bombs—16. Use of special combat ammunition—only with permission of the supreme commander of the Unified Armed Forces.

8. Air Defense

7th Air Defense Army of the country—2nd and 3rd air defense corps.

Combat tasks:
- in cooperation with air defense forces of the Front and the air defense of the neighbors in the unified air defense system of the Warsaw Treaty countries, to repel massive enemy air strikes by concentrating main efforts in the direction Karlsruhe, Prague, Ostrava.
- not to allow enemy reconnaissance and air strikes against our groups of forces, especially in the area of the Czech Lands, against aircraft on the airfields, and against important political and economic centers of the country, as well as communications centers. The main effort should be concentrated on protecting the areas of Prague, Ostrava, Brno and Bratislava;
- upon the beginning of combat actions, troops of the Czechoslovak Front, with anti-aircraft missile forces, to continue to defend the most important areas and objects of the country, with fighter aircraft forces to defend objects at the Front following the advancing troops.

Air Defense troops of the Front

Combat tasks:
- Upon the beginning of combat action at the Front, to take part in the general air defense system of the Warsaw Treaty countries with all forces and resources to cover the main group of the Front's troops.
- During the operation, in cooperation with the 7th Air Defense Army, units of the 10th and 57th Air Force and the air defense of the 1st Western Front, to cover the troops at the front from enemy air strikes as they pass over the border mountains, and also during the crossing of the Neckar and Rhine rivers to cover the missile forces and command and control centers.

9. The 22nd airborne brigade is to be ready to be deployed from the region of Prostějov, Niva, Brodek to the region north of Stuttgart on D4 or to the region of Rastatt on D5, or to the region to the east of Mulhouse on D6 with the task of capturing and holding river crossings on the Neckar or Rhine rivers until the arrival of our troops.

10. Reserves of the Front.

The 3rd, 18th, 26th, and 32nd mechanized rifle divisions of the Southern Group of Forces, and the 14th and 17th tank divisions are to concentrate in the regions designated on the decision map in the period from D3 to D5.

The 6th engineering brigade by D3 is to be concentrated in the region of Panenský Týnec, and Bor, past Slaný, to be ready to ensure forcing of the Neckar and Rhine rivers by the troops at the Front.

The 103rd chemical warfare battalion from D2 is to be stationed in the region of Hluboš, past Příbram, past Dobříš. The main effort of radiation reconnaissance should be concentrated in the region of Hořovice, Blovice, and Sedlčany.

Objects of special treatment should be deployed in areas where command and control centers at the Front and the 331st front brigade are deployed, as well as in the regions where reserve divisions at the Front are concentrated.

11. Material Maintenance of the Rear. The main effort in the material maintenance of the rear of the troops of the Front should be concentrated throughout the
entire depth of the operation in the area of the 1st Army's advance.

To support the troops of the 1st Army, the 10th and 57th Air Forces should deploy
to the forward front base number 1 and the base of the 10th Air Force in the region
to the West of Pilsen by the end of D2; troops of the 4th Army should deploy the
forward front base number 2 in the region to the south of Pilsen.

A field pipeline is to be deployed in the direction of Roudnice, Pilsen, Nuremberg, and Karlsruhe and used to supply aircraft fuel.

The rebuilding of railroads should be planned in the directions of Cheb-Nuremberg
or Domažlice-Schwandorf-Regensburg-Donauwörth.

Two roads should be built following the 1st Army, and one front road throughout the entire depth of the operation following the 4th Army.

The ČSSR Ministry of National Defense will assign material resources, including
full replacement of ammunition used during the operation for the troops at the
Czechoslovak Front.

Support for the 57th Air Force should be planned taking into account the material resources located in the territory of the ČSSR for the Unified Command.

Use of material resources should be planned as follows:
– ammunition—45,000 tons
– combustible-lubricating oil—93, 000 tons
– including aircraft fuel—40, 000 tons
– missile fuel:
– oxidizer—220 tons
– missile fuel—70 tons

Automobile transportation at the Front should be able to supply the troops with
70, 000 tons of cargo during the operation.

Transportation for the troops should be able to carry 58,000 tons of cargo. By the
end of the operation the troops should have 80 percent of mobile reserves available.
In D1 and D2 a hospital bed network for 10-12,000 sick and wounded personnel is
to be deployed.

By the end of the operation the hospital bed network should cover 18 percent of
the hospital losses of the Front.

12. Headquarters at the Front should be deployed from "X" plus 6 hours—5 kilometers to the east of Strašice. The axis of movement—Heilbronn, Horb, Epinal.

Reserve Command Post—forest, to the north of Březová
Advanced Command Post—forest 5 kilometers to the east of Dobřany
Rear Command Post—Jince-Obecnice
Reserve Rear Command Post—past Dobřany, Slapy, past Mníšek
Headquarters of MNO—object K-116, Prague.

Minister of National Defense of the ČSSR
General of the Army [signed] Bohumír Lomský

Chief of the General Staff of the Czechoslovak People's Army
Colonel General [signed] Otakar Rytíř
Head of the Operations Department of the General Staff
Major General [signed] Václav Vitanovský
October 11, 1964
[...]

Executed by Major General Jan Voštera
[signed] Gen. Voštera
October 14, 1964

[*Source: 008074/ZD-OS 64, pp. 1–18, VÚA. Translated by Svetlana Savranskaya and Anna Locher.*]

Document No. 28: Warsaw Pact Intelligence on NATO's Strategy and Combat Readiness, 1965

This paper by the Intelligence Department of the Czechoslovak General Staff examines the United States' flexible response strategy under consideration by NATO. President John F. Kennedy had introduced the new strategy soon after entering the White House in 1961, intending to replace the doctrine of massive retaliation. Although it would take NATO until 1967 to make the switch, the Warsaw Pact assumed that this would eventually happen and began to prepare for what was to come. This paper, obviously based on Soviet materials and marked for restricted circulation, concludes that the appearance of the new strategy is an indication that massive retaliation has failed. The authors see the new approach as clearly more aggressive, since massive retaliation implied a defensive reaction whereas the new strategy, they point out, aims at exploiting the weaknesses of the East European communist countries. They warn that the Warsaw Pact should be prepared for a general war unleashed by the West. The unstated conclusion is that the more aggressive new policy justifies the Pact's own offensive strategy. In other words, no change is required from current posture.

[...] The NATO Command holds that regarding the current correlation of forces between the socialist states and the capitalist ones, not only an all-out nuclear war but also a limited one is possible. In accordance with that, a theory of limited warfare has been elaborated, which has been reflected in the operational preparedness of the Allied armed forces in the Central European theater, particularly during the last few years.

[...] Limited warfare represents a twofold issue. On the one hand, adequate forces must be assigned in order to reach their given assignment with sufficient speed. On the other hand, armed forces must be employed in such a way that the risk of extension of a limited war into a general one is to be avoided as much as possible. Since the West has not deployed enough conventional forces in Europe, the necessity of a limited nuclear strike during the forthcoming war has been [seriously] considered.

[...] The limited war concept, as advanced by the United States in particular, should ensure the gradual attainment of military and political goals with minimal risk of launching a general nuclear war, as the U.S. Command has been increasingly aware of its destructiveness.

In NATO's opinion, a general nuclear war may be launched following a shorter or longer period of increasing international tension; or else quite suddenly, should an advantageous military and political situation arise. One of these advantageous conditions for launching such a war could be an aggravation of political conflicts and economic problems in the states of one or the other coalition leading, for example, to an enforced restriction of the armed forces. Another eventuality, considered as the most probable lately, would be the transformation of a limited war into a gen-

170

eral nuclear one due to the gradual abandoning of particular restraints. Such transformation might also be caused by a disproportional reaction to the measures applied by one of the countries waging war, by a misunderstanding of signals, or by human or equipment failure. The launch of a surprise general nuclear war [now] takes priority in the plans of NATO's command.

[...] The clash is supposed to be a response to the direct or indirect threat to national security, when no other option would offer hopes of reaching the requisite political goals. This—rather vague—definition implies that the NATO Command, and the United States in particular, still reckon with the eventuality of a general nuclear war, which would be launched by themselves.

The present strategic concept of so-called "flexible response", which includes waging limited wars and—under advantageous or, on the contrary, hopeless conditions—a general war is obviously aggressive, hazardous and, in its consequences, dangerous from the military and political points of view. The theory of limited war itself seems rather inconsistent, full of theoretically unclear issues, in particular with regard to the political and military aims of the war, the assignment of forces and means, and the choice of targets. The NATO Command is obviously uncertain on issues relating to the proper mechanisms of such warfare in a theater where even in peace time strong formations from both camps face each other. Here, even a partial failure would probably be evaluated as a good reason to abandon any limitations that were intended at the beginning. The issue of employing nuclear weapons during a limited war has not been completely resolved yet. The NATO Command principle of first-use of nuclear weapons during a conventional conflict if their troops were to suffer serious losses, or if important land areas were to be lost, or generally, if the intended political goals could not be reached by means of conventional warfare, make this theory highly problematic, in particular if applied to conditions in the Central European theater. [...]

As opinions on the possibilities of launching a war and on warfare itself have been undergoing changes, and following the FRG and other European NATO members' initiatives, a new concept was adopted in 1963 called "Forward Defense". This concept covers, more or less exclusively, the territory of the FRG only. In essence, this concept includes the elaboration and application of the new principles to conditions in the European theater. The intention is to wage active warfare already from the FRG's eastern border to avoid the loss of its territory and to create conditions for launching offensive operations, and to transfer fighting to the territories of the GDR and ČSSR within short periods of time.

[...] The Impact of Strategic Concepts on the Operational Preparedness of NATO's Armed Forces.

The operational preparedness of the Allied armed forces also revealed their adoption of a strategic concept oriented toward the option to launch both a general nuclear war and local wars with the use of conventional or nuclear weapons. [...]

More extensive exercises until *circa* 1960 were conducted on the "Massive Retaliation" concept based on mass application of all kinds of nuclear weapons in case of any armed conflict between the two camps, on waging a flexible defense aimed at gaining time for mobilization, on the concentration of reserves, and on preparations for the transition to a counterattack. The air force was almost the sole means of conducting a nuclear attack. [...]

All exercises at that time were aimed at training for defensive operations. That corresponded with the then-existing concept, mission and tasks of the NATO ground forces. Their scenarios presumed an extended period of growing threat of war, which allowed the timely assumption of combat readiness by the troops, the implementation of certain mobilization measures, and the preparation of a pre-planned operational configuration. As the air force dominated among the strategic means of nuclear attack, any eventuality to initiate war with complete surprise was effectively excluded. [...]

[...] Major changes in exercise scenarios appeared as the "Massive Retaliation" concept was abandoned in favor of the "Forward Strategy." These exercises resulted from NATO's concept to wage limited war in the European theater, at least temporarily. Hostilities had usually been started and carried on for a shorter period of time as defensive operations. At this stage, exclusively conventional weapons were used; in later stages, however, nuclear weapons of operational-tactical and tactical range were employed, usually from several hours up to several days after the initiation of operations. The NATO armed forces usually employed nuclear weapons in case the opponent delivered a nuclear strike first.

At that time, the period of growing threat of war was much shorter. Accordingly, time schedules for combat readiness were shortened as well. The decrease in the time necessary for preparation and achievement of combat readiness offered a chance to avoid early detection and application of countermeasures by the enemy, thus facilitating an operational surprise.

With the adoption of "Forward Defense," the operational formation of troops has changed substantially as compared with exercises carried out prior to 1960, in particular by the Central Group of Armies [...]. The front echelon consists of two armies (7th U.S. Army, 1st French Army), while instead of the former, second echelon reserves are being formed, consisting of one or two groups. Other significant features include the commitment of French groupings (3rd Mechanized Division, 1st Armored Division) with the front echelon in the zone facing the ČSSR, or the operational subordination of the 2nd West German Army Corps to the 1st French Army. These measures have substantially reinforced the right flank of the Central Group of Armies in both the Pilsen—Nuremberg and in the Linz—Munich directions.

These conceptual changes have been reflected in the operational conduct of the initial combat period as well. Although the allied NATO forces initially practiced a mobile defense during these exercises, their troops were considerably more active and the entire combat phase was shorter (2-3 days). The intended depth of retreat was considerably reduced, too (120 km maximum). Although a kick-off into counterattack was not trained for, the defensive phase was terminated with strong counter-strikes with the intention to initiate the counterattack much earlier than before.

[...] The Limited War concept has been trained for in the Central European theater since 1962, initially within the framework of an army group (exercises "Grand Slam" I and II), in 1963 within the framework of the overall Central European theater ("Lion Ver" exercise) and in 1964 in Europe as such (Fallex-64 maneuvers).

172

Before 1964, NATO forces employed nuclear weapons only after their use by the enemy. In 1964, nuclear weapons were employed first to eliminate the breach in their defenses and the successful initiation of a hostile attack. The enemy's response—unlimited usage of nuclear weapons as retaliation—resulted in general nuclear war.

[...] Nuclear weapons were employed in 1962 during Day 3 (46 hrs) of combat operations to halt the enemy permanently 50 to 150 km from the border; in 1963, it was only 10 hours after the initiation of combat activities, with the intention of equalizing the adverse ratio of forces. The enemy's attack was halted after an advance of 30 to 100 km. In the ČSSR, their success was negligible. During the 1964 fall maneuvers, nuclear weapons were used some 34 hours after the outbreak, as the front defensive line was broken through to a depth of 30-80 km from the borders.

[...] The completed exercises indicate that the Allied armed forces are not capable of waging combat activities successfully for a longer period without employing nuclear weapons. This is due to the adverse ratio of forces, which would become even more apparent during the opening days of conventional warfare. NATO command therefore considers the readiness of its forces to wage a general nuclear war as one of the important conditions for waging a limited war successfully.

[...] Summary, Conclusions

[...] Among the national staffs, those prepared best are the U.S. Army staffs in Germany, who carried through intensive preparations throughout the year. Aside from their participation in Allied exercises, they carried out extensive exercises as a national army.

The West German army staffs achieved the objectives of operational preparedness. During the Allied exercises, they demonstrated their ability to fulfill their tasks within the framework of the Allied forces. The higher staffs are mostly manned with officers of the former Hitler army who possess extensive combat experience; their advanced age will soon become a problem, however. Their level of operational preparedness is the closest to that of the U.S. Army.

The best prepared staffs of the French army are those of its 1st Army. The preparedness of the staffs on French territory has been rather intense lately. The intention is to eliminate the deficits caused by many years of colonial wars, plus to reach the level of preparedness common among the American staffs. However, they also possess enormous experience in the organization and direction of combat activities under special conditions.

[*Source: MNO-GŠ/05, 1965, sg. 31/1–8, VÚA. Translated by Marian J. Kratochvíl.*]

1. The Soviet delegation arriving to the meeting in May, 1955, where the Warsaw Pact was signed. First row from the second person on the left to the right: Bolesław Bierut, First Secretary of the Polish Communist Party; Nikolai A. Bulganin, Chairman of the Council of Ministers of the USSR; Marshal Ivan Konev; Viacheslav M. Molotov, Minister of Foreign Affairs and Vice-President of the Council of Ministers of the USSR; Marshal Georgii K. Zhukov, Minister of Defense of the USSR.

2. May 14, 1955, András Hegedűs, Hungarian Prime Minister signs the official document establishing the Warsaw Treaty Organization.

Na důkaz toho zplnomocněnci podepsali tuto Smlouvu a při-
ložili k ní pečeti.

Z plné moci Presidia Lidového shro-
máždění Albánské lidové republiky

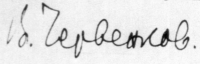

Z plné moci Presidia Lidového shro-
máždění Bulharské lidové republiky

Z plné moci Presidia Maďarské lidové republiky

Z plné moci Presidenta Německé demo-
kratické republiky

3. May 14, 1955, Signatures from the Czech version of the official document establishing the Warsaw Treaty Organization.

4. German Democratic Republic, October 29, 1965. "October Storm", a war game of the Warsaw Pact countries in the southeastern part of the GDR. From right to left: Erich Honecker, secretary of the National Defense Council of the GDR; Willi Stoph, Chairman of the Council of Ministers of the GDR; Walter Ulbricht, General Secretary of the Socialist Unity Party of the GDR; Marshal Andrei Grechko, Supreme Commander of the Warsaw Pact; Heinz Hoffmann, Minister of National Defense of the GDR; Paul Verner, SED official; Professor Albert Norden; Professor Kurt Hager; Marshal Marian Spychalski and General Bohumír Lomský, Minister of National Defense of the Czechoslovak Socialist Republic.

5. Erfurt, October 29, 1965. Parade at the end of a Warsaw Treaty war game.

6. 1968. Demonstrators surrounding a tank in Košice.

7. July 29–August 1, 1968, The Čierna nad Tisou talks take place between the CPCz CC Presidium and the CPSU CC Politburo. Among others: Josef Smrkovský, Chairman of of the National Assembly of the Czechoslovak Socialist Republic, Leonid Brezhnev, General Secretary of the Communist Party of the USSR, Alexander Dubček, First Secretary of the Communist Party of the Czechoslovak Socialist Republic, Nikolai Podgornyi, President of the Presidium of the Supreme Soviet, Aleksei Kosygin, Chairman of the Council of Ministers of the USSR.

8. This map depicts a 1974 Warsaw Pact exercise in the Baltic Sea known as VAL-74. A command and staff exercise, its purpose was to plan for a scenario in which the unified Baltic fleets would destroy combined enemy naval forces, gain control of the Baltic, support the capture of Denmark and ultimately close the Danish Straits. The title reads: "Initial Conditions and Decisions of Fleet Commanders." Warsaw Pact Supreme Commander Marshal Ivan I. Iakubovskii directed this iteration of the exercise.

9. Czechoslovakia, June 25, 1968, Czechoslovak and Soviet military officers at a Warsaw Treaty exercise.

10. Moscow, January 12, 1982. Delegates to the meeting of the Council of Ministers of Defense of the Warsaw Pact countries visiting Lenin's former study in the Kremlin. From left to right: in the first row, Florian Siwicki (Poland), second from the left, Lajos Czinege (Hungary), behind him Anatolii I. Gribkov, the Warsaw Pact chief of staff, Martin Dzúr (Czechoslovakia), behind him Constantin Olteanu (Romania), Viktor Kulikov (USSR), Dobri Dzhurov (Bulgaria) and Heinz Hoffmann (German Democratic Republic).

11. Budapest, February 25, 1991. Czechoslovak Minister of Defense, Luboš Dobrovský, signs the documents officially ending the military functions of the alliance by March 31.

12. Budapest, February 25, 1991. Romanian Minister of Defense, Victor Stănculescu, signs the agreement terminating the military aspects of the Warsaw Pact.

13. Budapest, February 25, 1991. Soviet Minister of Defense, Dmitrii T. Iazov, adds his signature to the document eliminating the military component of the alliance.

PART TWO

The Crisis

Document No. 29: Albanian Note to the Political Consultative Committee, January 15, 1965

The Albanian government sent this note to other Warsaw Pact members in advance of a PCC meeting. The note was presented as a substitute for the Albanians' presence at the session. In it, the Albanians declare that Khrushchev, who was recently deposed, violated the principles of the Warsaw Pact by arbitrarily obstructing their participation in the alliance, and argue furthermore that the Soviet Union broke bilateral treaties with Tirana. They particularly criticize the Soviet military for appropriating eight submarines the Albanians claimed were theirs. For this and other breaches, the Albanians appeal to the PCC to condemn Moscow, and ask that various conditions be put in place to guarantee full and equal participation for all alliance members. These conditions include restitution by the Soviet Union of all damages arising from the rupture of relations and termination of economic assistance as well as the resumption of diplomatic relations. Intriguingly, the Albanians also demand annulment of the 1963 Nuclear Test Ban Treaty between the Soviet Union, United States and Great Britain on the grounds that it had been signed without consultation with Warsaw Pact members. The memo also asserts that the Warsaw Pact must defend the GDR and that a separate peace treaty with it should be concluded, rejecting what it calls Khrushchev's "capitulationist" policy on this issue. Another interesting demand is that, as a counter-measure to the Multilateral Force (MLF) project that envisaged the sharing of U.S. nuclear weapons among the NATO allies, the Warsaw Pact should allow for similar sharing by all its members. Far from being sympathetic, the PCC responded by excluding Albania from participation in all future deliberations of the alliance.

Comrades!

The government of the People's Republic of Albania has received the note of January 5, 1965, in which the government of the People's Republic of Poland—as the government of the host country of the PCC meeting—invites the People's Republic of Albania to attend the meeting of the Warsaw Treaty's Political Consultative Committee taking place in Warsaw on January 19, 1965.

The government of the People's Republic of Albania considers it necessary to explain its point of view in this context: [...]

Following the orders of the Soviet government under N. Khrushchev, the People's Republic of Albania had been, completely arbitrarily as well as illegally, *de facto* excluded from the Warsaw Treaty since 1961.

[...] In order to join meetings of the Warsaw Treaty [...] it is necessary for the Albanian government that the following legitimate demands be met in advance:

I. All arbitrary violations of the stipulations and spirit of the Warsaw Treaty which the Soviet government has committed against the People's Republic of Albania must be acknowledged as illegal and hostile actions, and condemned. [...]

II. The Albanian government demands that the Soviet government return immediately all armament and other military equipment belonging to the People's Republic of Albania, and reimburse the damage the Albanian economy has suffered in order to guarantee the defense of the People's Republic of Albania and of the socialist bloc. [Albania also demands] restitution of the damage caused by unilateral cancellation of loans, agreements, and various economic arrangements. The Soviet government immediately and courageously must amend the disastrous error of breaking diplomatic relations with Albania. [...]

III. [...]

IV. The Albanian government rightfully requests:

a) Original copies of minutes of meetings in which the unlawful decisions against the People's Republic of Albania were discussed and made [...]

b) For the purpose of their complete information: all minutes and decisions which were taken in the meantime during public and internal meetings of the member-states of the Warsaw Treaty and its political and military bodies.

c) [...] For the purpose of complete information, the Albanian government demands copies of all reports, contributions and decisions on all these questions which have been taken up by the leading organs of the Warsaw Treaty during the four-year period in which Albania was arbitrarily deprived of its right to participate in meetings of the member-states.

d) The Albanian government demands to know whether the Moscow treaty banning nuclear tests in the atmosphere, in outer space and under water, signed by the Soviet Union, the United States of America and England on August 5, 1963, was based on a collective decision of the member-states of the Warsaw Treaty [...]. The Albanian government attributes crucial importance to this question, for if there was a collective decision it is unlawful [...], because it would outrageously contravene the Warsaw Treaty as well as the common policy and line of the socialist states. [...]

The Albanian government attaches utmost urgency to the rectification of the disastrous errors of the Soviet government, first and foremost in [the following ways]:

a) *A peace treaty with the German Democratic Republic must be signed as soon as possible. [...]*

b) *The organization of the Warsaw Treaty must proclaim publicly that, in the event the United States of America provides Germany with nuclear weapons as part of the Multilateral Force, as a countermeasure all socialist countries would be equipped with nuclear weapons.*

c) *The Moscow [Limited Nuclear Test Ban] Treaty must be revoked as quickly as possible by the Soviet government and the signatory governments of the socialist countries [...]*

The government of the People's Republic of Albania calls on the friendly governments of the member-states of the Warsaw Treaty to denounce the policy of surrender to American imperialism which the Soviet government under N. Khrushchev attempted to impose on the Warsaw Treaty, and to adopt a true Marxist–Leninist policy as soon as possible. [...]

[*Source: ZK SED, DY/30, 3388, SAPMO. Translated by Karen Riechert.*]

Document No. 30: Minutes of Discussion at Political Consultative Committee Meeting in Warsaw, January 20, 1965

This gathering of the PCC turned out to be the most contentious to date. It was the first session after the downfall of Khrushchev in June 1964, and also the first to be convened at the initiative of a member other than the Soviet Union—the GDR. One of the controversial subjects of discussion was non-proliferation. This was an important issue because it represented the next phase in the process of establishing some control over nuclear weapons following the 1963 Limited Test Ban Treaty. The matter had particular resonance for the Warsaw Pact in the context of the MLF, since the acceptance of the principle of non-proliferation by all sides would have had the important effect of denying West Germany access to nuclear weapons. Perhaps more importantly, given that the MLF was practically moribund at this point, the issue also related to China, which had exploded its first atomic bomb in 1964. The question was how and whether Beijing's nuclear program could be constrained in view of the opposition by the Chinese, as well as the French, to any restrictions that would not also be binding on the superpowers.

Within the Warsaw Pact, Romania took the lead in opposing the draft of the Non-proliferation Treaty (NPT) the Soviets had been preparing to negotiate with the United States. In doing so, the Romanians were basically taking the Chinese position, making the case that the Treaty currently being negotiated by the superpowers did not take account of the interests of others, and should be opposed as a violation of the principle of equal national sovereignty.

This meeting offers valuable insight into how complex relations had become within the Pact, how far Moscow's authority among its members had declined, how the Sino-Soviet rift influenced intra-bloc ties, and how far Romania was willing to go in adopting a position that was opposed by the Soviet Union.

[...]

[*Gheorghe Gheorgiu-*] *Dej:* Please allow me to say a few words, although I will not say anything new that I have not already said at our meeting. It has to do above all else with the idea of the nonproliferation of nuclear weapons and the inclusion of a relevant formulation in the Communiqué [from the meeting]. We already spoke of our position regarding the nonproliferation of nuclear weapons. It is true that today many countries, including the USA, are coming forward regarding the nonproliferation of nuclear weapons. And not only the USA. Other countries as well (e.g. India) which want to exploit this idea with the goal of linking it to a definite campaign, having as its goal the condemnation of China for the tests it conducted with an atomic weapon. The Indian government, as far as we know, gave instructions to its representatives in other countries to sound out the situation, along with the stance of these countries regarding the aforementioned problem, because it seeks to bring its campaign before the United Nations assembly. It is directed against People's

179

China. [...] The government of India wants to demand a harsh condemnation of People's China at the U.N.

The question arises whether it is useful for us at this time to link the matter [of the Multilateral Force, MLF] with the question of nonproliferation of nuclear weapons [...] when all our exertions are directed against the creation of multilateral nuclear forces. We can think about it, or even better, establish contacts with representatives of China, Korea, Vietnam and other socialist countries and bring them over to our side, to a position opposed to the creation of the MLF. We would achieve in this way at the very least a unity of stances among the socialist countries on this very important international issue. We are not presenting the issue in a way that would oppose the campaign directed against third countries. For us it has to do with the actions of the Indian government, with which our countries maintain good relations; we should use them to influence [India] not to use the tribunal of the U.N. against People's China. It cannot be ruled out that this is connected with the stance of the USA, which is also presenting the matter of China in the very same way. [...]

Right now, the government of India is expanding its efforts. We have expressed our regret about this, and it is an unpleasant surprise that the Indian government is undertaking such efforts. Why is it not so sensitive, for example, with regard to the MLF, the question of prohibiting nuclear weapons, or the arms race? Nevertheless, it wants to create a scandal at the U.N. out of the Chinese matter. This will lead to a worsening of relations between China and India and—it cannot be ruled out—to other unpleasant things. For both the former and the latter country are beginning to engage each other in this way. We have to think out what we should do, [and] we have to appeal to the governments of other countries, in order to calm [the situation] and to approach sensibly the [...] resolution of controversial problems. [...]

I would like to declare with total conviction that we will be making a mistake if we include in the communiqué such a formulation [i.e., supporting nonproliferation]. The government of India will not fail to exploit it, and we will not be able to oppose it. [...]

Ulbricht: We have to be guided by the fundamental danger. And the fundamental danger now is the USA–FRG atomic bloc. In this regard we must take into account that the Bonn government is the only one putting forward revanchist demands. This does not concern India or any other states. That is, the danger of proliferation of atomic weapons lies in the fact that the FRG will receive such weapons, which it will use for its revanchist goals. That is where the main danger lies that we should come out against.

The Romanian comrades, however, are trying to skirt the problem and turn attention to India's initiative. [Dej tried to respond at this point.]

Let me finish, Comrade Dej, I did not interrupt you.

The attempt to skirt the fundamental problem represents a great danger for the countries of the Warsaw Pact because it would mean that they are not coming out against the proliferation of atomic weapons. The FRG will receive the right to jointly decide upon the use of nuclear arms, and we are supposed to just declare that we are in favor of a treaty on the non-use of such arms?

Currently, the fact of possession of nuclear arms creates a specific situation in itself, and leads to certain activities. This is a very complex problem. We believe that the most realistic move is to strive for the nonproliferation of nuclear weapons.

The USA possesses nuclear weapons and the most important question now is in what way and under what conditions it will give the Federal Republic of Germany access to them, how broad of a right the FRG will have to use these arms. In this lies the main danger.

I am certain that the Chinese comrades will support our stance. They told us that they are against multilateral nuclear forces among the NATO countries, that they are against the proliferation of nuclear weapons by the USA and their transfer to the FRG, and I believe that this is the most proper point of view. I do not doubt that we will easily be able to agree with the Chinese comrades, because this is not a matter that is open to discussion.

Dej: If the Chinese comrades respond in the affirmative, then I will carry out a self-criticism not only before you, but also before the Chinese Comrades.

Ulbricht: But we have come together here as the countries of the Warsaw Pact to talk about a concrete enemy. We cannot consult about all our resolutions in advance with every country. After all, we have a treaty that was concluded by certain states. In signing it, we agreed to a particular order that we have to abide by.

We believe that the formulation on the nonproliferation of nuclear weapons must be added to the communiqué. If we do not include this formulation, it will mean that we are not against the West Germans receiving atomic weapons.

If we come forward only later—after the FRG receives these weapons—with a proposal forbidding the use of these weapons, it will not be any policy. The Chinese comrades will not do that, they will not sign.

I ask you, Comrade Dej, are you in favor of our going on record in the communiqué that we are against the proliferation of nuclear weapons in the form of the MLF—which would mean that the West Germans will receive the right to participate in the use and concentration of these weapons or, to put it bluntly, will mean the joint atomic armament of the USA and the FRG?

Should we go on record in the communiqué in this fashion? What do you think?

Dej: We completely agree that it be recorded in the communiqué that we all believe that the Germans should not achieve access to nuclear weapons. But we cannot link this idea with the nonproliferation of nuclear weapons. For that is a much broader idea. We can link it to the regime established in Germany on the basis of the treaties concluded after the Second World War.

Ulbricht: You speak of the Germans—which Germans do you mean?

Dej: The Federal Republic of Germany.

Novotný: We should specify certain things. The Americans, for example, also assert that the FRG cannot receive nuclear weapons. We do not want that—they say—and for that very reason we are organizing joint nuclear forces.

For us, it has to do with the West Germans not receiving nuclear weapons in any form.

Dej: We should write in the communiqué that the FRG cannot receive nuclear weapons in any form.

Novotný: Such a situation has now developed that we must take a stance. Either accept it as it is, or work to change the situation. And the question here does not apply just to Germany.

Gomułka: Clarifies the Polish stance regarding the MLF. We assess the multilateral nuclear forces as a proliferation of nuclear weapons to states that do not yet possess them. That is why we are coming out against these forces, without limiting the question to the FRG and the NATO states.

The Romanian comrades—and as Comrade Dej assert—also the Chinese comrades speak only of the FRG and NATO.

Dej: It has to do only with the FRG and preventing it from gaining access to nuclear weapons.

Gomułka: For us the term "MLF" is a synonym for the term "proliferation." Tell us yourselves: If German units join the multilateral nuclear forces under an American command that receives nuclear weapons—is that not a proliferation of nuclear weapons? And 25 battleships?

After all, these are only the first steps. Schooling German units in the USA and preparing them to handle nuclear weapons—is that proliferation?

[Ion Gheorghe] Maurer[1]*:* Of course.

Gomułka: For me it is a matter of not dividing these matters, that the MLF be treated as a proliferation of nuclear weapons. We are against that. The Romanian comrades agree with us in our assessment of the MLF, and if they agree—they should also come out against the proliferation of nuclear weapons.

But you, Comrades, apply this only to the FRG and not to all the NATO countries. I think that you would also not want other NATO countries—e.g., Turkey, Belgium, Holland, etc.—to possess nuclear weapons. You should also specify this.

If we proceed only with that proposal—that will be our weakness, because when they ask us about other countries, we will have nothing to say.

Second, for some reason, Comrade Dej has not taken into account the fact that the current situation is somewhat different than several months ago. Before the experimental detonation of an atomic weapon in China, the idea of nonproliferation of nuclear weapons was also leveled directly against the Chinese Republic. Now, this problem no longer exists. China counts itself among the nuclear powers, and we are not coming out against China. This means that there is a different situation.

Let us see now what the intentions of the Chinese comrades are in this regard, to which countries the People's Republic of China would like to proliferate nuclear weapons. I do not know which [countries], and I think that the PRC absolutely does not want to proliferate these weapons. But the danger lies in the fact that such countries as Japan and India—i.e., the very two countries that are coming out against the PRC—can produce atomic weapons with relative ease. If every state accepted a treaty banning nuclear weapons, that would also lie in the interest of People's China and the entire socialist camp. That is the second matter that Comrade Dej should take into consideration.

Third matter: we can find many documents—our declarations and statements, adopted together with the Chinese—in which we expressed our coordinated stance

[1] Premier of Romania.

regarding the nonproliferation of nuclear weapons. Those are declarations from the Warsaw Pact and from the international conferences of the communist and workers' parties.

We all stand in favor of the nonproliferation of nuclear weapons and under new conditions we are reaffirming our old declarations.

The fourth matter that I would like to touch upon is linked to the communiqué. In our discussions, Cde. Dej came out in opposition to the draft treaty that Cde. Ulbricht proposed to bring before the U.N. in the name of the socialist countries. That matter is closed. [The question] no longer has to do with whether the members of the commission can argue about the text of the treaty. There will not even be time for precise study of all of its provisions. We also have comments regarding the contents of the treaty.

But at this moment, the discussion is not about the draft [nonproliferation] treaty, but about the communiqué, about whether we should add to it a formulation stating that we are declaring ourselves to be opposed in general to the proliferation of nuclear weapons to new countries. We have already declared ourselves against the MLF.

I cannot understand why you are opposed to such a general formulation. If you were against the treaty, that would be understandable, but your opposition to the communiqué is not understandable.

Now—regarding the U.N. You are saying that India will be coming forward with its proposal. But there are more countries that might come forward with proposals directed against the PRC—e.g., Ireland, which preceded even India and presented a proposal signed by Sweden, Norway, Brazil, Burma, the USA, England, Canada, and other countries coming forwards with proposals on the nonproliferation of nuclear weapons. It is a matter of course that such a proposal will be presented at the U.N.

Novotný: The entire world knows that we are consulting about this now.

Gomułka: And now we are supposed to come out at the U.N. in opposition to the idea of the nonproliferation of nuclear weapons!?

After all, this is a matter of our entire policy. We should orient ourselves to what sort of treaty it is that they are proposing. [...]

[...] It is clear to us that achieving a ban on the use of nuclear weapons will be a very difficult matter and at the current stage of development of the international situation, the West will not agree to it. We are presenting more far-reaching demands—the destruction of stockpiles of these weapons and even—this is already a new stage—universal disarmament.

Thus the question of nonproliferation of nuclear weapons lies, so to say, as the first and easiest step. The second step might be a ban on their use.

I do not have anything against your talking with the Chinese comrades, but don't we have our own minds, can't we evaluate the situation? We are not coming out here in opposition to the interest of the People's Republic of China.

If our initiative is rejected and the NATO states create an Atlantic, or some other kind of multilateral nuclear forces, then the problem will be different. Then we will assemble again and confer about how to proceed in the changed situation. Could it be that we will decide whether or not to give nuclear weapons to the Warsaw Pact states? In other words, then the situation will be different.

You think the same as we do, but you are afraid that this will create further differences between us and the Chinese comrades, that it might inflame the situation? But after all, parties can mutually influence each other. We may also be able to influence the views of the Chinese comrades.

Maurer: [...] The problem of nonproliferation of nuclear weapons is a broad matter of universal character and affects all the states of the world. There are both advocates and opponents to the idea. Currently, we have found ourselves in a situation in which we are supposed to take a stance on this problem, to declare ourselves either for or against it.

The Romanian delegation is guided by the following fact: the Political Consultative Committee of the Warsaw Pact states decided to gather in order to declare itself against the danger of nuclear war on the part of West Germany. Cde. Ulbricht's entire speech, as well as all of your speeches, mainly had in view this same goal, and that is normal. [...]

Why are we against a formulation on the nonproliferation of nuclear weapons and its placement in the communiqué? Because several socialist countries to not support the idea. It would be good to add that idea to our fighting arsenal only after we are certain that all socialist countries will support us.

You, Comrade Gomułka, have expended much energy and employed good logic in order to prove that the Chinese comrades—and not only they—will support your point of view. It seems to me that it would be easier to simply discuss the matter with them. Moreover, we will not only need the consent of the socialist countries, but also non-socialist and even developing capitalist countries. Do you believe, for example, that France will be in favor of the formulation on the nonproliferation of nuclear weapons? Gomułka: Yes, that's what I think. We should be certain of that. France is one of the leading states in the struggle against the atomic armament of the FRG. [...]

Gomułka: I have one question. Do you consider our earlier declarations regarding the nonproliferation of nuclear weapons to be invalid?

Maurer: I did not say that. The Romanian position can be reduced to the idea that we always link the question of nonproliferation of nuclear weapons with the much broader question of concluding a treaty on nuclear disarmament.

[...]

Brezhnev: First of all, I want to clarify and ask Cdes. Dej and Maurer whether what you are saying—to refrain from such a formulation at this time—is the personal opinion of the Romanian Workers' party, or whether you are subordinating [your opinion] to an understanding with the Chinese comrades? I would like to clarify why I am posing this question. Our party has always had and does have its own opinion regarding the nonproliferation of nuclear weapons, and we do not intend to retreat from that opinion. [...]

So much depends on the clarification because it is important for my further presentation that I know—I repeat—whether the stance voiced by you is the principled position of your own party, or whether you want to consult with the Chinese comrades as well.

If you are in favor of the nonproliferation of nuclear weapons as a matter of principle, we are glad, and we do not have anything against your seeking the opinion of the Chinese comrades.

In my address I said that it would probably be useful to bring up the question of the non-armament of West Germany with nuclear weapons in the U.N. assembly, to the extent that People's China will associate itself with such an initiative.

If I understand you well, you have your own stance, and your party declares itself to be in principle in favor of [...] nonproliferation. [...]

Maurer: Our stance is as follows: We are in favor of the nonproliferation of nuclear weapons as a first step, closely linked with nuclear disarmament. We support the idea of nonproliferation of nuclear weapons because it is a good idea, but we oppose adding it to the communiqué from a tactical point of view; in the interests of better organizing our struggle, we oppose adding it to the communiqué.

Brezhnev: [...] I am speaking in the name of the CC of the CPSU. Nobody is against universal disarmament, but it seems to me that there was mention in the Declaration and Statement from the Moscow conferences of the international communist movement of 1957 and 1960 that we should strive for disarmament by various means, including the nonproliferation of nuclear weapons. We all signed those documents then, including the Chinese comrades.

On this question, there are no differences between us. Another matter, and this is already a separate issue, should we add such a formulation to the communiqué?

In our opinion, repeating and accumulating all our old positions in a document does not strengthen the document. The document should be short, sharp. [...]

[...] We are sitting in the headquarters of the Central Committee of the Polish United Workers' Party at an extremely important historical juncture. [...] Simply remember how it was before and compare it with what is being done today. The Potsdam Agreement? It has been dissolved. Step by step, the imperialists are preparing for war. The revanchists dream of revenge. The Americans want to exploit this force [...] of over 30 million revanchists.

There has also been a process of secret armament. The Americans are openly selling atomic fuel for West German reactors. Officially, they say that it is for peaceful uses. But it is clear to specialists that the uranium that is being burned in them can yield plutonium, which is indispensable for atomic missiles. The Germans assert that they are preparing rockets for space research and similar goals. But I seriously doubt that the West Germans are truly interested in outer space. It is revenge that interests them.

We should demonstrate flexibility and courage and take steps that will demonstrate our readiness to give it to the imperialists in the teeth. We cannot permit ourselves to lag behind public opinion, [we] cannot permit ourselves to lose its trust.

If we do not affirm our stance in favor of the nonproliferation of nuclear weapons now, the imperialists will say: "They lacked courage and will swallow the proliferation of nuclear weapons." [...]

Should we add to the communiqué a formulation regarding the nonproliferation of nuclear weapons? Personally, I am for it, although there may be other forms. What is important is that you say that the Romanian Workers' Party supports nonproliferation in principle. Hence, we can discuss the issue of whether to add the formulation [on nonproliferation] [...] to the communiqué or not, and we can also think up a number of other forms.

The USSR, for example, might come forward with a relevant proposal at the U.N. assembly, and the other socialist countries—not as members of the Warsaw Pact, but as [individual] states—can voice their support for it. [...] Otherwise, the initiative might slip from our hands, and we might find ourselves left behind. Yes, it is a question of prestige. [...]

Maurer: I would like to ask, why must we decide today whether to present to the U.N. a joint proposal on the nonproliferation of nuclear weapons, and why can't we speak about it after consultations with other fraternal parties?

Brezhnev: Because we gathered together for exactly that, to decide the matter now. Do we have to assemble again in two weeks? We all agreed, after all, to inform them. But even if they do not agree, that will not cause us to change our opinion. Similarly, if the Romanian comrades have their own principled opinion, it will remain unchanged, regardless of any consultations. We cannot after all postpone our decisions until we consult with other countries— e.g., with Indonesia, which is also affected by the issue.

[...]

Novotný: [...] We might of course reproach the German comrades for viewing the matter too narrowly, linking it to German interests. You might demand a change in their formulations. But one party [...] is putting the issue forward, and we all came here to discuss it. We believe that reducing the issue of the nonproliferation of nuclear weapons to only the FRG is politically unacceptable. It's not just the FRG that is being discussed. It has to do with a general ban against the proliferation of these weapons. [...]

[...] Let the Romanian comrades forgive me, but if we proceed in accordance with their suggestion, then the entire world will know that we did not achieve an understanding, that we did not come to a unified stance through the fault of the Romanian comrades. We are here in a close circle, among communists. So we can state things bluntly. The whole world is waiting for a reaction. The entire Western press is expecting the Romanian delegation to arrive with a different stance. I am putting this bluntly and ask the Romanian comrades not to be insulted.

Dej: Public opinion around the world expects us to declare ourselves against multilateral nuclear forces—that is, we will declare ourselves regarding matter for which we have now gathered.[...]

Gomułka: It is already 1:00 p.m. We have little time left. We talked about whether to add to the communiqué the issue of nonproliferation of nuclear weapons which will be brought before the U.N. assembly. You [the Romanians] were against it, and we will not include the addition regarding the U.N. in the communiqué. But we are participating in our session as members of the Warsaw Pact. Comrade Brezhnev presented the stance of the CPSU, which we all support—you as well—including [the idea] that we should contact the other socialist states that are not members of the Warsaw Pact and coordinate with them. It cannot be ruled out that they will oppose bringing the matter to the U.N., but this does not mean that one of the socialist countries or several countries will not present it at the U.N. That is their sovereign right. We are thus finished with the first issue.

Let us turn now to the second issue arising from our discussion. The Romanian comrades have proposed consultations here on a broad range of subjects. Consultations between the member countries of the Warsaw Pact are thus all the more necessary. Comrade Ulbricht came forward with a proposal, supported by the Soviet comrades, calling for our acceptance of an internal statute that would obligate the ministers of foreign affairs of the Warsaw Pact states to come together periodically for consultations.

This arises from the resolutions of the Warsaw Pact, in which there is mention of consultations. We are also a Consultative Committee. But it would be difficult for us to gather three times a year. Our ministers of foreign affairs should systematically gather and consult on current questions. We should charge them with such a responsibility by means of an internal statute, which will not be subject to publication.

Maurer: We already responded to that some time ago when Khrushchev wrote to us on the matter. We are fundamentally opposed to the creation of such an organ because the Political Consultative Committee is already an organ of a permanent character.

Gomułka: We are not interested in the creation of such an organ. We will order the ministers of foreign affairs to gather for consultations to the extent that it is necessary.

Maurer: There is a great lack of clarity here and a confusion of ideas. The Political [Consultative] Committee was created on the basis of the Treaty, which was signed by representatives of all the member countries, which received the necessary mandate from their countries' governments. In this way, the Political Committee was created as the forum that signed the treaty.

In the Political Committee, government delegations participate. That can be ministers of foreign affairs, other ministers, or special representatives. Nothing prevents the ministers of foreign affairs from gathering when the need arises. But why do we need to create yet another organ—beyond the Political Consultative Committee—with a permanent character that would give orders to other representatives.

Gomułka: The ministers possess the powers granted to them by their governments. A meeting of ministers is not a permanent organ that would replace the Consultative Committee. For example, in preparation for our current conference, the deputy [foreign] ministers gathered earlier. [...]

Dej: Nobody is preventing our ministers from gathering and exchanging views. Why is a special statute necessary for this matter?

Brezhnev: In order to give expression to our unity and our striving for more consolidated work.

Dej: Neither the ministers of foreign affairs nor their deputies will define the policy of our countries; they will carry out the directives they receive. If any of our countries comes forward with such a proposition, we should define why we are calling the meeting and for what issue.

Gomułka: Of course, we would demand that, for we believe that there are too few consultations among us. They are necessary for the sake of working out a common line. For example, Khrushchev did not consult with us about his desire to go visit the FRG. And after all, that affected all of us. Or a second example: Rapacki came forward at the U.N. with a proposal related to the question of European security. We feel guilty that we did not consult with the other socialist countries on this issue, although the proposal was presented in a very general form. Now, we would like to consult about its concrete contents. If you do not want to participate, we will consult with those countries that want to. Many events occur in the international arena. Don't you think that we should exchange views on these subjects?

Dej: Fine, but why a statute?

Gomułka: And why shouldn't we approve a statute? Until now, there was no statute, and count—how many consultations were there?

Dej: And what guarantee do you have that they will take place now?

Gomułka: If we approve the statute and the Romanian government demands—a Romanian minister presents such a proposal—then we will be obligated to participate in such a consultation.

Dej: If it has to do with imposing moral obligations, there is no need to approve a statute. […]

Ulbricht: In the course of the last year-and-a-half, no consultations occurred; that is, we did not carry out the resolutions of the Warsaw Pact, despite the fact that individual states had a number of [political] initiatives. We want to insure that the resolutions of the Warsaw Pact are carried out by regularly convening such meetings. […]

Dej: We would ask that these issues be left aside because we want to have time to reflect upon the text of the communiqué.

Gomułka: I want to be precise. You are opposed to approving a statute regarding regular meetings of the [foreign] ministers?

Dej: Yes, we are opposed to a statute. […]

[*Source: Archiwum Akt Nowych, KC PZPR, 2662, pp. 152–190. Translated by Douglas Selvage.*]

Document No. 31: Plan for Hungarian Command-Staff War Game, May 1965

This war game involving Hungarian army action on the southwestern front provides valuable detail on Warsaw Pact expectations of Budapest's role. The Hungarians were to participate in an operation first directed at confronting NATO in Germany by advancing through Austria (which would represent a violation of that country's neutrality), and then into northern Italy. The game posited that at least three major cities— Vienna, Munich, and Verona—would be either totally destroyed or largely devastated by nuclear attacks. But in an example of utterly unrealistic thinking—what might be called nuclear romanticism—the planners presumed this would in no way prevent alliance forces from advancing on schedule.

[...]

The "Westerners" have started direct preparations for a surprise attack on the Soviet Union and the other socialist countries under cover of various exercises.

In the ensuing situation, the "Easterners" strive to ease international tensions and prevent war. At the same time, they increase all types of intelligence activities (and secretly conduct partial mobilization) [...]

The "Westerners" ("South" army group) advance their main forces after nuclear strikes, under cover of the Austrian armed forces north of Vienna and east of Graz and the 5th independent tactical air force and carrier aviation of the 6th Fleet, and mount an offensive to destroy the main groupings of the "Easterners" in Southern Czechoslovakia and Western Hungary, cross the Danube from movement, and later extend combat towards the borders of the Soviet Union and Romania.

The "South" army group directs its main thrust in the direction of Trnava, Lučenec and another thrust in the direction of Szombathely, Székesfehérvár, Cegléd (assignments of the troops—according to the map).

During the first nuclear-missile strike, 30 nuclear weapons are used.

[...]

The "South" army group is provided with 130 nuclear weapons, with a yield of 7,654 kilotons, including 55 nuclear weapons for the 5th independent tactical air force. Additionally, in the zone of the "South" army group, the carrier aviation of the 6th Fleet delivers 10 nuclear strikes and the "Polaris" submarines deliver five.

In the direction of Berlin and Prague, the "Center" army group assumes the offensive.

[...]

The "Easterners"

The Southwestern Front secretly prepares an offensive operation. After the nuclear strikes, it assumes the offensive from movement from the permanent barrack stations, its assignment being, by delivering the main strike in the direction of Vienna, Linz, and another strike in the direction of Szombathely, Graz, Villach, to complete the destruction of the advancing groupings of the Austrian troops, the 2nd Army group (FRG) and the 3rd Army (Italian), to reach the area of Passau, Salzburg, Hermagor on the 5th–6th days of the operation, and to eliminate Austria from the war.

Later, concentrating its main efforts in the direction of Munich, it must destroy the enemy's operational reserves in the southern part of the FRG and the eastern part of the Lombard plain, occupy the areas of Stuttgart, Singen, Bregenz, Brescia, and Bologna on the 11th–13th days of the operation, and create conditions for expanding the offensive to Italy and eliminating it from the war.

From the left, the Western Front assumes the offensive with its main strength in the direction of Frankfurt and with part of its strength in the direction of Nuremberg. [...]

To carry out the offensive operation, the Southwestern Front receives 125 nuclear weapons, with an active yield of 6,140 kilotons, including 50 airborne weapons. Additionally, Headquarters executes 15 nuclear strikes in the front zone, on the enemy's main targets West of the area of Munich, Innsbruck, and Venice.

[...]

X. PLANNED ORDER OF COMBAT

In view of the "Westerners'" offensive preparations, the commanders of the army corps and higher units of the Southwestern Front reach an enhanced level of readiness between 19:00 on June 21 and 7:00 on June 23. [...]

After receiving warning of an imminent enemy attack and following the initial advance of the 2nd Corps (FRG) and the 3rd Army (Italian), the Front Headquarters puts the troops on a state of total combat readiness by 7:00 on June 23, orders the deployment and advance of various units, and assumes the offensive in the prescribed directions.

Once the commencement of the "Westerners'" nuclear strikes has been ascertained, the commanders of the army corps and higher units take measures to prevent enemy strikes. [...]

[...]

16:00 on June 23–16:00 on June 24 [...]

The front troops deliver a strike against units of the Austrian army defending the frontier, press forward to a depth of 80–120 km and thrust forward, engaging in close combat with the forces of the 2nd Army Corps (FRG) and the 3rd Army (Italian), which are advancing in the direction of Vienna and Villach.

[...]

At 15:00 on June 24 [...]

The front troops destroy the main forces of the 2nd Corps (FRG) and the 3rd Corps of the 3rd Army (Italian), according to the decisions on close combat.

The front commander makes his decision about completing the destruction of the enemy's Munich grouping in cooperation with the troops of the Western front and about spreading the offensive in the direction of Northern Italy.

The front staff formulates the commander's decision, forwards assignments to the

190

troops and organizes control of their activities. The army and higher-unit staffs organize combat of the subordinate troops according to the assignments received.

At 8:00 on June 25 [...]

The front troops on the right wing, in cooperation with the higher units of the Western Front, have started pursuing the remnants of the enemy's destroyed Munich grouping, and reached the Lombardy Plain on the left wing.

[...]

The end of the war game is at 19:00 on June 25.

[...]

[*Source: Hungarian People's Army Headquarters First group Directorate 1969 Unit 68/014/185, War History Archive, Budapest. Translated by Attila Kolontári, Zsófia Zelnik, and Brian McLane.*]

Document No. 32: Transcript of Ceauşescu–Deng Conversation, July 25, 1965

This account of a meeting between Nicolae Ceauşescu and Chinese Politburo member Deng Xiaoping describes aspects of Soviet policy toward the Warsaw Pact, but also gives telling indications of China's and Romania's viewpoints on the subject. Ceauşescu informs Deng that the Soviets want to reorganize the Warsaw Pact's command structure to tighten its centralized control but that Romania's position aims at making the alliance into a framework for more genuine collaboration between independent countries. Deng responds that the Chinese fully agree and expresses the hope that Romania could serve as an intermediary between Beijing and the other East European countries. He suggests that Moscow should be made to apologize to the Albanians and allow them to rejoin the Warsaw Pact—which the Romanians subsequently tried to do but without success. The two leaders also discuss Vietnam at some length. Deng informs Ceauşescu that the Chinese are sending a letter to the Soviets concerning problems of Soviet–Chinese cooperation in North Vietnam. One of Beijing's concerns is that a recent Soviet idea that both North and South Vietnam become neutral countries arose from an agreement between Moscow and Washington, of which the Chinese disapprove, and which Deng sees as evidence of a Soviet desire to isolate China.

[…]

Comrade Nicolae Ceauşescu: [...] An issue raised by the Soviet comrades was the issue of the Warsaw Treaty Organization. In their view, toward the end of the year, a meeting of the Consultative Committee should take place due to the need to make some improvements regarding the organization of the military high command, with a view to ensuring broader participation by representatives of the other socialist countries in this high command. We told the Soviet comrades that we shall see. Since we have a common high command, it is to be assumed that the leadership of the current high command will also be joint. But the leadership of the current high command is Soviet. We shall see what proposals will be made. We had told them on other occasions that within the framework of this organization one must ensure that each army is independent, that each socialist country has an army of its own.

Comrade Ion Gheorghe Maurer: The relationships should be one of collaboration, of cooperation, not of subordination.

Comrade Nicolae Ceauşescu: We will analyze the proposals that will be made on that score.

Comrade Deng Xiaoping: This means the Soviets want to strengthen their control over the others.

Comrade Nicolae Ceauşescu: It is hard to say. The criticisms made so far were only about the fact that this command is Soviet. Naturally, they want to ensure a broader representative basis of the command, but we do not want only that and, mainly, not a [purely] formal representation, but really the organization of the command on a new basis—not as a unified command, but as an organ of collaboration between independent countries.

Comrade Ion Gheorghe Maurer: This means that we want to act in such a way that no supranational control over these countries exists. But let us see how things will pan out.

Comrade Kang Sheng: On this score I would like to say that a book with the title Military Strategy, edited by [Marshal Vasilii D.] Sokolovsky, was published in the Soviet Union. In the second edition of this book some modifications have been made, but the book is used as basic material in Soviet military academies. In it, it is stated that if there is a war against the imperialists, then all the socialist countries will have to act in common and all the armies of the socialist countries will have to be under the command of the Soviet Union. This is their strategic conception.

Comrade Ion Gheorghe Maurer: If each one of us devises such a conception, things will go really well!

Comrade Nicolae Ceaușescu: The fact is that this [conception] exists not only in handbooks; actually, in the organization of the Warsaw Treaty Organization and that of the unified command, the armies of the other socialist countries of Europe are subordinated. We want to do away with this state of affairs.

Comrade Ion Gheorghe Maurer: This is very important because a big issue arises. The COMECON was such a big issue and maybe it will be again; now comes the Warsaw Treaty Organization, an issue which is emerging. Maybe it will not be easy, but at any rate we must see.

Comrade Nicolae Ceaușescu: Of course, we understand that in case of a war against imperialism we will have to act in common, but these actions—which require the mobilization of all the people—must be performed on the basis of close cooperation, with the independence of each country being observed and the participation of each army as an independent army, as a national force. This will ensure that the effort of each country will really be an effort from all viewpoints.

Comrade Deng Xiaoping: We wholly agree with your opinion. We acted like that during the war in Korea. We can tell you that, together with the Korean comrades, we drew up a battle plan, but on the basis of the principles put forward by comrade Ceaușescu just now. We cannot accept that Vietnam and Korea would be subordinated to our country because China is a bigger country. But your experience is richer than ours because you came across such problems within the framework of COMECON and of the Warsaw Treaty Organization. We know that you have fought and think that there are many people who agree with you.

Comrade Nicolae Ceaușescu: We imparted our opinion to comrade Ulbricht because he also raised this issue. He said: it goes without saying that we must make improvements since we do not want things to happen as in 1962, during the crisis in the Caribbean Sea.[2] If we are a pact intended for defense and fight in common, the steps that are to be taken must be the result of everybody's will. It is with this issue in mind that we want to confer when we meet the Soviet comrades in Moscow in autumn. We agreed to debate these issues and proposed to the Soviet comrades to

[2] The Cuban missile crisis.

bring the Albanian comrades to the Consultative Committee session as well—not only to the session, but also to its preparatory session. The Soviet comrades agreed with this proposal. It goes without saying that we will have to see to it that the Albanian comrades participate. Albania is a member of the Warsaw Treaty Organization and it would be good for it to take part [in the session]. If there are more of us, we will be able to obtain better results.

Comrade Deng Xiaoping: Regarding the Albanian issue we discussed it with [Aleksei N.] Kosygin when he passed through our country on the occasion of his visit to Vietnam. Comrade Mao Zedong told Kosygin that the Soviets speak about the unity of the socialist camp, but why do they not want to solve the Albanian problem similarly? The problem is not difficult to solve. If they admit that they made a mistake regarding Albania, that will be enough for the problem to be solved. If they do not say that they made a mistake, the Albanian comrades will not come to the session even if they are invited. At the 22nd Congress of the CPSU a strong action against Albania was launched. If the Soviet Union does not solemnly admit that it erred, how can the Albanian comrades accept the invitation? We are convinced that you will approach this issue fairly within the framework of Comecon and within the framework of the Warsaw Treaty Organization, and then fairness will be on your side.

[…]

[*Source: CC PCR, Chancellery, dossier no. 105/1965, pp. 2–15, Romanian National Archives. Translated by Viorel Nicolae Buta.*]

Document No. 33: Hungarian Proposals for Reform of the Warsaw Pact, January 18–19, 1966

The next several documents (Documents Nos. 33–35) are proposals from key East European countries relating to reform of the Warsaw Pact. In January 1966, the Soviets had sent their own ideas on the subject to the other member-states, but in part because Moscow's conception amounted to reform from above, a number of them were unreceptive and decided to present counter-proposals. The first document reproduced here was written by Lajos Czinege, the Hungarian defense minister, and sent to the Hungarian Politburo for consideration before being submitted to an upcoming meeting of Warsaw Pact defense ministers. This particular version is a draft and so it is not clear whether the Soviets received the proposal in this exact form. Nonetheless, it is interesting as a reflection of the views of Hungarian military leaders. In brief, the proposal urges a unified system of military preparedness and standardized regulations in peace time. It calls for a unified command, but only in war time and in a form that would ensure real participation by member countries in command matters. It also appeals for the creation of a collective military body that would be subordinate to the PCC. In effect, Czinege's idea mirrors the NATO Military Committee. Other East European states expressed similar concerns about being drawn into a war, especially a nuclear one, without the ability to influence the policies that might lead to it.

Written one day after Czinege's proposal, the second document below, by Hungarian Foreign Minister János Péter, also proposes reorganization of the Warsaw Pact, and was intended for an upcoming foreign ministers' meeting. It seems clear that Hungary's leaders, along with those of other East European countries, solicited opinions from the relevant ministries. Péter's conception envisages the PCC as the highest body of the Warsaw Pact concerned with both political and military matters—following the model of the NATO Council. He argues that it should meet annually but also hold special sessions if any members so desire. The Pact should also create a council of foreign ministers and a permanent secretariat, both of which would be subordinated to the PCC—again as in NATO. The Hungarians' particular interest in a council of foreign ministers stems from their desire to provide input into the Soviet bloc's foreign policy decisions. The Eastern alliance never established a permanent secretariat, which was always an important brain center for NATO.

a) Proposal by Minister of National Defense
   (Lajos Czinege) to the HSWP Political Committee [...]
   January 18, 1966

[...]

Proposal concerning the command system of the
Unified Armed Forces to be made at the meeting of the ministers of
national defense of the member-states of the Warsaw Treaty.

In order to further improve the command of the Unified Armed Forces of the Warsaw Treaty the agreement must ensure—taking into account the sovereignty of the member-states—a more effective harmonization of their military efforts in the following areas:

1. In times of peace:
   – a uniform assessment of the military–political and strategic situation and the expected activity of NATO;
   – coordinated planning of military operations of the armed forces;
   – coordination of a well-balanced and systematic development of the armed forces;
   – standardization of the structure of the armed forces and of the principles of military operations and strategy;
   – coordinated development of the armament system and harmonization of the development and production of military technology;
   – establishment of a unified system of military preparedness of the armed forces and the effective deployment of the troops;
   – a unified system of requirements for the training of commanders, staffs and troops, and regular training in cooperation between the armed forces of the member-states;
   – necessary standardization of regulations concerning preparation of the seat of military operations in the territory of the member-states, mobilization of the armed forces, provision of material supplies, etc.;
   – coordination of research work in the field of military sciences and generalization of scientific results;
   – supervision of implementation of rules and regulations made jointly by the member-states.

2. In time of war:
   – effective utilization of all available military resources;
   – effective and coordinated reconnaissance of the enemy;
   – a unified command of air defense systems of the member-states;
   – a unified command of military operations in the European seat of operations;
   – constant cooperation among the armed forces of the member-states;
   – mutual assistance in supplying forces with material and technological resources, in sanitary provision, in the transportation and mobilization of troops and in telecommunications.

II.

Today the command system of the Unified Armed Forces cannot yet meet all the above requirements in every respect and in many ways fails to reflect the changes that have taken place in the course of the development of the Unified Armed Forces. Therefore, with a view to further improvement, the following matters must be clarified:

- questions concerning the legal status of the leading military organs of the member-states and the Supreme Command and their relationship;
- interpretation of the structure, mechanism and methods of command;
- structural conditions for improving the command system.

[...]

At the moment neither the ideas of the Supreme Command nor those of the other states is known. At the same time we do not have mature views on some aspects of the problem either (for instance on the coalition command system of the armed forces in time of war). With a view to this we have requested authorization from the Politburo to represent the following position as a starting point at the next preparatory meeting—with the intention to endorse the ideas that are the most desirable in our view.

In order to turn the Supreme Command into a truly collective body of military command, to ensure real participation of the member-states in the command of the troops belonging to the Warsaw Treaty, and to regulate the relationship between the Supreme Command and the high military commands of the member-states, the following regulations must be implemented:

1. A collective military command body must be established working under the guidance of the Political Consultative Committee, which is capable of making adequate military proposals to the Political Consultative Committee and based on the Committee's decision can take the necessary practical measures. [...]

With a view to this goal the highest military body of the Warsaw Treaty, the "Military High Council," must be established, consisting of the ministers of national defense of the member-states, the chiefs of staff, the supreme commander and the chief of staff.

2. The Supreme Command of the Unified Armed Forces must be transformed in a way that enables it to accomplish the following tasks in time of peace:
- make strategic plans for the use of troops under its jurisdiction;
- work out requirements for military operations and training, coordinate and supervise training, and plan and conduct joint military maneuvers;
- coordinate the war supplies of troops;
- develop modern military technology;
- coordinate work concerning command (telecommunications, ciphering), and any other activities requiring joint command and coordination.

[...]

Based on the resolutions, decisions and requirements of the Military High Council, the Supreme Command works out the necessary plans and directives for troops deployed in the Unified Armed Forces, issues the necessary orders, the execution of which is then ensured by the respective ministers of national defense.

[...]

In time of war the Supreme Command must be capable of accomplishing all the tasks assigned to it by the Political Consultative Committee and the Military High Command. The full elaboration of the wartime military command system requires further work.

* * *

The organization of the Supreme Command must include: the supreme commander, his deputies, and the joint staff working under the supreme commander.

a) The supreme commander of the Unified Armed Forces must be a person who does not fulfill any function in his own national army.

b) Deputies must be appointed to assist the supreme commander who should represent the military leadership of the member-states, instead of the current common practice that the ministers of defense of the member-states are at the same time the deputies of the supreme commander, and thus, in a military sense, his subordinates.

c) The unified staff must be a working team—not subordinated to the military leadership of the member-states—consisting of generals and officers delegated by the member-states of the Warsaw Treaty. [...]

[...]

b) Proposal by the Foreign Minister János Péter re:
the Strengthening of the Political Structure of the Warsaw Pact
January 19, 1966

[...]

I request authorization from the Politburo to present the following organizational proposals at the meeting of the foreign ministers of the member-states of the Warsaw Treaty. [...]

I.

1. The highest body of the Warsaw Treaty is the Political Consultative Committee (henceforth PCC) both in a political and in a military sense.

2. Participants of the meetings of the PCC are: first secretaries of communist and workers' parties, prime ministers, ministers of foreign affairs and ministers of national defense of the member-states.

[...]

3. The PCC holds one regular meeting annually, which lasts usually for one or two days. Invitations to attend the regular meeting of the PCC must be sent out 14

days before the time of the session. Preparations for regular sessions of the PCC are made by the Council of Foreign Ministers, the Military Council, the Permanent Secretariat, and the Unified Command. The agenda of the meetings is decided by the PCC.

[...]

4. The PCC holds a special meeting if proposed by any of the member-states because of some internationally significant situation or for some other important reason, and if the member-states endorse this proposal. The member-state, which makes the proposal also volunteers to organize the special session. The agenda of this special session includes only that issue for which the meeting was convened.

[...]

5. The functions of the chairman and the vice chairman of the meetings of the PCC are fulfilled by the leaders of the delegations of the member-states in rotation,

[...]

6. At its meetings, the PCC may adopt a resolution and issue a joint communiqué. A unanimous decision is needed for the adoption of a resolution and the approval of a joint communiqué.

7. The working language of the sessions of the PCC is Russian. Where simultaneous interpreting is provided, the representatives of the member-states may also speak in their native language.

8. Generally the meetings of the PCC are confidential. The joint communiqué adopted at the meeting is made public.

[...]

II.

Subordinated to the Political Consultative Committee, the following political bodies must be established:

1. The Council of Foreign Ministers, whose main task is to make preparations for the upcoming meeting of the PCC and attends to all other matters which are delegated to its scope of authority.

2. The Permanent Secretariat, which is a permanently functioning political body of the Warsaw Treaty. The Secretariat is headed by the first secretary. The costs of establishing and maintaining the Permanent Secretariat are provided for by each of the member-states in proportion to their national income.

[...]

János Péter

[*Source: M-KS-288.f. 5/385 ő.e., Hungarian National Archives. Translated by Andreas Bocz.*]

Document No. 34: Polish proposals for Reform
of the Warsaw Pact, January 21 and 26, 1966

Much like their Hungarian colleagues (see Documents Nos. 33a and b), the Poles also prepared proposals for reorganizing the Warsaw Pact. The diversity of views evident in these documents was not apparent to the outside world during the Cold War. While not necessarily directed against the Soviet Union, these propositions by essentially loyal allies are at the same time explorations of how far they could go in defining room for independent action within the alliance. In the first example below, Polish Foreign Minister Adam Rapacki's sophisticated submission presents several arguments. He agrees that the Warsaw Pact needs reorganization. In military matters, he concedes that the Soviet Union should retain primary responsibility, but in the political arena the focus should be on consultation and working toward common positions on both principle and policy. Among his numerous proposals for action is the creation of separate decision-making and advisory bodies which would help institutionalize a more equal role for the allies in both areas of internal Pact activity.

The second proposal reproduced here, from the Polish Defense Ministry, is informative at two levels: it not only presents views of the military but also provides considerable detail about Soviet goals, gleaned from informal consultations with Soviet officers. While the unnamed authors of the document are just as intent on securing Poland's interests, their report lacks the forcefulness of Rapacki's submission. Naturally, their arguments center around aspects of the Warsaw Pact's military activities and command structure, including the question of whether nuclear weapons should remain under exclusive Soviet control—an idea the Polish military hopes to discourage.

a) Proposal by Foreign Minister Adam Rapacki
   January 21, 1966
   […]

III.

The Soviet initiative to improve the instruments of the Pact's operation is coming at the right time, when a greater need for strengthening the unity of action of the member-states is emerging. In the present circumstances the elaboration of a common political line for the Pact, which would take into account the positions of all interested parties, calls for systematic and frequent consultations and contacts.

IV.

The Warsaw Pact has created a Political Consultative Committee for consultations among member-states and for consideration of questions arising from the Pact's operation. According to the Pact's provisions, each state is to be represented in the

Consultative Committee by a member of the government or another especially appointed representative. The Committee may set up such auxiliary bodies as are deemed necessary. In practice, however, that Committee has been transformed into summit meetings, convened sporadically and generally not properly prepared, which adopt spectacular resolutions (declarations, communiqués).

In fact, this is inconsistent with the consultative tasks of the Committee, with its originally intended composition (government members), and with its name (to whom is a gathering of top party and government leaders to be advisory?). In such circumstances, meetings of the Political Consultative Committee cannot be held with proper frequency the way meetings of party and government leaders, by their very nature, are held when there are very important matters to be considered or decided upon. (Reminder: a resolution of the Committee from January 1956 called for meetings of the Committee at least twice a year, not counting extraordinary meetings.)

Thus, as the Committee has transformed itself into a Council, there is no body which would ensure the opportunity for systematic and frequent consultations among member countries, despite the fact that they were suggesting such a need.

V.

To improve and rationalize the operation of the Pact consistent with the existing needs, it would be proper to specify the decision-making as well as consultative and advisory bodies.

1. This objective could be achieved by setting up a Pact's Council, which would take over functions heretofore exercised by the Political Consultative Committee. The Council would be holding meetings at the summit level; it would decide on key issues, with the rule of unanimity. It would be hearing and approving reports of the Unified Command. It would be meeting whenever needed.

2. The Political Consultative Committee should be restored to its original character provided for in the Pact. It could thus become a flexible forum for consultations of foreign ministers, in some cases, when needed, with the participation of defense ministers. In particular cases the ministers might delegate their deputies. This Committee would become a consultative and advisory body, preparing positions for the governments, or the Council. The Committee should be meeting at least 2–3 times a year. In this way consultations which are now difficult to hold or which are held only as a result of arduous procedures, would acquire an institutional character.

3. A Permanent Secretariat of the Pact should be set up at a proper level and with proper composition. It is necessary to properly prepare meetings of the Council and the Political Consultative Committee, to ensure regular liaison among member-states during the intersession periods, for providing continuity of coordination and information on matters related to the decisions adopted, or the ones that should be submitted for discussion. The shortcomings resulting from the lack of such a body have been felt frequently. To be sure, according to the Resolution adopted by the Political Consultative Committee in 1956 (Prague), a United Secretariat of the Committee, composed of a General Secretary and his deputies, one from each country, has been set up. This Secretariat, according to the Resolution, functions only during the meet-

ings of the Political Consultative Committee. In practice, deputy minister of foreign affairs of the USSR served as Secretary General. His activity as a Secretary General was limited to organizational functions and only during the sessions of the Political Consultative Committee. During the inter-session periods neither the Secretary General nor the Secretariat is in practice performing any functions. The fact that up to now the Secretary General was not disconnected from state functions in his own country was in some situations causing even political difficulties (e.g. in the case of inviting Albania to the meeting of the Political Consultative Committee in Warsaw in January 1964, Poland took over functions which should have normally belonged to the Secretary General). To satisfy the needs mentioned earlier in pt. 3, the institution of the Secretary General and the Permanent Secretariat should be organized and set to be able to:

a) provide a steady organizational link among member-states during the inter-session periods;

b) perform functions connected with the preparation and servicing of meetings of the Council and the Political Consultative Committee;

c) provide current information to the member-states on the implementation of adopted resolutions and decisions, as well as on matters calling for consideration. Circulate documents relating to the activities of the Pact;

d) submit to the member governments motions regarding consultations, convening meetings of the Consultative Committee and in exceptional cases also the Council;

e) submit proposals for consultations on working levels regarding matters of lesser importance (e.g. preparations for U.N. sessions, the Disarmament Conference in Geneva, etc.);

f) organize an exchange of information among foreign ministries of the member-states regarding assessment of the political situation in the area of analytical and research work carried out by the foreign ministries of member-states.

The position of the Secretary General should be situated in such a way that he would be able to stay in touch with member governments at the highest levels (prime ministers, foreign ministers) and obtain the necessary information. He should not be combining this function with any other state function in his own country. He should be nominated by a resolution of the Council for a period of 2–3 years. The headquarters of the Permanent Secretariat should be in Moscow. The Permanent Secretariat should be staffed by representatives from all member-states, including the country of the Secretary General. They would be cooperating and fulfilling the role of liaison officers between the Secretariat and member governments (foreign ministries) and the Secretary General. Such representatives could be responsible employees of member countries' embassies. The Permanent Secretariat should also have its own small, but indispensable and qualified staff.

VI.

In our opinion the new measures in the area of organizational improvement of the Pact should be made public (published). It would emphasize the political vitality of the Warsaw Pact.

[...]

[*Source: KC PZPR 2948/48–53, Archiwum Akt Nowych. Previously published in the* Cold War International History Project Bulletin, *no. 11 (Winter 1998): 238–240. Translated by Jan Chowaniec.*]

b) Proposal by the Polish Defense Ministry,
   January 26, 1966

[...]
In connection with a letter by Comrade Brezhnev to Comrade Gomułka regarding improving and ameliorating the bodies set up by the Warsaw Pact and proposing to call a conference of defense ministers on the reorganization of the command and general staff, it is known to us that the Soviet side—unwilling to impose its proposals upon the leadership of other countries—does not intend to put forward any preliminary proposals on the organization of the command and general staff of the Unified Armed Forces, but instead expects such proposals from the countries concerned.

From unofficial talks with Soviet comrades it looks as though that their position can be outlined as follows:

1. There is no intention either to change or amend the Warsaw Pact provisions, but rather to base [any changes] on art. 5 and 6.

2. The intention is to set up a command and general staff of the Unified Armed Forces with the prerogatives and real possibilities of coordinating defense efforts of member-states relating to forces assigned to the Unified Armed Forces in the operational, training, organization and technical area.

It is intended to position more properly than up to now the status of the Supreme Commander and the general staff of the Unified Armed Forces, and to define the place of commanders of troops assigned to these forces. A need is also seen for a different, more independent positioning of defense ministers of member-states vis-à-vis the Supreme Commander of the Unified Armed Forces.

3. It is also expected that a Military Advisory Council is to be established within the Political Consultative Committee—as an advisory body to the Committee.

Such Council would be composed of defense ministers and the Supreme Commander of the Unified Armed Forces, on an equal footing. The Secretary of the Council would be the chief of staff of the Unified Forces. Chairmanship of the Council meetings would rotate consecutively among all its members. The Council would consider general questions of development and readiness of the Unified Armed Forces, and prepare proposals for the Political Committee and recommendations for the national military commands. The issues will be dealt with according to the rule of full equality.

4. The Supreme Commander of the Unified Armed Forces would coordinate operational-training preparedness of the Unified Armed Forces, as well as matters relating to the enhancement of their development and military readiness.

The Supreme Commander and the chief of staff of the Unified Armed Forces would be relieved of their functions in the Soviet Army.

5. Strategic weapons will not be included in the Unified Armed Forces of the Warsaw Pact, and operational plans will be developed by the General Staff of the Soviet Army, as well as by general staffs of member-states in the areas of concern to them.

6. It is envisaged that in peace time the staff of the Unified Armed Forces, employing about 600 people, will be in charge of coordinating preparations of the military for the realization of tasks assigned to them.

However, the position of the general staff of the Unified Armed Forces as a command organ in war time is still a matter too premature to be considered, as there is, among other things, a need to maintain the current procedure of working out strategic and operational plans, the rules for using strategic weapons, as well as [a need to] to maneuver forces and equipment from one war theater to another.

7. The general staff of the Unified Armed Forces will be composed of the representatives of all armies in proportion to the number of forces assigned to them. It is assumed that Soviet participation in the staff will be percentage-wise smaller than their actual contribution to the Pact.

8. The following are projections of a new percentage share in the command budget of the Unified Armed Forces:

Percentage share in the budget

Countries	Currently		Proposed	
Bulgaria	7	%	9	%
Czechoslovakia	13	%	13.5	%
GDR	6	%	10	%
Poland	13.5	%	16.5	%
Romania	10	%	11	%
Hungary	6	%	9	%
USSR	44.5	%	31	%
	100	%	100	%

9. In the organizational structure of the command and general staff the following positions are envisaged: supreme commander, first deputy, chief of staff, air force commander, two deputies for naval operations (for the Baltic and the Black Seas), deputy chief of air force, an inspector and a quartermaster at the rank of deputies, a deputy for technical questions and chiefs of military formations: rocket and artillery, engineering and chemical. Also included into the command as deputies to the supreme commander would be commanders of assigned forces of member-states.

Key positions, such as supreme commander, chief of staff, chief of air defense, deputy chief of air force, quartermaster, deputy for technical questions, would be staffed by representatives of the Soviet Army.

In view of this purely tentative recognition, one can state the following:

The Soviet side, initiating the question of improvement of the bodies set up by the Warsaw Pact, so far has not presented any specific and official preliminary materials in this regard.

Therefore, during the forthcoming conference of ministers of national defense it would be useful to obtain in the first place the Soviet position on the following questions:

a) Defining the role and competence of the chief command of the Unified Armed Forces in the event of a threat of war and during a war period;

b) The scope of participation of member countries' political–military leadership in drawing up strategic–operational plans for particular war theaters;

c) The subordination of the supreme commander of the Unified Armed Forces. It is now difficult to foresee what kind of position the Soviet side and other interested states will take on the above questions. Nevertheless, the Ministry of National Defense is presenting the following point of view, which, if accepted, might be the basis for our position at the conference of defense ministers and for further work on proposals for detailed solutions:

1. It is proposed to set up an Advisory Committee for Defense as a body of the Council, which is the top organ of the party and government leadership.

The Advisory Committee should be composed of ministers of national defense of the Pact members, the supreme commander and the chief of staff of the Unified Armed Forces as its secretary.

The rule of rotation should be introduced in chairing Committee meetings.

In addition, it would also be advisable to set up a Consultative Commission of the chiefs of staff, which would deal with operational planning and the resulting tasks for preparing the armed forces.

2. The Supreme Commander of the Unified Armed Forces, his deputies and the chief of staff should be appointed by the Pact's Council, with the Supreme Commander and the chief of staff being relieved of their duties in the armed forces of their country.

The Supreme Commander is to be subordinated to the Council and carries out its decisions. In the inter-session periods he personally coordinates with members of the Council basic questions requiring joint decisions, or does this within the Advisory Committee for Defense.

In peace time, the command and chief of staff of the Unified Armed Forces should play the role of a coordinating body, preparing the designated military forces, while in war time they should take command of those forces in the European War Theater. The Supreme Commander and the staff of the Unified Armed Forces should participate, based on a common defense strategy of Pact members and jointly with their general staffs, in developing plans for the particular strategic directions of the European War Theater. On the basis of such plans the Supreme Commander is coordinating and preparing the staff of the Unified Armed Forces and the designated forces for the execution of tasks facing them. Thus, he is carrying on proper operational and training activities, as well as coordinating organizational, technical-manufacturing and scientific-research activities.

The internal structure of the command and general staff should correspond to the needs of directing activities in the particular strategic areas. The position of Polish representatives in the chain of command and the general staff of the Unified Armed Forces on the Western front should correspond with the place and tasks of the Polish armed forces scheduled to be deployed in that area.

The organizational structure of the staff of the Unified Armed Forces should ensure realization of the above tasks in peace time and constitute a nucleus of proper organs envisioned for a period of war. A preliminary assumption is that these tasks could be tackled by a staff of approximately 200 professional workers. But, it should be assumed that most of the key positions will be staffed by representatives of the Soviet Army.

Development of the command and the general staff of the Unified Armed Forces for a war period should be carried out through the inclusion of the proper channels from the general staff and other institutions of the Soviet Army, provided for in the operational plan for use in the European War Theater. It is also assumed that the backup and support units for the command and general staff of the Unified Armed Forces should be assigned from the Soviet Army within their peacetime activities and consistent with a plan for their deployment in case of war. The command and the general staff of the Unified Armed Forces should continue to be headquartered in Moscow.

3. There is a need in all Warsaw Pact countries, without exception, to clearly define commands in charge of forces assigned to the Unified Armed Forces, as well to define both the formations and size of those forces.

The strategic assault forces are still to be at the disposal of the Soviet Army. Their use is being planned by the general staff of the Soviet Army. However, the commander of the Unified Armed Forces should be included in planning their use in favor of forces entrusted to his command. It also seems necessary to define an obligatory scope and method for use of the strategic assault forces for the common defense of the Pact members.

Ministers of national defense and the general staffs of the Warsaw Pact states are to fully exercise their superior command and leadership role with regard to formations assigned to the Unified Armed Forces. They are to be held responsible for their moral–political condition, their mobilization and fighting readiness, for their operational and tactical preparedness and completeness in terms of numbers, arms and equipment.

4. Together with establishing broader tasks and new organizational structures of the command and general staff of the Unified Armed Forces there is a need to fix the size and percentage share of contributions borne by the USSR and other countries of the Warsaw Pact.

It is suggested that this question should be considered in terms of proportional efforts resulting from the threat that we face in the European War Theater.

The population, economic and military potential of the NATO states in Europe is, in comparison with the potential of the people's democracies, clearly unfavorable to us. Creation of the indispensable superiority for defense and defeat of the enemy can be ensured by the engagement in this theater of the proper Soviet forces in the dimension of approximately two-thirds of total Warsaw Pact potential.

The above indicator of the USSR's indispensable share corresponds with the real place and potential of that country. It reflects both the probable size of its armed forces provided for the European War Theater, as well as its population potential (counted for the European area of the USSR) and its share in the production of basic raw materials and strategic materials. The share of the above factors can roughly be estimated at 65–90 percent in relation to the total potential of all other Warsaw Pact countries.

Moreover, the relative weight of the USSR is determined by its strategic assault power on behalf of the whole Warsaw Pact.

In view of the above statements it does not seem feasible to accept unofficial suggestions regarding the percentage share of the USSR in the budget of the command of the Unified Armed Forces (merely about 31 percent).

In the opinion of the Ministry of National Defense the share of member-states in the command of the Unified Armed Forces should:

 – correspond percentage-wise to the share of positions held in the command and the general staff the Unified Armed Forces (this indicator with regard to the Soviet Army representatives should be 50 percent as a minimum);
 – remain basically within the actual percentage share kept in the budget up to now;
 – take into consideration national income per capita in the particular countries;
 – take into consideration a particular country's effort in the development of its territorial defense and its contribution to securing the redeployment of allied forces, thus bringing relief to operational forces.

Taking into consideration these premises, Poland's share should not exceed the present 13.5 percent, and we should be trying to obtain from our point of view more justified numbers—e.g. a minimum of 50 percent for the Soviet Union, and for the remaining Pact members also about 50 percent. With this assumption our share would amount to 1/5 of the share of all people's democracies, which would be about 10 percent of the total budget.

However, this proposal may encounter strong opposition, based, among other things, on current membership contributions to the CMEA, which for the USSR amounts to only 32.25 percent.

[…]

[*Source: KC PZPR 2948/27–36, Archiwum Akt Nowych. Previously published in the* Cold War International History Project Bulletin, *no. 11 (Winter 1998): 240–243. Translated by Jan Chowaniec.*]

Document No 35: Czechoslovak Proposal for
Reform of the Warsaw Pact, February 1966

This Czechoslovak document offers another East European perspective on the subject of Warsaw Pact reorganization. While still fairly accommodating of the Soviet position, the Czechoslovaks by now were already experiencing a liberalizing trend that would shortly lead to the Prague Spring, and their views here are not as submissive and pliable as they once were. The general staff officers who composed the document propose allowing national armies to be directed without the intercession of the Warsaw Pact command. They also complain that the Soviets are being excessively secretive about important matters such as the supreme commander's exact role and the scope of his authority during a war. More generally, they point out that Moscow has not been consulting with its allies about its plans to make use of Warsaw Pact forces, an approach the Czechoslovaks argue hampers effective preparations for war. Still, the tone of the document is somewhat muted, which suggests that some dissension existed within the ranks of the Czechoslovak military.

[...]

Comrade Brezhnev's letter implies that specific measures to improve the structure and mechanisms of the Treaty and its military bodies in particular must be taken [...]

The fundamental problem to be resolved first: [...] "How to ensure the full responsibility of all Treaty members for the comprehensive defense of the entire bloc that gives them the right jointly to decide the main issues concerning the preparation of our states for war."

As the following lines suggest, this is not the case today. We are convinced that without a major change, no proposed re-shuffling of the UAF Staff would achieve the goals desired in the reorganization of the Unified Command.

Every member of the PCC should be reassured that his country's share within the Unified Armed Forces truly safeguards the inviolability of state frontiers, and must have the opportunity to assess realistically the measures through which this is safeguarded. Since the very existence and future of the nation are at stake, the responsibility of each of our parties and governments for the final success in a possible war requires certitude about the correctness of the measures being taken in peace time.

[...] Individual states build their armed forces and make other war preparations, not only without any possibility of cooperating in the elaboration of the general concept, or of evaluating it, but without even any knowledge of the particular measures adopted by all the other participants. This makes it impossible for them to be certain about their respective contributions to the common cause and about all that has been done to ensure its success.

We believe that, for instance, the cooperation of states concerned with formulating the strategic concept for the conduct of war in the European theater is indispensable for creating the conditions necessary to fulfill the principle cited [at the beginning of this document]. [...] That has not been the case so far. The previous overall strategic concept, which directed our armed forces to "firmly cover the state border [and] not allow penetration of our territory by enemy forces...'" was changed [...] and the Czechoslovak People's Army was assigned an active task."[3]

[...]

The supreme commander in a rather peremptory manner usually decides the size and composition of forces. The member-states, without knowing the actual requirements, are not in a position to completely justify their proposals. And this is the way the share of each country in the common measures that are taken is determined. These are measures that not only are vital for the defense of the country and the entire bloc, but also influence fundamentally the methods and possibilities for the further development of socialist society—all this without proper evaluation and decision by the respective party and government.

[...]

All documents concerning the rights and duties of the supreme commander show clearly that he has the right to directly command and suggest different measures only to the troops assigned to the Unified Armed Forces. Nevertheless, at numerous talks, he has exceeded his authority by making decisions on the development of all our [Czechoslovak] armed forces. For instance, during negotiations in Moscow on February 1–3, 1960, the supreme commander emphasized that the Unified Command " ... insists that 16 all-purpose divisions be formed during a war." At that time, however, the ČSSR had only 11 divisions assigned to the Unified Armed Forces.

This shows that the supreme commander is interested (and perhaps rightly so) in the overall capacities of the country during war; however, his duties and the duties of his staff in war time have never been formalized.

II.

[...]

Before starting to work on a draft specifying the role and responsibilities of both the Political Consultative Committee and the Staff of the Unified Armed Forces, it is necessary to answer unambiguously the question of what would be expected from both of these bodies in war time.

The point is to decide whether in war time the Supreme Commander and his staff would constitute the command headquarters of the Unified Armed Forces of the Warsaw Treaty, or whether this function would be performed by someone else (for instance, by the Soviet Army General Staff directly). Only after this question has been answered is it possible to discuss what competencies this organ [the Supreme Commander and his staff] should have in peace time.

[Source: GŠ-OS, 1966, 0039042/1, VÚA. Translated by Marian J. Kratochvíl.]

---

[3] The reference is to an offensive operation.

Document No. 36: Statement by the Romanian Chief of Staff on Reform of the Warsaw Pact, February 4–9, 1966

The controversies over Warsaw Pact reorganization, revealed in the previous several documents, were the most fundamental the alliance faced in the latter 1960s. Of the various forums for hammering out these issues, perhaps the most important were the meetings at the deputy level of the defense and foreign ministries. This record from a meeting of Warsaw Pact chiefs of staff—who simultaneously served as deputy ministers of defense—is representative of the kinds of working-level sessions that focused primarily on military affairs. (See Document No. 37 for an analogous record of discussions in the political sphere.) Of particular interest is the detailed exposition of the Romanian viewpoint, which shows that Bucharest's aim was its complete independence in deciding its own military issues, and simultaneously reducing the powers of any Warsaw Pact agencies to the minimum. Even in case of an attack on the alliance, Romania reserved the right to decide whether and under what conditions its forces should enter the conflict. The Romanians also insisted that their armed forces should not be subject to inspection by the Warsaw Pact, and furthermore that no permanent representatives of the supreme commander should be installed on Romanian territory. To further complicate matters for Moscow, by insisting on the principle of unanimity the Romanians claimed the right to veto any Warsaw Pact decisions. Each of these rights they claimed not only for themselves but for all member-states. Not surprisingly, a sharp discussion ensued, and the meeting finally ended without an agreement—much to the consternation of the Soviets.

[...]

The principles of the statute [of the Unified Command] are obviously contradictory to the principles of cooperation and mutual assistance, based on sovereignty, national independence, and nonintervention in internal affairs. [These principles] are embodied in the treaty and concern substantial rights held by our governments. All these regulations, as well as their application, would make the supreme commander superior to the governments and transform the Supreme Command into a supranational body. [...]

[...]

Several examples to follow should demonstrate to what extent existing regulations contradict the provisions of the treaty. In 1961, during the Berlin events, the Supreme Commander, without consulting us, ordered that certain measures be adopted to increase the combat readiness of our country. These included, for example: mobilization of certain units and corps, which resulted in a temporary increase in force levels of 12,000 troops; exercises by armed forces and staffs; the redeployment of some units from their garrisons to other areas; etc.

Similar measures were applied during the Cuban crisis, too. Without any preliminary consultation with the defense minister, without any consent by the national governments of the Warsaw Treaty signatories with respect to Art. 4 of the treaty, the supreme commander issued an order to increase the combat readiness of troops assigned to the Unified Armed Forces. The governments of the treaty signatories thus confronted a situation that could well have resulted in a state of war without the ability to make proper decisions as supreme bodies exercising executive power.

[...]

The lack of consultations was manifested even during certain joint exercises led by the Unified Command—for instance during the 1962 exercise in Hungary, or the 1963 exercise in Bulgaria. Although our command and our troops participated, the Romanian Ministry of Armed Forces had not been consulted; the Ministry did not participate in elaborating the exercise's goals, planning concepts, or reconnaissance, or in the preparation of [after-action] assessments.

[...] We maintain that the statute and other relevant documents which regulate command and staff activities must be in compliance with the treaty and with organizational principles of relations between the socialist states.

Comrades!

In view of this, our delegation shall present certain proposals, which concern issues crucial to Supreme Command activities:

1. The statute and other documents, which define the duties of this Command, must follow the principle, according to which the party and government of each country, exclusively, are fully responsible for the command, organization, armament and preparedness of all [that country's] armed forces, both in peace and in war time.

2. With the intention to improve the organization of the Unified Command, to ensure the participation of representatives of all Warsaw Treaty signatory states in [the Pact's] activities, we propose the formation of a Unified Command Military Council. The Council shall be constituted as a body empowered to adopt decisions on the principle of [unanimous] consent. The Military Council shall judge which issues are under the competence of the Command. The Military Council should include the supreme commander as its chairman, along with his deputies and chief of staff as its members. Its motions and decisions shall be subject to approval by the governments of the treaty signatories. [...]

3. [...] All plans, documents, activities and measures resulting from this appointment may be implemented only after their approval by the governments of the Warsaw Treaty signatories.

4. In compliance with Art. 5 of the treaty, each country shall assign the forces that will carry on the joint activities, following the consent of the signatories. The coordination and engagement of these forces must be stipulated precisely by rules approved by the Warsaw Treaty signatories. Their engagement in war may be decided exclusively by the country to which these forces belong, while the national commands are charged with their command. [...]

[Source: GŠ-OS, 1966, 0039042/19, VÚA. Translated by Marian J. Kratochvíl.]

Document No. 37: Summary of Discussion at Conference of Warsaw Treaty Deputy Foreign Ministers, February 17, 1966

As the previous document description indicates, Warsaw Pact officials at the deputy minister level carried out some of the most crucial work involving such highly contentious issues as Warsaw Pact reorganization. This deputy foreign ministers' meeting, held in Berlin, was a forum for hashing out the various political counter-proposals presented by the East European member-states. Hungarian and German records of the session also exist, but the Polish version is the most informative.

Soviet Deputy Foreign Minister Leonid Ilichev opened the session with a speech that acknowledged the need to improve Warsaw Pact organization. On one of the key issues of debate—whether to create a secretariat and in what form—the Soviets favored its establishment as a permanent body but wanted to limit its role to handling technical matters, such as preparing for meetings, rather than deliberating over substantive political issues—the function filled by NATO's Secretariat.

The Romanian presentation made for a fascinating counterpoint. Emphasizing the principles of sovereignty and noninterference, Deputy Foreign Minister Mircea Maliţa invoked the danger of the PCC becoming a supranational organ that would usurp the powers of national governments (implicitly in favor of the Soviets). He argued that the current requirement that participation at PCC meetings should be at the very highest levels was too inflexible and had led directly to the elimination of Albania as a member because of its government's refusal to send party leader Enver Hoxha. (Romania wanted the Albanians to be reinstated, so that it would gain another ally against the Soviets.) In these and other respects as well, Romania's views contradicted those of other East European members. Eventually, the Soviets, East Germans and Poles caucused in an attempt to break the deadlock created by the Romanian representative. But the move fell short, and the meeting failed to produce the unanimity necessary for passing a concluding resolution.

[...]

I.

The point of the talks was to strengthen and improve the structure and mechanisms of the Warsaw Treaty.

In the first phase of talks, the Romanian delegation already disagreed with this formulation of the session agenda. It [Romanian delegation] requested limiting [the formulation] to "exchanging ideas on the matter of improving methods of consultation between member-states of the Warsaw Treaty," arguing that it [Romania] is authorized only to discuss matters involving the work of the Political Consultative Committee.

[...]

II.

The PPR delegation presented the view [...] that in accordance with specifications established during the meeting at Comrade Premier's [Józef Cyrankiewicz's], we did not bring up the concept of establishing a Treaty Council and reducing the Consultative Committee to the role implied in its name. However, we presented a view [...] [in favor of] establishing a permanent Council or a Committee of Foreign Ministers, which would convene not less than twice a year. [...]

The Ministers Council or Committee would convene as needed at the minister's or deputy's level, would be a support institution for the Consultative Committee, and would have a consultative character.

[...]

III.

The stance of Romanian delegation:

1. The party and government leaderships of all states are responsible for their own foreign policy, therefore we should respect the principles of sovereignty and equality and not interfere in the internal affairs of other countries.

2. Consultation, based on the rules specified in the Treaty itself, is a proper form of cooperation between member-states of the Warsaw Treaty.

3. The system of consultation within the framework of the Political Consultative Committee should be improved, especially when it comes to steps which may involve the interests and obligations of other member-states of the Treaty.

Because of that, the Romanian delegate reminded [us] that matters as important as the introduction of missiles to Cuba, a program of universal and complete disarmament, and lately the draft of a treaty on non-proliferation of nuclear weapons required prior consultation.

Consultations do not limit the rights of states to take initiatives in foreign policy.

[...]

4. [...]

5. [...]

6. The Romanian delegation opposes the establishment of a rigid frame of reference for the Political Consultative Committee and defining its statute or regulations.

7. In the past, the Political Consultative Committee has exceeded its competences as a consultative institution. It has done so by making decisions on certain political and military issues. [...]

The representative of Romania, in his presentations, consistently repeated the view he presented previously. It was obvious that he had been given very inflexible and specific instructions.

8. In this situation it became clear that reaching any kind of agreement was not possible.

[...]

[...] During the session, the chairman (GDR) acting on "quiet" suggestions from the USSR proposed accepting a formal protocol. But the Romanian delegate did not even agree to include a sentence [in the protocol] about the need for further exchange of views on the matters discussed previously. At a meeting initiated during a break, the chiefs of delegations engaged in a quite dramatic exchange of words. The Romanian was urged not to close the door to the prospect of continued discussion about such a loosely formulated proposal. He declined, pleading a lack of mandate.

[...]

The Romanian arguments were spurious and some were even ludicrous (i.e. the supposed lack of authority of foreign ministers to participate in the activities of the proposed Committee of Ministers). An analysis of those arguments leads to an evident conclusion—that they were pretexts.

The real motives behind Romania's stance—with an incessant emphasis on the necessity of consultations and with a peculiar understanding of the principle of sovereignty—were: ensuring for itself full freedom of conduct, not committing itself to any new organizational ties, and attempting to loosen existing ties. The Romanians strive to paralyze the Treaty and transform its institutions into non-committal discussion clubs. The present session showed further undesirable evolution of the Romanian position.

* * *

In view of the situation that had been unfolding for some time, I raised—on behalf of our leadership—the following matter during a talk with Cde. [Leonid] Ilichev after the conclusion of the session: without doing anything that could weaken the Warsaw Treaty from our side, it would be wise to think about concentrating efforts to coordinate the activities of the four states most interested in this matter—due to their geographic position— (the USSR, Poland, Czechoslovakia, and the GDR).

More frequent consultations between these states regarding the problems of European security could lead to the establishment of a regional pact of the four, within the framework of the Warsaw Treaty. I have emphasized that so far this is only a preliminary consideration at the level of the Ministry of Foreign Affairs.

The Soviet comrades considered the matter with great attention, and have declared that they will refer it to their leadership.

M[arian] Naszkowski

[*Source: KC PZPR, 2948, pp. 64–69. Translated by Magdalena Klotzbach for the National Security Archive.*]

Document No. 38: Study of Special Features of a Surprise Outbreak of War Prepared for the Hungarian Military, February 22–23, 1966

This document is rare among the publicly available materials dealing with the possible consequences of a Western nuclear strike. Its unusual aspect is in the admission that there is really no defense against such a strike. The text does not say this outright but clearly indicates there is no realistic possibility of defense. The authors of the study predict that Western-launched Polaris missiles would reach Hungary in 8–10 minutes. Some 20–30 minutes later, tactical air force strikes would ensue, followed some six hours later by strategic bombers taking off from the United States. Local air defenses, particularly fighter aircraft flying at twice the speed of sound, would be partially successful but unable entirely to repel such a large-scale assault.

[...]

With the simultaneous launching of air and space-based attacks, the first manifestation over Hungarian air space may be of Polaris-type ballistic missiles, 8–10 minutes after their launching from submarines patrolling in the Mediterranean. Some 20–30 minutes later—after take-off—strike forces of tactical aircraft (belonging to the 4th and 5th Allied Tactical Air Headquarters) and 1.5–2 hours later, tactical bombers located in Europe (Spain) may reach the borders of the country. Some 6–8 hours after take-off, we can expect strikes by strategic bombers taking off from United States territory and the return of the tactical aircraft participating in the action.

[...]

Our air-defense forces (airborne missile defense units and fighter planes) will be able to destroy the enemy's means of air attack, flying at 1.7–2 times the speed of sound, from altitudes of 500 m and lower up to 27,000 m, at any time of year or day.

Radar units will be able to detect the means of air attack at 60–70 km distance from the country's borders at altitudes of 500 m, and at 200–250 km at altitudes of 16,000 m. This detection potential (assuming 960 km/h as the cruising speed) means that air targets are detected about 4 minutes before they reach the borders of the country if they are flying at low altitudes, and 13–15 minutes beforehand at high altitudes.

[...]

Detection of intercontinental ballistic missiles by the reconnaissance facilities of the Unified Air-defense Headquarters will probably take place 25 minutes before impact, in case of a trajectory of about 10,000 km. At this time, there may still be 9–10 minutes left before the launching of Polaris-type missiles and the take-off of tactical aircraft. The Polaris can be expected to appear 17–20 minutes later (counting 8–10 minutes flying time). Some 10–15 minutes after impact, NATO tactical aircraft will reach the furthest limit of detection by the Hungarian People's Army's radar (assuming a distance of 350–450 km, traveling at speeds of 960 km/h and low altitude.)

[...]

Under the most unfavorable conditions described, with no prior indication that the enemy is preparing for combat, and when therefore preliminary regulations cannot be implemented, the command post of the national air-defense troops will be able to raise the alarm for the Hungarian People's Army and notify Civil Defense and participating air-defense forces about 15–20 minutes before the Polaris missiles land.

[...]

It can be concluded that there is only partial provision for fending off the first massive strike by the enemy in the event of a complete surprise [attack]. With respect to tactical aircraft, many more air targets can be expected within 20–30 minutes than the means in place will be able to repulse.

[*Source: 68/014/186, pp. 19–31, War History Archives, Budapest. Translated by Attila Kolontári, Zsófia Zelnik, and Brian McLaine.*]

Document No. 39: Memorandum of the Conference of Defense Ministers, May 27–28, 1966

After two earlier meetings of Warsaw Pact deputy defense ministers and deputy foreign ministers had ended in deadlock (Document Nos. 36 and 37), Moscow communicated informally with some of its allies, particularly the Poles, to make them come up with generally acceptable proposals for reorganizing the alliance. The main obstacle, of course, was the Romanians, who had previously raised a variety of challenges to the Soviet position. This document records a subsequent meeting of the Pact's defense ministers where the new proposals were discussed in an attempt to find a compromise. Among other points of interest, it gives a more detailed sense of the differing perspectives of the East European partners. The Poles had helped draft the proposals. The Hungarians for the most part agreed to them, while the East German, Bulgarian and Czechoslovak ministers had little of substance to add. However, the Romanians refused to budge. Although some progress was eventually made, the participants failed to come up with a final resolution. The dispute over reorganization of the alliance continued through the late 1960s.

[...]

On May 27–28, 1966, a conference of army representatives from the member-states of the Warsaw Treaty was held, at the level of Defense Ministers, in Moscow. It was dedicated to jurisdictional and organizational matters and enhancement of the work of military institutions of the Warsaw Treaty. [...]

[...]

Basically all comments made by the Polish side during both the period preceding it and during the conference deserve emphasis, but especially:

- currently accepting as fundamental the organizational structure of the main military institutions of the Unified Armed Forces with a reduced number of participants (about 200 people);
- establishing an appropriate share for each country in the composition of the main military institutions of the Unified Armed Forces and their budget (with 13.5 percent of Polish contribution it will be approximately 500,000–600,000 rubles annually);
- accepting the formulation which grants the General Staff of the Soviet Army the power, to present appropriate proposals for planning the operational use of forces instead of giving recommendations to defense ministers and general staffs;
- from the decision about the deployment of national forces to the Unified Armed Forces, removing the formulation [which states] that it covers the entire force of every country.

[...]

The Bulgarian, German, and Czechoslovak delegations, while fully approving the draft documents, basically did not make remarks of substantial significance.

Also the Hungarian delegation, in general, approved the discussed drafts. However, by raising quite numerous, but not very precise observations on details during the first phase of the conference, it introduced non-constructive elements to the discussion, and by doing so made it easier for the Romanian delegation to increase the number of its reservations.

[...]

In a sense it was to the surprise of the Soviet hosts, who as a result of talks held recently at the highest political level and working contacts, expected much fewer objections of the Romanian side.

The Romanian stance on the following issues deserves special attention:

- questioning every decision of the statute draft in which the Political Consultative Committee is mentioned, and demanding that only the government institution act in all these instances. The Romanian delegation, while negating previous practice based on the spirit of the protocol to the Warsaw Treaty from May 14, 1955, expressed the view that the Political Consultative Committee cannot be a political institution with the right to resolve mutually established general problems concerning the defensive capabilities of member-states of the Warsaw Treaty.

  Taking into consideration their inflexibility and persistence on this issue as well as the emphasis placed on the significance of the problem that should be resolved on an appropriate level, one can anticipate that the Romanian side will attempt to lower the standing and powers of the Political Consultative Committee, and possibly even question the existence of this type of institution.

- disagreeing with the establishment of the Military Consultative Council composed of defense ministers from individual states and the supreme commander of the Unified Armed Forces, and demanding the establishment of a military council for the Supreme Command, the composition of which would include the supreme commander and his national deputies.

  In this situation, based on a petition from the Soviet side, a compromise solution was reached, which assumed that instead of establishing a Military Consultative Council, meetings of Warsaw Treaty defense ministers would be convened as needed. Despite this concession, it was impossible to persuade the Romanian delegation that there was no purpose in establishing a military council for the Supreme Command. Despite that, the Romanian delegation no longer considers the council to be a decision-making institution but a consultative one. [The Romanians'] consistency regarding this matter, as well as certain remarks made about the competences of the supreme commander, allow for speculation that the underlying reasons are to restrain his authority and the possibility of carrying out individual work.

- categorical opposition to the existence of institutions for permanent representatives of the supreme commander which would be attached to individual armies. The Romanian side was not satisfied even with the proposed formulation that these representatives would only be attached to the armies of those states that considered it necessary. The obvious attempt to impose a unilateral stance on other delegations prompted a wide-ranging discussion, during which the defense ministers appealed to the Romanian delegation to accept the proposal for a fully flexible formulation. After their appeal failed, the chairman of the Polish delegation considered it appropriate to point out the gist of the problem by stating that the Romanian delegation wanted to introduce the principle that the stance of one Treaty member-state should apply to all members. However, in our understanding, genuine democracy in inter-allied cooperation gives the right to not accept a specific solution by a partner who does not accept it; in no circumstances should this limit the rights of the remaining [partners] to accept decisions which they agree with, or which undermine elements of our mutual defense.

In light of this thesis, it was decided that the Romanian side will present its particular stance on this matter as well as on two previously discussed issues in a special appendix to the protocol.

[…]

[*Source: KC PZPR, 2663, pp. 234–39, Archiwum Akt Nowych. Translated by Magdalena Klotzbach for the National Security Archive.*]

Document No. 40: Memorandum of the Conference
of Foreign Ministers, June 14–15, 1966

Because of the lack of consensus on how to improve the functioning of the Warsaw Pact, the Soviets decided to shelve the issue temporarily in order to focus on other pressing matters at the important foreign ministers' conference recorded here. One priority was the question of a conference on European security. The Soviets had prepared a declaration on the subject but had not been able to build a consensus among the partners. At this meeting, the issue became intermingled with reform of the Warsaw Pact when Soviet Foreign Minister Gromyko submitted a draft declaration on European security and the Romanians responded with the demand to add several paragraphs on contentious matters such as the withdrawal of foreign troops. A related dispute arose over Romania's insistence that any statement avoid strong condemnation of West Germany, with which Bucharest was about to establish diplomatic relations. This predictably angered the East Germans, who only backed down after the Soviets warned them not to press the issue. Moscow wanted to ensure at least a modicum of agreement among the partners. Other sharp differences surfaced, for example, between the Romanians and the Poles, and according to different accounts the Soviets, though firm at first, later went to considerable lengths in trying to forge a compromise. In the end, Romanian intransigence once again determined the outcome, and a final resolution on substantive issues was put off until the meeting of the PCC in early July.

---

a) Session of June 14

[...] Many specific proposals for the improvement of the Warsaw Treaty organization could not be discussed in detail since the Romanians took a negative stance towards the institutionalization of the Treaty, which the six remaining delegations saw as a way to increase its effectiveness.

[...] Romanian delegate Cde. [Corneliu] Mănescu: [...] We have carefully studied the proposals of our German comrades. We have also concluded that the GDR intends to renegotiate the issues that had already been dealt with in Berlin. The views of individual delegations are already well known after the exchange of opinions that took place in Berlin. Therefore, I do not intend to go into detail on our standpoint here. I only wish to mention some principal considerations.

The GDR proposal no longer mentions the Political Consultative Committee (PCC) Statute; instead, it states the necessity of creating fundamental norms for PCC activity. Cde. [Mircea] Maliţa's arguments against adoption of the Statute as presented in Berlin correspond in full with those against the so-called fundamental norms. The term is not important; what is important is the proposal to modify PCC activities. We do not consider it an effective or necessary step. The institutional framework formed by means of these fundamental norms would not comply with the

Warsaw Treaty, since its consultative character would be impaired. We are convinced that the PCC can be successful under conditions of strict adherence to the principles and all provisions of the Warsaw Treaty. This should form the basis of relations among the socialist states.

The GDR proposal brings us to a reconsideration of the issue concerning the representation of countries at PCC meetings. We maintain that every country should be represented at PCC meetings on a level, which would be agreed upon during the preliminary consultations with respect to the nature of the topics to be discussed. Each state is entitled to decide independently at what level it would be represented at [a particular] PCC meeting. To adopt the rule that PCC meetings must be attended by first secretaries and prime ministers would be contradictory to Article 6 of the Treaty.

We have already mentioned that we do not agree with the establishment of a Permanent Commission on Foreign Political Affairs as a PCC auxiliary body. We are in favor of consultations among the foreign ministers or consultations on the occasion of various international conferences; we do not consider it necessary to constitute a Permanent Commission from the participants at these consultations, however. The introduction of organizational rules for our consultations would result in a loss of flexibility and operational spirit. The fact is that during the past ten years our mutual consultations have been carried out informally, not within the framework of a Permanent Commission. This demonstrates that there is no need to establish such a body.

So far as the Secretariat is concerned, Romania suggests a Technical Secretariat with an exclusively technical character. Its staff should consist of a few persons only. On technical matters, the Secretariat will cooperate with the Ministry of Foreign Affairs of the country that would be hosting the forthcoming PCC meeting. The Secretariat should distribute a preliminary draft of the conference agenda, plus relevant materials for the forthcoming session. We do not consider it expedient to form a joint Secretariat.

Finally, let me point out that, in our opinion, an essential precondition for cooperation is acknowledgement of the principle, according to which the leadership of each country should elaborate and manage its foreign policy, take necessary measures and bear full responsibility for them. As to mutual consultations among the Treaty signatories, their forms may differ both in manner of these consultations and in their content. Be it issues of foreign policy or of the military, any subsequent consultations may only follow a joint agreement of the states concerned.

[...] The USSR Minister of Foreign Affairs Cde. A[ndrei A.] Gromyko pointed out that our conference was dealing with important issues. He stated that the current situation would be rather precarious if any of the participants believed that nothing needed to be done. The importance of issues connected with Warsaw Treaty Organization activities is greater since many of them have not been regulated yet. No rules have been set so far for PCC activities; no auxiliary PCC bodies have been constituted yet. [...]

The activities of the PCC are not organized. It is not expedient to arrange every single PCC meeting in advance. If there is no unity on convening a meeting, none will be convened. Then, a situation may arise which calls for a debate on urgent issues, but because of disagreement about the level of representation, the PCC would not be able to discuss these issues. Political issues would thus become subordinated to organizational ones. A certain kind of order must be adopted that would be acceptable to everyone.

[...] For the sake of efficiency, the PCC should make decisions. Should the PCC meetings confine themselves to an exchange of opinion, PCC activity would not be effective. Since there are different opinions about this matter there is all the more reason to try to find common ground. I would like to point out NATO practices. Their people continue to try hard to make organizational matters clear. They are obviously after different political goals; nevertheless their organization scheme works automatically. I will not call for mimicking their practices; we should realize, however, that the Western leaders are not their own enemies. If their organizational measures were of no use to them, they would have dropped them long ago.

There are no regulations concerning the activities of PCC auxiliary bodies either. A resolution was adopted to constitute the Permanent Commission on Foreign Political Affairs; the Commission does not operate, however. There was an opinion voiced that an institution would not be necessary; mere consultations would do just as well. These consultations have not taken place until now. Apparently, if there is no appropriate institution, [its absence] has consequences. True, the consultations may be conducted bilaterally. There are issues, however, that are of interest to everyone. Should these be negotiated bilaterally between the signatory states, it would be rather clumsy. How many days have we been working here and no agreement on the final document has been reached so far? For instance, if this document were to be negotiated bilaterally it would be impossible to reach an agreement.

We must act more flexibly. The present state of affairs cannot be called a flexible one; on the contrary, it contradicts effectiveness. That concerns the entire Warsaw Treaty mechanism. The better we fix the issues resulting from the situation, the better our organization will function in the organizational sense and the more effective will be our results. This is how we understand effectiveness and flexibility.

The GDR proposal corresponds with these goals. Some fine-tuning of this proposal may perhaps be needed; if we want to act more effectively, however, no objections should be raised against it. This is no attempt to impair the sovereign rights of the states. Everything proposed here is fully compatible with state sovereignty.

So far as the Secretariat is concerned, we understand that this body cannot assume more powers than it is given by the PCC. It seems to me that we have reached a certain degree of mutual understanding on this issue. Let us try to find, therefore, a common language on this issue.

Comrade Gromyko finally expressed his hope that the Romanian comrades would review their position and agree with our opinion, according to which certain organizational forms must be found that would improve the effectiveness of Warsaw Treaty activities. The GDR proposal serves a useful objective. It is not a question for us having to agree on either everything or on nothing. [...]

Comrade Mănescu was the next to speak. He said: [...] The speeches of other speakers included remarks on our standpoint. I suppose therefore that matters have not been made completely clear yet. That is why I want to come back to certain points in order to explain our standpoint thoroughly.

Concerning the level of representation at PCC meetings, we quoted Article 6 of the Warsaw Treaty. According to this article, every state may be represented at PCC consultations by any person whose appointment is deemed expedient, from the [party] first secretary and premier down to any other representative. We do not exclude [the possibility] that states shall be represented by their first secretaries and/or prime ministers. We maintain, however, that this level of representation should not be an exclusive one. We received a reply, which we do not agree with: the Warsaw Treaty provisions must not be interpreted rigidly. I repeat again that on this issue we stick strictly to the provisions of Article 6 of the Treaty.

[...] We repeat again that the PCC is a consultative body, not a decision-making body. The letter and spirit of the Warsaw Treaty clearly give the PCC the character of a consultative body.

[...] The Polish representative, Comrade [Marian] Naszkowski [...] suggested that the delegations think over once again the proposals that have been submitted, as well as the views expressed. A working group should be formed to confirm the points that have already been agreed upon. [...]

A shorter discussion followed with the participation of Comrades Gromyko, Naszkowski, Bashev and Mănescu. It was agreed that the working group would include representatives of all delegations. Its work will commence after lunch. [...]

b) Session of June 15

[...] Comrade Gromyko referred to the tabled material, which in fact reveals the extent of our disagreement on many highly important issues. The material demonstrates how different the conceptions of the tasks and mechanism of the Warsaw Treaty are. [...] We have not made a single step forward in our work [said Gromyko].

Nothing is said in the material about a Commission of Ministers of Foreign Affairs. But this is an issue of importance. It is not the title that matters but actual consultations among foreign ministers.

As to the Secretariat, the resolution has been adopted already. Even if we adopt the idea of a Technical Secretariat, the former resolution remains valid. It would be wrong not to respect our own resolutions. We agree, however, to constitute a smaller Technical Secretariat, although this does not solve the problem. Maybe we shall agree upon a larger secretariat later. [...]

Comrade Mănescu spoke next. He stated: All our delegations had their representatives in the working group. The group compiled a list of issues on which there was agreement. The document also reveals concessions, which the respective delegations made during negotiations. Now, it seems that the agreed issues are being repudiated.[...]

As to the 1956 resolutions,[4] I repeat again that these issues remained open for 10 years. We ask why the resolutions were not implemented in 1956, 1957, or in 1958.

---

[4] Resolutions of the first PCC meeting providing for the creation of additional institutions.

In our opinion, the reason was that life had shown that these resolutions were unnecessary. We solemnly declare that we value the improvement of Warsaw Treaty activities. However, we have in mind improvement based on strict adherence to the articles of the Treaty.

An issue has arisen here as to whether the document should emphasize the necessity of consultations. I have nothing to add except for what is [already] included in Article 6. This article clearly deals with consultations as well as with the level of representation at PCC meetings. There is no other document, which would deal with these issues. That implies that an improvement of activity would be possible if based on adherence to the Treaty and its consultative character. Creating a decision-making body would bring no improvement.

As to the further process, either the working group shall set about their work, or draft an agreement as intended by Comrade [Václav] David.[5] The Romanian delegation is in favor of the second option.

Comrade Gromyko replied, stating that adherence to the Treaty was beyond any discussion. However, Article 6 includes a provision according to which the PCC may constitute its auxiliary bodies. A resolution was adopted calling for the constitution of two auxiliary bodies. That is in accord with the Treaty. Therefore, we are much more in favor of adhering to the Treaty, including the resolutions that had been adopted on its basis. It seems that the Romanian delegation does not doubt that the Permanent Commission and Joint Secretariat are PCC auxiliary bodies. In view of that, their standpoint is [rather] inconsistent. [...]

Comrade Gromyko came back to the issue of the Permanent Commission. He pointed out that the Romanian delegation was against the Permanent Commission on the one hand, while nobody was against consultations on the other hand. All of us feel the necessity for consultations. The protocol might include, therefore, [a provision] that the foreign ministers would meet regularly twice a year, or else upon request of any [signatory] country, without constituting any kind of body.

Comrade Mănescu rejected this proposal, having pointed out Article 3 of the Treaty where consultations among its signatories were described in a comprehensive fashion.

Comrade Gromyko replied that Article 3 did not cover in full all forms of these consultations. Among the most effective ones, he included personal contacts.

Comrade Mănescu stressed that the Romanian delegation was not renouncing consultations, but wanted them to observe previously existing patterns. Or, their form may be negotiated on a case-by-case basis. Comrade Bashev then suggested that the protocol could simply include a statement to the effect that the foreign ministers agreed, in accordance with Article 3, to meet regularly.

Comrade Mănescu repeated his point of view.

[...] The conference adjourned without any agreed-upon conclusions. [...]

[*Source: 0071/66, AMZV. Translated by Karel Sieber.*]

---

[5] Czechoslovak Minister of Foreign Affairs.

Document No. 41: Minutes of Summit of Warsaw Pact Leaders in Bucharest, July 5–7, 1966

After a series of unproductive meetings of the allies, this PCC session finally produced agreement on certain issues important to the Soviets. The relatively free-wheeling discussion prompted a senior Romanian official to later comment that this was the first high-level gathering where widely divergent views were both discussed and accepted. The issue of Vietnam prompted loud arguments between the Soviets, Romanians and Poles. At one point, Brezhnev became so upset at Ceauşescu —who had proposed 20 separate amendments to a Soviet declaration on the Vietnam War—that he threatened to sign the document even without Romania. Ceauşescu retorted that he would then publish his own declaration. Eventually the Poles and the Romanians agreed to remove some of their revisions and the document was finally signed.

Another major topic was European security. Again, the sides managed to reach a compromise that incorporated Romania's calls for the removal of foreign troops and bases and the dissolution of military blocs. The final agreement, the so-called Bucharest Declaration, did not invite United States participation in a planned European security conference, but did not explicitly exclude it either. Other subjects discussed in Bucharest included principles of exchanging information among Warsaw Pact partners and relations with China, including a recent meeting between Ceauşescu and Chinese Premier Zhou Enlai.

Record of the Statements of the Delegation Chiefs at the
Unofficial Meeting of first Secretaries and Premiers of the
Governments of Member-States of the Warsaw Treaty.

[...]

Brezhnev: [...] This morning we had an exchange of opinions regarding the possible inclusion in the text of the Declaration of a formulation proposed by Cde. Novotný regarding the accountability of the United States for damages due to the aggressive activities of the U.S. The Soviet delegation supports this proposal. Such a formulation would include two ideas. First, that all of us together with the Vietnamese nation run a ledger regarding losses inflicted on Vietnamese cities, villages, and industrial facilities, etc. from American bombings. And that the world society together with the Vietnamese nation will present such a bill to the American government, to the American aggressors.

Second thought—that world public opinion will come out with a political accusation against the American aggressors as war instigators, similar to the case of the Second World War against the Hitlerites.

Novotný: Stating his proposition precisely, said: We present the bill for material and human losses.

Brezhnev: One does not present a bill for humans, there is no price for a human life. We can talk about accountability for war and material losses inflicted on Vietnam.

Ceauşescu: We can connect the first idea with the second, saying that the Americans should take responsibility as war instigators for crimes committed against the civilian population as was the case after the Second World War.

Brezhnev: One can exclude the DRV [Democratic Republic of Vietnam]—it is not conducting a war, it is defending itself. And that is why one should formulate this sharply.

[...]

Gomułka: It would be best if our document had a more concrete character. It should be in the form of a note rather than a resolution. Besides, I think that we should avoid a formulation such as "we are presenting a bill."

[...]

Ceauşescu: The declaration we adopt should be a very strong document, it cannot have the character of a diplomatic note. It should reflect the determined will of the socialist countries that sharply condemn American imperialism; it should demand an immediate condemnation of the aggression. If they continue their aggressive activities we will also be obliged to take other steps.

As far as the matter of solidarity with Vietnam, it must be an appeal to all governments of the world and to democratic movements, so they develop a broad movement in defense of Vietnam. This meets the Vietnamese comrades' plea and the appeal of the National Liberation Front published today, which called on socialist countries to support Vietnam.If we did not publish such a declaration, the world would not understand why the party first secretaries and government premiers assembled. This has meaning not only for Vietnam. This will be an expression of our decisiveness also toward the German problem and generally to world problems. After all, it is the first time in a long time that the representatives of seven socialist countries have assembled in order to adopt a statement regarding a serious matter. And here one does not need a diplomatic note; a note can be sent and we do not need to assemble for that purpose. This is not what the international communist movement awaits, but a statement that will be a help to it.

[...]

Gomułka: [...] We are in favor of a most determined, sharp, powerful, and concrete document. And that is why we think that it should not be in the form of a resolution such as one adopts during rallies or in the form of a newspaper article. [...] Here I have the latest Chinese statement in front of me. To make no mention of its content, I think it serves as an example of how one should write such a statement [...] I am not assuming a position toward it, but the form is good and we should give our Declaration a Chinese form, but put our content [in it].

[...]

Ulbricht: [...] The statement we adopt here will have particular meaning for both German nations. It should help us to strengthen the protest movement in the FRG against support for American imperialism. We agree with the proposal of Cde. Brezhnev and Cde. Novotný: let the editorial board work on the statement draft; it will be easier for us to discuss a concrete text.

Ceaușescu: I am sorry that I am speaking for the second time, but because Cde. Gomułka expressed himself regarding the Romanian proposal in the form that he did, I want to say that I do not share his opinion. We did not want to evaluate a Polish proposal, we also have our opinion about it, but we did not gather here to mutually evaluate our drafts. (Gomułka: I do not claim that our proposal should be deemed the best one since we had only two hours to work on this project). But, if we were, at least, to take the last three points of the Polish draft, then this is contrary to our [...]; one could understand this as capitulation to American imperialism. [...]

Gomułka: [...] I would also not be forced to speak again if Cde. Ceaușescu would not force me to it due to his statement in which he evaluated the stance of our CC, our party and government, included in the Polish draft, as capitulationist. We categorically reject this. With what right, on what basis, does Cde. Ceaușescu insinuate such an assessment that we are calling for capitulation to American imperialism?! Toward American aggression? Our party, government, and people have never capitulated to American or any other imperialism.

[...]

Did we insult you, because you [should] tell us that what I said is not acceptable to you? Speaking of your draft of the Statement we did not assess the position of your CC, or your government; we only talked about the tone of the document. I called it a "rally resolution" and I expressed our opinion that the document should be more concrete, [there should be] a more serious format and that is why I talked about the [form of the] note. What is insulting about that? And you insulted me. To say that a party like ours, the government and the Polish people, capitulates to American aggression—this is insulting to us! Surely, Cde. Ceaușescu, as the host of the meeting, has not learned how to conduct talks in such circles as he has managed to assess our party, our nation, in this way. And I hereby declare an official protest against such formulations of Cde. Ceaușescu—that we are capitulating to American aggression!

[...]

Ceaușescu: I would like to say to Cde. Gomułka that it surprises me that from the discussion of a concrete document it has come around to discussion of the position of the PUWP. This is not the subject of our negotiations and when Cde. Gomułka was talking about our draft, I understood that he was not talking about the position of our party. If that were the case, I would approach things differently.

But if one side condemns a document, then in turn, it should listen to the opinion of the other side about its draft. Cde. Gomułka also characterized our draft in a form that is unacceptable to us.

Gomułka: We characterized your draft as a rally resolution and you as us capitulating before the Americans. We did not insult you, but you insulted us.

Brezhnev: I think that we should respect our resolutions. Yesterday at the evening session [...] we came to an understanding that the ministers of foreign affairs will take all three drafts and will try to give the joint Declaration a more governmental character since seven countries are assembled [here]. [...] And this is the first thing which I wanted to say.

Second, [...] I would not like to start polemics with Cde. Ceaușescu, but when he mentioned capitulation it sounded like he was talking about the Polish party, and

Cde. Gomułka could have felt insulted. After all, we all know that the Polish party has never capitulated.

It appears from the statements of all comrades that such a document is needed, but do we need to ponder over whether this is to be a note or a statement right now? Would it perhaps be better if it were a Joint Statement addressed to governments?

Gomułka: I did speak for it to being in the form of a note.

[...]

Brezhnev: Cde. Ceaușescu brought up the matter possibly withdrawing from the 18-member Committee [...] His point is not a formal and documented withdrawal from the Committee, but a practical step.

Ceaușescu: [...] I consider it necessary that socialist countries participating in the work of the Disarmament Committee [in Geneva] no longer take part in this work until the American aggression in Vietnam is over. It is after all difficult to conduct discussions on disarmament when the war in Vietnam is being escalated at the same time.

This would have great political significance and it would show assertiveness and determination on the part of the socialist countries as well as positively influence other anti-American movements.

[...]

Novotný: This is a very important issue, which is not connected to the current conflict in Vietnam. One has to think. [...] Are we withdrawing from the Committee or are we stating that we will not be participating for now?

Ceaușescu: We would like to propose this formulation—that we will not participate.

Novotný: The point is not to play into their hands. Here the problem relates to Europe and borders, and since this is a new issue allow us to think about this, give us time to think and consult with the appropriate organs in our country. We may possibly come to an understanding to meet at an appropriate time and discuss this topic.

Gomułka: We are not prepared to discuss this issue. My personal opinion is that one cannot exclude the fact that such a situation may arise, but one has to wait for the results of our Declaration regarding the issue of European security because there is a certain contradiction here: on the one hand we are proposing steps towards disarmament, and at the same time we are leaving the Committee.

[...]

Brezhnev: One has to be reminded of the fact that in this Committee socialist and neutral countries comprise two-thirds, and the capitalist countries, on which we are exerting pressure, only one-third. If we leave the Committee, the neutral countries will be left without any help. (Kosygin: And after all, the Committee itself was created at our request.) And all of this has to be taken into account. And the most important is the situation at the present time, which as I said, we do not know in detail.

[...]

Ceaușescu: In principle, our government thinks it right not to participate in the work of the Committee any longer.

At this, the meeting of delegation heads ended deciding that the ministers will

228

gather once more on the same day and the results of their work will be presented at the meeting of first secretaries and government premiers.

The course of the evening meeting of the ministers was very short. [...]

The next day, July 6, 1966, at 7:30, the ministers assembled again having already before them a draft prepared by the Polish delegation which took into account the Polish remarks, both substantive and structural. Despite the fact that all delegations, except for the Romanian one, stated that the draft had been improved due to the Polish corrections, Minister Mănescu nevertheless stated that this was an entirely new draft, this time a Polish one, and he demanded that one be worked out based on the previous draft.

In this situation, [Foreign] Minister [Adam] Rapacki stated that he did not see any possibility of continuing this meeting of the ministers. Further discussion did not change the view of the Romanians and the ministers found themselves at an impasse, about which each delegation informed its leadership.

2. Meeting of the delegation chiefs regarding CMEA—July 6, 1966, 10:00.

[...]

3. Meeting of delegation chiefs regarding the Statement on Vietnam: July 6, 1966, 11:30.

Texts of the statement were distributed at the beginning.

a) A text worked out on July 5 as a combination of the Russian and Romanian draft.

b) A text based on the above-mentioned draft, but including Polish corrections.

Ulbricht: [...] We gathered here in order to reach understanding on the issue of the statement on Vietnam. The meeting of the ministers, which found itself at an impasse, was chaired by Minister János Péter. I will ask him to inform us about the state of the work on the joint draft.

Péter: [...] In connection with the quarrel over procedures our work was interrupted. The quarrel over procedures boiled down to the following points: before yesterday the Working Committee, appointed by the ministers, had prepared a draft document for the ministers. The ministers submitted a series of remarks, which were included in the document in writing. The remarks were submitted in part by the Romanian comrades and in part by the Polish comrades. In addition, some ministers of foreign affairs warned that they had a series of comments on this draft.

This morning, the Polish comrades prepared a new draft taking into account all proposals. And one must say that indeed all the proposals were included in this draft: both the remarks submitted in writing yesterday by the Romanians and Poles as well as the wishes of the Vietnamese comrades. Also, what was discussed yesterday at the plenary session was also included. The six ministers of foreign affairs acknowledged that a new document should serve as the basis. [...] Cde. Mănescu, the minister of foreign affairs of Romania, insisted that yesterday's draft be adopted as a basis.

[...] Therefore, our work found itself at a dead end.

[...]

Novotný: Cde. Péter stated that this is a new draft. I read the previous draft and I think that the formulation "new" does not correspond with reality. This is a further development of the old draft, to which remarks were included and in which there were certain editorial improvements. This is how we understand this draft.

Péter: (confirms.)

Ceauşescu: [...] This draft is unacceptable to us since it represents a step backward in relation to the previous draft, and we propose that the draft worked out yesterday by the committee comprised of the ministers of foreign affairs be adopted as the basis. [...]

Gomułka once more explained that what is called "the Polish draft" is not a new draft. [...] When it comes to the issue of substance, then it includes all proposals: Soviet, Romanian, Polish and all others that were submitted by the ministers. It also includes entirely new points, which were suggested by the Vietnamese side. A significant majority of the ministers stated that the Polish corrections improved the text and supported it. Cde. Gomułka appealed to the Romanians not to be petty, to rise to the situation as it exists, and guided by our main goal, that is, providing support to the Vietnamese nation, accept the proposed draft without discussion as a joint draft by our delegations, the Warsaw Pact nations.

Kádár: I propose ending the formal discussion [...] and before we break up to give appropriate directives to our ministers to finish work on the draft.

Brezhnev: With regard to the fact that Cde. Ceauşescu broached the issue of procedures at the first plenary session and, as far as I understood, due to this the document cannot be adopted, I am forced to return to the history of this problem.

At the request of all of you, the Foreign Ministry of the USSR received an assignment to work on a draft of a document which was to become the basis for discussion. We completed the assignment and while coming to the meeting we did not think that a Soviet draft, or a draft by any other party, would be discussed. Having discussed this at the Politburo, we counted on the fact that comrades would pay appropriate attention to this elaborated document, and that they would unquestionably add their remarks, which would improve it.

However, the circumstances turned out to be different: the Romanian comrades on their own initiative wrote their own draft. We had nothing against this, especially since there were no fundamental differences between these drafts. The Polish comrades also had the right to make their remarks. After all, everyone has such a right.

That is why we assigned the ministers of foreign affairs [...] to work out a joint text. We did not have any intention to say entirely whose draft would be adopted [...] We are working on examining the collective effort of the ministers of foreign affairs. And in no document will the author of this draft be written. [...] Therefore the arguments of Cde. Ceauşescu are not convincing. Why such minutiae? [...] We think that the draft is very good, it entirely reflects the essence of the problem, and the ministers were able to include in it everything submitted by the delegations. [...]

Maurer: [...] On behalf of the Romanian delegation Cde. Ceauşescu stated that this draft is unacceptable to us. And he said that this was not due to procedural or formal reasons. We want to assure Cde. Gomułka that we have many comments pertaining to this document, which relate not only to the organization of the material, and even this in a certain sense shows shades of difference—very important ones—which I think Cde. Gomułka did not notice given all of his great experience.

We oppose some of the ideas included in this document [...] We understand that every socialist country is providing material support to Vietnam in its fight against American aggression. We know that in this field the most significant and effective is the assistance from the Soviet Union. And we do not doubt that if the Vietnamese comrades were to turn for help to any of us we would not refuse them any help.

But here there is talk about the political support Vietnam needs. Instead, in our opinion, in the draft of the statement that was provided in the morning, some opinions have been presented in a different way from which the Vietnamese comrades would like to see them. And this is not only their wish, but ours also [...]

Ceauşescu: [...] We have many comments with regards to the morning draft. Adopting this draft as a basis means that we should start our work from the beginning. [...]

The point is to solve the issue pragmatically. We do not have anything against the fact that the Polish comrades submitted their remarks. But since Cde. Gomułka said that the new draft included all previous propositions, then to facilitate the work we propose to use yesterday's draft as the basis and let the Polish comrades say what corrections should be introduced. This will facilitate our work and we will not have to start the work over from the beginning.

[...]

Ulbricht: When Cde. Ceauşescu says that one should simply take the old draft and add to it the two Romanian corrections, it is not "simple" because after all over 20 Romanian corrections were already taken into account and included in this draft by the ministers of foreign affairs. The old draft also takes into account our corrections and I think that the same applies to other delegations [...] I would propose to appoint a small group comprised of Brezhnev, Gomułka and Ceauşescu, who could find a way in the shortest amount of time.

Ceauşescu: I have a question for Cde. Gomułka. As I understood it, that evening remarks were received regarding your draft from all the misters of foreign affairs. Were remarks also received from the Romanian minister of foreign affairs?

[...]

Gomułka: Asking [deputy foreign] Minister [Marian] Naszkowski to give an explanation.

Naszkowski: Explained that nobody was consulted and that is also why Mănescu was not being consulted. The text worked out by the Polish delegation was sent out before the morning meeting to all ministers along with a cover letter in which there was a mention of the Polish corrections.

Ulbricht: Clear and let us end the discussion.

Brezhnev: We cannot end since we have not come up with anything and the point pertains to fundamental issues. Perhaps Cde. Ceauşescu would tell us what his fundamental objections are.

Ceauşescu: [...] We do have remarks concerning the draft and one has to delegate to the ministers to discuss everything page by page. We would like to move some ideas from the old text to the new. We agree that there are a series of good and new things in the new draft, but we have reservations about some formulations. We agree that the ministers started their work, but let the ministers do this, not us, because otherwise we will transform ourselves into an Editorial Board. We will give them until afternoon and let them present what they have come up with.

[...]

Gomułka: Let Minister Mănescu give concrete remarks on the morning draft because we have already been sitting over this for two days and now the matter has risen to a higher level.

Brezhnev: (became aggravated). We cannot sit here indefinitely. Our country is suffering due to natural disasters which have come upon us recently. Earthquakes, floods, etc. In Tashkent about 2,000 buildings have been destroyed, Krasnoiarsk is under water, Kuban—demolished homes in Kabar—an earthquake, and we are sitting here and thinking: a committee or a sub-committee! [...]

Here lies a letter before me from the Vietnamese comrades—absolutely everything is in this document. I have read the document twice and the letter from the Vietnamese. Comrades, we need to treat one another with respect. In the end even six countries can sign.

Ceaușescu: If the six of you want to sign, nobody is stopping you from doing so, but in the form in which this document exists, we cannot sign it.

This kind of pressure cannot be tolerated among communist and workers' parties. Please write this down. We will send out our position to all of the parties. We think that the principles of equality and mutual respect should exist among communist and workers' parties. We reject similar attempts at pressure. Maintaining unity, which is so desired, is only possible when we abide by the principles of equality and mutual respect. People are suffering in Vietnam and we are not providing Vietnam with full political and diplomatic aid, which we can afford! We are not discussing the issue of whether we should remain in the Geneva Committee[6] or not while the Americans are bombing Vietnam. What disarmament negotiations can be conducted with the Americans in such a situation?

We also want the statement to have mobilizing power, that it address the nations and communist parties, and that it help Vietnam. That is why we wanted and agreed to having such a Joint Statement. Why are you portraying the issue in such a way that if Romania does not agree than we would sign it without her? Please, go ahead and sign. Then we will publish our Declaration.

Ulbricht: We have a proposal from Cde. Brezhnev that the Romanian comrades submit their remarks in writing as to the draft.

Novotný: I propose to make one last effort. Let us give time to the ministers beginning at 14:00, and at 17:00 we will assemble once more, we will discuss the issue and we will make a decision on what to do in such a situation.

[...]

Brezhnev: I categorically and decidedly reject the statement that there was any talk of pressure in my speech. I made statements several times and while sitting next to Cde. Ceaușescu I told him several times about our concern about the situation in the nation and our impatience due to being outside the country at such a moment. And Cde. Ceaușescu is throwing such accusations at me. And in addition he threatens

---

[6] Eighteen-Nation Disarmament Committee of the United Nations.

us with writing to all the fraternal parties. This is a threat. And what is it that you are going to write? Let us end this, I accept Cde. *Novotný*'s proposal.

[...]

At the ministers' meeting, which lasted not until 16:00 [...], but which dragged on until 19:00, Mănescu announced over 20 comments to the draft. As a result of the discussion he withdrew a few remarks, and about 10 remarks were taken into account in a compromise formulation. However, the following matters were left to the decision of the leaders of delegations due to the fact that the Romanian delegation absolutely did not agree with the opinion of the six remaining ministers:

- referring to Nuremberg
- a formulation about "systematic violations of the Geneva Accords" on disarmament
- the repercussions of spreading the war in Vietnam by the U.S. on relations with other governments
- contacts and consultations between interested countries on the issue of helping Vietnam
- providing assistance to Vietnam "until final victory"
- an appeal to communist parties and social movements instead of to governments.

4. Meeting of the delegation chiefs on the issue of the statement on Vietnam, July 6, 1966, at 21:00.

As a result of the discussion, Ceaușescu withdrew most of the above-mentioned stipulations; on the other hand the Polish delegation withdrew its proposal regarding contacts, emphasizing that it was doing this only as the last resort since holding on to its proposal would create a situation in which the Romanian comrades would feel they could not sign the text. Some formulations were included in the nature of a compromise. [...]

The same evening celebratory signings of the statement regarding the U.S. aggression in Vietnam took place.

[...]

The next day, July 7, 1966 [...], at the plenary session, [...] Cde. Brezhnev informed the assembled that in the course of talks between delegations the view was expressed that it is worthwhile to take this opportunity to exchange information regarding the current situation in the respective countries, and especially the visits which have recently taken place. In this connection, it was decided to hold yet another unofficial meeting of the leaders of delegations [...]

5. Meeting of heads of delegations devoted to a mutual [exchange] of information. July 7, 1966, at 15:00.

[...]

A report was read by Marshal Malinovskii regarding the current state of war in Vietnam, after which Brezhnev turned to Ceaușescu so that he could inform those assembled about Romania's problems and visits. Ceaușescu began to make excuses that perhaps it was not worth starting, that it was time to go to a celebration, etc. Then Brezhnev asked directly: You would not be willing to tell us, of course as much as you can, about the visit of Zhou Enlai? Ceaușescu, once again, began to make excuses saying that there was no time [to discuss this].

Ulbricht then spoke: Come on, tell us something about the talks with Zhou Enlai [...] An unpleasant silence set in. Brezhnev said: Well, you don't want to, you don't have to, we do not insist.

Only after this Ceaușescu stated:

We had very long talks, so I will only talk about their conclusion. The view of the Chinese comrades on many issues regarding the international situation was in accord with our joint assessment of these problems. The same refers to the necessity of fighting American imperialism and assistance to Vietnam. On a series of other matters of a more general nature, they have different opinions from ours. These are the kind of matters that can be discussed and do not pose obstacles to reaching a mutual understanding.

We spoke a lot about the international situation, about relations with socialist countries and communist parties. We expressed our opinion, and they on the other hand expressed their views on some issues. For example, on the issue of relations with socialist countries. In the final analysis they agreed as to the necessity of strengthening unity, but they raised the issue that they do not find understanding from the side of the socialist countries, and particularly from the Soviet Union. Finally, he said that if those who criticized them publicly admit that they were acting incorrectly, then they could talk. This was the conclusion of his statement.

[...]

As a general conclusion since we have not yet analyzed it, I think that if the socialist countries show more patience, we will try to develop these contacts. There are possibilities to find ways for the development of these contacts. But we will say to you openly: the Chinese bear a lot of distrust towards us. They do not think that we, as socialist countries, are ready to do everything to help Vietnam. We are convinced that the statement regarding Vietnam will have an influence on them (Gomułka: I doubt it), as well as a series of other measures from our side, which will help to dispel this distrust.

[...]

We informed them that we wanted to come out with a joint statement at our conference. They answered: It will be good if there is a good statement. Let us now see what they will say about our statement once they read it. I think that it will please them and that the Vietnamese comrades will also like it

[...]

The meeting of party leaders of communist and workers' nations, the members of the Warsaw Pact on July 7, 1966.

[...]

Cde. Ulbricht: We are continuing our conversation. The ministers of foreign affairs worked very hard. As a result we have a joint document from the ministers, a draft of the statement on Vietnam. I have a question: do the leaderships of delegations think that this draft can be approved? [...]

Cde. Gomułka: I would like to explain what we had in mind while formulating our correction. We had in mind, foremost, consultations between socialist countries and the members of the Warsaw Pact, as well as the countries remaining outside the Pact. For example, the DPRK [Democratic People's Republic of Korea, North Korea],

234

Cuba and Mongolia, without excluding China. Our next point is that foremost all over the world, and especially in the so-called Third World (e.g. Egypt, Algeria, and others) there exists an enormous outrage against the American escalation of the war. The point is to take advantage of this outrage and to announce a broader offensive against the aggression. This is what guided us while proposing our correction.

The Romanian comrades are against such a formulation. They are actually limiting the entire issue when they say that first one has to consult Vietnam. It is hard to adopt that only on condition of a consultation with Vietnam. And besides, they limit the consultation to the countries of the Warsaw Pact.

Cde. Gromyko: This restricts very much.

Cde. Novotný: I propose to change and write: with the DRV government and with other interested countries.

Cde. Ceauşescu: I would like to say why we think that this formulation is not good. It can set off a series of discussions. Comrades, you know that a range of countries exists which are coming out with proposals regarding various peace talks. Having left this formulation we are encountering opposition from the Vietnamese comrades who will accuse us of wanting to conduct talks behind their backs. That is why we propose that the main role be bequeathed to Vietnam.

Cde. Gomułka: And what is your attitude towards the proposal of Cde. Novotný?

Cde. Ceauşescu: If we erase: […] and with other interested countries, then agreed.

Cde. Brezhnev: The point here is to exclude Great Britain and the United States of America. They can comment on this formulation in a variety of ways.

Cde. Gomułka: In this case, perhaps one can formulate it as follows: […] and with other countries, which support the liberation war.

Cde. Kosygin: We are not able to take any steps without the consent of the Vietnamese.

Cde. Ceauşescu: In this case we propose to erase this point.

Cde. Brezhnev: That's a pity.

Cde. Gomułka: I think that the Vietnamese would be in favor of leaving this point.

Cde. Kádár: We think that it is necessary to aid Vietnam along political and diplomatic lines. The addenda do not give us the opportunity to do so. However, it is a pity that one has to erase this point. I want to propose a correction, similar to the one which was formulated by Cde. Novotný.

Perhaps one could write: with the DRV government, among one another…and further in the way proposed by the Romanian comrades.

Cde. Novotný: I agree with Cde. Kádár's proposal.

Cde. Brezhnev: I propose: […] among one another and with other peace-loving countries, which feel the need for consultation while giving assistance for the purpose of repelling American aggression.

Cde. Ceauşescu: But the Vietnamese do not want to talk even with the Yugoslavs. Why create difficulties?

Cde. Kosygin: I propose to formulate this as follows: among one another and with the DRV as well as with other interested countries, which express readiness to fight American aggression.

In this way we will avoid what could also be referred to America and Great Britain.

After all the Americans are looking for the opportunity for consultation; the same refers to [British Prime Minister Harold] Wilson. But we do not want to consult with them.

Cde. Kádár: First: the DRV government, then among one another, and after that what Cde. Kosygin said.

Cde. Ceauşescu: I do not think that one needs to refer to all the countries. Besides, one has to state clearly that we will consult only when a necessity arises, and the Vietnamese comrades will express their consent.

One can formulate this as follows: [...] contacts among one another, after coming to an understanding with the DRV they will consult regarding new undertakings, which will have the indispensable objective of providing support in the struggle of the Vietnamese nation.

Cde. Brezhnev: If we want to consult with you we will have to ask them for consent?

Cde. Ceauşescu: If we want to call a conference regarding Vietnam or consult with others, then one has to ask them.

Cde. Brezhnev: I propose to erase the third point.

Cde. Ceauşescu: Erase it.

Cde. Ulbricht: How about other comrades?

Cde. Gomułka: I will consent to this only as a last resort, namely, if the Romanian comrades would, due to this, refuse to sign the statement. Then there would be a situation without an exit.

Cde. Ceauşescu: Erase it.

[...]

(Cde. Brezhnev congratulates Cde. Wiesław[7] and then Cde. Ceauşescu).

Cde. Ulbricht: Therefore, we can say that the statement has been unanimously accepted by everyone. We have finished our work.

[...]

[*Source: KC PZPR 2663, pp. 281–314, Archiwum Akt Nowych. Translated by Małgorzata Gnoińska for the George Washington Cold War Group.*]

---

[7] *Nom de guerre* of Gomułka.

Document No. 42: Transcript of Gathering of Warsaw Pact Leaders in Karlovy Vary, April 25, 1967

This conference of Warsaw Pact leaders at Karlovy Vary, Czechoslovakia, received significant attention in the West at the time, but it was only recently that the transcript of most of the sessions became available. Officially, it was not a Warsaw Pact meeting, but it dealt extensively with socialist bloc political strategy vis-à-vis NATO. Significantly, the Romanians refused to attend, allegedly because Ceauşescu had not been properly consulted, but in reality because he did not want to commit to what the Soviet Union would dictate on behalf of the other member-states. Ceauşescu also wanted to avoid being associated with an anti-NATO policy since he was already trying to improve relations with certain members of the alliance himself. The thrust of the session was to call publicly for the dissolution of NATO and ejection of the United States from Europe, a move which Western observers regarded as the start of a broad campaign against the Atlantic alliance. Some analysts, such as Marshall Shulman[8], saw the declaration as amounting to the creation of a northern tier within the Warsaw Pact comprising Poland, East Germany and Czechoslovakia, strategically the most important members of the bloc.

TOP SECRET

Notes of Conversations of First Secretaries
of CC Communist and Workers' Parties in Socialist Countries
at the Meeting in Karlovy Vary

[...]

Brezhnev: First of all, I would like to inform the comrades about the purpose of our meeting. [...] Cde. Gomułka put forth an idea, to which we adhere. Namely, whether we, as communist parties of socialist countries, should approach the Chinese leadership with a letter. The main thought was to invite the Chinese for joint agreed-upon actions in the fight against American imperialism in the defense of Vietnam. And not only in general words, but to try to present certain matters concretely while complementing the aspect of political unity:

1. Taking into consideration the danger of the Americans breaking Haiphong, we asked the Chinese to designate their ports for the transfer of supplies to Vietnam.

2. The capacity of the rail [system] should also be increased, since there is much congestion over there at the moment.

[...]

---

[8] Marshall Shulman, a political scientist at Columbia University, was a specialist on the Soviet Union who later became special adviser to Secretary of State Cyrus Vance for Soviet affairs from 1977 to 1980.

3. We would ask the Chinese to perhaps make their airports, which are located near the border, available [to us]. The planes will be ours; we can also send our own staff.

4. We, the Soviet Union, could also provide China with locomotives for Vietnam; the idea itself is important and, if we were to reach a basic agreement, we could delegate 1–2 parties to draft such a letter, as well as to dispatch it, or hand it personally to all those interested, have it signed and find ways to deliver it directly to the leadership of the CCP. [...]

If this letter were accepted, this would be our joint success. [...]

On the other hand, if this letter were badly received, if they were to give a bad answer, then this would expose them in the eyes of the Vietnamese. And subsequently we could send their letter, along with our response, to the fraternal parties and to whomever we deem necessary. This would contribute to further unveiling the essence of Mao Zedong's policy, towards [the goal of] further isolating China. [...]

Gomułka: [...] As Comrade Brezhnev was saying, if the Chinese were to accept our proposal, this would restrain them from attacking the USSR. It would be a great international event. [President Lyndon B.] Johnson would find himself under pressure of public opinion.

If the Chinese were to reject our proposals, then we would have, in the presence of the entire international movement [and] all the parties, a document pointing to the source and causes of why we cannot stop the bombings of the DRV.

[...]

Brezhnev: [...] We have to do this with the utmost caution, while maintaining top secrecy in order not to give them any reasons to feel offended, since by inviting them to cooperate we are [...] I spoke to [CPSU Politburo member Mikhail] Suslov yesterday, and today with Kosygin. They support this idea. I assume that Mongolia will sign the letter. We should also turn to the Romanians, [since] it is a socialist country. We will tell them about our initiative and I don't know exactly how they could refuse.

I, personally, spoke twice to [North Korean leader] Kim Il Sung (he sent two battalions of pilots to Vietnam). We have to approach him. Indeed, it will be difficult for him to sign, but maybe he will.

Gomułka: If Kim Il Sung were not to sign, I doubt whether it would be worth approaching the Mongolians. Mongolia will not be able to help very much.

The justification is that it is the Warsaw Pact countries which are coming out with a request, and if Kim Il Sung signed then perhaps we could even get Mongolia.

[...]

Ulbricht: The proposal of Comrades Brezhnev and Gomułka is very good and it spurs us on. I consider it correct for the CPSU to work on the draft of the letter. We should try very much to have both Korea and Mongolia sign the letter. It is very important from the political point of view that two Asian countries take part in this and that we are not coming out with this alone as European nations. If Korea were to take part in this, it would have great political weight.

[...]

As far as the Romanians, in view of their reaction to our meeting, I don't think it is necessary to open up the curtains. And our argument would not affect them. It would be better to put the matter in this way: It is we, the first secretaries, who met and came to an agreement; where and how is not their business. Let them think what they want, but formally it is not necessary to inform them about this because they will immediately say that they were not consulted, etc.

We have to give the impression that we are discussing this matter with them in a preliminary way, and that we are only now beginning to come to an understanding between one another. [...]

Gomułka: I think that we should begin differently—from Korea, since this is, to some degree, what the content of our letter depends upon. If Kim Il Sung's response is positive, then we would have to draft a letter, consult with all the countries, and with Romania in the end. Why? Not only because they will spread the news immediately, but also because they will have many corrections, proposals, etc. And if we say that we already have the consent of Korea, Mongolia, and [other] socialist countries, it will be easier to agree on the content of the letter.

Let the CPSU take care of this. It will send out people to us in order to personally deliver the draft of the letter and let each country take a position on it. Afterwards, we will work out the final version of the letter. And as for the Romanians, we should not send them the first draft, but only the draft that has been agreed upon.

Ulbricht: No. It is our private business what we agree upon. If the Romanians find out that we have already agreed on everything, then they will refuse due to official reasons.

[...]

Gomułka: Yes, but first we will coordinate among ourselves; we will not tell them; this is our private matter.

Kádár: [...] I think, however, that a point of departure should be the fact that we gathered in Karlovy Vary, which to the Romanians is after all not a secret, and that this was an appropriate moment to talk about this. While approaching this with caution, we don't have to say that we have already agreed on anything, but simply that we met and here is how this idea came up [...] We should treat the Warsaw Pact as a point of departure.

[...] We should approach the Romanians and then Korea and Mongolia. Depending on the answer from the Romanians, we will be able to expand this to the Asian countries. And if it does not work out, we will stay within the framework of the Warsaw Pact. No matter what "tricks" we try, the answer of the Romanians will be either "yes" or "no."

[...]

Gomułka: Let them find out 2 days prior to such a letter coming out, but let's not give them 3 weeks.

Kádár: It is worth pondering, but the Romanians will find out earlier than the Chinese. Such a danger exists. And even if they find out last they will drag it out. And it will leak out. The Yugoslavs and the Chinese will find out. [...]

Brezhnev: [...] If the Koreans don't go for the letter, then our letter will assume the character of a Warsaw [Pact] document. If they agree, it means that the fraternal parties of socialist countries, which want to jointly defend Vietnam, are approaching [them with such an initiative]. Our next moves will depend on this.

I would propose such a plan: [...] We will prepare two versions: counting on Korea and as the countries of the Warsaw Pact. Afterwards, our responsible secretary will go to you; we will designate two representatives and we will give them 1–2 days in order to agree on the two versions of the letter. If we get such a request, I can send [KGB head Yuri] Andropov to Korea. I will come to an understanding with Kim Il Sung to receive him as if on a personal matter. He will fly in secret. First, without showing the letter, he will present the idea to him orally, and if Kim Il Sung supports it, then he will show him the letter. If he does not support it, he will not show the letter. He will say, "Oh well, we wanted to strengthen our solidarity, etc., etc." [...] If Andropov says it didn't work out, that version will be dropped. The second one will remain in effect, the Warsaw one.

[...]

Brezhnev: This would be the first variant. But where the author of the letter is the CPSU, Ceaușescu will be digging out points in order to say that he is against it. He will state that in order to take a stand on such a letter, we will have to meet [and] discuss the matter, etc. And then he will start his song—to stop the work of the Committee of the 18th, to strengthen the political campaign against the Americans, to pressure Johnson, etc. How to avoid this?

[...]

And now we have a situation in which Romania stands in our way. But if we send the letter earlier that means we would mess things up. They will notify the Chinese and, in general, they will be against [it], because it is not their initiative.

[...]

Brezhnev: It looks as if, with a heavy heart, Andropov or I would have to go to them and say: Comrades, members of the Politburo, I have instructions from the CC to relay to you this idea. The war is going on, we are passing many documents, but this is not everything. Even though relations with the Chinese are bad, nevertheless this is a socialist country. It would be good if all of us approached the Chinese with such-and-such a matter. And here we would let them understand what constitutes the content of our letter without showing the letter itself. (Gomułka: This will not work). Ceaușescu will respond: We will discuss it at the Politburo, if not at the CC. This means that it will take 3–4 days, and maybe even a week. And we will have to go there for a second time. He will not provide an answer the first time. He will think of what to come up with.

[...]

Gomułka: The Romanians maintain good relations with the Bulgarians, but even if Cde. Zhivkov goes to them in person, they will not sign it even then.

Zhivkov: Yes, I think they would not agree. We need to take advantage of the time.

Gomułka: They will say that they have to consult on it and coordinate with the Chinese comrades, etc.

[...]

Brezhnev: At the first stage we will do the following: we, along with the PUWP, will work on the draft given that [there are] no ciphers, no ambassadors; the responsible secretaries of the CC will go in person. We will consult with the Koreans as to whether they fundamentally support such an idea. We can present to Kim Il Sung the essence of our proposal. If he says "no" because he is dependent on [this or that], etc. (he told me about it), then our internal variant remains.

[…]

Gomułka: There is still one more thing—in what language is it to be written? The Romanians will say they will only sign if it is in Romanian. I think we can write it in Russian and include copies in all languages. The copies could also be signed, because the Romanians will not sign a Russian text.

[…]

Kádár: […] First, Cde. Brezhnev will dispatch his personal representative, Andropov, to three parties: the Korean, and on the way back to Tsedenbal and Ceaușescu, given that he will not go on behalf of the Politburo, but that he will be your personal envoy. Let him say: I would like to hear your personal opinion. One can conclude from the reaction of the interlocutor what his attitude towards the matter is.

And afterwards, the second level. If Ceaușescu does not agree to the idea itself, then we have nothing to talk about. And then in order to avoid unpleasant consequences, we will come out, not as the Warsaw Pact, but as six parties which support this idea. If, however, the idea is acceptable to him, then we can take the second step.

[…]

Kádár: We don't need to mention the Warsaw Pact. And if the Romanians do not agree, then we will come out as six parties. This is our holy right to come out jointly.

[…]

[*Source: Archiwum Akt Nowych, KC PZPR XI A/13, Warsaw. Translated by Małgorzata Gnoińska for the George Washington Cold War Group.*]

Document No. 43: East German Analysis of the NATO "Fallex 66" Exercise, 1967

Each autumn, NATO held a major command post exercise known as "Fallex." This East German analysis of Fallex 66, carried out on West German territory, provides an interesting perspective of NATO capabilities from the point of view of the adversary. One of its main conclusions is that the Western alliance showed an impressive ability to defend the Federal Republic. According to the scenario of the exercise, Warsaw Pact forces would be able to penetrate up to 110 kilometers inside the country before being forced to retreat and deal with a counter-offensive on East German and Czechoslovak territory. The study found that the West's use of tactical nuclear weapons would be particularly effective, especially in destroying enemy aircraft before they could take off. Interestingly, some Western records of Fallex 66 were only recently published by a German Social Democratic parliamentarian who wanted to expose NATO's plans for extensive use of nuclear weapons, which he argued underlined the impossibility of defending West Germany by conventional means.[9] Clearly, the East Germans were less skeptical. The level of detail in their analysis, furthermore, shows that they had access to very sensitive military information. This is supported by the testimony of a former Stasi analyst who has written that East German intelligence was receiving information directly from its agents on the spot.[10] Unfortunately, this kind of detail is usually unavailable from official Western sources.

The exercise "Fallex 66" is divided into the preliminary and the main exercise; the main exercise consisted of three independent parts.

The 5-day preliminary exercise was carried out with reduced numbers at the locations and was essentially meant to prepare for the main exercise. During its course the first phase of the NATO states' transition from peace time to war time was developed by the staffs in their areas of exercise.

The first part of the [main] exercise, called "Top Gear," followed the pre-exercise and included the immediate preparation and conduct of a limited war, including the limited deployment of nuclear weapons. (Duration of this stage of the exercise: 5 days.)

During the second part of the [main] exercise, called "Jolly Roger," the organization, maintenance and conduct of operations of NATO troops was practiced under the condition of the initial phase of a general nuclear war.

This exercise started from the same initial position as the previous partial exercise. The participants were supposed to proceed from the previously practiced assum-

---

[9] Wolfram Dorn, *So heiss war der Kalte Krieg: Fallex 66*, ["This Hot Was the Cold War: Fallex 66"] (Cologne: Dittrich, 2002).

[10] The analyst, Heinz Busch, worked in the office of Markus Wolf. Unpublished manuscript provided to Bernd Schaefer.

ption of a limited nuclear war, assume the original initial position and start conducting operations according to the plans for a general nuclear war.

The partial exercise "Full Moon" concluded the exercise. From D-30 to D-36, it served to practice, during six days following the massive use of nuclear strikes by both sides, the resumption and implementation of measures aimed at the overall consolidation of NATO forces by the transfer from overseas, and the reorganization and overall consolidation of NATO troops in Europe.

The first two partial exercises were intended as a defensive exercise of ground forces with a subsequent transition to a counteroffensive.

They started from the same initial position. This situation was based on the assumption of a several-month period of tensions followed by one month of covert warfare. It was further assumed that the NATO forces had initiated hostilities with essentially unchanged peacetime strength, and that both sides had assumed their starting positions by the beginning of hostilities.

[...]

The idea behind the partial exercise "Top Gear" was that a limited war breaking out in the South European theater of war, extended to the West European theater of war after one day. Both sides fought with limited intensity at the beginning.

The "Orange" side enters West Germany in several areas up to 50 kilometers with a troop strength ranging from regiments to divisions. After a limited and selective use of nuclear weapons by the "Blue" side, the "Orange" side withdraws its troops. Their negotiations do not bring any results.

The war is in danger of entering a new, higher level.

At this point the partial exercise was called off.

The idea behind the following partial exercise "Jolly Roger" was that both sides would lead massive surprise nuclear attacks.

In the course of simultaneously opened operations by different units, the "Orange" side manages to partly enter West Germany up to 110 kilometers. At this point the attack of the "Orange" side is brought to a halt by a flexible defense, including the use of nuclear weapons.

After bringing in reserves, the troops of the "Blue" side started to destroy the "Orange" groupings and broke through to the territories of the GDR and the ČSSR with a counterattack. In this situation the partial exercise was called off.

[...]

The massive deployment of nuclear weapons started with the beginning of a general nuclear war (partial exercise "Jolly Roger"). It was assumed that the "Orange" side started the war with a massive first nuclear strike directed simultaneously at targets within the combat zone to the full depth of NATO territory (150 nuclear weapons [delivered against] the United States and Canada, as well as an unknown number against France, Great Britain, and the Benelux countries). Although, during the exercise, the first massive nuclear strike was assumed to come from the "Orange" side, a directive concerning the actions of NATO forces at the beginning of a war implies that in the case of a general nuclear war the deployment of nuclear weapons will be ordered immediately after zero hour. The decision as to what extent this is a general nuclear war is left to the NATO authorities.

In "Fallex 66" the first massive strike of the nuclear attack of the European NATO forces was triggered 15 to 20 minutes after the first strike of "Orange".

This is a relatively long span of time and is inconsistent with the real potential of NATO and the previous experience of its alert checks and command post exercises.

According to those [factors] the first strike of a NATO nuclear attack was triggered 5 minutes after the first strike of the "Orange" side at the latest.

[Source: VA-01/21906, pp. 1–18, BA-MA. Translated by Karen Riechert.]

Document No. 44: Report on the State of the Bulgarian Army in the Wake of the Middle East War, October 7, 1967

The June 1967 Arab–Israeli war came as a shock to the Warsaw Pact. Because Israel was armed and backed by the United States, the performance of the Israeli army in its crushing defeat of the Arabs was seen as indicative of how NATO might perform in war time. At least two high-level meetings evaluated the war's impact from the military, political, and economic points of view. At a July 11 conference of party chiefs, Brezhnev complained about Middle Eastern clients he could not control: "It's not Europe, where we have the iron thumb."[11] The document presented here, from the Bulgarian archives, is an assessment of the state of the Bulgarian army in light of the recent conflict. Its firm conclusion is that the army would be entirely unprepared for any such engagement. Extrapolating the Middle East experience to a scenario the Bulgarians might face, Defense Minister Dobri Dzhurov declares that particularly in the case of a surprise attack from Greece or Turkey, his army would be unable to counter in either direction. This view contrasted with NATO estimates from the 1950s, according to which the Greek army was in such a poor state that it would be unable to hold back a Bulgarian assault even for a short period.[12]

Protocol "B" No. 8 of the meeting of the Politburo
of the Central Committee of the Bulgarian Communist Party
October 17, 1967

Agenda:
On the status of the Bulgarian Armed Forces in light of events in the Middle East.

Decisions:
1. The report of the leadership of the Ministry of People's Defense on the status of the Bulgarian Armed Forces has been approved.

The considerations of the Ministry on enhancing the combat readiness and combat capabilities of the armed forces, and the proposals made in this respect during the Politburo meeting shall be taken into account by the Ministry of People's Defense in its future activities.

---

[11] Record of meeting, Budapest, 11–12 July 1967, in *The Soviet Bloc and the Aftermath of the June 1967 War: Selected Documents from East-Central European Archives*, ed. James G. Hershberg for the conference, "The United States, the Middle East, and the 1967 Arab–Israeli War," Department of State, Washington, 12–13 January 2004, pp. 12–52, at p. 23.

[12] John O. Iatrides, "Failed Rampart: NATO's Balkan Front," paper presented at the conference, "NATO and the Warsaw Pact: Intra-Bloc Conflicts," Kent State University, 23–24 April 2004.

2. Based on the agreement in principle between Cde. Todor Zhivkov and Cde. Leonid Brezhnev on the role, tasks and development of the Bulgarian Armed Forces, Cde. Dobri Djurov, after specifying the strength of the Bulgarian Armed Forces with the State Defense Committee, shall put forward the issue to the respective Soviet bodies to solve the problems resulting from this.

Signed: (Todor Zhivkov)

Report
on the status of the Bulgarian Armed Forces
in light of events in the Middle East

[...]
This report will deal with the status of intelligence, combat and mobilization readiness, training of commanders, staffs and troops, and the political and morale status, discipline and logistical support of the Bulgarian Armed Forces. In our opinion, these are the main factors having an impact on the combat readiness and combat capabilities of the armed forces. As seen from the analysis above, serious failures in those areas caused the defeat of the Arab countries.
[...]

1. Status of intelligence in the Bulgarian Armed Forces
[...]
I need to report, however, that we have not yet reached a turning point in our effort to enhance intelligence to the level of modern requirements and it does not meet the demands of the armed forces and the country.

Strategic intelligence meets the most urgent peacetime demands of supplying information related to the composition, organization, grouping, armament and operational–tactical concepts of the Turkish and Greek Armed Forces. [Our] intelligence, however, has no sources available to reveal the enemy's intentions for unexpected invasion, which, taking into account the experience of events in the Middle East is of paramount importance for the defense of the country.

In addition, the main source for supplying information about our enemy is the intelligence service personnel, working under cover in our official missions abroad. We will not be able to rely on them in a complex situation or in time of war, and thus we will lack the necessary intelligence information at the moment we need it most.
[...]

2. Combat and Mobilization Readiness
[...]
Due to restricted numbers of personnel, the army's peacetime combat staff is not sufficient for the achievement of the tasks set. The border with Greece is actually open.

Land forces formations and units on alert are not sufficiently developed as far as structures and manpower. As a matter of fact, army peacetime formations and units have been closed. The organizational structure of the ministry of defense, army staffs and armed forces is underdeveloped, as well. Our armed forces do not have sufficient

246

numbers of combat ready units to ensure forcing water obstacles and high frequency communications. A particularly weak spot is air defense among the troops, since divisions, brigades and regiments have very few artillery weapons.

Current air force personnel are not capable of ensuring either a successful counterattack against the enemy in the air, or the necessary support to army and navy units. The problem of direct anti-air craft defense of airfields has not yet been solved. Reserve airfields are not supplied with fuel, lubricants and ammunition.

The Navy is based at two naval bases only—Varna and Burgas—which allows for easy destruction.

Military personnel in most of the wartime formations in all services have been downsized to the extreme, which prolongs their mobilization term and weakens their combat capabilities.

The issue of civil defense in the country is still on the agenda. Civil defense has almost no peacetime materiel and equipment, due to which combat readiness does not meet modern requirements.

The leadership of the Ministry has already reported to the Politburo on the above-mentioned issues and has pointed out the fact that their solution is beyond its capabilities. We certainly hope that after increasing the strength of the armed forces and receiving the support needed in armaments and combat equipment from the USSR, these shortcomings will be overcome.

3. Preparation of officers, staffs and management of the troops

[...]

The joint command of the Warsaw Pact Unified Armed Forces is another problem to be solved. The current headquarters in Moscow with its personnel, structure and prerogatives, is not capable of ensuring command of the Unified Armed Forces. This is absolutely unfavorable for the Bulgarian People's Republic and the Bulgarian Armed Forces, taking into consideration their special position in the Balkans. In our view, it is urgent to put forward the question of establishing an efficient body to control the Warsaw Pact Unified Armed Forces.

Drawing [conclusions] from the shortcomings stated above and the experiences of the hostilities in the Middle East, we are taking necessary steps to further enhance the preparation of officers and headquarters.

[...]

4. Quality of combat training at the unit level

[...]

The main weak spot in the training of air force and air defense units is their insufficient capability to attack air targets at low altitude, using anti-missile maneuvering and radio interference. I am obliged to report now that for the past few years we have been training our air force and air defense units to attack low flying targets over ground and sea. Until recently we considered as low flying targets objects flying at an altitude between 150 and 200 meters. Experience from operations in Vietnam and the Middle East shows that our enemy's aviation used low altitudes of 30–50 meters, whereas our aviation was not prepared for this. We have started enhanced training and we have achieved some success. However, this task has not been completed yet. Fighter-bomber crews have not been trained sufficiently to fly at low altitude and to take off from grass airfields.

In the Navy, the problem of air defense on naval bases and ships at sea still exists, as does the problem of overcoming obstacles during airborne operations operations over unprepared areas of the coast.

[...]

When unexpectedly attacked with nuclear weapons, peacetime land forces units of the Bulgarian Armed Forces, even with some difficulty, by taking advantage of the strike results of Soviet strategic aviation, are capable of managing the offensive in the Bulgarian–Turkish direction. The defense of the Bulgarian–Greek line, however, has not been secured, which raises serious alarms in the Ministry of People's Defense.

When suddenly attacked without nuclear weapons, on a local or world conflict scale, the peacetime land forces units will not be capable of taking the offensive in ether direction. In this case, defense of the Bulgarian–Greek line remains the weakest spot.

[...]

[*Source: 64/367, Central State Archives, Sofia. Translated by Greta Keremidchieva.*]

Document No. 45: Memorandum of Results of the
Chiefs of General Staff Meeting regarding Reorganization
of the Warsaw Treaty, March 1, 1968

Since 1965 the Soviets had been trying, without much success, to bring about greater institutionalization and a tightening of controls within the Warsaw Pact. By the end of 1967, the matter had taken on added importance with NATO's recent steps toward greater consolidation following recommendations made by the Harmel Report[13] prepared by Belgium's former foreign minister. As a result, Moscow convened several important meetings of its allies, one of which is summarized in this memorandum. A key issue in reorganization of the Pact was the creation of a Military Council, which was supposed to be the counterpart to the NATO Military Committee. The meeting concluded without concrete results.

[...]

During February 29–March 1 of this year a meeting was held in Prague on the level of army defense ministers' deputies of member-states of the Warsaw Treaty concerning the establishment of principal institutions of the Unified Command.

Marshal Iakubovskii—the Supreme Commander of the Unified Armed Forces, directed the meeting, and the armies of individual states were represented by delegations with chiefs of general staffs as their leaders. [...]

[...]

The organizer of the meeting, the Command of the Unified Armed Forces, used as a focal point, repeatedly emphasizing it, that the matter of establishing the Staff of the Unified Armed Forces and the Committee on Technology was agreed upon at the conference of defense ministers in May 1966. Therefore, the fundamental object of this meeting was to coordinate a draft statute for the Military Council.

Bringing up the issue of the Military Council during the talks meant contradicting the stance of the Romanian side, which has demanded the establishment of such an institution during previous meetings. At that time, disapproving the Romanian proposal on this matter was a result of the fact that it [the Romanian side] assumed that the Military Council would function on the principle of unanimity (actual "veto rights"). Because the Romanian comrades, during preparatory talks led by the Supreme Commander during his recent visit to Bucharest, supposedly decided to abandon the idea of unanimity, grounds emerged for elaborating to a document, which in this case would be an expression of bilateral compromise. [...]

---

[13] For details, see Helga Haftendorn, *NATO and the Nuclear Revolution: A Crisis of Credibility, 1966–1967* (Oxford: Clarendon Press, 1996), and "The Future Taks of the Alliance: NATO's Harmel Report, 1966/67," ed. Anna Locher and Christian Nünlist, http://www.ethz/php/collections/coll_Harmel.htm.

Every delegation—except for the Romanian—has expressed their full support for the proposed draft and once again has validated the need to establish principal institutions of the Unified Armed Forces. [...]

The Romanian delegation has definitely avoided taking a fundamental stance in the matter of the draft statute about the Military Council, as well as [in the matter of] the proposal to establish the Staff of the Unified Armed Forces and the Committee on Technology. According to the Romanian comrades the main and principal problem is defining the overall position of the Unified Command, its relation to the governments of member-states of the Warsaw Treaty and the Political Consultative Committee, a method of nominating the Supreme Commander, etc. According to the Romanian delegation these matters should be expressed in the statute of the Unified Command, in which detailed competences of the Military Council, the Staff, the Committee on Technology of the UAF [Unified Armed Forces], and others should also be settled. In this case, there would be no need to work out a separate statute for the Military Council.

When it comes to the Staff and the UAF Committee on Technology, the Romanian delegation believes that despite the fact that the, essentially, accepted protocol on this matter was signed by every defense minister (including Romania's then-Minister of Armed Forces) in May of 1966—it is still an open matter. As was declared, the above-mentioned protocol was evaluated by the Romanian leadership as a [protocol] which does not concern relations that should exist between our socialist countries, and for that reason it [protocol] cannot be treated as binding. The Romanian delegation has also opposed the institution of the representatives of the Supreme Commander for individual armies, regardless of the fact that this problem was not included in the matters under discussion. To rationalize its standpoint, [the Romanian delegation] has stated that an institution of representatives warps relations between socialist countries and leads to negative comments both from within the country and abroad, which, among other things, harms the Soviet Union in particular. Furthermore, the Romanian delegation has also declared that it is not necessary to include the political preamble in a possible future statute of the Unified Command because the appropriate political targets are defined in the Warsaw Treaty itself.

Essentially, one can recognize that the Romanian stance is becoming more and more inflexible with the objective of not recognizing the Unified Armed Forces. The Romanian comrades use as a tool the letter of the Warsaw Treaty, which de facto does not contain this kind of literal definition [of the Unified Armed Forces]. For that reason, there is no doubt that in case of further discussion, as demanded by the Romanian side, to establish "general matters," one has to take into account the disclosure of principal contradictions with regard to the substance of the Unified Armed Forces.

Due to the distinctive stance consistently held by Romania, which does not bode well for reaching a common view at the working level, it seems reasonable to discuss specific proposals about the establishment of principal institutions of the Unified Armed Forces at the highest level, and subsequently, to have them be approved by the sides interested in a positive resolution to this matter. For the Romanian side, if it continues to maintain its previous stance, there will be an open opportunity to join and participate in the established institutions whenever it [Romania] recognizes this [joining and participation] to be appropriate. This view, expressed in a general manner by the Supreme Commander of the Unified Armed Forces, was also represented during unofficial talks by all delegations which held positive views on the matters that were discussed.

[*Source: 2663/366–80 KC PZPR, XIA/104, AAN. Translated by Magdalena Klotzbach for the National Security Archive.*]

Document No. 46: Czechoslovak Report on the Meeting of the Political Consultative Committee of March 6–7, 1968, March 26, 1968

This meeting of the PCC is interesting in several respects. It was the first to be convened at Romania's initiative, the Romanian goal being to discuss both the ongoing conundrum of Warsaw Pact reorganization and one of the hot issues of the day—nonproliferation of nuclear weapons. The meeting also revealed aspects of the internal dynamics underway in Czechoslovakia at a time of growing political ferment in the country. As with earlier meetings, the Soviets were unable to achieve any satisfaction on alliance restructuring and the delegates once again shunted the matter off to higher levels. Romania's main problem with Moscow concerning the Non-Proliferation Treaty (NPT) was that the proposed document unduly favored the superpowers, which were already in basic agreement on the treaty's text. Bucharest also claimed that the NPT failed to offer sufficient safeguards for other countries because it did not commit the superpowers strongly enough to reductions of their nuclear stockpiles and did not include security guarantees for non-nuclear states, such as all the Soviet Union's Warsaw Pact allies. A contributing factor in the Romanians' opposition was their interest in closer ties with China, which also opposed the treaty as unduly advantageous to the Soviet Union.

At the head of the Czechoslovak delegation was party leader Alexander Dubček, who at the time was struggling to keep up with the wave of reforms sweeping through all levels of Czechoslovak society. What is notable is the fact that although reform of the Warsaw Pact was being debated internally within the Czechoslovak military and political leaderships, and even high-ranking officers held reservations about the way Moscow had been running the process, Dubček did not register any disagreements whatsoever at the meeting, choosing instead to show full support for the Soviet position (see Document No. 55 a). Prague radio nevertheless broadcast commentary about this meeting claiming that the Czechoslovaks had joined Romania in expressing doubts about the Soviet nuclear umbrella and drawing a comparison to French President Charles de Gaulle's criticism of the value of the U.S. nuclear commitment to his country's security. However, there are no records from the conference indicating that any such comments were made. It is possible that the ongoing debates led the commentator, liberal-minded journalist Luboš Dobrovský, to believe that objections to Soviet plans would be raised and wanted to report that they had been before receiving confirmation. In any case, the political leadership, very likely Dubček himself, clearly overruled any such notion, no doubt deciding that the wiser course, on this subject as on the NPT, would be to avoid giving Moscow further cause to question Prague's loyalty during a very fluid period.

[...]

The Warsaw Treaty PCC summit met
in Sofia from March 6–7, 1968. [...]

[...]

The agenda as approved earlier included the following issues:

1. The Non-proliferation treaty,
2. Vietnam,
3. Constituting and forming the Staff and Military Council of the Warsaw Treaty Unified Command.

Com. Ceaușescu expressed his reservations about the formulations of agenda Pt. 3. He requested the point be entitled "military questions." He denied that any agreement had been reached on naming this point during preparatory meetings for the PCC summit. The Romanians' objections reflected their desire to ensure that the title would not express objectives to which Romania had reservations. An exchange of opinions followed. The term was not modified. The summit then opened discussion on the non-proliferation treaty. An exchange of opinions on this issue was the main, even sole, subject of the presentations by the respective delegations, since the "Declaration on the Threat to Peace Resulting from Extension of American Aggression in Vietnam" had been prepared by an expert group, ultimately on the foreign ministers' level. [...]

I. NON-PROLIFERATION TREATY TALKS

All participating delegations paid major attention to this issue since the PCC summit had been convened upon a Romanian request to discuss approaches by the Warsaw Treaty states to the proposed non-proliferation treaty.

The Sofia summit was preceded by consultations by the deputy foreign ministers of the Warsaw Treaty states, which took place in Berlin from February 26–27, 1968. Most of its participants agreed the deputy ministers should prepare the Sofia summit agenda and, in addition, they should provide a preliminary assessment of the opinions and approaches of the respective countries concerning the proposed non-proliferation treaty. Then, an attempt to find a common solution should be made that would facilitate the PCC's work, plus contribute to the successful course of the Sofia summit in the interests of the unity of the Warsaw Treaty member-states. However, the Berlin meeting was not able to complete this task. The Romanian delegation merely brought forward all its previously known reservations to the treaty draft while stating that proper discussion of the topic should be (exclusively) reserved to the PCC Sofia summit. Under these conditions, the delegations of six of the Berlin participants could do nothing more than present their principal viewpoints on the non-proliferation treaty, as well as on the individual Romanian remarks. The course of the Berlin meeting reconfirmed the identical positive approach of six of the European socialist countries on the non-proliferation treaty. At the same time, it demonstrated that Romania insisted on her reservations to the treaty draft.

The Sofia PCC summit thus began talks on the non-proliferation treaty but the differences in approach to the proposed treaty by six delegations on the one hand

and the Romanian one on the other hand were not surmounted; during the preliminary meetings, they were merely confirmed. Moreover, in addition to the previous Romanian remarks, another Romanian proposal to amend Article III of the draft (concerning inspections) appeared. The summit participants received that proposal a few days prior to the summit's commencement.

The Eighteen-Nation Disarmament Committee [ENDC] in Geneva was concluding final talks on the non-proliferation treaty at the same time the Sofia PCC summit was convened. The question was whether the Geneva Committee's work would be completed before March 15, 1968, as provided for by the resolution of the XXIIth U.N. General Assembly. To a great extent, this fact affected the course of discussion in Sofia as most participants realized that the Sofia summit should not jeopardize in any way the work of the ENDC, or presentation of the report on the draft non-proliferation treaty to the U.N. General Assembly in due time.

Therefore, Comrade Brezhnev, head of the Soviet delegation, in his opening speech emphasized that time was of the essence. A loss of this favorable moment for signing the non-proliferation treaty could negate the possibility that now exists. That would produce adverse consequences for the further course of European events, in his opinion. He addressed his appeal for a joint effort by all socialist states and uniform support for the accelerated negotiation and adoption of the treaty in this sense, too. Other delegations, except Romania's, raised similar demands.

The appearance of the head of the Romanian delegation confirmed, however, that Romania did not intend to alter in any way its critical approach to the proposed non-proliferation treaty. Romania ignored the urgent reasons shared by the other socialist states in favor of urgent passage, particularly due to the danger of the FRG's eventual nuclear armament. While pushing through their maximized demands, Romania proceeds from the unrealistic assumption that the U.S. with their allies could be still forced to make further major concessions. That was also demonstrated in Ceaușescu's appearance. Cde. Ceaușescu informed the PCC at the same time that he had instructed the Romanian delegation to the ENDC to have these remarks on the non-proliferation treaty draft submitted as an official document. Cde. Ceaușescu's appearance revealed that Romania was not only unwilling to alter its attitude toward the non-proliferation treaty any time soon but was also ready to press its reservations during further negotiations in the ENDC and later on at the U.N. General Assembly session. (The Romanian delegation to the ENDC formally presented its amendments on March 11, 1968.)

Although the Romanian delegation in Sofia agreed with the importance of the non-proliferation treaty, by its rigid and unrealistic approach it objectively played into the hands of its opponents who have been trying to delay and ultimately prevent its conclusion by constantly submitting new reservations. These concerns were immediately confirmed on March 6, when the FRG government delivered a memorandum to the ENDC. In trying to influence its members, this memorandum contained reservations similar to these presented by Romania and refers even to the interests of "other" countries in substantially altering the treaty.

Unlike Romania, the other summit participants assessed the importance of the treaty and the necessity of adopting it as soon as possible in light of the existing inter-

254

national situation and the danger that lurks in the possibility that a nuclear weapon might come into the hands of militarist and revanchist circles in the FRG, or other reactionary circles in certain other capitalist states. That was the specific reason for stressing the time factor; early adoption of the non-proliferation treaty would represent, no doubt, a major achievement for the socialist states in their struggle to decrease the danger of the outbreak of a nuclear conflict; the treaty's opponents would be unable to organize any resistance or to escalate pressure against the treaty.

When evaluating the Romanian remarks to the draft treaty, the Sofia summit participants agreed that:

- Some amendments are unrealistic, as they require that the non-proliferation treaty resolve the entire complex of nuclear disarmament [issues]; they go beyond the framework of the treaty. Such amendments may only succeed in preventing agreement on the treaty.
- The Romanian proposal for guarantees to the non-nuclear nations has no chance of being accepted by the U.S. That would constitute an insurmountable obstacle to adoption of the treaty. The socialist states have emphasized that they consider a solution to the issue outside the framework of the treaty as sufficient. As far as the security of the European socialist states is concerned, they see the guarantees of their security in the Warsaw Treaty and in the nuclear forces of the USSR.
- Other Romanian remarks, concerning enforcement of and withdrawal from the treaty, do not strengthen but weaken the treaty. As such, they might be misused in the future to the disadvantage of the socialist states.

The delegations of six Warsaw Treaty member-states, taking into account the forthcoming conclusion of the Geneva meeting and the Romanians' decision to make their separate standpoint public, as well as because the Sofia final communiqué does not reflect Romania's dissenting attitude, have therefore agreed to formulate their common position in the interests of the peaceful goals of the socialist states. At the meeting of the delegations of Bulgaria, ČSSR, Hungary, the GDR, Poland and USSR on March 7, the text of a declaration was drawn up and approved in which these six states clearly stated their support for a speedy conclusion of the non-proliferation treaty, declared their support for the Soviet treaty draft dated January 15, 1968, and called on the other states to resolve this issue in positive way. The document, which was signed by the first secretaries of the communist and workers' parties along with the prime ministers, was made public by mutual agreement on March 9. Cde. Ceauşescu, head of the Romanian delegation, was informed of the forthcoming declaration of the six countries by Cde. Zhivkov.

Talks concerning the non-proliferation treaty held in Sofia during the PCC meeting did not result in any change in original approaches by the individual participants. The Romanians did nothing during the summit that might evidence even the slightest goodwill toward finding a uniform standpoint for the socialist states by means of multilateral discussion of the non-proliferation issue. It is to be expected, therefore, that the Romanian delegation would not present itself as being in accord with the other socialist countries during the U.N. General Assembly session.

II. THE VIETNAM PROBLEM

The PCC Sofia summit unanimously adopted the "Declaration on the Threat to Peace Resulting from Extension of American Aggression in Vietnam."[14]

A group of experts from all participating states has been negotiating the draft of this Declaration since March 5. Their talks were based on a proposal elaborated jointly by Bulgaria, the USSR and Poland in accordance with the resolution of the Berlin meeting of deputy foreign ministers.[15] In preparing the resolution, the position and suggestions of the Democratic Republic of Vietnam, presented shortly before the meeting by the Vietnamese comrades, were also taken into account. Following the DRV request, the original text of the declaration was amended [to include] [...] support for the DRV's four points[16] and the National Liberation Front's program,[17] condemnation of U.S. maneuvering at the so-called peace talks, [...] etc. The individual delegations addressed numerous comments to the text of the declaration. Most of them were resolved by means of compromise formulations. The remarks of Czechoslovak experts leading to greater specification and improvement of the text were accepted in principle. The final text was approved during the last foreign ministers' meeting. All of the PCC summit participants signed the declaration during the final session on March 7, 1968.

The declaration forcefully denounces U.S. aggression in Vietnam, gives a high appraisal of the heroic struggle of the Vietnamese people both in the south and north of the country, [provides] serious warnings to the U.S. government, and [offers] support for the views of the DRV and NLF concerning the solution of the Vietnam issue. The declaration represents important support for the struggle of the Vietnamese people against American aggression; it is, at the same time, a promise that full support and any necessary aid shall be granted to the DRV and the Vietnamese people as long as is necessary for the victorious rebuff of imperialist aggression. [...]

[14] For the text, see http://www.isn.ethz.ch/php/documents/collection_3/PCC_docs/1968/1968_-33.pdf.

[15] The meeting took place on February 26–27, 1968.

[16] On April 8, 1965, the Hanoi government proposed a formula for ending the war that included recognition of Vietnamese independence and territorial integrity, a prohibition against foreign bases and military alliances in either zone of the country, application of the National Liberation Front program for South Vietnam, and the reunification of North and South Vietnam on peaceful terms.

[17] Formed on December 20, 1960, the NLF was a Hanoi-backed coalition of mostly Southern Vietnamese guerrilla and opposition groups whose 10-point manifesto sought reunification, independence, democracy, and neutrality, among other goals.

III. THE CONSTITUTION OF THE STAFF AND MILITARY COUNCIL OF THE WARSAW TREATY UNIFIED COMMAND

Point 3 of agenda was to deal with the issue of reinforcement of military bodies of the Warsaw Treaty; within its framework, the Military Council, Staff and Committee on Technology were to be constituted.

Because of the specific views of the Romanian representatives on documents that had already been agreed to relating to the military section of the Warsaw treaty, and with the intention not to aggravate the contentious issues of the Sofia summit, the delegation heads agreed to listen to the report of Supreme Commander of the Unified Armed Forces Marshal of the USSR Cde. Iakubovskii but not to discuss this question and to postpone its resolution until the next PCC meeting.

[...]

The resolution was approved unanimously with the provision that it not be published in the press and that the proceedings be considered secret.

[...]

[*Source: AÚV KSČ 02/1, 4011/26, Central State Archives, Prague. Translated by Marian J. Kratochvíl.*]

Document No. 47: Remarks by the Czechoslovak Chief of Staff on the Theory of Local War, March 13, 1968

These remarks by Chief of General Staff Gen. Otakar Rytíř are one of several examples of the critical views of various Czechoslovak military and party officials toward the overall Soviet strategy being imposed on the Warsaw Pact. Rytíř's comments are compelling not only because of his blunt language but also because he was not a reformer. His criticism of Moscow's position is based on the belief that its policy undermined the interests of both Czechoslovakia and the Soviet Union. For one thing, the defensive tasks assigned to Czechoslovakia within the framework of the Warsaw Pact were, he believed, beyond the economic capacity of the country. For another, the alliance had failed to create effective common institutions for the previous 10 years, and had been particularly negligent in elaborating a military doctrine for the Warsaw Pact. His implication is that the Soviets have their own doctrine and simply presume that other member-states will follow suit.

Rytíř recalls with approval the "doctrine" propounded by Khrushchev, namely that in the event of war the Soviets would be ready to carry out a nuclear strike that would destroy Europe and United States; the result of this plain-spoken warning, he believed, was that no war had broken out. In response, however, the West developed the theory of limited war, which Rytíř refers to as "local war," as a way to circumvent the Soviet threat by allegedly not relying on nuclear weapons in battle. But this new theory "deceived our Soviet comrades," he asserts, because if implemented it would require the application of high technology and highly trained manpower at a level only the West could afford. Speaking presciently, he declares: "This competition we cannot win."

[...]

We are under great pressure; we lack space, material, people. We are in a situation where the task as given to us is beyond the capabilities of our state, be it human or economic resources. Where is the cause, comrades? The cause is, I think, at the heart of the Warsaw Treaty. We have been bargaining for ten years already. Nevertheless, we cannot agree on constituting some kind of entity—a military body of the Warsaw Treaty, i.e. the staff and the Military Council. These bodies should then make an assessment of the Warsaw Treaty military concept as their major issue.

We cannot do without a certain concept. Such concepts must not originate from the Soviet General Staff exclusively, however. Such concepts, since these are coalition concepts, must originate from the alliance. That is to say, the signatories of the Warsaw Treaty must also participate. This is the principal question, comrades. Excuse me, I cannot discuss it widely and in detail for I would be digressing, would be getting into strategic operational plans, and this is what I cannot do by all my, so to speak, efforts, and believe me, sincere efforts, to reveal to you the complexity of this issue.

This is the point, comrades. We could agree on this issue if a body had been constituted. Within this body, we could push through our voice to be heard. We would have been heard (and listened to). Today, our voice comes out as our viewpoints, our opinions, but of course not as pressure. For we have no legal basis to intervene. Therefore, through the Unified Command, which in fact does not exist, through the Unified Command as a transit station, come the tasks for our army in case of an eventual war. Naturally, I do not doubt that this task is based on the economic and human resources of the Soviet Union, so far as the Soviet Army is concerned. But it is not based on our economic and human resources. And this is not just our case, it is the case of all our neighbors.

Such is the situation, which we cannot stand any longer, we must get to it. Up to now, we have not, although we had been drawing their attention to both the Soviet representatives and ours. Let us pose just a small question, comrades. Look, there was a doctrine a long time ago—maybe it will be a more complex problem for certain comrades, but allow me to break it to you—there was a doctrine, under Khrushchev: There would be war, seven strikes would hit Germany, Germany would be liquidated. Sorry, eight strikes, I got a bit confused. So-and-so many strikes shall devastate America. Comrades, it is hard to say that all that was wrong; that is hard to say. Look, comrades, maybe I am mistaken; I would sum up the situation as follows: thank God that we have nuclear weapons. In my opinion, because of them, there has been no third world war. I think that—I beg you, I am just expressing my opinion and I gave my opinion to the Soviet comrades as well—I think our potential enemies over there got it. And what did they come up with? They came up with the theory of local war. Because for them, the threat of a nuclear strike was a real threat. And they were really threatened. There was panic there. Not just among the public. There was panic on the staffs, too. They realized that in reality, and they took Khrushchev literally—maybe there was 89 percent posturing in Khrushchev's words—so they took it word for word and said: When you rub us this way, then we are going to rub you another way, with the theory of local war. The local war theory allows for warfare without nuclear weapons. With this theory, they—in my opinion, to put it bluntly—cheated and deceived our Soviet comrades a bit. And they took the bait—I mean the local war theory. Maybe from the viewpoint of the Soviet Union that local war theory conveys to them. But from the viewpoint of our republic this theory does not suit us. Why doesn't it suit us, comrades? Because the local war theory means what? An orientation to classical warfare. Classical war means what? It means saturating units with high technology, with high numbers of personnel. Only the capitalist system can afford that under present conditions, under [the existing] economic situation of the two camps, the socialist and the capitalist. Because its economy—whether we like it or not—is on a higher level, it has greater possibilities. Today. Maybe ten years later it will be different. But such is the situation today. That means we conceded to what, comrades? We conceded—if we accept the local war theory—the start of a competition with the West in the [conventional] armament of our forces. Well, that contest we cannot win, comrades. Because their economy is much stronger than ours. We say today: Let us take care not to lag behind. We can naturally put forward the slogan: draw even and surpass the Western states in technology. But [...] we would be walking about in birch-bark shoes, [or] barefooted, comrades.

For we cannot hold out in such a competition. This is a fundamental question of our lives, comrades. And if we take the position of our Republic, and we as the general staff, defense ministry, we must protect the interests of our army, even if we agree with our duties of international friendship within the Warsaw Treaty. But we must protect our interests.

[...] I had tough disputes with the Unified Command when they came and requested an increase in the number of divisions. And it took me two days, two [full] days it took me before I convinced one army general of the economic and human resources of our Republic. Unfortunately, we must admit, comrades, that our political officers do not pay due attention to these issues. And these are issues of basic importance. And here I see somehow that this point, that is to say more independence in foreign policy—I refer to policies within the Warsaw Treaty—not simply the West, and Western Germany.

We must achieve equal status within the Warsaw Treaty.

[*Source: Sb. KV ČSFR, A 666, Institute for Contemporary History, Prague. Translated by Marian Kratochvíl.*]

Document No. 48: Record of Gomułka–Iakubovskii Conversation in Warsaw, April 19, 1968

Because of the continuing stalemate over Moscow-backed reforms within the Warsaw Pact, the Kremlin sent Supreme Commander Ivan I. Iakubovskii to Eastern Europe to lobby each country's party leader. This is a record of his meeting with Władysław Gomułka in Poland, the first stop on his tour. Iakubovskii brought with him a Soviet draft of several proposed new statutes regarding the Military Council, the unified command and the unified air defense system. By this time, the reform movement that came to be known as the Prague Spring was in full stride in Czechoslovakia, a situation that alarmed Gomułka because of its potential to stir up political difficulties in neighboring Poland. The Polish leader described a chaotic situation in the Czechoslovak army which he claimed was leaving the borders with West Germany "practically open." It was time, he said, for the Warsaw Pact to consider military occupation of the country—a position he and other hard-line leaders would repeat in the coming months. Later in the discussion, both Gomułka and Polish Premier Józef Cyrankiewicz voiced their opposition to using East German troops in any military intervention in Czechoslovakia. Iakubovskii listened to Gomułka's suggestions but was noncommittal.

[...]

Marshal Iakubovskii: [...] stated that in accordance with the decision of the Political Consultative Committee in Sofia in March of this year, [...] the Staff of the Unified Armed Forces has compiled draft statutes: concerning the Unified Armed Forces, the Military Council of the Unified Armed Forces, and a common air defense system for all member-states of the Warsaw Pact. Drafts of the documents mentioned above have been sent to the governments and to defense ministers of member-states of the Warsaw Pact, except for Romania.

Marshal Iakubovskii would like to receive the preliminary positions and opinions of the governments and defense ministers during his trip, which he has begun by paying a visit to Poland. He also plans to visit the GDR, Bulgaria, Hungary, and Czechoslovakia. He does not exclude the possibility of visiting Romania.

[...]

Cde. Gomułka: stated that Romania, despite its declaration to do so, has not yet presented its own draft for improving the operations of institutions of the Supreme Command of the Unified Armed Forces, and for that reason he doubts that Romania will agree to accept drafts of documents assembled by the Staff of the Unified Armed Forces. He also believes that due to Romania's negative stance on this issue, which was demonstrated in several previous talks, there is no need for further delay on this matter, and he emphasized the urgency of quickly implementing the documents even without Romania's participation.

[...]

After evaluating the situation in the ČSSR, Cde. Gomułka stressed that this situation is highly troubling despite Cde. [Alexander] Dubček's assurances that the CPCz Leadership will have it under control. Counterrevolutionary forces clearly aim to change the state existing in the ČSSR to a bourgeois democracy, as proven by the following: the desire to change the constitution and electoral law; the demand to hold an extraordinary session of the CPCz Congress in order to change even the present Central Committee; disturbing political ambitions of other parties and their slogans for legal opposition; the initiation of contact by a peasants' party with the Vatican; slogans and intentions to convene national councils and the leadership of workers' union organizations without the communists; proposals to reactivate a social-democratic party; etc.

The visits and talks by various Czechoslovak delegations—of scientists and journalists, among others—in the FRG and also in Israel basically open the way now only to the formal engagement of diplomatic relations with these countries.

Official assurances about alliance and brotherhood with the USSR and other socialist states do not find full practical support. In connection with [Jan] Masaryk's death[18] some speak of the responsibility of Soviet advisers. In trade contacts the ČSSR would like to receive the maximum from the USSR and simultaneously have unlimited freedom of trade with the West. Lately, more and more in the press, on the radio and on television in the ČSSR criticism of Poland is present. Various resolutions and protests, especially from student, scientific, and cultural circles, are being delivered to the PPR embassy in Prague.

It is no wonder that Poland is being attacked by Zionist and reactionary circles in the West. However, we cannot agree with the criticism coming from a socialist country with which we are tied by a pact of friendship. The helplessness of the ČSSR leadership and the lifting of limitations on publications have prompted the emergence of active and uncontrolled forces. Hence, our three protests in Prague. The behavior of Czechoslovak activists stimulates reactionary forces in our country. These forces, in the name of demands for "democracy and freedom" attempted to create chaos, but currently are in a crouch and no doubt are tying their hopes to the further reactionary course of events in Czechoslovakia. Our interests are without any doubt connected with the situation in Czechoslovakia. The disorganization of their army leaves the border with the FRG practically open, and a possible provocative strike even by a small group of forces from West Germany could bring incalculable consequences. Hence, there is a reason to keep Soviet forces in Czechoslovakia, within the framework of the Warsaw Pact.

[...]

Referring to drafts of documents, Cde. Gomułka emphasized: the need to strengthen and improve the activity of institutions of the Supreme Command of the Unified Armed Forces; the unity of activity of the Warsaw Pact states and their armies; and

---

[18] Czechoslovakia's non-communist Foreign Minister, Jan Masaryk, was found dead in a courtyard outside his second-storey Ministry apartment on March 10, 1948, just two weeks after the communist coup. Czechoslovak authorities ruled the death a suicide but many have long suspected he was murdered for political reasons using the notorious technique of defenestration. Although the facts remain somewhat obscure, in early 2004 Czech police concluded he had been pushed out of his window.

[the point] that the supreme commander should have a greater say on raising the attack readiness of the Unified Armed Forces. He further stated that the leadership of Poland, which actually initiated Marshal Iakubovskii's current trip, will accept the drafted documents, and informed the supreme commander that the conclusions of the PPR minister of national defense came from the instructions of the party leadership. These instructions were directed towards guaranteeing the supreme commander tools that are indispensable for solving the basic problems of the Unified Armed Forces. Moreover, he considers it justified to mention the following in the drafts of documents: unequivocally to talk about the military forces assigned to the Unified Armed Forces and their development, keeping in mind the economic potential of each country, and to extend the capabilities of the Committee on Technology in the field of coordination and unification of armament systems, technical equipment, arms co-production, and scientific-research works.

Marshal Iakubovskii: recognized the statement of Cde. Gomułka to be an instruction to act. At the same time he stated that proposals and corrections to the documents are accurate in merit and editorially progressive. He then presented to Cde. Gomułka the idea of carrying out a command post exercise with designated troops on the territory of the ČSSR in May of this year. The following would participate in the exercise: two army commands with designated troops from the Czechoslovak People's Army as well as one army command with designated troops from the Polish Army, the NVA, the Group of Soviet Forces in Germany, the Southern Group of Soviet Forces, and the Transcarpathian Military District.

Cde. Gomułka: approved the participation of Polish Army staffs and units in the exercise and proposed not to introduce NVA troops onto the territory of the ČSSR.

Cde. [Józef] Cyrankiewicz: recognized that the exercise could cover part of the territories of several countries, which would cause the armed forces of the GDR to operate only on their own territory.

Cde. Gomułka: regarding drafts of documents, he underlined the need to make current the status of the Political Consultative Committee so that it would be a full decision-making institution, and its decisions would be binding for all members.

Marshal Iakubovskii: stated that Yugoslavia is actively interested in the situation in the ČSSR as well as in the March incidents in Poland. Moreover, [Yugoslavia] is evidencing special worries about the Mediterranean, protesting the presence of U.S. and Soviet fleets in that area. This is distinctive because [Yugoslavia] did not raise official protests when only the U.S. fleet was in the Mediterranean.

Cde. Gomułka: emphasized the bankruptcy of Yugoslav conceptions up till now. The increase in unemployment, sending workers to labor in western countries (mainly the FRG), working with western firms (among others with "Fiat" on a profit-sharing basis), the uneven development of federal republics without a uniform, general plan, all prove the economic regression of that country. Today, Tito unifies Yugoslavia—it is difficult to foresee what may come after his departure.

[...]

[Source: KC PZPR, 2663, pp. 412–17, AAN. Translated by Magdalena Klotzbach for the National Security Archive.]

Document No. 49: Report to Nicolae Ceaușescu on the Meeting of the Political Consultative Committee in Sofia, June 3, 1968

After his visit with Gomułka in Poland (Document No. 48), Soviet Marshal Iaku-bovskii traveled to East Berlin and Budapest to try to win support for Moscow's plans to reorganize the Warsaw Pact. Given the problems raised by Romania at earlier meetings (see, for example, Document No. 45), he deliberately bypassed Bucharest. The Soviets did send a copy of their proposal to Romania, however, and this letter from Defense Minister Ion Ioniță to Nicolae Ceaușescu reflects the Romanian military's positions on the matter. Ioniță believes it is quite possible other allies will accept the Soviet proposals, in which case Romania should not consider itself bound by any agreements infringing on its sovereignty. He proposes various stances Romania could take. One, clearly with the French example in mind, is to leave the military structures of the Pact. An alternative approach would be to agree with the Soviet documents but with reservations, particularly concerning the right of the supreme commander to deploy troops on the territory of member-states. Ioniță's letter shows how much more extensively the alliance's members debated fundamental issues about its functioning in the 1960s than they did in later years.

[...]

1. In accordance with what was established at the Conference of the Political Consultative Committee that took place in Sofia, Marshal of the Soviet Union I.I. Iakubovskii sent to the [Romanian] Ministry of Armed Forces, along with letter No. 104704 of May 24, 1968, the drafts of the following documents drawn up by the Unified Command:
    – Statute of the Unified Armed Forces [...];
    – Statute of the Military Council [...];
    – Statute of the common system of air defense [...]; and
    – Organizational diagrams of the leading organs of the Supreme Command [...] and the Committee on Technology.

[Iakubovskii] asks for the documents to be analyzed by the Ministry of Armed Forces and [for the results of the analysis] to be brought to the notice of the Romanian Communist Party's leadership and of the government.

At the same time, [Iakubovskii] indicates that soon he will come in person to the Socialist Republic of Romania, so that together with the [Romanian] minister of armed forces he can bring to the notice of the general secretary of the Central Committee of the Romanian Communist Party and of the president of the Council of Ministers the above-mentioned materials, along with the observations and proposals concerning these materials made by the ministries of armed forces of the Polish People's Republic, the German Democratic Republic, the Bulgarian People's Republic, the Czechoslovak Socialist Republic, and the Hungarian People's Republic.

2. I report that the discussions regarding the improvement of the Unified Command began in 1966 at the initiative of the Soviet side. At two conferences, in February 1966 at the level of the chiefs of general staffs, and in May 1966 at the level of ministers of defense [...], a draft statute of the Unified Armed Forces Command was discussed and drawn up, on which the delegation of the Ministry of Armed Forces agreed, except for a number of objections that were included in the protocol of the conference of the ministers of armed forces, which took place in Moscow in May 1966.

These objections referred to:
- the role and functions of the Political Consultative Committee;
- the need to create the Military Council of the Unified Command, with a consultative role;
- representatives of the supreme commander of the Unified Armed Forces in the armies of the Warsaw Treaty states, whose presence was not deemed advisable.

On the occasion of the meeting of the Political Consultative Committee in Bucharest, in May 1966, the Romanian side drew up its own draft statute, which it handed over to the ministers of defense of the states taking part in the Warsaw Treaty Organization. As you know, the draft statute of the Unified Command was not discussed any further at this conference of the Political Consultative Committee.

In February 1968, another conference at the chief-of-general-staff level took place in Prague; at this conference the issues of creating the Military Council of the Unified Command and of approving the statute thereof, as well as a draft statute of the Unified Command, were discussed. The delegation of the Ministry of Armed Forces did not agree with the provisions of the protocol concluded on that occasion, expressing a different view, in which it was specified that "it is of the opinion that general issues and issues of principle must first of all be solved and finalized, and only then is the statute of the Unified Command—where its attributions are established—to be submitted to the governments of the Warsaw Treaty states for consideration and approval; afterwards, one may proceed to the creation of its various organs..."

After the Prague conference, these issues were included on the agenda of the conference of the Political Consultative Committee in Sofia, in March 1968, which established that the ministers of defense of the Warsaw Treaty states are to analyze and put forward, in six months' time, proposals concerning the statute of the Unified Command, as well as the creation of the general staff, the Military Council, and the Technical Council.

3. It was apparent from the documents sent by the Unified Command and analyzed beforehand by the collegium of the Ministry of Armed Forces, that in these documents some of the proposals the Ministry of Armed Forces made at previous conferences were included, such as those referring to the creation of the Military Council; the appointment, by the governments of the Warsaw Treaty states, of the chief of staff and of the supreme commander's deputies in charge of air defense and equipment from the ranks of the armed forces of each state; direct subordination of the troops which make up the Unified Armed Forces to the ministries of defense (practically, however, due to the rights of command and control granted to the supreme commander and to the general staff, this [direct subordination] is only fiction); pro-

portional representation of the armies of the Warsaw Treaty countries within the framework of the Unified Command, etc.

Issues were also included, however, that contradicted the point of view approved by the state and party leadership [of Romania] and supported by the delegations of the Ministry of Armed Forces at the previous conferences.

In connection with the aforementioned issues, we paid special attention to the fact that some provisions in the present statute of the Unified Command, which refer to the right of the supreme commander to command, control and give orders to the troops comprising the Unified Armed Forces, were again adopted, in spite of the fact that they were abandoned and were no longer included in the draft statute of May 1966. However, now there is a proposal to create a body whose commander has the right to command and control, not only rights of coordination and cooperation, [but of] examination and recommendation, as the delegations of the Ministry of Armed Forces have proposed at all the conferences that have taken place so far.

Below, I will bring to your attention the main issues included in the draft documents sent, and the proposals of the Ministry of Armed Forces.

a) In the draft statute of the Unified Armed Forces it is stipulated that the Political Consultative Committee has the task of settling general issues commonly agreed upon, which are directed towards strengthening the defense capability of the Warsaw Treaty states, and improving the structure of the Unified Armed Forces; appointing the supreme commander; making decisions and giving instructions with regard to the activity of the supreme commander, the latter being required to inform the Political Consultative Committee about the results of his activity.

Concurrently, the Political Consultative Committee is given the right to make decisions as to troops of the Unified Armed Forces moving to the stage of high and complete combat capability, and to analyze and approve plans linked with the development of the Unified Armed Forces (it is true that such rights are granted to the Political Consultative Committee or the governments of the Warsaw Treaty states).

Granted such rights to the Political Consultative Committee is in contradiction with the provisions of the Warsaw Treaty, Art. 6 of which states that the Political Consultative Committee was created "with the purpose of carrying out—between the signatory states—the consultations provided in the present Treaty..." and, therefore, it is a consultative organ.

The right is granted to the supreme commander to command and control the armed forces of the Warsaw Treaty states. According to the draft statute, the supreme commander can issue orders, directives, dispositions, and even deploy troops of the Unified Armed Forces on the territories of the Warsaw Treaty states, and to relocate them to other points, depending on the situation and corresponding to the needs of mutual defense. To confer a legal aspect on this right, it is stated that the deployments are to be conducted in keeping with the "decisions of the governments of these states."

The right is also conferred on the supreme commander to control the development of operational and combat preparations, and the level of combat capability of the troops and fleets composing the Unified Armed Forces, in compliance with both the general plan of the common activities and his own assessment. Such control attributions are also provided for the general staff of the Unified Command.

In this way, the provisions of the draft statute contradict the principles of collaboration and mutual assistance based on respect for sovereignty and national independence, and nonintervention in internal affairs, thus negatively affecting the essential attributes of the governments of the Warsaw Treaty states. All these rights place the supreme commander above the national governments and turn the Supreme Command into a supranational command and control organ, instead of a coordination and cooperation organ, the activity of which is based on the principles of organizing relationships between socialist countries with equal rights.

Another fact deserving special attention is the proposed denomination of the draft statute: "Statute of the Unified Armed Forces of the Warsaw Treaty states."

The argument that "the Unified Armed Forces are created in accordance with Art. 5 of the Treaty of Friendship..." is not correct; Art. 5 provides that "The contracting parties have agreed on the creation of a Unified Command of the armed forces...," and not on the creation of the Unified Armed Forces. It is logical, therefore, to draw up a statute of this command, and not of the Unified Armed Forces. I emphasize the fact that the present statute approved by the Political Consultative Committee in 1956 bears the title "Statute of the Unified Command of the armed forces of the Warsaw Treaty states."

Besides in the title of the draft statute of the Unified Command, its contents, and the drafts of the other documents sent, the "unified armed forces" are often referred to. This is something we cannot agree with since the armed forces of the Warsaw Treaty states are not unified; they remain subordinate to the national commands, and the way they are used can only be decided by the party and state leadership of the state in question.

b) The draft "Statute of the Military Council of the Unified Armed Forces of the states participating in the Warsaw Treaty Organization" stipulates that the Military Council is a military organ of the Unified Armed Forces, with functions of consultation and recommendation. The recommendations and the proposals are to be adopted, however, by the Military Council, on the basis of a simple majority of votes. The Military Council is composed of the supreme commander, his deputies in the armies of the Warsaw Treaty states, the chief of the general staff of the Unified Armed Forces, the deputy in charge of air defense, the deputy in charge of equipment, and a secretary appointed by the supreme commander.

Concomitantly, it is mentioned that the chief of staff of the Unified Armed Forces "organizes control over the fulfillment of the supreme commander's decisions regarding the proposals and recommendations adopted by the Military Council."

The Military Council's adoption of proposals and recommendations by a simple majority of votes is a principle applicable within the internal framework of the parties and states, and I think it cannot be extended to relationships between parties and states. Its application to international relationships is not acceptable.

c) Together with the draft statute of the Unified Armed Forces and the draft statute of the Military Council of the Unified Armed Forces of the Warsaw Treaty states, I have also received a new "Statute of the common air defense system of the states participating in the Warsaw Treaty Organization."

267

It is apparent from the analysis of this draft statute that the common air defense system joins together all the air defense troops of the Warsaw Treaty states, and on the part of the USSR the air defense troops deployed on the territories of the Soviet Socialist Republics of Latvia, Lithuania, Belorussia, Ukraine, and Moldavia.

It is stipulated that command of the common air defense system be exerted by the commander of the air defense troops of the Warsaw Treaty states, the command organ being the chief of staff of air defense of the state from which the commander was appointed.

[...] The adoption of such a statute for air defense troops would lead, practically, to their subordination to the commander of air defense troops of the Warsaw Treaty states.

The existence of representatives of the supreme commander in the armies of Warsaw Treaty states, an issue vigorously debated at previous conferences, and—as a result of a proposal by the Ministry of Armed Forces—no longer included in the draft statute drawn up at the conference of ministers of defense in May 1966, is included again in the draft statutes received, the purpose being to make their existence permanent. [...]

4. In conclusion, a study of the documents sent by the Unified Command has brought out in particular the obvious change of position of our Soviet partner, in the sense that it has again introduced provisions in the documents, which grant the supreme commander, the General Staff, and the commander of the air defense troops of the Warsaw Treaty states the possibility of commanding and controlling troops intended to act jointly. The fact is also significant that in the draft statute of the Unified Command drawn up at the Conference of the Ministries of Defense in May 1966 as a result of proposals by the Ministry of Armed Forces, such provisions were no longer included. All of the delegations—including the Soviet one—agreed that the Unified Command should be an organ of coordination and cooperation, not of command and control.

5. Taking into consideration the things I have brought to your attention, I think that at discussions at future conferences of the ministries of defense aimed at drawing up proposals for the Political Consultative Committee, the Ministry of Armed Forces delegation must set forth the following point of view:

- to further support the point of view and the draft statute of the Unified Command drawn up by the Ministry of Armed Forces and approved by the party and state leadership in 1966, [...];
- to agree with the draft statute of the Military Council, with the observation that the recommendations and proposals of the Military Council should be adopted on the basis of unanimity, not a simple majority of votes. [...];
- to support the idea that the draft statute referring to the air defense system of the Warsaw Treaty states should be drawn up in accordance with the same principle as in the draft statute of the Unified Command drawn up by the Ministry of Armed Forces; [that draft] assigns air defense the role of coordinator of joint activities to the command of air defense troops of the Warsaw Treaty states.

[...] Taking into account the experience acquired so far, and the viewpoint expressed at previous conferences by the delegations of other countries, it is quite possible that the point of view of the Ministry of Armed Forces may not be accepted. In such a situation, the other delegations might express agreement with the draft documents drawn up by the Unified Command, and put forward a common point of view to the Political Consultative Committee.

If the situation develops as I described above and the conclusion of a protocol is proposed, the delegation of the Ministry of Armed Forces should express its divergent viewpoint about the issue of the documents drawn up by the Unified Command, stating that the Ministry of Armed Forces will not work in compliance with the provisions of these documents since they infringe on the principles of equality between states, alliance, independence, national sovereignty and nonintervention in the internal affairs of other countries, and they turn the Political Consultative Committee and the Unified Command into supranational bodies.

As a follow-up to this position, the Socialist Republic of Romania, without declaring that it is leaving the Treaty places itself outside of the integrated military organs of the Warsaw Treaty Organization.

There could be another solution, namely, that—in the event the other delegations do not adopt our point of view, which is in fact the most probable situation—the delegation of the Ministry of Armed Forces would finally agree with the draft documents drawn up by the Unified Command, except for the provisions referring to the existence of representatives of the supreme commander in the framework of the armies of the Warsaw Treaty states, to the right of the supreme commander to deploy and redeploy troops of the Unified Armed Forces on the territory of Warsaw Treaty states, and to the adoption of recommendations and proposals in the Military Council on the basis of a simple majority of votes.

Expressing this point of view, the delegation of the Ministry of Armed Forces should declare that the Socialist Republic of Romania reserves the right to review the number of tactical and operational units and large units of all the categories of armed forces, which are to be included in the structure of the Unified Armed Forces with a view toward] reducing them.

[Source: *Arhivele Militare Române (henceforth AMR) [Romanian Military Archives], fond V2, vol.3, dosar 12/35, ff.53–63. DR, vol.1, pp. 399–409. Translated by Viorel Nicolae Buta.*]

Document No. 50: Memorandum of the Academic Staff of the Czechoslovak Military Academies on Czechoslovakia's Defense Doctrine, June 4, 1968

Sometimes referred to in Western literature as the Gottwald memorandum, this document was prepared by the staffs of the Klement Gottwald Military Political Academy in Prague and the Antonín Zápotocký Military Technical Academy in Brno. Its authors were official theoreticians who by this time had become reformers, and as such had moved in their thinking much farther than the Dubček leadership. Although the memorandum was originally intended for party leaders, it also was published in the newspapers on July 2, which must certainly have alarmed the Soviets because its ideas were quite unorthodox. Despite the use of Marxist jargon it contained some very common-sense judgments, many of which were ahead of their time. Among its noteworthy points are the argument that nuclear deterrence was irrelevant to small countries like Czechoslovakia that were not in a position to implement it; the statement that future security policy should be European-based and aimed at reducing tensions; and the view that crises such as in Berlin and Cuba must be avoided because of their adverse economic effects quite apart from the terrible military threats they engender.

Formulation and Constitution of Czechoslovak State Interests in the Military Area

The draft of the action program of the Czechoslovak People's Army poses with particular urgency the question of elaborating the state military doctrine of the Czechoslovak Socialist Republic. In our opinion, the point of departure ought to be the state interests of Czechoslovakia in the military area which, however, have not yet been formulated and constituted.

The signatories of this memorandum, who are scholarly associates working for the Czechoslovak armed forces, wish to contribute to the scientific examination and formulation of those state interests. In sections 1 and 2, they express their position concerning the present state of our military doctrine and military policy. In sections 3 and 4, they outline the procedure for a theoretical examination of the data aimed at the formulation of doctrinal conclusions. In section 5, they justify the necessity of using scientific methods to solve these problems.

They are sending this memorandum to provide the basis for an exchange of opinion. They consider a dialogue necessary for the development of scientific research.

Prague, May 1968

1. Political and Military Doctrine

1.1. The political doctrine of a socialist state is primarily influenced by the choice of wider goals within the international community and its relationship with the diverse forces representative of social progress.

The principle of socialist internationalism is organically linked with the national responsibility of a sovereign state. This is normally more important as well as more difficult the smaller the physical power of the state. The choice cannot solely depend on "national interest," which cannot be defined in a pure form—neither as an interest of one's own state, nor as an interest of the leading state of a coalition. The interest of the societal movement, of which sovereign states are a part, is decisive, specifically the interest of European socialism and its dynamic development. Mere defense of what has been accomplished fosters stagnation and degeneration; the wrong choice of an offensive strategy has a destructive effect on the progress of the whole societal movement.

1.2. Military policy as an aggregate of actions in military matters implements military interests and needs through a chosen strategy. In regard to national interest, the military doctrine of the state can be described as a comprehensive formulation of its military interests and needs.

The doctrine is a binding theoretical and ideological base for the formulation of military policy and the resulting measures as well as for negotiations with the alliance partners. It amounts to a compromise between the maximum requirements and actual resources, between the dynamics of the evolving military knowledge and the findings of the social sciences, between the development of technology and the requirement of an effective defense system corresponding to the military circumstances at any given time.

1.3. The formulation of the state's military doctrine influences retroactively its political doctrine and strategy. It substantially affects its capability to project itself internationally by nonmilitary means. Giving up one's own military doctrine means giving up responsibility for one's own national and international action. A surrender to spontaneity, this entails the de-politicization of military thought, which in turn leads to a paralysis of the army. It is the fundamental source of crisis of the army organism by tearing it out of society. It disrupts the metabolism between the army and the society. It deprives the army of its raison d'être for the national community by limiting the interaction between national goals and the goals of the socialist community.

2. The Past, Present, and Future of Czechoslovakia's Military Policy

2.1. The foundations of Czechoslovakia's present defense systems were laid at the beginning of the 1950s, at which time the responsible political actors of the socialist countries assumed that a military conflict in Europe was imminent. It was a strategy based on the slogan of defense against imperialist aggression, but at the same time assuming the possibility of transition to the strategic offensive with the goal of achieving complete Soviet hegemony in Europe. No explicit reassessment of this coalition strategy, by taking into account the potential of nuclear missiles, has ever taken place.

2.2. The Czechoslovak army, created with great urgency and extraordinary exertion, became a substantial strategic force by the time Europe's political and military situation had fundamentally changed. Although in 1953 we noted a relaxation of international tension and in 1956 introduced the new strategy of peaceful coexistence, no formulation of Czechoslovakia's own military doctrine or reform of its army took place. Invoking the threat of German aggression, the alliance continued to be tightened up. Increasingly, the threat of German aggression has taken on the role of an extraneous factor employed with the intent to strengthen the cohesion of the socialist community. Once the original notions about the applicability of a universal economic and political model had to be revised, military cooperation was supposed to compensate for insufficient economic cooperation and the inadequacy of other relationships among the socialist countries.

2.3. In politics, there is a lack of clarity about the probable trends of development in the progressive movement to which we belong. There is a prevailing tendency to cling to the obsolete notions that have become part of the ideological legacy of the socialist countries. There is a prevailing tendency to try to influence all the segments of the movement, regardless of the sharply growing differences in their respective needs resulting from social and economic development.

In 1956 and 1961, we proved by our deeds that we were ready to bear any global risks without claiming a share of responsibility for the political decisions and their implementation. By doing so, we proved that we did not understand even the European situation and were guided not by sober analysis but by political and ideological stereotypes. (Hence also the surprise with regard to Hungary in 1956 and the inadequate response in 1961.)

2.4. Our military policy did not rest on an analysis of our own national needs and interests. It did not rest on our own military doctrine. Instead it was a reflection of the former sectarian party leadership, which prevented the party from conducting a realistic policy of harmonizing the interests of different groups with national and international interests for the benefit of socialism. The development of the army was deprived of both rational criteria and an institutionalized opposition. Military policy was reduced to the quest to optimally match our resources with the demands of the alliance. Devoid of principles, it was bound to create contradictions and crises within the army.

Inevitably the twenty years of deformed development affected the ability, or rather inability, of the cadres to overcome the deformations. Theoretical backwardness in military theory and the formulation of a military doctrine has been a great obstacle to the overcoming of past errors.

2.5. Czechoslovakia's military policy will continue being built upon the alliance with other Warsaw Treaty partners, above all the USSR. At the same time, however, it will be a policy based on state sovereignty, and designed to provide our input into developing the alliance's common positions. A modern conception of the Warsaw Treaty can only have one meaning: the increased external security of its member-states to foster the development of both the socialist states and the states of Western Europe. Our military policy will not shun global risks, but only in the role of a partner rather than of a victim of a development that it cannot influence.

272

It will essentially be a European security policy, supportive of international détente in Europe, all-European cooperation, and Europe's progressive forces. It will serve as an instrument of a broader, but not self-serving policy. A military policy that needs to construe and exaggerate an enemy threat fosters conservative tendencies in both socialism and capitalism. While in the short run it may seem to "strengthen" socialism, in the long run it weakens it.

2.6. Czechoslovakia's military policy must rest on a scientific analysis of a whole range of possible war situations in Europe, formulate its own sovereign interests and needs accordingly, estimate its military capabilities in particular situations within the framework of the coalition, and act on its own scientifically elaborated strategic doctrine.

3. The Contemporary War–Peace Situation

3.1. The naively pragmatic realist approach considers relations among sovereign states from the point of view of either war or peace. In actuality there is a whole range of situations whose common denominator is the availability of instruments of armed violence but which differ in the manner of their use. As a result of substantive social and political changes and the scientific–technological revolution in military affairs, such a range of situations is considerably more complex and diverse not only in comparison with the situation before World War II but also with the situation in the early fifties.

Yet, at this very time of incipient gigantic transformations of a social and political as well as scientific and technological nature, our military policy and doctrine applied the Soviet model as universally valid.

3.2. The above-mentioned range of possible situations may be summarized as follows:

- absolute war (in different variations),
- limited wars (of several types),
- a situation between war and peace resulting from the long-term legalization of an originally temporary armistice as a result of which the adversaries are no longer fighting but peace treaties have not been concluded either,
- potential war, i.e. indirect use of instruments of armed violence as a means of foreign policy,
- peace among potential adversaries,
- peace among allied sovereign states,
- peace among neutrals,
- absolute peace through general and complete disarmament.

This description is a distillation of specific situations, which are in turn combinations of an indefinite number of possible situations that make sovereign states and military coalitions implement their foreign and military policies.

3.3. The stereotype of class struggle, with its dichotomy of friends and foes, has reduced substantive political distinctions among sovereign states to basic class antagonism, with pernicious consequences for our political strategy and tactics. Yet the Leninist postulate of specific analysis of a concrete situation differentiates according to actual distinctions.

At the very least, the typology should consider:
- actual and potential allies,
- neutrals,
- potential adversaries,
- actual adversaries,
- war enemies.

Czechoslovakia's state interests and needs require doing justice to different situational variants while rejecting illusions and dangerous simplifications.

4. Possible Formulation of Czechoslovakia's Military Interests and Needs Related to the War–Peace Situation in Contemporary Europe

The doctrinal formulation and constitution of Czechoslovak military interests and needs first requires a substantive analysis of particular war–peace situations, especially in Europe. Our own military interests and needs should then be formulated accordingly. This should be the point of departure for practical measures in accordance with the doctrine. Following is a brief outline of how one might proceed in some of the basic situations.

4.1. Absolute war in Europe

Given the accumulation of nuclear missiles by both major military coalitions, the possible outbreak of such a war in Europe is fraught with catastrophic consequences for most of its European participants. At the same time, the permanent lead time in the offensive rather than the defensive deployment of nuclear missiles, as well as our unfavorable geographical position, make it impossible to substantially limit the destructiveness of enemy first strikes against our territory to an extent compatible with the preservation of our national and state existence. It must be said openly that the outbreak and conduct of a global nuclear war in the European theater would be tantamount to national extinction and the demise of state sovereignty, especially of the frontline states, including Czechoslovakia. The futility of such a war as a means of settling European disputes, as demonstrated by the development of the so-called Berlin crisis of 1961, of course does not exclude its possibility.

In such a situation, we consider it appropriate to formulate Czechoslovakia's military interests and needs as a matter of primary existential importance:
- preventing the conduct of a nuclear war on our territory is a fundamental existential need of our society;
- Czechoslovakia has a strategic interest in actively contributing to the reduction of the real possibility of absolute war in Europe.

Our fundamental needs and interests in the event of such a war should determine a foreign policy aimed at limiting the possibility of a nuclear attack against Czechoslovakia. The appropriate measures are, for example, the conclusion of a nuclear non-proliferation treaty, the creation of a nuclear-free zone in Central Europe, and supplementary guarantees of the status quo in Europe.

4.2. Limited war in Europe

Analysis of the possible scenarios in Europe obviously starts with recognition of the growing danger of such a war and its growing strategic and political significance.

In recognizing the futility of limited war as a means of Czechoslovak foreign policy and in emphasizing our interest in eliminating it as a means of settlement of European disputes, we assume the necessity of purposefully waging war against an attack in a fashion conducive to limiting its destructive effects on our territory and population.

The formulation and constitution of Czechoslovakia's particular interests and needs will determine the practical measures to be taken:

- Preparation of Czechoslovakia's armed forces and its entire defense system within the framework of the Warsaw Treaty for the different variants of enemy attack with the goal of repelling it, defeating the adversary, and compelling him to settle peacefully.
- Reduction of the real possibility of war by reciprocal military and political acts of peaceful coexistence aimed at eliminating the use of force as a means of the settlement of disputes.

4.3. Situation between war and peace in Europe

This is the situation resulting from the failure to conclude a peace treaty with Germany and from the great-power status of Berlin inside the territory of the GDR. Herein is the possibility of a sudden deterioration leading to severe military and political crisis. At the present time, such a crisis would have catastrophic consequences for our economy, as happened during the 1961 Berlin and 1962 Cuban crises. This would substantially worsen our strained economic situation, with overly negative consequences for our development in a progressive direction.

These characteristics determine our approach to the formulation of Czechoslovakia's interests and needs, namely:

- our primary strategic and political need to prevent such a military and political crisis at the present time,
- our interest in reducing the possibility of a transition from the absence of war to a limited war while searching for a solution to the German question as the key question of contemporary Europe.

This further postulates measures to be taken in both military and foreign policy, above all through the Warsaw Pact, with the goal of normalizing relations between Czechoslovakia and the Federal Republic of Germany.

4.4. Potential war in Europe

At issue is the indirect use of the potential for armed violence as an instrument of foreign policy, as implied in the policy of deterrence, practiced especially by the nuclear powers. Czechoslovakia cannot use deterrence against the Western powers. Its deterrence posture is declaratory and politically ineffective if it is not supported by strategic measures against potential adversaries geographically distant from us. At the same time, the use of deterrence against Czechoslovakia by some of its potential adversaries forces us to respond in kind.

These characteristics determine the formulation of Czechoslovakia's needs and interests, namely:

- our temporary need to use the potential for armed violence against the adversary that uses it against us,
- our lack of interest in using it as a matter of equivalent reciprocity, i.e. our interest in its exclusion as an instrument of foreign policy.

In this situation, we aim at the conclusion of legally binding agreements with potential adversaries that would ban the use of the threat of force in mutual relations. This can be realized in relations between Czechoslovakia and Austria, Czechoslovakia and France, and Czechoslovakia and the Federal Republic of Germany.

4.5. Peace among potential adversaries in Europe

This is the situation obtaining in Europe among potential adversaries who have no mutually exclusive interests and do not apply the policy of deterrence against one another.

Here Czechoslovakia's interests and needs lie in the legal codification of the state of peace with a growing number of potential adversaries.

Our practical goals should be the conclusion of non-aggression treaties and arms limitation agreements with such partners. In this way, we can contribute to the reduction of tensions between potential adversaries, the growth of peace in Europe, and the reciprocal gradual neutralization of instruments of armed violence.

4.6. In other possible peace situations in Europe, as enumerated earlier, military interests and needs represent a share in Czechoslovakia's overall interests and needs. The closer the peace, of course, the lower the share. Absolute peace entails the abolition of the material and technological base for war, and thus also of the base for military interests and needs.

In view of Czechoslovakia's current foreign and military policy predicament, our main task is the formulation and constitution of its military interests and needs pertinent to the situations referred to in points 4.2 through 4.5.

If the formulation of Czechoslovak military doctrine is to be more scientific, the main question is that of choosing the right approach and avoiding the wrong ones.

5. Systems Analysis and the Use of Modern Research Methods

5.1. In constituting a Czechoslovak military doctrine, the most dangerous and precarious approach is the one-sided use of simple logic and old-fashioned working habits.

If Czechoslovakia is to be preserved as an entity, giving absolute priority to the possibility of a general war in Europe that involves the massive use of nuclear weapons makes no sense, for this entails a high probability of our country's physical liquidation regardless of how much money and resources are spent on its armed forces and regardless even of the final outcome of the war.

5.2. For each of the variants under 4.2, 4.3, 4.4, and 4.5, systems analysis and other modern methods of research allow us to determine the correlation between, on the one hand, the material, financial, and personnel expenditures on the armed forces (assuming perfect rationality of their development) and, on the other hand, the degree of risk of the state's physical destruction and the loss of its sovereignty, while taking into account the chances of a further advance of socialism, or even the elimination of the threat of war.

At issue is the attainment of pragmatic stability in national defense and army development, corresponding to political needs and related to foreign policy by striving to avert war through increasing the risks for the potential adversary while preserving the sovereign existence of the Czechoslovak Socialist Republic, thus giving substance to its contribution to the coalition in fulfillment of its internationalist duty.

Managing the development of our armed forces solely on the basis of simple logic, empiricism, and historical analogy, perhaps solely in the interests of the coalition without regard to one's own sovereign interests, is in its final effect inappropriate and contradicts the coalition's interests.

Besides the reconciliation of our own and the coalition's interests in our military doctrine, we consider it necessary to utilize systems analysis and all other available methods of scientific prognosis, including model-building. Thus the preparedness of our armed forces in different variants can be assessed and related to the evolving political needs and economic possibilities. This concerns not so much tactical, operational, and organizational issues as the confrontation of political and doctrinal problems with reality.

We regard systems analysis as the new quality that can raise the effectiveness of our armed forces above the current level.

5.3. At the most general level, we can see two possible ways of managing our army's development:

- The first way is proceeding from the recognition of the personnel, technological, and financial limitations imposed by society upon the armed forces toward the evaluation of the risks resulting from the failure to achieve desirable political goals under the different variants of European development described in the preceding section. The decision about the extent of acceptable risk must be made by the supreme political organ of the state.
- The second way is proceeding from the recognition of the acceptable risk as set by the political leadership toward the provision of the necessary personnel, technological, and financial means corresponding to the different variants of European development.

Either of these ways presupposes elaboration of less than optimal models of army development for each of the variants, applying the requirements of national defense regardless of the existing structure of the system. Confrontation of the model with the available resources should then determine the specific measures to be taken in managing the development of the armed forces and their components.

The proposed procedure would not make sense if we were to keep the non-systemic, compartmentalized approach to building our armed forces without being able to prove to the political leadership that the available personnel, financial, and technological means are being used with maximum effectiveness to prepare our armed forces for any of the different variants of European development rather than merely show their apparent preparedness at parades and exercises organized according to a prepared scenario.

5.4. Increasingly, strategic thought has been shifting away from seeking the overall destruction of all enemy assets to the disruption of the enemy defense system by destroying selected elements, thus leading to its collapse. In some cases, such as in the Israeli–Arab war, the theory proved its superiority in practice as well. Its application in developing our army, elaborating our strategy, and designing our operational plans can result not only in substantial military savings but also increased effectiveness for our defense system. In case of a relative (but scientifically arrived at and justified) decrease of those expenditures, it may help limit the consequences of the exponential growth in costs of the new combat and management technology. Most importantly, it may help impress on the armed forces command and the political leadership the best way of discharging their responsibilities toward both the state and the coalition.

5.5. The proposed procedures and methods toward the constitution of Czechoslovak military doctrine can of course be implemented only through a qualitatively new utilization of our state's scientific potential. We regard science as being critically conducive to the implementation of working methods that practitioners are inhibited from using because of their particular way of thinking, their time limitations, and reasons of expediency. We regard science as a counterweight that could block and balance arbitrary tendencies in the conduct of the armed forces command and the political leadership. In this we see the fundamental prerequisite for a qualitatively new Czechoslovak military doctrine and the corresponding management of our armed forces.

[*Source: Sb. KV ČSFR, D II/73, Institute for Contemporary History, Prague. Translated by Vojtech Mastny.*]

Document No. 51: Action Program of the
Czechoslovak Army, June 11, 1968

During the Prague Spring, no segment of Czechoslovak society, not even the military, was immune to pressures for reform. As seen elsewhere (Document No. 47, for example), elements of the Czechoslovak Army wanted to move much farther than the delegation to the PCC meeting in March was willing to go. This draft action program, prepared within the Defense Ministry, offers interesting details of the reformers' thinking. It shows the authors' clear interest in demonstrating fundamental loyalty to the Warsaw Pact. Thus, the program reflects support for structural and statutory changes in the alliance and for the proposed Military Council. But it also insists that in view of the nuclear weapons in Soviet hands, Moscow should thoroughly discuss and share its intentions with its allies. The document argues that there should be consultations within the Pact about a strategic concept and a military doctrine for the coalition. Furthermore, the authors assert that Czechoslovakia should not only elaborate its own military doctrine but also develop its armed forces on the basis of national principles and provide for direction of the country's defense by parliamentary and governmental commissions rather than by party-appointed bodies. Despite references to the desirability of full integration into the Warsaw Pact, these were innovations that the Soviets loathed.

[...]

The existence of the Czechoslovak People's Army (CzPA) is one of the basic attributes of sovereignty of the Czechoslovak state, and a basis for the successful development of its socialist establishment. In the interests of society, the army must be built upon democratic traditions. [...]

[The Communist Party] saw the safeguards of the security of the state in the strengthening of political and economic power of the people's democracy as well as in the firm international position of our Republic. The alliance with the Soviet Union was adopted as the guideline for Czechoslovak foreign policy. The Soviet army became a pattern for building our democratic and antifascist army.

However, the CzPA was being built amid the complex interaction of external and internal influences. It has been influenced by the development of our national democratic and socialist revolution, the distribution of class and political changes and their evolutionary trends, the international setting, the interpretation of patterns of contemporary warfare, as well as the overall development of military affairs.

Under the pressure of the danger of an early war, all the socialist countries tried hard to increase their defensive capabilities in the 1950s. The increased pace resulted in certain mistakes and inconsistencies in its development, however. For instance, the purge in the officers' ranks, which should have gotten rid of reactionary and politically unreliable cadres, was accompanied by serious violations of socialist law and order. The purge affected numerous people dedicated to socialism, too. Wide-scale army recruitment could not always ensure the principle of quality first. New commanding officers could not be trained properly; the level of professional military preparedness decreased.

The thesis on the sharpening of class struggle influenced the army's development in a negative way, too. Internal army life was subject to distortions, as was the role of the army in society. Legislative and public control of the army was abandoned. Army management tended to centralize political power in practice, the CPCz's [Communist Party of Czechoslovakia] role was changed unfavorably, and the differences between party and official [government] activities gradually disappeared.

Mistakes were also committed during the CzPA's integration with the armed forces of the world socialist system. The automatic adoption of the Soviet pattern of the army's formation and management resulted in the neglect of specific conditions both in theory and practice. The continuity with previous army development was disrupted pointlessly. National specifics were neglected or underestimated, our own military traditions disdained and, above all, high-quality creative work in the military sciences stagnated.

These circumstances shaped both positively and negatively the CzPA's characteristically extensive model of development. Since 1953, this gradually came to contradict the requirements of warfare as well as the capacities of the Czechoslovak economy. These contradictions became one of the causes of a disconnect between the army and the people.

After the XXth CPSU Congress,[19] which amounted to a turning point in the military policy of the communist parties as well, attempts were made to abandon some of the negative consequences of the CzPA's extensive build-up. No decisive turning point in the army's development took place, however. The build-up of the army was determined too much by short-term and often one-sided premises based on simple logic, theory and historical analogies. Instead of a purposeful formation of a comprehensive system, an inadequately coordinated development of individual components took place.

The development in warfare has acquired brand new qualities in the meantime. These call for fundamental changes in all branches. It became obvious that the optimal army model could only be the result of a systemic approach to its formation.

The XIIIth CPCz Congress,[20] which posited the build-up of uniform defense systems and the substitution of extensive methods of army work with intensive ones, inaugurated an era of analytical and synthetic conceptualization. At issue was the solution of topical problems related to national defense, combat readiness, and army life. A comprehensive plan for the development of the CzPA was tackled, questions of a national defense system were addressed, and the possibilities of enhancing the combat readiness of troops as well as of improving the system and methods of their training were explored. Certain questions of management and command were elaborated, along with the role of science in the CzPA; changes were also introduced in cadre preparation at military academies.

---

[19] The congress, which took place from February 14 to 25, 1956, was the venue for Nikita Khrushchev's secret speech denouncing Joseph Stalin and his policies.

[20] The congress met from May 31 to June 4, 1966.

Despite the efforts at conceptualization, the process of decision-making and implementation is very slow. The improvements reached previously are rather insignificant. Tensions between new ideas and efforts on the one hand and conservative views and working habits [on the other hand] are growing. CzPA issues are still handled in an extensive fashion. Partial corrections do not ensure the desired reform; they merely increase the complexity of the situation and intensify the inner contradictions. Doubts concerning the correctness of the prior build-up of our armed forces are appearing in all basic spheres—military, technical and social. As a result of the disproportions mentioned, successes in troop preparedness are often gained at the cost of maximal psychic and physical stress on the part of army personnel.

[...]

The tasks of our army derive from its operational and strategic position and the tasks delegated by the Warsaw Treaty. The doctrinal conceptualization of the issues of life and development of our army within the coalition and Soviet military doctrines has not yet responded satisfactorily to the specifics of our development, organization and training. We are facing the task of elaborating the military doctrine of the ČSSR.

[...]

Under the complicated conditions of the current development of our society, our membership in the Warsaw Treaty guarantees the safety of our state and victory for socialism in our country.

During the existence of the Warsaw Treaty, a certain improvement in the military potential of this coalition has been attained. From the very beginning, the CzPA has participated effectively and actively in increasing the combat forces of the allied troops. The combat readiness and general preparedness of staffs and CzPA troops have been demonstrated in numerous allied exercises or other training missions. [The troops] have acquitted themselves during several serious military–political events as well.

The CzPA is eminently interested in the structural and statutory strengthening of the Warsaw Treaty's military bodies. Our continuing efforts in this direction stem from a situation that no longer meets the requirements of current development, thus hampering the solution of major issues concerning the prospects for development and preparedness of the Czechoslovak armed forces.

Major efforts must be developed to increase the role of the military bodies of the Warsaw Treaty, in particular:

- demand the establishment of the Military Council of the Unified Forces Staff and Committee on Technology, as per the relevant documents;
- as a first priority of the Military Council, elaborate a more precise Statute of the Unified Command, specifying its relations with the Political Consultative Committee, the governments, and commands of the member-states in both peace time and under conditions of military preparedness of the state; and prepare material for PCC discussion of coalition military doctrine;
- In the second phase, clarify the role and status of the coalition's military bodies in war time while striving to deepen their activities in peace time.

[...]

In 1968, the Party and government bodies should strive for a thorough discussion in the PCC of the international situation, its development, and the USSR's intentions in the military–political area.

On this basis, it will then be necessary to consult jointly on the strategic concept of the Warsaw Treaty, including the main conclusions with regard to coalition doctrine. Following these negotiations, parts of today's military doctrine must be revised and reconciled with our capabilities to the extent necessary for proceeding with urgent tasks in the development of the Czechoslovak armed forces, even before the elaboration of a comprehensive national doctrine.

[...]

We believe it necessary to point out that further development of the army shall follow from Czechoslovak military doctrine, from comprehensive and objective analyses, and from the defense requirements of our state in accordance with its needs and possibilities. At the same time, the integrated defense system of the Warsaw Treaty, as well as the positive results of army development since 1945, shall be respected.

[...]

[*Source: MNO, sekr. MNO, 1968, j. 0262000 z 27.5.1968, VÚA. Translated by Marian Kratochvíl.*]

Document No. 52: Czechoslovak Central Committee Study of Security Policy, June 24, 1968

At the same time that elements of the Czechoslovak army were pressing a nationally oriented reform agenda with respect to the Warsaw Pact, upper layers of the Communist Party put forward an even more controversial critique of the alliance. Prepared by the Eighth [Defense and Security Policy] Department of the Central Committee, this study of Czechoslovak security policy was sent by the head of the CC State Administration Department, Gen. Václav Prchlík, to Dubček for discussion by the Presidium. However, before that debate could take place, Defense Minister Martin Dzúr objected that the study was "politically incorrect"[21] and should not be submitted to the leadership. The study makes a number of points that are worth noting. It argues that 20 years of building up the army at great cost, even during periods of détente, had showed that the Warsaw Pact's commitment to peaceful coexistence was only verbal. It also points out that the practice of invoking the threat of German militarism was nothing but a rationalization for tightening controls within the alliance and requiring higher defense expenditures. Going further, the study declares that the drive to expand military ties among socialist countries was needed only because not enough basis existed for greater cooperation in other fields. Among several other points, the document states that any kind of nuclear war in Europe would be senseless and only bring about the physical destruction of Czechoslovakia. Consequently, it asserts that the nation's primary military purpose must be to sustain Czechoslovakia's existence and sovereignty.

Although the study never reached the Presidium, the Soviet Embassy in Prague obtained a copy and later forwarded it to Moscow with a note that it had been prepared by the "infamous Gen. Prchlík."[22]

[...]

The Czechoslovak Army has been built up for almost twenty years through the exertion of a maximum of both human and material effort, often at the highest pace and to the detriment of other vital social needs. This proceeded even when the relaxation of international tensions was being proclaimed and the political line of peace-

---

[21] Dzúr to Dubček, August 2, 1968, in *Vojenské otázky československé reformy, 1967–1970: Vojenská varianta řešení čs. krize (1967–1968)* [Military Issues in the Czechoslovak Reform, 1967–1970: The Military Option in the Solution of the Czechoslovak Crisis], ed. Antonín Benčík, Jaromír Navrátil, and Jan Paulík (Brno: Doplněk, 1996), p. 249.

[22] Comment by Ambassador Stepan Chervonenko, November 11, 1968, ZIS-195, Institute for Contemporary History, Prague. Over the course of a lengthy army career, Gen. Prchlík served as chief of the Main Political Directorate from 1958 to February 1968, when the Prague Spring was already underway. He was also a long-time member of the Central Committee, heading the CC State Administration Department from February to July 1968. His notoriety, from the Soviet standpoint, reached its pinnacle as a result of a meeting with journalists in Prague on July 15, 1968, during which he expounded even more critically on the same themes laid out in this internal CC study.

ful coexistence was gradually being formulated. One can say that only lip service was being paid to these new phenomena. In the military arena, the earlier approaches have been retained, with certain modifications. Coalition relationships have been further strengthened, primarily with a reference to the acute threat of German imperialist aggression. In reality, this unambiguous threat has been presented more than once an additional reason—an external factor—in part for strengthening ties within the socialist commonwealth, and in part to justify the extraordinary human and material requirements of the armed forces. The military factor has been compensating more and more for inadequate economic cooperation and the slow development of other relations between socialist countries.

Such an approach has become the source of political and ideological attitudes that have not respected the differences in the historical and social–economic interests and levels [of advancement] of particular countries. More than once, for example by taking part in the events of 1956 and 1961[23], we undertook every risk in global politics without vying effectively for a role in those decisions and measures.

Consequently, the party's military policy has not reflected an analysis of the real needs and interests of our national and state community. [...]

One of the key reasons for the failure of the document on the Czechoslovak defense system[24] has been the fact it has not reflected a Czechoslovak military doctrine or basic formulations of a Czechoslovak political and military strategy. It has adopted an incorrect—inverse—procedure for deriving the [defense] system and its constituent elements as well as its support from the operational mission that exceeded both the cadre and material capabilities of our state. Giving up the formulation of our own military doctrine has meant relinquishing our own responsibility in this substantial area of the state life, in both the national as well as international context. Consequences of this have been the growth of the armed forces by its momentum and the divorce of military thinking from politics. Henceforth, the basic source of the crisis of the Army has been created by culling it out of the structure of the society; [the army] was losing its national justification and thus even a sense of its social usefulness. This condition has been further underscored by the above-mentioned exclusive control, from which all representative and executive bodies of the state have been excluded. In practice, the direct management of the armed forces by the party (in fact by only a narrow party-state body and an individual) could not but have had adverse effects even for the party itself and its internal life. [...]

Fulfilling existing commitments to our country's defense means that, despite extraordinary exertions, we cannot keep up with the level of our potential adversary's armies. At the same time, a number of essential army elements are in a state of collapse even now. Up to the year 1970, the operational mission and the resulting requirements for the army's build-up are determined by the Warsaw Pact protocol. If no change is made, tensions will not only endure, but also deepen. [...]

The military doctrine should reflect a balance between all the possibilities and

---

[23] The Hungarian revolution and Berlin crisis.

[24] Resolution of the party presidium on the Czechoslovak defense system of February 14, 1967.

needs of our state, of its dynamic development, as well as of the interests of European socialist development. [...]

It is no longer acceptable that the requirements of the Czechoslovak defense system be derived from the pre-approved operational mission of the Czechoslovak Army. Overestimating the military point of view, with its in adequate assessment of the personnel and material possibilities of our state in particular, has resulted in an insoluble dilemma between the requirements of the armed forces and the possibilities of securing them, with serious, adverse consequences for the further development of society as a whole.

In its consequences, the [new military] doctrine will continue to reflect the alliance ties with the Soviet Union and other Warsaw Pact partners. At the same time, it will establish a policy of introducing considerations based on our own conditions and possibilities into common decisions of the alliance. It [the doctrine] does not aim to renounce global risks. But it must not merely submit to them passively.

In its essence, the Czechoslovak defense policy aspires to be a European security policy, a policy promoting the process of relaxing international tensions in the world, a policy of friendly cooperation with all who express a sincere interest in that. It strives to be a policy of close cooperation with all progressive powers. So it would become a valuable instrument of overall Czechoslovak policy. It will not simply construct or exaggerate the danger posed by the adversary, which ultimately only promotes the conservative tendencies in both socialism and capitalism. [...]

Dwelling on the absolute inevitability of a general war in Europe with the massive use of nuclear weapons makes no existential sense to Czechoslovakia. This option entails a high probability of the physical annihilation of the ČSSR, regardless of the amounts spent and the means applied to the build-up of the armed forces, and notwithstanding even for the final result of the war. [...]

[*Source: Sb. KV ČSFR, D II/60, Institute for Contemporary History, Prague. Translated by Karel Sieber.*]

Document No. 53: Reports on the "Šumava" Exercise, July 1968

These three documents relate to the "Šumava" maneuvers, which became the military cover for the Soviet invasion of Czechoslovakia. The first item is a memo by Gen. Tadeusz Tuczapski, one of Poland's more outspoken military officers. Tuczapski does not try to hide the difficulties or problems that emerged during the exercise, which was intended to intimidate the Dubček leadership, although it did not entirely succeed. The maneuvers resulted in near chaos when Polish movements interfered with an ongoing Czechoslovak reconnaissance exercise. Soviet Marshal Ivan Iakubovskii's intervention created a "very unpleasant atmosphere" and delays ensued. Other problems arose, partly because the Soviets shrouded their plan of action in secrecy. The exercise showed that the forces on which the Soviets intended to rely did not in fact function very well.

The second document is a report by two Hungarian generals and is also quite candid. It makes clear that the exercise was organized for political reasons, to impress the Czechoslovak with the combined strength of Warsaw Pact forces. However, the plan backfired, according to the Hungarians, creating a "tense, nervous, and antagonistic atmosphere." Iakubovskii contributed to the difficulties by parading his mistrust of the Czechoslovaks representatives, who in turn tried at length to convince the Soviets of their reliability. The Hungarians' conclusion was that the maneuvers mainly highlighted the "shortcomings, irregularities, and inadequate provisions in the Warsaw Pact." If not corrected, they warned, these problems would drain Soviet credibility and weaken the alliance.

Finally, the East German view presented here is by Gen. Fritz Streletz,[25] in the form of an information report on a conversation with Soviet Gen. M.I. Kazakov on July 5. Kazakov described the exercise to Streletz (who obviously had not attended) in order to be sure the East Germans were aware of their role in case of an invasion. One of Kazakov's comments was that the combat readiness of the Czechoslovak army had so declined that its ability to operate with other Warsaw Pact armies was in doubt.

---

a) Memorandum by Gen. Tadeusz Tuczapski, July 4, 1968

[...]

I report that on June 18–July 2 a command post exercise (cryptonym "Šumava") was carried on the territory of the Czechoslovak Socialist Republic.

The exercise was led by the Supreme Commander of the Unified Armed Forces—Marshal of the Soviet Union Ivan Iakubovskii. [...]

---

[25] Gen. Streletz later became deputy defense minister and chief of the general ("main") staff in 1979. After the collapse of the GDR, in the early 1990s, he was sentenced to prison for his role in the shoot-to-kill practice against citizens attempting to escape across the East German border.

Participating in the exercise were:
- the command and staff of the Northern Army Group of Poland—as the command and staff of the Front;
- the staffs of two armies together with staffs of two divisions from the Czechoslovak People's Army;
- the staffs of two armies together with staffs of four divisions and four regiments from the Soviet Army Group from the GDR and the Carpathian military district;
- the staff of one army and one division from the Hungarian People's Army;
- the staff of one army and one division from the GDR National People's Army (deployed on the territory of the GDR);
- the command and staff of Silesian military district, the and 10th Sudeten Armored Division—as the army staff and one division [staff].

[...]

The Czechoslovak side, until the commencement of the exercise, was against deployment of the staff and units of the Polish Army on the territory of the ČSSR. Only after Marshal Iakubovskii's intervention at the highest authorities of the ČSSR on June 19, that is, already after the commencement of the exercise, did they agree to allow the staff of our army and staff of one division without troops to enter the territory of the ČSSR. However, the practice range "Mimoň" in the northwestern part of the ČSSR was enforced as a location for the deployment of training staffs of the Polish People's Army, which was not in accordance with the expected operational direction of our army. On June 24, a reconnaissance battalion of the Czechoslovak People's Army had been operating near the location where our division and army staff were deployed, which [because they were] carrying out a tactical exercise and shooting from tanks in the immediate vicinity of our staffs clearly disrupted the work of both our army staff and division staff.

Discussion of this subject between Marshal Iakubovskii; Premier of the ČSSR government Cde. [Oldřich] Černík; and Minister of National Defense Cde. [Martin] Dzúr took place in a very unpleasant atmosphere.

As a result of this discussion the reconnaissance battalion was removed from the area of the army's deployment on July 2.

The plan for the duration of the exercise, which was delivered to operational groups of individual armies, projected concluding the exercise on June 29, and discussing it on July 7.

The plan of the exercise was implemented with much delay, particularly because of operationally unjustified delays in playing out specific situations. As a result of pressure from the Czechoslovak side, attempts by the Soviet comrades to prolong the exercise were torpedoed, and the exercise ended on June 30.

Also, the review of the exercise, which was planned [to take place] after July 6, after another change resulting from talks on July 1 between CPCz CC First Secretary Cde. [Alexander] Dubček and Marshal Iakubovskii, was carried out on July 2, 1968—in accordance with the initial plan.

President of the ČSSR Cde. Gen. [Ludvík] Svoboda, [who was] present during the exercise when the first reports were heard, subsequently hosted a dinner for the directors of the exercise. During this dinner the president raised two very cordial toasts and emphasized in the first toast the role of the Soviet Union in our camp. He also stated that without the Soviet Union our nations and our states could not exist.

[...]

On July 1, the chief of the directing staff, Army Gen. Kazakov declared to representatives of individual armies participating in the exercise that after going over the exercise, the staffs and units would return to their garrisons. However, several hours later Marshal Iakubovskii voided this declaration, and decided that staffs would remain on ČSSR territory, without defining the date of departure of forces from the ČSSR.

[...]

The staff of our army and division, during their stay in the ČSSR, organized and held many meetings with civilians. These meetings—despite the fact that an official representative of the political department of the Czechoslovak Army district, who was supposed to facilitate contacts with local party and administrative authorities, was attached to the army staff—were in all cases inspired and organized by the political department of the Polish army that was taking part in the exercise. During every meeting (mostly organized in the form of a visit to work institutions) the Polish soldiers were greeted only by the representatives of the local administration.

[...]

During the meetings, the people of the ČSSR (mostly workers) generally showed sympathy to our troops and much interest in them. However, in a single case, when a larger number of our troops than initially planned went to the "Škoda" plant—that "surplus" was not allowed in the plant, and only a delegation of 18 persons was received. The atmosphere during the meeting at this plant was not the best.

Significantly, during every meeting, the Czechoslovak comrades scrupulously avoided discussion of current subjects with regard to the ČSSR.

[...]

Characteristic of the atmosphere of the "Šumava" exercise were the tense relations during the whole time between the comrades from the Czechoslovak People's Army and the Soviet directors of the exercise. The state of tension was caused by both sides. During the initial stages, the Czechoslovak comrades took the view that the exercise should be shortened significantly, and toward the end of the exercise demanded that it be finished in accordance with the plan. They also desired guarantees that troops and staffs would leave the ČSSR immediately after the exercise.

The Soviet comrades hoped to extend the duration of the exercise to its maximum beyond what had been agreed with the Czechoslovak side, and they kept secret the real plan of action, without giving concrete answers to questions about the departure date of staffs and forces taking part in the exercise from the territory of the ČSSR.

Another reason for the Soviet leadership's dissatisfaction was the information given by the press, television, and radio of the ČSSR about the conclusion of the exercise—because it was put out unilaterally and had not been discussed with the leadership of the exercise.

The state of tension has significantly intensified during July 1–3 as a result of Marshal Iakubovskii's intervention with regard to the deployment of the Czechoslovak reconnaissance battalion near the staff of the Polish army that was taking part in the exercise.

The intensification of the tense situation was also caused by the fact that the Czechoslovak side did not agree to introduce additional Soviet detachments and repair shops onto ČSSR territory, as well as by a letter from ČSSR Deputy Minister of National Defense Gen. Lt. Mucha to the Chief of Staff of the exercise, Army Gen. Kazakov. [The letter] restricted the free movement of Soviet army units at Czechoslovak army training ranges on the alleged grounds that shooting was being practiced there.

We need to take into account the further intensification of the state of tension due to the prolonged stay of Soviet and Polish forces on the territory of the ČSSR. Already, one can notice increased uneasiness and discomfort on the Czechoslovak side, which has been pointing out the continued further presence of allied forces spurs the appearance and spread of anti-Soviet feelings, including in the Czechoslovak army.

[...]

[*Source: KC PZPR 2663, pp. 419–24, Archiwum Akt Nowych. Translated by Magdalena Klotzbach for the National Security Archive.*]

b) Report by Generals István Oláh and Ferenc Szűcs
   to the Hungarian Politburo, July 5, 1968

The Supreme Chief of the Warsaw Pact's Joint Armed Forces organized strategic–operational military command-staff exercises under the codename "Šumava," which started on 18 June 1968. Most of the exercises were held on the territory of the ČSSR, with some on the territory of the GDR, Poland, and the Soviet Union. Soviet, Czechoslovak, Polish, German, and Hungarian army and division staffs took part in the exercise: in total, these included the staff of one front, the staffs of seven combined-arms armies, one air force army staff, one air defense army staff, and the staffs of nine divisions, as well as subordinate intelligence and rear services units together with lower-level formations. Originally, it was not planned to include the Germans but in the last phase of preparations they joined on the basis of decisions of which we were totally unaware. The Hungarian People's Army was represented by the staffs of the 5th army and the 11th tank division (altogether approximately 800 persons and 260 vehicles).

Romania and Bulgaria, under the command of their deputy chiefs of the General Staff, took part with three persons each, at the invitation of the Supreme Commander.

The exercise was organized essentially for political reasons and with political objectives, on the basis of an analysis of the situation worked out at the Dresden and Moscow conferences. The exercise and the preparation of the highest-ranking staffs were to serve as a kind of camouflage.

The objective of the exercise, its content and procedure, and above all the methods used in carrying it out revealed the extent and implications of the conflicting assessments of underlying facts. As a result, a tense, nervous, and antagonistic atmos-

289

phere arose in which views held by Czechoslovakia clashed with those of the exercise commanders, the Soviet comrades.

On the basis of statements by the exercise commanders, the information they provided, and their activities, as well as on the basis of our own experience, the objectives of the exercise can be summed up as follows:

a) With regard to foreign policy, this was decidedly a demonstration of the strength and unity of the Warsaw Pact and a warning to the imperialists that speculation about the events in Czechoslovakia or about similar internal political developments elsewhere, as well as all provocative attempts, would be doomed from the very start.

b) With regard to domestic policy, the exercises were intended to influence the Czechoslovak events in the sense that a show of the strength and determination of the Warsaw Pact states would paralyze and frighten enemies at home; the exercises would also intimidate wavering elements (especially intellectuals) and bolster and safeguard true Communists dedicated to the revolution and to socialism.

c) Extensive meetings between senior military commanders and the staff participating in the exercise as well as members of units with the Czechoslovak people are to strengthen friendship and shore up the authority of the Soviet Union and the Warsaw Pact.

d) The exceptionally important strategic–operational exercises are designed to enable multinational army staffs to acquire greater experience in planning, organizing, supervising, and cooperating in military operations.

* * *

These planned objectives guided the exercise command in determining the scope of the exercises (the number of those involved), the timetable (making the exercises as long as possible), their content (deploying huge enemy and domestic forces against the ČSSR or for its defense), as well as the means to carry all this out.

The objectives of the exercise were determined by the position of the Soviet comrades in assessing internal political events in Czechoslovakia. They proceeded from the conviction that there is a counterrevolutionary situation in Czechoslovakia or, to be more accurate, a situation on the verge of counterrevolution [...]

The assessment of the Czechoslovak comrades of their internal situation as well as their vision of the exercise and its requirements differed from everything that has been said above. They essentially agreed to the exercise after being convinced that all activities would take place on the basis of a mutual agreement, with Czechoslovakia's active participation and within the framework of specified military objectives.

But this did not happen, and that is why there was a tense atmosphere at the exercise from the very beginning. They were taken aback when they learned that although the exercise was not supposed to be held until the second half of June, some of the Soviet intelligence units and General Kazakov's preparatory staff had arrived on Czechoslovak territory as early as the end of May and beginning of June.

Moreover, during his stay of more than two weeks, Cde. Kazakov was unable or unwilling to inform the Party, government, and military leadership of the objectives of the exercise, the dates of its commencement and termination, the forms it was to take, the planned progression and time schedule of the individual phases, and the size of the armies and staffs arriving on Czechoslovak territory. According to the Czechoslovak comrades, he merely informed them of requirements, especially with regard to intelligence activities. Referring to adequate information, he pointed out that this was the responsibility of the Supreme Commander, who was due to arrive on 10–11 June. This disconcerted the Czechoslovak political and military leadership, and they increasingly pressed for sufficient information, but to no avail. As a result, each demand of the Soviet comrades to increase the number of units and formations triggered conflicts and heated discussions. This gradually increased the mistrust that was already present at the outset.

[...]

The tension increased still further when the Supreme Commander delayed his arrival from the 10th or 11th to the 14th, and then finally arrived on the 18th, the day before the start of the exercises.

The arrival of the Supreme Commander further increased the tense atmosphere surrounding the exercises. The leadership of the Czechoslovak Party again got no answers when it raised questions about the exercises.

[...]

The date of the termination of the exercise was a constant problem not only for the Czechoslovak comrades, but for us as well. On this point the Supreme Commander kept everyone in a state of maximum uncertainty.

The repeated insistence by the Czechoslovak side that the exercise be terminated and that the armies be withdrawn made certain Soviet comrades ask the following question: If these commanders are truly friends of the Soviet Union, why do they object to a Soviet presence that, after all, is there for their benefit as well? Insinuations were made that the presence of Soviet units and military organs had been a problem in the past for Imre Nagy, though not for Cde. [János] Kádár. (The Czechoslovak events were in general terms compared to the Hungarian counterrevolution.)

[...]

As we have pointed out, the Czechoslovak military leaders assessed their domestic situation as well as the objectives of the exercise and the need for it differently from the Soviet comrades. That is why they tried their utmost to ensure that the exercise would not go in the direction it did.

In our opinion, there is no counterrevolutionary situation in the country.

[...]

The experience of the entire exercise unfortunately confirmed that there are unacceptable shortcomings, irregularities, and inadequate provisions in the Warsaw Pact. All this clearly demonstrates that sooner or later these deficiencies will erode the dignity of the Soviet Union and undermine the Pact.

If such results are to be averted, the following steps are necessary:
- the text of the Treaty must be made more specific on the basis of the Politburo resolution, as we had planned;

– in connection with the organization and conduct of the so-called joint exercises, matters of substantial and fundamental importance and their observance must be specified in advance.

On the basis of our experience during the past 20 days and prompted by a feeling of responsibility for the common cause, I take the liberty of proposing to use acceptable methods in explaining to the leaders of the Soviet Party and Government that the unprofessional, crude, and insulting behavior of certain Soviet military commanders is objectively detrimental to the authority and reputation of the Soviet Union and to the unity of the Warsaw Pact.

[*Source: Archives of the Hungarian Defense Ministry, 5/12/11. Translated by Mark Kramer.*]

c) Information Report by Gen. Fritz Streletz to the
   GDR National Defense Council, July 5, 1968

On July 5, 1968 I was received by Army General Kazakov for a conversation in which he told me the following:

The relocation of Soviet and Polish headquarters and troops is taking place at a time currently not specified.

1. The leading Soviet comrades are pleased and satisfied to recognize the politically clear and principle-based position of the Army leadership of the National People's Army.

The National People's Army is maintaining its discipline with regard to the instructions given by their superiors.

In contrast, the Czechoslovak and Polish armies have begun their troop relocations without orders from the leaders of the exercise after the evaluation of the exercise on July 2.

The Polish comrades are also now pushing for their troops and headquarters to relocate as quickly as possible to accommodations on Polish territory.

[...]

2. In the course of the day on July 4, Marshal Iakubovskii was given a document signed by Defense Minister Dzúr. Speaking for the Czechoslovak Party and national leadership, the document called for a plan for troop relocation from the territory of the Czechoslovak Socialist Republic by 20:00 hours of the same day.

This was the occasion for a discussion between Marshal Iakubovskii and Minister Dzúr, which began at 19:00 hours and ended toward 20:00 hours.

Marshal Iakubovskii clearly laid out the Soviet opinion and described how he personally evaluated developments in the ČSSR.

Minister Dzúr responded that the Soviet comrades had not correctly evaluated the process of democratization and that the Communist Party of Czechoslovakia and the working class of the ČSSR had power firmly in hand.

The exercise as such had helped the party and national leadership of the ČSSR a lot. What would now play itself out after the exercise does not help the advanced forces, but rather hindered them in their work.

Marshal Iakubovskii did not agree with this opinion. He pointed to the fact that the USSR had helped and is helping the ČSSR in general.

The genuine danger of the counterrevolution must be recognized and the suggested measures must be taken.

Minister Dzúr would not turn over the relocation plan. He was informed that the Czechoslovak document had been sent onward to Moscow.

In closing, Army General Kazakov expressed the basic idea that the Czechoslovak comrades had gotten stuck in their democratization process, that they themselves no longer knew what they really wanted.

After that, Army General Kazakov informed me that implementation of the most varied field excursions was planned for 6–7 July for staff officers as well as for enlisted officers and soldiers.

[...]

There were no instructions from Moscow about how and whether things would go forward in the next weeks.

[...]

[*Source: DY/30/3618, pp. 81–85, SAPMO-BA. Translated by Paul Spitzer for the National Security Archive.*]

Document No. 54: Transcript of the Meeting of Five Warsaw Pact States in Warsaw, July 14–15, 1968

The July 14–15 Warsaw meeting involving the leaders of the USSR, Poland, East Germany, Hungary and Bulgaria was the venue at which the so-called "Warsaw Five" came to a consensus on the likely need for military intervention in Czechoslovakia. This excerpt from the minutes of the session[26] shows that the Soviets at the time believed they could not rely on the Czechoslovaks (for obvious reasons), the Romanians or the Albanians when the time came to act. Polish leader Gomułka was the most vocal in his criticism of Czechoslovakia at the meeting. He feared that the spillover effect of the reform movement would cause serious control problems in his own country, weaken the Soviet bloc, and possibly change the entire correlation of forces in Europe. Among other lengthy speeches by each leader, Bulgaria's Todor Zhivkov noted that the only solution was the use of external force. Brezhnev, who had shown some reluctance toward the idea of an invasion up till now, expressed support for Gomułka's evaluation of the situation.

[...]

Cde. Gomułka: There is obviously a danger that our bloc would be weakened. All political questions are being decided today on a world-wide scale. I would not consider it possible that socialism would give an unambiguous reply to capitalism, or capitalism to socialism, in the form of some kind of neo-capitalism. Problems are not being solved on the scale of a single country, they are being solved on a world-wide scale. Well, this is quite obvious, and the development of power, of our communist movement, depends on that. We are living through an unfortunate period now. Many tendencies exist within our movement, many anarchistic concepts, many eccentric concepts. This is the big weakness of our movement. We have all sorts of things—anarchism, revisionism etc., anything you want, comrades—may be found within our international movement. We, the Warsaw Treaty countries, have up to now represented the decisive force of internationalism and socialism. We are the force that represents socialism in the world. Neither China, nor Cuba, nor even Korea represent the true picture of socialism. The Warsaw Treaty states are the showcase of socialism. Socialism is what we represent. Such is the case with our level of force, too. It exists in direct proportion to our internal unity. The GDR, Hungary or Bulgaria do not represent our power. These countries do not represent the decisive power factor, it is our Soviet brother who represents this force! The Soviet Union and the power of its nuclear weapons keep the imperialist world in check.

Comrades, [our] problems are not of the sort where everything can be decided by means of power. If everything could be decided by power, military power would be

---

[26] For other excerpts of this important session that relate more specifically to the Czechoslovak crisis, see Járomír Navrátil *et al*, *The Prague Spring 1968* (Budapest: CEU Press, 1994), pp. 212–233.

decisive. However, moral strength and the impact of socialism on our position among the socialist states are decisive for the unity of our countries; they are also decisive for our keeping tight together in line.

What is happening in Czechoslovakia now should change the correlation of power in Europe.

[...] We have long been aware of the fact that no declaration from West Germany or any guarantees on paper shall ever secure the safety of our borders. Only our common and united action may secure them. This is not a matter of borders; this is a matter of socialism. This is not a simple attack on our borders; it is an attack on socialism and our unity. When observing the present Czechoslovak approach, their contacts with West Germany, the various delegations [that are formed] and meetings that are held, all these official or unofficial invitations, we have to conclude that the Czechs in effect repudiated the resolutions that we had adopted last year during the Warsaw conference of ministers. We agreed there, didn't we, that all conferences would be held jointly, on a common basis? And where did they take counsel? Apparently, with all their democracy, they wanted to keep silent for weeks—they invited a representative of parliament, for instance. The Czechoslovak deputy chairman of parliament traveled to Bonn. They gave various pledges as to what they would say about it or the kind of negotiations they would they lead. [...]

I am therefore convinced that the Czechoslovak comrades have already abandoned their alliance with us. They have broken our bilateral or multilateral resolutions. They have ceased to consult with us on matters of importance.

[...]

This is the third time we have met to consider the questions of interest to us today. The first time was at the meeting in Dresden [on March 23, 1968], together with the Czech comrades. The second time was at the discussions of the problem in Moscow, without the comrades from Czechoslovakia. And finally we are gathered here for the third time, having invited the Czech comrades to take part only to find that they rejected the invitation and said in response that they would recommend bilateral meetings. At Dresden our assessment of events in Czechoslovakia was one and the same. Together we stated then that the events in that country are of an anti-socialist and even counterrevolutionary nature. Not all the Czech comrades accepted that position, although they acknowledged that certain things had been occurring over which they had no control... There were no major differences of view, although the Czech comrades rejected the notion that the underlying process was counterrevolutionary. They wanted to disavow this assessment. At the meeting in Moscow there were divergent viewpoints, and our position was not so unified.

[...] What is the current situation in Czechoslovakia? What is the nature of events there? We believe that the country is being peacefully transformed from a socialist state into a bourgeois republic. At the current stage the process is still in its initial phase. Our second basic point might be put as follows: In Czechoslovakia a process is under way whereby the CPCz is abandoning the precepts of Marxism–Leninism and is being transformed into a social democratic party. This process is already far advanced, and its main stage will occur with the Extraordinary CPCz Congress scheduled for September. Fundamental changes in the nature and complexion of the Party will be a prerequisite for the transformation of the country into a bourgeois republic. Without such changes, the transformation of the country would be impossible.

Our conclusion is that novel events are under way, with no parallel in the whole history of the socialist countries. No parallel at any rate in terms of scale. A new process has begun—a process of peaceful transition from socialism to neo-capitalism. Until recently this problem hadn't even been conceived. As a result there had repeatedly been superficial approaches to the very concept of the process of counterrevolution. The whole essence of our understanding of the danger of counterrevolution was inappropriate. Today we are not talking about a return to capitalism in the classical sense, that is, in the way we understood it during the interwar period. To look at the problem only in this way would lead us down the wrong track. [...]

[...] It would be difficult to maintain that in Czechoslovakia today the same methods could be used as were used in Hungary in 1956. The Hungarian events in the fall of 1956 were of the classical counterrevolutionary type—armed counterrevolution. When speaking about the process of counterrevolution, many people operate on the basis of old assumptions; they think that the process will develop in the same way as in the past. Those who still rely on these old assumptions will not grasp our assertion that today the process is different. The means used now are different, and so are the methods of using them. The methods are meant for the longer term. The sort of counterrevolutions we had in the past won't occur today; they will transpire differently. This is a process that might last many years. [...]

In the socialist countries class antagonisms have been suppressed. That applies to Czechoslovakia, too. There are no social classes right now capable of restoring the old order. However, reactionary forces are present. There is a social basis for counterrevolution. This is particularly true among the intellectuals and the whole mentality of broad social circles. [...]

[...] I think that a dominant majority of the leadership of the Czech Party have become captives to revisionism. And it is always the case that when a government is taken over by revisionists, they first of all do away with all their ideological enemies. [...]

[...] We must frankly say that what is going on in Czechoslovakia could have grave consequences. The whole system of socialism is in danger of being weakened. Today if you take account of matters not from the standpoint of one country, but from the standpoint of the whole world, a single fundamental question still looms: Who will win out over whom?[27] We are living through very difficult times, when the international workers' movement has been beset by various negative and centrifugal tendencies: revisionism, nationalism, and even strands of anarchism. We can be a real force in the world only if there is unity among us. We must remember that those of us gathered here bear a special responsibility. Our countries are the fist of the socialist system. We provide an example of socialism to the world. It is we who provide that example—and not China, Korea, Cuba, or Vietnam. We are the showpiece of

---

[27] *Translator's note:* In Polish (and Russian) this is "*kto kogo*," the phrase coined by Vladimir Lenin in the early days of the Bolshevik Party. The phrase amounts to a stark zero-sum conception of politics.

socialism, and the working masses of the entire world look up to us. The greater our strength, the greater our unity. [...] We Poles are well aware that our borders can be safeguarded effectively only if the countries of the socialist commonwealth maintain a united stance. And this by no means applies just to our own borders; every attack on these borders is an attack on the whole of international socialism.

Cde. Kádár: [...] If you consider the matter from the standpoint of the existing situation, the basic question is whether you would call what is going on there a counterrevolution or whether it should be called something else. The crux of the matter is whether the entire process can be uniformly regarded as counterrevolutionary... In my view the whole process has dangerous tendencies within it. I would not say, however, that the Party there is being transformed into a social-democratic party.

[...]

In reaching a decision we must remember the Hungarian events of 1956. We must recall the experiences of that period. The problem we are discussing, the struggle over the changing situation in Czechoslovakia, is of an international character, since that struggle also has come under scrutiny at the international level. During the struggle over Hungary in 1956 all the fraternal Communist Parties took part in lending us support. The question is to find what support we can provide now.

The situation in Czechoslovakia is steadily deteriorating. It is much more alarming than it was during our meetings in Dresden and in Moscow. Back then we expressed the wish that in Czechoslovakia itself forces would emerge that would be able to turn the situation around. Now this task is more urgent than ever. It is urgent to find Marxist-Leninist forces in Czechoslovakia, to whom we ought to provide full support.

Cde. Ulbricht: Our Political Bureau supported the idea of calling today's meeting. We had assumed that the CPCz CC Presidium would send its own representatives. We had hoped so because we observe that the situation in Czechoslovakia has given rise to new, negative elements. It therefore was appropriate and justifiable for us to want an exchange of views with them. However, the CPCz CC Presidium refused to take part in our meeting today and proposed bilateral meetings. ...With the publication of the reactionary "Two Thousand Words" Manifesto, the leadership of the Czechoslovak Party is not in a position to find a solution on its own. The only way is to find a solution jointly.

Cde. Kádár recounted his discussions with Dubček, which he called different things. They want to wait for a general disruption. Dubček does not grasp the situation. I am amazed by the analysis that Cde. Kádár offered. Do you not see, Cde. Kádár, that the question is not only about Czechoslovakia. Cde. Kádár said that we are dealing with revisionist forces there. I can't agree with that. The question is about counterrevolutionary forces. The "Two Thousand Words" Manifesto expresses their goal: to destroy the Party's power. If the "Two Thousand Words" Manifesto is not counterrevolutionary, then certainly there is not a counterrevolution. The reality of the situation in Czechoslovakia indicates that there is a counterrevolutionary underground. There is a gradual shift toward bringing this underground counterrevolution to the surface. ...

The Czechs' plans for counterrevolution are obvious. There can be no further doubt about this matter. The counterrevolutionaries want to prepare the Party Congress in such a way that they can crush and eliminate the Marxist–Leninists. The "Two Thousand Words" is unambiguously counterrevolutionary. They next will move to multi-party elections and try to get rid of the Party, and will then want to change the constitution.

I don't know, Comrade Kádár, why you can't grasp all this. Don't you realize that the next blow by imperialism will take place in Hungary? We can already detect that imperialist centers are concentrating their work now on the Hungarian intelligentsia.

In my view, Cde. Gomułka gave a principled and accurate assessment of the situation in Czechoslovakia. The interference by imperialism in Czechoslovakia is being carried out within the framework of a long-term global strategy, a strategy spanning at least ten years.

[…]

An idea has been floated to create a trilateral alliance among Czechoslovakia, Romania, and Yugoslavia. This is an old idea, which was first conceived during the time of Masaryk [President of Czechoslovakia in 1918–1937], who wanted to set up the so-called Little Entente consisting of those three countries. Back then this concept was aimed at establishing the "special authority" of Czechoslovakia in the framework of this alliance. Today the concept is intended to separate socialist Czechoslovakia from the Soviet Union and the whole commonwealth of socialist countries. Ceauşescu and Tito support it and have even given their official backing.

[…]

Cde. Zhivkov: The representatives of our Central Committee and Political Bureau of our Party share the view of the situation in Czechoslovakia presented by Cde. Gomułka and Cde. Ulbricht. Unfortunately we cannot agree with the view offered by Cde. Kádár, nor with his conclusions. We want to depict things accurately and call a spade a spade.

[…]

There is only one appropriate way out—through resolute assistance to Czechoslovakia from our Parties and the countries of the Warsaw Pact. We cannot currently rely on the internal forces in Czechoslovakia. There are no forces there that could carry out the types of tasks we wrote about in our letter. Only by relying on the armed forces of the Warsaw Pact can we change the situation.

In Czechoslovakia we must restore the dictatorship of the proletariat, which has been trampled underfoot. All the state and Party organizations have been taken over by revisionists and counterrevolutionaries. The Party Congress must be derailed. It is essential that we reestablish the Party and restore the Marxist–Leninist content of its activity. We must prevent the social-democratization of the Party. A decree must be prepared to dissolve the various counterrevolutionary and bourgeois organizations. There is no other way out.

[…]

Cde. Brezhnev: […] Like all the other delegations present here, we understandably regret that the Czechoslovak comrades, whom we invited, are not taking part. No matter how their absence is explained by the CPCz CC Presidium, one cannot help thinking, comrades, that this is typical of the current situation whereby the

Presidium does not wish to heed the advice and suggestions of its friends. It openly rejects the possibility of collectively assessing matters that not only concern Czechoslovakia itself, but also affect our common interests.

[...]

The delegation of the CPSU Central Committee fully endorses the assessment of the situation in Czechoslovakia presented by Cde. Gomułka at our conference. We agree that the events taking place there are dangerous not only because they are openly directed against the socialist gains of the Czechoslovak people, but also because they undermine the positions of socialism in Europe and are playing into the hands of imperialism throughout the world. This is the essence of what Cdes. Ulbricht and Zhivkov said as well.

What is happening in the ČSSR passed long ago beyond a purely national framework and is now impinging on the fundamental problems of the vitality of the entire socialist system. One might say that Czechoslovakia has become one of the focal points of the bitter ideological and political struggle between imperialism and socialism. The attempt being made by the anti-socialist and counterrevolutionary forces to bring about the downfall of the Communist Party of Czechoslovakia and remove it from power is essentially an attempt to strike a blow against our common ideological platform, the great Marxist–Leninist teachings, and thus to compromise the very principles of socialism.

One cannot help seeing the other side of the question as well. By jointly exploiting the ongoing events for their own purposes, the internal counterrevolutionary forces and the imperialist reactionary forces are counting on being able to turn Czechoslovakia back along a capitalist path, to weaken the strength of the Warsaw Pact, and to annihilate the unity of the socialist system and of the entire world communist and national liberation movement. It goes without saying that if the international reactionary forces succeed in carrying out their plans, there will be a direct threat to the security of our countries. That's why we agree it is essential to do everything possible to prevent such a development from arising.

[...]

Based on a sober analysis of the facts, and taking account of the experience of our own and other fraternal parties, we seriously warned the Czechoslovak comrades about the menacing course of political developments in the ČSSR and about the existence there of a certain social milieu that is conducive to the activities of anti-socialist and counterrevolutionary forces. We urged them to be aware of the danger of taking a conciliatory approach to attacks made against the Party and the socialist gains of the Czechoslovak people.

Not only did we express our concerns; we gave them comradely advice about a number of measures that could be taken to improve the situation. We recommended steps that might prevent things from developing in an undesirable way. The Czechoslovak comrades agreed with these suggestions, and they spoke about their own plans and about how the CPCz leadership is determined to put an end to the activities of counterrevolutionary elements and to assert control over the course of events.

Unfortunately, these proposals and plans were not carried out. The situation in the country has deteriorated as far as it can.

[...]

It is necessary, in my view, to give special consideration to still another question.

Nowadays, on television and radio in Czechoslovakia, certain prominent figures are referring to our recent meeting as some sort of interference in the internal affairs of the ČSSR. This question, comrades, must be made more precise. When the plenum of the CPCz Central Committee recognized the necessity of removing Cde. Novotný from the post of first Secretary and then of dismissing him from the post of President, we said nothing in regard to these changes. That was the internal affair of a fraternal party and country. When there was a change of Secretaries of the Central Committee and of members of the Central Committee's Presidium, and also a change of ministers, we again, as you recall, said nothing about it (I mean we said nothing openly in the press). We believe that this is the internal affair of a fraternal Party, its Central Committee, and its National Assembly.

However, comrades, when the situation has developed into an open political massacre of all Party cadres, when exhortations are made to change virtually the whole Party leadership from top to bottom, when one hears ever louder voices calling for a reorientation of the CPCz, and when the fate of the whole Party and of the socialist achievements of the Czechoslovak people is under challenge, then this is a different matter. If there exists a real threat that the political content of the CPCz will be transformed into some sort of new organization—in the best of instances into a social democratic one or perhaps even into a petty bourgeois character—then this, I repeat, affects the interests not only of Communists in Czechoslovakia and not only the people of Czechoslovakia, but the interests of the entire socialist system and of the whole world Communist movement. We would be correct to regard such a turn of events as a direct threat to the world position of socialism and a direct threat to all our countries.

Any attempt to thwart such a process cannot be considered interference in internal affairs. This is an expression of our international duty to the whole Communist movement and our international duty to the Communists and working people of Czechoslovakia. Confronted by the growing danger that socialism will be dislodged in one of the countries of the socialist commonwealth, we cannot shut ourselves off, comrades, into our own national apartments. That would be a betrayal of the interests of Communism.

Communism develops and exists only as an international movement. All its victories and all its achievements are related to this. Anyone who departs from internationalism cannot consider himself a Communist. Our countries are linked to the ČSSR by treaties and agreements. These are not agreements between individual persons but mutual commitments between friends and states. They are founded on the general desire to defend socialism in our countries and to safeguard it against all and any hazards.

No one has the right to dissociate himself from his international commitments or his allied obligations. It must be emphasized that the demagoguery we hear about this nowadays is out of place.

We respect the right of every Party and the right of every nation. We recognize the idea of specific national forms of socialist development in different countries. But we also believe in a common historical fate. The cause of defending socialism—that is our common undertaking. Our Parties were united in their understanding of this at the meeting in Moscow at the beginning of May. We are certain that such unity characterizes our meeting this time as well.

There has never been a case in which socialism triumphed and was firmly entrenched, only to have a capitalist order restored. This has never happened and we are certain it never will. The guarantee of this is our common readiness to do whatever is necessary to help a fraternal Party and people defeat the plans of counterrevolution and thwart imperialist plans in relation to Czechoslovakia.

Our delegation declares that the Communist Party of the Soviet Union, our government, and our people are fully ready to offer Czechoslovakia all necessary assistance.

[…]

[*Source: KC PZPR 192/24/4, Archiwum Akt Nowych. Translated by Mark Kramer and Marian J. Kratochvíl.*]

Document No. 55: Czechoslovak and East German Views on the Warsaw Pact, July 1968

The two documents reproduced here show the different perspectives held by the Czechoslovak reformers and the conservative East Germans. Both records are from July 1968, when the Czechoslovak crisis had already escalated. The first document precedes the crucial July 14–15 Warsaw meeting of Warsaw Pact members—minus Czechoslovakia and Romania—at which the remaining five countries' leaders reached a consensus on the probable need for military intervention in Czechoslovakia (see Document No. 54). The memorandum is intended to preempt the spreading criticism of Czechoslovakia as being disloyal to the alliance. It apparently resulted from a conference of representatives of reformist and conservative groups within the armed forces held in Bratislava. It summarizes the position which the reformist group thought Czechoslovakia should take in the Warsaw Pact—acting as not only a disciplined and responsible, but also a creative and active, member of the alliance.

The second item below, an East German document, was prepared on July 29, after the so-called Prchlík affair (see footnote 22 for Document No. 52) and the summit of five Warsaw Pact member-states in the Polish capital (Document No. 54). That meeting resulted in the transmittal of the so-called "Warsaw Letter" warning the Czechoslovak leadership of possible military action if the reform movement were not terminated swiftly. The document below is an analysis and interpretation of the Warsaw Treaty, and is obviously intended to justify the forthcoming intervention. It says specifically that by not taking part in the Warsaw meeting, Czechoslovakia has violated provisions of the alliance requiring consultation in the event other signatories perceive a danger to their security. At best, this view could be said to represent a loose construction of the alliance treaty, if not an outright distortion.

a) Czechoslovak Reformist Memorandum
   on the Warsaw Treaty and Czechoslovakia,
   July 1968

The government of the ČSSR has been deeply convinced of the historic importance of the founding and existence of the Warsaw Treaty on friendship, co-operation and mutual assistance among our countries, as well as of the establishment of the Unified Armed Forces of the countries participating in the Pact. The Pact is our common response to the activities of the aggressive imperialist forces, the NATO military grouping in particular.

[...]

Currently, we are once again seeking to increase our active share in the joint defense of the Warsaw Treaty states, as we do not want to be a mere passive member.

This fundamental line arises from both the action program of the Communist Party of Czechoslovakia, and the programmatic declaration of the ČSSR government.

In the CPCz action program, it is explicitly declared that:

"The basic orientation of Czechoslovak foreign policy, born and affirmed in times of the national liberation struggle and in the process of the socialist reconstruction of our country, is toward the alliance and cooperation with the Soviet Union and other socialist countries. We will be striving to further intensify relations with our allies—the countries of the world socialist community—on the basis of mutual esteem, sovereignty and equality, respect and international solidarity. In this sense, we will contribute to joint activities of the Council for Mutual Economic Assistance and the Warsaw Treaty, in a more active way and with a well thought-out conception."

In the program declaration of the ČSSR government, it is also stated that:

"As long as NATO exists, we will co-operate to secure the Warsaw Treaty, strive for the Czechoslovak People's Army to become a firm link in this alliance and develop greater initiative to intensify the work of the Unified Command."

This stand of the ČSSR is confirmed by our deeds, through which we honor the respective resolutions of the Warsaw Treaty and the instructions of the supreme commander of the Unified Armed Forces, as evident from the solution of problems concerning the build-up of the Czechoslovak armed forces, from their combat readiness, and the fulfillment of assignments during alliance exercises, and from combat and political preparation in general.

The baseline of securing the Warsaw Pact has finally been manifested in the efforts of the ČSSR in implementing the Soviet Union's suggestions, which were included in the letter to the Central Committee of the Communist Party of the Soviet Union of January 7, 1966, in which it is also stated that:

"The basic sense of these suggestions, as we see it, is to make the Warsaw Pact more flexible and operational, and also to contribute to improving the efficacy of the efforts exerted by all our member-states to secure the integrity and tenability of the socialistic countries of Europe. This exchange of opinion entitles us to conclude that the issue of improving the Warsaw Treaty has ripened and seeks a practical solution."

[...]

The stand of ČSSR was also manifested in the general solution of this problem as early as in 1966, and then on March 6–7, 1968, at the conference of the Political Consultative Committee in Sofia. Then, Alexander Dubček, Czechoslovak delegation leader and first secretary of the Central Committee of the Communist Party of Czechoslovakia, was prepared to negotiate and ratify the relevant documents, which refer to strengthening the military bodies of the Warsaw Pact and which were proposed by I[van] I. Iakubovskii, marshal of the Soviet Union and supreme commander of the Unified Armed Forces.

[...]

All these facts conclusively demonstrate our strong resolution to strengthen the allied ties within the Warsaw Treaty and to secure, in unity with its other members, the defense of the entire socialist community.

[*Source: MNO-1968, sekr. min. 2/1–9, VÚA. Translated by Stanislav Mareš.*]

b) East German Remarks on the Warsaw Treaty,
July 29, 1968

Generally it must be stated that the preamble, as well as article 8, of the Warsaw Treaty stress accordance and compliance with the principles of respect for the independence and sovereignty of states, as well as for non-interference in their domestic affairs. Those are also the paragraphs of the treaty, which the anti-socialist and counterrevolutionary elements have constantly been invoking in their polemics against the staff exercise.

Besides, articles 3 and 5 fully warrant necessary measures by the signatory states with regard to one of the member-states.

[...]

By refusing to join the Warsaw meeting, the party leadership of the CPCz and the government of the ČSSR have clearly violated article 3: The "guarantee of the joint defense, the maintenance of peace and of mutual security" has to be discussed immediately, if one or more of the member-states believe that "danger is ... imminent;" not only after an imperialist attack has already occurred.

The second sentence of article 5 states that, in addition to the creation of a Unified Supreme Command, other agreed measures necessary for strengthening the defense of member-states can be implemented; in order to protect the peaceful work of their people, to protect the inviolability of their borders and territories, and to guarantee protection against potential aggression. However, this is also about the borders and territories of the member-states. Their security cannot be guaranteed once a possible aggression has occurred, but is rather supposed to preempt an [act of] aggression.

[*Source: ZPA NL 182/1233, SAPMO. Translated by Karen Reichert.*]

Document No. 56: Report by East German Defense Minister on the Invasion of Czechoslovakia, August 22, 1968

This report by East German Defense Minister Heinz Hoffmann deals with the invasion of Czechoslovakia. It is an internal report addressed to his country's National Defense Council and although it is undated it clearly was written very soon after the intervention had begun. Of particular interest are Hoffmann's comments about NATO's attitude toward the invasion and about the role of East German forces in the operation. He reports, accurately, that NATO intelligence and command staffs were completely taken by surprise, but he cautions that this does not mean NATO has poor intelligence capabilities. Both remarks are fully consistent with what is known from the NATO side.[28]

[...]

In case of a so-called "break-away" by the ČSSR from the community of social-ist states, NATO would, aside from the resulting political effects, gain the possibili-ty of deploying its military units deep in the flanks of the socialist camp.

NATO would thus be in the position to threaten the GDR and the People's Republic of Poland at their southern borders, to split up the compact territory of the European socialist states, and to expand its sphere of control as far as the Carpathians.

According to the plan of the Unified Command and due to the evolving, severe political situation in the ČSSR, which is known to you in detail, a series of staff com-mand and troop exercises of the Unified Armed Forces took place between mid-June and the beginning of August 1968. Staff commands, troops, and special forces of the National People's Army participated in these exercises as well.

[...]

In connection with the counter-revolutionary developments taking place in the ČSSR, which were characterized by the active appearance of revisionist and anti-socialist forces, we had to realize with concern in the past few months that the inten-sity of operational and combat education in the Czechoslovak People's Army, which holds a responsible place in the strategic lineup of the Unified Armed Forces, had fallen considerably.

Furthermore, the safeguarding of the state border between the ČSSR and West Germany has slackened to an extent that abetted the unhindered infiltration of sub-versive and other counter-revolutionary forces.

[...]

Under conditions in which the NATO states, particularly West Germany, are con-tinually increasing their readiness to commit aggression, these are circumstances that

[28] See, for example, records of the meeting of the U.S. National Security Council on August 20, just hours after the start of the invasion, in which the secretary of state, Dean Rusk, opens the meet-ing by declaring: "This surprises me." Navrátil, *The Prague Spring 1968*, pp. 445–448. See also Vojtech Mastny, "Was 1968 a Strategic Watershed of the Cold War?" *Diplomatic History 29*, no. 1 (2005): 149–77.

could lead to a weakening of the readiness of the Warsaw Pact states to react against a surprise imperialist aggression.

This corresponds with the strategic concept of the enemy to gradually paralyze the Warsaw Pact as a precondition for a desired change in the status quo in Europe, and therewith a change in the global correlation of forces in its favor.

[...]

The party and state leaderships of the five socialist countries have been anxious to bring about a political solution to the situation in the ČSSR by granting manifold fraternal socialist help.

The consultations in Dresden, Warsaw, Čierna nad Tisou, Bratislava and Karlovy Vary are known to all of you. In this connection, I may recall the great efforts of our Soviet friends, who have undertaken everything to grant any imaginable help and support to the Czechoslovak comrades.

After influential circles of the Czechoslovak party and state leadership clearly indicated that they would not enforce the commitments assumed in Bratislava, and after counter-revolutionary intrigues kept increasing, the leadership of the communist and workers' parties as well as the governments of the Soviet Union, the GDR, the People's Republic of Poland, the People's Republic of Bulgaria and the Hungarian People's Republic decided to execute appropriate military measures.

This was the moment when a political solution was no longer possible and when peace in Europe was acutely threatened.

The goal of these military measures was and is to support the progressive forces in the ČSSR and protect the socialist achievements of the Czechoslovak people against the intrigues of the internal and external counter-revolution. This meant that everything possible had to be done to firmly secure socialism, and thus peace, in Europe.

To accomplish this goal, mixed operational groupings have been formed in the southern areas of the German Democratic Republic and the People's Republic of Poland, as well as in the southwest of the Soviet Union and the northern part of the People's Republic of Hungary, out of the formations of the fraternal armies, which have been taking part in the most varied joint educational measures of the Unified Command of the Unified Armed Forces.

[...]

On the territory of the German Democratic Republic, units of the Soviet armed forces in the GDR and of the National People's Army have been deployed with the task of taking over the safeguarding of the state border between the ČSSR and West Germany, and to be ready for the break-up of the counterrevolutionary forces in the area of the capital of the ČSSR, Prague.

The operational grouping established on the territory of the People's Republic of Poland has included troops of the Soviet Army stationed in Poland and troops of the Polish Army. Detachments of this grouping were assigned to secure the border between the ČSSR and Austria while the bulk of its forces were kept on reserve to support them.

The Eastern grouping, created from units of the Soviet Army and troops of the Bulgarian People's Army, got the task of waiting in the wings in the Eastern Slovak

306

area, and of preparing for actions against counter-revolutionary elements, and serve as a reserve for the entire contingent of the Unified Armed Forces.

From the territory of the People's Republic of Hungary, the grouping composed of Soviet and Hungarian troops was assigned to form a line[29] to secure the state borders between the ČSSR and West Germany and Austria and to be ready for actions against the counterrevolutionary forces in the central Czechoslovak area.

In accordance with these short-term tasks and upon the decision of the party and state leadership of the five fraternal countries, the units of the four operational groupings began their deployment under cover of night on August 20, 1968, in their rear areas in immediate proximity to the border of the ČSSR, which they crossed with their frontal units between 11:30 pm and midnight.

At the same time, airborne troops were deployed in Prague to provide effective support and help to the progressive forces in the capital of the ČSSR as quickly as possible.

The troops fulfilled their tasks in the directions of their planned assignments with high precision, so that the counter-revolutionary forces, as well as the NATO intelligence and command, were taken completely by surprise.

[...]

Having executed all the measures with precision and caught the enemy by surprise should not, however, lead us to assume that NATO's and, especially, the Bundeswehr's intelligence is poor.

On the contrary, we do not underestimate the adversary and will continue to increase our vigilance since we know that we face a brutal, perfidious, and determined enemy in NATO and in particular in West German imperialism.

[...]

[*Source: AZN 32921, 2–18, BA-MA. Translated by Thomas Holderegger.*]

---

[29] The Soviets deployed these troops a certain distance from the West German border—not so close as to provoke a Western response—while positioning them to strike against the Czechoslovak Army in the interior of the country if necessary.

Document No. 57: Record of the Meeting between President Ludvík Svoboda and Czechoslovak Army Officers, August 28, 1968

This internal Czechoslovak record of a meeting following the August invasion shows genuine confusion among senior Czechoslovak military and civilian officials over the reasons for the Soviet-led move. Throughout the Prague Spring, the country's leaders had repeatedly claimed that the party was loyal to Moscow and the socialist camp, and had no intention of leaving the Warsaw Pact, unlike the Hungarian leadership in 1956. (See Document No.3) However, newly available Warsaw Pact records show increasing suspicion of Czechoslovak motives on the part of Brezhnev and his colleagues to a point where they concluded Dubček was simply trying to deceive his Warsaw Pact allies. The fact that several key Czechoslovak leaders including Dubček were actually sincere, as evidenced by Prime Minister Černík's plaintive remarks in the document below, illustrates the importance of perceptions and misperceptions during such crisis.

Cde. President opened the meeting, saying: "I invited you at this very difficult time to inform you of my viewpoint concerning the events of the past days. First, I would like to express my thanks, for the army behaved well, was disciplined and discharged the orders of the minister of defense, as well as mine, very well. Our army units did not come out against the Soviet Army. In such a case, the situation would have been very bad. It is good therefore that the army did not contribute to a deterioration of the situation. I would like to be informed by the respective Military District commanders and army commanders about the course of events with respect to their units and what the situation is like nowadays."

[...]

Gen. [Stanislav] Procházka, commander, Western Military District: "The command post exerted enormous efforts to avoid conflicts. We succeeded. Commanding officers, staffs and troops alike discharged the orders of Cde. President of the Republic and Minister of Defense. They were convinced that we had been assaulted without reason, that an injury had been committed." [...]

[...]

Gen. [Jozef] Kúkel: "The troops discharged your orders. Only the final point of the minister's order has not been obeyed—regarding assistance to the Soviet Army (order No. 1). All airfields are manned; elsewhere the situation is really on edge. The danger is that foreign troops do not allow any maintenance of advanced aircraft technology and airfield equipment, so there is a danger of serious damage." [...]

[...]

Gen. [Karel] Peprný: "The Border Guards have been discharging their orders from the very beginning."

Cde. President: "Are you the one who is securing the border?"

Reply: "Yes, except for the departments of border control. From the very beginning, foreign troops exhibited certain tendencies to offer assistance for control of the border. We rejected all offers. In three cases, they required arms to be laid down. However, our commanding officers did not put them down. There is peace in the units, although we must calm down and persuade some individuals. The Border Guards never gave any provocation. Foreign commanding officers turned up with objections concerning the security of the borders. We are confronting them with arguments. [...]

Gen. [Juraj] Lalo: "Our commanding officers and troops have been backing your orders from the very beginning. Emotions rose as the news got around that the Hungarian troops were disarming our units." (He describes the assault on the Štúrovo barracks at 01:00 am. The soldiers, dressed inadequately, were chased out of the barracks; the officers were detained and interrogated one after the other until noon.)

[...]

Gen. [E.] Chlad: "At the Prague garrison, the situation is very complicated. Nevertheless, no case of conflict has arisen until now. The garrison command was occupied by force; they requested arms to be laid down. We were not disarmed, though. The battalion bears these events with hardship, as does the entire nation." [...]

[...]

Cde. President: "I have full respect for those who could not avoid their emotions, those who were perhaps swearing yesterday and disagreed with the communiqué. The conduct of our people gave us proof of their high patriotic conscience. Nowadays, however, we must take the path of [common] sense." [...]

Cde. President then proposed a toast.

[...] Cde. President then concluded, saying: "I would like to tell you the following today: Do not allow a single shot from one gun to be fired at a Soviet man. This has not occurred so far and I do hope it will not happen in the future." [...]

Cde. President explained the present situation, saying: "You know better than I how foreign troops invaded the country. We all declared that nobody had invited them—neither I, nor the government, nor the Presidium of the Central Committee of the Party. We expressed this fact and the whole world knows it. The reality is, however, that they are here. Truth and moral right are on our side.

"I had a talk with Cde. Brezhnev as early as the first day and I took some measures. Before I flew to Moscow, I was summoned before a certain group of people who brought up the proposal to disband the government and to form a new 'revolutionary' government instead. Obviously, I could not accept this. I told them I would rather fire a bullet into my head. I demanded categorically that the constitutional bodies start their work. I demanded that [Alexander] Dubček, [Oldřich] Černík and the others be set free; we can start normal work solely by legal means. They responded they could not resolve that matter here: they had their orders from Moscow. I demanded the negotiations with Moscow. We had agreed on that with the government. My request was accepted at 7 a.m. [...]

"The representatives of the other four [political] parties were invited, too, and the Soviet officials had talks with them. They turned up later and required the formation of the 'revolutionary government' again. We categorically rejected their requests and they finally gave way. [...]

"What we wanted—to set Dubček and Černík free—was also done upon our request. That they gave their consent for these comrades to lead [official] bodies and to join the negotiations also was the result of our proposal. The comrades could see how Brezhnev congratulated me, saying that all this happened thanks to me.

"We could hardly have expressed it better in the communiqué. There is a word [there] about friendship. We could have given it up, but it is a historical reality. It is not true that we surrendered, not in the least—no. We obtained approval of the conclusion that all foreign troops shall leave our country. We achieved recognition of our existing constitutional bodies and our government. The government shall set up commissions and these commissions will further consider the issue of evacuation."

[…]

Premier Cde. Černík arrived at the invitation of Cde. President. The commanders repeated their reports. Cde. Černík then said: "[…] From the first day, we—and all people in this country—had to ask ourselves: What have we done? Why did they intervene? We did not want anything other than to live decently and build socialism under conditions we considered optimal. We had no intention to secede. For our nations, for our small state, it was an obvious necessity to stay with the Soviet Union. And it was not a mere necessity; it was also a question of heart. Where else does the Soviet Union enjoy such love and historically rooted confidence as she enjoyed here, among our people?

"We know very well that the ČSSR belongs to the Soviet sphere and we agree with that. Everybody knows that the Americans will not fight for Czechoslovakia, because they would lose all of Europe. Our nations, which survived centuries of oppression, can appreciate their freedom, and they appreciate their allies, too. So why? An article in *Literární listy*[30] or some Club of Engaged Non-Party Members, etc., cannot justify what has been done to us.

"Look where the first attack was directed. It was not against some counterrevolutionary center, it was directed against the Party leadership. The first captives were the Party leaders—Dubček, Černík, [Josef] Smrkovský and others. This is awful, such a shame.

"We are well aware of the fact that a small nation can protect itself solely with its intellect, not by means of force. This is not collaboration. We must seek avenues to build up our own country under given conditions. What would those who come after us say if we waged a fight and thus brought upon us occupation for several decades?

"We must get away from the given situation, which is the result of World War II. Spheres of influence were created and the powers respect them. Whether we like it or not, each of these spheres has its center. Whether we like it or not, the existence of a center sometimes implies certain subordination. We cannot simply jump out. As a small nation, however, we may create our own space within this framework by means of clever policy."

[…]

[*Source: Č.j. 0781/68, Military Office of the President of the Republic, Prague. Translated by Marian J. Kratochvíl.*]

---

[30] The main reformist weekly in Czechoslovakia.

Document No. 58: Letter from the East German Deputy Defense Minister to Erich Honecker about His Conversation with Marshal Iakubovskii, August 31, 1968

This letter from Gen. Heinz Kessler to GDR leader Erich Honecker provides a per-spective on the delicate matter of East German participation in the Czechoslovak invasion. The issue was sensitive given the Czechs' memories of German occupation during World War II. In a conversation between Kessler and Warsaw Pact Supreme Commander Iakubovskii about how to treat the NVA's participation in public, the Soviet marshal decided, apparently on his own initiative, that it should be mentioned only in general terms, and not include any references to specific deployments. Iakubovskii reveals that reconnaissance and transport units were in fact deployed on Czechoslovak territory. (See also Document No. 56.) In his conversation with Kessler, Iakubovskii leaves open the possibility that those units earmarked for possible deploy-ment but not yet used—one rifle division and one tank division—may still be called upon and should remain on alert.

[…]

As ordered, I asked Cde. Marshal of the Soviet Union Iakubovskii his opinion on the following questions:

1. In which framework it appears to be appropriate to give, with the help of press, radio, and television, a public account of the participation of formations and units of the National People's Army in the joint undertaking "Danube."

2. Whether the possibility of an assignment of the formations and units of Military District III (11th Motorized Rifle Division, 7th Tank Division) in the ordered direc-tions on Czechoslovak territory is still being considered.

Cde. Marshal of the Soviet Union Iakubovskii explained that a public reporting met his full approval. The National People's Army in general and the formations and units designated for the joint undertaking "Danube" have to be seen as a component for the solution of the assigned tasks; and, in this context, a public account in press, radio, and television was possible and desirable.

He asked not to announce the specific areas of deployment and the direction of the actions. The same principle had been established during the past few days for all four armies involved in the measure.

Furthermore, he explained that, contingent on the development of the political situation, it was still necessary to strictly maintain the ordered combat readiness, and that it was possible that the 11th Motorized Rifle Division would be deployed as planned in the direction of Karlovy Vary and the 7th Tank Division in the direction Děčín–Prague.

[…]

[*Source: VA-01/23454, BA-MA. Translated by Thomas Holderegger.*]

Document No. 59: Report by the East German Defense Minister on NATO's "Fallex 68/Golden Rod" Exercise, November 21, 1968

Defense Minister Hoffmann's report on NATO's "Fallex" maneuvers in October 1968 reveals the interesting notion that Warsaw Pact leaders felt the need to provide further justification for the intervention in Czechoslovakia. The interpretation Hoffmann offers, clearly reporting what the Soviets have told him, is that NATO had been preparing to take advantage of internal developments in Czechoslovakia to interfere in the country's affairs, and was only prevented from doing so by the Warsaw Pact action. (See also Document No. 56.) Thus the argument now is that there were military as well as political reasons for invading. Since this was not a public document but an internal report addressed to the East German National Defense Council, it was obviously not intended for propaganda purposes. In the months leading up to the intervention, no internal documentation reflected this concern. Nor is there any indication whatsoever from Western sources that this entered into the thinking of NATO member-states.

What was the "Fallex 68" exercise about?

The main political goal was apparently to prove the necessity of the further existence and rapid stabilization of the NATO Pact. The rationale behind it was the thesis of an alleged "threat from the East".

[...]

The assumed political starting position of "Fallex 68" again clearly demonstrated the link between the United States' and West Germany's counterrevolutionary Ostpolitik, as well as between NATO's military strategy of flexible response and the U.S. global strategy. Linking in principle the political assumption of the exercise with events in the ČSSR suggests that, depending on how the situation developed, NATO did not exclude the possibility of rehearsing for, or even initiating, Czechoslovakia's departure from the socialist camp.

The main political requirements imagined for triggering an aggression were:

- splitting the ideological and organizational unity of the community of socialist states, especially separation from the Soviet Union.
- an internal "softening" of individual socialist states. This year's "Fallex" exercise again confirmed the intentions of the Bundeswehr leadership to capitalize on the already existing potential for influencing NATO decisions, and to increase it further. The result was the acceptance of West Germany's opinion on the early, selective and gradual, as well as general, deployment of nuclear weapons against countries of the Warsaw Treaty.

This was indicated by layout of the exercise. In it NATO for the first time not only deployed nuclear weapons selectively within the scope of a limited nuclear war, but started a general nuclear war.

What were NATO's main military goals during the exercise?

The goal was to assess the particular deployments of NATO forces as specified within the framework of an overall plan during the course of the year 1968, and based on decisions of the NATO Ministerial Council to officially confirm the strategy of flexible response from December 1967.

[...]

What are the most important results?

1. The "Fallex 68" exercise has confirmed the opinion of our party and government leaders on potential types of war, as well as on the methods of unleashing a war of aggression by NATO in Europe, especially against the German Democratic Republic.

NATO's intention to immediately gain the initiative by the early surprise deployment of nuclear weapons in a limited war, as well as in a general nuclear war, has clearly been confirmed.

The role of a limited war was heavily emphasized, since it promised partly to achieve certain political goals for the enemy in individual socialist countries in case conditions are politically favorable to the enemy.

It demonstrated that NATO is aiming to achieve certain success by means of a limited war in Europe—obviously also due to the evaluation of experiences with psychological warfare in ideologically softening socialist countries. However, NATO still attributes the decisive role in achieving its goals to a general nuclear war.

2. The different types of aggression, from covert to limited and finally general nuclear war, were not practiced separately during the exercise, but as stages of a gradually escalating war.

The war was preceded by a period of continuously increasing tensions, during which covert warfare was escalated to open military actions that finally turned into a limited war.

This exercise concept aimed at:

a) assessing the possibility of military escalation in order to achieve political goals
b) testing different military actions as a form of political pressure against the states of the Warsaw Treaty
c) testing the overall NATO concept of crisis management during all its stages of escalation

[...]

Starting from the conception that success through limited military action requires the subversion of the socialist community of states and the "softening" of individual socialist states, NATO leaders attempted with "Fallex 68" to test useful models for the realization of this theory under various conditions.

[*Source: DVW1/39492, pp. 13–26. Translated by Karen Riechert.*]

Document No. 60: Czechoslovak–Soviet Agreement on the Stationing of Soviet Nuclear Forces, November 13–14, 1968

This document is a report by Chief of Gen. Staff Rusov to President Svoboda about the secret agreement governing the stationing of Soviet nuclear missiles in Czechoslovakia. The issue of Soviet nuclear deployments on the territory of other Warsaw Pact states was one of the most sensitive that arose within the alliance.[31] With respect to Czechoslovakia, the Soviet-led invasion added a new twist. A Czech author, Jiří Fidler, has asserted that one of the main reasons for the invasion was to force Czechoslovakia to accept the Soviet missiles.[32] In fact, the two countries had signed agreements on the matter well before 1968, reflecting the view of certain senior Czechoslovak military and political leaders that having those weapons stationed on their territory provided additional security against the West. Although it is highly probable that the missle deployments occurred, there is no conclusive evidence on this point as yet.

INFORMATION REPORT

for the President of
the Czechoslovak Socialist Republic,
Comrade L. Svoboda

1. Based on the Agreement between the Governments of the Union of Soviet Socialist Republics and the Czechoslovak Socialist Republic, dated December 15, 1965, three facilities garrisoned by Soviet troops with special tasks will be established on our territory to ensure full combat readiness of the Czechoslovak People's Army (codeword project "Javor" [Maple]). Issues connected with the implementation of the project were communicated to you on October 23, 1968, and you have voiced your full approval of it.

2. At the moment, specific measures are going to be taken to hand over some of the facilities and buildings to designated Soviet special units.
Between November 13 and November 14, 1968, the General Staffs of the Armed Forces of the USSR and Czechoslovakia prepared a "Protocol" finalizing all issues related to the above project. The Czechoslovak side has succeeded in asserting all interests of the Czechoslovak Socialist Republic and the Czechoslovak People's Army in the Protocol.

---

[31] Cf. Mark Kramer, "The 'Lessons' of the Cuban Missile Crisis for Warsaw Pact Nuclear Operations," *Cold War International History Project Bulletin* 5 (1995): 59, 110–15, 160.

[32] Jiří Fidler, *21.8.1968: Okupace Československa: Bratrská agrese* [August 21, 1968: The Occupation of Czechoslovakia: A Fraternal Aggression] (Prague: Havran, 2003), pp. 106–10.

Contrary to the existing concept, which I mentioned in my report of October 23, 1968, the Protocol contains some changes resulting from the temporary stationing of other Soviet troops on our territory, namely:

a) Given that there is now a new situation on Czechoslovak territory, trying to deny and conceal the presence of Soviet troops in the above-mentioned facilities would be illogical and inappropriate from the viewpoint of secrecy; however, the utmost must be done not to disclose the true nature of the facilities by sticking to an adopted cover story (the same approach will also be adopted vis-à-vis the Headquarters of Soviet troops temporarily stationed in the Czechoslovak Socialist Republic);

b) Insofar as garrison duties, disciplinary matters, etc. are concerned, the Soviet troops stationed in the above-mentioned facilities will be subordinated to the Commander-in-Chief of Soviet troops temporarily stationed in Czechoslovakia; as to professional matters, they will continue to be subordinated directly to the General Staff of the Soviet Armed Forces;

c) Insofar as Subparagraphs (a) and (b) are concerned, the Czechoslovak side will basically not be responsible for a number of duties vis-à-vis the Soviet troops stationed in the above-mentioned facilities (logistical support, guarding, training, etc.)—these duties will be handled in the same way as with other Soviet units and formations temporarily stationed in Czechoslovakia.

Thus, only the following planned measures are to be accomplished by the Czechoslovak party:

– maintaining the nature of the facilities in question in secrecy (including necessary contacts with representatives of Czechoslovak local government bodies, in particular insofar as the maintenance of special parts of the facilities is concerned);

– provision of quarters in the spirit of the basic Agreement of December 15, 1965;

– provision of reliable communications with the General Staff of the Czechoslovak People's Army and, through the latter's exchange, also with the Headquarters of Soviet troops temporarily stationed in the Czechoslovak Socialist Republic;

– participation of Czechoslovak troops in extraordinary measures taken to ensure full protection and defense of the facilities in question;

– other issues, if necessary and appropriate (the extent of which will be limited), since especially the Jince facility is fairly far away from General Maiorov's formations, and because no Soviet command offices are expected to be established there.

The Czech side will meet its obligations outlined above by allocating just 3 to 5 professional soldiers per facility, plus a minimum number of officers at the General Staff; the other numbers of professional soldiers and civilian employees that have been considered so far will be cancelled. The stationing of the above-mentioned Czechoslovak liaison personnel outside the facilities will be discussed by the Joint Technical Commission.

3. The meeting also resulted in an outline of further steps to be taken, namely:
   – as soon as you approve the contents of the Protocol, it will be signed by the Chiefs of General Staffs of both parties concerned;
   – since early December, the Joint Technical Commission, including representatives of Soviet units, will gradually start taking over the facilities in Mimoň and Jince, the aim being to complete the process by (the end of) December. Early in January 1969, the facilities will be taken over by a state commission, and the Soviet troops manning the facilities will arrive in full strength (460) by the end of January;
   – the third facility (Bílina) will be handed over in a similar manner at the end of 1969.

4. I am hereby requesting that you kindly approve the measures outlined above.

[*Source: VS, OS-OL, č.j. 00671/12, VÚA. Translated by Jiří Mareš.*]

Document No. 61: Czechoslovak General Staff Study on the Warsaw Treaty, December 21, 1968

The Czechoslovak General Staff prepared this study about the role of the country in the military organization of the Warsaw Pact four months after the Soviet intervention. As such it presents a somewhat different point of view from critiques prepared only months before during the height of the Prague Spring, although it also tries to preserve some of the ideas from that period (see Document Nos. 51 and 52). This study argues that Czechoslovakia has always played a major role in the Warsaw Pact, and should continue to do so. It emphasizes that the country has been second only to the USSR in promoting the strengthening of the Pact's military organs, and it asserts the need to move toward greater institutionalization of the organization, as had taken place in NATO.

[...]

From the viewpoint of organization and lines of responsibility, the Warsaw Treaty has always been too loose a bond, failing to utilize all the potential to which it is entitled by certain provisions, and has not yet reached its desired condition in terms of the statutory and structural consolidation of its parts. In this sense, it cannot compare to the organizational refinement of NATO, in spite of the more forward-looking social order it is built upon.

In [our] political circles, the fear is sometimes expressed that by striving to strengthen mainly the military bodies of the Warsaw Treaty we may leave an impression of insincerity about our efforts to achieve a European security system, as mentioned in Art. 11 of the Treaty.

It needs to be stressed here that by strengthening these bodies, we would not even reach the organizational level of the NATO military bodies, and the aforementioned argument can thus be regarded as unsubstantiated.

In fact, accomplishment of the measures in question would make possible the attainment of the objectives set by the Warsaw Treaty and increase the effectiveness of the Treaty itself. This path also appears to offer the best way to eliminate the drawbacks in the way the Treaty has operated in the past; it would fully meet the needs of strengthening cooperation among socialist countries, so urgently needed in the current state of international affairs. This applies especially to the military bodies of the Warsaw Treaty. [...]

It must be said that these questions have been addressed at conferences of the coalition's defense ministers and chiefs of general staff, and at consultations of representatives of troops and services; largely, however, they had to do with the urgency of a particular problem, not an attempt to examine systematically certain statutory principles.

At such occasions, the leading officials of the Czechoslovak People's Army have always been among those who have taken the most initiative. [...] They were regarded as a pillar of the coalition and as a counterpoise to certain detrimental endeavors, which have been manifested since 1964 mainly by the Socialist Republic of Romania.

Romania's standpoint arose from a narrow perception of state sovereignty and a slightly different evaluation of the political situation, of the Federal Republic of Germany in particular. Besides that, Romania was interested in a relatively substantial adjustment in the power assigned to the supreme commander of the Unified Armed Forces of the Warsaw Treaty. On the other hand, Romania's attitude revealed a statutory lack in the military organization of the coalition, i.e. a vagueness concerning the rights and duties of both the supreme commander and the General Staff, as well as concerning the influence of coalition members on their activities.

According to some coalition members, this factor leads on the one hand to excessively lax conduct by the coalition's leading member-state, while on the other hand it fails to define precisely the rights and obligations of individual coalition members, which can in the worst scenario benefit even harmful endeavors.

[...] From a legal standpoint, proceeding from the principles of sovereignty, there is no doubt that whatever measure is to be adopted in the scope of a joint defense activity, it must be approved beforehand by the government of each nation in question. This principle, surely unambiguous from a legal point of view, collides, however, with certain difficulties of a pragmatic nature. There are measures, which cannot be discussed with individual governments due to time constraints or efficiency imperatives, but which must be effected immediately.

This is so, e.g., in the case of a swift and efficient reaction to a surprise attack, the coordinated operation of an anti-aircraft system, an instant triggering of certain coalition defensive actions and equipment, communication and security measures, the deployment of troops according to temporary circumstances, etc. In these cases the group in command—here the supreme commander and his Staff—must be able to act with no delays and to direct the combat activity in all its dimensions, benefiting the entire coalition and all its members. The necessary power must be grounded in statute in advance and defined in the most precise way, with the consent of all the member-states' governments.

As concerns the influence of the member-states' military bodies on the systematic handling of the coalition's military problems, it has been regarded as a drawback that the supreme commander does not yet have a permanent advisory council, which would ensure this kind of systematic operation. [...] It is indeed true that the primary questions have always been dealt with at conferences of the coalition's defense ministers or chiefs of general staff, but these groups assembled when there was an immediate need, usually following a Political Consultative Committee session or a mutual agreement, and they did not operate in a systematic fashion, as is so necessary for the operations of the supreme commander and his staff.

[...]

The problems relating to the statutory and structural consolidation of Warsaw Pact bodies, military bodies in particular, are finding their way onto the agendas of conferences of chiefs of general staff of the allied armies and the member-states' defense ministers, and are gradually expanding to become their central topic. Besides that, they are also on the agenda at Political Consultative Committee sessions, if only as one of the activities of this supreme coalition authority. [...] In the past three years, the problems in question have been discussed several times in the Political Consultative Committee and at conferences of chiefs of general staff and of defense ministers.

Not even the events of 1968 in Czechoslovakia have had a substantial impact on the development of these problems. The General Staff of the Czechoslovak People's Army clearly realized that the Warsaw Treaty is the country's only guarantee of security, that no change in our obligations in foreign policy or military affairs is to be allowed, and that an all-round consolidation of the coalition is to be strived for.

[...]

The views of individual member-states have been unified by means of the supreme commander's visits with their party, government and military officials, while allowing for careful preparation by the general staffs and respecting specific approaches of the individual parties to a particular solution of the problem.

In the current stage, the effort in question has not yet been completed. We can, however, safely assume that it will ripen in due time to a state where the relevant statutory document could be submitted to the Political Consultative Committee for approval.

Such an act, however, cannot be regarded as the last word in this area. Only after it is committed can we approach a practical solution to an entire range of problems on the military side of coalition, including the establishment of principles for carrying out defensive tasks in concert with [the requirements of] politics and economics, which basically means creating a coalition doctrine, even though it is uncertain whether this exact term is to be used.

[...]

It may be assumed that the development has reached a qualitative turning point which, however, should not be regarded as static. There is no doubt that the military organization of the coalition will continue to develop along with the political concepts of the socialist camp. The pace of this development, however, will depend on the scope of the coalition as well as the international and domestic political changes in and out of it.

[*Source: MNO/OS, 1968, kar. 43, sig. 13/5, č.j. 0018361, VÚA. Translated by Stan Mareš.*]

PART THREE

The Alliance at Its Peak

Document No. 62: New Secret Statutes of the Warsaw Pact, March 17, 1969

The March 1969 Political Consultative Committee meeting was a watershed for the Warsaw Pact. After years of trying, the Soviet Union finally managed to achieve agreement on the reorganization and consolidation of the alliance, which would have far-reaching consequences in coming years. The statutes of the new institutions approved at the session are reproduced here. The first item is the statute of the Committee of Defense Ministers, one of the new entities created at the meeting. The ministers had held meetings before but these were now to be regularized, following NATO practice.

The second document aimed at responding to deficiencies in the assignment of authority to the Warsaw Pact supreme commander. Moscow's allies had repeatedly criticized the original formulation, in effect since 1955, for being too vague and delegating unwarranted power to the commander, who was always a Soviet officer. The new document was more detailed, specifically delineating the commander's authority in peace time. The document reproduced here still vested the commander with considerable powers but at the same time incorporated concessions to the East Europeans such as codifying certain rights of national governments, particularly with respect to deployments of troops on their territories. This was, of course, partly a result of the events in Czechoslovakia. An additional statute, spelling out his powers in war time, was planned but remained very controversial, and was not actually approved until 1980 (Document No. 86).

---

a) Statute of the Committee of Ministers
   of Defense in Peace Time

1. On the basis of Article 6 of the Warsaw Treaty the Committee of the Ministers of Defense will be constituted to elaborate agreed recommendations and suggestions on issues concerning the defensive capabilities of the member-states of the Warsaw Treaty, as well as on the creation and increase of the readiness for action of the unified forces and [it will be constituted] to prepare matters which have to be discussed in the Political Consultative Committee.

The Committee of the Ministers of Defense is a military organ of the Treaty. Its members are the Ministers of Defense of the member-states, the Supreme Commander and the chief of staff of the Unified Armed Forces.

2. It is the task of the Ministers of Defense
a) to examine the situation of the likely opponent, his strategic plans and the trends in his forces' development
b) to elaborate recommendations and suggestions for matters concerning the perfection of the defensive capabilities of the member-states

c) to discuss the recommendations and suggestions concerning the creation and development of the Unified Armed Forces as well as the increase of their readiness for action

d) to examine matters which are related to the activities of the leading bodies of the Unified Armed Forces

e) to examine the condition of the theaters of war and give recommendations for their preparation

f) to examine the condition of the command resources for war time and to take the necessary steps for their perfection

g) to discuss other military matters that require joint coordination.

3. The recommendations and proposals of the Committee of the Ministers of Defense concerning the most important military and politico-military matters that require jointly discussed decisions will be presented to the governments, or else to the Political Consultative Committee, for consideration and appropriate confirmations.

The decisions of the Committee of the Ministers of Defense concerning matters which are within the jurisdiction of the Ministers of Defense will be accepted for implementation by the Ministers of Defense and the Supreme Commander The meetings of the Committee of the Ministers of Defense will be held once or twice a year. The Ministers of Defense chair the meetings alternately. Each minister of defense who is chairman is responsible for convening the meeting.

An extraordinary meeting will be convened by each chairman at the request of one member of the committee provided that at least 50 percent of the members of the committee agree. [...]

b) Statute of the Unified Armed Forces and
   Unified Command in Peace Time

GENERAL STATUTES

[...] In case of an armed attack in Europe on one or more participating states of the Treaty by any state or group of states, every member-state of the Treaty immediately will help the attacked state or states by exercising the right to individual and collective self-defense, either individually or by arrangement with other member-states of the treaty, with all methods it considers to be necessary, including the use of armed force. The member-states will immediately consult each other concerning joint steps, which must be initiated to restore and preserve international peace and security.

With this aim in view the member-states of the Treaty created the Unified Armed Forces and take the necessary steps to strengthen their power and constantly increase their readiness for action and [they] coordinate their joint defense efforts to defend peace and socialism in Europe.

To exercise the command of the Unified Armed Forces and ensure the coordination of their duties, the Unified Command headed by the Supreme Commander of the Unified Armed Forces was created pursuant to Article 5 of the above-mentioned treaty.

I. The Unified Armed Forces of the member-states

1. The Unified Armed Forces of the member-states are understood to be those forces and equipment which according to the agreement of the member-states are assigned for joint activities as well the joint Military Councils which were created in accordance with Article 5 [...]

2. The Unified Armed Forces of the member-states consist of the national units, provided for joint military operations in accordance with the decisions of each country's governments, tactical and operational units of all services, these contingents, security detachments, front and rear commands, as well as the commanding bodies of the Unified Armed Forces.

The total strength of the forces-in-being in peace time and war time, the order of battle of the units, sub-units, rear and front commands, their structure, armament and equipment as well as the extent of materiel reserves and the steps toward operational preparation of the national territories will be laid down by the government of each state in view of the recommendations of the Supreme Commander of the Unified Armed Forces and on the basis of the decision of the Political Consultative Committee, depending on the available resources and economic possibilities. These matters will be determined by special agreements which will be signed by the Supreme Commander of the Unified Armed Forces and the Ministers of Defense of each state and confirmed by the governments of the relevant member-states.

3. In peace time the troops and fleets belonging to the Unified Armed Forces remain in direct subordination to each ministry of defense; their activities will be governed by the laws, statutes and service regulations of each state.

The ministries of defense are fully responsible to their governments for the condition, armament, equipment, combat readiness, political indoctrination, and military training of their troops, as well as for the stocking of the prescribed material and technical reserves.

In war time the organization of the command of the Unified Armed Forces, the activities of the Unified Command as well as the mutual relations of the Unified Command and the national commands will be governed by particular statutes.

4. For the joint management of the air defense of the member-states, a unified air defense system was created.

5. Operational planning for troops assigned to the Unified Armed Forces for war time will be carried out by the Ministers of Defense and the general (main[1]) staffs of the member-states taking into consideration the recommendations of the Supreme Commander of the Unified Armed Forces and the suggestions made by the general staff of the armed forces of the USSR, and if necessary jointly with the other armies. Strategic operations plans for the forces-in-being of each country for war time will be signed by the Ministers of Defense and the Supreme Commander of the Unified Armed Forces and will be confirmed by the relevant governments of the member-states.

[1] The East German general staff was officially called "main staff."

II. The Unified Command, highest service positions and leading bodies of the Unified Armed Forces

6. The following service positions will be established within the Unified Command:
   - the Supreme Commander of the Unified Armed Forces
   - the chief of staff of the Unified Armed Forces and the first deputy of the Supreme Commander
   - deputies of the Supreme Commander of each member-state in the rank of, either to the minister of defense or chief of the general (main) staff
   - deputy of the Supreme Commander for air defense
   - deputy of the Supreme Commander for the air forces
   - deputy of the Supreme Commander for the navies
   - deputy of the Supreme Commander for armaments and chief of the Committee on Technology.

7. For the command of the activities of the Unified Armed Forces the following agencies will be created:
   - the Military Council
   - the Staff
   - the Committee on Technology.

8. With the consent of the governments, Liaisons of the Supreme Commander of the Unified Armed Forces can be appointed in the armies of the member-states. They will follow guidelines approved by the Ministers of Defense and confirmed by the Supreme Commander.

III. The Supreme Commander

9. In accordance with the decision of the governments of the member-states the Supreme Commander will be appointed from among the marshals (generals) of any of the member-states for 4–6 years.

10. In his activities the Supreme Commander will be guided by the decisions of the governments of the member-states and the instructions of the Political Consultative Committee.

In agreement with the Ministers of Defense and if necessary with the governments, as well as with the help of his deputies and the staff, he organizes and implements measures aimed at increasing combat and mobilization readiness.

The Supreme Commander reports periodically to the Political Consultative Committee and the governments of the member-states about his activities and the condition and development of the Unified Armed Forces.

11. In agreement with Article 10 of the statutes, the Supreme Commander:
   - coordinates operational plans for the employment of the troops and naval forces assigned to the Unified Armed Forces.
   - issues directives for increasing readiness for operational and combat training; lays down the annual joint activities of the Unified Armed Forces (exercises, war games, training, conferences, consultations, discussions and others) and is in charge of their implementation.

- prepares proposals for the improvement of armament, preparation of the battlefield, and stockpiling of matériel.

12. In accordance with Articles 10 and 11, the Supreme Commander has the right:
- in implementing the decisions of the governments of the member-states or the Political Consultative Committee, to give instructions concerning the transition of troops to a heightened or total readiness for action.
- in realizing the plan agreed upon with the defense ministers, to participate in controlling the combat and operational preparation as well as the level of combat readiness of the troops and naval forces assigned to the Unified Armed Forces.
- together with the Ministers of Defense of the member-states, to sign draft versions of operational plans, agreements, plans and other documents, which concern the development of the Unified Armed Forces and to present these documents to the relevant governments for review and approval.
- to consult the Ministers of Defense or the governments of the member-states as well as the Political Consultative Committee in all matters concerning the Unified Armed Forces.
- in agreement with the Ministers of Defense of the member-states to suggest candidates for the following positions to the governments for consideration:
- chief of staff of the Unified Armed Forces and first deputy of the Supreme Commander
- commander of air defense troops of and deputy of the Supreme Commander
- deputy of the Supreme Commander for the air force
- deputy of the Supreme Commander for the navy
- chief of the Committee on Technology and deputy of the Supreme Commander armament
- in agreement with the Ministers of Defense and on the basis of Article 8 of these statutes, to name the representatives of the Supreme Commander in the armies of the member-states
- in conformity with the prescribed numerical strength of the personnel of the staff, the Committee on Technology, and other agencies of the Unified Armed Forces, and in agreement with the Ministers of Defense, to confirm and determine the career tables of the generals, admirals, and officers of the leading agencies of the Unified Armed Forces and to give instructions for their use in their positions.

IV. Deputies of the Supreme Commander

13. In agreement with Article 6 of these statutes, the Supreme Commander has the following deputies:
- the chief of staff of the Unified Armed Forces and first deputy of the Supreme Commander
- the deputies of the Supreme Commander who are at the same time either deputy Ministers of Defense of the member-states or chiefs of the general (main) staffs
- Each government of a member-state names the deputy of the Supreme Commander who carries out his duties in its country. To treat and solve problems

of mutual interest, the Supreme Commander consults periodically with his deputies.

- the commander of air defense troops of the member-states and deputy of the Supreme Commander
- the deputy of the Supreme Commander for the air forces
- the deputy of the Supreme Commander for the navy
- the chief of the Committee on Technology and deputy of the Supreme Commander for armament.

14. The chief of staff, the commanders of air defense troops and of the navy, and the chief of the Committee on Technology will be appointed for a period of 4–6 years by mutual agreement of the governments from among the staff of the forces of any member-state.

15. The deputies of the Supreme Commander are guided in their activities by the present statutes, the statutes of the military council and the instructions of the Supreme Commander as well as the Ministers of Defense of each state. The deputy of the Supreme Commander and commander of the air defense troops are also guided by the statutes on the unified air defense system.

V. The military council

16. The military council deals comprehensively with current issues concerning the condition and development of the Unified Armed Forces.

The activities of the military council are of a consultative and advisory character. They are regulated by special statutes.

17. The military council ... consists of:
- the Supreme Commander as chairman
- the chief of staff
- the deputies of the Supreme Commander deputies of the Ministers of Defense or the chiefs of the general (main) staffs
- the commander of the air defense troops
- the deputy of the Supreme Commander for the air force
- the deputy of the Supreme Commander of for the navy
- the chief of the Committee on Technology.

VI. The chief of staff

18. The chief of staff supervises the work of the staff of the Unified Armed Forces and coordinates the activities of all leading agencies of the Supreme Commander. He personally participates in the elaboration of issues related to the operations of the Unified Armed Forces in war time. He deals with [other] matters concerning the Unified Armed Forces, reports to the Supreme Commander, and supervises the implementation of his decisions.

19. On instructions from the Supreme Commander, the chief of staff together with the general (main) staffs coordinates the joint activities of the Unified Armed Forces. Together with the general (main) staffs he determines the distribution order of doc-

uments of informative character and maintains correspondence with the general (main) staffs on matters within his area of responsibility.

20. The chief of staff has the right to issue orders to the staff and to confirm regulations for the administration and departments of the staff, plans and other working documents. Furthermore, he has the right to use the diplomatic pouch and other means that exist within the countries.

21. The chief of staff has deputies in the rank of deputy chiefs of the general (main) staffs appointed by the ministries of defense of the member-states. They work permanently in the staff while representing there the general (main) staffs. They ensure continuous cooperation between the staff and the general (main) staffs of the member-states and participate in the operational planning for their troops.

VII. The staff main [executive] agency of the Supreme Commander

22. The staff of the Unified Armed Forces is the leadership organ of the Supreme Commander of the Unified Forces.

23. The staff is responsible for the examination and evaluation of the politico-military and strategic situation, the elaboration of proposals concerning combat and mobilization readiness of the troops and naval forces, their operational and combat training, the development of forces, structures and weapons systems, the equipping of the troops and naval forces with weapons and [other] military technology, as well as for the preparation of theaters of war and the formation of necessary reserves.

24. The staff analyzes data about the likely adversary, his strategic plans, structure, weapons, military technology, and other matters concerning NATO and other imperialist military blocs, and on this basis prepares proposals for the Supreme Commander and, at his instruction, informs the general (main) staffs of the armies of the member-states.

25. In accordance with Article 11 of the present statutes, the staff plans the annual activities of the staffs and troops of the Unified Armed Forces (exercises, war games, training, conferences, consultations, discussions). In agreement with the general (main) staffs of the armies of the member-states, it presents [the plan] to the Supreme Commander, and after his approval, prepares and carries out the activities.

26. It analyzes, interprets, and disseminates proposals for how positive experiences, new methods and procedures could be used in training the troops. It analyzes and interprets the results that have been achieved.

To analyze the experiences and condition of the troops, as well as to provide support on the spot, generals and officers participate in joint activities of the troops and naval forces assigned to the Unified Armed Forces (exercises, trainings, war games).

[*Source: AZN 32854, BA-MA. Translated by Rebekka Weinel for the National Security Archive.*]

Document No. 63: Appeal for a European Security Conference, March 17, 1969

One of the issues discussed at the March 1969 PCC meeting was an appeal for a European security conference. This appeal was important because it eventually opened the way to the Helsinki conference and the adoption of the Helsinki Final Act in 1975. The Soviets had raised the idea time and again in previous years but always under conditions that were patently unacceptable to the West, such as excluding the United States or requiring restrictions of West Germany. This time Moscow issued the appeal without preconditions. It was still controversial, as Romanian President Ceauşescu's later comments indicate (see Document No. 64), but the public call was sufficiently open-ended that some Western countries believed it could be taken seriously. (The question of American participation remained unclear for a time, but by the end of 1969 the Soviet Union had accepted that there was no sense discussing the issue without U.S. involvement.) These materials on the CSCE show that the idea of a security conference was important for the Soviets. There were certainly differences within the Eastern alliance over the nature and details of the conference, as later documents in this collection show, but there was enough of a consensus to allow the process to move forward in a manner that would fundamentally influence the way security would be defined and received by both East and West to the very end of the Cold War.

It was almost three years ago that the Warsaw Pact member-states proposed in Bucharest an all-European conference to discuss questions of European security and peaceful cooperation. Personal contacts that have taken place since then prove that not a single European government opposes the idea of an all-European conference and that realistic possibilities exist for holding such a conference. All of the European states have not met since World War II, even though there is a series of questions which they should examine at the negotiating table.

[...]

The Warsaw Pact member-states reaffirm their proposals directed against division of the world into military blocs, the arms race, and threats to people's peace and security. They also reaffirm other measures embodied in the 1967 Bucharest declaration on the strengthening of European security and peace.

[...]

The prevention of fresh military conflicts through the strengthening of economic, political, and cultural relations among states and on the basis of respect for the equality, independence, and sovereignty of countries is a question of vital importance for the European peoples. [...]

The inviolability of existing borders in Europe, including the Oder-Neisse border and the frontier between the GDR and the German Federal Republic, is a fundamental requisite for Europe's security, as is recognition of the existence of the GDR and the Federal Republic of Germany. The Federal Republic of Germany should renounce its claims to representing all German people and to possessing atomic weapons in whatever form and declare that West Berlin has a special status and does not belong to West Germany.

[...]

A practical step toward strengthening European security would be an early meeting of officials of all interested European states at which they could jointly fix the procedure for convening the all-European conference and define questions to be placed on its agenda. At the same time we are ready to examine any other proposal concerning the method of preparing and calling such a conference.

States taking part in the Political Consultative Committee session address this appeal to the countries of Europe: Cooperate in convening an all-European conference and in creating conditions required for its success and for fulfillment of the hopes people have pinned on it. In the interests of putting this important initiative into effect, which would be an historic event in the life of the continent, those taking part in the session address a solemn appeal to all European states to strengthen the atmosphere of trust and thus to refrain from any action which would poison the atmosphere of relations between states. They appeal to the states of Europe to proceed from general statements about peace to concrete actions and measures serving a relaxation of tension, disarmament, cooperation among people, and peace. They appeal to all European governments to exert joint efforts to make Europe a continent of fruitful cooperation between nations and of equal rights and a factor in the stability, peace, and mutual understanding of the world at large.

[*Source: Open Society Archive, Budapest, Radio Free Europe/Radio Liberty collection, 80-1-109. Translated by Radio Free Europe/Radio Liberty.*]

Document No. 64: Report by Ceauşescu to the Romanian Politburo on the PCC Meeting in Budapest, March 18, 1969

Despite the main import of the March 1969 PCC session (see Documents Nos. 62 and 63), Nicolae Ceauşescu in this very colorful report to the Romanian Politburo chooses to focus on areas where disagreements took place, and on which the Romanian delegation managed to have an impact. One example was an appeal for holding a conference on European security (later known as the CSCE), which the Soviet Union wanted the PCC to issue. But Ceauşescu objected, complaining that the appeal's tone toward the West was far too harsh. In another example, Romanian opposition blocked a Polish proposal to reject West Germany's claim to West Berlin. The Romanian leader again got his way when he insisted that the ongoing Sino-Soviet border clashes should be discussed bilaterally with China and not within the framework of the PCC. Politburo member Emil Bodnăraş, duly complimenting his boss's performance at the PCC, makes the interesting observation that if Soviets are faced with a tough position they tend to back down.

Stenographic Record of the Meeting of the Executive Committee
of the Central Committee of the Romanian Communist Party
March 18, 1969

[...]

Cde. Nicolae Ceauşescu: Let me inform you in a nutshell, comrades, about what happened in Budapest. In fact, you have read the communiqué and the appeal, so this is the whole result.

The discussions were held within the framework of the committee, especially with the comrades who were there before, and—to some extent—in the evening; then Monday morning with some of the delegations.

The main concern was that of the Soviet [delegates], and also of some of the other [delegates], who wanted to include as a first issue in the communiqué the incidents with China and reach solidarity against China. Besides other expressions in the communiqué, which referred to the increase in the aggressiveness of imperialism, in the number of aggressive actions, and the imminent danger of war, there was also the necessity of strengthening the fighting force of the Warsaw Treaty so that it can crush any oppressor on any frontier. Isn't that so? The last formulation was something to that effect.

The appeal was somewhat better but again with many such tendencies. Let us call for the achievement of security, but if you don't come they'll beat the living daylights out of you. The meaning of the appeal was something like this: you'll get into hot water whether you come or not! [Smiling]

Those persons who were more active in the committee, in the sense of having adopted harsh positions, were the Poles, who really had the harshest positions.

The comrades said nice words to one another at about two o'clock in the morning but it seems that these words also eventually did some good.

Cde. Emil Bodnăraş: Afterwards they entered into the zoological field.

Cde. Nicolae Ceauşescu: You see, [Mircea] Maliţa [...] [said] this in the following way: if people don't help one another in all respects, then what kind of an alliance is it if you don't act in both the East and the West, the South and the North?

Naturally, something was obtained, especially due to the appeal in the commission, but practically speaking nothing was obtained until the delegations came, and an understanding was reached.

We arrived there the day before yesterday. The reception was correct, as it was with all the others; nobody was received differently. We went to the hotel on Margaret Island, where all the delegations—except for the Soviet one—were accommodated. The Hungarians told us that no program had been envisaged for Sunday evening, that each delegation was free to do as it wished. We set about playing chess, and agreed to pay a visit to the embassy.

[Ion Gheorghe] Maurer went downstairs to go for a short walk, and in the meantime the Soviets came and the discussions began. We went downstairs, too, and stopped. Among other general topics of discussion, [the Soviets] raised the main issue. Let's discuss serious things to see what we have to do. They said they wished the meeting to yield good results, and achieve unity [of opinion]. We told them that we wanted the same thing. But, as they surely knew, it was difficult to reach a result regarding the communiqué.

Dear gentlemen, to our knowledge the appeal is in a more advanced form and maybe a short communiqué would be good, but it should reflect all of the points of view.

They said: Vietnam should be [included].

We answered: we agree that it should be.

They said: European security?

We answered: we agree.

They said: what about the Middle East?

We answered: we agree, but let's not start making history.

At any rate, the first discussion went something like that.

They said: then let's talk with the other delegations and issue a communiqué, where all of these issues would be raised. We'll go and talk with the other delegations as well, and then will come back again and talk with you.

We went to the embassy and at about 12 o'clock at night they finished the discussions with the others and came to us—Brezhnev and Kosygin—and told us: we held discussions with all the others. Of course, everybody has his own opinion, and everybody wants a more comprehensive communiqué. We have to take a stand. The main point, however, is that we cannot help taking a stand and include in the communiqué the issue of border incidents with China, that this is the main issue. [They added] that it would be inconceivable for us to meet and discuss other things and not discuss the most serious issue.

After they repeated their story again, that we have to raise the issue of European security, that we have to raise the issue of the Middle East—things that they had repeated the day before—they told us: look what Nixon did, he demanded the strengthening of NATO, of course, in one form or another; he declared that Germany could not remain divided forever, and that it would have to be united [in the long run], and then he spoke in favor of the peaceful solution of issues, but only in general terms. [They added] that [the Western countries] were strengthening NATO, and we have to factor in this fact.

[Later] they spoke about Vietnam again, the Middle East, and the FRG; and the last outstanding issue was China.

We listened in silence, and did not interrupt them at all.

The main issue is China and we have to discuss it.

Cde. Emil Bodnăraş: This was a result of their consultation with the others.

Cde. Nicolae Ceauşescu: I listened to them in silence, I did not interrupt them at all. I let them finish what they had to say, and I briefly told them all the issues, and it was also with the European security issue that I began.

It is just. We must speak about European security, and we take the view that we must include it [on our agenda], and we commit ourselves to act for strengthening European security. It is true that Nixon paid this visit but we must not forget that Nixon's partners in NATO spoke in favor of emphasizing ways of understanding our socialist countries, and of taking the road of peace not of tension—especially France and even other partners—and we must take this into account when we collaborate in our policy.

Regarding the FRG, I said we agreed that there were revanchist and neo-Nazi forces, but it was also true that there were progressive forces wanting a different policy, that there were the trade unions, and the youth. Consequently the working class is getting stronger. [I also told them] that nevertheless, the communist party was created and it was functioning legally, which means that these forces have their say in the FRG. In addition, one has to take into account the outcome of the elections, the fact that Gustav Heinemann was elected president and that after the elections he declared that [the possibility of the] FRG leaving NATO had to be considered. We must take all these facts into account and encourage these forces to act for the purpose of dissolving this aggressive bloc, as we have always agreed.

Concerning Vietnam, we told them we agree.

Concerning the Middle East, we agree. Obviously, there is no point in our making history in the Middle East, but concerning ourselves with what we have to do now.

As far as China is concerned, of course, we told them that we were worried by these events but we did not think they could be discussed within the framework of their Political Consultative Committee, and that we had not gathered there for that purpose. Moreover, we told them that if they wished—outside the meeting and on a bilateral basis—we were ready to listen to them. We were willing to let them know our considerations if they were interested in them.

They said: OK.

[We said]: we are in full agreement with everything, except [the China issue]. All the outstanding issues are OK with us.

They said: how can we go home and tell our Politburo that we came here and did not speak about this issue, that we get information every two hours that the situation is changing that so-and-so took over command of the troops, that [the Chinese]

334

are mobilizing their agricultural communes, etc. Why do we keep discussing the FRG […] I can spit on the FRG, but China is the main danger.

I was about to tell him, my dear Sir, you are smart, it is true, but you cannot spit on the FRG anytime you feel like. But I did not.

I told them: we do not agree to discuss [the China issue].

[They said]: what? Are we not going to discuss anything? Is this issue so…?

Here Maurer cut in to clarify things: however, we agree to discuss—we can discuss anything but let it be clear to you, we will not sign any communiqué and will not tackle this issue!

Whereupon we parted company.

[…]

This is how we parted; then we went to bed without a worry in the world.

We did not sleep very well, it is true… [Laughs]

Cde. Emil Bodnăraş: What time did you leave?

Cde. Nicolae Ceauşescu: It was 2:00 a.m.

I also called them (the comrades who had participated in the meeting), and told them not to waste their time there any longer. Then they said that they would see the following day [what should be done.]

Meanwhile, Kirpichenko[2] came, too. [He said]: you see, we did not understand, we do not want to include this issue in the communiqué at any price. However, we want to discuss this issue about China because Kosygin made a mistake when he said he did not mean to touch on the issue other than in the communiqué. Naturally, this would create a bad impression (he told the boys), it would be detrimental to bilateral and multilateral relationships.

They conversed all morning long, to all appearances with the Poles and the Germans; they also had discussions with the Czechs for a short while.

In the meantime, the comrades worked on this appeal.

Eventually, only the discussion of an amendment of ours and of one of the Poles' remained outstanding, and the Poles asked us for a meeting. We went downstairs, into a hall there, and they raised the issue of their amendment. It was an amendment dealing with the recognition of boundaries. We had something clearer but ultimately they proposed a formulation/wording which we accepted—however without West Berlin, because they wanted to put down in writing in the amendment that the FRG's claim on Berlin should be rejected, a formulation we could not accept since this would have meant that we were the ones to decide who Berlin belonged to. But this was something we could not decide there. We could only say that Berlin had a special status and it was not part of the FRG. With that we agreed. The rest … more … we should decide who Berlin belonged to … this would be established when we arrived at peace.

And there was also our proposal, whereby we requested—in the interests of peace—that an end be put to demonstrations of force and military maneuvers. [The Soviets] did not agree with this. We did not cherish any illusions that they would accept it but they had the Poles reject it on their behalf. Then we proposed an acceptable formula: one should act to increase trust or one should abstain from undertaking any

---

[2] Soviet Politburo member Aleksei I. Kirpichenko.

actions that could poison interstate relationships. We added to the interpretation: no maneuvers are to be performed any longer. With this, the communiqué was ready.

In the meantime, the Soviets worked on a shorter communiqué which they did not show to anyone, and proposed to us to meet at 2:00 a.m., Budapest time. But only the first secretaries and the chairmen of the Councils of Ministers [met], before the official meeting began, because [that meeting] was postponed until 15:00.

We met, they showed us the communiqué, and we had only one observation to make: that it was not the Political Consultative Committee that decided whether to adopt documents but the participating states. We agreed with the appeal and went to the conference.

Cde. Emil Bodnăraş: The Chinese issue did not appear any more.

Cde. Nicolae Ceauşescu: It did not appear in any way whatsoever, although Kosygin had said that if we gave up, others would raise the issue because they were very upset. The Soviets said that no one was to take the floor at the conference; we gathered together and listened for about 20 minutes to the supreme commander who gave us an account of the documents that had been drawn up for the past year, and told us how good the work of the defense ministers was, and then we moved on to the signing of the documents.

I asked: my dear Sir, we have not clarified things in the draft decision yet (because they had maintained the old formulation, where it was stipulated that it was the Political Consultative Committee that decided on the adoption of documents, not the participating states). I said that we did not agree with the old formulation, and instead we should say: the participating states.

We all agreed but since the documents had already been typed [we proposed] to sign them in that form and afterwards to have the respective page retyped. (They had had the document laced up with string and showed up with it all prepared.) When they brought the document for us to sign, in order to be sure that that page would be retyped, I crossed it out by pen to cancel it. [Laughter] Well, what was I to do if they acted like that?

Cde. Emil Bodnăraş: That is why you were laughing when you signed?

Cde. Nicolae Ceauşescu: We had decided in advance that the respective page would be retyped, but to be sure that they would not forget to do so, I crossed it out.

Cde. Emil Bodnăraş: Well done, very fine.

Cde. Nicolae Ceauşescu: Then I signed. Afterwards, in the end we remembered that in fact the pages should have been initialed so that none of them could be changed. That is why I requested that the documents be initialed.

We all agreed and this operation was performed right away.

Then this appeal was brought in, and I signed it, but as there were no photographers around I waited until the photographers came.

With this, we finished. We congratulated one another for having done a good job. Brezhnev thanked us. When I went out with Brezhnev, he said he thanked me because we had succeeded in reaching a very good result, and this was a very important thing.

He said we should find the right moment to sign the Treaty since they did not have more amendments. I told him we did not have any amendments either.

With this, all was finished.

336

We had dinner there, without problems.

[János] Kádár made a speech, a general one, and proposed a toast.

There were no other problems and we said goodbye and came home. We parted company last night in a fairly good atmosphere.

That was about all.

Cde. Ion Gheorghe Maurer: And a conclusion: when people face a firmly supported position, they cave in.

Cde. Nicolae Ceaușescu: This is a just conclusion.

Cde. Ion Gheorghe Maurer: They have no other choice, so they give in. They did not give in because they are wise but because this is what the situation requires. This is an especially important thing to remember.

Cde. Nicolae Ceaușescu: We discussed things with the Czechs a little longer. Over dinner, we held discussions to some extent with János Kádár, and we arranged to have a meeting. We discussed matters with Todor Zhivkov, too. He remembered that work at the hydroelectric power station on the Danube was behind schedule, and that we had to meet.

Cde. Emil Bodnăraș: How glad all the others were the morning after!

Cde. Nicolae Ceaușescu: It seems that the Hungarians were a little concerned. The Czechs told us that they did not see either, but I do not know whether they told this to the Soviets. We did not discuss this issue with the others. During the discussions last night, when the conversation inadvertently digressed to Yugoslavia, [Jenő] Fock said we had to start getting rid of it.

We think that both the communiqué and the appeal are good.

[...]

Cde. Paul Niculescu-Mizil: Everything is good.

Cde. Nicolae Ceaușescu: It is good that we did not agree to discuss the issue of China because this would not have been of any help and would have contributed, in a way, to the aggravation of the situation.

Cde. Emil Bodnăraș: We cannot but express our admiration for the way our delegation presented itself, including the crossing out of that page. It was a formidable initiative.

Cde. Nicolae Ceaușescu: It was Maurer's initiative.

Cde. Emil Bodnăraș: This is something we must remember: that if [the Soviets] come to face a just and firm position, they are compelled to cave in; they have no other options. This is also valid for Cde. Niculescu-Mizil, who is about to leave for Moscow.

As regards the communiqué, we have to see.

Cde. Nicolae Ceaușescu: We can at most make recommendations regarding the state of readiness, and take measures for the equipment [of the armed forces].

Cde. Ion Gheorghe Maurer: The only trouble you can have here is the fact that it forces you to make expenses.

Cde. Emil Bodnăraș: I think that this fact, that it is the participating states not the Political Consultative Committee, has a qualitative aspect. This is valid as it extends to any relationships.

Cde. Nicolae Ceaușescu: They said: the states participating in the meeting of the Political Consultative Committee. We proposed a different formulation, but afterwards we agreed.

Cde. Paul Niculescu-Mizil: In 1956, after an hour-and-a-half of discussions, [the Soviets] said they did not understand what this issue was all about.

Cde. Nicolae Ceaușescu: Now they understand. They said they have nothing against it, and the others said the same thing.

Cde. Emil Bodnăraș: And we saved the other socialist states from having to commit themselves.

Cde. Nicolae Ceaușescu: I do not know whether we saved them because they can commit themselves.

Cde. Emil Bodnăraș: I am sure that as in our country the Executive Committee was informed beforehand about the issues to be discussed. And so, with certitude, given the scope of the issues, all of the Central Committees or the central organs were informed that the communiqué was to be signed, and what the position on the Chinese issue was. Now they will go back home and have to explain why they did not sign.

Cde. Nicolae Ceaușescu: Brezhnev said: how can I go home and say that I did not discuss this issue?

Cde. Emil Bodnăraș: And when they arrive home, many will breathe easily. Here the adventurous spirit was stopped, [as were] the formulations about Europe that were very bellicose, and the spirit of European security built on the spirit of August 21.[3]

Cde. Nicolae Ceaușescu: With this we can end the meeting, comrades.

[*Source: 40/1969, f. 2, 4–13, PCR-Cancelarie, ANIC. Translated by Viorel Nicolae Buta for the PHP.*]

---

[3] A reference to the 1968 Soviet-led invasion of Czechoslovakia whose purpose was to crush the Prague Spring.

Document No. 65: Polish Army Report on East German Misbehavior during the "Oder–Neisse-69" Exercise, October 22, 1969

Despite efforts at the leadership levels to find common ground within the Warsaw Pact, relationships among the supposedly fraternal parties at lower echelons were often quite raw. This Polish report describes with some feeling a variety of transgressions committed by German soldiers on Polish territory during the recent "Oder–Neisse" exercises. The document, from the Main Political Administration of the Polish Armed Forces, mentions that the East Germans still have a guilt complex about the last war but also show scorn for Polish organizational abilities and suspicion that the Poles are seeking rapprochement with West Germany over their heads. East German officers, the report complains, boast of a special relationship between Berlin and Moscow and show considerable lack of tact, for example by relishing the fact that some of their troops crossed over the Polish border on the anniversary of Hitler's invasion. Specific misdeeds ranged from the petty—throwing candy to children and taking pictures—to the serious, including a charge of rape, undoubtedly recalling some of Poland's bitter experiences at German hands during World War II.

[...]

During the "Oder–Neisse" maneuvers, [...] the attitudes of the NVA[4] GDR officers and conscripts serving on the territory of the PPR were dominated by guilty feelings caused by the previous historical period. [...] The German comrades have very strongly emphasized their ideological and spiritual allegiance to the defensive union of the Warsaw Treaty's socialist states. During the "Oder–Neisse-69" exercise, the above-mentioned guilty feelings of the NVA GDR units operating on PPR territory were replaced by distinct self-confidence.

One can conclude from our finding that the NVA GDR comrades put a lot of effort into the organizational and propaganda preparations of the military for the exercises. However, it is noteworthy that these preparations were directed almost solely at popularizing the GDR and its political and economic achievements. [...]

[...] According to our finding, during the preparation period for these exercises among the NVA GDR units, a special briefing took place during which peace initiatives of the party leadership and government of the PPR were not always accurately interpreted, especially in relation to the FRG. Proposals by the Polish side were represented as an attempt to establish relations between Poland and the FRG, excluding the GDR. These theories were conveyed by a number of the NVA GDR officers during conversations with Polish citizens. For example, during a meeting of the leadership of the orchestra representing the Neubrandenburg Military District with the factory council and directors of the porcelain factory in Chodzież, the leader

---

[4] Nationale Volksarmee (National People's Army).

of this orchestra appealed to those gathered that "the government of the PPR should not engage in talks with West Germany."

During talks with Polish Army officers, comrades from the NVA GDR were skeptical about the PPR's agricultural policies. They stressed that in their opinion a better solution in this matter would be to adopt the GDR's agricultural policies as a model. They have frequently boasted about the GDR's economic successes and high living standards. They have credited these achievements to politics of the SED and industriousness of the German nation. [...]

During their stay on the territory of PPR, especially during the first phase of the exercises, comrades from the NVA GDR displayed excessive levels of self-confidence as mentioned above, particularly by overestimating their own and underestimating our organizational skills. [...]

[...]

Some officers of the NVA GDR political apparatus have committed blunders of substantial significance through their actions. These officers have over-emphasized the bond between the GDR and the USSR, repeatedly omitting their partnership with the entire socialist camp. Their attitude has troubled the Soviet comrades. This stance seems to arise from the fact that due to the GDR's strong economic standing, politically less mature officers of the NVA GDR consider their country to be the main partner of the USSR. [...]

In their contacts with the Polish side, certain comrades from the NVA GDR did not always display adequate political tact. This may be demonstrated by the NVA's proposal to have some of their training units cross the PPR border at dawn on September 1 of this year—precisely on the 30th anniversary of Hitler's invasion of Poland. [...] Also symptomatic is the fact that during official meetings NVA GDR officers making presentations have never used phrases that address Poland's historic title to its western and northern lands. There is no doubt that this is a result of many years of subjecting NVA GDR soldiers during political training to the theory that "Hitler lost these territories."

In some comments to us by comrades of the NVA GDR one could detect hidden traces of malice. For example, due to condensation in the air state emblems fell off a few GDR flags displayed in small towns, which local authorities immediately tried to fix. The German comrades scrupulously picked up on these sporadic incidents, and informed us that in "town 'x' the FRG flag is being displayed." [...]

The behavior of several representatives of the NVA GDR during their stay on Polish territory was not always in accord with existing rules of military conduct on this matter. NVA GDR soldiers have frequently left the training areas without authorization, attempted to exchange marks for złotys, bought alcohol, gotten drunk, etc. In particular, a practice of throwing sweets to children and photographing these youngsters while they pick up the sweets caused unpleasant feedback and reminiscences among civilians. [...]

[...]

On September 20 at 19:00, a Poznań garrison command patrol stopped a group of eight officers, non-commissioned officers, and privates of the NVA GDR, who under the influence of alcohol disgusted people who were walking on the streets of the city.

340

On the same day at 24:00, a group of drunk NVA GDR officers broke into a private apartment on Mierzyński St., and disturbed the peace of nearby residents.

On September 21 around 21:00, chief petty officer Alfred Schell, a crew member of the NVA GDR guided missile cutter, raped citizen Matylda Oleś from Chorzów, who was vacationing in Ustka. The person responsible [for the rape] was delivered to the NVA GDR Military Prosecutor.

On the night of September 21, Col. Leisner, deputy commander of the 9th Armored Division of the NVA GDR, after binge drinking in the town of Charzyków, and missing his shoes and uniform, attempted to break into the room of Soviet typists, which required intervention.

[...]

[Source: Departament I, Spis 28/74, Wiązka 6, AMSZ. Translated by Magdalena Klotzbach for the National Security Archive.]

Document No. 66: Speech by Marshal Grechko at the "Zapad" Exercise, October 16, 1969

This speech by Defense Minister Andrei Grechko at the end of the annual "Zapad" ("West") exercise shows that since the onset of détente little had changed in Warsaw Pact military planning. As always, the exercise began with a NATO conventional attack. Even with French participation, the offensive succeeded in penetrating only 10–70 kilometers into Warsaw Pact territory before being repulsed all the way back to the Rhine. According to the scenario, the West would prepare to use nuclear weapons while the East would try to prevent their use.

Speaking about the international situation, Grechko admits that no immediate threat of Western attack exists but warns that it could arise suddenly. Here again, apparently little had changed in the détente era. Grechko's conclusion is that there is still a need to prepare for both nuclear and conventional war. He says that the USSR in principle will not be the first to use nuclear weapons but if the enemy chose to strike, the Soviets would not back away from their use. This was similar to the Western approach, except that no-one in the West spoke quite so openly about it at the time.

Evaluating generally the military and political situation in Europe we believe that today there is no immediate threat of attack against our countries. But one could appear suddenly. [...]

Under the current conditions one should take into consideration the possibility of waging a war with as well as without the use of nuclear weapons.

We are guided in this respect by the principle, which our party is implementing, not to use nuclear weapons first. But this does not mean that in a certain military and political situation, when the enemy reveals his aggressive intentions, we will not use our might in order to remove the threat of attack. [...]

In terms of the deployment depth, the forces of the NATO and the Warsaw Pact countries are in roughly similar positions. Thus, the divisions of the first echelon of both sides are located at most one day's march from one another. However, the "East" has considerably more of these forces, and this is their advantage. For example, at the depth of 100 km from the FRG border, the "East" has 1.5 times more divisions, and at the depth of 500 km—1.6 times more. Therefore, increasing military forces at the theater level must always happen with the "East's" overwhelming superiority, and the correlation of forces must turn more and more in their favor.

During our game, the deployment of military forces began with bringing them into a state of battle readiness. At the same time, the two sides began to do this practically simultaneously, and this allowed us to compare and evaluate the military capabilities of the "West" and the "East" at the start of the war.

The "Western side"

The calculations made by the "West" confirmed that the NATO command is capable of relatively quickly filling up its forces, mobilizing and deploying them at the starting positions for the conduct of military activities. This must be taken into account seriously. But NATO's capabilities should also not be overstated. In any case, the "West's" supposition that they can deploy 11 new West German divisions in the space of six days can hardly be recognized as realistic.

The thing is—the FRG's depots, according to the information we have today (I stress today because tomorrow the situation may change), do not hold a sufficient quantity of heavy weaponry. The formation of such a quantity of new divisions is only possible in case the existing divisions are downsized and the troops and heavy weaponry made available thereby are used as the nucleus of the new formations. But this would require 8–10 days.

The General Staffs and their intelligence directorates should attentively examine the real meaning implicit in the staffing of 25,000 and 18,000 West German divisions. The FRG military command hardly commits a mistake by creating such cumbersome and hard-to-direct divisions.

Most likely, the training and the reserve brigade battalions of these divisions are the people used for the covert deployment of new motorized infantry divisions.

The "West's" preliminary calculations regarding the advancement of forces into starting positions also appear quite unrealistic. From the 28 divisions which acted in the first echelon, just over half could be deployed by 5:00 a.m. on October 12. Also doubtful is the operational expediency of introducing mobilized German divisions into the first echelon and the assignment of 1 Belgian, 1 English and 7 American Corps into the second echelon. Such a complicated redeployment could not and cannot go unnoticed by the "East" and they, naturally, would not ignore this. One would suppose that the "West", preparing the attack, would try to keep their cards close to the vest for as long as possible, so as not to give the "East" direct cause for appropriate counter-actions.

Finally, the last issue. It is difficult to agree with the "West's" decision to first launch a 600 km-deep offensive with decisive aims without the use of nuclear weapons. They did not have the forces and the means for this, and the correlation of forces was not in their favor. By October 12—that is, by the beginning of hostilities—the "West" had 1.5 times fewer land forces and aviation than the "East." Moreover, for the offensive they would have to introduce a considerable part of the rapidly mobilized divisions and advance them 300–400 km, while the "East" by this time would have a much greater number of fully staffed and completely battle-ready divisions located near the border. Besides, the "West" had to redeploy American tactical aviation from the British Isles, as well as Belgian, Dutch and French aviation detachments to the FRG territory, and this, according to our information, requires no less than 4–5 days.

The "West's" decision to launch an attack to carry out their plans could be justified to some extent if they immediately delivered a nuclear first strike. But in this case, too, it is difficult to say what would result, because the "East" would immediately respond with even more powerful nuclear strikes.

The "Eastern side"

During the game we had the opportunity to check and test some aspects of [the process of] bringing the military forces of the "East" into a state of full battle readiness. Preliminary conclusions can be drawn as to some of them. During the game, as the chief of the General Staff, Marshal of the USSR M[atvei] Zakharov reported, the commands of the fronts, the navies, air forces and military supply and service regiments were realistically mobilized. Generally, mobilization was completed in an organized fashion. Supply of human resources and automobile transport by the civilian economy was completed on time. The quality of the mobilized recruits may be regarded as satisfactory. In general, the game confirmed the realism of our plans and calculations as to the transfer of the staffs of the fronts to the [mode of] organization and [mode of] staffing in war time.

At the same time, one cannot help but mention that even with the small volume of mobilization serious shortcomings took place. For example, the district military committees [*voenkomaty*] of the Carpathian Military District failed to send draft cards to a large number of draftees. In connection with this, resources had to be transferred from other district military committees to staff the deployed regiments. Military committees have a poor knowledge of questions of operational accounting for draftees sent to the military units, and as a result measures were not always taken in time to fill the vacancies that arose. There are still many shortcomings in the work of the reception points.

There were some shortcomings in mobilization at the Northern and the Southern fronts, as well as in the National People's Army of the German Democratic Republic. [...] In particular, in the Polish Army, the transfer of forces to a state of heightened battle readiness entails filling up many units and groupings with reservist draftees. At the same time, in the Soviet Army, in the National People's Army of the GDR and in the Czechoslovak People's Army this is done at the time of introduction into full battle readiness. It is desirable that in all the countries of the Warsaw Treaty, the introduction of forces into a state of battle readiness be done by common signal and to the same extent. [...]

The deployment of forces of all fronts at the military theaters. As I already said at the beginning of the report, each front of the first echelon has its peculiarities in the deployment of forces. The Northern front, in the space of 2–3 days, had to gather forces practically from the entire territory of Poland, regroup them at a distance of 200–800 km, move them beyond the Oder r[iver], concentrate them in the starting region to the northwest of Berlin, introduce them into the first echelon and prepare them for both attack and defense against enemy strikes. [...]

The conditions of deployment of forces on the Central and Southern fronts were different. They had to move armies in the direction of the forthcoming activities, regroup divisions of the first echelon at a distance of 50–200 km, and place second echelons and reserves within the corresponding [army] groupings.

At the same time, the Central and the Southern fronts had to provide operational cover for the deployment of the entire grouping of the "East's" military forces within the borders of the GDR and Czechoslovakia.

The tasks that were put before the fronts of the first echelon were generally implemented correctly by them. But I must say that it is very important for us to attain a further reduction in the time it takes to regroup forces, especially those of the Northern front. The earlier the fronts are ready to launch an attack, the more favorable is their position in relation to the enemy. Therefore, one must strive to win literally every hour in deployment, insistently search out possibilities for regrouping in a shortened time period, and with a lesser number of marches. [...]

[T]he "Eastern" navy in the Baltic [Sea] today has an overwhelming superiority over the enemy's navy in all types of vessels, especially in missile-armed vessels, torpedo boats and submarines, as well as in naval aviation. The Unified Baltic fleet is capable of launching 25–30 times more missiles at one time than the enemy. In tactical–technical terms—autonomy, range of fire and the firepower—the "Eastern" forces in the Baltic also exceed the means available to the "West." It would be incorrect not to use this in the early hours of war.

Under such conditions the "West's" decision to actively use surface ships in the central and eastern regions of the Baltic Sea would be a risky one. The possibility of the "West" staging the landing of a major force on the "East's" coast also remains improbable. Of course, one must not exclude the possibility of the "West" landing substantial special forces from the sea in order to destroy bridges, command centers and other sites or sea-borne troops up to a battalion to carry out particular tactical tasks. The struggle against this type of landings should be the responsibility of both the sea and the land command. However, one would hardly need to commit major forces to this. [...]

[T]he tasks of fighting against the enemy's aircraft in the Eastern Atlantic must, firstly, be solved by the Northern Fleet in cooperation with the long-range air force and those submarines of the Baltic Fleet, which could be moved to the Atlantic in peace time. Of course, the possibility of activity by the air force of the Baltic Fleet against enemy aircraft carriers in the Atlantic must not be excluded in such necessary cases as determined by the Supreme Command [*Stavka*].

Another task of the Unified Baltic Fleet is to take control of the straits zone. Implementation of this task will allow the deployment of forces of the Baltic Fleet for the war in the Atlantic. But this is possible [on condition of] close interaction with the forces advancing across the Jutland peninsula, as well as by means of conducting a landing operation and deployment of airborne troops on the islands with the involvement of major air power. The conduct of such an operation requires covert and serious preparation; the timing and means of conducting it will differ depending on the concrete requirements of the situation.

Calculations indicate that the greatest danger for the landing force will not, evidently, emanate from the sea, but mainly from the air. Therefore, when planning a landing operation, one should provide for more reliable air cover for the landing force. [...]

Finally, we believe that when the war starts the Unified Baltic Fleet can and must cut all of the enemy's naval transportation in the Baltic Sea. [...]

A few words about the liberation of West Berlin. In the game, this task was entrusted to the command of the National People's Army of the GDR. The West Berlin garrison, as we know, consists of about 30,000 troops, including the police, 90 tanks and 150 artillery pieces. But this is not the main thing. West Berlin is a large, modern city and the battle for it could take on a protracted and stubborn character, if it were done without appropriate preparation. This task must be solved quickly, I would say with lightning speed [*molnienosno*]. The last war gives us many useful examples of the successful capture of cities. They should be used. [...]

On the basis of the analysis of the capabilities of both sides and the probable plans of the NATO command, I submit that with actions excluding the use of nuclear weapons, a critical situation in the Central European T[heater of War] will already materialize on the 2nd–4th day of the war. In our game we took up the matter concretely on the morning of the 4th day of military hostilities.

By that time, the directions of the concentration of the main forces of the two sides had been mainly determined. The "West" and the "East" attained some results in different directions. The breakthrough of the tank grouping of the "East" into the region of Marburg [an der Lahn and] Fulda created the threat of cutting off the forces of the "West" and the crossing of the Rhine. At the same time, the "West" was successful in the Berlin direction. However, the question of taking the strategic initiative had not yet been solved. Everything depended on the actions taken by the two sides further on.

When making decisions, commanders and staffs had to take into account first of all that the front of military actions increased from 750 to 1600 km. Spaces of 70–80 km formed in the operational disposition.

On the other hand, the presence of reserves had a great influence on the nature of subsequent actions. In this respect, the position of the "East" was more favorable and advantageous. They had twice as many divisions in the rear, of which 40 percent could be moved into battle within a day, whereas the NATO command in the next two days could increase their push by bringing in [only] limited reserves from the rear.

As a result, with the arrival of the Reserve and the Western Fronts, the correlation of forces changed considerably in favor of the "East." This important circumstance was not appropriately evaluated by the "West," and as a result they considered it possible to continue to advance for another 2–3 days in the main directions without the use of nuclear weapons.

It would probably be more expedient to use the defense lines that had been prepared, create strong counter-attack groupings and stop the "East" by using nuclear weapons. Such a decision would correspond with the principles of the exercises conducted by the NATO command in the last 5–7 years. But the "West" chose a different road in our game. I do not want to say that this was a bad road, but, probably, not the best one.

[*Source: VS, OS-OL, krab. 2915, 999–154, č.j. 18004, VÚA. Translated for the National Security Archive by Sergey Radchenko.*]

Document No. 67: Hungarian Foreign Ministry Memorandum of Soviet–Hungarian Consultations on the European Security Conference, October 18, 1969

Between March and October 1969, the Soviet-bloc appeal for a European security con-ference made considerable progress; several West European countries responded favor-ably and Finland offered to host the preparatory meetings (although it is still not entire-ly clear whether this was a Finnish or Soviet initiative). During the Fall, the Kremlin engaged the Hungarians more and more in contrast to the Poles and East Germans who were each espousing proposals for the conference that for different reasons made Moscow decidedly uneasy (see Document Nos. 68 and 69). The document below gives an idea of the issues on which the various sides disagreed. For example, Berlin insist-ed that a foremost priority of the conference should be diplomatic recognition of the German Democratic Republic—an idea Soviet Deputy Foreign Minister Vladimir Semenov likened to "choking an infant in a cradle" (the infant being the conference on security and cooperation itself).

This memorandum also provides important evidence of Moscow's greater willing-ness after August 1968 to pursue consensus among the allies through persuasion rather than coercion. Contrary to standard interpretations that hold that once the Soviets had restored order in Czechoslovakia they could do more or less as they pleased within the alliance, Brezhnev and most of his colleagues seem to have recognized they could no longer rule by diktat but had to treat the East European regimes more like partners. Finally, this memo also shows how political rather than military issues came to domi-nate discussions within the Warsaw Pact during this early period of détente.

MEMORANDUM FOR THE POLITBURO

On October 17, the Soviet Deputy Foreign Minister [Vladimir Semenov] suggested that we conduct an informal exchange of opinion the next day in Moscow on prepa-rations for the European security conference. With the approval of comrades Kádár, Fock and Pullai the meeting took place on October 18. (At this time, deputy minis-ters from the Soviet Foreign Ministry were holding similar bilateral talks with rep-resentatives from the Foreign Ministries of Poland, Czechoslovakia and Romania.)

In the course of the talks we touched upon the following issues:

1. The standpoint of the Western powers concerning the conference

According to comrade Semenov, the situation is complex. We cannot say that we have the conference in our pocket. Though the general public received the idea very well the world over, significant forces are working against it more and more actively.

The leaders of the United States, England, West Germany and Italy clearly see that the conference would serve to recognize the realities resulting from World War

II, including the *de facto* recognition of the GDR, the easing of European tensions and the loosening of ties between NATO countries. Therefore, they endorse it with their words, but they are working against it in the background.

The French attitude is rather reserved. The French leaders concede that their major political endeavor, the simultaneous weakening of the European position of the two opposing camps, could hardly bear fruit at the conference, so their attitude is characterized by reserve and disinterest.

Some activity can be observed among the leading circles of certain smaller European nations (Belgium, Finland).

Based on the above analysis, the Soviet leaders have concluded that we can reasonably reckon with the possibility of this conference only if, as a first step, we propose a rather general agenda acceptable to all. This would be served by two Soviet procedural motions, of which the first would declare a renunciation of force, the other the need to improve economic cooperation in a general way.

[...]

2. The standpoint of the member-states of the Warsaw Treaty concerning the preparations and agenda for the conference.

With the exception of the Romanians, there is consensus that the foreign ministers should meet in Prague on October 30–31. The Romanian side agrees with that date, but they still propose Bucharest as the site of the meeting. The Soviet comrades told the Romanians that in addition to political reasons there was a procedural motive for choosing Prague: the last time representatives of the Warsaw Treaty met in Prague was in January 1956, while they last met in Bucharest in the summer of 1966. I indicated that the Hungarian side supported Prague.

There is also consensus that the security conference should have the two items proposed by the Soviet side on the agenda. However, some countries proposed amendments to the agenda which would automatically make the conference impossible to hold.

Thus, the Polish side proposes amendments to the first item on the agenda under the heading of a collective European security treaty (territorial status quo, *de jure* recognition of the GDR and its borders), which would effectively turn the security conference into a peace conference, making it impossible to hold because the Western countries would not be willing to discuss such issues.

Supplementary proposals by the Romanian side demand the elimination of the existing blocs, the withdrawal of foreign troops from European countries, the abolition of foreign military bases, and renunciation of demonstrations of force. These proposals are not acceptable to the NATO countries. If pressed hard, they would torpedo the conference.

The amendments proposed by the GDR are of a structural nature, but in reality they are aimed at the recognition of the GDR by the conference.

The Bulgarian and Czechoslovak sides agree with the Soviet proposals.

So now there is a danger that the conference agenda at the meeting of Warsaw Treaty foreign ministers on October 30–31 will be modified in a way that is similar to choking an infant in a cradle, thereby losing the positive results of our preparatory efforts.

Therefore, comrade Semenov and his colleagues requested that the Hungarian side assist in making the foreign ministers' meeting more constructive. Though in their opinion the Hungarians' supplementary proposals that were on the Politburo agenda correspond generally to the common interests of the socialist countries, for tactical reasons they suggest that we not submit them now but at a later phase of the security conference. They asked us to assist them this time in disarming the rather excessive Romanian and Polish proposals.

[…]

4. Concerning the preparations for the European security conference, I propose:

In order to establish a stance shared by the members of the Warsaw Treaty, we should support the Soviet proposals for the agenda of the security conference at the foreign ministers' meeting in Prague. We should counter the excessive Polish, Romanian and East German standpoints.

[…]

Károly Erdélyi[5]

[*Source: M-KS-288.f. 5/501. ő.e., Hungarian National Archives. Translated by Andreas Bocz.*]

---

[5] Hungarian Deputy Minister of Foreign Affairs.

Document No. 68: Polish Proposals for the Conference on Security and Disarmament, October 24, 1969

The Warsaw Pact member-states held numerous meetings to discuss a common strategy for the CSCE conference, including how to sell it to the West. But before anything could be agreed, the Poles prepared their own unilateral proposal without prior clearance from Moscow. (Ever since the Rapacki Plan,[6] security of its western border had been a particular concern for Poland.)

This proposal, which was not just an idea for a conference but a draft of a treaty, is reproduced here. Among its features is a provision for compulsory consultation among signatories (including smaller countries), which could be read as putting constraints on the Soviet Union. The Poles' ultimate goal, as implied in this document and elsewhere, was to soften the division of Europe and enhance Poland's international status and influence.

The second document, on disarmament, proposed freezing nuclear weapons at current levels on the territories of non-nuclear states. The authors obviously had in mind not just NATO stockpiles but Soviet weapons in Poland, East Germany, Czechoslovakia and Hungary, but they also called for the gradual reduction and withdrawal of these weapons, proposing negotiations under international supervision, thus removing the issue from the superpower context. Needless to say, the Soviets summarily rejected these ideas and prevented the Poles from actually submitting their proposal.

Draft Principles of a Treaty on Security
and Cooperation in Europe
[...]

II. The discretionary part of the Treaty
would contain a decision based on the following rules:

1. Acceptance of obligations:
   - non-use of force or threat of its use against the sovereignty, territorial integrity or independence of any country, or in any other way incompatible with the goals and rules of the United Nations Charter;
   - acceptance and respect of existing state borders in Europe;
   - non-intervention in the internal affairs of other countries;
   - resolution of any disagreements which may arise between signatories of the treaty only through peaceful methods in accordance with the United Nations Charter in such a way as not to threaten peace and security in Europe.

---

[6] On October 2, 1957, Polish Foreign Minister Adam Rapacki proposed a nuclear-free zone in Central Europe (Poland, Czechoslovakia, West Germany and East Germany). The plan never reached fruition but served as a model for further discussion.

2. The obligation of signatories to hold consultations when, according to any one of them a situation which can threaten peace in Europe or lead to a military attack against one or several European member-states of the Treaty will arise. The point of these consultations would be to take necessary steps consistent with the United Nations Charter (steps which would be assumed adequate and effective) to remove the threat and maintain peace and security in Europe.

3. The obligation to refrain from providing the aggressor any kind of political, military, economic, or moral help even if signatories of the Treaty are tied to it by military or any other agreement.

4. Confirmation of the right of an attacked member-state of the Treaty to individual or collective self-defense (in accordance with Art. 51 of the United Nations Charter) including the use of military force of one or several member-states of the Treaty with which it is tied in bilateral or multilateral allied agreements. All sides would be obligated to inform the U.N. Security Council about the individual or collective self-defense steps taken and would act in accordance with specific decisions of the United Nations Charter.

5. Agreement that after the implementation of the Treaty and assessment of its effectiveness, member-states of the Treaty would hold a conference to discuss the possibility of dissolving the political–military groups existing in Europe—NATO and the Warsaw Pact—and to add to the Treaty legal–international obligations to provide mutual assistance based on the rule that a military attack in Europe against one or more member-states of the Treaty would imply an attack on all member-states of the Treaty.

6. [...]

7. Acceptance of obligations:
a) the conduct of negotiations in the area of disarmament, and the execution in good will of all obligations in order to lead to universal and complete disarmament under strict international control;
b) the effort to use adequate and effective means of regional disarmament in Europe, which would support prevention of an arms race, especially nuclear arms but also other weapons of mass destruction, and which would facilitate universal and complete disarmament: these means would be subject to separate agreement or agreements.

8. Obligation for:
   – the development of universal European economic, social, scientific–technical, cultural and other forms of cooperation based on principles of equality and mutual benefit;
   – the use, especially, of all means leading to the removal of existing barriers and limitations to the development of economic relations between all Euro-

pean countries on the basis of bilateral and multilateral agreements, including also within the framework and with the mediation of the U.N. European Economic Commission. Detailed agreements on issues of European economic, social, scientific–technical, cultural, and other forms of cooperation would be subject to separate agreements between European countries.

9. Acceptance by the signatories of the Treaty of their obligation to hold periodic, and when necessary extraordinary, conferences to examine all issues, which may arise due to the implementation of decisions adopted in the treaty.

10. For the realization of goals and tasks arising from this treaty, the parties would establish commissions for matters of security and disarmament and all-European economic and social as well as scientific–technical and cultural cooperation. A task of these commissions would be to discuss problems of security and disarmament in Europe and issues of European economic, social, scientific–technical, and cultural cooperation. [...]

Draft Principles of Steps Toward
Disarmament in Europe

[...]
The government of the PPR presents the following proposal to freeze nuclear weapons on the territory of the specified group of non-nuclear European states:

1. The freeze would include territories of the specified group of European states which belong to either political–military group—the Warsaw Pact or NATO.

2. The object of the freeze would be all types of nuclear and thermonuclear weapons, regardless of modes of use or transport (artillery shells, bombs, torpedoes, warheads, etc.).

3. States with military forces on territory where a nuclear weapons freeze is proposed would undertake not to increase the quantities of nuclear and thermonuclear weapons on the territories of non-nuclear European member-states to the agreement where these weapons are currently located.

4. States with military forces on territory where a nuclear weapons freeze is proposed would in the next phase begin to gradually decrease the quantities of nuclear and thermo-nuclear weapons located on that territory until complete disarmament is achieved.

5. Non-nuclear states covered by the proposed agreement would confirm their obligations, which are based on the decisions of the treaty on non-proliferation of nuclear weapons, not to acquire and not to produce these weapons, and also to take responsibility for ensuring that obligations concerning a weapons freeze on their territory would be observed.

6. Considering the general military–political situation, the issue of freezing the means of nuclear weapons transportation within non-nuclear European countries and their relocation to territories of the nuclear powers could be considered during the next phase.

7. Control and authority over the execution of decisions contained in the agreement would be determined using, among other things, the experiences of the International Atomic Energy Agency in forming a control system for implementing the treaty on non-proliferation of nuclear weapons. The membership, structure, and work methods of the institutions of control and authority would be subject to detailed discussions and agreements.

The government of the PPR proposes that implementation of the agreement be accompanied by a binding declaration of the nuclear powers that they will not use their weapons against the territories of member-states of the treaty, obligating themselves in this way to maintain the status of this territory as free of nuclear weapons.

[...]

[*Source: KC PZPR, XIA/106, 24–30, AAN. Translated by Magdalena Klotzbach for the National Security Archive.*]

Document No. 69: East German Evaluation of Polish Proposal for a European Security Treaty, November 13, 1969

In this reaction to the Polish proposals on European security and disarmament (see the previous document), the East Germans clearly grasped what the Poles were up to, concluding that if their proposal were implemented it would be much more onerous for the Soviets and the Warsaw Pact than for the United States and NATO. The discussion over what exactly the CSCE should look like continued mainly because the Soviets themselves were unsure of what they wanted or believed they could accomplish. The initial Soviet idea was for a conference that would make general statements essentially confirming the territorial and political status quo in Europe, but deal with no specifics. However, during the four years before the signing of the Helsinki Final Act, the West, especially West Europeans, managed to maneuver the Soviets into discussions about highly specific issues, non-military ones such as human rights in particular.

During pre-consultations of the Warsaw Treaty's deputy ministers of foreign affairs on October 24, 1969 in Moscow, the People's Republic of Poland presented a draft proposal of "Basic Principles of a Treaty on European Security and Cooperation." The Polish side stressed that the draft of this document was supposed to aid long-term discussion of problems of European security.

However, it should be presented as a document at the European Security Conference. [...]

Despite repeated requests by Cde. [Stefan] Jędrychowski, the document was not discussed at the Warsaw Treaty foreign ministers' conference on October 30 and 31, 1969 in Prague. Cde. Winzer and Cde. Mănescu stated that the party and government leadership of their countries will examine the draft and will inform the Polish side of their statement.

Cde. Jędrychowski stressed that the Polish side will not take any steps to publish the draft before a statement by the member-states of the Warsaw Treaty. [...]

[...] attention must be paid to the following issues:

a) The goal of the [...] consultation requirement lies in the implementation of measures to eliminate the existing threat. Such consultations, to be undertaken upon request of an individual member state, could be used by imperialist states to interfere in matters pertinent to the mutual relationship of the socialist states. Therefore they would be part of the internal affairs of the community of socialist states. (As is known, the imperialist states have regarded support for the fraternal ČSSR by the five socialist states as a threat to peace in Europe.)

b) The listed obligation to enter into negotiations on disarmament, and to attempt to "produce adequate and effective regional measures in the field of disarmament in Europe, contributing to ending the arms race especially with regard to nuclear weapons, but also concerning other weapons of mass destruction," as well as to conclude separate agreements on those, seeks disarmament limited to Europe. The USSR would be included, but not the main military power of capitalism, the United States. Therefore, maintaining this suggestion should be contingent on the Americans simultaneously signing this treaty.

c) For the same reason, the creation of a Commission of European States for Security and Disarmament proves to be problematic for the socialist states. In the long run, it would be acceptable to create a Commission of European States for Security and Peaceful Cooperation.

[...] *Summary:*

On the one hand, the basic orientation of the Polish draft proposal on "Basic Principles of a Treaty on European Security and Cooperation" goes far beyond the agenda for a first European security conference as proposed by the Prague conference of foreign ministers. On the other hand, important elements of socialist European security policy are missing. The principles of the current Polish proposal would require a number of corrections and additions if they were to be used in a document for general discussion of questions of European security.

A Polish proposal on organizing a system of collective security in Europe could generally entail positive effects in that the discussion of the overall subject of European security would be kept alive beyond the first European security conference. [...]

This is counterbalanced by several, potentially negative, effects of the diplomatic use and publication of the proposal at the current stage of preparation of a European security conference. Right now, realistic conditions do not exist for a number of proposals that require agreement. Therefore it does not seem appropriate to spell out the proposals in a document for the first European security conference of states and to declare them as official subjects of negotiation. They would divert attention from realistic proposals made by the Prague conference of foreign ministers.

Including the Polish draft proposal in diplomatic exploratory talks with West and North European countries could result in:

1. questioning and delaying the first European security conference, possibly scheduled for the first half of 1970, by Western powers due to the complex and multifaceted nature of the Polish proposal;

2. NATO states and neutral countries using the Polish draft to justify their intentions to propose a large catalogue of issues (e.g. the demand for a balanced reduction of troops, or discussion of the so-called "German question", etc.) for negotiation at the first European security conference, and to delay the opening of the conference because of the complexity of such issues.

Also it cannot be ignored that a separate Polish proposal on European problems might be used by the other side to instigate differences in socialist attitudes towards European security issues.

All in all, it must be expected that the additional Polish proposal would make it more difficult for the socialist offensive to realize a first European security conference.

[*Source: G-A 556, 161–68. MfAA. Translated by Karen Riechert.*]

Document No. 70: Speech by Grechko at the First Meeting of the Warsaw Pact Committee of Ministers of Defense, December 22, 1969

Soviet Defense Minister Grechko's speech at the first meeting of the recently created Committee of Ministers of Defense can be regarded as representative of Soviet military thinking during the early period of superpower détente. Clearly uncomfortable with the new approach, Grechko believed (as his hard-line counterparts in the United States did about the Soviet Union) that the West was using the cover of a relaxation of tensions to build up its military capabilities for limited wars and subversion, primarily in the Third World, but possibly in Europe as well. At the same time, Grechko seems to contradict himself on the threat to peace. Notwithstanding his warnings, he acknowledges that both the superpowers are in a position to deliver crippling nuclear strikes against each other, which means that neither side is likely to initiate a nuclear exchange. He also admits that a conventional surprise attack by NATO is improbable because of the Western alliance's significant weaknesses. Nonetheless, his message is clear—there should be no reduction of vigilance.

[...]

Marshal of the Soviet Union [Andrei] Grechko started with a description of the present military–political situation, which he assessed to be still complicated.

In order to counter the decline of its influence in the world, imperialism has been increasing its aggressiveness against the national and social liberation movements developing in Africa, Latin America, and Asia, which have been further restricting its base.

Since it is getting harder for imperialism to reach its military–political goals, it has been forced to modify its strategy in the direction of preparing and conducting limited wars as well as in the direction of political diversion. Yet imperialism's main goals are not achievable with the help of a so-called indirect strategy. Imperialism thus is still trying hard to boost, modernize, and further develop its military forces.

[...] Both the U.S. and the Soviet Union possess a substantial potential of strategic nuclear weapons, which enables both sides to inflict devastating strikes upon each other, regardless of who might use these weapons first.

The fear of the existing military superiority of the socialist states, both in the field of nuclear armaments and in conventional warfare, has forced the U.S. to the negotiating table in Helsinki. The negotiations on limiting strategic armaments have been characterized as a mutual feeling-out, in which no side is willing to put its cards on the table.

Marshal Grechko affirmed that there is presently no immediate danger of an outbreak of war against the socialist states, although the danger of a world war may emerge at any time given the expansion of conflicts in the Middle East, U.S. aggression in Vietnam, and other sources of danger.

The policies of the Chinese leaders hold dangers for peace, too. China is trying to feign a negotiation position. The politics of the Chinese leaders amount to the preparation of war against the Soviet Union.

Yet the main danger for peace in Europe is the aggressive NATO bloc, particularly its main powers, the U.S., which comprises more than 90 percent of the strategic and 70 percent of the tactical nuclear capabilities of NATO; and West Germany, where the new government has not changed the direction of aggressive West German politics.

[...]

The NATO strategy of Flexible Response, which rests on the old strategy of Massive Retaliation, is a conception afflicted with many weaknesses.

The difference between the two strategies consists in the recognition of the possibilities of limited war by the strategy of Flexible Response, although its main focus still is on the massive deployment of nuclear weapons.

[...]

Passivity and inner inconsistency, which do not allow predetermined activities, have been the weak sides of the strategy of Flexible Response. Therefore, the U.S. and NATO aim at taking the strategic initiative in any case, thus actually preparing for a preventive war with the use of nuclear weapons immediately or after two to, at most, six days following the initiation of war.

[...]

The initiation of a surprise attack under conventional conditions with available forces and means has been considered unlikely.

[...]

For conditions involving the use of conventional weapons, the operational planning of NATO thus temporarily envisions the conduct of defense in particular directions. According to NATO views, the shift to offensive action is possible only after massive nuclear strikes aimed at creating a favorable ratio of forces. This assessment has been made on the basis of the deployments, characteristics, and scenarios used in NATO's most recent major strategic exercises, including "Fallex 68."

Aside from the operational planning for defense, NATO also maintains plans that envisage the immediate use of nuclear weapons and the beginning of ground force attack operations, yet only together with the use of U.S. strategic nuclear arsenals.

[...]

NATO has succeeded in creating a situation of encirclement for the states of the Warsaw Treaty.

[...]

The main weakness of NATO consists in the fact that, despite all its efforts, it remains inferior in both forces and equipment to the states of the Warsaw Treaty. [...]

[...]

[*Source: AZN 32855, 18–28, BA-MA. Translated by Thomas Holderegger.*]

Document No. 71: Hungarian Report of Warsaw Pact Summit on Policy toward West Germany, January 7, 1970

This Hungarian report of a meeting of Warsaw Pact heads of state deals mainly with policy toward West Germany in the wake of Willy Brandt's election as chancellor and the initiation of Ostpolitik.[7] The meeting provides another example of Moscow's changed approach toward alliance members. Rather than simply announcing its decision, the Kremlin found it advisable first to consult about the meaning of the new FRG policy and how to respond, in hopes of gaining maximun support for its preferred policies. The document, which is typical of the high quality of Hungarian diplomatic reporting, records a rather lively debate at the meeting. The general consensus is that any change on Bonn's part was mainly tactical but should nevertheless be pursued, in part for the economic and trade benefits for the socialist bloc. Standing in opposition to closer ties was the GDR's Walter Ulbricht who flatly declared that nothing had happened to ameliorate Bonn's revanchist instincts. Soviet leader Brezhnev then announced that Brandt would visit Moscow in a few days for negotiations, but declared that the time was not right to discuss the establishment of diplomatic relations. He acknowledged Ulbricht's charge that the new chancellor may only want to drive a wedge into the Warsaw Pact but he added that for the time being there was no better alternative to Brandt. Brezhnev's overall tone was somewhat skeptical about détente, even though it was Moscow's idea to pursue it, which indicates that the Soviets were not yet convinced they would get from it what they wanted.

[...]

Cde. Brezhnev opened the conference, which had been called to determine our joint policies towards the FRG. After this, Cde. Ulbricht presented the position of the German Socialist Unity Party's Central Committee; next to speak were Cdes. Kádár, Ceaușescu, Zhivkov, Husák, Gomułka and Brezhnev, in that order. At the end of the conference two documents were endorsed: a communiqué about the meeting and—at the request of the Vietnamese comrades—a statement in support of the struggle of Vietnam. No documents were produced for internal use.

The debate reflected an appropriate assessment of the position and politics of the FRG [...] The speakers primarily studied what actual possibilities the new elements in West German politics could offer to the socialist countries for improving current relations. Considering the complexity of the problem, the exchange of views failed to produce a complete agreement. The countries representing the extreme positions were the GDR on the one hand, and Poland and Romania on the other—while Hun-

---

[7] Willy Brandt was West Germany's chancellor from 1969 to 1974. His *Ostpolitik*, or "Eastern Policy," aimed at normalizing relations between the two Germanys and generally improving ties with the rest of the Soviet bloc ("change through rapprochement"). While not abandoning the idea of German unification, his goal was to reduce tensions so long as Europe remained divided by the Cold War.

gary, Bulgaria, Czechoslovakia and the Soviet Union assessed the situation essentially identically and reached basically similar conclusions.

In his speech, Cde. Ulbricht underlined that the political line taken by [Konrad] Adenauer, [Ludwig] Erhard and [Kurt Georg] Kiesinger[8]—characterized by the objectives of salvaging the dominance of monopolies in West Germany, changing the European status quo and penetrating the socialist countries of Europe—was also W. Brandt's line; therefore the overall situation in West Germany remained essentially the same. For this reason, we must follow without fail the old, harmonized course of action set in 1967 in Warsaw. First and foremost among our demands is the full recognition of the GDR in international law, which all the fraternal countries must earnestly support. Generally speaking, the GDR is skeptical about bilateral talks between the socialist countries and the FRG, as the latter looks upon bilateral agreements as a temporary measure until the signing of a German peace treaty, which will settle these problems once and for all, according to the FRG. In this way, the FRG can at any time cast aside the bilateral agreements signed with the socialist countries. Cde. Ulbricht explained that Soviet–American talks about the renunciation of force could only be useful if the GDR could also sign a similar agreement with the FRG, fully based on international law. In addition, he pointed out that there was no need for separate talks between Poland and the FRG about the Oder–Neisse Line, because the Oder–Neisse Line constituted the eastern border of the GDR. If Poland wanted to negotiate with the FRG, it should make a treaty with the latter, in which the FRG would guarantee Poland's territorial integrity.

Cde. Ulbricht informed the participants that the GDR was resolved to present the FRG with a draft international treaty on mutual recognition and the establishment of diplomatic relations. This would form the basis of the settlement of the two German states' relations. Until then the GDR would negotiate with the FRG on matters of mail, transportation and travel, but these negations would only aim at the collection of old debts and the guaranteeing of conditions for future, regular payment. The socialist countries of Europe should wait to establish diplomatic relations with Bonn until the FRG recognizes the GDR. Addressing some criticism to the press of certain socialist countries without actually mentioning names, Cde. Ulbricht next made the point that right now it was not the unification of the two German states, but the affirmation of their parallel existence and the lending of support to the GDR that had to be their concern. The unification of the two German states was only possible on a socialist basis and in all likelihood would take place only during the lifetime of future generations.

In Cde. Ceaușescu's assessment, the statement made by the Brandt government expressed certain rational views and some shift towards a more flexible political line, regardless of its inconsistencies. This was an important, positive step forward, he said, calling attention to the point that Brandt's failure would imply the transfer of power to a reactionary government. He stressed the need for every socialist country to dev-

---

[8] All three politicians, members of the right-of-center Christian Democratic Union (CDU) party, served as chancellor of the FRG prior to Willy Brandt: Adenauer from 1949 to 1963, Erhard from 1963 to 1966, and Kiesinger from 1966 to 1969. Kiesinger headed a coalition government that included Brandt and his left-of-center Social Democratic Party.

elop and normalize relations and establish diplomatic links with the FRG. This should not be conditioned on the existence of diplomatic relations between the GDR and the FRG. We should develop economic, technological, scientific, cultural and other relations with the FRG, because that would lend support to the progressive forces. We should support the GDR. He agreed with Cde. Kádár's proposal to encourage the admission of both German states to the U.N.

Cde. Gomułka stated that the conditions set in Warsaw in 1967 had been appropriate to the situation that had existed then. The recent changes in the FRG have opened up possibilities that we must try to exploit. The strategic objective is the full recognition of the GDR under international law. The FRG's *de facto* recognition of the GDR constitutes the step that immediately precedes its recognition *de jure*. Putting pressure on the FRG to recognize the GDR under international law would seriously set back the cause of the conference on security in Europe.

Cde. Gomułka also mentioned that the Polish side was going to start negotiations with the FRG in the near future about recognition of the Oder–Neisse border, in the course of which they intended to honor the harmonized socialist position and planned to conduct consultations with the other socialist countries. The Oder–Neisse border forms the starting point in Polish–German relations vis-à-vis both German states, which requires that the FRG, too, recognize the border, which is incidentally in the joint interests of all the socialist countries.

The Polish side supports negotiations between the Soviet Union and the FRG aimed at the renunciation of force; they also find it useful that the Soviet Union is conducting talks about the status of West Berlin. In Cde. Gomułka's opinion, Czechoslovakia, too, is entitled to conduct bilateral negotiations with the FRG about the abrogation of the Munich agreement[9]; he then went on to stress the importance of developing economic links with the FRG, which was in our joint interest. Therefore, Poland has already been conducting negotiations with the FRG about long-term trading of goods, as well as regarding economic, technological and scientific cooperation.

The socialist countries must follow a united political line towards the FRG based on principles, forcing it into acceptance of preconditions for security in Europe. At the same time, they should exploit every tactical opportunity.

- The full text of Cde. *Kádár's* speech, in which he put forward the Hungarian position, is enclosed.
- The speech made by Cde. *Brezhnev*, the last person to speak, was aimed at summing up and synthesizing the exchange of views, as well as toning down the extreme elements that were contained, to a lesser degree, in the East German position and, to a larger degree, in the Romanian and Polish views.

In assessing the situation, he started out by declaring that the elections in West Germany did not constitute a major turn, and that the FRG continued to be one of

[9] The September 29, 1938, agreement betwen Germany, Italy, Great Britain, and France, whereby Czechoslovakia was compelled to cede its predominantly German-inhabited borderlands to Germany. The abrogation of the agreement *ab initio*, i.e. ruling that it was never valid, meant that the "Sudeten" Germans who were summarily expelled from that afterWoedII had never lost their Czechoslovak citizenship and were therefore not entitled to claim compensation under German law for their property confiscated by Czechoslovakia.

In assessing the situation, he started out by declaring that the elections in West Germany did not constitute a major turn, and that the FRG continued to be one of the bastions of imperialism. In that regard, Cde. Ulbricht's argument merited some consideration. At the same time, however, one must not forget what Lenin had said about the importance of exploiting the shades of difference between certain representatives of imperialism.

The ousting of CDU–CSU from power constituted an important event; this undermined the positions of the most aggressive wing in West German imperialism. Brandt expresses certain demands that have been in the air for some time now. Since at the moment we do not have a better alternative to the Brandt government, we must take advantage of the positive aspects in its policies in order to undermine the positions of the revanchist forces and to have those of our demands accepted, to which the West-German public is the most favorably disposed.

At the same time, we must not overlook the most important element: the changes in the FRG are of a tactical, rather than a strategic, nature, and it would be a mistake to overestimate their importance. Of all the social democratic parties, Brandt's party is among those that are farthest to the right. It is clear that Brandt's program is a mixed bag and that he has already backed off on a number of issues. In most of the decisions associated with his government, including the signing of the nuclear test ban treaty, he has acted under pressure from the socialist countries, rather than at his own discretion. Through his discriminating politics, he aims to divide the socialist countries and isolate the GDR.

Our only reaction to such politics is to stand united on a shared platform and to judge Brandt by his actions.

We should not, however, give a one-sided interpretation to these phenomena. Undoubtedly, the social democrats' rise to power could, in due time, bring substantial changes to West German politics. Therefore, we must be active, we must continue the political struggle relentlessly, and we must keep up the pressure on the FRG, because it is clear that they will only yield when they have no alternative left.

Cde. Brezhnev announced that the Soviet Union would start negotiations with the FRG on the renunciation of force on December 8 in Moscow. In connection with this topic, in line with the spirit of the Budapest and the Bucharest declarations, (see Documents Nos. 63 and 41) the Soviet Union was going to address all fundamental issues relevant to the cause of security in Europe:

a) Recognition of European borders in the form of a treaty, rather than by declaration. This is likely to be the result of a long and arduous battle.

b) The GDR's recognition by the FRG under international law. This should be accompanied by efforts to have the GDR recognized by some other states, too, such as Finland and India.

c) Ratification of the nuclear test ban treaty, along with blocking all channels through which the FRG could acquire nuclear weapons.

d) Recognition of the invalidation of the Munich agreement.

This negotiation will be the first test of the Brandt administration's true motives and designs. In all probability, the most important issues will be settled only gradually.

In principle, the Soviet Union supports the idea of establishing diplomatic connections, but putting it into effect immediately would amount to a unilateral concession. For this reason, we should return to the problem after the establishment of relations between the GDR and the FRG on the basis of equal status.

In discussing cooperation between socialist countries in general, and without mentioning specific names, Cde. Brezhnev criticized the Romanian and Polish approaches to the FRG. He underlined that in their politics towards the socialist countries, the Western powers harmonize not only their principles, but also their various concrete steps, both in NATO and in the Common Market. We must do the same. He warned certain socialist countries of the danger of their overestimating the significance of economic ties with the FRG. He recommended that we increase the frequency of political consultations and mutually improve the flow of information between ourselves.

Summary: The discussion of the political line towards the FRG was useful. Although the exchange of ideas has failed to produce complete agreement on either the assessment of the West German situation or the political line to be taken towards it, we can nevertheless be hopeful that participants will take into account the views put forward here in their future building of relations. Basically, the view that carried the day (and this was accepted by every side except the East German delegation) made room for negotiations with the FRG on any reasonable subject, naturally after mutual consultation and exchange of information with the other Warsaw Pact members.
[...]

János Kádár's Speech at the Moscow Meeting
[...] From an international viewpoint, the tactical changes introduced in the political line taken by West Germany have been made necessary above all by changes in the international balance of power in favor of the socialist countries, by the political and economic achievements made by the socialist countries in general and by the GDR in particular, and by the socialist countries' consequent politics towards the FRG. [...]

Demonstrating our patience, we should assess the Brandt government on the basis of its actions, criticizing its negative moves but responding positively to its positive steps. [...]

a) We must keep constant pressure on the Brandt government to facilitate the following changes:
- The FRG's new government should renounce the foreign political objective inherited from the previous governments, which aimed at annexation of the GDR; it should fully recognize the GDR under international law. They should accept the fact that, as a result of the developments of long years and the different social evolution of the GDR and the FRG, the reunification of Germany has become impossible. The FRG should abandon its ambition to represent the entire German people.
- The FRG should recognize the present European status quo, most notably existing borders, including Poland's borders as well as the one between the GDR and the FRG. When the FRG renounces all territorial demands, it must make it clear that it means the FRG within its present borders and that it desists from demanding border changes, renouncing its program of revising the borders.

362

- It should declare the Munich Treaty to be invalid *ab initio*.[10]
- The FRG should withdraw from all claims to West Berlin.
- We must exclude the possibility of the FRG coming into possession of nuclear weapons in any roundabout way.
- Ties between the FRG and the USA and NATO should weaken.
- Propaganda from Radio Free Europe against our country should be suspended or limited (especially in view of the fact that the agreement between RFE[11] and the FRG will expire in 1970).
- They should cease support to Hungarian fascist émigrés, whose activities should be terminated.

b) [...] We must make further efforts to have the GDR recognized under international law primarily in third world countries (India, for example), but also in some developed capitalist countries (e.g. Finland).

Parallel with these efforts, we must aim to get the GDR accepted by as many inter-governmental organizations and specialized U.N. branches as possible; we must also work to get both the GDR and the FRG invited to the U.N. simultaneously and with equal status.

c) We do not see the establishment of diplomatic ties with the FRG as a timely proposition. [...]

d) After eliminating the negative elements, which serve to underline the continuity of the old political line, we must try to incorporate the positive elements of the Brandt government's program in interstate treaties. [...]

e) In the area of Hungarian–West-German relations, [...] the following options are available:

aa) Interstate agreements

- Signing long-term commercial agreements, of 5-year duration if possible. With regard to its applicability to West Berlin, we should work towards an agreement that is more favorable to us than the previous one.
- *Treaty on economic–industrial–technological cooperation:* in accordance with our long-term economic plans.
- *Treaty on proprietary rights:* in the interests of pending financial matters (the compensation of people persecuted under Nazism on the basis of the BRüG and BEG Laws of West Germany,[12] etc.).
- *Commercial and shipping treaty* on principles, which could be used to obtain most-favored-nation status. [...]

  In view of the prominent role the FRG plays in subverting the socialist countries, it would be unwise to regulate our cultural relations with the FRG in the form of an agreement. Judgment on a case-by-case basis seems more appropriate.

---

[10] i.e., invalid in the first place.

[11] Radio Free Europe, based in Munich.

[12] The Bundesrückerstattungsgesetz (Federal Restitution Law) of July 19, 1967, provided for material restitution of property to the victims of the Nazi regime. The Bundesentschädigungsgesetz (Federal Compensation Law) was a series of three laws, finalized on September 14, 1965, which privied for financial compensation to the victims of the Nazi regime.

bb) The organization of ministerial meetings in areas (foreign trade, finance, transport), where the outcome could be advantageous for us.

– In this regard, we should focus on international ministerial conferences, which could be attended by both the GDR and the FRG, so as to give a boost to the GDR's international recognition.

One such event could be the conference of transport ministers for Eastern and Central European states, scheduled to take place within the next two years.

cc) To foster a better understanding, and also to influence the West German government, it would be useful to have an exchange of views between the politicians of the two countries.

– The same consideration should lead us in providing extra support to the left-wing forces in the FRG. For this reason, we should develop relations with the two communist parties (DKP, KPD[13]), the trade unions, the youth organizations under left-wing control, progressive individuals and certain social-democratic leaders.

dd) Our attacks should be concentrated on the extreme right wing and the neo-Nazi forces in the FRG, as well as on certain reactionary political leaders (for example, Strauss[14]).

[...]

[*Source: MOL M-KS-288.f. 5/509. ő.e. Translated for the PHP by the Open Society Archive.*]

---

[13] Deutsche Kommunistische Partei, Kommunistische Partei Deutschlands.

[14] Franz Josef Strauss was a member of the conservative Christian Social Union (CSU), the Bavarian sister party of the CDU. He held several ministerial portfolios under previous CDU governments and was a vocal critic of Brandt's *Ostpolitik*.

Document No. 72: Minutes of Romanian Politburo Meeting Concerning the Ceaușescu–Brezhnev Conversation, May 20, 1970

Several of the documents in this volume illuminate Romania's unique role as maverick within the Warsaw Pact. This report by Nicolae Ceaușescu to the Romanian Politburo about a meeting with Leonid Brezhnev gives a fascinating look—albeit from one side—at the personal relationships between the Romanian and Soviet leaders, and at Romanian opinions of the Soviets. Although he may tend to embellish his account, Ceaușescu probably also felt a need to be reasonably accurate in conveying such important information to his colleagues.

Not surprisingly, Brezhnev's main purpose at the meeting was to complain about Romania's position within the Warsaw Pact and its foreign policy in general. In his version of events, Ceaușescu refuted each point and regularly put the Soviets on the defensive. At one point, a Romanian official says, they turned green. The Romanians' contempt for the Soviet leadership comes through most starkly in the comments of Politburo member Emil Bodnăraș, who says they looked "pathetic" and displayed "complete incompetence and weakness," proving that they are "prisoners of the apparatus" and incapable of thinking independently.

This almost verbatim account of the Politburo discussion gives a vivid sense of the free-flowing, almost rambling quality of Ceaușescu's speech and shows how he dominated the discussions behind closed doors.

[...]

Cde. N. Ceaușescu: [...] We spoke first and, for a little more than an hour we spoke, in the spirit of our discussion here in the Executive Committee, regarding some of our general concerns; of course, stressing economic problems. [...] Then Brezhnev started speaking. He began with a history of the relationship between the CPSU and the PCR, saying that there were many positive elements: he mentioned the exchanges of delegations in the past year—seven from us, participation in ideological reunions by them. There were also exchanges of technical documentation—they gave us 3,000 pages and we gave them 1,200—as well as cultural exchanges, what we gave them and what they gave us. [Brezhnev said] there are issues of common interest, that both they and we appreciate the leading role of the party. After that he said that there are also a number of disagreements, especially as concerned the political realm. And he began by saying that that is a consequence of the fact that Romania's position is opposed to that of the socialist countries. Of course, it is the right of every party to establish its own general political line, the direction of its foreign policy, but that on vital issues we should come to a consensus. There are instances in which Romania took a common position, but there are issues on which Romania did not act in common and even acted demonstratively.

Cde. Ștefan Voicu: Twice or three times he underlined "demonstratively."

Cde. N. Ceauşescu: And he began with the Federal Republic of Germany; that it is true that at the consultative meeting in 1966[15] it was discussed that, after all, the establishment of diplomatic relations would serve as an encouragement to the FRG government, that, of course, maybe you had economic incentives. [But that] underlines more the policies of [West German Chancellor Willy] Brandt and not of the GDR, and that in the future it will be necessary for us to consult in the spirit of what had been decided in December 1966.

After that, he mentioned the issue of the Middle East. He began again with the causes of the conflict with Israel, that we did not qualify Israel as an aggressor state, that, after all, this was encouraging the aggressor. [He mentioned] that we did not participate in the meeting in Prague,[16] that they have information that a lot of Jews are emigrating from Romania, some of them young males who are eligible for military service; that Romania received credits from Israel, etc. More so, the formalization of the relationship with Israel shows that Romania is distancing itself from the class position on this issue.

Then there was Nixon's visit[17]—that this was a slap in the face for the progressive movement. That at a time when there was a war in Vietnam, when the Americans were doing this and that in Vietnam, that was the time when we received him, that we received him right before the [party] Congress and that we even postponed the Congress in preparation for this visit. Considering this, how was he [Brezhnev] supposed to come to Romania. I did, among other things, complain that he did not visit Romania.

[Brezhnev said] that he knows we used to help Vietnam but that at this time he does not know if we still do; that this might imply that Romania is "getting cozy" with imperialism.

Cde. Paul Niculescu-Mizil: That this has the characteristics of "getting cozy" with the leaders of imperialism.

Cde. N. Ceauşescu: Then he said that he does not know what Romania is getting from the Americans, what economic incentives, but that he has to say that this has hurt Romanian prestige, that this is the reason why some foreign delegates at the Congress had taken a number of positions, and that these actions are proof of a certain isolation from the other socialist countries.

After that, he started talking about European security, of course. After he mentioned that we are all in favor of security, that this was decided even in 1966 but that Romania came up with the initiative of organizing a conference. The agreements reached at that conference had also been violated, and the fact that these proposals did not accomplish anything was also detrimental to Romanian prestige. He was very preoccupied with Romania's prestige.

[15] The reference is probably to the Bucharest meeting of the Warsaw Pact Political Consultative Committee on July 4–7, 1966. For its records on the PHP website, see http://www.isn.ethz.ch/php/documents/collection_3/PCC_meetings/coll_3_PCC_1966.htm.

[16] An apparent error. The conference of Eastern European party chiefs, without Ceauşescu, convened to agree on a common position toward Israel after its victory in the Six-Day War of June 1967. The leaders met on July 11–12, 1967, in Budapest.

[17] Richard Nixon visited Romania from August 2–3, 1969, during a trip to Asia.

Then he said that we raised objections to the conference of foreign ministers on the subject of European security and was quite insistent on this subject of European security, of military blocs, including the policy of dissolving alliances; thus also of dissolving the Warsaw Pact.

[He mentioned] that NATO discusses all issues, and that we too have the right to discuss all issues, and to hold summits; that it would be a good thing if the foreign ministers met after the NATO foreign ministers meet in May.

Then he talked about differences in regard to issues in the communist and workers' movement, that in this case Romania is not seeking [a solution] to some of the common problems; rather it is following some kind of social interest. He began with some problems—that we said at first that we would not participate at the consultative meeting [of the communist and workers' parties] but that we participated in the end. Then he talked about the participation of the Chinese Communist Party, that the materials of the conference were not widely publicized in Romania, and that this should be done since these are common materials, not just from one single party, and that they have great importance everywhere.

[He said] that the publishing of the journal *Problems of Peace and Socialism*[18] is being done tendentiously, with some articles being taken out or some passages being censored. Yet this is a common journal.

[He said] that Romania did not want to participate in the meeting to prepare for the world anti-imperialist congress. As a matter of fact that was just an introduction since he then went on to discuss the issue of China, our position vis-à-vis the Chinese, that Mao does "I don't know what," and that we are adopting a position of neutrality.

Cde. E. Bodnăraș: That the position of our party is not consistent with the danger of Maoism.

Cde. N. Ceaușescu: That we had published in Romanian newspapers some pictures from the Sino-Soviet border conflict, in a unilateral fashion, using only Chinese sources while censoring the [Russian] sources.

That in regard to the Warsaw Pact we carry out a policy of duplicity, that we agree with all the documents but in reality we do not enforce the decisions. Then he raised the problem that we do not want to participate in exercises, that we are generally raising the issue of doing away with military exercises, and [he asked] how can we argue for such a thing—look at what happened when the Arabs no longer carried out military exercises—that the imperialist [forces] had maneuvers.

That Romania is advocating the immediate dissolution of military blocs but that the Warsaw Treaty was established as a response to the establishment of the imperialist military alliances and that we do not make any distinction between [who is] rattling the weapons.

He said then that we had refused proposals for the formation of a commission of foreign ministers. Then, or at some other time, he raised the issue that, after all, the Warsaw Treaty has a clause requiring consultation with regard to issues like this, such as diplomatic relations, and that we have violated the terms of the treaty. Thus,

---

[18] Multilingual international communist ideological journal, controlled by Moscow, with editorial offices in Bucharest.

are all those facts aiding the strengthening of the alliance or leading to its weakening? Maybe Romania does not want to be a member of the Warsaw Pact and in this case it should openly say so—and we can say this: it was suggested that it would be better if we were to leave the Warsaw Pact.

He also mentioned the relationship of Romania with the socialist countries. Even though in the beginning he gave us some figures—that we get 90 per cent of our coke [and] that we also get 40 per cent of our cotton from them. Afterwards he began saying that relations have greatly diminished, that they are not growing, that COMECON decisions are not being respected, that international organizations and joint ventures are resisted and that we do not want to participate; that for example we did not want to participate in interchim,[19] the organization for computing technology. [He added] that we are experiencing an adjustment in Romania's economic relations toward the West, that we are establishing joint ventures with Western countries, such as with respect to copper with countries like Italy, France and Great Britain, and at the same time we refuse to participate in proposed joint ventures [with socialist countries]. He came up with a quote from a foreign correspondent who said, after I received Schiller[20], that Romania decided to accept [foreign] investment. [He said] that this economic policy is not in the national interests of Romania, since this will create problems; that [we have] already taken credits; that there is a negative balance; that he can show us that other countries passed through the same pains; that maybe the Romanians desire to reorient themselves toward the West.

Cde. P. Niculescu-Mizil: That Romania should make this clear.

Cde. N. Ceauşescu: When I responded to this, he said that he did not say such a thing, that there is no way his words could be interpreted this way.

Then he said that he would like very much to hear about good relations between our two parties and two peoples, but that, unfortunately, various scholars, historians—he even gave some names […]—are trying in different ways to reassess the relationship between Russia and Romania, to play down Russia's role in the Balkans. Also, there are attempts to negate Romania's participation in the anti-Soviet war. There are also attempts with regard to the events prior to World War II. And here he went back and forth regarding the politics of 1939.

[He said] that the role of the Soviet Army in the war and in the liberation is being underestimated. Of course, this did not have any connection with the previous idea, that he liked very much what has been done with the reconsideration of certain historical events.

Cde. P. Niculescu-Mizil: [He] shares the preoccupation of Cde. Ceauşescu with regard to some issues that have been reconsidered.

Then he started talking about the plenary[21], that it would be positive if everything that was good in the past were maintained, that the class characteristics of past regimes must be taken into consideration.

Then he said that a series of Soviet cultural institutions [in Romania] have been

[19] As rendered in original.

[20] West German Minister of Economics Karl Schiller.

[21] An apparent reference to the Tenth Congress of the Romanian Communist Party on August 6–12, 1969, which envisaged creating a "developed socialist society" in the country.

closed, for example the Muzeum, the Russian–Romanian Institute at the [Romanian] Academy, the Maxim Gorkii Institute and book store; that the activity of the ARLUS[22] has been reduced, but that at the same time there are new libraries opening up in cooperation with western states. He gave the example of the U.S. library. [...]

[He said] that there are now antagonistic inscriptions on the Soviet embassy [in Bucharest].

These were, in general, the issues raised. He ended by mentioning that graffiti.

Then he raised the issue of the Romanian position with regard to Czechoslovakia. After all, by the position it had adopted, Romania had caused damage, etc. [He said] that he does not understand where Zhou Enlai got the idea that there is a threat directed toward Romania, when they, who are neighbors with Romania, did not know of any such threat. Of course, a lot of time has passed since then and one can draw the conclusion that we [the Soviets] have acted justly in helping Czechoslovakia, since now the Czechoslovak people are thanking us.

Cde. E. Bodnăraș: [He said that] the Romanian comrades, even though so much time had passed, are still criticizing the actions of the socialist countries, even during the congresses of other parties.

Cde. N. Ceaușescu: And of course, this only complicates the relationship among our people. Of course, [he said], the reasons for these disagreements must be sought in the past.

Cde. E. Bodnăraș: He then listed the causes.

Cde. N. Ceaușescu: That before there were friendly relations [between the Soviet Union and Romania], but that some differences appeared during Khrushchev's leadership, since he spoke more freely and did not have a lot of self-control, but that all that should have been resolved long ago.

Maybe the Romanians want to obtain some economic advantages by bringing up all these issues. It would be great if they said so. After all, you [Romanians] should not take [economic aid] only from the Americans, we [the Soviets] would also offer [aid]. Of course, this cannot lead to collaboration and in the West there is the hope that Romania will lean towards the West, that a chain is being created that we do not want to simplify. The Romanians will appreciate Soviet patience in relation to this issue, that we [the Soviets] want to develop this relationship and that we will respect equal rights, mutual advantage, and the sovereignty and national interests of Romania. Of course, we do not believe that it runs counter to Romania's interests to have relations with the Soviet Union and the other socialist countries. We believe that this meeting, today, can represent a turning point in the development of this relationship between our two countries. It is necessary to carry out an advantageous trade [policy] and it must be understood that in recent years Romania has no longer supplied [the Soviet Union] with a series of goods, copper, but at the same time it wants from [the Soviet Union] goods [worth] hard currency. that Romania needs hard currency, but we also need it. [...]

After the break we responded to the points made by Brezhnev. We too began with history. From the very beginning I said that, in his speech, Brezhnev made a series of

---

[22] "Romanian Association for Relations with the Soviet Union."

accusations, insinuated a number of things with regard to the Romanian Communist Party, with which we do not agree. We reject them and we hope that we are going to discuss things openly, and say what we mean, that if they are to start accusing us, branding us, there can be no friendship.

Then I spoke about all these issues regarding history, regarding what we are doing now and that we too, as much as they, appreciate the role of the party and the state. But you will see that in the minutes of the conversation.

Cde. Emil Bodnăraş: As far as that statement that Romania is isolated, we showed him how [much that is not] true.

Cde. N. Ceauşescu: On all these issues where Romania has taken positions which oppose those of the socialist community, that [Romania] has taken unexpected positions, I replied that I must say that these statements cannot be accepted since they are not true. On the contrary, Romania is guiding its actions on the basis of unanimously adopted documents, and here I too began with the Declaration of 1957.[23] [I said] that in all our agreements, including in 1966, we chose to act for the development of relations with the FRG, and that not only did we put that in writing, but, even more so, in all our discussions we determined to act towards this goal. [I said] that we had discussed this issue in November as well; that [the Romanians] did inform [the Soviets] that we were moving ahead with negotiations. Other [countries] were even farther ahead with their negotiations, but no one made an issue out of that. Not only did Romania not violate [previous agreements], but it acted constantly in support of the documents and declarations we agreed upon. I explained to him that the stability of relations did not harm, but aided [the socialist camp], including the GDR. He said that is isolating the GDR, and gave me the example of the Zeiss factory[24], of the lawsuit.

Cde. Ion Gheorghe Maurer: Meaning that from the perspective of the law, the FRG is in the right in this case, and that the [lawsuit] was postponed so that we do not have to make a decision.

Cde. N. Ceauşescu: We will send someone to see. I told him that, on the contrary, we have helped by [adopting] these positions. As we agreed in Moscow, [the communiqué said] that there was a positive change in the government of the FRG. It is true that the paragraph was introduced at our request, but they signed it.

We are the only socialist country that spends the most time concerned about relations with the GDR, and some members of the [SED] Politburo thanked us for the diplomatic help we gave.

As far as the war in the Middle East is concerned, we presented once more our position, why at the time we thought it wise not to accept that declaration and what our position is now; that it is surprising to us that [the Soviets] do not trust Romania and that they view us with suspicion, that faith is being placed in very reactionary Arab circles.

I told him that as far as our relationship with Israel is concerned, they are not at

---

[23] The November 19, 1957, "Peace Manifesto" of the Moscow conference of 64 communist parties.

[24] Optical factory in Jena, East Germany.

370

all more extraordinary than with other countries, even among those countries which broke relations with Israel. Moreover, we have even more developed relations with the Arab nations and it surprises us that so much weight is placed on what some reactionary circles are saying.

With regard to Nixon's visit, if there are to be questions about what was discussed there, then many things could also be questioned. For example, we could question what is being discussed between the Soviet Union and the United States in Vienna, since we do not know what is being said there and we have not been consulted.

Cde. Ştefan Voicu: They turned green.

Cde. Paul Niculescu-Mizil: Yes, but we do not ask that question.

Cde. N. Ceauşescu: When they heard that we are not about to ask that they breathed easier.

As far as Vietnam (DRV) is concerned, I went on, we have given and we are continuing to give the most aid after the Soviet Union and the People's Republic of China. [I told him] that we told Nixon that [the U.S.] must leave Vietnam and that our position was also clearly expressed in the declaration about Cambodia.

If there are questions about what Romania is receiving, we must say that relations between Romania and the U.S. are not as developed as those of some other socialist countries, which have even received credits. [That] includes the GDR, which has a gross trade balance with the U.S. far greater than that of Romania.

[I said] that we are pleased to see that Comrade Brezhnev is so concerned with the prestige of Romania, but that Romania's prestige has not suffered at all, that it is very great, and that he must not worry himself on this account.

As far as the Congress is concerned, [his perception] of this problem is once again false. There were 70 delegations present at the congress in Bucharest. We also received 14 messages [from other parties]. With regard to the fact that [some delegations] raised the problem of Nixon's visit, we have copies of the speeches they prepared before their arrival, which do not contain a single word about this thing; we also have copies of the speeches they gave after they visited the embassy of the Soviet Union.

Cde. P. Niculescu-Mizil: Basov[25]

jumped up and said that nothing was worked on at the embassy. Afterwards however he recognized that a meeting had been held at the embassy.

Cde. Ghizela Vass: With the Czechs.

Cde. N. Ceauşescu: With regard to the issue of European security we have expressed our position, starting with 1966.

As far as a meeting of foreign ministers is concerned, we raised this issue in Prague and in Budapest; [the Soviets] never gave a response at the time, saying that they will inform the governments, but nothing came of it. After that, when Macovescu went to Moscow he received an answer on this [issue], but the other socialist countries have not received an answer to this day. We all agreed with respect to a meeting of the European nations that all interested countries should participate. And this is against what we have decided must be done—not [negotiations] between [alliances] but all countries interested [...] Of course, Romania had made its point of view known,

---

[25] Soviet Ambassador to Bucharest A.V. Basov.

informing the European governments, stating that Romania is ready to participate in any meeting.

We are surprised that such a clear-cut issue is being described in this way—that Romania is against a meeting of foreign ministers to discuss this issue. On the contrary, Romania has had a different position, and I do not understand who has an interest in presenting this issue in such a way. We have raised objections to the fact that there were three meetings of foreign ministers, [and] a meeting of first secretaries in December, where a communiqué was made public, and, because we are concerned for the prestige of the foreign ministers, we wondered what they would be discussing if they had another meeting. In any case, we said at the time that if they plan to meet in May our foreign minister will not be able to participate since he will not be in the country, but that we will send his deputy as our representative. However, from this one cannot draw the conclusion that we are against this meeting. We support [the idea] that the foreign ministers meet as many times as is necessary, but we would like to set an agenda. We are not opposed to them meeting and conferring after the NATO [foreign ministers] meet.

As far as the Warsaw Treaty is concerned, it is written in the documents that if the other alliance bloc is dissolved, so will it be. Romania is only acting in the letter and spirit of our joint documents and positions. Why, after all, did we participate in the Moscow conference?[26]

After that I said that we have published, generally, the materials concerning the conference, even the fairly long summary. [Brezhnev] replied: yes, but you did not [publish] everything that was said against China. I said: of course, only what we considered [correct].

With regard to *Problems of Peace and Socialism*, I said that we agreed, when it was created, that this would be a journal [for facilitating] an exchange of ideological opinions, that it would not [be a spring board] from which to attack other parties. We would like to keep it that way. However, as long as it continues to attack other parties, we will not agree.

With regard to the anti-imperialist congress, I said that this was another issue that has not been thoughtfully described. Why are facts presented falsely, when it was Romania that called for the participation of all parties who would like to take part in preparations, and opposed a [non-representative] commission? And, after all, there was no final decision. In any case, Romania was not part of the commission as it was proposed, and thus it could not participate in a commission of which it was not a part. We are for participating in this congress and have supported this participation.

Then, I went to the issue of China. I said that it is true that the situation worries us; that something must be done so an agreement is reached, that differences are smoothed over. [I said] that this is not a question of neutrality, that we are not at all neutral. We criticized the Chinese when they intervened in the internal affaires of other parties. We believe that through our action we are doing a good thing, and that the time will come when [the Soviets] will be grateful to us. We desire that an agreement be reached, and we believe this to be the duty of every communist party. I told

---

[26] The October 21, 1966, meeting of Warsaw Pact party chiefs with Brezhnev.

him that I do not know and I would like him to provide us with the newspaper in which Chinese photographs were published. Later it was proven that that was all just a misunderstanding on their part.

[...]

We said that we are standing firm on the line of the Warsaw Treaty as far as military readiness is concerned, with regard to the preoccupation with introducing military equipment, of receiving military equipment. But, at the same time, we are taking into consideration the fact that we have to take action in the direction of reducing military forces. I raised the issue of military exercises, with the rattling of weapons, that this is in agreement with our common position. Again I brought up the declarations made in 1957 and 1966, including the proposals for arms reductions made by the Soviet Union. Thus, we are only acting in support of this. Just like yourselves, we are proposing arms reductions. Of course, we do not believe that this can be done unilaterally, and as long as this [goal] will not be reached, we must take some measures.

Since the issue of military exercises was raised here [...] this very month three [sic] military exercises were organized: one with the naval forces, two for the air forces and one for the air defense system.

As far as the military exercise that Cde. Katushev[27] is speaking about, this is once again false. Not only were we not opposed, but we were [one of the] organizers. We sent our chief of staff, we gave him the power to sign, so that the military exercise could take place, and he was told that they cannot go on with the exercise. Thus, it was not the Romanians who were opposed to this military exercise. However, as you well know, we have told you since 1966 that we will not participate in such military exercises except on the basis of government-to-government agreements.

As far as this commission of the foreign ministers, this is an issue that is still being discussed, beginning with 1959–1960. We do not consider it to be of any value. The foreign ministers could meet, and are meeting even now often enough. They stay two months at the U.N., they have [plenty] of time to talk. At this, [Andrei] Gromyko replied that he spends less time there.

Once again we said that we do not understand this issue: that Romania should make its position known on whether it would like to participate or not in the Warsaw Treaty Organization. This issue makes no sense, especially considering the position of Romania.

Then I moved on to the COMECON, to this issue of international organizations. I explained that we have contacted [the Soviets] and other socialist countries. There are many issues still in negotiation. We had an agreement with the Poles with regard to copper, and they said that they are negotiating with the French, that for coke they are negotiating with the Japanese. Then we too made inquiries in other parts. For us it is more sound to take coke, copper, gas and oil from you [the Soviets]. But you said that you couldn't give us any oil so we had to look somewhere else; we asked for gas and you said that you cannot see how that would be possible.

Cde. P. Niculescu-Mizil: [We said] that you are giving [oil and natural gas] to other [countries].

---

[27] Konstantin Katushev was secretary of the CPSU Central Committee.

Cde. N. Ceaușescu: I said: you are exporting [oil and natural gas] to Bulgaria, you can also export it to [Romania]. Of course, I did not want to say that they are exporting to the FRG.

As far as participation in a series of [international] organizations we talked, debated it, and came to the conclusion that we should maintain the position we agreed on a year ago. We are for participating [where] we think it would be justified. Of course, along the way, [Brezhnev] said that they did not say this or that, that we misunderstood their position. With regard to this organization for computer technology I told him that we had reached agreement on all issues but that we have been stumped by some organizational problems. They said that they only raised the issue, that it is up to us if we want to participate or not, that they are not criticizing us.

We said that we would be satisfied to import from socialist countries, we even handed them a list [of goods], but they told us that some of those are not available. Then, of course, we will take from where we can. In any case, we have decided to ensure the future development of the Romanian economy, and if we cannot resolve it with the socialist countries, we will resolve it through any means available to us.

After that, I told them that all these joint ventures are on the principle of equality, that they do not have any political conditions, and we will not accept, under any circumstance and from no one, any sort of political conditions. [I said] that one cannot talk about and we cannot agree with what was said, that there is some sort of economic orientation by Romania toward the West.

I would like to thank Cde. Brezhnev for his preoccupation regarding Romania's economic condition, that it is not in Romania's national interest. I must say, however, that the situation is not as he described, that we have accepted these credits deliberately, that we could easily solve this problem by reducing the volume of investment. That, however, would be a mistake. Then Podgornyi[28] said: it would be a mistake to a do so. [I said] you should not concern yourself with Romania's balance [of payments] since [Brezhnev] alluded that at some point we too, just like others, will come begging.

We will have our own program to insure that the balance will also show improvement, but over time so that we can ensure future development. Then I said that I do not understand what Cde. Brezhnev wanted to say when he said that maybe the Romanians want to re-orient toward the West. If I were to think more about it, I said, it would mean that Romania should re-orient itself toward a market economy, but then he said no, he did not say such a thing.

Cde. P. Niculescu-Mizil: [Brezhnev] said: why are you interpreting [my words] this way? I never said that.

Cde. N. Ceaușescu: As far as bilateral relations are concerned, I said that they were always good, but that historians can always interpret one event or another, and that this is their role. While we do not negate the role of the Russian army in the Balkans, one cannot negate the role of the Romanian army there either, that we have cemeteries of fallen Romanian soldiers there as well as the letter asking for

---

[28] Chairman of the Presidium of the Supreme Soviet Nikolai V. Podgornyi.

help.[29] After all, of course everyone can interpret in their own way. But I find it surprising that we are talking here about the progressive role of the Tsarist government, that I do not want to start quoting Lenin here with respect to this role. Suslov[30] then intervened and said [they are saying that about Tsarism] only at this time, generally, [referring] to the Balkans.

Cde. Ştefan Voicu: [They said] that the Balkan Wars had a class dimension.

Cde. N. Ceauşescu: After that I said that we do not try to negate the participation of bourgeois Romania in the anti-Soviet war, but it is a known [fact] that the communists opposed the Romanian bourgeoisie. The Romanian communists were the ones who organized the fight against this war, and the fact that Romania switched sides in this war underlines the indictment of the Romanian bourgeoisie for its participation in the war.

I said that we appreciate the participation of the Red Army, of the Soviet Union [in the liberation of Romania]. Unfortunately, it cannot be said that as far as Romania is concerned the facts are truthfully presented, even though its role is known, and that the king of Romania [Mihai I] was among the few state leaders who received the Star of Victory for [Romania's] contribution [to the war effort].

As far as the Muzeum is concerned, we took those measures in order to better show the value and establish some order. In our own history museum there is an exhibit, which displays our relations with Russia and relations with the CPSU.

With regard to the Russian language, instead of [maintaining] an institute with poor results, we have incorporated the study of Russian language and literature in the university.

As for ARLUS, they have a palace in [Romania], and in some of the bigger cities they have some cultural centers and I do not know if in the Soviet Union there is an equivalent thing. As far as I know, there is not. I told him that ARLUS publishes a newspaper that is sold in bookstores, in the Russian Book [section]. After all, Cde. Brezhnev mentioned that in Romania there were 20 million books published. As far as the libraries are concerned, we have contacted all the socialist countries, just as we do in France and in other countries. We are interested that libraries be opened in Romania and that we open up [libraries] in other countries. To this they said that they understand and raise no objections.

Then we discussed the issue of the graffiti. I told him that I do not know how this happened, that only 15 days before this meeting someone placed graffiti on the fence of the embassy, that I don't even know how someone found a spot to write on the fence since the fence is made of iron bars. But even if we admit that there is such a someone, he is a madman, and what does this prove? We never said that a number of Soviet officials are saying this publicly. We believed that these were occasional problems and that it is not worth wasting time on them.

---

[29] After a failed Russian attack on the Turkish fortifications of Plevna (Bulgaria), Grand Duke Nikolai, commander of the Russian Army, sent a letter to Carol I, Prince of Romania, on July 19, 1877, in which he asked that Romanian troops cross the Danube River and join the Russians in the fight against the Ottomans.

[30] Soviet Politburo member Mikhail A. Suslov.

On the issue of Czechoslovakia, I don't want to talk about it. I must say that we, even now, hold the opinion that the intervention in Czechoslovakia [in August 1968] was a mistake, that not only have things not gotten back to normal but they continue to grow in complexity. We would like very much for things to get back to normal, but as far as we know things are a far way from normal. I also emphasized that, of course, all this is making bilateral relations more complicated, and that it would be better to ask ourselves what the causes of the differences and misunderstandings are. [I said] that, in my opinion, they cannot be limited or reduced to the idea that Khrushchev had problems controlling himself. Of course, we had our own problems with Cde. Khrushchev. Many we have discussed [before]. But those are not the causes. Here we are talking about the idea that beginning with 1960, 1962, a new type of relationship was introduced among socialist states—the idea of economic, political and military integration, which means supranational organizations, which Romania cannot and will not accept. These are the causes which led to this situation and this is why it is necessary to bring clarity. We are for cooperation, [in a form] to which we have agreed, but we will not accept, and Romania will never sign such agreements.

As far as what the West thinks [...] If we are to think about what the West thinks, there are many things being said about the Soviet Union, but we believe that we should not discuss what the Western media or the West thinks [in general], when we are discussing any disagreements among ourselves.

Then I said that I did not understand and do not understand what Cde. Brezhnev referred to when he said that the Romanians will appreciate the patience of the Soviet Union on these issues.

[...]

He replied that he did not say this here. Rusakov[31] also jumped in and said [that Brezhnev] was referring to the Chinese. I told him: you said this to both the Chinese and [to us]. He replied that there are minutes of the conversation, you will read and you will see that I said no such thing.

After that I praised Brezhnev's declaration regarding respect for equal rights, respect for sovereignty and independence. [I said] that for collaboration it is necessary to have mutual respect and [only] on this basis can [parties] act, and that we want to act, to discuss, to come to an agreement. We would like to see this meeting become a turning point towards the normalization and future development of relations. I said that we agree with the idea that trade should be advantageous, that we can't even think of it in a different way. We understand that not even the Soviet Union can sustain a [disadvantageous] trade [policy]. We agreed that Maurer and Kosygin[32] should meet.

With regard to the issue of gathering information, I told them that I was thinking of dropping the issue, but that the comrades in the delegation are insisting that I tell them. I asked what is the reason behind the fact that a number of Soviet officials are contacting Romanian citizens and requesting information on various issues? You know very well, and we told you this in 1964, and even after that, if you have any

---

[31] CPSU CC Secretary Konstantin V. Rusakov.
[32] Soviet Premier Aleksei Kosygin.

questions, ask through official channels and we will tell you everything. [I told them] that we do not like being forced to take measures against various citizens.

Cde. P. Niculescu-Mizil: To this they replied: we don't even have something like that in China. There was a decision of the [CPSU] Politburo on this issue and we do not practice such things.

Cde. N. Ceaușescu: He replied right away. As a matter of fact this was the only time when Brezhnev interrupted me in the middle of a sentence. I told him: we are asking you to ask your citizens—we will do the same—indications [sic] to no longer do such a thing.

This was the end. Of course, I also gave another ending, I could not very well end the conversation talking about the agency. We took another 20-minute break. They consulted among themselves.

When they returned they began by saying that I tackled some of the issues based on the notes I took [during Brezhnev's speech] and that it is likely that I could not take down all the ideas, everything that was said, but that after I read the minutes of the conversation I will see that some things that I responded to were never said by him. [They said] that this is understandable, that I took notes during the time he spoke but that I could not write down everything, that after I read the minutes of the conversation I will reconsider some of my conclusions.

[They said] that for relations to improve we must liquidate everything which might affect their relations. That I said that all the problems are connected to the issue of protocol, including the Nixon visit. Based on that [they said], one could draw the conclusion that we [the Soviets] are mistaken in everything and that you have been right in everything. We could understand if you came and said, of course, comrades, we have our own weaknesses, but we will analyze, we will think about [them]. However, instead of this, you came over and rejected everything.

Cde. P. Niculescu-Mizil: [They said] that we see in some things normal protocol issues but that they see those same issues from a political perspective.

Cde. N. Ceaușescu: [They said:] We see them from a political [perspective] while you see them as issues concerning protocol, organization. These are the differences. In regard to China, we understand your relations with them but we see them from a political perspective. In India you have relations with two [communist] parties.

Cde. P. Niculescu-Mizil: They would like to see how Romania views China. This is what they want to know: whose side is Romania on?

Cde. N. Ceaușescu: And then they came back to the information-gathering issue. [They said] that they do not carry out such activities anywhere and that if we catch a Soviet or Romanian provocateur, we can take any measures we want against them.

Cde. P. Niculescu-Mizil: [They said:] Take note of the declaration [of the CPSU Politburo], that there were instructions given out that there are to be no more such activities. If you catch a Soviet or Romanian provocateur, take measures.

Cde. N. Ceaușescu: With regard to Czechoslovakia, [they said that] of course, there are complications, that what the opportunists and the counterrevolutionaries have done in a year-and-a-half cannot be undone [overnight] and that of course they should be helped.

Cde. P. Niculescu-Mizil: [They also said] that the Romanian Communist Party should no longer use its point of view as propaganda.

Cde. N. Ceaușescu: With regard to economic issues, they said that they are not thinking of putting any type of pressure on Romania, that they want to develop bilateral relations. After that we came to an agreement on the meeting between Maurer and Kosygin. [Brezhnev] brought up the issue of the Treaty of Friendship and Mutual Assistance, that we should sign it, and we came up with a number of dates. Finally we settled on June 6. They first said June 22, but we said that we cannot [since] Maurer leaves for West Germany and then the Padishah [sic] of Iran comes [to Romania].

[The discussion] ended in a relaxed atmosphere, making jokes and [talking] about hunting.

Cde. Ștefan Voicu: Podgornyi from time to time intervened with jokes, relaxing [the atmosphere].

Cde. Emil Bodnăraș: After that they organized a dinner.

Cde. N. Ceaușescu: We agreed, again upon departure, that we should accomplish what we had agreed upon.

We believe that the way things developed [from beginning to] end was positive. Of course, at first they attempted, as they have always done, to start from an unyielding position. When they saw that nothing can be accomplished that way, they changed their tune and declared themselves in accord, that the most important thing is to learn from the past and to look to the future. As Podgornyi said, let's get back to the old friendship. Very well, I said, we agree. This is how we ended.

I don't know, do the comrades who were part of the delegation have anything more to add?

Cde. P. Niculeascu-Mizil: This was indeed a very successful visit for our party. It led to a discussion in which we made our position clear and it created the possibility for developing the relationship in the future.

Cde. Ceaușescu gave a response to all issues. The fact that the response was immediate, the fact that he responded firmly yet at the same time maintained complete calm, but especially since our positions were supported with arguments—[these] were extremely important [factors]. They presented some things, came up with facts which were easily disproved. We could have proved at any time that our newspapers did not publish any Chinese pictures. On some things they recognized that we were right.

Cde. E. Bodnăraș: It was a heavy hit, pathetic for those who were putting so much faith in what the apparatus provided them, that their arguments were disproved on the spot and that their complete incompetence and weakness were proven. The competence and clarity of the presentation by Cde. Ceaușescu, who, unlike them, had the advantage of having a good grasp of all the issues, was a major surprise for them. As much as they are the prisoners of the apparatus, they found themselves before a party leader who had a good grasp of all issues, and immediately [was able to] quote the date and the year, what one or another said, what happened. This was the most valuable part of the discussion. Also, the uncompromising resolve, especially where the analysis of causes was concerned. There [it was] pointed out: here is the cause, the re-orientation of the nature of the relationships among socialist countries, in the [attempts to] integrate [them] politically and economically. We are for cooperation

378

but we are unequivocally opposed to integration and we will not sign any document on economic, political or military integration.

Cde. P. Niculescu-Mizil: We understand the idea of open discussions, but even in these open discussions it is inadmissible that such accusations can be used, such insinuations against a party. There must be trust.

Cde. Ştefan Voicu: They put together a big file, which took them weeks or months, with things that happened over the years and which, presented in such a way, after their own liking, to show a position without [a basis] in the class [struggle], to show that Romania is not taking a class position. The replies and arguments made by Cde. Ceauşescu disappointed them, as we say in Romanian, it burst their bubble, since it was a very logical argumentation, [delivered] immediately. It was probably better that we did not go to the embassy. That showed the ability of the [Romanian] Party and of its leader to immediately adopt a position. Cde. Ceauşescu spoke for three and three-quarter hours with perfect logic, [raising] issues that could not be argued against on the spot. What they wanted to contest immediately was the issue of information gathering, but they were unable to. Gromyko was restless for over two hours but could not say a thing. This was a very important thing [that they said], well, you say you have no fault, only we are at fault.

Cde. E. Bodnăraş: Of course, I left with a bit of sorrow leaving behind a collective that was behind [the times].

[…]

[*Source: Collection Central Committee of the Romanian Communist Party, folder 59/1970, pp. 2–3, 5–27, A.N.I.C. Translated for CWIHP by Mircea Munteanu.*]

Document No. 73: The Surrender of Hannover according to the Polish Army's "Bison" Exercise, April 21–28, 1971

Among the many documents now available about Warsaw Pact exercises, this Polish example provides a particularly optimistic depiction of what was planned. For example, in describing the aftermath of the surrender of Hannover, West Germany, it was anticipated that the Polish army would establish a loyalist administration in cooperation with the Social Democrats, traditionally reviled by communists. This account also shows the level of detailed planning that went into these exercises.

[...]

Due to the capitulation of the Hannover garrison, the Command of the Front has decided to provide assistance to the 5th Army by restoring the city to full function. For this reason, for the disposition of the command of the 5th Army, we direct:

- one military police company from the NVA;
- one company for the protection of public order from the Army Security Service;
- a group of civilian party aktiv members from the SED (20 members);
- a group of press and radio journalists from the GDR (8);
- specialists in typography and radiophony (12);
- part of a front group to secure special propaganda (24 officers, ensigns, and non-commissioned officers).

The groups mentioned above will report for the disposition of the command of the 5th Army today at 6:00 p.m. In the following days the government of the GDR will direct other groups of specialists to the city of Hannover. Each time, the arrival of these groups will be signaled.

Responsibilities of the 5th Army command include:

a) to organize the Hannover Garrison Command and appoint one of the senior officers from the 6th Armored Division as commandant of the Garrison;

b) to assign specified forces and equipment from the above-mentioned formations to the commandant of the Garrison. Simultaneously, with the support of democratic forces, to organize the regular police;

c) to organize quick and efficient press and radio information for the people;

d) to form a temporary camp for prisoners-of-war from the crew of the surrendered garrison;

e) to provide full protection and defense for depots and storehouses (both civilian and military);

f) to bring water-works, power plants, and heating plants into operation;

g) to assist the leadership that is being organized with the distribution of foodstuffs from local supplies;

h) to establish a united front municipal government recruited from activists from the KPD [German Communist Party] and the SPD [German Social Democratic Party];

i) as the removal of the ruins progresses, to bring industrial plants into production.

[...]

After a general assessment of the state of food reserves as well as the state of medical needs for civilians and prisoners, report specific requests to the staff of the Front by 11:00 a.m., April 29, 1971.

[...]

[*Source: Collection Political Administration of the Military District of Silesia, File 152448/74/42. Archives of the Ground Forces, Wrocław. Translated by Magdalena Klotzbach for the National Security Archive.*]

Document No. 74: Transcript of Romanian Politburo Meeting on Ceauşescu's Trip to Asia and Moscow, June 25, 1971

In this set of minutes, the Romanian Politburo discusses Ceauşescu's recent trip to China and Moscow. At the time, the Chinese factor was becoming increasingly important for the Warsaw Pact, as well as divisive since it did not have the same immediate significance for Eastern Europe as it did for the USSR. Not surprisingly, Romania differed from Moscow more than the other partners did. During his meetings with the Chinese, Ceauşescu explained the Romanian position on the Warsaw Pact, specifically Romanian opposition to the transformation of the alliance into a supranational entity. He also told the Chinese that they were not without blame for what the Pact had become since they had participated in its establishment, if only as observers. On his way back from China, Ceauşescu stopped in Moscow, where top Soviet leaders reprimanded him for various transgressions, including allegedly making anti-Soviet statements.

Comrade Nicolae Ceauşescu: [...] The way we were welcomed in Beijing was especially good. [...] During the visit we met Mao Zedong and Lin Biao[33]; Kang Sheng[34] was also there.

[...] From among the activists, practically all participated, beginning with Zhou Enlai, the chief of the General Staff, Li Xiannian, who leads the government's activity, the secretary in charge of propaganda, Mao Zedong's son-in-law, Yan Yuan.[35] [...]

At the third meeting, it was Zhou Enlai who spoke; as to the duration, he spoke about as much as we did. They also told us about the difficulties they had had to overcome, about the fact that there had been a fight between two lines, about the fact that a dangerous frame of mind had been created, that there were a lot of the old landlords, feudals who also held executive positions, that an attitude of kowtowing to foreign countries and a certain bourgeois mentality had appeared, and that the whole activity consisted in uprooting this mentality, in arranging things in such a manner that people would be able to understand the revolutionary principles and become educated by work.

Of course, within the framework of this activity two lines appeared: some cadres—headed by Liu Shaoqi[36]—wanted this state of affairs to be preserved; then they told

---

[33] Lin Biao, a prominent military and political leader in China, had by 1970 emerged as Mao's second-in-command and designated successor. Just three months after this meeting, he died in a plane crash in Mongolia under mysterious circumstances, and was later officially accused of having plotted to assassinate Mao. A more probable explanation is that he was trying to save himself from Mao's plot against him.

[34] Kang Sheng was an alternate member of the Politburo of the Chinese Communist Party.

[35] Probably Yao Wenyuan, member of the politburo in charge of the Propaganda Department, reputed to be Mao's son, later disgraced as one of the "Gang of Four."

[36] China's head of state, deposed in 1966, mistreated during the Cultural Revolution and left to die in 1969.

us about Peng Zhen and Peng Dehuai[37]; that armed conflicts had taken place. Both in the universities and in the regions we were told that two camps had formed and even armed conflicts had occurred between them, but now—in general—things were normal again, the situation had been restored and they are now concerned with the problem of using a number of people, of cadres.

Afterwards, they very briefly—only for about ten minutes—told us about the way the talks with the Soviets were getting along, but without abusive language, level-headedly enough. They said they did not want to revise the treaties, but only make some corrections and establish the borders on a sure basis; that they wished to conclude with the Soviets a treaty of respect and non-aggression, and wanted to proceed to improvement of state-to-state relations. Surely, the talks are not going smoothly, the Soviets do not agree. The Soviets, in their turn, say that the Chinese do not agree. But everything is level-headed enough. Surely, the Chinese said, ideological problems cannot be solved now, it takes time; as Mao Zedong said, it would take 8,000 years.

They told us that they wanted to normalize relations with the other socialist countries as well. In actual fact, they had already sent ambassadors to all the socialist countries; they said they would send an ambassador to Mongolia, too. They said they intended to act in the same way in the future. Everything was level-headed enough and, frankly speaking, I was surprised because I expected them to be harsher. [...]

The discussions with Mao Zedong were general. With him it was apparent that he said the same things the Soviets did. He said as follows: the Soviets swear at us, insult us, and—in spite of all this—they want unity with us. Well, with whom do they want unity, with those who are agents of the Americans?! We cannot unite with them; how could they unite with us? Generally speaking, the discussions were general enough, nor was he violent. From this point of view, one can see they have a preoccupation, in fact they emphasized it several times, with improving state-to-state relations, and the wish to reach an understanding with the Soviet Union at the state level. At the party level that kind of understanding is not possible now since we have ideological differences and they will last a long time, 8,000 years. Then I also told him: there may be problems after 8,000 years, too; the problem is, how are we going to hold these talks? They said: we do not swear at the Soviets, they swear at us; the only thing we do is say what Lenin said about social-imperialism, and if they are social-imperialists, we are not guilty. Mao Zedong said, however, that they wished to normalize relations at the level of state and economic issues.

As regards the problem of relations with other states, a point we insisted upon a lot, they said: we will negotiate with each party individually, we will judge each party by the way they behave in battle, because only in battle can one see whether it is Marxist–Leninist, revolutionary, and anti-imperialist; we are against conferences, and centers, and against the conferences convened by Moscow, and against a leftist

---

[37] Peng Zhen, Chinese politburo member and Liu Shaogi's associate, purged during the Cultural Revolution, but later rehabilitated. Peng Dehuai, a prominent Chinese military leader, commanded Chinese troops in the Korean War and later served as minister of defense. Disgraced in 1958, he was accused of plotting with the Soviet Union and suffered persecution during the Cultural Revolution.

conference. They were probably referring to the Albanians because the latter requested such a conference. We are against any center; we want bilateral relationships; we
will have, by degrees, bilateral relationships, we will analyze each party, and we will
establish relations depending on their position; if they do not swear at us any longer
and if in battle they prove their position is Marxist–Leninist, revolutionary, and anti-
imperialist, we will develop relationships.

[...]

They spoke a lot about the situation in Japan, about Japanese militarism.

They spoke hardly at all about Vietnam's problems. We put forward our considerations and, in connection with the negotiations, we said that there were favorable
conditions, and so on. They never said either yes or no, which means closer to yes.
Of course, they did not say they agreed either.

As to the problem of European security, they did not say anything. We told them
what our opinion was. Eventually, they agreed to write in the communiqué that they
supported our position on this problem. Afterwards, they told us that this would
mean backing the Soviets, and so on.

Concerning the Middle East issue, they actually do not know the first thing about
it; they spoke about Israel's aggression, but we noticed that they had set up direct
telephone lines with the aggressors.

In general, they were level-headed enough. The only criticism was directed at the
Americans, but especially for the fact that the Americans wanted to leave the Japanese
in their place in Asia. They told us that they were willing to welcome [President]
Nixon, but the main issue was Taiwan.

In connection with the United Nations, they thanked us for our support (this was
written in the communiqué as well) and said that they wanted to go to the U.N.
Generally speaking, they thanked us for lending them a helping hand with the development of their relations with other countries they are interested in. They also told
us that up to then they had been concerned with their internal problems and could
not deal with international issues as well, but now they can deal with these issues, too.

[...]

They told us that since 1960 they had not had any links with the parties, with the
socialist countries and now they had to see how they behaved. This proves that they
are serious people, not—now we swear at each other, now we kiss and make up. It
is clear that it will be difficult for them to forget the Soviets' offenses.

From a bilateral viewpoint, they practically declared they wanted to normalize all
relations.

[...]

They asked us about Comecon. We told them; we also told them about this integration program. We told them about the Warsaw Treaty Organization, too: how it
was established, how we look upon it, and that the aim was being pursued of achieving a supranational organ, [of achieving] political, economic, and military integration. We told them that we were not partial to these formulas but we wished to collaborate in the spirit of the treaty provisions and of the statute we have. They said
this was a just point of view. We said that they were also guilty [for the conclusion]
of this treaty since they had agreed to it; they, too, were observers at the time. We

said to them that they might want to join Comecon as well; neither they nor the Vietnamese nor the Koreans wanted to; the Koreans told us there are pressures there. We told them that, according to the laws of physics, if they came too, the pressures would disperse to some extent. They considered our position to be rational, but neither praised us nor criticized these organs; they only registered what we said.

They criticized this craving for domination, superpower chauvinism, and social imperialism.

That is about all [I have to say] about the discussions.

[...]

In Korea we were also well received both by the leadership and the population. Everything was organized, a kind of festivity, just like in China; well organized from this viewpoint.

The discussions were good. As regards bilateral issues, we agreed to develop cooperation. I had Cde. [Manea] Mănescu speak to a vice president. We proposed that from the amount of 27 million roubles provided for 1975 to reach an amount of over 50 million roubles. They are interested, and I think we can achieve good things. We had no problems. They also emphasize the development of industry, of agriculture. Pyongyang is completely rebuilt. Other towns, too. They work hard, there is discipline everywhere, everything is very beautiful.

[...]

I look upon the visit to Korea as being good from the economic, bilateral, and political points of view as well.

The way we were received in Vietnam was correct, but they have a different situation, they are at war. A sizable number of people went out in the streets. Generally speaking, my impression is that they are disorganized. Consequently, a good reception, good discussions, mainly in connection with the situation in Vietnam. We put forward our concepts and they totally agreed with them.

[...]

They told us that through their agency we could get into Indochina. They, too, hoped to play a major part in Indochina. Even in the event of reunification, Vietnam would have an important role in Indochina. From this point of view, therefore, we understood each other very well, political issues included.

As regards relations between the socialist countries, they said: we have also received help from both the Soviet Union and China and we wish to receive such help in the future. They told us that they had had discussions with both the Soviets and the Chinese. They were not partial to taking part in any international conference without China. [...]

They, too, have good development prospects, but it is my impression that they have not set to work properly so far. The situation in Korea is different: there they set themselves the task of becoming a model for the South. According to their conception, the Vietnamese must first solve the unification problem by means of war and then start rebuilding their country. In their view the predominant idea is that they should first achieve unification and afterwards construction, while the Koreans speak of everything in comparison with the South. I have not seen any such preoccupation in the Vietnamese, but it is likely that they will arrive at such an understanding themselves.

[...]

In Mongolia the reception was good and the first toasts were good; there were no problems. The communiqué issued was good. The meeting was not so good because they inserted a remark in their speeches—although we had agreed they should not—that the imperialists wanted to divide the socialist countries, that they were using the weapon of ideology for this purpose, and that the duty of socialism was to fight back with all available means.

During the talks they told us about China, about their historical relationships with China, about the fact that Manchuria had oppressed them for three hundred years, and that China now wanted to swallow them, that Mao Zedong himself had said that Mongolia belonged to China. In fact, in 1924, the Soviet Union signed a secret agreement with Chang Kai-shek, which stated that Mongolia belonged to China. We told them that we had our history, too, that we were under the Turkish yoke, the tsarist yoke, and the Austro-Hungarian yoke. We also told them about our gold in Moscow. We told them that since we were sure they would inform [Moscow] accordingly.

Afterwards they told us about Czechoslovakia, that the imperialists had wanted to occupy it and that the five countries had saved Czechoslovakia. Then I asked him [my interlocutor], where did you learn that? He told me that he heard it from the Poles. I retorted: I did not come here to listen to your lecture about Czechoslovakia, for you to give me lessons, because we know better.

Afterwards, [he spoke] about the fight against imperialism, about China—the same old story all over again.

I told them a few things about the situation in our country; I spoke to them about bilateral relations. They said they would think it over and then would see [what to do].

Then the meeting took place. Except for the first part, he kept speaking about the Soviet Union: when it was born, that it was the bastion of peace and so on and so forth. I told him: this question of Czechoslovakia is not in order; either we must say that we do not agree and explain how things stand to the participants or you take it out permanently. Afterwards, he referred to the fact that the member-states of the Warsaw Treaty Organization, which was the main guarantee of peace and security for the entire socialist system, struggle collectively in support of European security. I told him this was inadmissible. He also referred to the fight against revisionism and left-wing dogmatism, against superpower chauvinism and against nationalism. I do not know what to say: the Chinese say that the Soviets are revisionist, the Soviets say that the Chinese are revisionists; others say that the Yugoslavs are revisionists and I do not know any longer who is [and who is not]. As regards the nationalists, some say that we are nationalist. Then I said: there are nationalists in Arabia, too; did the Soviet Union not conclude a pact with the Arabs, with the nationalists?! I cannot have an argument with the Arabs over this [issue]. He suggested that he read only part of the speech and give the remainder in writing. Then we decided not to make speeches, but to say a few words of greeting only. Very well, and that was all there was to it. I think that, from this point of view, the visit was not of much use because here the Soviets cut in and required them to put in certain things. [...]

On the way back we stopped in Moscow. We have required that, when we come back we will inform them—if they wish—about where we were and what we did where we were. We were met by Kosygin, Suslov and others from the Section; they invited us to have a meal at the airport. We informed them succinctly about the Chinese idea to develop relations with the socialist countries. [...]

It was Kosygin who began by saying that [...] the fact that in China there was no discussion about the community of socialist countries damaged the community of socialist countries; that in Cde. Ceauşescu's speech, an appeal was made for the unity of small and medium-sized countries, and what kind of unity can exist with Saudi Arabia, where there are slaves [?] Afterwards, in Cde. Ceauşescu's speech, references were made to superpowers and superpower chauvinism. In fact, Zhou Enlai said this, not me. But did the Soviet Union threaten somebody, did the Soviet Union threaten you? After all, 70 percent of the Soviet Union's trade is with the socialist countries. Nothing was said about helping the COMECON countries, only China's 200 million in aid was mentioned; in fact, what does 200 million mean for the Soviet Union and Romania! Then, he said, you talked about the superpowers; after all, Romania borders only the Soviet Union, Bulgaria, Hungary, and Yugoslavia. That means, therefore, that only the Soviet Union threatens Romania. Maybe the United States of America threatens you, but not the Warsaw Treaty Organization, which is an umbrella [organization], and so on. Maybe China threatens you, but that should have been said. Afterwards, you talked about the Cultural Revolution. The Cultural Revolution has its international part, too, and he took a booklet out of his pocket: look, by accepting the Cultural Revolution you accepted the anti-Soviet position, anti-so-and-so, anti-so-and-so. Look, while you were there they issued a poster—and he takes a poster out of his pocket. But we have always strived to improve our relations with Romania, we are in the Comecon, and so on.

Suslov also cut in and picked up this idea that the visit had the effect of worsening the divergences and that it was directed against the socialist countries.

After they were finished, I began: I am amazed at the way Cdes. Kosygin and Suslov have approached the issues and we reject such an interpretation. If the Soviet comrades have some issues to discuss, they must discuss them with us, because we did not discuss the issue of big and small countries in China, but set it forth several times, including on the 50th anniversary of the founding of the party; it is a reality that there are small countries, middle countries, powers, and superpowers. And in connection with the superpowers, was it not comrade Brezhnev who said—at the 24th Congress [of the CPSU]—that the Soviet Union was a superpower? But China is a superpower, too. The Chinese did not say that they were a superpower; Zhou Enlai says that he will never conduct a superpower policy. Consequently, there are superpowers, big, middle, and small countries. Then Kosygin says: about Romania I do not even say that it is a middle country, for fear of hurting you. Then I told him that Romania was a small country and as regards Saudi Arabia—that there was slavery there, but there was exploitation in other countries as well. Marx and Engels spoke a lot about the exploitation of the labor force. Then, if we decided not to collaborate with countries where there was exploitation, we should not collaborate with a lot of countries. It is all the same to me if there the labor force is sold for life, and elsewhere it is sold by the day, it is still exploitation. If you wanted to discuss this problem with us, you could discuss it with us, not wait to connect it with our visit to China. Then I told him that we did not go there to discuss others. He said: we negotiate directly with China, not through go-betweens; I do not mean Romania. Then I told him: rest assured that we spoke only a little about you; we were busy dealing with our relationships, not yours. You said that this poster had been published, but why did articles directed against China appear in *Izvestia* and *Krasnaya Zvezda*? Why did you publish this brochure and write a review of it? Why did the Romanian-speaking and Chinese-speaking radio stations transmit two anti-Chinese conferences? We told you and the Chinese comrades that an end must be put to your swearing at each other. Then he says: look what the Chinese say—that capitalism is being restored in our country! Start talking to the Chinese for a change.

We think that, generally speaking, such vituperation must stop. You surely have your bilateral problems, but what we are concerned with here is the fact that unity must exist between the socialist countries, and what is detrimental to unity is precisely this continual swearing. When I spoke about doing away with differences, they said: but we have good relations with all the socialist countries. As if the whole world did not know. I told myself, if you only knew what the Koreans said! I told them, we did not go there to tell them about Comecon when nobody wants to hear about Comecon. We spoke there and uttered words of appreciation about the Soviet Union. Says he: only two passages! Practically speaking, they had nothing to tell us.

I told him that the fact surprises me that he links this issue with economic relations. I told him, I have more experience in politics, but how can others interpret the fact that, in connection with this visit, you question the economic relationships, the commercial relationships and so on. I understand, I cannot make interpretations, but others may understand something else. After all, we wanted to inform you in a comradely manner, for we could have informed you through our ambassadors. Either he understood or he did not, but suddenly he jumped up and said: what did you say, what issues did you want to raise through the embassy?! I told him, we cannot accept the kind of discussion and affirmations you have made here; on the contrary, we think that the visit served the unity of the socialist countries. This is our position and, of course, we will inform the Executive Committee and the Central Committee about your position. And, in connection with this, he said: what, you will inform both the Central Committee and via the embassy?! We said, just as between friends; we told you all this only because there are good, friendly relations between us; we told you so that you might know our opinions, too. Why did we thank the Chinese? Well, because 200 million means something for us; for the Soviet Union it is little, true; but they granted us credit, gave us help and we thanked them. If tomorrow you also give us a credit, we will thank you as well.

[…]

They realized that our favorable opinions about China would exert a good influence. They have this position and that is why they tried to raise the issues in the way they raised them. They prepared [Mongolian leader] Yumjaagiyn Tsedenbal as well, maybe some others, too. It seems, however, that things in their country have also evolved gradually because four days earlier they had let us know that they would have us stay and we would go to the villa, but in the end Kosygin and the others came to the airport. Maybe they also have different discussions and opinions and reached the conclusion that it was better to go on this way, to test their force. This means that they are still prisoners of the old policy, that they are more willing to try to reach an understanding with the United States and with others than with China. They are not afraid that the Chinese will attack them—in fact the Chinese told us that they did not have such intentions—but they fear that Chinese influence in the world will increase.

[...]

[*Source: ANIC, Central Committee of the Romanian Communist Party, Chancellery, file no.72/1971, ff.10–58. Translated by Viorel Nicolae Buta for the Parallel History Project.*]

Document No. 75: Comparison of Warsaw Treaty and NATO Positions concerning the European Security Conference, December 1, 1971

At the time this document was written, preparations for the European security confer-ence had been underway for almost two years and the respective positions of the Warsaw Pact and NATO had crystallized. Those positions are reflected clearly here and point to some very different conceptions of the CSCE and its purpose. The Soviets wanted to convene the conference soon, whereas the Western side favored discussing the agenda first, and proposed adding to it a range of subjects including human rights. For its part, the East wanted to limit the agenda to security issues but excluding arms control nego-tiations. In the end, preparatory discussions would not start until the following year, and the conference itself would not meet until 1975 in Helsinki. So the West ultimately achieved much of what it wanted: delays, a broad agenda and a process that would con-tinue past the conference itself. Importantly, the Western representatives also won the right to review how the other side was observing the agreement, a practice that turned out to be very much to Moscow's disadvantage.

Comparison of the Warsaw Treaty and NATO Positions on Issues Concerning the Conference on Security and Cooperation in Europe

Position concerning the idea of the CSCE:

Warsaw Treaty: Is the author of the proposal whose formal expression was "An Appeal to all countries of Europe" adopted at the PCC meeting in Budapest on March 17, 1969. The proposal was further developed during the following PCC ses-sions and meetings of foreign ministers of the Warsaw Treaty states, including the last one, held in Warsaw (November 30 to December 1, 1971).

NATO: Believes that at the present phase of general European dialogue, con-vening the Conference has become inevitable.

Proposed topics:

Warsaw Treaty: Formulated in a Memorandum approved during the meeting of foreign ministers of the Warsaw Treaty states in Budapest (June 22, 1970)

a) assuring security in Europe and abandoning the use of force, or threat of its use, in mutual relations between states in Europe;

b) widening, based on equal opportunity, trade, economic, scientific–technologi-cal and cultural relations which lead to the development of political coopera-tion between European states;

c) establishing, during the European conference, an institution for matters of secu-rity and cooperation in Europe.

NATO: Formulated on the basis of the report of the NATO Permanent Council [which was] examined during the session of the NATO Ministerial Council (Brussels, December 1971)

    a) problems of security, including policies regulating relations between states and certain military aspects of security;

    b) free movement of people, information and ideas, and cultural relations;

    c) cooperation in the fields of the economy, applied sciences, technology, and pure science;

    d) cooperation aimed at improvement of the human environment.

Participants:

Warsaw Treaty: All European countries with full and equal rights, including the GDR and the FRG, and also the USA and Canada.

NATO: In effect accepts the proposal for the Conference participants presented by the Warsaw Treaty. Assumes that the participation of the GDR will not be understood as its international recognition by the West, if by the time the Conference is convened, this problem is not resolved.

(This problem may lead to tendencies which would limit the full and equal rights of the GDR during the Conference).

Demands participation of the EEC[38] representative in the Conference (possibly other international organizations as well).

Level:

Warsaw Treaty: High, equal to the level of problems considered during the Conference.

NATO: Mentioned as possibly at the level of foreign ministers.

Time:

Warsaw Treaty: The earliest possible. The year 1972 is officially proposed, however, in reality 1973 is predicted.

NATO: Not before 1973; after meeting specific conditions, and "thorough preparations." France declared [it is] working toward convening the CSCE in 1972.

Place:

Warsaw Treaty: In accordance with the offer of the Finnish government – Helsinki. Possible location in a different neutral country (i.e.: Geneva or Vienna) is not excluded.

NATO: No strong support for, but also no objection to Helsinki.

Permanent institution:

Warsaw Treaty: Proposal for establishment of an institution for matters of security and cooperation by the European Conference. Such institution should assure the continuation of the process of shaping European security, perform the function of an inter-conference body and create a mechanism for preparing future conferences.

---

[38] European Economic Community ("Common Market").

NATO: Lack of unanimity, with the majority accepting the need to establish a permanent institution.

Possible demand to establish an institution, which would prepare the Conference: Great Britain suggested a Permanent Commission, which could possibly replace the Conference. France suggested establishing, as a result of the first session of the Conference, one or a few Commissions (i.e. for matters of security, economic cooperation and cultural cooperation, with headquarters in Geneva).

Preliminary conditions:

Warsaw Treaty: No preliminary conditions. (A demand to synchronize the date of the coming in to effect of the Berlin agreement as well as the USSR's and Poland's treaties with the FRG, which in the context of NATO's conditions is interpreted by the West as a preliminary condition).

NATO: Positive conclusion of negotiations on West Berlin—interpreted as signing the final protocol to the four-party agreement from September 3, 1971—considered to be a condition for participation in multilateral preparations for the Conference.

Preparations:

Warsaw Treaty: Acceptance of the Finnish proposal from November 1970 for preparatory consultations in Helsinki, binding to lead to multilateral phase of discussions. Flexibility on the part of the participants with regard to the level of participation in the multilateral meeting (proposed phrase: "plenipotentiary representatives").

NATO: Acknowledgment of the Finnish proposal and initiation of contact with the Finnish government. (A multilateral phase of consultations in Helsinki is possible after the coming into effect of the Berlin agreement.) Suggestion for preparatory talks at the level of chiefs of accredited missions in Helsinki (assumes a lower status for representatives of the GDR and the FRG).

CSCE and the problems of regional disarmament:

Warsaw Treaty: Supports the idea of separate (outside the Conference forum) consideration of problems of regional disarmament in Europe. Assumes the possibility of considering certain disarmament matters by the institution established by the European Conference (i.e. reduction of foreign forces in Europe).

Assumption that disarmament negotiations should not be led on an inter-bloc level.

NATO: Demands including in the Conference agenda "certain military aspects of security." Interpretation of this demand is not unequivocal.

Tendencies in favor of inter-bloc discussion on the subject of disarmament (pressing the Brosio mission[39]).

[*Source: KC PZPR, XIB/171, pp. 1–4, Archiwum Akt Nowych. Translated by Magdalena Klotzbach for the National Security Archive.*]

[39] Proposed visit to Moscow by NATO Secretary General Manlio Brosio.

Document No. 76: Hungarian Memorandum on the Deputy Foreign Ministers' Meeting in Moscow, February 3, 1975

This memorandum from Hungarian delegate József Marjai on the meeting of Warsaw Pact deputy foreign ministers in Moscow from January 29 to 30 is of interest mainly because it shows how the split between Romania and its allies had widened. Eventually it reached the point where it was impossible to hold joint celebrations of the twentieth anniversary of the Pact. The Romanians had objected to the event because they opposed virtually all joint activities, favoring national celebrations instead. In this case, they proposed a meeting of parliamentarians to discuss the issues of security and cooperation in Europe. The absence of celebrations had no military significance but it showed the extent to which Romania had managed to obstruct political unity within the Pact.

By decision of the Warsaw Pact's Political Consultative Committee (PCC) at the meeting in Warsaw in April 1974, a Joint Secretariat was appointed and made responsible for elaborating suggestions regarding the preparation and organization of celebrations commemorating the 20th anniversary of the Warsaw PCC. The Polish People's Republic was charged with coordinating the work of the Joint Secretariat with the cooperation of the PCC's Secretary.

In mid-January of this year, S[tanisław] Trepczyński, Poland's deputy foreign minister, sent the member-states the summary plan of action prepared on the basis of contributions by the heads of delegations during the PCC countries' last meeting and [on the basis of] supplementary suggestions made later. The summary plan of action also incorporates suggestions for developing mechanisms of cooperation within the Organization.

II.

1. The summary plan of action was discussed on January 29–30 in Moscow under the auspices of the Joint Secretariat established during the April 1974 PCC meeting.

[...]

It became apparent during the discussions and in finalizing the minutes that the member-states, except the Romanian comrades, agreed with the suggestions. Except for holding the Political Consultative Committee meeting on the occasion of the anniversary and setting the date at a later time, the Romanian delegation objected to any suggestions that would have demonstrated the unity of the Warsaw Pact countries and the strengthening of their cooperation; their recommendations were aimed at changing the political content of the actions.

[...]

Since it did not seem possible, even after repeated attempts, to work out a text acceptable to the Romanian comrades, by agreement with them, their objections and modifying suggestions were amended to the minutes, using their own words, after the text was discussed and accepted by the other member-states and modified in some respects.

2. The meeting participants reached agreement on the establishment of the Foreign Ministers' Committee and the Joint Secretariat. However, due to the Romanians' opposition, the details of the mandate, constituency and functions of the established organizations could not be defined. In the discussion concerning organizations for political cooperation the following has become apparent: the Romanian party accepts the establishment of a Committee of Foreign Ministers (not of foreign policy), but currently only as a body that is not continuously active and does not have the necessary working [elements]; instead, it is a [formal] representative, body, which would not meet more often than the foreign ministers' meetings are held at present.

3. In his outspoken speech delivered at the plenary session, the Soviet deputy foreign minister, in agreement with the other delegations, criticized the behavior of the Romanian deputy foreign minister and his colleagues after the Romanians repeatedly declined to endorse the joint standpoint that had been developed with their agreement.

4. The closely cooperating member-states have developed an agreement, following the endorsement of the Central Committees, to implement the actions recorded in the minutes, even without the Romanians' consent. An understanding was reached that the Romanian comrades would later join these actions (or most of them) as soon as they are finalized.
[...]

[*Source: MOL, M-KS-288.f. 5.cs.657. ő.e. Translated for the PHP by the Open Society Archive.*]

Document No. 77: Iakubovskii Report on the State of the Unified Armed Forces, December 31, 1975

In an earlier account of a meeting between Ceauşescu and Brezhnev in 1970 (Document No. 72), the Romanian leader boasted that he had easily prevailed over the Soviet general secretary one-on-one. But in the larger picture Moscow ultimately had the upper hand over Bucharest. In this document, Warsaw Pact Supreme Commander Iakubovskii reports on the state of the Unified Armed Forces. He indicates that operational plans and the coordination of forces are being handled without Romania's participation, and that while Pact members have signed agreements to develop their forces over the next five years (1976–1980), this plan excludes Romania. By 1975, therefore, Romania for all intents and purposes was no longer a member of the military structures of the alliance. France was in a similar position with respect to NATO except that President Charles de Gaulle had taken the initiative in withdrawing from the organization's military structures, whereas Romania found itself isolated by its erstwhile partners.

[...]

During the course of the year, a new operational plan of combat use and plans for joint action by Unified Armed Forces of the Warsaw Treaty were perfected in practice. Troops from the Army of the Socialist Republic of Romania were excluded.

[...]

In most of the Allied armies supplies of material resources, excluding certain types of ammunition and fuel, have reached agreed levels.

At the same time, notwithstanding the generally successful fulfillment of the protocols, a significant quantity of military equipment and armaments remains outdated among the troops and fleets of some of the allied countries, including tactical–operational missiles, tanks, aircraft, and combat ships. There remains a lag in the stockpiling of supplies of material resources. The construction of hangars for aircraft at permanent airfields continues to proceed slowly. There have also been a series of shortfalls in the preparation of communications and contacts. All of this to a definite extent lowers the combat preparedness and fighting capacity of the Unified Armed Forces.

The unified and national commands considered these deficiencies in elaborating the protocols for developing the army and naval forces of the Unified Armed Forces for the new five-year plan.

As of January 1, 1976, the protocols for the years 1976–1980 were signed by all the allied armies except the Army of the Socialist Republic of Romania, and were approved by the appropriate party and state organs of the countries of the Warsaw Pact.

[...]

The mobilization plans are closely tied to the plans for making the troops ready for action and constitutes a common system for transferring the armed forces from a peacetime to a wartime footing. Last year's exercises with practical mobilization of forces provided great practice for the formations and units of all branches of the Armed Forces in fulfilling the measures for mobilization, and allowed us to verify whether the mobilization plans are realistic and to map out concrete measures for the further perfection of troop mobilization.

[...]

In 1975, more than 40 major joint measures were carried out in the Unified Armed Forces, including 20 exercises of differing scale. Of these, the most prominent were: the "Soiuz-75" operational command-staff study on maps in the Western theater; two front and four army command-staff exercises; and a special tactical exercise involving railroad troops of the Polish and Soviet Armies, which bore practical significance for the preparation of the theater of military actions.

[...]

[*Source: KC PZPR, XIA/587, Archiwum Akt Nowych. Translated by Malcolm Byrne for the National Security Archive.*]

Document No. 78: Evaluation of the Helsinki Final Act by the Czechoslovak Party Presidium, April 28, 1976

While the West won a number of concessions in the lead-up to the 1975 Helsinki conference (see Document No. 75), the Warsaw Pact believed it had achieved much of what it wanted out of the process, as this Czechoslovak evaluation of the Final Act shows. Written half a year after the signing of the Act, the document may be regarded as close to the Soviet position since it originated with a staunchly conformist regime and was based in part on discussions held in Moscow during the intervening period. An important aim of the document was to outline a strategy for implementing the final agreement. In particular, the Soviets wanted to supplement the Act with a series of bilateral consultative agreements with each Western country. To break the unity the West had shown during the preparatory stages of the CSCE, the Warsaw Pact plan was to assign each member-state the task of promoting relations with particular West European countries. The document does not reveal any concerns as yet over the Basket III human rights issue, but those would soon materialize.

By its resolution of August 22, 1975, the CC CPCz Presidium has decided to prepare an assessment of the results of the Helsinki conference for specific sectors and to consult and coordinate it with other socialist countries. [...]

Fulfilling the results of the CSCE conference will be a long-term process. Its focus will be primarily in the area of bilateral relations with the capitalist states. In this way, implementation of détente and the strengthening of positive elements in relations between states with different social systems will be guaranteed.

In particular, at issue will be first of all the further strengthening of the meaning, effect, and deliberate fulfillment of the Final Act, especially of the Declaration on Principles Guiding Relations between European States, which is to be approached as a single whole, thus maintaining and reinforcing its fundamental political importance. Concerning matters of a military character following from the so-called confidence-building measures that are a part of the first basket, we will only implement them by taking account [our] political needs in a fashion that would not jeopardize the overall results of the CSCE and to an extent that would in no way go beyond the framework of the specific provisions of the Final Act. Such an approach has been made entirely feasible by the adoption of the principle of voluntary fulfillment of these provisions. However, we will actively exploit the provisions applying to disarmament in negotiations about it.

With regard to the second and third baskets, two views must be considered: On the one hand, to exploit the maximum possibilities embodied in the Final Act for the more offensive assertion of our particular economic as well as ideological and political interests and needs in relation to capitalist Europe, the United States and Canada; on the other hand, concerning the parts or specific provisions of the Final Act that have been adopted as a result of the Western states' efforts, to proceed in a way that does not give the West needless excuses for weakening the CSCE's general political results. At the same time, [we should] not allow the capitalist states to misuse provisions of the second and the third baskets [to justify] intervening in others' internal affairs.

In further deepening the process of détente, one of the major areas of the social-ist countries' initiative will be complementing political détente by military détente. In this sense, the Czechoslovak Socialist Republic together with other fraternal countries will continue to struggle for the positive development of negotiations on the reduction, and later the cessation, of the arms race, and for further advances toward general and complete disarmament thus reducing the military confrontation in Europe.

Simultaneously, we will broadly support the application of the positive results of the Conference on Security and Cooperation in Europe to influence developments in other parts of the world, especially in Asia.

We assume that the conference has created and, in its way, even institutionalized, for the first time on a broad continental scale, a political platform of international relations among countries with different social systems, which is based on the principles of peaceful coexistence and recognition of an objective need to further continue and deepen the process of détente and make it irreversible. [...]

I.

In the area of European security affairs, we will [...]
- attempt, if possible, to include in every agreement and treaty with the European capitalist states a general reference to the CSCE Final Act, primarily to the Declaration on Principles Guiding Relations, so that the international validity and weight of this Declaration is strengthened and the idea is promoted that the CSCE's results are landmarks in the development of Europe; [...]
- proceed similarly in negotiations with the non-European states so that the political *relevance of the CSCE's results is extended beyond European boundaries as well*, thus stimulating favorable conditions for similar solutions in other parts of the world, especially in Asia;
- with the exception of Austria (in regard to the State Treaty on neutrality and the risk of establishing a precedent for the consolidation of political relations between Austria and the FRG), seek *bilateral declarations between the ČSSR and the other participants in the Conference* to include all the European capitalist states; they are to be based on the Declaration on Principles Guiding Relations with the purpose of strengthening the importance of the Declaration by applying it to bilateral relations and, at the same time, giving our foreign policy another instrument with which to develop diplomatic initiatives through such relations; [...]
- implement the so-called *confidence-building measures* in accordance with the letter of the Final Act, our interests and the interests of the socialist common-wealth, in close cooperation with the Warsaw Pact allies; [...]
- With regard to disarmament, which is only mentioned indirectly in the Final Act, it will be especially necessary: [...]

– to take an active part in *asserting the common policy of the socialist countries at the Vienna negotiations* on the reduction of armed forces and armaments in Central Europe,[40] with the aim of reaching particular results;
– with respect to the importance of trying *to convene a world conference on disarmament,* to exert pressure by bilateral negotiations, primarily on countries that continue to question the usefulness of such an action or oppose it;
– in close coordination with other socialist countries, to actively assist in *increasing the effectiveness of the Geneva Disarmament Committee,*[41] where actual prospects have opened up for an early conclusion of an international convention prohibiting the misuse of environmental modification techniques in a military or any other way, as well as a partial agreement on a chemical weapons ban;

II.

In the area of the second basket, we will [...]
– use the appropriate provisions of the Final Act on trade policy to expand and improve contractual law in mutual relations, thus advancing conditions for bilateral and multilateral economic, scientific and technical cooperation in the spirit of equality, respect for sovereignty, and non-intervention in internal affairs;
– considering that the Final Act does not provide enough support for eliminating the remnants of the discriminatory practices of the developed capitalist states toward the socialist commonwealth in international economic relations, *discuss the interpretation of the results of the CSCE in the COMECON* with the aim of actively using them to defend and safeguard the interests of the socialist commonwealth in the further development of economic relations with the capitalist states. [...]

III.

In the area of humanitarian and other affairs, [we will] proceed aggressively in every direction wherever there are conditions to do so. Refer to the fact that the final document of the Conference sets clear criteria for cooperation [in this area], which is to lead to the strengthening of peace and security while respecting the agreed principles of interstate relations, primarily the principles of non-interference and a respect for the laws, traditions and customs of every state. In developing cooperation in these areas, [we will] proceed in the spirit of the Final Act by applying the rule of reciprocity. [...]
– With regard to family visits, [*we will*] enlarge the category of people who will be allowed to travel abroad to the capitalist countries in order to meet relatives living there legally, so that visits will be permitted for both spouses at the

[40] Mutual and Balanced Force Reduction talks (MBFR).
[41] Conference of the Committee on Disarmament (CCD).

same time; persons of retirement age will also be allowed to travel abroad to the capitalist countries without regard to the number of trips in one year or their duration;

- With regard to *family reunification,* in 1975–1976, [we will] process applications of underage children to emigrate from the ČSSR on condition that the applicants personally settle the necessary formalities at Czechoslovak embassies. [We will] treat in a similar fashion some applications by spouses of émigrés who are living alone in the ČSSR. [...]
- With regard to information exchange, the Final Act provisions have an advisory character that presumes implementation by later agreements. In their negotiation, it will be necessary to consistently assert our interests and strive for conditions that would allow us to act aggressively toward the West and placing the maximum limitation on ideological penetration from the West.
- With regard to *printed information,* [we will] strive by bilateral negotiations with the Western states that the university libraries, the departments of Czech, Slovak and Slavic studies, as well as other institutions, according to local conditions, subscribe to the Czechoslovak press. For possible wider subscription, [we will] select Western press titles least harmful by their content. [...]
- With regard to *information exchange,* the major Czechoslovak dailies, the Czechoslovak Press Agency and specialized journals will establish closer contacts and conclude agreements on cooperation primarily with *progressive* partners in the West, with the aim of creating conditions for informing the Western public objectively about the ČSSR. [We will] invite to Czechoslovakia progressive and other respected journalists and columnists who are guaranteed to provide more or less objective information about socialist Czechoslovakia. [...]

[We will] review and propose amendments to the existing *cultural agreements with non-socialist countries.* [...] *In doing so, we will try to foster above all* contacts along institutional lines. [...]

[We will] *systematically train persons being sent abroad within the framework of cultural, scientific, scholarly and medical contacts with foreign countries,* [will] give them specific state propaganda assignments, and provide them with appropriate informational and propaganda materials; likewise [we will] raise the political standards of the Czechoslovaks receiving their foreign counterparts in the ČSSR; [...]

In implementing the results of the CSCE, we will assume that in today's world, divided according to class, the implacable struggle between socialism and capitalism goes on, and its focus is shifting more and more to the ideological arena.

In the fight between two adversarial ideologies in connection with the process of détente and the CSCE, our propaganda and agitation will also effectively foster the promotion of foremost political interests of the socialist countries while at the same time helping to broaden the material base of détente, thus making it permanent and irreversible. It will be a matter of efficient and active agitation and propaganda utilizing all the successes of the really existing socialism, such as the safeguarding of the rights and living standards of workers, social achievements, economic results, the development of science, education, and culture, thus promoting more effectively the socialist ideas in the West. At the same time, [it will be necessary] to unmask and fight attempts at distorted interpretation of the CSCE's results, especially in the area of so-called humanitarian affairs, by the opponents of détente, as well as against the anticommunist, anti-Soviet and anti-peace activity of the Communist Party of China's Maoist leadership.

Such an approach will undoubtedly place much higher demands on the ideological front, which presupposes taking particular steps leading to increased effectiveness in ideological work both domestically and abroad. For this purpose, it will also be necessary to improve the overall efficiency of the mass media and increase their political and professional standards and responsiveness. This will be the direction of our propaganda and agitation work as well.

[*Source: AÚV KSČ 02/1/2/2 62/23, SÚA. Translated by Karel Sieber.*]

Document No. 79: Czechoslovak Analysis of the "Soiuz 77" Exercise, March 21–29, 1977

One of the themes that has become apparent with the recent availability of East European military files is that Warsaw Pact exercises often operated on fundamentally unreasonable assumptions. Thus, the 1977 "Soiuz" (Unity) exercise in Czechoslovakia and Hungary presumes, as usual, a NATO attack, this time making use of Austrian territory. As early as the second day, the Warsaw Pact is already in a position to start a counter-offensive and push the enemy back. This is particularly surprising given the signals Soviet bloc intelligence was receiving about NATO's growing conventional and nuclear capabilities at the time. It also seems clear that the Soviet General Staff, in order to justify the Warsaw Pact's own offensive strategy, held fast to the ideologically conditioned basic premise that NATO would be the one to initiate hostilities.

According to the "Staff of the Unified Armed Forces Plan of Joint Measures for the Czechoslovak People's Army in the 1976–1977 Training Year" and the "Calendar Plan of the CzPA Measures in the 1976–1977 Training Year," an allied, unilateral, multi-level, strategic–operational command-staff exercise, "Soiuz 77", has been conducted on the territory of the People's Republic of Hungary and the Czechoslovak Socialist Republic from March 21 to 29, 1977.

The staff of the Unified Armed Forces and operational staffs of the Hungarian People's Army, Soviet Army and the Czechoslovak People's Army under the command of Unified Armed Forces of the Warsaw Pact Supreme Commander Marshal of the Soviet Union V. G. Kulikov took part in the exercise. [...]

The exercising sides presumed that an armed conflict had been initiated by surprise on March 20 by the "Westerners" using conventional means of destruction while maintaining nuclear weapons in constant readiness for use.

The Central Army Group [...] prepared a major strike [...] in the direction of Regensburg, Tábor, Katowice with the task of destroying the "Easterners'" main grouping in the area of Karlovy Vary, Strakonice, Prague. [It intended] to fulfill the nearer assignment by reaching the Wrocław–Katowice–Lučenec line on the sixth or eighth day of the operation.

On the right wing, the main grouping of the Central Army Group [was] to attack by violating Austrian neutrality with the aim of striking in the direction of Brno, Ostrava, to come to the flank of the Central Front striking group and in cooperation with the major forces of the Central Army Group to encircle and destroy the "Easterners'" forces in the area of Bohemia and central Moravia.

The "Easterners:" were planning to fend off the aggression and go on the attack. The Central Front [...] prepared to fend off the "Westerners'" aggression and mount an offensive operation in the Prague–Stuttgart direction with the aim of destroying the opposing "Western" groupings and reaching the German–French state border. The main strike [was to be] led in the direction Nuremberg, Stuttgart. [...]

In accordance with the intention of the exercise, at 8 a. m. on March 20, NATO armed forces carried out surprise concentrated air strikes on "Eastern" military and industrial objectives and moved on to attack the territory of the ČSSR and GDR with assault groupings of land forces. At the same time, the NATO armies violated Austrian neutrality.

After two days of fighting, [...] they broke through to the depth of 35–50 kilometers to ČSSR territory in the Karlovy Vary and Pilsen directions.

The "Easterners" repulsed the enemy's aggression on March 20 and 21 and moved on to attack in several directions. The Central Front concentrated all of its effort to stop the principal advance of the [...] major forces and carried out retaliatory air strikes on the nuclear facilities, command posts, airfields and land force grouping of the enemy forces. With a part of its troops, it moved on to attack in the Munich and Vienna operational directions.

[*Source: VÚA, VS, OS, 1987, č.j. 75150. Translated by Karel Sieber.*]

Document No. 80: Description of Activities of an East German Spy inside NATO, April–May 1977

Much has been written about the murky world of espionage on both sides of the Iron Curtain during the Cold War. It is well established that East and West tried, and often succeeded in, placing "moles" (double agents) inside each other's camps. Rarely, however, is there hard evidence of their operational activities. This excerpt from the memoir of East German intelligence officer Heinz Busch gives an example, offering an absorbing, if brief, account of the exploits of Ursula Lorenzen, alias "Michelle", an agent who operated inside NATO for years, extracting some of the Western alliance's most closely held military secrets. She was only one of a number of such agents who provided the East Germans and their allies with a vast and detailed picture of Western capabilities and intentions.[42]

[...]

Since the late 1970s, HVA [*Hauptverwaltung Aufklärung*[43]] agent "Topas,"[44] identification no. XV/333/69, was the agency's most important source inside NATO headquarters in Brussels. His British wife also worked for HVA in NATO, under the pseudonym "Kriemhild" and "Türkis" (registration no. XV/144/71). Until that time, the IM[45] couple "Michelle" [...] and "Bordeaux," under changing identification nos. XV/962/60, XV/797/61 and, after the recall to the GDR, XV/4188/83, had been covering HVA's information needs from NATO headquarters.

[...]

"Michelle" had been recruited in 1962 by a personal acquaintance, an agent initially sent by HVA from the GDR to the West as a recruiter, working under the pseudonym "Bordeaux." He placed her within NATO through a position at the West German Embassy in Paris that lasted several years and was not particularly rewarding in terms of intelligence gathering. On January 16, 1967, she assumed her work within NATO as an assistant to the director for operations in NATO's international secretariat, where she stayed until the GDR recalled her in March 1979. As time went by, she got security clearance up to documents classified as "top secret Atomal."[46] [...] The deliveries of agent "Michelle" to NVA headquarters consisted of a large

---

[42] For details, see Bernd Shaefer, *The Warsaw Pact's Intelligence on NATO: East German Military Espionage against the West*, IFS Info No. 2/2002 (Oslo: Institute for Defence Studies, 2002), also at www.isn.ethz.ch/php/documents/collection_17/texts/schaefer.pdf.

[43] Main Intelligence Administration (East German military intelligence).

[44] Rainer Rupp.

[45] Inoffizieller Mitarbeiter (unofficial agent).

[46] "Atomal" is a special NATO classification grade conerning either U.S. information classified undeer the Atomic Energy Act of 1954 or British nuclear information released to NATO. Atomal could be at any of the four general classification levels; the reference here is probably to the highest level, "Cosmic Top Secret."

number of NATO documents of high or highest classification. Usually, she took the documents home in the evening, where "Bordeaux" sifted and photographed them and sent them off; on the next day, sometimes also with somewhat longer delay, [Michelle] brought the documents back to their proper place, including the safe of her boss. [...] The topics were manifold and comprised materials and reports prepared for meetings of the leading bodies; plans on force levels, armament, and infrastructure; internal documents about disarmament problems and intra-bloc relations; long-term defense plans, etc. [...] From all the documents on NATO's nuclear planning and nuclear sharing process (political consultation procedures about the use of nuclear weapons, requirement procedures of the MNC[47] for the clearance of the release of nuclear weapons, and interrelated provisions) that were drafted and authorized in the 1970s, this agent obtained those that were interesting for the Warsaw Pact. [...] This became apparent with the delivery of April/May 1977. It included the entire documentation on NATO's strategic command-staff exercise, "Hilex 7," the secret NATO document PO/76/91 including all proposals and concepts for the defense ministers' meeting (DPC and NPG)[48], the bulky study no. 47 of the Nuclear Planning Group, the secret NATO document AC 281-DS(77)3 containing the minutes of the meeting of the Council's executive working group about the alliance's study AD-70 ("Defense Problems of NATO in the 1970s"), extensive correspondence between NATO entities and national leaderships about the strategic staff exercise Wintex/Cimec 79 (!), two secret documents concerning external reinforcements for the command area Europe, decisions of the Defense Planning Committee meeting of December 1976, extensive, almost complete documentation on the strategic staff exercises Wintex 77 and Hilex 8, and some equally important, but less voluminous documents.

[*Source:* Heinz Busch, *"Militärspionage der DDR,"* manuscript, Berlin 2001, pp. 223–27. Translated by Thomas Holderegger.]

---

[47] Ministerial Council
[48] Defense Planning Council, Nuclear Planning Group

Document No. 81: Marshal Ogarkov Analysis of the "Zapad" Exercise, May 30–June 9, 1977

The 1977 "Zapad" ("West") maneuvers, which took place in East Germany, were intended to assess the Warsaw Pact's ability to counteract the marked progress in NATO's combat readiness. The Western alliance had recently completed the comparable "Wintex" maneuvers, the largest ever, and according to an East German report, the results showed the Pact falling short of its objective.

Adding to the significance of "Zapad," the scenario assumed that NATO would initiate hostilities under the guise of maneuvers (such as Wintex). This theme appears with greater frequency in the late 1970s. Warsaw Pact intelligence was well aware of NATO's actual plans, but that did not entirely quell uneasiness over the presence of so many troops on maneuvers in the immediate vicinity. In his closing remarks following the exercise, Nikolai V. Ogarkov, chief of the Soviet General Staff, is fairly candid about the shortcomings revealed by "Zapad", as is Marshal Dmitrii Ustinov, the minister of defense and the exercise's commander. Ustinov notes that the Pact needs to acquire completely new (conventional) weapons systems to counter the West's growing superiority in advanced technology. During the 1970s, Soviet bloc analysts realized that the gap in military technology continued to widen and might never be bridged.

As always, the "Zapad" exercise ended on an upbeat note with the East eventually launching an offensive deep into the FRG and winning the war, despite Ogarkov's acknowledgement that not a single division had fulfilled its task.

REPORT

The exercise had three characteristics:

First, the exercise was distinct from previous ones in its large, spatial scope. The commanders and headquarters of the allied armies worked in locations with realistic space for administrative field stations and transfer points with great distances between them, and they worked through the questions under study during the entire exercise within a realistic timeframe using the "real time" method.

Second, it was carried out on the level of operational–strategic exercise, based on one of the possible variations of joint military action of the Warsaw Pact member-states for repelling aggression in the Western Theater. At the same time it also included significantly adjusted, realistic military staffing and initial positioning of the opposing sides. This was done deliberately in advance so that the commanders and headquarters could work from actions according to a realistic plan and so that they would show more creativity and initiative in their search for the best means to solve complex operational tasks.

Third, for the first time in the practice of our mutual undertakings, we studied in detail the use of armed forces in battle as a strategic operation in the continental war theater using a group of troops from the coalition staff and with the creation of a General Command Headquarters in the theater. The role of that headquarters was carried out by the directors. However, this does not exclude the fact that in the future the General Command Headquarters in the theater might also be under study.

[...]

The initial conditions were set up on May 31, that is, 3–4 days before the beginning of the war. The national boundaries used ran from Rostock to Leipzig to Pilsen, 100–150 km eastward from its actual location.

The "Western Forces" by that time had finished covert mobilization and, under the pretense of an exercise, implemented operational deployment in the Central European Theater (CET) and on the Atlantic. Altogether in the CET there were 85 divisions deployed as well as 3,700 fighter planes and more than 450 warships in concentrated groups.

A powerful grouping was concentrated in the first operational echelon on the territories of the Federal Republic of Germany and Denmark: 60 divisions, more than 15,000 tanks, and 9,500 units of artillery, which represented more than 70 percent of all its forces and materiel deployed in the CET.

The Western Forces had 25 divisions from various NATO countries on reserve in the CET. The Eastern Forces, having ascertained that the Western Forces were preparing to unleash the war, began covert mobilization and deployment of their troops and flotilla on May 28.

Having approximately the same number of troops and amount of materiel in its own forces in the western part of the theater as the Western Forces had, the Eastern Forces concentrated only 40 percent of their troops in the first echelon on May 31. The remaining troops were located 300 to 1200 km behind, while the 45th Army was 1,500 km from the areas of operation.

Thus, with an almost equal number of forces, generally speaking, the Western Forces created a 1–1/2 times advantage over the troops of the first operational echelon of the Eastern Forces (2nd and 3rd Fronts and the 28th Army), and a three- or even five-times advantage in its own shock troop formations.

[...]

Taking into account the overall situation, the two sides planned as follows [...]:

The Western Forces, under the guise of a large-scale strategic exercise, and while carrying out the deployment of troops of its operational groups, planned to attack the opposing troops of the 2nd and 3rd Fronts and the 28th Army with sudden, massive surprise attacks on a broad front until the approach of Eastern operational reserves. Then, developing an offensive approach, they planned to take control of the territory of East Germany as well as of the western regions of Czechoslovakia and Poland by the sixth or seventh day. Simultaneously, aerial attacks, paratroop attacks, and diversionary and reconnaissance groups would not allow movement into the areas of action along the Front of the second echelon of the Eastern Forces. Further, with the accumulation of forces making it favorable to introduce operational reserves into battle, using attacks by two basic groups from the area west of Gdańsk and from the region west of Liwiec River in the general direction towards Brest, and with part of the forces headed toward Kaliningrad and to Lvov, they planned to completely defeat advancing Eastern operational reserves in head-on clashes, and to reach the western border of the Soviet Union.

By May 31, the Eastern Forces had completed mobilizing their land and naval forces and, with the goal of stopping the aggression, went ahead with their operational deployment by advancing the main groups of the 4th and 5th Fronts into the western regions of Poland and Czechoslovakia.

The plan of the Eastern Forces envisaged repulsing the attacks of the Western Forces, then introducing into battle the reserve fronts and armies to take the lead and defeat the groups of the first operational echelons of Western Forces which had invaded their territory, and move into counter-attack.

They further planned to inflict defeat on the advancing and newly formed operational enemy reserves and to completely defeat the aggressor on his own territory.

[...]

On the eighth day of operations, conditions became more complicated when the Eastern Forces repulsed enemy invaders and went on to attack in the direction of Hamburg, Hannover, Frankfurt, and Munich. Within 3–4 days they had advanced 100–150 km. At the same time, they successfully battled for control of the Baltic Straits. Only in the area toward Prague did the Eastern Forces still face a complicated situation. Troops from the 3rd Front fought hard for Prague in that area.

[...]

On the whole, the situation for the Eastern Forces turned out favorably: They became proficient in taking the strategic initiative, actually cut off groups of Western Forces, created favorable conditions for defeating them, and took control of West German soil.

The Western Forces fought difficult defensive battles, attempting not to have their main forces defeated. Near Hamburg the troops of the first Dutch Army Corps found themselves surrounded. In the Hannover region, as the result of the Eastern Forces making deep inroads toward that area, the Western Forces were threatened with being cut off in the theater of action and being defeated unit by unit.

Under these circumstances, on June 10 the Western Forces made the decision to use nuclear weapons. They began immediate preparation for a massive nuclear attack. In conjunction with this, at 9:30 on the 11th, General Headquarters sent a directive to all Fronts and to the Unified Baltic Fleet whereby the Supreme Command, based on confirmed data, warned the troops and fleets that the enemy was preparing for a nuclear attack.

Under these conditions, the commanders and headquarters staff of the Eastern Forces were supposed to quickly ascertain the deadlines for the beginning of an enemy nuclear attack and to carry out reconnaissance of important targets as well as prepare aerial forces, rocket troops and artillery to the highest level possible, all the while making arrangements for a first nuclear strike on the enemy.

Simultaneously, it became necessary to take steps to increase their own troop readiness, to assist them to recover from a nuclear attack, and after the assault to remove the aftermath and restore administrative systems and the combat-readiness of troops with the goal of preventing the enemy from engaging in active operations following the nuclear attacks. Along with this, under such complex circumstances, there remained the task of leading the 5th Front into battle at the appropriate time.

These tasks were generally solved correctly at the Fronts and in the armies, although at the same time there were some shortcomings.

First: discovery of preparations for and the beginning of a nuclear attack.

At most of the Fronts and in the armies, the commanders understood that the Western Forces, having lost the initiative, were preparing to use nuclear weapons. […] For the last 30–40 minutes before the Western nuclear attack began, all nuclear weapons at the Fronts were placed at Battle Alert #1 and aerial forces were dispatched at the front. The preparatory steps taken by the Eastern Fronts and fleets on the whole allowed them to refine their plans and to launch the first nuclear attack at the Western Forces at the appropriate time.

Second: maximum weakening of enemy nuclear forces and recovery of our own troops from nuclear attack.

We can all well imagine, theoretically, the difficult after-effects of a massive nuclear attack if measures are not taken to lessen the enemy's nuclear capacity as much as possible and to lead our troops to recover from nuclear attack.

However, these two related tasks were not given sufficient attention by field commanders at the front and in the armies. The necessary measures were not taken to lessen the strength of the enemy's nuclear attack, especially those needed to uncover hidden nuclear rockets.

While reconnoitering for enemy targets before launching the nuclear attack, they found administrative posts, rocket and artillery divisions and aircraft at airfields within reach of our firepower, capable of attacking these targets with conventional means. Unfortunately, neither aviation forces nor artillery nor even tactical rockets with warheads were used for this purpose. Although theoretically we all know that all important targets, if they can be attacked, must be destroyed immediately by conventional means at the commanders' request—and even that of the division commanders—we should not wait until there is the possibility of attacking them with nuclear weapons.

Another effective way of weakening the enemy's nuclear attack is through a concentrated blow to his administrative systems using nuclear weapons at the beginning of the nuclear strike. This measure was correctly planned and implemented by the 2nd Front headquarters.

[…]

At the same time, at many other headquarters there was no planning for the replacement of regional concentrations of troops, deployment areas of missile brigades and battalions, nuclear artillery, or for airfields serving as bases for transport planes and command posts, a fact which under real conditions is unacceptable and would lead to dire consequences.

Third—launching the nuclear attack in time.

When the threat of nuclear attack by the Western Forces was imminent, the commanders and headquarters at the Fronts and in the Armies concentrated their greatest attention on refining their plans for a first nuclear strike and on bringing their nuclear weapons up to the highest level of combat-readiness.

During this time, all the field administration of the unified forces worked with great intensity and focus. At the 1st, 2nd, and 3rd Fronts, in the 9th Army of the National People's Army of the German Democratic Republic and in the 28th Army, this work was particularly well-coordinated and was handled directly by the commanding officers. The refinement of plans for the first nuclear strike and for the preparation for launching such a strike was carried out in time at all the Fronts. During this work, however, the groups for nuclear planning in the 19th and 30th aerial forces were not well coordinated. They did not work closely enough with the headquarters for artillery and rocket launchers at the Fronts.

We cannot avoid discussing the methods used during this period at the administrative posts at the Front, and their equipment. Take, for example, the 2nd Front. Here, during the first nuclear attack, they planned to use about 300 nuclear warheads. Many targets to be attacked were mobile, and their positions changed constantly. To refine the plan for a first nuclear strike and move those nuclear weapons from certain targets onto other targets would have meant carrying out a tremendous amount of work in a short period of time.

Without the use of computers and some decentralization of leadership, it would be difficult to resolve this problem, we were all convinced. Thus the question arises about the necessity of developing such automation at the front field administration.

Fourth Problem—the nature of troop activity at the start of nuclear strike launches by the opposing forces.

Having determined that the Western Forces were going ahead with preparations for launching a nuclear attack, the Eastern Forces began launching a first nuclear attack on the Western Forces at 11:29. Almost simultaneously, at 11:30, the first enemy nuclear strike occurred. In essence, putting the nuclear bombs into action took the form of a counter-attack.

By general calculation, the Western Forces launched 680 nuclear strikes at the troops on the Front and the Unified Baltic Fleet, and 400 strikes went deep into the country, to the western regions of the USSR.

The Eastern troops suffered significant losses. Only 36 percent of its formations maintained their fighting capability. In all, 31 percent of the divisions lost their fighting capacity.

The remaining formations ended up severely limited in their fighting capacity.

Twenty-four percent of rocket formations and units and 70 percent of aerial units suffered a total loss of fighting capacity. Along the front lines, huge areas of contamination, destruction, and fires developed.

The first nuclear strikes of the Eastern Forces were equally effective. Fifteen divisions of the Western Forces totally lost their fighting capacity. There was total destruction of 300 divisions of operational–tactical and tactical rockets (35 percent), 14 divisions of anti-aircraft rockets, 23 percent of tactical aircraft, and 25 percent of the joint command posts. The Western Forces lost a quarter of a million of their personnel.

In general, the two sides suffered equal losses; however, the Eastern Forces lost almost twice as many divisions. This situation could be explained by the fact that, with an approximately equal balance in nuclear forces, the Western Forces had a certain advantage in tactical nuclear capabilities. This is why, before the nuclear strikes

410

begin, it is very important to inflict the maximum amount of damage on the enemy's tactical nuclear capabilities during battle with conventional weapons.

Despite the complexities of the situation, the commanders and staff headquarters worked in an organized manner at this stage. The field administrations, particularly those of the 2nd and 3rd Fronts as well as in the 23rd Army, did all they could to make full use of the results of their nuclear strikes and to keep the enemy from going into active battle. It is true that not everyone was able to figure out the consequences of their work equally. This work was best organized at the 2nd and 4th Fronts. Over the course of two-three hours the headquarter staffs of these Fronts collected the basic facts of the situation and refined the tasks for the troops.

Based on the circumstances that developed, the troop commanders made the following decisions:

1st Front—on the morning of June 12, go into action, launch the main strike at Schwerin and Lübeck. On the morning of June 13 have the 17th Army attack toward Jutland and, together with the Unified Baltic Fleet, defeat the enemy in the Baltic Straits area.

2nd Front—continue attacking, launching the main strike into the Ruhr industrial area from the north. Putting the 11th tactical army into battle, launch an attack in coordination with the 1st and 4th Fronts to defeat the main groups of the central and northern NATO troops.

4th Front—renew the attack with army formations of the first echelon which have maintained their fighting capacity. From June 11–12 use the second echelon troops for a follow-up attack and continue carrying out their tasks along with the 109th airborne division, which pushed ahead into the area of Fulda on June 11.

3rd Front—on the morning of June 12, combat-ready formations should attack. Have the 32nd army corps increase its forces and help them succeed in the area toward Mainburg. Include the 4th Army, the 32nd army corps and the 7th Army in the first echelon, and in the second echelon, include the 5th Army.

[...]

We must note that the 5th Front during this time was in a very difficult situation. First, the Front came under serious aerial attack while it was in the final stages of deployment to its appointed regions. The circumstances were such that the aerial attacks, paratroop landings, and diversionary-reconnaissance groups destroyed the main bottlenecks on the routes where the Front troops were heading out, and they destroyed almost all the stores of fuel and heating supplies.

Under such complicated circumstances, the troop commanders, field command and Front headquarters staff took energetic measures to search for possible ways to replenish the necessary materiel by using current reserves from neighboring Fronts in the Polish People's Republic and the Czechoslovak Socialist Republic, [and] by delivering fuel by air from the rear base. They also enabled the Front troops—albeit with some tardiness—to re-group and head out to their appointed positions.

At that time the commanders planned to send the troops into battle. Their decision envisaged that the 5th Front would go into battle alongside the 28th Army, which at that time was given over to its staff. The attack on the right wing was planned for two armies, the 18th and part of the 28th, and on the left wing, the 43rd. The 13th

tactical army was located in the second echelon of the Front. They considered sending the 13th into battle to increase their chances of success. Just when the Front Troop
Commander had planned and organized sending the troops into battle, there was an
enemy nuclear attack, and he had to change his decision in many ways, since, as a
result of the nuclear rocket attack, the 18th Army lost nearly all its fighting capacity. Not one of its divisions could fulfill its appointed tasks. Within the 13th tactical
army one division lost its fighting capacity entirely, while a second division ended up
with limited fighting capacity and only a third was battle-ready. Under such circumstances the Front Troop Commander made an entirely correct decision to send the
troops into battle and fulfill their appointed tasks by launching an attack with the
28th Army strengthened with formations and units which had retained their fighting
capacity after the nuclear strike.

    [...]

During the time when the enemy's threat to use nuclear weapons increased, the
General headquarter staffs of the Polish Army, the Czechoslovak People's Army and
the Main Headquarters of the National People's Army of the German Democratic
Republic notified their territorial troops and put into effect local civil defense measures aimed at recovery from enemy nuclear attacks. They took measures to maintain constant communications with their troops and with government administrative
organs.

With the launch of nuclear attacks, data collection about the attack on the troops
and the countries was organized; local civil defense forces were put into action to
clean up the remains of the enemy's nuclear attacks; and measures were taken to
restore the fighting capacity of their troops as well as to render the necessary assistance to the Soviet Fronts.

[*Source: VS, OS-OL, 1977, krab., 29-999-155, č.j. 22013/23, VÚA. Translated by
Paul Spitzer for the National Security Archive.*]

Document No. 82: Report by Marshal Kulikov on the State of the Unified Armed Forces, January 30, 1978

In 1977, Marshal Viktor Kulikov had taken over as Warsaw Pact supreme commander. Here he reports on the condition of the Pact during a period when the alliance was taking steps to counter what it perceived to be a shift in the military balance in NATO's favor. He places particular emphasis on combat readiness and modernization of armaments of all kinds. By 1978, détente had already begun to deteriorate over a variety of issues from the SALT process to conflicts in the Third World, notwithstanding the interest of both superpowers in reducing tensions.[49] The Kremlin's main response was to increase military preparedness and intensify planning for the possibility of war in Europe. This record is one indication that those preparations had begun as early as January 1978.

The activities of the Unified Armed Forces of the member-states of the Warsaw Pact and their administrative organs in 1977 took place under conditions of continuous growth of the might and international authority of the countries of the socialist commonwealth.

[...]

The decisions made by the member-states of the Warsaw Pact at the Political Consultative Committee meeting in November 1976 had important meaning for the further improvement of the Unified Armed Forces. These decisions concerned the creation of separate units (subdivisions) in each allied army, equipped with the most advanced types of weaponry and [other] military hardware; the further strengthening of the common air defense system; and improvement of the activities and organizational structure of the administrative organs of the Unified Armed Forces. These decisions are being implemented. [...]

Work has continued in the Unified Armed Forces to implement the bilateral Protocols on the development of ground and naval forces in 1976–1980. Some strengthening of the military composition of all types of military forces took place, the organizational structure and the bringing to full strength of groupings and units improved, and their battle readiness and battle capabilities increased. Plans for the mutual supply of hardware and weaponry and equipping of ground troops and fleets in the past year have mainly been implemented.

---

[49] Much new material on the collapse of détente emerged in the 1990s, largely through a multinational collaborative research undertaking known as the Carter–Brezhnev Project, organized by James G. Blight and janet Lang of the Thomas J. Watson Institute at Brown University. The documentary record, including many declassified Soviet, East European and U.S. documents, and transcripts of oral history conferences involving former policy-makers from the U.S. and USSR is available at the National Security Archive, one of the contributors to the project. Documents and analyses have appeared in print in the *Cold War International History Project Bulletin* and in a volume edited by Odd Arne Westad, *The Fall of Détente: Soviet–American Relations during the Carter Years* (Oslo: Scandinavian University Press, 1997).

As a result, the Unified Armed Forces took a new step in their development. [...]

The outfitting of the land forces in 1977 increased: in terms of operational–tactical and tactical missile systems—by 8 percent, tanks—by 4 percent, armored personnel carriers—by 37 percent, multiple launch missile systems—by 21 percent, anti-tank guided missile systems—by 39 percent.

The outfitting of forces with modern types of short-range air-defense systems, such as "Kub", "Krug", "Strela-1M" and "Strela-2M", increased considerably.

The modernization of T-54 and T-55 tanks and of some artillery systems continued. In all, by the end of 1977, 55 percent of tanks had been modernized. [...]

The outfitting of groupings and units of the individual countries' *air defense forces* with new types of weapons, which had better battle capabilities and fire power, continued: with MIG-21bis planes, S-75M "Volkhov" and S-125M "Neva" surface-to-air missiles, as well as with modern radar stations and "Almaz-2", "Vozdukh-1M" and other automated guidance systems.

[...]

In the fighter fleet at the front, as a result of the replacement of obsolete aircraft with aircraft of the MIG-23bn and SU-20 type, the relative presence of modern aircraft increased somewhat. [...]

In 1977, 22 percent of ships slated for replacement in the next 5-year plan had been replaced. In some fleets, attack helicopters were introduced for fighting against small-scale surface targets. The training of crews for new coast guard ships and re-training of pilots for MI-14pl anti-ship helicopter had been organized. Preparation has begun for the introduction into the military of modern coastal missile systems. [...]

The combat and mobilization readiness of the Unified Armed Forces on the whole provides for the fulfillment of tasks aimed at repelling aggression. In all types of military forces, the time needed to bring units and groupings into full combat readiness had been decreased.

The air defense forces have cut the time it takes to bring surface-to-air missile battalions into launch readiness.

In some fighter squadrons in the air defense and air forces, the time it takes to prepare aircraft (helicopters) for a battle mission had been cut by 10–20 percent. The technical readiness of air force equipment is kept at a level of 90–93 percent of what is available in the units.

[*Source: KC PZPR, XIA/589, Archiwum Akt Nowych. Translated by Sergey Radchenko.*]

Document No. 83: Soviet Statement at the Chiefs of General Staff Meeting in Sofia, June 12–14, 1978

As part of the continuing effort to establish a war time chain of authority and procedures within the Warsaw Pact, Soviet Gen. S.F. Romanov tries to explain to his counterparts why a statute on these matters is needed. His statement starts with a repetition of the standard Soviet view that a future war will be a decisive confrontation between the two systems, that it will most likely be fought with all available weapons and that the goal of the Warsaw Pact side will be complete victory. (By this time NATO had already abandoned that goal in favor of terminating war as quickly and advantageously as possible.) Among other points, Romanov emphasizes the importance of centralizing command in one person—naturally a Soviet officer—who would have the right to issue binding orders. The responsibility of national military commands, he says, is to fulfill operational tasks, secure materiel and provide technical support. As a sign of Moscow's eagerness to satisfy the interests of loyal allies, the Soviets incorporated numerous changes into the final text. The Poles alone reportedly presented as many as 60 amendments for consideration.

[...]

In conformity with the resolution of the Political Consultative Committee, the Committee of the Ministers of Defense of the member-states of the Warsaw Treaty decided in December 1977 [...] to work out draft principles for the Unified Armed Forces of the member-states of the Warsaw Treaty and for their unified command (in war time).

[...]

A comprehensive analysis of the problems of *common defense* [...] leads to the conclusion that a future war, if unleashed by an imperialist aggressor, becomes a pivotal conflict between the classes of the two opposing social systems, the capitalist and the socialist one.

[...]

Most likely, the full arsenal of available means of destruction will be used in such a war.

[...]

In the course of a modern strategic operation, it is possible to successfully counter an aggression by the enemy, to annihilate his main units on the territory of the entire theater of war, while delivering strikes on a wide front, conducting combat operations with all modern components of the armed forces, aggregating efforts concerning goal, place, and time, ensuring their steadfast leadership, and maintaining continuous cooperation. The use of strategic and tactical nuclear weapons can be the main instrument to annihilate the enemy.

Within the Soviet military forces, this new form of strategic action has been elaborated and analyzed for more than 15 years. During these years, a number of strategic command post exercises were conducted and a certain experience was gained. The strategic command post exercise "Zapad 77", which took place under the direction of the minister of defense of the USSR, Marshal of the Soviet Union [Dmitrii] F. Ustinov, and in which operational staffs of all allied armies in the western theater participated, received special importance in this connection. The ministers for national defense, the army generals [Wojciech] Jaruzelski, [Heinz] Hoffmann, and [Martin] Dzúr, actively participated in the conduct of the exercise.

[…]

In addition, in the past few years, the Unified Command of the member-states of the Warsaw Treaty has been very busy analyzing the problems of strategic operations in the continental theater of war.

It will suffice to name such exercises as "Shield 76," "Soiuz 77," "Wal-77," "Soiuz 78," and others that have been conducted under the leadership of the supreme commander of the Unified Armed Forces, comrade Marshal of the Soviet Union [Viktor] Kulikov. All of them generated rich material for general and practical conclusions. At present, one can say that the views about goals, character, and methods of leading a strategic operation in a theater of war have emerged in essence. The main tasks of the Unified Armed Forces in a strategic operation in a theater of war are defense against aggression by the enemy, the thwarting of his nuclear strike, achievement of the strategic initiative by destruction of the main groupings of nuclear missiles, ground, tactical air, and naval forces of the adversary in the theater of war, and achievement of complete victory over the enemy.

[…]

It seems appropriate that *the first paragraph* of the draft of the principles in war time should reflect above all the material base, that is, define in what composition and at what time the Unified Armed Forces are at the disposal of the Unified Command.

[…]

We have already stated that a future war will demand the utmost exertion of all military, economic, and spiritual forces of the socialist coalition. Objectively, the conduct of such a war will only be feasible through a single body, equipped with full political, administrative, and military power, that is, through the highest politico-military leadership of the coalition.

Accordingly, the leadership of the Unified Armed Forces in strategic operations in a theater of war has to be centralized and has to be exercised by one person, who is directly responsible to the highest politico-military leadership.

[…]

According to our view, this person should be the supreme commander of the Unified Armed Forces in the Western and Southwestern theaters of war.

[…]

In this context, we must not overlook the high degree of readiness of the leadership bodies and systems of our likely enemy, the NATO forces, which have been developed and functioning for years.

[…]

416

I merely allow myself to point out that at the regular NATO Council meeting of May 30 and 31 of this year in Washington, NATO's heads of state and government, during their survey of the extensive and long-term program for the increase of armaments in Europe, paid close attention to the enhancement of what they call the command level, coordinated leadership of the allied forces, and improvement in the work of the staffs deployed in Europe.

At the same time, a series of specific recommendations has been accepted for the improvement of the communications and automation systems and particularly for the initiation of the second stage of NATO's comprehensive intelligence system.

[...]

The principle of centralized leadership of the armed forces in a strategic operation implies the right of the supreme commander of the Unified Armed Forces in the theater of war, starting from the moment of his appointment to the official position, to give commands, directives, orders, and instructions, the fulfillment of which is mandatory for all the troops and fleets belonging to the Unified Armed Forces in the theater of war.

In other words, the Supreme Command of the Unified Armed Forces in the theater of war must exercise the immediate and direct leadership of the fronts, the fleets, the separate armies and operational and tactical units, for which it is directly responsible, regardless of which allied state has assigned them to the Unified Armed Forces.

[...]

[*Source: VA-01/40363, pp. 90–108, BA-MA. Translated by Christian Nünlist.*]

Document No. 84: Speech by Brezhnev at the Political Consultative Committee Meeting in Moscow, November 22, 1978

Addressing his fellow Warsaw Pact leaders, Brezhnev reflects an increasingly dour view of the world situation, deploring the deterioration of détente with the United States. He notes that among other things the Western allies are increasing their military spending, which he ascribes to the correlation of forces turning against them. He is troubled by indications that China and NATO may be starting to develop closer economic and military cooperation, and he invokes the socialist camp's "sacred duty"—not to disturb the equilibrium of military power. As the decade of the 1970s came to a close, Brezhnev was not alone among Soviet and other Warsaw Pact leaders in his concern for the direction of events, particularly the arms race and the hardening of U.S. policy, but he has no clear answer at this point for what to do. The meeting decided to press for a statute for command in war time.

The strengthening of the positions of socialism in the world in recent years is an incontrovertible fact.

Our countries' defenses have become even stronger. Today we are not weaker than the imperialist powers and their main military alliance, which is aimed at the socialist world—neither on land, nor in the air, nor on the high seas.

Others might not, but you and I know well that the countries of the Warsaw Treaty have not done anything and are not doing anything [presently] above what is called for by the requirements of a reliable defense of the borders of socialism. However, even the tentative parity in armaments and armed forces is perceived quite nervously in the ruling imperialist circles. In those circles—especially in the USA and in the ruling leadership of NATO—they obviously do not want to let go of the hope of achieving some kind of breakthrough, of overturning the existing correlation of forces, and of gaining an opportunity to impose their will [and] their ways on the rest of the world.

Washington's defense budget is 130 billion dollars in the current financial year. They are working on new systems of weapons of mass destruction—we know this very well—in closed American engineering and construction offices. I have in mind not only the neutron bomb, but also laser weapons, genetic, infrasound weapons, and so on.

The Americans are pushing their allies toward the path of unrestrained growth of military expenditures. The Washington session of the NATO Council is a clear expression of that. The NATO bloc presented a certain "gift" to their people, who had been following the special U.N. session on disarmament with hope—an additional program to increase armaments over ten years. They earmarked an additional 80 billion dollars over and above the gigantic military outlays that had been planned before.

The Western politicians are practically beside themselves also because the sphere of the imperialist dominance is shrinking as a result of the victories of the revolutionary movements in the former colonial countries.

[...]

The situation in the developed capitalist countries does not make the bosses of imperialism any happier.

[...]

In this atmosphere, one could anticipate a massive attack against détente, against the policies of the socialist states.

The U.S. government is doing everything possible to discredit and to conceal the successes of socialism, to push back the positions of the socialist commonwealth.

[...]

In their efforts to counter the growing ideological influence of socialism with something, the Carter administration unfolded a hypocritical campaign around imaginary "violations of human rights" in the socialist countries. This campaign represents an attempt at an impudent interference in the internal affairs of the socialist countries. It was calculated to sow mistrust, and to impede mutual understanding between countries with opposing social systems. The firm and principled position of our states has undermined their calculations considerably.

Unfortunately, imperialism has now acquired an ally—today's China. Beijing's policy, directed against the Soviet Union and other countries of the socialist commonwealth, makes it a very attractive partner for world imperialism. They have already begun to feed today's China, to supply it with weapons, and to push it toward hostile excursions against the socialist countries, as was done some time ago in Europe during the years of the shameful Munich policies.

The economic and military cooperation between NATO and China, directed against the socialist commonwealth and the progressive forces of the entire world, is taking on more and more real dimensions. The one who does not understand that understands very little in the current international situation.

The political agreement that Japan recently signed with China, to applause from Washington, is also a potential step in the same direction. The placement of pieces on the chessboard of world politics today is such that one cannot exclude a banding together of U.S. and Japanese imperialism with militant Chinese chauvinism, regardless of the significant contradictions between them. I believe I do not have to explain what it would mean in terms of the aggravation of the entire global situation.

[...]

We oppose the arms race; we do not plan to attack anybody, and we are always prepared to dissolve the military blocs. However, as long as the West is acting in another direction, our sacred duty to our own peoples, to the cause of socialism, is not to allow imperialism to break the correlation of forces, which has been achieved at the price of many sacrifices, and which in itself represents the most important guarantee against nuclear war in the present times. As expensive as it might be, we have to continue to make sure that the defenses of the socialist commonwealth remain at the appropriate level.

The NATO countries coordinate their actions carefully in the military sphere. And it would be unforgivable if we did not do everything necessary to ensure precise coordination among the Warsaw Treaty countries on defense issues.

Let me now speak about some basic directions in our efforts to improve the international situation, and in particular about the development of relations with the countries of Western Europe, and also with Japan.

Objective reality is such that notwithstanding the general class solidarity of the bourgeoisie of the USA, Western Europe and Japan, the interests of these three main centers of imperialism do not always coincide completely, and often contradict each other.

[...]

We can rightfully list the relatively stable [position] of Western Europe on questions of détente among our achievements. In our persistent, long-standing struggle for lasting peace on the European continent, we have never separated our own security from that of Europe as a whole.

[...]

However, whatever our successes in the development of economic and other ties, the peace will not be lasting, nor will détente be reliable as long as the arms race goes on.

[...]

One should probably consider the negotiations between the USSR and the USA on the new agreement to limit offensive strategic armaments to be the most important [negotiations] at the present time.

Today the American administration, it seems, has come to the conclusion that from the point of view of [their] domestic calculations, it would be expedient for them to sign the SALT agreement this year. The positions of the sides on the remaining issues are so close now that such a perspective does exist. (That is of course if Carter is not unexpectedly swayed in another direction). If everything proceeds normally, it might be expedient for me to meet with Carter in the nearest future in order to sign that agreement, and to try to introduce a positive current into the development of Soviet–American relations once again.

Negotiations on reductions of conventional forces and armaments in Central Europe remain an important area. Here you and I have made serious steps toward accommodating the Western position in the name of achieving an agreement. And they have not even responded to our proposals so far.

[...]

And what should we do in terms of new initiatives in the sphere of disarmament?

It seems to me that there is no need to take some grand, universal steps. As I have already mentioned, we have introduced many good proposals, which together make up an almost comprehensive package. Still, of course it would make sense to make concrete proposals on separate issues.

Here is an issue, for example.

In 1976, our countries introduced a proposal that member-states of the European conference would undertake an obligation not to be the first to use nuclear weapons against each other. The NATO countries are moving away from that now. They claim that accepting our proposal would give an advantage to the members of the Warsaw Treaty, because we allegedly have a disproportionate advantage in the sphere of conventional weapons.

If that were the only problem, then we, of course, could propose to the NATO countries and to other participants of the European Conference that we conclude an agreement on no-first-use of nuclear as well as conventional weapons; in other words, a kind of non-aggression pact. As you know, some time ago, we already introduced a similar proposal. But in general, obviously, we should feel out the position of the Western powers on this entire issue further.

Here is one more problem. Politicians in West European countries have spoken often recently about the danger they see in the increases in reserves of intermediate-range nuclear missiles and other similar kinds of armaments in the European theater. In particular, FRG Chancellor [Helmut] Schmidt was telling me about that.

It is true, these kinds of nuclear missiles are not part of the Soviet–American negotiations on the limitation of strategic weapons, neither are they touched upon in the Vienna negotiations. They ended up being in the "in-between" zone, or as they say in the West, in the "gray zone."

In principle, we are not against their limitation by both countries, including of course analogous kinds of weapons in West European countries. I told Schmidt directly that there are no armaments about which we are not ready to negotiate—of course, on the principle of reciprocity, and not inflicting any damage to either side. However, it is clear that one can only consider this problem seriously together with the question of American bases in Europe, which are targeted at the socialist states.

[…]

[*Source: KC PZPR, XIB/127, AAN. Translated by Svetlana Savranskaya for the National Security Archive.*]

Document No. 85: Minutes of the Romanian Politburo Meeting, November 24, 1978

These Romanian Politburo minutes deal largely with a recent PCC meeting where the USSR had pressed for affirmation of the rights and prerogatives of the Warsaw Pact supreme commander in war time. In 1969, the alliance had approved a similar statute for peace time (Document No. 62b), but the war time equivalent had been postponed for several years because of ongoing objections by member-states.

As this record shows, the Romanians continued to oppose the idea. They argued that there was no trend toward war, as the Soviets were insisting, and demanded cuts in military spending instead. They specifically criticized "Soviet militarist circles" and objected to the member-states' obligation to bear the costs of Moscow's "adventurous" policy. Finally, Ceauşescu remarked that the difference between the two alliances' determination to pursue the current arms race was that "NATO's decision is public, and ours is secret." Romania's objections continued to delay final adoption of the statute until March 1980 (see Document No. 86).

An interesting fact that emerged from this episode was that the PCC by this time had evolved into a venue where military matters were increasingly being discussed— a different situation from the early 1970s when it was a forum mainly for political matters such as the CSCE.

Cde. Manea Mănescu: [...] I want to refer to the intervention—firm, principled, bearing special patriotic and revolutionary responsibility for the present and the future of our country, and, I would say, for the other socialist countries as well— which Cde. Nicolae Ceauşescu made at the Conference of the Political Consultative Committee of the Warsaw Treaty states regarding the Report on the military situation, and the decision related to this report.

[...] After Marshal [Viktor] Kulikov presented the report, Cde. Nicolae Ceauşescu took the floor and criticized the working procedures, and the technique of drawing up materials of special significance, which commit the states participating in the Warsaw Treaty on crucial issues of peace and war, the arms race, disarmament, and international détente.

Cde. Nicolae Ceauşescu pointed out from the very beginning that the report and the decision did not result in a comradely collaboration of the states participating in the Warsaw Treaty, and that a decision can only be made on the basis of common agreement, in accordance with the provisions of the acts and norms that guide the activity of the Political Consultative Committee. Cde. Nicolae Ceauşescu also pointed out that the estimates of the ratio of forces are made on the basis of erroneous, even false data, that issues are raised as if a world war were imminent, which is in total contradiction with the first document and the debates that took place on it.

In fact, Cde. Nicolae Ceauşescu drew very serious attention to the responsibility we have to analyze the present situation objectively, make correct political assessments, and not fall prey to militarism, which would bring about incalculable consequences for the future of mankind. (It would force the Warsaw Treaty states to make investments and incur exorbitant material and financial costs, which would constitute a heavy burden for the people, with negative consequences for economic and social development, and for the living standards of the people). On the contrary, as Cde. Nicolae Ceauşescu showed in his first exposé, our countries have to lead by example as far as measures for reducing military expenditures, independent of the measures the NATO countries take, since this would have a highly positive influence on the peoples' fight for peace and détente in the world.

Actually, the Report is an emanation of Soviet militarist circles, which are pursuing a policy of excessive armament by replacing current weapons, involving the Warsaw Treaty states in a dangerous arms race, and having them bear the costs arising from this adventurous way of acting. The Report included conclusions intended to justify the so-called necessity course; namely, in case of necessity, command of Warsaw Treaty troops should be transferred to the Soviet General Staff, with all the consequences deriving from this fact regarding the independence and sovereignty of our country and of other socialist countries participating in the Warsaw Treaty. This would give the Soviet Union the possibility to interfere in the internal affairs of our countries.

I must tell you that Cde. Nicolae Ceauşescu was listened to with a good deal of attention by all the participants in the conference. The other speakers who took the floor after Cde. Nicolae Ceauşescu only referred to the fact that the report and the decision had to be approved because Cde. Nicolae Ceauşescu's arguments were so strong that there was not even a slight attempt at formulating counter-arguments to what Cde. Nicolae Ceauşescu had shown when he raised the content of the report for discussion. [The report] was obviously subjective and created for the purpose of justifying the arms race, the so-called necessity of allocating high investments, convert the armaments in all sectors as soon as possible, and involving the economic potential of all the countries taking part in this arms race.

[...] It was clearly apparent that things had been agreed to in the sense that the report was [deemed] good and a decision had to be taken.

Cde. Nicolae Ceauşescu: In the decision it was stated that expenditures should be increased, and investments should be increased. It is not stated that measures are to be taken, only that expenditures should be increased substantially. And, in comparison with the current five-year period, to stipulate that the investments should be increased.

Cde. Paul Niculescu: And in the Declaration it is stated that we clearly declare ourselves against the armament policy. How can this be explained?

Cde. Leonte Răutu: It is a decision to stimulate the arms race, and to stimulate NATO to do the same thing.

Cde. Nicolae Ceauşescu: The difference lies in the fact that NATO's decision is public, and ours is secret.

Cde. Manea Mănescu: It is a bellicose decision.

Cde. Nicolae Ceaușescu: We said that we agreed to provide the measures to be taken; we did not reject any measures.

We said that we agreed that a Statute would be drawn up, but we were not in a position now to establish how this Statute would look based on what a general or a marshal said since we did not even discuss this issue.

[...]

Cde. Paul Niculescu: During the [Second] World War there was an anti-Hitlerite coalition also comprising capitalist states, but they did not choose this solution. The General Staffs of the respective states collaborated.

Cde. Leonte Răutu: Particularly since we are not now in war time.

Cde. Manea Mănescu: It is not possible for their General Staff to draw up such materials, and align all the others.

[...]

Cde. Ion Coman: I would like to show the Political Consultative Committee how these materials were brought to Bucharest. On Saturday, at 13:00, Marshal Kulikov called us up and told us he wanted to come to Bucharest with the report's theses and the decision. I told him to send us the materials in advance so that we could translate them with a view to discussing them. He said he would not send them but bring them with him. When he came with the materials, I told him at least to wait until we translated them but he did not agree this time either. This is the way the materials for the meeting of the general secretaries were prepared.

[...]

Cde. Nicolae Ceaușescu: Of course, it is clearly pointed out in the Treaty that the decisions are to be adopted by common agreement. In the Committee of the Ministers of Defense as well, decisions on recommendations and proposals concerning the main military issues are made by common agreement and afterwards are submitted to the governments and the Political Consultative Committee for consideration and approval. Consequently, even the proposals and recommendations of the Committee of the Ministers of Defense are subject to common agreement. They cannot be adopted on a majority basis.

[Source: Dos. 89/1978, f.2–6, 6–12, 14–25, ANIC. Translated by Viorel Nicolae Buta for the PHP.]

PART FOUR

The Incipient Decline

Document No. 86: Statute of the Unified Command in War Time, March 18, 1980

The statute of the Unified Command in war time finally won approval by the Warsaw Pact members after nearly a decade. In part, the delay grew out of its members' concerns that any steps that might be taken to prepare for war could become a self-fulfilling prophecy. By late 1978, however, the international situation had deteriorated, détente was foundering, and the West appeared to be taking a more aggressive stance, mainly through its conventional rearmament program. Even then, Romania continued to oppose the statute, and never actually signed it, the main objection being that it gave the supreme commander too much discretion over use of the resources of member-states. Interestingly, according to Polish General Antoni Jasiński, the statute was never really put into effect.[1] Obviously war never broke out, but there were also problems within the Soviet military command. Chief among them were ambiguities over divisions of responsibility and authority, particularly between the supreme commander (who of course was a Soviet officer), and the chief of the Soviet General Staff. Normally, the former would be subordinated to the latter. But Marshal Kulikov and Marshal Ogarkov were not on good terms, and many details of how to function in an emergency remained unresolved. Thus, while the supreme commander may have enjoyed enormous authority with respect to Eastern Europe, in Moscow he was a secondary figure.

[...]

GENERAL RULES

Theater of Operations

[...]

3. The present Statute defines the composition, the purpose and rules of functioning of the UAF and their administrative bodies (the Highest Supreme Command, the UAF Supreme Commands in the Western and Southwestern theaters of war and the Commands of the Unified Baltic Fleet and the Unified Black Sea Fleet), the rules of commanding air defense, the organization of political work, logistics and engineering–technical supply for the UAF in the theater of war, mutual relations between administrative bodies of the UAF and the national military–political leadership of the Warsaw Pact member-states, and also the provision of financial means.

[...]

---

[1] See the section "The Chain of Command: The Soviet General Staff and the Warsaw Pact" in the collection of interviews with Polish generals on the PHP website, http://www.isn.ethz.ch/php/-documents/collection_9/texts/Chain_Command.htm.

1. The Unified Armed Forces of the Warsaw
Pact Member-States.

[...]

6. *Strategic groups* are comprised of land forces, naval forces, administrative bodies, and a support group dispatched to the Unified Armed Forces of the Warsaw Pact member-states subordinated to the Supreme Commands of the UAF in the Western and Southwestern theaters or subordinated directly to the Highest Command.

[...]

All remaining military formations, training centers, administrative bodies, and rear areas remain under the supervision of the national military–political leadership and are used in accordance with their plans. Based on mutual agreement between the national military–political leadership and the Highest Supreme Command, if necessary, the force and means of these military formations, administrative bodies, and rear area forces may be used in the interests of and in accordance with the plans of the Highest Supreme Command and Supreme Command of the UAF in the theater of war.

7. The composition of the UAF during peace time is defined by special protocols in accordance with general military–political goals which are strategically selected by the military–political leaderships of the Warsaw Pact member-states. The protocols are usually prepared for a period of five years and are signed by the UAF supreme commander of the Warsaw Pact member-states and the defense ministers of all states, and are approved accordingly by the governments of the Warsaw Pact member-states. Depending on the military–political situation, the combatant composition and the number of forces and fleets dispatched to the UAF may be specified and changed: during peace time by the national state leaderships at the suggestion of the UAF supreme commander of the Warsaw Pact member-states, and during a war period by the Highest Supreme Command of the UAF and Supreme Commands in the theater of war in consultation with the national military–political leadership.

8. Depending on the situation, when member-states of the Warsaw Pact consider it necessary, the Unified Armed Forces respond to orders of the Highest Supreme Command [e.g.] in case of an unexpected armed attack by an aggressor on one or more member-states of the Warsaw Pact. At the same time, the UAF Supreme Command in the Western and Southwestern theaters and the Commands of the Unified Baltic and Unified Black Sea War Fleets will be activated.

9. The Unified Armed Forces move from peace to war status by decision of the Warsaw Pact member-states in accordance with the guidelines of the Highest Supreme Command, and if it has not yet become binding, in accordance with the guidelines of the UAF supreme commander of the Warsaw Pact member-states.

In case of unexpected aggression against one or more member-states of the Warsaw Pact the armed forces and the fleet will be moved to war status by the national military–political leadership which will at the same time immediately inform the Highest Supreme Command or the UAF supreme commander of the Warsaw Pact member-states (the UAF Supreme Commands in the theater of war) and also the national military–political leadership of the Warsaw Pact member-states about that move.

II. The Highest Supreme Command of the Unified Armed Forces of the Warsaw Pact Member-States.

10. The only Highest Supreme Command is appointed in order to centrally command the Unified Armed Forces of the Warsaw Pact member-states during the war period. The highest supreme commander of the Unified Armed Forces is appointed and the composition of the Highest Supreme Command is determined by the decision of the Warsaw Pact member-states. The General Staff of the USSR Armed Forces is the administrative body of the Unified Armed Forces Highest Supreme Command.

11. The Highest Supreme Command administers war activity through the unified national bodies administering armed forces and fleet forces. [...]

III. The Supreme Commands of the Unified Armed Forces in the Western and Southwestern Theaters of War Activity.

12. The Supreme Commands of the UAF in the Western and Southwestern theaters administer the strategic groups of armed forces and fleets in theater activity and are directly subordinated to the Highest Supreme Command of the Unified Armed Forces of the Warsaw Pact member-states.

They participate in operational and strategic planning; organize operational cooperation between army groups, fleets and operational units of the UAF armed forces in the theater of war as well as the utilization of the Highest Supreme Command's reserves, which are dispatched at their disposal; and command coalition groups of armed forces and fleets at appropriate theaters. Together with the national military–political leadership of the allied states they undertake actions to strengthen the combat ability of armed forces and fleets and to provide their universal supply.

13. The Supreme Command of the UAF in the Western (Southwestern) theaters comprises the following:
- the UAF supreme commander in the theater;
- the UAF chief of staff in the theater—the first deputy of the supreme commander;
- the chief of the UAF Political Administration in the theater;
- deputies of the UAF supreme commander in the theater of each allied state whose armed forces and fleet forces are part of the UAF in the theater;
- deputies of the UAF supreme commander in the theater for matters concerning the type of armed forces, rear areas, and armaments;
- commanders (chiefs) of armed forces type and other official persona.
[...]

14. The War Council of the Unified Armed Forces in the theater is established beside the UAF supreme commander in the Western (Southwestern) theaters.

The War Council comprises the following: the UAF supreme commander in the theater—the chairman of the War Council, the UAF chief of staff in the theater of war—first deputy of the supreme commander, the chief of the Political Administration, deputies of the UAF supreme commander in the theater of each allied army. [...]

The War Council deals with problems of the state and actions of the armed forces and fleet forces which are part of the UAF in the theater.

The decisions of the War Council are introduced by orders and directives of the UAF supreme commander in the theater.

15. The UAF supreme commander in the Western (Southwestern) theaters is subordinated to the highest supreme commander and is endowed with full powers in the administration of actions of army groups (from specific forces) subordinated to it, Air Defense formations, Air Forces, forces of the Unified fleets and other formations in the theater. It can directly turn to the military–political leaderships of allied states in all matters relating to the UAF in the theater.

16. The UAF chief of staff in the theater—the first deputy of the supreme commander directs the work of the Staff and coordinates the work of all administrative bodies of the UAF Supreme Command in the theater.

[...]

17. The chief of staff of the Unified Armed Forces in the Western (Southwestern) theaters is the main administrative body of the UAF supreme commander in the theater.

The UAF Staff in the theater controls the movement of armed forces and fleets dispatched to the UAF in the theater from peace to war status, and commands them during operational development.

[...]

18. The deputies of the UAF supreme commander from allied states participate in working out a proposal for the armed utilization of national formations, planning their war activity, organizing cooperation among coalition groups, and exercising control over the execution of tasks given to them.

[...]

[...]
IV. The Unified War Fleets.

29. The Unified Baltic Fleet comprises of the following: the USSR Baltic Fleet, the People's Navy of the German Democratic Republic, and the Navy of the Polish People's Republic.

The Unified Black Sea Fleet comprises of the following: the USSR Black Sea Fleet, the Bulgarian People's Republic Navy, and the Romanian Socialist Republic Navy.

30. The commander of the Unified Baltic Fleet is the commander of the Baltic Fleet of the USSR; and the commander of the Unified Black Sea Fleet is the commander of the Black Sea Fleet of the USSR.

[...]

[...]
V. The Principles of Air Defense.

36. The UAF supreme commander in the theater commands the air defense forces in the theater and organizes cooperation through his deputy for matters concerning the air defense.

The coordination of combat activities of all forces and means of air defense deployed in the Western and Southwestern theaters lies in the hands of the Highest Supreme

Command which does it through the commander of the air defense forces of the Warsaw Pact member-states.

[...]

VI. The Principles of Commanding the Unified Armed
Forces in the Theater of War.

38. The development of the administrative bodies and communications systems of the UAF Supreme Commands in the Western and Southwestern theaters and their position on the prepared commanding points are carried out based on special ordinance (guidelines) of the Highest Supreme Command, which is supported by plans prepared during peace time by the Staff of the Unified Armed Forces, and are consulted on with the national military leaderships of appropriate member-states of the Warsaw Pact.

[...]

41. The armed forces and fleets which are part of the UAF in the theater of war receive their tasks through operational directives and orders given by the Highest Supreme Command, the UAF Supreme Commands in the theater and the commands of appointed War Fleets.

[...]

42. When the Unified Armed Forces move to war status the representatives of the UAF supreme commander of the Warsaw Pact member-states from allied armies, which are in peace [status], become the representatives of the Supreme Command in the theater beside the national military–political leadership, and beside the remaining cells are the relevant representatives of the administrative bodies.

In order to secure cooperation and to raise efficiency in the command of the armed forces and fleets, the UAF Supreme Commands in the theater and the Commands of the Unified War Fleet direct operational groups to the remaining allied armies and fleets. Their number, composition, work and selection method during peace time is defined by the UAF Staff of the Warsaw Pact member-states. The dispatch of assault groups occurs according to the guidelines of the UAF Supreme Commands in the theater.

VII. The Basics of the Organization of Political Work.

43. The Central Committees of communist and workers parties from allied states direct the party-political work in the national operational and tactical formations and units dispatched to the Armed Forces of the Warsaw Pact member-states through appropriate political bodies from their armies.

[...]

VIII. The Principles of Securing the Rear.

47. Securing the rear of the national operational formations that are part of the UAF in the theater is organized based on directives from the Highest Supreme Command and decisions of the UAF supreme commander in the theater.

It is accomplished with the forces and means of the rear of the national operational formations and the rear from the center of the Warsaw Pact member-states Armed Forces. It also comes at the cost of forces and means dispatched on direct orders of the UAF supreme commander in the theater of war and strategic reserves of forces and means of the rear established during peace-time and developed by the Highest Supreme Command at the beginning of war activity.

[...]

IX. The Principles of Special-Technical Security·

52. Special-technical security of the UAF in the theater is organized based on directives from the Highest Command and on decisions of the UAF supreme commander in the theater, and utilizes (in an agreed scope) the national resources of each Warsaw Pact member-state army of a specified type.

53. Keeping armaments, technical means and ammunition in a state of readiness for use on the battlefield; and the evacuation, repair and restoration of damaged and inoperative armaments and technical means are carried out with the forces and repair-evacuation means of national armed forces.

Assigned bodies from the national military–political leadership of the Warsaw Pact member-states are responsible for securing armaments, means of war technology, ammunition, spare parts and military technical equipment.

54. Reserves of armaments, technical means, ammunition, spare parts and military technical equipment are accumulated during peace time appropriate to the operational objectives of the national operational and tactical unions.

Additional forces and means of special-technical security for allied armed forces sent to regions of anticipated operational development on the territory of a specific country, and also the utilization of material resources and potential of national industry to repair armaments, technical means and ammunition of all kinds are defined based on mutual agreement between the UAF Supreme Commands in the theater and national military–political leaderships of relevant member-states of the Warsaw Pact.

55. When necessary, special-technical security for the armed forces which are a part of the operational formations of different nations may be implemented by forces and means of the operational formations of which they are a part. In such cases, national forces and repair-evacuation means, indispensable ammunition and military technical equipment reserves are put at the disposal of that formation. Restoration of supplies used by these armed forces is carried out at the cost of this country's own resources.

56. The UAF supreme commander in the theater (after consulting with the national military–political leadership and keeping in mind the situation) can conduct maneuvers with the forces and means of special-technical supply and with ammunition reserves between national operational (tactical) formations, and also reach out to local reserves and national industrial plants to perform repairs and restoration of armaments and technical means.

X. Mutual Relations between the UAF Commands in the Theater and the National Military–Political Leaderships of Warsaw Pact Member-States.

57. The UAF Supreme Commands in the Western and Southwestern theaters and national military–political leaderships of relevant allied states are guided by the decisions of the Warsaw Pact member-states and directives and guidelines of the Highest Supreme Command in the battle field.

Close cooperation, which is still strengthening, exists between the UAF Supreme Commands in the theater and the national military–political leaderships.

58. When the UAF Supreme Commands in the Western and Southwestern theaters take charge of the armed forces and Unified War Fleet, the orders, directives and ordinances delivered to them become binding for all groupings, units, troop formations (ships), formations, commanding bodies administrative bodies and administrative organs in the rear that have been assigned by the allied armies to the UAF in the theater.

59. The national military–political leadership of each member-state of the Warsaw Pact ensures the full and timely execution of the Supreme Command's decisions, and a high level of combat readiness on the part of the armed forces and fleets dispatched to the UAF in the theater, together with the national reserves; it maintains an established level of personnel, armaments, technical equipment, and all kinds of material and technical means. [It also] carries out the supply of reserves, and the completion and restoration of the combat capability of national operational and tactical formations, and units (warships) that are part of the UAF in the theater. It engages in activities to raise the moral–political condition of the personnel of the national armed forces and fleets and to mobilize them to perform combat tasks assigned to them; it ensures the introduction and operational development of operational and tactical formations of allied armies on the territory of one's own country (in the air and on water).

60. The commanders of national operational units (groupings and troop formations) dispatched to the Unified Armed Forces of the Warsaw Pact member-states and directed to the disposal of the Highest Supreme Command and the UAF Supreme Commands in the theater bear full responsibility for maintaining an established level of combat readiness by the armed forces subordinated to them, and for the completion of tasks given to them. [They] plan and organize their combat activity, and command subordinate operational and tactical formations, and units (battleships).

61. The national military–political leadership of the Warsaw Pact member-states appoints generals, admirals, and officers to positions in administrative bodies of the UAF Supreme Commands in the theater according to their organizational structure and posts.

During war, the national military–political leadership (after consultations with the UAF Supreme Commands in relevant theaters) appoints and deploys the commanders of the national operational formations and their deputies, and also determines the commanders' staff in administrative bodies of the UAF Supreme Commands in the theater.

All remaining cadre problems in the allied armed forces that are part of the UAF in the theater remain within the competence of national commanders.

62. Jurisdiction over the UAF military cadre is defined based on agreements between member-states of the Warsaw Pact.

XI. Financial Arrangements.

[...]

64. The percentage of input into the budget of the Supreme Commands in the Western and Southwestern theaters is defined in compliance with the decisions of the Warsaw Pact member-states (on percentage of inputs to the Unified Command budget) made at the Political Consultative Committee meeting on March 17, 1969. It is as follows:

- in the Western theater: GDR—16.2 percent, PPR—23.1 percent, USSR—44.5 percent, ČSR—16.2 percent;
- in the Southwestern theater: BPR—16.9 percent, HPR—14.3 percent, RSR—24.1 percent, USSR—44.5 percent.

[*Source: AZN 32854, BA-MA. Translated by Magdalena Klotzbach for the National Security Archive.*]

Document No. 87: Ceauşescu's Speech at the Political Consultative Committee Meeting in Warsaw, May 14–15, 1980

At this meeting of the PCC, Romania found a great many things to disparage, including its handling of the MBFR[2] and its criticisms of China, West Germany and the Camp David accords.[3] Ceauşescu proposes to proceed toward dissolving both the Warsaw Pact and NATO, and meanwhile requiring unilateral cuts in military spending of 10–15 percent by 1985, as well as a reduction in conventional forces and abolition of foreign bases on the territories of Warsaw Pact member-states. He also asserts that it was not necessary for the Soviet Union to send troops to Afghanistan and that Romania would be willing to assist in a political solution that would lead to the withdrawal of Soviet forces and, in his view, add to Soviet prestige. For the sake of the appearance of unity, the Soviet Union decided not to publicize these disagreements or to push through any documents Romania did not want to sign.

N. *Ceauşescu* (Romanian Socialist Republic):

Dear Comrades!

[...]

International events have demonstrated and continue to demonstrate with force that the existence of military blocs is a source of perpetuating tensions, and therefore, more than before, it is necessary to confirm again decisively the position of the socialist countries that have signed the founding act of the Warsaw Treaty concerning the simultaneous dissolution of the NATO and Warsaw Pact blocs. In order to achieve this goal, we consider it necessary to move toward decreasing the military character of these blocs, creating suitable conditions for their simultaneous dissolution and realizing European security on a new basis—full equality, and respect for the independence and sovereignty of all states.

[...]

This meeting of member-states of the Warsaw Pact is taking place under particularly complicated international conditions, when tensions are deepening and the imperialist policy of force and dictation, and of consolidation or spheres of influence is becoming strongly apparent. Tendencies toward a return to the "cold war" are deepening, and a serious threat hangs over détente, cooperation, and peace around the world.

[...]

The serious exacerbation of the international situation is a direct result of the accumulation of complex issues that were not resolved at the right time, and of the appear

---

[2] Mutual and Balanced Force Reduction talks about NATO and Warsaw Pact conventional forces in Europe.

[3] The September 17, 1978, Egyptian–Israeli agreement that led to Israeli withdrawal from the Sinai Peninsula and a peace treaty between the two countries.

ance of new conflicts and areas of tension. One can say that a basic factor in the exacerbation of tensions and the increased threat of war is the unceasing growth of the arms race and the huge rise in military spending. It must be stated candidly that armaments have reached such a level that they have ceased to serve the defense of security but are becoming ever more a factor for destabilization and danger, placing peace and the lives of the people, and the very gains of human civilization, under threat.

The world economic crisis is also furthering the complication of the international situation. [...]

At the same time, the deepening rift between wealthy and poor countries as a result of the policies of the imperialist and colonial states, and the struggle for a new international economic order constitute another serious issue in contemporary international life.

[...]

There is no doubt that the imperialist countries bear a major responsibility for the situation that has developed; however, our countries cannot be content with that statement.

[...]

In fact, Europe continues to play, one may say, a determining role in the development of current international conditions, if one considers that the most powerful military forces, and armaments of all kinds, including nuclear, are concentrated on this continent. The military blocs of NATO and the Warsaw Pact face off against each other in Europe. Speaking in seismological terms, one may say that such destructive forces have piled up in Europe that the epicenter of a future world war, placing all of civilization under threat, is located here. That is why the realization of European security, the development of cooperation among all the states on the continent—on the basis of full equality, respect for independence and national sovereignty, non-interference in internal affairs, and rejection of the use or threat of force—are decisive factors for the peace of nations, for security and détente throughout the world.

We must openly state that after the Conference on Security and Cooperation in Europe, a historic moment in the life of the continent, too little was done to implement the Helsinki Final Act. As a matter of fact, nothing was done to move toward measures to reduce military opposition and disarmament. [...]

[...] It is necessary to do everything to prevent the deployment of new kinds of missiles or, at least, to delay those decisions in order to move towards negotiations aimed at an agreement to eliminate intermediate-range missiles from Europe. In this regard, we propose that the Warsaw Pact member-states put together a concrete proposal concerning initiating negotiations as soon as possible. We should not wait for the deployment of missiles; we should not wait for them to be used.

[...]

Freezing military budgets at 1980 levels would also have special significance, followed by gradual decreases in military spending of at least 10–15 percent by 1985.

At the same time, we consider that reaching agreement on limiting the numbers of foreign troops on the territory of other European states, as well as setting a time limit for their complete withdrawal, would have an entirely positive effect.

436

It is also necessary to act with all firmness to liquidate military bases, to establish nuclear-free zones in Europe, and to create conditions for the simultaneous dissolution of military blocs. [...]

The socialist countries bear major responsibility before their own people, before the European people, and before all the peoples of the world for putting forward decisive, concrete measures aimed at implementing a policy of détente, of independence, and of disarmament and peace both in Europe and on a global scale.

[...]

Speaking out in favor of European security, the implementation of disarmament and the establishment of a new international economic order, we must also keep in mind that a range of difficult issues exists in the world, which contribute to the further complication of international political life.

[...]

Among these issues is the question of Afghanistan.

I want to declare at this conference that the Romanian communist party and the Romanian Socialist Republic support in every way the struggle of progressive forces in Afghanistan for the liquidation of feudal backwardness, and for a revolutionary democratic transformation; and we are ready to extend broad cooperation to the progressive forces of Afghanistan. We well understand that the realization of such transformations meets with opposition from internal reactionary forces and that these forces receive support from the side of reaction outside [Afghanistan]. We believe that before the revolutionary and progressive forces of Afghanistan stand the tasks of delivering a decisive blow to the reactionary forces, securing the triumph of the democratic revolution, and creating conditions for the transition to building a socialist society.

Proceeding from this, I again want to confirm the opinion of our party, according to which it was not necessary to send Soviet forces into Afghanistan, and that it was necessary to find other forms of support for the revolutionary forces of Afghanistan. It is well known that this has created a highly complicated situation in the world, and has given the United States and other reactionary circles powerful grounds for strengthening the campaign against the Soviet Union, other socialist countries, socialism in general, and the international communist and workers' movement. We are by no means indifferent to the anti-Soviet campaign currently being carried out, or to the fact that in a number of international forums, beginning with the United Nations, the socialist countries have found themselves more than once in isolation. Therefore, we believe that we should move with full determination toward a political resolution in Afghanistan capable of bringing to a halt all outside support to the reactionary, antigovernment forces, and at the same time bringing about the withdrawal of Soviet military units.

[...]

[*Source: KC PZPR, XIA/590, k. 171–291, Archiwum Akt Nowych. Translated by Malcolm Byrne for the National Security Archive.*]

Document No. 88: Summary of the Deputy Foreign Ministers' Preparatory Meeting for the CSCE Madrid Conference, July 8–9, 1980

The purpose of this meeting of Warsaw Pact deputy foreign ministers, held at Soviet initiative, was to prepare a joint strategy for a CSCE follow-up session in Madrid. That session would begin in 1980 and drag on for over three years. The Soviets' basic goal in Madrid was to weaken NATO politically and undermine support in Western Europe for the Atlantic alliance's military reorganization program. Within the Eastern bloc, this strategy was known as military détente. Moscow was most interested in emphasizing Basket I issues, namely, the basic political–military aspects of East–West relations, and shifting attention away from Basket III, with its human rights content, which was a particularly sensitive issue in the wake of the Soviet intervention in Afghanistan. This and similar documents show that much of the detail work in hammering out strategies within the Warsaw Pact took place at the level of deputy ministers.

On July 8–9 a consultation of the deputy ministers of foreign affairs of the Warsaw Pact member-states took place in Prague. The purpose of this consultative session, called at the May Political Consultative Committee meeting, was to exchange views and experiences concerning the preparations made to date for the Madrid meeting and to get clarification on the main directions of the next coordinated advance. [...]

All the participants [...] agreed on the character of the intentions of the capitalist states who are preparing to level sharp criticism of the socialist states at the Madrid meeting, in particular of the Soviet Union, based on the provision of international aid to Afghanistan and on the alleged failure to satisfy the Final Act especially in the area of human rights and freedoms. The United States will go farthest in this sort of confrontation while other West European countries with the possible exception of Great Britain and the Netherlands will be interested in not having the confrontation exceed the threshold, which would endanger the essence of détente—in which they are to some extent interested. The participants in the consultation agreed that it is necessary to exploit the non-integrated Western stand on the Madrid meeting and, in this regard, to pay primary attention to the neutral and non-aligned countries, but also to some NATO countries as well as France.

The head of the Soviet delegation, Cde. A. Kovalev, emphasized in his speech that in a situation where the United States and several other countries such as Great Britain were prepared to give the meeting a confrontational character, it would be important, as suggested in Cde. L. I. Brezhnev's proposal at the Political Consultative Committee, to concentrate, in the course of the meeting, on one or two of the most topical items in every part of the Final Act that serve our interests and can become of interest to other countries as well. [...] Among these matters are:

In the first basket

1. Convening a conference on military détente and disarmament in Europe as the Warsaw declaration of the Warsaw Pact Political Consultative Committee[4] session suggests. This question will be a priority for the Warsaw Pact member-states. Unlike the enemies of détente such as the United States, which are against convening such a conference, the Warsaw Pact member-states must endeavor to determine not too narrow a mandate, but a broad and flexible one that would create a wide space for assessing all the proposals submitted (by France, Finland and Sweden, e.g.) concerning confidence and security-building measures and disarmament initiatives, and would not set any preliminary conditions that could *a priori* influence the course and final result of the conference. [...]

If the Western position on this question is positive, the Soviet Union will have no objections to including several confidence-building measures in the final document of the Madrid meeting. [...]

2. Recommending that the principles governing relations between states, included in the first part of the Final Act, be embedded by the signatory states in the legislative (constitutional) provisions that conform to the procedural norms of each of the states. [...]

Concerning the standpoint of the Romanian Socialist Republic its representative repeated familiar views and proposals. However, he did not aggravate the negotiation. [...]

In the second basket

The Soviet Union will not be able to overlook the severe violation of the Final Act in this area by the United States, especially its introduction of new discriminatory measures. However, it is ready to consider matters concerning:

1. Convening an all-European conference on power engineering;

2. Building up the role of the U.N. Economic Commission for Europe and forming a Center for Industrial Cooperation within its framework;

3. Joint representation of foreign companies that would make possible broader participation by small and medium-size companies;

4. Convening a second Scientific Forum[5];

5. Foreign migratory workers, of particular interest to the Mediterranean countries.

Beyond these initiatives, the Bulgarian People's Republic delegation intends to submit a proposal on water resources management. The German Democratic Republic delegation is paying attention to the subject of abandoning attempts to misuse economic relations for political pressure. [...] The Romanian Socialist Republic delegation is the only one that has also mentioned the matter of making forms of cooperation between European and developing countries more effective and of supporting the creation of a new international order.

---

[4] http://www.isn.ethz.ch/php/documents/collection_3/PCC_docs/1980/1980_11_I.pdf. See also Document No. 87.

[5] To follow the first forum, which had met from February 18 to March 3, 1980, in Hamburg.

In the third basket

Taking into account the principle of non-interference in internal affairs and of sovereign equality, and in line with the rule according to which the development of cooperation in the area of culture is possible assuming the growth of mutual confidence and other improvements in relations between participating states, the Soviet Union is ready to assess matters concerning:

1. Measures guaranteeing the security of citizens on foreign territory including persons traveling on business;

2. The facilitation of family reunions and marriages betwen citizens of different states;

3. Acceleration of the granting of visas, for example to businessmen; [...]

6. Cultural exchanges and widening cooperation between press agencies, radio, television and motion picture [activities];

In the third basket, the Romanian Socialist Republic intends to recommend convening an experts' meeting to elaborate rules of conduct for foreign journalists. It recommends convening a Forum for Art and Culture. The proposal for holding an all-European meeting on cultural affairs is also being considered by the German Democratic Republic, and the Bulgarian People's Republic is working on a proposal to realize an all-European youth rally. [...]

As far as procedural matters are concerned, the head of the Soviet delegation pointed out that it is necessary to pay substantial attention to them and prevent a repeat of the negative experience from Belgrade. When negotiating conditions, it will be necessary to abide by the letter and spirit of the Final Act rigorously, and not to allow its disparagement. It is essential not to let matters come to the so-called "accounting," where advantage is taken of the meeting for propaganda purposes hostile to our countries.[6] [...]

The German Democratic Republic delegation recommended that the socialist states put forward their proposals as early as the beginning of the meeting to make the Western states discuss them and to prevent Western attempts to divide the meeting into two phases where the first one is mainly misused for the purpose of attacking the Soviet Union and other socialist countries. [...]

The head of the Polish People's Republic delegation spoke against excessive institutionalizing and automation of meetings, referring to the aspiration of some Western countries, especially the United States, to misuse them for propaganda purposes and for confrontation.

[*Source: 8736/24, AÚV KSČ, SÚA. Translated by Karel Sieber.*]

---

[6] The reference is to the review of implementation that Western representatives insisted should precede the discussion at CSCE follow-up meetings.

Document No. 89: Bulgarian Report on the Defense Ministers' Meeting in Bucharest, December 8, 1980

Bulgarian Gen. Dobri Dzhurov's report, not terribly informative on its face, is interesting precisely for that reason—because of what it reveals about Warsaw Pact thinking about the Polish crisis at this time. At bottom, even during this critical period, the alliance was still undecided about what to do. According to the CIA informant, Polish Col. Ryszard Kukliński, Soviet-led forces were finally supposed to intervene against Solidarity on December 8, the day this report was written. But the Warsaw Pact summit of December 5 ended with the decision not to take military action for the time being. In fact, an exercise began near the Polish borders at about this time, but it was abruptly terminated on December 9, even though the plans continued in effect and the assembled units remained in a state of readiness. Tellingly, the Polish military representatives at the Bucharest meeting supported the eventual use of force—but for simple reasons of personal survival.

During my visit to Bucharest I had meetings and talks with a number of Soviet and Polish comrades on the situation in the Polish People's Republic. Their views and assessments tend to be the following:

1. There are two sources of power in the Polish People's Republic. The "Solidarity" trade unions are winning more and more recognition as a dominant power in the country. The party and the state leadership, and partially the government, in spite of the fact that they have the armed forces and the security authorities under their control, lack the courage to take the necessary measures to win recognition as the only legal power in the country.

2. It is considered that due to weak agitation and propaganda almost nothing has been achieved to accomplish the main task that was assigned at the Sixth Plenum of the Central Committee of the Polish United Workers Party—strengthening of the party ranks. The party is not being led by the necessary class positions.

3. The second task set by the Plenum—to put up resistance against the anti-socialist elements—was not present in the activities of the party and the state either, which has resulted in a strengthening of the counterrevolutionary forces, whereas the government and the party have become weaker.

4. The comrades from the Polish Armed Forces think that "there is no way to retreat, the gallows are behind [us]." They can see two ways to overcome the crisis—a political solution, which was accepted as the general line at the Sixth Plenum, and the use of force. The first one has practically failed, therefore the second one remains.

5. Regarding the work during the Seventh Plenum of the Polish United Workers Party (based on incomplete information) the following conclusions could be drawn:

Kania's[7] report is not critical enough; it lacks a class approach to what is happening in the country.

Comments at the Plenum, which numbered over 40, were aimed at the mistakes made by individual party leaders, without bringing up for discussion the general issue—what should be done to resist the counterrevolutionary forces and take the country out of the difficult crisis.

Organizational changes, whose result was to remove some leaders from the Politburo and the Central Committee, aim at ensuring the integrity of the Politburo of the Polish United Workers Party.

[*Source: 35/606-80, TsDA, Sofia. Translated by Greta Keremidchieva.*]

---

[7] Polish party General Secretary Stanisław Kania.

Document No. 90: The Soviet Military's Attempts to Gain Polish Leadership Cooperation to End the Polish Crisis, January–April 1981

The first document below is a letter from East German Defense Minister Heinz Hoffmann to SED leader Erich Honecker reporting on a telephone conversation Hoffmann had with Warsaw Pact Supreme Commander Viktor Kulikov. During that conversation, Kulikov described the Soviet military's position on Poland at the time. Moscow was still interested in staging maneuvers on Polish territory to get rid of Solidarity but wanted to do so by involving rather than ignoring the Polish army. Kulikov had therefore been trying to persuade Kania and Jaruzelski to hold joint exercises, and to include East German participation, but the Poles were evasive and held out instead for command post exercises of military staffs that would not involve large numbers of troops or fleets. Kania's evasiveness would cost him his post later in the year.

The second document is an East German report about a Warsaw Pact Military Council meeting in Sofia at which Marshal Viktor Kulikov related his ongoing efforts to work with the Polish leadership to stamp out the Solidarity opposition. A month after the Bydgoszcz crisis[8], the public outcry caused by that event still has the Polish party and military on the defensive. Kania and Jaruzelski in particular, Kulikov reports, are hesitant to act assertively. Instead they have asked that the Warsaw Pact set up a special command center at the Soviet base at Legnica. Their plan is to raise the threat of a possibly imminent Soviet-led intervention and thereby strengthen their hand with Solidarity. After the Sofia meeting, according to Ryszard Kukliński, hard-line Polish General Eugeniusz Molczyk, who may have been conspiring with the Soviets, remarked to the party leadership in Warsaw that if socialism were to be defeated in Poland steps might have to be taken to keep the country in the Warsaw Pact.[9] This may have been a deliberate signal from the Soviets, and therefore part of a new Soviet strategy to prod the Poles into action by making them believe there was a danger of intervention when in reality the Politburo had already secretly ruled it out. Certainly by May, if not April, this was the case.

---

[8] On March 19, 1981, communist thugs beat up Solidarity activists with police support in Bydgoszcz.

[9] "Col. Ryszard Kukliński's Interview, Washington, October 28, 1997," material prepared for the conference, "Poland 1980–1982: Internal Crisis, International Dimensions," Jachranka–Warsaw, November 8–10, 1997.

a) Letter from East German Defense Minister Heinz Hoffmann
   to Erich Honecker regarding Conversation
   with Marshal Kulikov, January 19, 1981

[...]

On January 19, 1981, the supreme commander of the Unified Armed Forces of the Warsaw Pact, Marshal [Viktor] Kulikov, called me and informed me of the following:

The previous week, Marshal Kulikov was in the People's Republic of Poland to carry out final negotiations on the development of the Polish army from1981–1985, and to sign the protocol.

The negotiations and the signing were carried out with much resistance.

[...]

The meeting with First Secretary of the Central Committee of the Polish Workers' Party Comrade [Stanisław] Kania illustrated that there were still significant difficulties in the People's Republic of Poland in all areas. As before, the Polish comrades are not prepared to take energetic steps against the counterrevolutionary powers. They show significant restraint and want to solve the problems through long-term measures without the use of force.

The Soviet leadership sees the situation in the People's Republic of Poland as very serious.

The trade union "Solidarity" is continually gaining influence in the factories and among the working class and is supported by the Catholic Church.

The Polish party leadership saw itself as unable to prevent [Solidarity leader Lech] Wałęsa's trip to Rome to see the Pope.

During his stay in the People's Republic of Poland, Marshal Kulikov also visited two divisions of the Polish army both in the garrison and during tactical exercises.

All in all, the impression was a positive one. The division commander and other leadership cadres made a good impression on him. Because of the short period of time, the soldiers' mood could not be assessed.

The idea of restraint in the deployment of state organs of power was noticeable everywhere at the officer level.

Comrade Kulikov once again sought to clarify conclusively the problems of a joint exercise. Only after many discussions was he able to get the agreement of First Secretary of the Central Committee of the Polish Workers' Party Comrade Kania. He declared himself prepared "to allow for a joint exercise at the given time with the participation of the National Peoples Army of the GDR."

At the same time, it was agreed that the joint command staff exercise under the leadership of the supreme commander of the Unified Forces should be carried out with staffs and active troops.

While the Polish comrades focus on the joint exercise as a theoretical exercise, the Soviet comrades' view is, as always, to link this exercise with practical elements.

Marshal Kulikov also sought agreement on the inclusion of the three Baltic fleets in this joint exercise. The Polish side has not yet agreed to this suggestion.

All problems related to the joint exercise are currently being worked out in Moscow.

After the conclusion of the preparations, all the exercise materials are being presented for approval to the GDR minister of defense. A particular time for the exercise could not yet be determined. ·

[*Source: AZN, 32642, 7–9, BA-MA. Translated by Catherine Nielsen and Karen Riechert.*]

b) East German Report of the Military
Council Meeting in Sofia, April 24, 1981

Before his departure from Sofia, Marshal Kulikov informed Comrade General [Fritz] Streletz in a private conversation that Comrades Kania and [Wojciech] Jaruzelski had approached the Soviet side with a request to again station and activate a collective leadership organ of the Unified Armed Forces on Polish territory, at Legnica.

It would help the Polish party and leadership with their work if it became known that the Soviet Army, the National People's Army of the GDR and the Czechoslovak army continued to be present on Polish territory.

Marshal Kulikov told Jaruzelski that the Soviet side would agree on condition that this leadership organ took part in the exercises and other training activities of the Polish army. This would require that the Polish troops would not simply remain in their barracks or be deployed for agricultural work, but rather would increasingly take part in exercises and extended deployments together with representatives of the three fraternal armies. These measures must also be properly publicized in the Polish press, radio and television.

The Polish comrades agreed to these suggestions.

[…]

[*Source: AZN, 32641, BA-MA. Translated by Catherine Nielsen and Karen Riechert.*]

Document No. 91: Report on Conversation between Marshal Kulikov and Senior East German Military Officials, June 13, 1981

In this colorful account of a conversation between Soviet Marshal Viktor Kulikov and East German generals in Dresden, Kulikov reveals a great deal about both Soviet military strategy and thinking toward Poland, and quite a bit about his own personal views as well. His reference to a Soviet operational group working at the base at Legnica is significant because by the following month there is evidence that it had been withdrawn, which indicates the timing of the Kremlin's decision to give up on a military solution, at least for the foreseeable future. On the personal side, Kulikov sprinkles his remarks with disparaging comments about Poland. He tells his audience how happy he is to see the orderly landscape of the GDR after the chaos in Poland, and alludes to the "Polish disease" of Catholicism and to the "misery" of Polish nationalism and argumentativeness.

[…]

At the beginning of his remarks, Marshal of the Soviet Union [Viktor] Kulikov explained why this meeting was taking place in the guest house of the 1st guard tank army in Dresden.

There are two reasons for it:

1. Since all his activities are being tracked by the Polish comrades, he wanted to avoid having this meeting with representatives of the National People's Army of the GDR and of the Czechoslovak People's Army become public.

2. He intentionally drove by car from Legnica to Dresden to break free from the Polish atmosphere and to see once again properly cultivated agricultural areas as well as cities and villages that make the heart jump.

Marshal of the Soviet Union Kulikov stressed that he was holding this conversation on behalf of CPSU CC Politburo member and Minister of Defense of the USSR Cde. Marshal of the Soviet Union [Dmitrii] Ustinov.

The goal of the meeting consists in giving information about the 11th plenum of the CC of the Polish United Workers' Party and in presenting recommendations on how to continue work regarding the Polish Army.

[…]

Marshal Kulikov currently assesses the *state of the Polish Army* as follows: He himself has had many meetings and encounters with the leading cadres of the Polish Army and is in permanent contact with Minister [Wojciech] Jaruzelski and all his deputies.

The higher commanders of the Polish Army know the situation in the country and are worried that the party and state leadership are not pointing the way out of this complicated situation.

[...]

The Polish Army's comrade-in-arms relationship with the Northern Group of the Soviet Army can be called normal.

However, there are preliminary indications of deficient supplies of products to the Northern Group, to which the Polish government is committed. Too little meat, eggs, and other products have been provided to the Northern Group in the last few days, so that the Soviet Union, among other things, is forced to provide supplies to all pilots of the Northern Group directly from the Soviet Union.

Lately, trends toward anti-Soviet behavior have emerged.

Discussions such as the following arise:

– what are the Soviet troops doing on Polish territory,
– it is time for their redeployment to the Soviet Union, and other utterances.

Furthermore, memorials to the Soviet Army are being defiled.

[...]

Addressing the situation in its entirety, Cde. Kulikov voiced [the following]:

To sum up, Poland is on the brink of a catastrophe. Attacks against the police are on the increase so that the army remains the only organized force.

Cdes. [Stanisław] Kania and Jaruzelski have not met their repeated promises to alter the conditions. This concerned both the registration of "Rural Solidarity" and the incidents in Bydgoszcz.

In a personal conversation, Marshal of the Soviet Union Kulikov pointed out to Cde. Jaruzelski that it would certainly be appropriate to discharge Deputy Prime Minister [Mieczysław] Rakowski from his position.

Cde. Jaruzelski answered that he agreed completely with Cde. Kulikov. Under normal conditions, Cde. Rakowski would have to be discharged from his function as deputy prime minister. But since he is a very skillful negotiator and often has very good ideas, it would not be appropriate to discharge him.

A general disease of the Poles is Catholicism. Ninety percent of all Poles declare themselves openly Catholic and, certainly, more than half of the remaining 10 percent are Catholics who just do not avow it openly.

The funeral service following Cardinal [Stefan] Wyszyński's death proved that the Poles live in the 16th century as far as religion is concerned. He stressed—not in the 17th or 18th but in the 16th [century].

While the funeral after Stalin's death in Moscow had lasted three hours, the services after Cardinal Wyszyński's death lasted six hours.

A further misery is [their] strong nationalism. It's always about "us Poles".

Unfortunately, where there are three Poles there are four points of view, as the 11th plenum has shown, too.

And certainly, the Polish comrades have also now assured themselves that socialism cannot be based on socialist industry and a kulak[10] economy.

With regard to the *further arrangement of cooperation* with the Polish Army, Marshal of the Soviet Union Kulikov recommended the following:

---

[10] A Russian term from tsarist times for a prosperous peasant, used disparagingly under communism. Kulikov is referring to private ownership in Polish agriculture.

1. It would be advisable to develop cooperation with the Polish Army in broader and more purposeful terms; it is presently the only organized force on which to count in Poland.

In doing so, consultations, exchanges of delegations, and joint exercises on the territory of the Soviet Union, the People's Republic of Poland, the GDR, and the ČSSR have to be conducted more intensively.

We should develop more activities to support the Polish Army in all fields. It is important to present the Warsaw Treaty in complex action.

2. Increased personal contacts between the leading cadres of the National People's Army and the Polish Army should be sought.

By virtue of his manifold experience, Cde. Colonel General [Heinz] Kessler should organize a meeting with the head of the political administration of the Polish Army in order to give him clues and advice toward further improving work in preparation for the party congress.

3. It is imperative that leading cadres of the military districts and forces of the National People's Army participate in all joint exercises on Polish territory in order to force a meeting with their Polish partners. These meetings are of particular importance for a thorough study of the leading cadres of the Polish Army and for a real[istic] assessment of who we can trust and where caution is advisable.

4. The documents for the exercise "Shield-81" (measures on Polish territory) have to be kept up to date.

It would be appropriate to carry out reconnaissance periodically and to check how the Group of Soviet forces in Germany and the National People's Army can cross the border into the People's Republic of Poland

In doing so, the construction of temporary border crossings at the Oder [river] should be arranged, and possible marching routes should not cross major cities.

Without exaggerating, one should be prepared for every eventuality at any time of the day or night.

5. All communications and command links must constantly be reviewed between:
– the National People's Army and the Group of Soviet Forces in Germany, and
– the Main Staff[11] of the National People's Army and the staff of the Unified Armed Forces, as well as the General Staff of the forces of the USSR.

Furthermore, the links and cooperation between the People's Navy[12] and the naval base of the Baltic Fleet in Świnoujście should be secured at all times.

The operational group of the staff of the Unified Armed Force and Marshal of the Soviet Union Kulikov remain in Legnica. [...]

[*Source: Die Bundesbeauftragte für die Unterlagen des Staatssicherheitsdienstes der ehemaligen DDR (BStU), Zentralarchiv, AIM 17164/81, Part II, Vol. I, pp. 79–88 Translated by Anna Locher.*]

[11] General Staff.
[12] East German Navy.

Document No. 92: Information by Marshal Ustinov on Soviet Strategic Offensive Forces, September 1981

In this statement during the annual "Zapad" exercises, Soviet Defense Minister Marshal Dmitrii Ustinov provides a description of the purpose of certain Soviet armaments, which basically confirms Western assessments that they were first-strike weapons. Specifically, he says that the SS-20 missile is meant for both first and subsequent nuclear strikes against strategic military targets in "all European NATO states and the adjacent seas." Ustinov underscores that the United States and NATO have no equivalent and that SS-20s are particularly secure because they are on mobile launchers. He also talks about the Kiev aircraft carrier, making it clear that it was designed to destroy U.S. and NATO attack carriers and missile submarines as well as provide support for troop landings. In short, he confirms Western concerns at the time about these offensive weapons, which the Soviet Union had been developing and deploying during détente.

During the "Zapad 81" exercise, the following systems of the Soviet Union's strategic offensive forces were explained to the ministers of defense of socialist states by [...] Marshal of the Soviet Union [Dmitrii F.] Ustinov:

1. the RSD 20 intermediate-range strategic missile system
2. the "Kiev" aircraft carrier of project 1143

Both systems receive major attention from strategic intelligence in the United States and all other NATO countries.

Their concealment from enemy intelligence is achieved through an effective system of safeguarding and deception at the locations of deployment as well as during transfer to areas of employment before and at the start of a possible war.

Comrade Ustinov asked to consider both those strategic systems top secret, and to inform only a limited number of people about them. Also, within the Soviet Army only leading cadres are informed about these two systems.

I. The RSD 20 intermediate-range strategic missile system
(NATO classification: SS-20)

Strategic goals

- Participation in the first and subsequent nuclear strikes by the strategic offensive forces of the Soviet Union (strategic missile units, nuclear missile submarines, long-range aircraft)
- Destruction of objects of military and strategic relevance on the territory of all European NATO states and adjacent seas.

Characteristics

- Since 1970, the missile system has been part of the strategic missile forces of the Soviet Union.

- It has long range, high flexibility, can be quickly deployed, and is very accurate; it is part of the third generation of this missile system.
- It can be aimed against both areas and specific targets.
- Currently, and in the coming years, the United States and other NATO states do not have a comparable missile system ready.

[...]

II. The "Kiev" aircraft carrier of project 1143

Strategic goals

The "Kiev" aircraft carrier operates in a possible war as part of the relevant naval groupings and fulfills the following tasks:
- Destruction of attack aircraft carriers of the United States [and] other NATO states on their way to, and within, areas of deployment.
- Search and destruction of nuclear missile submarines of the United States and other NATO states on their way to, and within, areas of deployment.
- Providing cover for our own nuclear missile submarines during their operations in areas of deployment and on their return to base.
- Support of our own naval amphibious forces troops during landing and seizure of coastal areas.

[...]

Since coming into service five years ago, the "Kiev" aircraft carrier has covered 240,000 km on the world's oceans and fulfilled all its tasks with good or excellent results.

[*Source VA-01/32641, pp, 1–6, BA-MA. Translated by Karen Riechert.*]

Document No. 93: Report on the Committee of Ministers of Defense Meeting in Moscow, December 1–4, 1981

At this meeting of the Committee of Defense Ministers in Moscow, the main topic is not Poland but the Reagan administration's proposal for a zero option on medium-range missiles in Europe. Soviet Marshal Dmitrii Ustinov declares that the correlation of forces is not in the Warsaw Pact's favor—except in the area of nuclear weapons; therefore the U.S. proposal is unacceptable. On the third day of the session, Poland is discussed. Polish Defense Minister Florian Siwicki asks the group to approve a draft communiqué regarding a declaration of martial law he has brought with him, refer-ring to the need for measures to ensure the security of the entire socialist community. The Polish argument adds that a strong statement is needed to help counter potential claims by the West that a crackdown was neither necessary nor supported by Poland's allies. But the underlying aim was to come up with a justification for the Polish people for instituting martial law. The discussion was contentious and the draft underwent several modifications. In the end, the desired communiqué was never issued.

[...]

Between December 1–4, 1981, the 14th meeting of the Committee of Ministers of Defense of the Warsaw Pact member-states took place in Moscow under the chair-manship of Marshal D[mitri] Ustinov, minister of defense of the Soviet Union. The participants at the meetings included all the members of the defense ministers com-mittee, except Army General W[ojciech] Jaruzelski, defense minister of the Polish People's Republic. The Polish People's Army (PPA) delegation was headed by Col. Gen. F[lorian] Siwicki, chief of General Staff and deputy national defense minister of the PPR. Each point of the agenda was discussed in the following order.

1. *Analysis of the state and developmental tendencies of the armed forces of the aggressive NATO bloc.*

The head of the Chief Directorate of Information and deputy chief of the USSR General Staff, Army General P.I. Ivashutin, in his introductory speech, thoroughly analyzed the current state of the international military and political situation. It was consistent with the appraisal made at the 26th CPSU Congress as well as the con-gress of fraternal socialist states.

PPA Chief of Staff Col. Gen. Siwicki said in his speech, among other things, that the complex socio-economic situation in the country might produce, in the near future, serious disturbances in arms and military procurement for the PPA as well as for the armies of the alliance. He then spoke about the significance of the state of the army's political morale. He noted that as a result of the situation in the country, fundamental changes were introduced in party and political work. More time had been spent on it. The quality of party and youth meetings had improved, including the intensity of

451

individual discussions. At this time, in party and political work, almost 60 percent of the [political training] is dedicated to explaining party and government policies. [He added] that these policies are aimed at bringing the country out of its complicated situation as well as to unmask the enemy activities of those opposed to socialism, especially "Solidarity's" extremist circles.

At the end of his speech, Gen. Siwicki said that "at least once a month, at the meetings of the Military Council, an assessment on the state of the military's political morale is conducted, which, at this moment, appears to be satisfactory. Thanks to this effort, the PPA successfully resists the attacks of the class enemy and plays an essential stabilizing role in the life of our country, despite the fact that the conscripts entering its ranks, who found themselves under the negative influence of Solidarity, preserved their own ideological and political character."

Gen. Siwicki said that the PPA activists support the party and state apparatus. He considers the defense of the socialist states, the snappy battle with manifestations of counterrevolution, to be his duty, to be his highest goal.

With regard to the situation in the PPR and its development, alarm was registered during the discussions concerning that point of the program in the speeches by the defense ministers of the USSR, Bulgaria, the GDR as well as the commander of the Unified Armed Forces.

2. *On the state and development of the air forces.*
A report will be given by a representative of the USSR Ministry of Defense.

3. *On the progress of the resolution passed at the 3rd and 6th meetings of the Committee of Ministers of Defense of the Warsaw Pact member-states on the subject of improving the command system of the allied armies.*
Information to be delivered by representatives of the PPR and Romanian ministries of national defense.

4. *On the program for the 16th Meeting of the Committee of Ministers of Defense.*
Draft to be presented by the chief of staff of the Unified Armed Forces of the Warsaw Past member-states.

The draft resolutions put forward on this point were unanimously accepted.

At the conference, the draft information text to the press, radio and television concerning the work of the 14th meeting of the Committee of Ministers of Defense was prepared for approval.

Before discussing the matter of the draft text, a supplement concerning the reaction to the situation in the PPR was put forward, which was sent by Comrade Jaruzelski to the Committee of Ministers of Defense with a request that it be attached to the text for the mass media with the following content: "The Committee of Ministers of Defense has expressed its alarm at the development of the situation in the PPR, resulting from the subversive activities of the anti-socialist forces, who are making it more difficult to fulfill the allied obligations of the armed forces of the Warsaw Pact member-states and result in the necessity of taking suitable steps aimed at ensuring the common security in socialist Europe."

Regarding this supplement, Minister of National Defense of the Romanian Socialist Republic Lieutenant-General C[onstantin] Olteănu did not express his consent. And he demanded that the text with the contents agreed upon before the meeting of the Committee of Ministers of Defense be accepted. The remaining defense ministers supported accepting the supplement.

A closed session of the Committee of Ministers of Defense, including only members, took place next, at which it was proposed that the Romanian defense minister and, if necessary, others who need to do this, consult about the problem mentioned above with their own political leadership.

On the draft supplement, I reported to you, honorable comrade general secretary and president, on the telephone on December 2, 1981, and I asked for your agreement.

After the consultations had taken place, Minister of Defense of the Hungarian People's Republic Amy-General L[ajos] Czinege, reported that the Hungarian side had agreed to the supplement only in the event of full agreement by all the defense ministers.

During the evening of December 3–4, 1981, the draft supplement was changed several times and its final text contained: "The Committee of Ministers of Defense expressed its alarm at the worsening situation in the PPR. The subversive activities of the anti-socialist forces, behind whom stand the aggressive imperialist circles, has a direct impact on the fulfillment of the allied obligations of the armed forces of the Warsaw Pact member-sates. Solidarity was expressed with the PUWP's battle, with all Polish patriots against counterrevolution, with the battle to bring the country out of its crisis. As a result, it was underlined that the Polish nation can rely completely on the support of the socialist sates."

During the early morning hours, on the last day of the conference, another closed session of the Defense Ministers Committee, including only members, took place, at which it was agreed that the prepared text for the mass media will not be supplemented; but that, apart from this, information will be published in the press by the defense ministers of all the countries, with the exception of the Romanian Socialist Republic. This course of action was agreed upon by all the defense ministers except the Romanian. Further details were to be talked over after the protocol was signed.

After the session ended, another session of the defense ministers committee, including only members, took place, where Comrade Ustinov familiarized them with the substance of Comrade Jaruzelski's request. He asked that in the current, very complicated, practically climactic period the Committee of Ministers of Defense express its displeasure with regard to the situation in the PPR and express its support for the present Polish leadership.

The chief of the PPA General Staff spoke next. He said that the situation in their country had deteriorated greatly, that the Front of National Unity could be organized and that the party was disintegrating. All this was utilized by enemy forces supported by the "West."

In this battle the Polish leadership needs support. Dissolving the firefighting schools was a minor success, to which the counterrevolution responded with very sharp demands to isolate further the party and to weaken the state authorities. It wanted to show its strength and to demonstrate that the entire Polish nation was following it. The "Solidarity" leadership turned to the Sejm so that it would overturn the decision of the government on dissolving the firefighting schools and show a vote of no-confidence in the government. Otherwise, they threatened to introduce strikes, including a general strike. It was also counting on an increase in the wave of discontent with the state of provisions, especially before Christmas.

For the above-mentioned reasons, Comrade Jaruzelski asked that the diversionary claims of the "West," according to which the PPR did not have the support of its allies, be denied. Comrade Siwicki expressed his conviction that supplementing the text for the press would be a cold shower for the counterrevolution and, at the same time, support the battle by the Polish leadership against reaction. He then asserted that the PPR still had enough power to resolve the situation. This was not about any concrete military steps but about moral and political support for the PPR's party and state leadership.

Comrade Ustinov asserted that the complex situation in the PPR was known and understood by us. That was why such moral support could be helpful and would not indicate the threat to use force. His outlook received the consent of the remaining members of the Committee of Ministers of Defense, with the exception of the Romanian minister of national defense.

The Hungarian defense minister asserted that he would give his consent to supplement the text for the mass media, but only if all the defense ministers agreed. The Hungarian side did not quite understand who was supposed to be helped, because after closing the firefighting school 20 counterrevolutionaries were arrested and then let go. Comrade Czinege turned to Comrade Siwicki with the following questions: Why does Comrade Jaruzelski not turn to the first and general secretaries of the fraternal parties with the request, since it was a political problem? Why did they not resolve the situation themselves? And who ought to be supported if they [Polish Party] are always on the retreat? He also added that if they [Polish party] resisted, even the counterrevolution would behave differently.

Comrade Siwicki said that they had a few scenarios planned against the counterrevolution. There is a scenario to ban strikes, to limit the freedom of citizens, to introduce military courts, and a plan to establish order in the country.

Further in the discussion, Comrade Czinege again asserted that the Hungarian side will give its consent only in the event that all the defense ministers agree. Given that two defense ministers would not give their consent, the discussion to accept the supplement ended.

After the discussion, a sharp exchange of views followed between the defense minister of the Hungarian People's Republic and the chief of the General Staff of the USSR armed forces, Comrade [Nikolai] Ogarkov, who asserted that the Hungarian comrades possibly forgot about 1956 and the bloodshed that occurred at that time. Drawing attention to this was seen by Comrade Czinege as an insult to Comrade Kádár and himself, and he voiced his astonishment as to how a marshal of the Soviet Union could come up with such a declaration. Comrade Ogarkov added that the Soviet comrades did not want the kind of bloodshed in the PPR that had happened in Hungary, and that was why they supported every effort to resolve the crisis in Poland.

In the talks with Comrades Ustinov and [Viktor] Kulikov, a suggestion emerged about the suitability of raising matters in connection with resolving the situation in the PPR at the meeting of the highest representatives of the communist and workers' parties of the Warsaw Pact member-states.

The 14th meeting of the Committee of Ministers of Defense ended with the signing of the protocol.

In his final speech, the chairman of the conference, USSR Minister of National Defense Marshal of the Soviet Union Ustinov underlined the significance of the concluded meeting for the strengthening of the defense capabilities of the Warsaw Pact member-states. He thanked the members of the Committee of Ministers of Defense for their participation in the conference and gave the last word to the minister of national defense of the Czechoslovak Socialist Republic, who will chair the 15th meeting of the Committee of Ministers of Defense in 1982 in Prague.

In my speech, I voiced my conviction that the 14th meeting of the Committee of Ministers of Defense added to the strengthening of unity and friendship, and to a deepening of cooperation between the fraternal armies. I thanked the chairman, Comrade Ustinov, for organizing and leading the conference. I underlined the strong feelings of the Soviet people with our nations and the decisive role of the Soviet Union in our common struggle, measured to ensure the defense of socialism and peace. I ensured all the members of the Committee of Ministers of Defense that during the preparations and execution of the 15th meeting of the Committee of Ministers of Defense in 1982 in Prague, we will take advantage of all experiences, most of all from our Soviet friends, for a prosperous conference proceeding.

[*Source: Andrzej Paczkowski and Andrzej Werblan, "On the Decision to Introduce Martial Law in Poland in 1981," Cold War International History Project Working Paper No. 21, November 1997, pp. 37–43. Translated by Leo Gluchowski.*]

Document No. 94: Transcript of the Soviet Politburo Meeting on the Crisis in Poland, December 10, 1981

This extraordinary document records a Soviet Politburo meeting just three days before the declaration of martial law in Poland. The main topic of discussion initially is Poland's economic situation and Jaruzelski's earlier request for economic assistance. It appears from the discussion that Moscow is not certain whether martial law is finally imminent. Of the many important points raised here, one of the more significant is the Soviets' indication that they have no intention of introducing forces into Poland to back up a Polish crackdown. This directly contradicts Jaruzelski's ex post facto rendition of events, in which he contends Moscow was poised for an outside military solution but that he managed to help avert its intervention. The full Soviet record is not yet accessible, and therefore the question of Soviet intentions remains open, but this document is powerful evidence against Jaruzelski's allegation that he was struggling to keep the Soviet Army at bay. Another interesting conclusion that can be gleaned here is that the Soviet formation since 1969 of a loyal Eastern European officer corps bore fruit in the Polish case—at least in the short term. In the long term, however, Soviet and communist control could not be maintained.

ON THE QUESTION OF THE SITUATION IN POLAND

Brezhnev: This question does not appear on our agenda. But I think this session of the Politburo must begin with this question since we sent Cdes. [Nikolai K.] Baibakov and [Viktor G.] Kulikov on a special mission to Poland to discuss urgent and pressing questions with the Polish comrades. On December 8, Cde. Kulikov provided information on the discussions he held in Warsaw, and yesterday, December 9, Cde. Baibakov reported from Warsaw that he held discussions with Cde. Jaruzelski. From these and subsequent discussions, it was apparent to Cde. Baibakov that the Polish comrades hope to receive additional raw and other materials during the first quarter of next year from the USSR and other socialist countries roughly in the amount of $1.5 billion.

[...]

And now let us listen to Cde. Baibakov.

Baibakov: following the instructions of the Politburo I left for Warsaw. I met there with all of the comrades with whom it was necessary to talk over the questions I was entrusted with.

First of all, I held a discussion with Deputy Chairman of the Council of Ministers Cde. [Janusz] Obodowski. In this discussion, the Polish comrades raised the question of economic aid.

[...]

The time is now approaching for Poland to repay its credits to the West European countries. For this, Poland requires a minimum of 2.8 million hard-currency rubles. When I heard what our Polish comrades were asking and how much all of this aid amounted to, I raised the question of bringing our mutual economic relations into balance. Along with that, I noted that Polish industry is falling short of fulfilling its plan by significant margins. The coal industry, which is a fundamental source of foreign currency, is essentially disorganized, necessary measures are not being taken, and strikes are continuing. Now that there are no strikes, coal extraction is still occurring at a very low level.

[...]

As is known, by decision of the Politburo and by request of the Polish comrades we are providing them with aid in the form of the supply of 30,000 tons of meat. Of these 30,000 tons, 16,000 tons have already been redirected abroad. It must be said that produce, meat in this case, is being supplied in dirty, unsanitized railroad cars used to transport ore, in a very unattractive condition. Genuine sabotage is taking place during the unloading of this produce at Polish stations. The Poles utter the most obscene words about the Soviet Union and the Soviet people, they refuse to clean the railroad cars, and so on. It is simply impossible to count all of the insults that pour out about us.

Realizing this situation with the state of the balance of payments, the Poles want to introduce a moratorium on the repayment of debt to the Western countries. If they announce a moratorium, then all Polish vessels in the waters of any state or at the docks, and all other property located in countries to which Poland is in debt will be seized. Therefore the Poles have now given orders to the captains of vessels to leave port and to remain in neutral waters.

Now I will say a few words about my discussion with Cde. Jaruzelski. He confirmed the requests made by Obodowski relating to the supply of goods. Then in the evening, along with the ambassador[13] and Cde. Kulikov, we again visited with Jaruzelski. Obodowski and the secretary of the Central Committee of the PUWP in charge of these questions also attended the discussion. Jaruzelski was in a highly agitated state. It felt as though he was under the strong influence of a letter from the head of the Polish Catholic Church, Archbishop [Józef] Glemp, who, as is known, promised to declare a holy war against the Polish authorities. True, Jaruzelski there and then answered that in the event of an outburst by "Solidarity," they would quarantine all hostile elements.

As far as primary party organizations, they have essentially collapsed and are inactive. And concerning the party as a whole, Jaruzelski said that it effectively does not exist. The country is going to pieces and local districts are not receiving reinforcements because the Central Committee and government cannot give firm and clear orders. Jaruzelski himself has turned into a man who is unbalanced and unsure of himself.

[...]

___

[13] Boris I. Aristov.

Rusakov: The day before yesterday they had a conference of secretaries of voivodship[14] committees. As Cde. Arestov [sic: Aristov] reported, the secretaries of the voivodship committees did not understand Cde. Jaruzelski's speech at all, which did not give a clear, precise line. No one knows what is going to happen in the next few days. There was a conversation about operation "X".[15] At first, the point was that it would be at night from the 11th to the 12th, then from the 12th to the 13th. And now they are already talking about it being around the 20th. The idea is that the chairman of the State Council, [Henryk] Jabłoński, will speak on radio and television, and announce the introduction of martial law. At the same time, Jaruzelski declared that the law concerning the introduction of martial law can only be invoked after it has been discussed in the Sejm[16], and the next session of the Sejm is set for December 15. In this way, everything is becoming very complicated. The agenda for the session of the Sejm has been published. The question of the introduction of martial law does not appear on it. But in any case, Solidarity knows well that the government is preparing to introduce martial law, and it in turn is taking all necessary measures [in the event of] the introduction of martial law.

Jaruzelski himself says that he is contemplating addressing the Polish people. But he will not talk about the party in his address, but will appeal to people on the basis of their patriotic emotions. Jaruzelski speaks of the necessity of proclaiming a military dictatorship as existed under [Marshal Józef] Piłsudski,[17] pointing out in addition that the Polish people will understand that better than anything else.

As concerns other figures, such as Olszowski, he has recently been acting more decisively and it must be said that at a Politburo session the decision to introduce martial law and to adopt more decisive measures against extremist figures in Solidarity was passed unanimously; no one expressed any objections. In addition, Jaruzelski intends to be in touch with the allies on this question. He says that if Polish forces cannot handle the resistance from Solidarity then the Polish comrades are relying on help from other countries, up to and including the introduction of armed forces on the territory of Poland. In addition, Jaruzelski refers to a speech by Cde. Kulikov who allegedly said that help from the USSR and allied states for the armed forces of Poland will be provided. However, as far as I know, Cde. Kulikov did not say so directly, he simply repeated words spoken by L.I. Brezhnev at another time, to the effect that we will not leave the PPR in trouble.

[...]

Andropov: From the discussion with Jaruzelski it is evident that he has not yet made a firm decision on the introduction of martial law and, notwithstanding even the unanimous decision of the Politburo of the PUWP CC on the introduction of martial law we have not yet seen any concrete measures from the leadership. The Solidarity extremists are attacking the leadership of the PPR by the throat. The Church in recent days has also expressed its clear position. It essentially has gone over to the side of Solidarity.

[14] Voivodship (*województwo*) is the unit of provincial administration.
[15] Intended proclamation of martial law.
[16] The Polish parliament.
[17] From 1926 to 1935.

And of course in these circumstances the Polish comrades must quickly prepare to move on "X" and carry out that operation. At the same time, Jaruzelski declares that we will move toward Operation "X" when Solidarity forces us to. That is a very alarming indication, even more so since the last session of the Politburo of the PUWP CC, and the decision on introducing martial law that was adopted there, testify that the Politburo is becoming more decisive; all the members came out in favor of decisive actions. That decision pressed Jaruzelski and he must now somehow extricate himself. Yesterday I spoke with [deputy minister of the interior Mirosław] Milewski[18] and asked him what kind of measures were being contemplated and when. He answered that he did not know about Operation "X" or about a concrete timeframe for its execution. In this way, it turns out that Jaruzelski is either hiding his plan for concrete actions from his comrades or he is simply abandoning [the idea] of carrying out that measure.

Now I would like to note that Jaruzelski is rather persistently placing economic demands before us and conditioning the implementation of Operation "X" on our economic aid; and I would even say more than that, he is raising the question, albeit indirectly, of military assistance.

[...]

As far as economic assistance, of course it will be difficult to do that on the scale they are requesting. Apparently something needs to be done. But again I want to say that the framing of the question about apportioning goods as economic aid carries an insolent character, and all of this is being done so that if later we do not supply them with something they can then shift the blame to us. If Cde. Kulikov actually spoke about the introduction of troops then I consider that he did so incorrectly. We cannot risk that. We do not intend to introduce troops into Poland. That is the correct position, and we must observe it to the end. I do not know how matters will develop in Poland, but even if Poland comes under the authority of Solidarity that will be one thing. But if the capitalist countries fall upon the Soviet Union, and they already have a suitable agreement, with various kinds of economic and political sanctions, then that will be very difficult for us. We must show concern for our country, for the strengthening of the Soviet Union. That is our main line.

[...]

Gromyko: Today we have been discussing the question of the situation in Poland very sharply. Very likely, we have never discussed it so sharply before. This is explained by the fact that we ourselves do not know the direction events in the PPR will take. The leadership of Poland itself feels power slipping through its hands. Kania and Jaruzelski, as is known, were counting on the support of neutrals. But now effectively there are none, there are no neutrals. Their position was defined rather clearly: Solidarity showed itself to be a patently counterrevolutionary organization, a pretender to power that has declared itself openly concerning the seizure of the power. The Polish leadership must decide the question: it will either surrender its position if it does not take decisive measures, or it will take decisive measures, introduce

---

[18] A pro-Soviet hardliner.

martial law, quarantine the extremists from Solidarity, and establish necessary order. There is no other way.

What is our attitude toward the Polish events? I completely agree with what the comrades have been expressing here. We can say to the Poles that we regard the Polish events with understanding. This is a measured formulation and there is no basis for changing it. At the same time, we will have to try somehow to disabuse Jaruzelski and other Polish leaders of their attitude with respect to the introduction of troops. There can be no introduction of troops into Poland.

[…]

Notwithstanding the rather unanimous decision of the Politburo of the PUWP[19] CC on the implementation of martial law, Jaruzelski is now taking a vacillating position again. At first he was somewhat heartened, but now he has grown soft again. Everything that was said to him before remains valid. If they exhibit vacillation in the struggle with the counterrevolution and beyond, then nothing will remain of socialist Poland. The introduction of martial law, of course, would impress upon the counterrevolution in Poland the firm intentions of the Polish leadership. But if the measures they intend to enact, are implemented, I think one may expect positive results.

[…]

Establishing order in Poland is a matter for the Polish United Workers' Party, its Central Committee and the Politburo. We have been telling the Polish friends and in the future we will tell them [again] that it is necessary to take firm positions and it would be impermissible to relax now.

[…]

Ustinov: The situation in the PPR, of course, is very bad. The situation grows more complicated day by day. In the leadership, in particular in the Politburo, there is no firmness, there is no unity. And all this has already affected the state of affairs. Only at the last session of the Politburo was a decision on carrying out martial law passed unanimously. Now everything hinges on Jaruzelski. How will he be able to carry off this decision. So far no one can speak openly about Jaruzelski's actions. Even we do not know. I had a conversation with [defense minister Florian] Siwicki. He said immediately that even we do not know what the general is thinking. In this way, the person who essentially fulfills the responsibilities of the minister of defense of the PPR does not know what is going to happen or what actions the chairman of the Council of Ministers and the minister will take.

As for what Cde. Kulikov supposedly said with respect to the introduction of troops into Poland, I can say with full authority that Kulikov did not say that. He merely repeated what Leonid Ilyich and we said about not leaving Poland in trouble. And he knows perfectly well that the Poles themselves requested us not to introduce troops.

As for our garrisons in Poland, we are fortifying them. I, perhaps, am also inclined to think that the Poles will not head towards a confrontation, and only if, possibly, when Solidarity seizes them by the throat will they act.

[19] Polish United Workers' Party.

The trouble is that the Polish leaders are not demonstrating decisiveness. As our comrades correctly expressed here, we should not impose on them any decisions about how to conduct a particular policy that we agree with. In our turn, we must ourselves be prepared and not take any action that we have not decided upon.

Suslov: I consider that, as is evident from the comrades' speeches, we all have a unanimous point of view toward the situation in Poland. In the course of the entire period of events in Poland we have displayed self-control and composure. Leonid Illyich Brezhnev spoke about this at the Plenum. We spoke about this in public and our people supported such a policy by the communist party.

We are carrying out great work on behalf of peace and we cannot change our position now. World public opinion will not understand us. We have conducted such major actions through the U.N. for the strengthening of peace. What an effect we have had from the visit of L.I. Brezhnev to the FRG, and from many other peaceful actions we have taken. This has made it possible for all peace-loving countries to understand that the Soviet Union is firmly and consistently defending a policy of peace. That is why it is impossible for us to change the position on Poland we have adopted since the very beginning of the Polish events. Let the Polish comrades themselves determine which actions they should take. We do not have to push them towards any more decisive acts. But we will say to the Poles, as we did earlier, that we regard their actions with understanding.

It seems to me that Jaruzelski is manifesting a certain cunning. He wants to cover his own back with requests which he presents to the Soviet Union. Naturally, we do not physically have the ability to fulfill these requests, but Jaruzelski will say later, well, I turned to the Soviet Union and requested help but I did not receive this help.

At the same time the Poles declare directly that they are against the introduction of troops. If troops are introduced that will mean a catastrophe. I think that we all share a unanimous opinion here that there can be no discussion of any introduction of troops.

[…]

[*Source: TsKhSD, Fond 89, Opis 42, Delo 6. Translated by Malcolm Byrne for the National Security Archive.*]

Document No. 95: Memorandum of Conversation with Marshals Ustinov and Kulikov concerning a Soviet War Game, June 14, 1982

This Soviet war game, described to East German Defense Minister Heinz Hoffmann by Soviet marshals Dmitrii Ustinov and Viktor Kulikov, envisioned several air and sea landings—on the Danish islands, in the Lower Saxony area of West Germany, and in France. Interestingly, one of the Soviet assumptions in this exercise, which took place immediately after the Polish crisis, was that Poland and Romania would want to leave the Warsaw Pact. The Russians pointed out that Romania had recently refused permission to Warsaw Pact troops to cross its territory in order to take part in an exercise in Bulgaria. Ustinov remarks that Ceauşescu either does not understand the current situation "or he may be out of his mind." Exercise planners also presumed that China had started a war against the Soviet Union.

[...]

On instruction of the general secretary of the Central Committee of the CPSU and chairman of the Defense Council of the USSR, Comrade Leonid *Brezhnev*, an operational–strategic war game involving the leading organs of the Soviet Army and Navy under direction of Comrade Minister *Ustinov* is taking place between June 10 and June 20, 1982.

[...]

The operational–strategic war game has been based on a most complex military–political and military–strategic situation.

In detail, there have been the following new aspects:

1. War was initiated in the Far East by China forty days ago, with the active support of Japan and Korea, reunified on a capitalist basis. So far, the U.S. is not yet participating in the war in the Far East.

A total of 290 divisions have been deployed in that area against the Soviet Union. The adversary managed to intrude onto the territory of the Soviet Union and of the People's Republic of Mongolia. Vladivostok has been taken by Chinese troops. Incursions were effected up to a depth of 500 kilometers in the direction of Ulaanbaatar.

On the 40th day of war, the Soviet troops formed for a counteroffensive in the Far East.

By unleashing war in the Far East, U.S. imperialism and NATO pursued the goal of averting the complete deployment of Soviet troops in the Western theater of war, and inducing the USSR to deploy troops in the Far East, so as to initiate a surprise attack in the European war theater as well.

In the Arab region, Saudi Arabia and Iran joined the hostilities on the side of the adversary. Two additional fronts were formed against this grouping.

2. In the Western theater of war, the adversary has deployed his forces using state-of-the-art technology.

A regiment of the 56th US missile brigade, equipped with 54 "Pershing-2" and 10 missile detachments with a total of 160 cruise missiles, has been deployed on the territory of Great Britain, the FRG, and Italy.

The adversary's air force consists of about 3,000 to 4,000 planes in the Western strategic direction.

For reinforcement of NATO, forces from overseas have been deployed. Greece and Turkey have left NATO.

3. Marshal of the Soviet Union *Kulikov* is acting as supreme commander of the Unified Armed Forces in the Western theater of war; Army General [Anatolii I.] *Gribkov* as supreme commander in the Southwestern theater of war.

In order to mislead the enemy, certain forces and means of the Soviet Army have been transferred from the European theater of war to the Far East.

The 160,000 members of the Soviet and fraternal armies marked for discharge have not been discharged.

The Group of Soviet Forces in Germany was made into a front.

The National People's Army of the GDR is operating as part of the Group of Soviet Forces in Germany, with two armies (11 divisions), one in the 1st, one in the 2nd echelon.

The Unified Armed Forces deployed 108 divisions, including 40 tank divisions, in the Western theater of war.

This grouping consists of:
- 29,000 tanks
- 25,000 artillery tubes
- 3,500 aircraft, including 50 percent nuclear-capable

The Soviet Army uses state-of-the-art technology such as aircraft of the type SU-24, MiG-28, and -29. All tank divisions are equipped with the modern T-72 tank.

The Soviet Army lands an airborne division and amphibious forces on the Danish islands.

In the Rhine region, the landing of an airborne division is planned in the Wesel area. It is planned to assign a third airborne division for the taking of Paris.

4. An extremely unstable situation has developed in *Poland* and in *Romania*, both states want to leave the Warsaw Treaty.

All forces and means of the Polish Army have been deployed within Poland. Also the Romanian forces perform tasks only within the Socialist Republic of Romania.

(One of the goals of this exercise obviously consists in testing whether the operational–strategic tasks of the Unified Armed Forces can also be accomplished without the Polish Army and the forces of the Socialist Republic of Romania.)

[...]

Furthermore, an exchange of views about the imminent joint maneuvers of the Armies of the member-states of the Warsaw Treaty, "Shield-82", took place in September of this year on the territory of the People's Republic of Bulgaria.

In this context, Minister *Hoffmann* informed about the results of the journey of the GDR military delegation to the Socialist Republic of Romania, and presented once more the Romanian point of view, particularly the comments of Comrade Ceauşescu about "Shield-82."

[...]

Comrade Minister *Ustinov* expressed thanks for the information about the results of the journey of the GDR military delegation to the Socialist Republic of Romania. In his opinion, the journey contributed to a clear picture of Comrade Ceauşescu and his policies. If he is such a great politician and statesman, as he presents himself, then he "should also make sure that NATO is dissolved tomorrow. After that, we are immediately ready to dissolve the Warsaw Treaty."

The findings of the military delegation reflected the old Romanian disease. One has to be bolder and tougher in talking to the Romanian comrades. At the next meeting of the Political Consultative Committee, all general secretaries and first secretaries should speak their minds clearly to Comrade Ceauşescu.

Those times when we always placated the Romanian comrades should belong to the past.

Comrade Ceauşescu is basing his judgment of the situation on no clear class position. He practically sells out the interests of the socialist camp. Either he does not understand what is going on or he may be out of his mind.

Addressing the international situation, Minister *Ustinov* stressed that the general situation and the political climate have not improved, but deteriorated. NATO, which keeps arming up, has to be assessed realistically.

The line of attack of U.S. President *Reagan's* Bonn and Berlin speeches was anti-Soviet and anti-socialist. Whoever does not understand this and does not see this correctly knows nothing about politics.

Many Western politicians talk nicely, but the actual content of their policies is more dangerous for us than ever. To his [Ustinov's] mind, also Federal Chancellor [Helmut] *Schmidt* had changed. Two or three years ago, he would not have dared to go to the Berlin Wall with *Reagan* and speak in such a tone as he did during Reagan's visit to Berlin.

Regarding anti-Soviet and anti-socialist policies, *Schmidt* today shares the points of view of [Franz Josef] *Strauss* and [Helmut] *Kohl*. Comrade *Ustinov* again explained at length his conversations with Chancellor *Schmidt* in Moscow.

We have to see *Reagan*, Schmidt, and [French President François] *Mitterrand* as standing side by side. It is about time to address NATO politicians in a different language than before. We should speak to them as they speak to the socialist camp, that is, we have to be harsher and more consistent to show them where they belong.

The implementation of NATO's decision to station cruise missiles and "Pershing-2" in Western Europe creates a new and very dangerous strategic situation for the Soviet Union. Once this decision has been implemented, the USSR will deploy an additional 200 to 300 SS-20 missiles. We will by no means allow NATO to surpass us in the nuclear field.

The US and NATO will not succeed in bringing us to our knees economically by using the arms race.

The slogan of Comrade Leonid *Brezhnev*, "*bread* and *defense*," still is of primary importance for us.

In certain areas, the adversary is superior to us in armament and equipment.

Yet the Soviet tank T-72 for example, which has been used in Lebanon, has proved to be superior to all American tanks.

In Israel's war against the PLO[20] and Lebanon, one has to assume that the U.S. is offering all-out support to Israel, and that this aggression contains a great danger for world peace.

We should assess the policies of the NATO leadership correctly and draw the necessary conclusions for our work.

In the political field, we have to be more aggressive than before and not work from defensive positions.

The ideological diversion by the adversary is increasing. We have to strengthen our political and ideological work to keep our soldiers steady in all situations.

[...]

[*Source: AZN 32643, 74–80, BA-MA. Translated by Anna Locher.*]

[20] The Palestine Liberation Organization.

Document No. 96: Report on Speech by Marshal Ogarkov at a Warsaw Pact Chiefs of Staff Meeting in Minsk, September 8–10, 1982

Speaking to a meeting of Warsaw Pact chiefs of staff in Minsk, Soviet Marshal Nikolai Ogarkov draws an alarming picture of the state of the world, comparing it to the conditions that immediately preceded the outbreak of World War II. Referring to the sanctions the West imposed against Poland and the USSR, he asserts that the United States has already declared war on the Soviet Union and its allies. The U.S. goal, he says, is to destabilize the Warsaw Pact countries through economic warfare while at the same time planning to wage limited nuclear war. The danger of war, he says, has never been so great, in part because the "leading imperialist circles" are so unpredictable. His remarks are a stark expression of the anxiety provoked by what Moscow regarded as the Reagan administration's twin military and political challenge.

[...]

At the beginning of his remarks, Cde. Marshal of the Soviet Union [Nikolai V.] Ogarkov elaborated on the policy of peace [conducted by] the Soviet Union and the countries of the Warsaw Treaty.

[...]

At the present time, the international situation is very serious and extremely complicated. It is only comparable to the situation in the 1930s, on the verge of the outbreak of the Second World War.

The advent of the [Ronald] Reagan presidency is evocative of the Fascist seizure of power. Indeed, the U.S. administration is organizing the struggle against socialism, particularly against the Soviet Union, in a similar fashion.

The Reagan administration has inaugurated open preparations for war. This can be seen every day in the political, economical, diplomatic, and military fields.

In saying so, it has to be considered that Reagan is only a puppet of the most aggressive circles of imperialism.

All instruments available to imperialism are being deployed against the Soviet Union and against the socialist camp.

The United States has in effect already declared war on us, the Soviet Union and some other states of the Warsaw Treaty. In several fields, the battle is already going on.

The goal of imperialism has always been the destruction of socialism.

Since the beginning of Soviet power, imperialism has always tried to liquidate the achievements of socialism with military power.

A pattern can be detected similar to the events in Hungary in 1956, to the events in the ČSSR in 1968, and to the present events in the People's Republic of Poland. We have to regard all these intrigues of imperialism as a single consistent policy.

The present stage is characterized by a global attack from imperialism against socialism on every front and in many forms and methods.

[...]

Thus, U.S. imperialism, supported by some other NATO countries, is presently conducting a major strike against the economy of the Soviet Union and the socialist camp.

In pursuit of that purpose, the various measures aimed at disrupting or cutting off normal trade relations have already called the viability of the entire international trade system into question.

This economic war aims at:

– destabilizing the situation in the Soviet Union and thus in the [whole] socialist camp, and

– fomenting widespread discontent with the policies in our countries.

[...]

At present, there are trouble spots on every continent.

They are the results of the aggressive policies of U.S. imperialism and serve the goal of separating the less-developed countries from the Soviet Union and the socialist camp, respectively.

A further goal of imperialist policy consists in perpetuating the current unstable situation in the People's Republic of Poland for as long as possible.[21] In doing so, imperialism is pursuing political as well as economic and military goals.

[...]

A second line that is being intensively followed by imperialism at present is its policy of lying, defamation, and agitation in order to shake the trust of the citizens of the socialist states in the party and state leaderships.

In doing so, the goal of [U.S. imperialism] is to destroy the unity and cohesion of the socialist camp and eventually break it.

At the same time, immense resources are provided by the imperialist states in order to improve and complete the material base of their aggressive forces in a previously unknown dimension.

The material preparations for war, as shown also by the current maneuvers of the NATO states, is not a game but deadly serious.

Imperialism incessantly undertakes every effort to improve its possibilities for conducting both a global and a limited nuclear war.

The new U.S. strategy of direct confrontation serves this goal.

[...]

The policy of the Reagan administration has to be seen as adventurous and serving the goal of world domination.

In the present stage, the risk of war is as high as ever before because the leading circles of imperialism are unpredictable, even though many people do not want to understand this. In 1941, too, there were many among us who warned against war

---

[21] Nine months after Gen. Wojciech Jaruzelski declared martial law—on December 13, 1981— to put down the nationwide Solidarity crisis, Poland continued to be ruled by emergency decree, a condition which lasted until December 1982.

and many who did not believe a war was coming. Therefore, since the danger of war was not assessed correctly, we had to make many sacrifices.

Thus, the situation is not only very serious, but also very dangerous.

[...]

It is also important for us as responsible military to draw the right lessons from previous wars.

World War I was a war of positions.

Since it was conducted in one dimension, defense was stronger than attack. The front spanned 10 to 20 kilometers and far-reaching means of destruction did not yet exist.

World War II was a war of movement. Due to the development of tank troops, artillery, air force, and airborne troops, this war was already conducted in two dimensions. It already covered big areas and fighting had a dynamic character.

World War III would, if unleashed by the imperialists, have to be waged already in three dimensions. Thus, control over airspace would play the most crucial role.

Only the side controlling airspace and outer space will be able to win a third World War, based on the status of development of technical weapons.

This war would be an armed conflict between the two world systems and would be led by coalition groupings. As a global war, it would cover each continent and outer space.

In World War I, 70 million troops fought, with 35 states involved.

In World War II, 110 million troops fought and 61 states belonged to the belligerent countries.

World War III would be a contest of life and death between the two world systems. The consequences for our planet would be devastating.

In this struggle, there would be no sitting on the fence. If there are politicians nowadays who say that we fight for and defend only our own territory, meaning that they only want to defend socialism on the national scale, then this can only be stupidity or a misunderstanding of the situation, and thus demagogy.

[...]

The most important theater of war in a future conflict is the Western theater. The outcome of the war will be decided there.

We have to consider that actions have to be conducted by coalition everywhere.

Thus, for example, the Soviet Union will act in Southeast Asia together with Vietnam, Laos, and Cambodia.

(This year, a war game will be conducted involving the leading bodies of the armed forces of these countries.)

In the Middle East, the Soviet Union and Afghanistan act together.

In the Western theater of war, that is, in the Western and Southwestern theater, the Unified Armed Forces of the member-states of the Warsaw Treaty will act. [...]

Within the training program planned in 1983, the war structure of the Western theater command will be developed.

[...]

[*Source: AZN 32643, 119–26, BA-MA. Translated by Christian Nünlist.*]

Document No. 97: East German Intelligence Report on the Operational Plan of the U.S. 5th Army Corps in War Time, December 16, 1982

At the beginning of the 1980s, the KGB's top priority was to acquire Western intelligence that could help warn of a surprise attack against the Warsaw Pact. The agency's head, Iurii Andropov, had been convinced for some time that nuclear war was a genuine possibility and he worried that advances in NATO technology and armaments would give the West a fatal advantage. The discovery of the U.S. Army and NATO operational plan described in this East German intelligence report provided invaluable information about Western strategies and objectives. Approved by the Department of the Army and adopted by NATO as of January 1, 1981, the general defense plan of the 5th Army Corps implements the strategies of flexible response and forward defense, aiming, inter alia, *at defeating invading Warsaw Pact forces, without reinforcements but possibly with the use of tactical nuclear weapons or mines. The plan also calls for strikes behind enemy lines, and provides for employing chemical weapons, although only in response to their use by the Warsaw Pact. Assuming the East Germans passed this information to the KGB, Andropov must not have been heartened to see how much more confident NATO had grown in its ability to cope with an attack since the 1970s.*

PREFACE

Through reliable intelligence we received knowledge of U.S. and NATO planning during crises and in war time for the V Corps/U.S. Army stationed in the FRG. It considers the secret operations plan (OPLAN) 33001 (GDP: General Defense Plan) for the V Corps/U.S. Army. Worked out by the Staff of the U.S. Army Europe, and approved by the U.S. Department of the Army, it has been incorporated into NATO planning after consultations. This OPLAN is the basis of action for the V Corps to lead the defense within NATO's Central Army Group (CENTAG). It consists of two parts, the so-called basic plan (OPLAN) and the attachments. Besides general information on intentions, goals and operational structure to defend CENTAG, the OPLAN has detailed instructions for the V Corps and its related combat and support troops, as well as general orders for cooperation and joint actions. Eighteen attachments with altogether 33 appendixes refer to the operational structure of the corps, boundaries of corps and divisions' areas for defense operations, and guiding principles to conduct the operation and ensure implementation of orders. Also they include guidelines for the use of nuclear weapons and chemical agents. In addition, there are appendixes on plans for outside reinforcements to the V Corps/U.S. Army.

OPLAN 33001 (GDP) came into force on January 1, 1981. For U.S. forces it has the security classification SECRET, and within NATO it is NATO SECRET.

This OPLAN is an important document of real NATO war planning. It allows drawing extensive conclusions on the perspective of NATO leaders regarding the character of an initial phase in a potential war, on the strategy of "Flexible Response," and on the principles of "Forward Defense" and defense operations in the European theater of war.

The plan is based on the assumption of a war starting unfavorably to NATO. According to this plan, Unified Forces of the Warsaw Pact begin a war after short preparation with conventional attacks. NATO has only 48 hours of advance alert to occupy defense lines, dig in and fortify them. None, or just parts, of the planned outside reinforcements are available.

CENTAG consists of V Corps/U.S. Army, VII Corps/U.S. Army, II and III Army Corps/FRG, and the II French Army Corps, provided there is a respective decision by the French government. CENTAG conducts its defense with the intention to destroy attacking forces of the Warsaw Pact already near the border areas, to maintain the integrity of NATO territory resp. restore it, to maintain a cohesive defense in conjunction with Northern Army Group (NORTHAG), and to prevent a breakthrough towards the Rhine.

Remarkable is NATO's intention to include the 12th Tank Division/FRG in the first line of defense within VII Corps/U.S. Army. This confirms existing information and conclusions drawn from exercises that in times of crises the 12th Tank Division will be released from the III Army Corp/FRG and integrated into VII Corps/U.S. Army.

Concerning the assessment of Warsaw Pact Forces there exists NATO's constantly updated "enemy assessment." It will be added separately to the OPLAN, supposedly on orders by NATO. Assessments about intentions and potential of Warsaw Pact Unified Forces, however, are evident in the appendixes. According to them, NATO expects in the defense area of V Corps/ U.S. Army about six to eight Warsaw Pact divisions in the first wave and additional three to four divisions during the second wave. Main attacks are expected in directions Eisenach–Bad Hersfeld–Alsfeld and Eisenach–Hünfeld–Schlitz.

[...]

The goal of the V Corps' defense (without external reinforcements) is to halt the attacking forces of the Warsaw Pact as near as possible to the FRG/GDR border, and to destroy forces that have penetrated NATO territory by means of counter-attacks or nuclear weapons. The focus is on maintaining a strong defense in the direction of the expected main attacks. The plan is to destroy the main forces of the first wave of attack to a depth of about 50 km east of Vogelsberg. With external reinforcements, the goal is to halt the first wave farther east and drive it from NATO territory by means of counter-strikes.

The operational plan foresees three phases for the defense—(1) the development of the Corps/actions by the covering troops of the Corps; (2) actions by the covering forces of the divisions and; (3) combat by the main forces. There will be two lines of defense, plus general reserves and covering troops in the battle zone. [...]

470

The deployment of the main forces of the Corps in the first line of defense and the massing of forces and material in front of the first line of defense are indications that NATO intends to put into practice the principle of "forward defense". The idea is to weaken the attacking groups of the Unified Armed Forces to the maximum extent possible and to keep them in check for at least 24 hours, in order to create favorable conditions for conducting counter-strikes. The goal is to destroy the first wave of attack while still in the vicinity of the border.

The defense area assigned to the Corps and the Divisions is, respectively, 70–80 and 40 km wide, and 120 and 60–70 km deep. This corresponds more or less to the norms applied in several troop exercises. The cover area in front of the first line of defense is to be 10–15 km deep.

The Corps' second line of defense is to take up its positions at a depth of 30 km, and the general reserves are to be placed behind the defense area of the divisions of the first line. The launching area for tactical nuclear weapons (LANCE) is to be located at a depth of 30–40 km.

A series of command lines are to run from north to south every 10–15 km from the FRG/GDR border to the rear of the Corps' defense area. Their purpose is to facilitate command of the troops, to ensure a rapid overview of combat developments, and to make it easier to organize cooperative actions.

Nuclear weapons are considered to be a means of fire support (nuclear fire support). They are to be put into action by the air force, the artillery and the engineers upon command, or after the go-ahead for nuclear weapons has been given (R hour). Particular importance is attached to nuclear mines (nuclear blocking ammunition) as an escalating element. [...]

The use of chemical agents is planned as a retaliatory measure following the first use of chemical agents by the armed forces of the Warsaw Pact. It is to be employed by the artillery and the engineers as fire support. The goal is to inflict high losses upon the enemy, to decrease their fighting power and to narrow the line of advance of the attacking groups, thus creating favorable conditions for their destruction, possibly also through the use of nuclear weapons. [...]

The following is the German translation of the operational plan.

[...]

[Source: Die Bundesbeauftragte für die Unterlagen des Staatssicherheitsdienstes der ehemaligen Deutschen Demokratischen Republik (BStU), Zentralarchiv, 626/84. Translated by Bernd Schaefer and Ursula Froese.]

Document No. 98: Speech by Andropov at the Political Consultative Committee Meeting in Prague, January 4–5, 1983

Iurii Andropov delivered this important speech to the PCC soon after becoming general secretary of the CPSU. His comments mark another stage in the Soviet leadership's endeavors to understand the changes in American and NATO policies from the Carter to the Reagan administrations. Andropov's interpretation is that the West is compensating for both recent losses in the Third World and the ongoing internal crisis of capitalism. At least the first part of the argument, though not the second, is directly in line with Reagan's own thinking. Implicitly criticizing the stagnant policies of his predecessor, Leonid Brezhnev, Andropov also asserts that the West is trying to exploit weaknesses in the socialist countries, including their indebtedness to Western creditors, inadequate food supplies and technological backwardness. He clearly believes the United States is out to achieve superiority, and is worried about what he believes is America's ability to maintain the arms race by simply cutting other expenditures as needed. Both of these views mirror the thinking in conservative Western circles.

Each of us, evidently, wonders what has caused the sharp turn in U.S. and NATO policy, which produced the current flare-up of tensions, and for how long this aggravation will last.

The essence of the matter, in our opinion, is above all the unfavorable changes in the world from the point of view of imperialism.

The 1970s were a time of further growth in the power and influence of the socialist commonwealth. We were able to achieve military–strategic parity with the West. This gave us an opportunity to conduct business on a par with it. Our dynamic policy of détente produced major positive developments in international relations.

Imperialism suffered noticeable losses in the wide zone of the so-called third world, upon control of whose resources the well-being of the West continues to depend. Revolutionary changes in Angola, Ethiopia, Nicaragua and other countries—and they were caused by objective factors—were taken by Washington, not without reason, as a defeat for American policy.

The Reagan phenomenon and his policy, however, has not only external but also internal causes. Symptoms of deep crisis—the fall of production, inflation, mass unemployment—have affected practically all capitalist countries. And the bourgeoisie, as a rule, looks for escape from such conditions by embarking on external political adventures.

But this is but one side of the coin. The other side is that the USA and NATO have seen their opportunity in the difficulties we all have been facing to one extent or another in our economic development. I have in mind the growth of foreign debts, the food situation, our technological lag in certain areas and a series of other bottlenecks. Internal political complications in some socialist countries have been appraised in a similar vein. Let us not close our eyes: for as long as these problems exist, our class enemies will try to turn them to their benefit; that is why they are class enemies.

The policy of Reagan and of those who stand behind him is nothing but an attempt to fight the laws of historical development, to cut by any possible means the further losses for the capitalist system. The sharp edge of this policy is directed against the Soviet Union and the entire socialist commonwealth. Washington's so-called differentiated approach to certain socialist countries is tactics that does not change anything in substance. The struggle unfolds in virtually all directions.

One cannot help notice the shamelessness with which the United States has been trying to complicate the economic conditions of the socialist countries. Just think of their actions against Poland! Or the notorious "gas pipeline" story, when the USA was willing to sacrifice the interests of even their closest allies.[22] The Americans, judging by everything, want to continue using trade relations as a weapon of political pressure. I am talking about the sharp limitation of our access to advanced technology, decreasing the volume of, and tightening credit, restrictions on foreign currency earnings of the socialist countries from exports, etc.

We all feel the increased activity of the ideological centers of imperialism. And this is not simply the renewal of a propaganda war, with which we are familiar from the past. A high-stakes wager has been placed—on creating a political opposition in our countries, and on manipulating it so as to unsettle the socialist societal order.

Especially dangerous is the military challenge thrown to us. Having set the aim of destroying the equilibrium in this area, Washington is inciting all [NATO] participants, and, as the December session of the NATO Council has shown, not without result, toward the relentless militarization of the NATO bloc.

The new round of the arms race, imposed by the USA, has major, qualitative differences. Whereas before, the Americans, in speaking about their nuclear weaponry, preferred to accentuate the fact that it was above all a means of "intimidation" and "deterrence," now, in creating modified missile systems, do not hide that they are really intended for a future war. From here spring the doctrines of "rational" and "limited" nuclear war; from here spring the statements about the possibility of surviving and winning a protracted nuclear conflict.

It is hard to say what is blackmail and what is genuine teadiness to take the fatal step. In any case, we cannot allow the military superiority of the USA, and we will not allow it. The equilibrium will not be broken. However, one has to take into account the fact that the escalation of the arms race could make the military–political situation unstable and uncertain. Such weapons appear, which are difficult, and maybe utterly impossible, to control with the help of national means.

On the whole, it will not be an exaggeration to say that we are facing one of imperialism's most massive attempts to slow down the process of social change in the world, to stop the advance of socialism or even to push it back in some places.

---

[22] The United States used the COCOM (Coordinating Committee for Multilateral Export Controls) rules on limitations of strategic exports to block the delivery of large-diameter pipes from Western Europe to the Soviet Union.

One should, naturally, consider in all seriousness the current change in the policy of the USA. But one should see that they are far from being entirely successful. The weaknesses and the miscalculations of their policy manifest themselves more and more clearly. Having planned to frighten us, Washington politicians sowed fear in their own country and among their own allies, and provoked a feeling of irritation among them. Apprehension is increasing in the West that people who came to power in America are capable of provoking a nuclear catastrophe.

Is it not symptomatic that, independent of the World Peace Council[23], a world antinuclear movement has emerged and is gaining strength in Western Europe and in the USA itself? This is already creating something of a political climate. The idea of freezing nuclear arsenals enjoys wide support in the Democratic Party of the USA. [The British] Labor [Party] is speaking out for nuclear disarmament in England. This is far from a trifle.

Of course, the NATO countries follow the United States and—some more, some less so—play along with the attacks on our policy. But the American goal of tough confrontation with the socialist commonwealth is far from being fully shared by their European allies, Canada, as well as, one could say, Japan. Quarrels and clashes on different questions—not only economic, but political as well—are not subsiding in the Western camp. Reagan's assertiveness in no way removes the contradictions between imperialists, on the contrary it aggravates them. [...]

Through the fault of the current administration, a kind of erosion of the top soil [*plodorodnogo sloia*] in Soviet–American relations has taken place. When Reagan came to the White House, he expressed himself to the effect that he, you see, had nothing at all to talk about with the Soviet Union until the USA achieved military superiority.

How did we respond to this? We could also say that we do not want to talk to a political thug, even if he heads the most powerful capitalist country. But the Soviet leadership has acted differently. It has confirmed its readiness for a serious, extensive dialogue with the United States, but, of course, for a dialogue of equals.

Words are now heard in Washington about the usefulness of more constructive relations with the Soviet Union. But we still have no reason to talk about a change of American policy in a better direction. Recent contacts, including my conversation in Moscow with U.S. Vice President [George] Bush and Secretary of State [George] Shultz, have been marked by a change in tone and nothing more.

The progress of Soviet–American talks in Geneva on questions of nuclear arms also gives no cause for excitement.

I can responsibly confirm that the total power of the armaments of the USSR and the USA is approximately the same. No matter how many times our specialists make necessary correlations, they necessarily come to the same conclusions: a more or less stable parity is evident. By the way, many serious people in the USA do not believe Reagan and his team when they insist on the contrary.

What is different is the structure of the strategic armaments of the USSR and the USA. The Americans are now trying to profit from this.

---

[23] A Soviet front organization.

The main core of our strategic forces is land-based ballistic missiles. This, one could say, is the bulwark of the security of the entire socialist commonwealth. But the Americans have a considerable superiority in strategic bombers. In addition, they have placed great emphasis on submarine-based nuclear weapons. Such a disproportion is in many ways a result of the difference in the actual geographic location of the two powers. The USA, located between two oceans, is one thing; our country is another. In the north we have permanent ice, and in the west and east outlets to the world's oceans pass through narrow, easily controlled straits.

It would seem that to try to fool or outsmart someone during negotiations on a problem as sensitive as defense is simply an unthinkable undertaking. But up to now the Americans are trying to conduct business precisely this way.

What are they offering? To limit and cut back on missile systems mainly, meaning our land-based ICBMs[24] in particular. Submarine-based delivery systems would also nominally face cuts, but only in a way that does not affect the work the Americans are doing to create a new submarine fleet equipped with more powerful and more precise "Trident-2" missiles.

And it is proposed to leave aside for now, or not even to touch at all, such strategic weapons as long-range cruise missiles, the numbers of which the USA plans to increase to many thousands. By hook or by crook, the Americans are trying to keep their superiority in strategic aviation as well.

Our point of view is such: limitations and cuts in strategic armaments should be implemented as a package encompassing land-, sea- and air-based means, without any kind of exceptions. It is absolutely necessary that the principle of parity and equal security be maintained strictly at every stage of the cut, so as not to allow a distortion in favor of one side or the other.

Let's suppose for a moment that we accepted the American proposals. We would have to begin immediately to disassemble our land-based missiles, that is—the main part of our strategic potential, which, as you know, was built up over decades. At the same time, the USA would have room to implement all the military programs announced by Reagan.

The matter is seriously aggravated by the U.S. administration's intention to deploy a hundred "MX" strategic missiles, each equipped with 10 warheads. As you understand, it is impossible for us not to react to the emergence of a new generation of missiles. We considered it necessary to declare openly that we will be forced to deploy our own similar system.

Facing a frankly destructive position on the part of the USA, however, we do not intend to slam the door; we will continue to look for ways to encourage the Americans to change their approach. At the talks and outside the talks we are proposing a realistic alternative to the arms race: to freeze strategic armaments now and agree to large-scale cuts. We can go a long way here. It is only important that the number of both countries' delivery systems for strategic weapons be equal, and that this equality not be undermined by other nuclear arms, for example, forward-based weapons.

---

[24] Intercontinental ballistic missiles.

The question of these weapons figures in the talks on intermediate-range nuclear weapons in Europe. Here, unfortunately, there has been no progress either. One cannot escape the impression that, using these talks as a cover, the Americans intend to present us with a *fait accompli* by having deployed their new missiles in Western Europe. Construction of the launch pads for these missiles is already in full swing.

The American administration, apparently, is counting on the fact that the seeming attractiveness of its "zero option" will continue to confuse the public. However, after a year of talks in Geneva the real meaning of the position of both sides is more and more exposed.

We are countering the U.S. line with considered, balanced proposals. They were publicly mentioned during the 60th anniversary celebrations of the USSR. Our readiness to cut back on intermediate-range nuclear weapons and after that not to have a single missile, a single aircraft more than the countries of the North Atlantic alliance has caused a cacophony in the West. The disparity of positions among official circles is unusually great: from the icy, emphatically negative position taken by the USA and England to the more or less reasonable stance of other NATO members.

I think there are grounds to believe that the new Soviet proposals have developed into a strong element of pressure on Washington.

During the course of negotiations one will have to continue to appeal to the statesmen and public opinion of Western Europe so that no one has any illusions about the real position of the USA.

Undoubtedly, as the time nears for the deployment of the American missiles, unease and protests in the NATO countries will grow.

If, however, in spite of everything, the Americans begin to deploy their missiles in Western Europe, the Soviet Union will find a way to respond. Evidently, we will have to return to this question later.

The other talks, in Vienna, where cutbacks of military forces and armaments in Central Europe are being discussed, are also dragging along. Here, too, the responsibility above all rests with the USA. We are thinking seriously about how to move the negotiations away from fruitless arguments about the number of forces, and how to make our [negotiating] partners get down to business at last. Perhaps this could help us to move forward not only in Vienna but in Geneva as well.

It is in our common interest to influence the American administration, to keep it from extremes. Time will tell whether or not their policies will be amended. The Soviet Union is for constructive relations with the USA, but we do not intend to beg for it. Such relations can only be built by both sides.

This is how the situation looks with America.

[...]

Comrades! At one time, when the question of overcoming the "cold war" was being determined, we began with the intensification of relations with Western Europe. Now the situation is similar in some respects. A broad, meaningful dialogue with the West European countries, strengthening cooperation with them, could give détente a second wind. Certain prerequisites are in place for this.

All of our countries traditionally have broad ties with France. Probably, one should develop them more actively, especially because this helps to strengthen elements of

476

independence in her policy. Of course, [President François] Mitterrand behaves unevenly, and makes frequent curtseys in direction of the Americans. But recently, one notices the French interest in reviving contacts with us, not only in the economic but in the political sphere. Several French ministers have already visited the Soviet Union. In the near future a visit by [Foreign Minister Claude] Cheysson is planned.

We do not consider the position of the FRG government to be entirely negative. It, of course, links its actions more tightly with Washington. And it will probably take considerable political skill, well thought-out diplomatic, propaganda and other steps to hold on to the maximum number of positive [aspects] of what has been accumulated in our relations with this country in the last decade, as well as to prevent it from a full retreat to the Reagan administration position. As always, much will depend on the coordination of our efforts.

We managed generally to take the right tone in addressing the [Helmut] Köhl cabinet. That is, to provide considered support for the realistic elements of Bonn's policy and, at the same time, principled, reasoned criticism of everything that leads to a departure from recognition of postwar European realities and to the violation of treaty obligations.

In general, there are possibilities for active work here as well. We proceeded on this basis when deciding on the visit of Cde. A.A. Gromyko to the FRG.

Noticeable events in European life are the victories of the socialists in Spain and Sweden. The number of states with parties of the Socialist International in power has increased. Our relations with them are, of course, specific. But as a rule it is preferable to do business with social democrats, especially on questions of the struggle for peace, in particular because in almost all of these countries the communists either give the ruling party parliamentary support or directly participate in the government.

I think it is useful to pay more attention to such European countries as Finland, Austria and Greece. Their positions on a range of questions are close to ours; one could come to an agreement with them.

This, in particular, is shown by the [CSCE] meeting in Madrid.[25] Acting jointly and in a coordinated fashion, we managed to direct the work of this meeting into a more productive channel. The USA clearly wanted to turn Madrid into a forum of, so to speak, pure confrontation. They could not do it. But it will also be very, very difficult to achieve those positive decisions, which would expand the all-European process begun in Helsinki, especially on the question of convening a conference on confidence-building measures and disarmament in Europe. However, together we have set this task and we should strive to achieve it.

[...]

Evidently, even under aggravated circumstances there is no need to change the strategic direction of our policy. A policy directed towards peace, towards the elimination of the nuclear threat—that is huge political capital for socialism. We should

---

[25] The most recent round of the Madrid meetings on European security, which took place from November 9–December 17, 1982, and involved 35 countries, ended in a deadlock primarily over interpretations of human rights.

continue to implement this policy consistently and purposefully. We do not want confrontations. Peaceful co-existence, disarmament, mutually beneficial cooperation—these are not propagandistic mottos, but the living essence of our policy.

We will not spare efforts to mobilize our peoples to resist the arms race, to expose the very ideology of militarism, not to leave room for views about the fatal unavoidability of a nuclear catastrophe, and to persuade them that détente is the future.

It is necessary to build up initiatives on the key questions of war and peace. This is a great task if for no other reason than that such initiatives force people to compare the two policies of NATO and the Warsaw Pact, and to draw conclusions—and, as a rule, in our favor.

A convincing example of this is the Soviet Union's commitment not to use nuclear weapons first. Western public opinion, as well as respected politicians, have valued its meaning. The impact of this decision turned out to be powerful and longstanding.

The further unfolding of the struggle against the militarization of space and for its use for exclusively peaceful aims, could yield a big political gain. This is a task of truly international importance. The socialist countries resolutely insist on the prohibition of deployment of any types of weapons in space. These efforts should probably be further developed, and ideas devised to back them up, including in the area of inspections.

Comrades!

Recently, attempts are being made in some quarters to treat our defensive military–political alliance and the aggressive NATO bloc on the same level. This is a strange view, particularly under current conditions. It is enough to compare how the Warsaw Pact and NATO have behaved themselves in different situations to be convinced that our alliance has always been a reliable counterweight to the forces of aggression and expansion. It has already played a progressive role in European and world affairs and will continue to play it. And if NATO has something to brag about, it is the ability to raise tensions.

While undertaking peaceful efforts we have considered and do consider it unquestionably necessary not to allow the balance of forces of both military groups to be upset. It would be a mistake if we did not respond to the strengthening of NATO and to the increase in its military preparations with appropriate care for our common defense capability.

We are not supporters of constant confrontation and competition between the two military groups. Our countries have expressed readiness more than once to disband their organization and the North Atlantic alliance simultaneously. In our opinion, one must not even speak about the unilateral disbandment of the Warsaw Pact. To seriously insist on the unilateral liquidation of our defensive alliance would mean to intentionally put the socialist countries in a difficult situation, where they would have to act alone against a well-organized enemy who is armed to the teeth. There is no doubt that the imperialists would judge this as a show of weakness, and would respond with even greater pressure on the socialist countries.

More than others, the Soviet Union probably feels the burden of the arms race, which we are being pulled in to. It is not easy for anyone to provide additional means for strengthening their military forces. For Reagan it is not a problem to take tens of billions of appropriations for social needs and pass them on to the military–industrial complex. But we cannot help but think about the well-being of workers.

But, unfortunately, today there is no other way out except to respond to the provocative actions of NATO with counter-actions that would be convincing to contemporary American politicians. Our peoples would not understand it if carelessness were displayed with regard to the NATO threats.

The highest awareness in our current harsh times would not at all be uncalled for. Joint defensive efforts are necessary for the security of each of our countries. Certain measures will probably have to be taken within the framework of our alliance, and by each of its members. [...]

I want to touch on one organizational question. Hasn't the time come to implement the decision taken at the meeting in Bucharest[26] to create a joint secretariat of the Warsaw Pact, and to think about its tasks and working order? Other proposals could probably arise regarding the working mechanism of our cooperation. If everyone agrees, appropriate powers could be given to the ministers of foreign affairs.

Further. The U.S. policy of aggravating the confrontation not only holds dangers for the states of the Warsaw Pact, it threatens the vital interests of other socialist countries. An important part of our policy entails mutual action with Cuba, Mongolia, Vietnam and Laos. Despite the known peculiarities of the positions of Yugoslavia and of the DPRK[27], we are paying appropriate attention to the development of relations with these countries. I suppose that in the forthcoming period it would be worth it to work even more actively in the direction of improving cooperation with the socialist states that are not party to our treaty. We are already acting as if along parallel lines when crisis situations occur, such as Israel's aggression in Lebanon.

It would probably be justified if, for a start, our dear Czechoslovak hosts in a general manner informed the countries of the world socialist system, including China, about the work of our current meeting. This would to some extent help to achieve a greater mutual understanding with them. In the future we can think about other steps in this direction.

[...]

We attach considerable significance to the proposal to conclude a treaty on the mutual renunciation of force and maintaining peaceful relations between the member-states of the Warsaw Pact and the member-states of the North Atlantic alliance. As we understand it, work toward advancing this proposal will assume a visible place among our common foreign policy efforts in the near future. [...]

[*Source: VA-01/40473, BA-MA. Translated by Sergey Radchenko.*]

[26] The PCC meeting of July 5–7, 1966. See Document No. 41.
[27] Democratic People's Republic of Korea (North Korea).

Document No. 99: Scenario of the "Soiuz-83" Exercise, June 9–August 2, 1983

Two excerpted descriptions of the "Soiuz-83" exercise appear below. The first document, a Czechoslovak military analysis, describes how the maneuvers fit with new Soviet military plans. It explains that the exercise presumed a Western ability to launch surprise attacks in all European theaters simultaneously. This same estimate of enemy capabilities can be found in early NATO and American documents from the 1950s where 175 Soviet divisions were believed to be ready to attack almost anywhere yet still remain capable of defending the homeland. A further assumption in the document below is that the West would resort to launching over 5,000 nuclear munitions if the initial assaults failed. In the second document, a letter to Czechoslovak Defense Minister Martin Dzúr, Marshal Viktor Kulikov provides a detailed break-down of how the exercise played out. He singles out the need to destroy the West's "intelligence and diversionary systems," which he describes as "qualitatively new means of warfare," even before the onset of military action, if the Warsaw Pact forces are to have any chance of success.

a) Analysis of the exercise, June 6, 1983

The "Westerners" planned to start hostilities by surprise on June 10 in the morning, and initiate strategic operations in all European theaters simultaneously. [They decided] to organize their main assault grouping in the Central European theater.

The goal of the offensive operation in the Central European theater was to destroy The "Easterners" nuclear missile grouping, ground, and naval forces on the territories of the GDR, ČSSR. and PPr and in the Baltic Sea, advance toward the borders of the USSR and sreate conditions for developing further attack.

If there were a danger that the attainment of the goals of the operation by conventional means would be frustrated, the "Westerners" presumed resorting to the use of nuclear weapons (more than 5,000 nuclear munitions, about 2,800 of which during the first strike).

[*Source: "Rozbor operačně-strategického velitelsko-štábního cvičení… 'Sojuz-83'" (Analysis of the Strategic Operational Staff Command Exercise… "Sojuz-83"), VS,OS, 1987, č.j. 75, 174/1, VÚA. Translated by Vojtech Mastny.*]

b) Letter by Marsal Kulikov to Czechoslovak Defense Minister
   Martin Dzúr, August 2, 1983

This exercise was carried out in accordance with the plan of joint activities of the Unified Armed Forces of the member-states of the Warsaw Treaty from 30 May to

9 June 1983 on the territories of the GDR, Polish People's Republic, ČSSR, and in the southern part of the Baltic sea on the subject: "The transfer of the Unified Armed Forces on the Western front from peace time to [active] military condition. The planning and conduct of the strategic operation in the theater of military operations."

[...]

The particular feature of the exercise was that the allied land and naval forces were brought into *heightened* combat readiness at the sending of a pre-determined signal through the "Monument" communications system and at the dispatch of an order from the Supreme Headquarters [of the Soviet Armed Forces] with the simultaneous subordination of the fronts (fleets) and armies to the Supreme Command of the Unified Armed Forces in the Western Theater of Military Operations. The next stage of combat readiness was achieved when, upon dispatch of appropriate signals and instructions of the Main Command of the Unified Armed forces in the Theater of Military Operations, the forces were brought into a state of combat readiness at their permanent stationing points. The transition of groupings and detachments onto the offensive from their permanent stationing points and the conduct of the air operation were carried out in real time by the "hour by hour" method. During the exercise, the methods of combating the enemy's forward intelligence systems were extensively practiced. [...]

Operational groups consisting of 10–12 generals and officers headed by the deputies of the supreme commander and of the chief of staff of the Unified Armed Forces in the course of the exercise worked on the fronts and in the armies. To work in the Staff of the Unified Armed Forces, the general staffs of the allied armies provided operational groups led by department heads of the general staffs and consisting of up to 15 people [...] and 5–10 vehicles. Besides, the general staffs of the allied armies provided to the Supreme Command special communication groups consisting of 40–50 people, 17–20 special vehicles, including the "R-140" radio station, and secure telegraph and telephone communications equipment. Special small-scale communications groups were dispatched from the Supreme Command to the fronts; there was an interchange between them as the fronts and armies interacted. In all, about 20 communications groups were dispatched, which provided for closed communications between the Staff of the Unified Armed Forces, general staffs, fronts and armies. [...]

The Staff of the Unified Armed Forces and the General (Main)[28] staffs of the allied armies will continue this work so as to have, by the end of 1985, common and uniform documents.

The method of counter-attack from permanent deployment areas, practiced during the exercises, showed that it requires intricate preparation, skilful organization and the performance of complex activities to provide for the timely advance of formations and units to the points of deployment as well as for strict coordination of the assignments and movements of the advancing forces at the front and army group levels. In addition, the missile forces and the artillery must come out to their predetermined position points and to their firing positions earlier than the main forces of the motorized rifle and tank formations. The deployment of formations and units

---

[28] The East German general staff was officially called the Main Staff.

at different distances from the state border does not allow for a simultaneous transition to attack as part of the assault groupings of the front. Therefore, it is necessary to determine a different time for initiating the advance of these detachments from their permanent stationing points, taking into consideration the [necessity of] their simultaneous passage to deployment points and the [simultaneous] delivery of a strike.

The exercise practiced extensively the deployment of the operational maneuver groups of the front within the armored army corps of the general purpose forces or within a separate army corps composed of brigades. The need to further improve their order of battle and organizational structure was confirmed, as was the need for securing more effectively their transition to combat and operations in depth.

Analysis of the practice of countering the enemy's intelligence and diversionary systems has shown that without the reliable destruction of these qualitatively new means of warfare, even before their introduction into action, it is hardly possible to achieve success in the operation. Therefore, the destruction of these weapons systems must be an integral part of the overall outgunning of the enemy before the military actions would actually begin.

[...]

An effective air operation [...] aimed at destroying nuclear missile, air force and air-defense formations and gaining air superiority was achieved by a massive concentration of the participating forces and equipment.

[...]

The operation was conducted in three stages with the delivery of six massive strikes at a depth of 600–800 km [and] a breadth of up to 1000 km. In the course of the first 24 hours, three massive strikes were delivered against the enemy's air defense sites, nuclear missile facilities and airfields. About 9,000 sorties were conducted. As a result, serious damage was inflicted on the nuclear missile formations, the air defense system and the enemy's administrative system, thus creating conditions for capturing the strategic initiative in the air and on land. [...]

The experience of planning an air- and seaborne landing showed that it is expedient to prepare for this within the front operating along the coast with the participation of the unified navy and under the direct command of the Supreme Command of the Unified Armed Forces in the Theater of Military Operations.

The actual performance of the unified naval forces and their equipment in landing seaborne troops confirmed once again that the whole fleet needs to have landing craft and hovercraft, as well as marine units. [...]

[*Source: VS, OS, 1987, č.j. 75174/1, VÚA. Translated by Sergey Radchenko.*]

Document No. 100: East German Summary of Warsaw Pact Summit in Moscow, June 28, 1983

The main purpose of this Warsaw Pact leadership meeting in Moscow was to assess the impending introduction of Euromissiles—intermediate-range missiles intended to counter the same kind of missiles already deployed by the Soviet Union—which by now was regarded as all but certain. If the missiles were deployed, the Soviet Union would have to live up to its stated intention to walk out of the Geneva talks, the only still ongoing East–West arms control negotiations. Andropov's message to his colleagues is that the Warsaw Pact must not allow the West to achieve military superiority through deployment of the new missiles. The question was what measures should be taken. Options ranged from deploying counter-missiles near the borders of Western countries that accepted Euromissiles to having individual Warsaw Pact member-states influence their NATO counterparts not to go ahead with the deployments. One conclusion that can be drawn from the second proposal is that by this time Moscow had become more dependent on its allies than in previous decades.

[...]

1. The Moscow meeting, which took place on initiative of the USSR half a year after the Prague session of the Political Consultative Committee of the states of the Warsaw Treaty, served:

   − to reassess the development of the international situation, particularly after the meeting at Williamsburg and the latest NATO meetings in Brussels and Paris;

   [...]

   − to discuss the necessary military and political counter-measures of the Warsaw Treaty states in case of the deployment of new U.S. intermediate-range ballistic missiles in Western Europe;

   [...]

3.a) The debate about the *defense measures* to be taken by the Warsaw Treaty states in case of the stationing of missiles in Western Europe took a central position. Cde. Andropov [...] reported, in addition to previous official Soviet statements, particularly the government declaration of May 28, 1983, that the USSR

   − refrains from its unilateral moratorium to deploy intermediate-range ballistic missiles in the Western part of the USSR;

   − also deploys wide range missiles;

   − is going to move Soviet tactical missiles closer to the borders of those NATO countries that deploy them.

Cde. Erich Honecker [...] explained the readiness of the GDR to make its territory available for stationing respective missile systems as a counter-weight to the planned [deployment of] U.S. nuclear weapons.

Cde. Husák remarked for the ČSSR (whose territory would also be affected) that it would actively contribute to the necessary measures. He explicitly supported the explanation of Cde. Erich Honecker.

Cdes. Jaruzelski, Kádár, and Zhivkov remarked that the military superiority of the United States and NATO must not be tolerated under any circumstances. [...]

4. The *SRR* [Socialist Republic of Romania] provided incorrect assessments and information, presenting them more arrogantly and more provocatively than earlier. The most comprehensive program of the struggle for peace is supposedly the declaration of the non-aligned New Delhi states. [Romania's] familiar divergent assessment of the reasons for the aggravation of the international situation has been connected to the claim that the defensive measures of the Warsaw Treaty states in the case of the stationing of new U.S. missiles would accelerate the arms race, increase the risk of war, and jeopardize the existence of the European peoples.

The SRR presented a series of proposals, which ran counter to the security interests of the Warsaw Treaty states, and which, on the question of intermediate-range nuclear weapons in Europe, amounted to support of the "zero or interim solution" of the United States. [...]

With reference to the proposals announced by Cde. Andropov, Cde. Ceauşescu demanded that the USSR not only inform the other states of the Warsaw Treaty about them, but also discuss such proposals with them in advance collectively at the highest level. In doing so, in his view, the elaboration of common positions, the consolidation of unity, cooperation, and solidarity among the fraternal countries could be served. [...]

Cde. Jaruzelski pointed out that the USSR was carrying the main burden of the defense of socialism and was also the shield of Poland's security and its borders. The PPR [Polish People's Republic] has been fulfilling its alliance commitments. At the same time, he referred to the fact that Poland suffered a direct deficit in the amount of 6 billion dollars and, in addition, an indirect deficit of almost 6 billion dollars because of the boycott policy of the imperialist states. Cde. Jaruzelski assessed the Pope's visit as having brought a certain degree of ideological damage. But the utterances of the Pope concerning peace and the borders of Poland corresponded to the common position of the Warsaw Pact states.

Cde. Kádár put special weight on the statement that the PRH [People's Republic of Hungary] stood in favor of enlarging the political dialogue as well as the bilateral relationship with capitalist states, particularly on economic and cultural grounds, regardless of the complicated international situation. For this purpose, the PRH was going to contribute its share with "its independent and autonomous foreign policy within the scope of the alliance."

8. At the end of the debate, Cde. Andropov proposed approving the *message to the leadership of the People's Republic of China*.

[...] Since the SRR rejected the draft, the message was not directly adopted at the meeting. Cde. Ceauşescu has been granted some days to think it over. The other fraternal countries agreed to pass the message—even if the SRR should not accept it— through the Soviet Foreign Ministry to the ambassador of the PRC [People's Republic of China] in Moscow within a short time.

[*Source: DC/20/ I/3/1950, SAPMO. Translated by Thomas Holderegger.*]

Document No. 101: Summary of the Committee of Ministers of Foreign Affairs Meeting in Sofia, October 20, 1983

One aim of this meeting of the Warsaw Pact's Committee of Foreign Ministers held on October 13–14, 1983, was to decide on ways to warn NATO against another round of the arms race. Most of the treatment of that subject focuses on a speech by Soviet Foreign Minister Gromyko who emphasizes the desirability of exploring "a convergence of interests between European socialist and capitalist countries" in order to influence U.S. policy. But this summary also devotes extensive attention to the problems Romania's persistent opposition to Warsaw Pact proposals poses for the Eastern alliance's own attempts to present a unified front to the West.

Work on the documents adopted by the Committee of Ministers of Foreign Affairs was affected by the fact that the Romanian delegation rejected the proposed texts prepared by the delegation of the People's Republic of Bulgaria following discussions with the USSR. [The Romanians] even submitted a virtually new alternative counterproposal. They persistently refused to accept the final text, which included both direct and indirect accusations that the USA and their allies are responsible for the current deterioration of the international state of affairs. They objected to wording, which implied that the Socialist Republic of Romania (SRR) was approaching international affairs in concert with other member-states of the Warsaw Treaty. It [Romania] refused to express support for the USSR's peace initiatives and suggestions for dealing with the issue of intermediate-range missiles in Europe. They even refused to positively affirm certain positions contained in the Prague Political declaration of the Political Consultative Committee,[29] in the communiqué from the April meeting of the Committee of Ministers of Foreign Affairs,[30] and in the Joint Declaration from June 28 in Moscow.[31] On the other hand, they backed language to the effect that the Warsaw Treaty affirms proposals for solving particular international issues that were submitted by collectives or individuals in the past. Approving this language would mean that the Warsaw Treaty as a whole accepts and supports various proposals submitted by the SRR on several occasions.

Romania advocated several times a text that could be interpreted as saying both the USA and USSR bear responsibility for the current state of affairs. It went furthest when demanding that the communiqué include a passage stating that the problem of intermediate-range missiles in Europe can only be solved by cutting the number of and destroying existing missiles (which would mean disposing of Soviet

---

[29] Declaration of January 5, 1983. See http://www.isn.ethz.ch/php/documents/collection_-3/PCC_docs/1983/1983_4.pdf.

[30] Communiqué of April 7, 1983, http://www.isn.ethz.ch/php/documents/collection_-3/CMFA_docs/CMFA_1983_I/1983_I_8.pdf.

[31] See document no. 100.

missiles, as demanded by the USA). Romania also failed to agree on expressing support for the USSR's policy at the Geneva negotiations or to label the USA's policy as not constructive, on the grounds of not being informed about the proceedings of the Geneva talks. Romania also objected to mentioning French and British nuclear capabilities.

Because of the Romanian delegation's resistance, efforts failed to include in the communiqué a direct response to the recent provocative appearance of [George] Shultz, [George] Bush and [Ronald] Reagan against the socialist bloc,[32] as demanded by the German Democratic Republic (GDR), Polish People's Republic (PPR) and Czechoslovak Socialist Republic (ČSSR).

For a long time, the SRR also refused to include in the communiqué a passage stating that the socialist countries had never sought military superiority but would never allow anyone to gain military superiority over them. In this context, the SRR maintained wording about deep responsibility for a new phase in the hectic arms race by those countries on whose territory the new missiles were stationed—allowing for an interpretation that would apply to both western and socialist countries (the ČSSR and GDR). Compared to the past, the SRR strongly demanded this time that the communiqué focus on the situation in Europe, excluding global and particularly non-European issues. It refused to include in the communiqué a detailed list of tension epicenters in the Near East, South Africa and Central America. These issues were therefore included in a more general form in item 5. The Czechoslovak delegation suggested including a paragraph in the introduction or conclusion of the communiqué stating that the current deteriorating international situation calls for broader cooperation, stronger unity and deeper coordination of activities in foreign affairs by the socialist countries. This suggestion was supported by the delegations of five countries, but rejected flatly by the SRR delegation, so that barely a single line was included in the communiqué on mutual cooperation among the Warsaw Treaty member-states.

The SRR delegation also demanded additional items in the communiqué, such as the usefulness of holding meetings between [Iurii] Andropov and Reagan, participation by other Warsaw Treaty and NATO members in the Geneva negotiations on intermediate-range nuclear missiles in Europe, and parallel talks with other European officials on the problems of Euromissiles with a view to aiding the advancement of the Geneva negotiations. None of these items was included in the communiqué.

The discussion of the communiqué sometimes proceeded in a very tense atmosphere, where it was not clear whether the SRR delegation wanted to agree on mutually acceptable wording or persistently assert its demands, and thus prevent the communiqué from being approved and as a result break up the meeting of the Committee of Ministers.

As the Romanian delegation refused to include these passages in the communiqué, compromise wording was only achieved on October 2 after backstage talks following the arrival of [Romanian Foreign] Minister S[tefan] Andrei.

---

[32] The reference is probably to the U.S. reaction to the downing on September 1, 1983, of a South Korean civilian airliner by Soviet military aircraft.

[...]

While preparing the communiqué text, a draft protocol of the meeting of the Committee of Ministers of Foreign Affairs was being negotiated. The greatest difficulties were connected with the Romanian request to include in the protocol a decision to set up a working group of experts in Bucharest, which would deal with problems related to nearly all negotiations on disarmament and coordinate the Warsaw Treaty member-states' respective proceedings. It was obvious that, by establishing such a group, the SRR wanted to gain access to information from these negotiations, especially in Geneva, and thus obtain the capability to influence the Soviet negotiating positions, or else claim to have such a capability). When this request was refused outright, the SRR disapproved of the establishment of any kind of working group. Later on, it proposed setting up a working group on nuclear-free zones in Europe. As there were some sensitive aspects to this problem, this proposal was not accepted either. To be fair, in denying the Romanian request, the Czechoslovak proposal to establish a working group on averting a nuclear war was deferred, too. It was decided to resolve through diplomacy which new working groups to set up in the region, and to submit the results for approval at the forthcoming ministers' committee meeting in April 1984 in Bucharest.

[...]

A confidential protocol from the meeting of the Committee of Ministers of Foreign Affairs in Sofia includes among other things a decision to approve the expert group recommendation on the problems of military budgets and of chemical weapons in Europe. It approves the results of an expert group on questions of the Joint Secretariat and improvement of the Warsaw Treaty working mechanism. As the SRR rejected new organizational forms of cooperation, such as the creation in Moscow of a standing group for the exchange of information, the state of affairs that ensued from the Prague PCC meeting has been confirmed. This entails a system of topical consultations of deputy ministers of foreign affairs and the establishment of working groups of experts to deal with particular issues [assigned by the deputies]. As a new feature, the post of the general secretary of the Political Consultative Committee is to be rotated in the future, the incumbent coming from the country that hosts the next meeting of the Committee. The Committee of Ministers recommended this material for approval at the following meeting of the Political Consultative Committee.

[...]

The actual meeting of the ministers of foreign affairs took place in the afternoon of October 13 and the morning of October 14. Comrade Gromyko appeared as the first speaker [...], stressing that the deployment of U.S. intermediate-range nuclear missiles right at the doorstep of the socialist community would create a severe breach of the military parity between the USSR and the USA, the Warsaw Treaty and NATO, a rupture of strategic stability and a steep deterioration in international affairs.

He alerted [the group] to the fact that a powerful peace movement in the West is growing in strength against Reagan's effort to drag the NATO allies into his militarist course against the USSR, a movement which must be taken into account by the respective governments as a serious political force. This is why ever more often, the sober voices of many politicians are to be heard. In Denmark and the Netherlands, it is a majority of parliamentarians. In Greece and Sweden it is the governments, in West Germany it is a large group of Social Democrats in the parliament. Many unconcerned countries are stepping in against the USA's current course, which resulted in Reagan's sharp invective against them at the current session of the United Nations General Assembly. The Prague Political Declaration undoubtedly played a positive role in disclosing the true culprits of the current sharpened international situation.

Comrade Gromyko then emphasized the need to focus our efforts on influencing those who are responsible for the foreign policy of the NATO countries, and to help the broad Western public become acquainted as thoroughly as possible with the perils of Reagan's aggressive course and to inspire it to [take] the most decisive actions.

He pointed out that not even in this crucial phase of the Soviet–American negotiations in Geneva on limitations of nuclear armaments in Europe did Washington bring anything new [to the table]. Despite the U.S.'s much trumpeted "flexibility" [its proposal] is still an unacceptable "interim" variant. The Geneva negotiations are a public deceit, while the deployment of U.S. missiles in Western Europe is indeed a reality. The Soviet Union is therefore assisting the United States' allies to increase the pressure on the Reagan administration with a view to negotiating seriously in Geneva over proposals to cut back on nuclear weapons in Europe. Referring to a difference in views between the USA and Denmark, Belgium, the Netherlands, Greece and West Germany, Comrade Gromyko said that there are yet reserves for our subsequent political work. He stressed that under these conditions it is utterly crucial for the socialist countries to let the USA know their common determination to step in against their dangerous plans, "so that the people of Washington and other NATO capitals hear that we speak one language..., that our countries are proceeding in a single direction, that they work alike, hard and decisively." He pointed out the serious risks that are imminent, should our adversary discover discord in our progress. He added that many times the Central Committee of the CPSU had discussed possible scenarios for both a political and military course of action in case the deployment of U.S. intermediate-range nuclear missiles came about after all.

As related to other problems, Comrade Gromyko stated that the USA and NATO had failed to contribute in any way to the continuation of the Vienna negotiations. We will strive so that our Western partners clearly state their opinion about our key proposals. On the question of control, he said that "the USA and NATO want control without disarmament while we insist on controlled disarmament."

He evaluated the results of the Madrid meeting positively, where socialist countries succeeded in hitting the "bull's eye" by correctly spotting the difference of opinions between the USA and the Western allies.[33] This shows clearly that "a convergence of interests between the European socialist and capitalist countries in continuing the East–West dialogue and preserving the fruits of détente has proved to be a factor that the United States cannot ignore."

[33] The Madrid review meeting of the Conference on Security and Cooperation in Europe, concluded on September 9, 1983.

[...]

Comrade Gromyko then provided information about bilateral relations between the USSR and other Western countries [besides the United States]. He remarked that such a level of tensions in relations with the USA as now exists has not been registered for a long time. U.S. foreign policy is boosting its propaganda against the USSR and "has broken all records in cynicism and lies."

After Comrade Gromyko, [Foreign] Ministers S[tefan] Olszowski, B[ohuslav] Chňoupek, State Secretary and First Deputy Minister H[erbert] Krolikowski, and on the following day P[éter] Várkonyi, S[tefan] Andrei and P[etar] Mladenov, stepped up. With the exception of S. Andrei, all the ministers expressed their approval of the assessment of the international political situation and of the primary tasks as laid down by A. A. Gromyko, with an emphasis on improving coordination in their implementation.

[...]

The extraordinary importance of the Sofia meeting of the Committee of Ministers of Foreign Affairs consisted in the fact that the meeting took place only a few weeks before the planned deployment of new U.S. intermediate-range missiles in certain West European countries. The communiqué, a document jointly adopted at the meeting, is one of our last warnings against this dangerous step and one of our last attempts to avert the deployment of these missiles. Although practical preparations for the deployment are already being undertaken, this document proceeds from the conviction that it is still possible to reach an agreement at the Geneva talks in the spirit of the USSR's proposals; it encourages the continuation of these talks and also appeals to the NATO member-states and other European countries to prevent the deployment of new intermediate-range nuclear missiles in Europe, and to contribute actively to the success of the Geneva negotiations.

[*Source: Č.j. 016.091/83, Archives of the Ministry of Foreign Affairs, Prague. Translated by Stan Mareš.*]

Document No. 102: Statement by Marshal Ustinov
at the Committee of Ministers of Defense Meeting
in Sofia, December 5–7, 1983

This meeting provided a forum for Soviet Defense Minister Marshal Dmitrii Ustinov to speak to his Warsaw Pact colleagues about the dangers posed by the West's decision to deploy Euromissiles.[34] He declares that the move calls for measures to preserve "equilibrium"—which ironically was the West's rationale for deploying them in the first place. This view was the Warsaw Pact's public position but was apparently genuinely believed by its leaders because Ustinov's remarks were made during a closed meeting. Commenting that the West is undertaking unprecedented preparations for war, he wonders aloud how the alliance should respond. He cites Soviet party General Secretary Iurii Andropov's instructions not to copy the enemy's armament program but to "go one's own way," and force the adversary to adjust accordingly.

In response to the aggressive actions of the Reagan administration and the governments of several other NATO countries, the Soviet Union has declared that it is lifting its voluntary moratorium on the deployment of intermediate-range Soviet nuclear weapons in the European part of the country. These weapons will now also be deployed at locations from which they could reach the territories of the relevant West European countries.

In coordination with the GDR and the ČSSR, preparations for stationing longer-range tactical missiles on the territories of these countries will be accelerated.

As regards U.S. territory, the necessary retaliatory measures will be taken. The Americans will not fail to notice the change in their situation after the stationing of their missiles in Western Europe. [...]

The above-mentioned measures are necessary for our security. American Imperialism has announced a "crusade" against Socialism. It is attempting to destroy Socialism as a social system and to establish itself as the dominant world power. Never before has the aggressiveness of American imperialism been so apparent. The American invasion of the small and essentially defenseless state of Grenada,[35] which constituted a breach of faith and was totally unprovoked, has demonstrated that the Washington administration brutally disrespects the norms of international law and is capable of the most irresponsible war adventures and crimes.

[President Ronald] Reagan's intention is to demonstrate to the Soviet Union, the

[34] The Pershing-2 intermediate-range missiles and cruise missiles to be installed in Western Europe to counter the already deployed Soviet SS-20 missiles targeted at the area.

[35] U.S. forces invaded Grenada on October 25, 1983, after former Deputy Prime Minister Bernard Coard, a hard-line Marxist, had seized power on the island in a coup. The move was part of the Reagan administration's campaign to contest perceived communist gains, particularly in Central America and the Caribbean.

other countries of the Warsaw Treaty, Cuba and countries like Nicaragua, Syria, Angola, Ethiopia and several others, that the USA is determined to apply military force against any state whose social and political system does not suit it, whenever it considers it to be necessary.

In its effort to gain control of positions of power in the world, the Washington administration together with its NATO allies is doing everything it can to attain military superiority over the socialist community.

The war preparations of imperialism have taken on truly unprecedented proportions. In the USA pressure is being applied to implement large-scale programs of military technology. So-called "pre-emptive strike forces" are being strengthened through the development of new tactical first-strike nuclear weapons, and also through the creation of guided systems of existing high-precision weapons. An all-encompassing missile defense system is being developed. The weapons race is being expanded to outer space.

U.S. military expenditures are growing at an enormous rate. Whereas in the past five years (1979–1983) they amounted to 850 billion dollars, they will more than double in the five years to come (1984–1988) and reach the astronomical amount of 1 trillion 800 billion dollars.

The ruling circles in the other NATO countries are also increasing military expenditures, building up their armed forces and militarizing their politics and economy. NATO forces are being reinforced in all the European theaters of war.

The growing aggressiveness of the USA and NATO is also evident in their new military strategy, which emphasizes conducting decisive attacks right from the first hours of the war. [...]

At the NATO meetings presently taking place, measures are being considered to push further ahead with war preparations. Also on the agenda are recommendations to begin working out plans for the deployment of the new American nuclear missiles to be stationed in England, Germany and Italy. The growing threat to the USSR and other countries of the socialist community is no illusion, but rather a brutal reality that we cannot afford to ignore.

It would be wrong to overlook the danger to freedom and socialism that arises from these war preparations of the USA and NATO. We do not have the right to allow the Unified Armed Forces of the Warsaw Pact to fall behind the NATO armies, especially not in the area of technical equipment. For this reason we will take additional measures to strengthen the defense of our states in 1983–1985.

In the implementation of our policy on military technology, we will be guided by the directives of comrade I.A. Andropov: "We will not run after our potential adversary and copy his armament program but go our own way, assert the initiave in the development of military technology, and force the adversary to adjust to us."

[*Source: VA-01/32870, pp. 88–97, BA-MA. Translated by Ursula Froese.*]

Document No. 103: Report on the Committee of Ministers of Foreign Affairs Meeting in Budapest, April 26, 1984

The main significance of this Czech summary of the foreign ministers' meeting is that it gives a clear picture of the concern that the Reagan administration's rearmament policy provoked within the Eastern alliance. Foreign ministers' meetings were generally characterized by very candid discussions. As usual, the Romanians created significant difficulties for the Soviets and their closer allies, in this case by effectively backing Reagan's proposal for an "interim solution" of freezing NATO Euromissile deployments at current levels while requiring the Warsaw Pact to remove all of its previous missile installations. This discussion came at a time when the Soviet Union and its allies were preparing for the Stockholm negotiations on confidence-building measures as part of the CSCE process. The Romanians wanted to focus on making missile deployments less threatening while the Soviets sought to undermine Western Europeans' support for further deployments.

On April 19 and 20, 1984, the 10th meeting of the Committee of Ministers of Foreign Affairs of the Warsaw Treaty member-states took place in Budapest. It was the first meeting after the deployment of new U.S. intermediate-range nuclear missiles in West Germany, Great Britain and Italy, after countermeasures on the part of the USSR, East Germany and the ČSSR, and after the failure of Soviet–American negotiations in Geneva.

[…]

The documents were proposed by the Hungarian side, after discussing them with the USSR. All delegations agreed to accept the Hungarian proposals as a basis for negotiations. The delegation of the Socialist Republic of Romania (SRR), however, raised several objections to all of the proposals, the acceptance of which would have resulted in the complete transformation of the documents' content.

THE COMMUNIQUÉ

In the introductory part—an evaluation of the international state of affairs—the SRR delegation refused to accept a passage, which accused the USA and NATO of [responsibility for] the current complex and tense situation, and pressed for adoption of more general language. In the passage on dialogue between East and West, the SRR surprisingly refused to agree to react positively to the NATO declaration of December 9, 1982, in Brussels—without giving acceptable grounds. Apparently it realized that a positive attitude would really mean supporting certain "differentiating processes" in NATO, or approaches by some Western European countries, which are not identical to those of the USA, and which we want to cultivate, not

492

ignore. In the end, however, the SRR agreed with modified wording of this issue in the communiqué's conclusion. The problems of intermediate-range nuclear missiles in Europe and Soviet–American negotiations are the key point of the entire communiqué. The SRR wanted wording that demanded an end to the further deployment of U.S. intermediate-range missiles in Europe, which would—according to the SRR's interpretation—be equivalent to a measure requesting withdrawal of previously deployed missiles. In the meantime, our countermeasures should be cancelled. This should create conditions for an urgent resumption of Soviet–American negotiations on disposing of nuclear weapons in Europe, both intermediate-range and tactical. This SRR proposal was really based on [Ronald] Reagan's "interim measure," without taking into account pronouncements by the USSR's leading officials and entirely ignoring the existence of U.S. intermediate-range missiles in Europe. The SRR representative stressed that without an idea for a way out of the current situation (Euromissiles, Soviet–U.S. negotiations), the Committee's meeting lacked sense because it is supposedly impossible to expect that the U.S. missiles would be withdrawn without prior negotiations. The SRR's standpoint was unacceptable to the USSR and the other delegations. After difficult talks, a complex compromise and mutually acceptable wording was negotiated.

THE PROTOCOL

Shortly before the Committee of Ministers meeting in Budapest, the SRR submitted for negotiations its own text of a nuclear weapons appeal. Because of the unacceptability of its contents from our point of view, negotiations on the matter were prevented. Not having accepted the Romanian proposal resulted in complications over completing negotiations on a proposal by the Warsaw Treaty countries to call on the NATO member-states to hold multilateral discussions on a treaty banning the use of force against each other. In the end, the call was successfully negotiated; because of the SRR's negative position, however, it was not distributed along with the communiqué on April 20, but was to be handed over to the ambassador of NATO countries in Budapest on July 7, 1984.

The most difficult talks were in the context of a proposal by Polish People's Republic (PPR) to establish a working group to prepare a protocol extending the validity of the Warsaw Treaty. This proposal was supported at all levels by representatives of all countries (special representatives, deputies and ministers), with the exception of Romania. Although the PPR submitted two other compromise proposals with the agreement of the other delegations, none of them was acceptable to the SRR. The SRR's representatives flatly proclaimed at all levels that according to the view of the SRR's leadership, this question could not be dealt with on any level but the highest. They refused to accept any written document on this topic, claiming that on this level (i.e. not the highest one) this question did not exist for the SRR.

[...]

The meeting of the Committee of Ministers of Foreign Affairs took place in the afternoon of April 19 (chaired by Comrade Chňoupek) and in the morning of April 20 (chaired by Comrade Mladenov).

[...]

Chňoupek justified the necessity of installing operational–tactical missile systems on the territory of the ČSSR as part of the counter-measures against the deployment of U.S. intermediate-range missiles in Western Europe. He stated that these measures were adopted in an agreement between the ČSSR and USSR to secure the defense capability of Czechoslovakia and our entire community and to sustain peace.

[...]

He further stressed that the ČSSR consistently exercises the agreed-upon policy of differentiation with respect to the NATO countries, which has already brought positive results. The West has once again had to realize that it cannot deal with us from a position of strength.

[...]

Várkonyi stated that the talks between leading representatives of People's Republic of Hungary (PRH) and some representatives of Western capitalist countries have proved that fears of the emergent international situation exist in many countries of Western Europe and that efforts are on the rise to soften the extreme manifestations of American foreign policy, to divert the dangerous course and to support a dialogue. The PRH regards such talks as useful and essential as they give an opportunity to convincingly explain and maintain the standpoints of the socialist commonwealth.

[...]

Mladenov provided information on the Zhivkov–Papandreou[36] talks in November of last year, which demonstrated identical views on several international issues, including that of transformation of the Balkans into a nuclear-free zone.

[...]

O[skar] Fischer [...] pointed out the necessity of building political barriers, which would prevent the Federal Republic of Germany from gaining access to nuclear weapons.

He did not mention in his speech the deployment of operational–tactical missile complexes on the territory of the German Democratic Republic.

S. Olszowski stated, while describing the current course of U.S. foreign policy, that the American worldview is accompanied by a peculiar concept of a "new economic order," based upon lawlessness and political arbitrariness, for this is the only way to describe the various forms of compulsion, constriction, illegal action, blackmail and other conduct exercised by the USA in many areas of international economic relations, even against their closest allies. It is this U.S. policy that Poland is constantly exposed to and suffers from.

S. Andrei stated in his speech that the primary objective of this meeting, which is the first one to follow the dangerous events of the turn of the year, is to introduce new political initiatives leading from confrontation and mistrust to a dialogue on disarmament.

---

[36] Andreas Papandreou, socialist prime minister of Greece.

He claimed that the SRR maintains the view that the European countries whose territories will be the first to host the deployment of intermediate-range missiles bear a special responsibility for the destinies of their peoples, for peace in Europe and the world. These countries must be the first to step in decisively to stop the pro liferation of U.S. missiles, to cancel the counter-measures and to resume the negotiations between the USSR and USA.

[...]

In the context of PPR's suggestion for an expert working group, which would elaborate a proposal for extending the validity of the Warsaw Pact, Andrei said that this question is of special political importance; it does not fall under the competence of ministers of foreign affairs and needs to be dealt with at the highest party and state levels. Therefore the SRR does not agree with the inclusion of this item in the Committee meeting's protocol. The matter will be discussed by the Presidium of the Communist Party of the SRR central committee, which will adopt an appropriate resolution.

[*Source: č.j. 012.352/84, Archives of the Ministry of Foreign Affairs, Prague. Translated by Stan Mareš.*]

Document No. 104: Transcript of Honecker–Chernenko
Meeting in Moscow, August 17, 1984

This remarkable set of minutes of a meeting between top Soviet and East German leaders shows how assertive the GDR had become by this time, and simultaneously the degree to which respect for Moscow's authority had eroded in some East European capitals. At the meeting, Erich Honecker faces sharp criticism from several Soviet leaders, including Mikhail Gorbachev, for allegedly succumbing to West German influence. But he defiantly answers the charges and manages to put Soviet party boss Konstantin Chernenko on the defensive. The bluntness of the exchanges is particularly striking for the GDR, which had started out as the most dependent of the Soviet satellites.

[*Konstantin*] *Chernenko:* [...] Comrade [Erich] Honecker, [...] the issue concerning development of the relationship between the GDR and the FRG is a question of our common global policy. This question directly affects the Soviet Union and the entire socialist community.

[...]

Comrade Honecker, you did not raise any doubts during the conversation in June. Then you said the GDR fully agrees with the Soviet Union on all international issues. [...] Despite that, there have been declarations about new measures facilitating contacts, and increasing opportunities for visits by FRG citizens and children. These measures are dubious with respect to internal security and represent a one-sided concession to Bonn. Thereby, they enjoy financial advantages, but these are only imaginary ones. In reality, for the GDR this means additional financial dependence on the FRG. [...] We should acknowledge the truth. While Bonn gained some edge on issues relating to the GDR and West Berlin, the GDR did not make progress on any of the big, vital questions.

[...]

It is difficult to understand, no matter how much the GDR has been saying so, how the development of relations with the FRG can possibly limit the damage caused by the deployment of American missiles.

Sure, there are anti-missile, anti-war, groups in the FRG. Even some politicians from the ruling circles hold rational views. However, this does not imply a solution by an all-German "coalition of reason."

[...]

You have complained how the publication in *Pravda* would have given the West reason to speculate about differences between the Soviet Union and the GDR. In reality the situation is different.

The origins of these speculations do not lie in our publications against revanchism, but in the absence of such publications in the GDR.

[...]

Regarding the visit to the FRG, of course, this is a matter to be decided by the GDR. We believe that you will again examine this issue collectively and comprehensively, with respect to the thoughts we have voiced. However, we want to tell you that the Soviet communists would receive it favorably if you would refrain from the visit during the current situation.

[...]

Comrade Honecker thanked Comrade Chernenko for his candid words on the issues mentioned.

[...]

Regarding the phrase "coalition of reason," it does not relate only to the FRG, but is intended to apply to the whole international situation and has global meaning.

[...]

Also, I want to remind [you] that during voting on the declaration and [other] documents from the session of the PCC conference of the Warsaw Treaty member-states, several proposed formulations were not adopted because of opposition by Comrade Ceauşescu, e.g. counter-measures against the deployment of intermediate-range missiles on the territory of the GDR and ČSSR.

[...]

You, Comrade Konstantin Ustinovich, have elaborated on the first and second article in *Pravda*. As far as the first one is concerned, I was informed [about it] and decided that we should publish it because it showed the GDR's position in conflict with that of the FRG. The second article we did not print because it was directed against some positions of our party's central committee. We believe that open polemics are not compatible with the norms that govern relations between our parties. We are against polemics with the CPSU, and can take care between us of any problems that exist. That's why I called you last Monday, to make it clear that open attacks should cease, since they do harm to our entire community.

[...]

Under any circumstance, I want to avoid giving the impression that there are differences of opinion and disagreements between us.

Maybe other comrades want to speak as well.

Comrade [Kurt] Hager: [...] For my part, I would like to state that the GDR is not a weak socialist state. One cannot compare it to Poland, or even say that concessions have been made. For many years we had to deal with millions of visitors from the FRG and West Berlin coming to us under the familiar agreements. This did not move the GDR closer to the FRG.

[...]

Comrade Gorbachev: [...] Also, Comrade Honecker, you have mentioned in your presentation, and previously in the car, that it is time to check our watches. Our meeting was supposed to lead to understanding and build confidence.

[...]

The draft program of the [U.S.] Republican Party says that the course of confrontation and pressure must be increased; the Soviet Union is presented as an unnatural state, and the central danger for the United States. Besides that, there are declarations by the FRG, e.g. the one of August 13 in West Berlin, and people gathered there who would have to welcome you in the event of a visit to the FRG.

[…]

When the missiles were stationed [in the FRG], [and] the Social Democrats voted for it, we declared that a new element had been added to the situation if nothing were to be done, and that things could not continue like that. This would also have an impact on relations between the two German states. And what is going to happen now? Contacts will be expanded, preparations for the visit will take place, loans will be granted. This does not comply with our declarations. The situation has changed in a way that makes it worth considering everything thoroughly.

[…]

Comrade [Herrmann] Axen: […] Our policy is meant to avoid confrontation at the border. […]

I want to emphasize one more point. There is not only an impact on the GDR by the FRG, but the GDR also has an impact on the FRG. And I think that today our impact on the FRG is bigger than vice versa.

[…]

Comrade [Dmitrii] Ustinov: […] I want to comment openly, so that nothing remains unspoken, that you are somewhat lacking in toughness in the relationship with the FRG.

[…]

Of course we know [Helmut] Kohl's declaration that no danger to peace should ever emanate from German soil. However, we know only too well that such a declaration is only hypocrisy and ideological camouflage.

[…]

Comrade Honecker: Comrade Ustinov, we know the issues you just mentioned very well. Only recently I gave awards to two female comrades who had served in NATO staff positions. We know pretty well how things are.

Concerning the FRG and the role of NATO in U.S. policy, I said the same to Comrade Ceauşescu who did not want to acknowledge reality. You may save any further remarks on that issue.

Comrade Ustinov: […] There are more facts. The West German army contributes 50 percent of NATO ground forces and 30 percent of its air forces. I only mention this to illustrate our point. You should not feel offended by that.

Comrade Honecker: I am aware of all that, Comrade Ustinov. And I have to deal with it daily.

[…]

Regarding the issues we have just dealt with, I think we could conclude that deciding the question of the visit to the FRG is the SED's business.

[…]

Comrade Ustinov: I want to point out that an increased danger of spying comes with the extended possibility for FRG citizens to enter the GDR. I also wonder whether there will be any impact on the soldiers when the door is opened wide.

Comrade Honecker: First, we did not open the door wide. Second, there is no linkage between loans and the easing of travel conditions.

Comrade [Erich] Mielke: Comrade Konstantin Ustinovich, above all I would like to say: You should trust us, us the GDR. We cannot fulfill our task as an intelligence institution if we do not have a clear policy. This clarity is provided by our general secretary and the Politburo of our party. And this is what our work is based on. And I do not want to claim this only for the organs of intelligence, but just the same for the organs of the People's Army, the organs of the Interior Ministry and our workers' militia.

By the way, Comrade Gorbachev, we also have this information. And you may even have gotten yours from us.

I also want to point out that I, too, received awards from the CPSU for working on important issues we accomplished. And one should not talk here about issues we pointed out more than 20 years ago. During my tenure, I have witnessed 12 Polish ministers in my field. For thirty years now we have been telling them they should be more concerned with political and ideological subversion. However, they have not been concerned. We have our experiences, and can say point blank that there is going to be no subversion of socialism in the GDR.

[*Source: DY 30/2380 (Büro Honecker), pp. 60–135. SAPMO. Translated by Karen Riechert.*]

Document No. 105: Report by the Head of Soviet Military Intelligence to the Committee of Ministers of Defense, December 3–5, 1984

As the political leadership in Moscow was on the verge of adopting "new thinking" under Mikhail Gorbachev, the Soviet military remained vested in presenting an alarmist view of the international scene. Here, Gen. Petr I. Ivashutin, head of Soviet military intelligence, gives his perspective on NATO's long-term armament program. The Western alliance by this time had successfully implemented the program adopted in 1979, which included the introduction of "smart" (high-precision) conventional weapons and the AirLand strategy of deep thrusts behind the lines of advancing enemy forces, along with its attendant build-up of military capabilities. Ivashutin argues that these developments show the enemy's determination to win. He implicitly holds up this threat as a warning against taking a softer line—a warning the Soviet leadership under Gorbachev would not heed.

[...]

In the past years, a new, even more dangerous phase of the North Atlantic Pact's militarization has begun, despite the fact that its military potential has for a long time exceeded reasonable defense requirements. The stationing of new American intermediate-range missiles in Western Europe continues, which is creating an additional strategic nuclear threat to the Warsaw Pact states. The [Western] alliance's long-term armaments program (through 1993) will be carried out at an accelerated pace in the hopes of gaining military superiority.

NATO's military spending in the period 1978–1984 is over 1.7 billion dollars.

The contribution by NATO's European member-states towards financing war preparations has increased significantly and represents over half of U.S. military spending. The contribution from countries such as Great Britain and France has increased by 80 percent and the FRG by 40 percent. Italy and Greece's contribution is 2.5 times higher and Turkey's is 9 times higher.

In this period, NATO's nuclear weapons potential in Europe has further developed. Troop placements in the theater have been strengthened; soldiers have been reequipped with new, modernized weapons systems and military tactics; the organizational structure as well as the leadership system and the military–technical support system are being improved; the mobilization base is being expanded and intensive operational training of the staff and troops is being carried out. [...]

1. *With respect to NATO member-states' nuclear weapons in the theater*, the number of nuclear-capable delivery vehicles has risen 25 percent and at present amounts to over 3,600. These could be used to launch over 4,200 nuclear warheads.

2. The formation of land forces has been strengthened with 6 newly deployed divisions (France 3, Great Britain, the Netherlands and Denmark 1 division each) and with 5 Spanish divisions.

Their combat potential has increased almost one-and-a-half times, and they have been quantitatively strengthened and qualitatively renewed through a supply of tanks, field artillery, missiles and anti-tank artillery, and through the introduction of automated command systems.

[...]

3. The number of *fighter jets* has increased by 18 percent. Almost a quarter of these are new models. Two-thirds of the fighter jets are multi-purpose fighter jets, approximately half of which are nuclear weapons carriers.

The combat potential of the air force has risen 60 percent.

4. The formation of the U.S. navy, which is to command fighting in the east Atlantic and the Mediterranean, has been strengthened considerably through the deployment of new surface ships, submarines and modernized battleships, as well as through the equipping of nuclear and conventional wing missiles for battling enemy ships.

In the navies of the NATO member-states, the development of highly maneuverable surface-to-air missiles as well as aircraft carriers in Great Britain and France has been resumed.

5. *The electronic means of warfare in the theater*, in particular in the air force and the ground forces, ensure signals and radio intelligence as well as interference capability in the entire frequency area of Warsaw Pact electronic devices.

6. *In the air defense system in the theater,* the anti-aircraft missile section of the "Hawk" anti-aircraft complex has been re-equipped with the "Improved Hawk" complex. One-third of interceptor jets have been replaced.

Its potential has increased 2–2.5 times. (It can fight against 1,000 targets simultaneously.)

7. Considering the changes outlined here, *the formation of NATO forces in the Western theater is currently as follows:* 46 divisions, 51 independent contingents, over 3,600 nuclear warheads, approx. 11,000 tanks, 9,800 field artillery guns, grenade launchers and missile launchers, 11,500 anti-tank weapons, 2,870 warplanes of the Air Force, approx. 3,000 aircraft and helicopters of the ground forces, and 480 ships first class. On average, 60 percent of the forces and artillery that NATO has in Europe is concentrated in this theater.

In case of mobilization, the combat level of the land forces could be doubled (primarily through the deployment of infantry divisions) and the combat level of the ground forces of the FRG, Great Britain and France could be increased by more than 30 percent.

NATO forces in this theater will be kept in high combat readiness. Virtually all of the divisions in the regular land forces are fully ready for combat; no more than 48 hours is necessary for their preparation. The navy needs the same amount of time for its preparations. The air force can achieve full combat readiness within 12 hours. The time needed to accomplish the steps necessary for "Simple Alert" and "Reinforced Alert" alarm levels has been shortened from 6 to 4 days.

Materiel reserves for 30 days have been established in the theater. For the American forces, reserves for 60 days have been set up. However, their air force will be supplied with the main types of ammunition for 90 days.

8. The NATO forces in this theater have a high level of training that has been achieved through *the improvement and intensification of operational and combat training.*

[...]

During this exercise, there was a realistic examination of the organization and leadership of the first strategic operation in the theater, taking into consideration the expected conditions and force potential of the end of the 1980s.

Strategic development was tested under a constricted time limit and with a restriction of the conflict period to 10 days. In the course of the operative development of the advance troops and force groups, the focus was on solving the problems of entering into conflict right after leaving the permanent garrison without covering the exit area [*ausgangsraeume*]. The staffs and troops have been trained to shift from peace time to assault groupings, and would be reinforced during hostilities.

In the course of this exercise, the question of the joint deployment of the air force and the ground forces in the course of the first strategic operation was examined. The focus was on the organization and execution of a comprehensive fight against the enemy firepower in the depth of his forces' operational buildup, taking into consideration existing and future weapons. The tactical and strategic fighter jets played a special role; they were the primary means for carrying out attacks on the enemy's advancing reserves and the second echelon. Airborne troop landings and the deployment of reconnaissance and diversionary tactics were carried out intensively. The problem of defeating and fording significant water barriers was practiced on a large scale. The timeframe for fighting without the use of nuclear weapons was 12 days.

Therefore, NATO forces in the Western theater are currently in a position [to exploit] considerable opportunities for the command of active and long-term fighting, both with and without the use of nuclear weapons. A NATO attack in this theater with available forces, without considerable prior strengthening, or with short-term mobilization, is possible.

Potential of the NATO forces in the Western theater

The primary development trend of NATO forces in the Western theater up to 1990 is in their further qualitative development without fundamental changes in combat readiness.

By 1990 the overall ability of nuclear forces in the NATO states in this theater to carry out a nuclear first strike will increase by 40 percent (up to 6,000 nuclear warheads), whereby an increase of 14 percent in the number of delivery vehicles (from 3,660 to 4,150) is planned.

The strategic situation in the theater will change drastically. The nuclear forces will gain the ability to carry out strikes against heavily protected and, especially, key targets within almost the entire Western theater as well as a significant portion of the territory of the USSR.

The fighting strength and firepower of the *NATO land forces in this theater* will be increased through their acquisition of new, highly effective weapons.

Almost half (45 percent) of the supply of tanks will be M 1 "Abrams," "Leopard 2,"

"Challenger" and AMX 30B 2. Troops will receive new cross-country armored personnel carriers and reconnaissance planes.

The range of the field artillery will increase from 30km to 40km or more. Its firing speed will increase 1.5–2 times and the effectiveness of its fire will be increased 3–5 times through the use of accelerated bullets and guided missiles ("Copperhead") as well as multiple-projectile and fragmentation munitions and new missile launchers.

The army corps will obtain qualitatively new abilities for encounters with armored targets up to 200km when the "Assault Breaker" reconnaissance and control complex is introduced at the end of the 1980s.

The regrouping and re-equipping of the 5th and 7th U.S. Army Corps as "Division 86" is complete. According to our calculations, the mechanized division and tank division of this new structure will exceed the combat potential of the current divisions by 70 and 40 percent, respectively.

By 1990 the combat potential of the NATO land forces in the Western theater will increase by more than 50 percent in comparison to 1984.

By 1990, 45 percent of *the NATO air force in the theater* will be comprised of F-15, F-16, A-10, "Mirage 2000," "Tornado" and other types of aircraft that will exceed the combat and flight performance of the previous generation by 2 to 3 times, in particular with respect to their payload. The combat potential of the air force will almost double.

Air force weapons the air force will include new, more accurate conventional air-to-surface missiles with a range of 600km. One of the purposes of these missiles will be the destruction of airfield runways. In addition, air-to-air missiles with a range of 75–280km and guided bombs and bombs with increased range will be supplied.

The establishment of the PLSS [*sic*][37] reconnaissance and control complex in the mid-1980s will significantly increase the air force's ability to decrease the effectiveness of the enemy's air traffic and control system through control of signal objects within a 500km range.

Therefore, by the end of the 1980s, the air force will be in the position, as NATO intends, to carry out far-reaching attacks with a large number of precision weapons, without aircraft having to enter the enemy's air defense zone, thereby cutting in half the number of aircraft lost.

[...]

The joint command systems of NATO's air defense, "NADGE,"[38] and "AWACS-NATO,"[39] will make it possible to increase the number of concurrent aerial targets by 3–4 times (from 1,000 targets currently to 4,000 by 1990).

The complete introduction of the complex automated *troop command system into the theater and at the operational–tactical level* as well as its combination with weapons-reconnaissance and electronic warfare systems will result in a reduction of the command cycle (through changes in the situation up until the initiation of countermeasures) in the units by more than three times (from 11 to 3 hours).

[37] PELSS (Precision Emitter Location and Strike System).
[38] NATO Air Defense Ground Environment System.
[39] Airborne Warning and Control System.

NATO's strategic development system will be further improved. The following exercises will be relegated:

- Maintenance of a daily full force level, training level and equipment level in the units and troop components that would make it possible to ensure the operational development of the army's first squadron within 48 hours, the army's squads and equal units within 4 to 5 days, and strategic formation in the theater within 8 to 10 days.
- By the end of the 1980s, the possibility to transfer by air and sea 6 divisions, 2 marine brigades and 60 tactical air squadrons (1,400 planes) from the U.S. to Europe within 10 days.

Further development of the early warning systems and the notification systems will be carried out almost in real time. The development of far-reaching radar and aircraft guidance systems as well as of a unified surveillance system in the inland and marginal seas will be completed.

Altogether, the analysis of NATO plans for the future outlined here is evidence of its [NATO's] goal to fulfill a high level of combat and mobilization readiness for its armed forces as well as to take the lead in strategic development. NATO is also pursuing the goal of giving the land, air and naval forces in the Western theater an offensive character and enabling them to carry out long-lasting operations, both with and without the use of nuclear weapons.

Southwestern theater

The increased attention given in recent years to preparations in the southwestern theater indicates a rise in the importance of the Mediterranean region in U.S. strategic plans.

They view it as a link that connects the responsibilities of the Supreme Command of U.S. forces in Europe with the newly created Central Command of U.S. forces in Southwest Asia.

The activities of these commands must be coordinated with Pentagon plans and are subordinate to a unified strategic goal, namely "the preservation of the Middle East and the Mediterranean region for the U.S. as an area in which American military power can be effectively used" in the interests of full-scale strategic actions against the Warsaw Pact and against the progressive Middle Eastern states.

In order to achieve this, the U.S.'s main efforts are focused on expanding its military presence in the Mediterranean region and on maximum mobilization of its allies' military resources, particularly the NATO states, in this region.

Connected with this is the modernization of Italy's military forces as well as those of Greece and Turkey, which has been done under U.S. and NATO pressure. They have been equipped with nuclear-capable carriers, modern tanks, artillery, aircraft and other technology from the militaries of NATO states in the Western theater. In addition, they have been furnished with their own models of the newest battle techniques.

This has allowed for an increase in the combat capability of the allied land forces of almost 12 percent and of the air forces of almost 30 percent (the Italian air force by 40 percent.)

The current level of forces in this theater is as follows: 27 divisions, 22 independent contingents, approx. 700 nuclear-capable delivery vehicles, over 4,500 tanks, more than 1,100 fighter jets and 330 battle ships first class.

The divisions in the first echelon can establish their combat readiness over the course of 48 hours. There are materiel–technical stores for 20 combat days.

The NATO states in this theater have significant human and materiel resources available that make it possible to increase by 30 percent on average the combat level of the land forces, air force and navy in the first 3–5 days of mobilization.

[...]

The formation of the Turkish forces in the direction of the Balkans will allow not only increased defensive but also offensive capabilities. This is evident in the character of the operational and combat training of their troops in recent years.

The focus during training will be not only on maintaining the Black Sea passage, but also on the command of resolute fighting on the front lines from the beginning of the war onwards.

Altogether, the combat potential of the NATO forces in the Southwest theater by the end of this decade will increase significantly in comparison with 1984, namely the land forces by 27 percent and the tactical aircraft by almost one-and-a-half times.

The information and assessment in this report on the character and modification of NATO's combat preparations are evidence that, as before, until 1990 the NATO command's main efforts will focus on the greatest possible development of the allied armed forces in the Western theater.

At the same time, the combat potential of the armed forces in the Southwestern theater will be mobilized at a further increased tempo on the level of the Western theater. In the end, the goal of threatening the socialist community to the south will be pursued.

Fulfillment of the main steps of the long-term armaments program in the framework of NATO will—according to the calculations of the U.S. and NATO leadership—ensure the achievement of a significant strategic advantage over the Warsaw Pact by the end of the 1980s. NATO assumes that the allied forces will then be able to carry out a successful global or limited war as well as a long- or short-term war with or without the use of nuclear weapons.

III. Changes in the military strategy of the NATO coalition

With a fundamental improvement in the quality of the military character, which is linked with the development and deployment of new homing and automated conventional weapons systems, and as a result of an immense increase in the combat potential of the armed forces, there have been changes in the military strategy of the coalition, which could have dangerous consequences.

Although for the 1980s their basis, as before, is the strategy of flexible response and the concept of forward defense, it must be taken into account that they are undergoing significant internal changes. The goal of the NATO troops holding the front line has not changed, but active combat would also be carried into the territory of the Warsaw Pact at the beginning of an armed conflict.

Connected with this is the ongoing search in the NATO armies for plans for strategic and operational–tactical applications.

In the U.S., the AirLand Battle Plan and the NATO FOFA Plan (Follow on Forces Attack = strikes against the second echelon) have been developed and were adopted by the Standing Military Planning Committee of the alliance in November of this year. They are organically connected with each other and reflect the current stance of the U.S. and NATO leadership on force deployment and general appropriations.

The goals of these plans should be achieved by using troops stationed in peace time to preempt the start of combat, and by simultaneously carrying out firefights or nuclear attacks against the enemy's first and second squadrons of the operative structure and operative and strategic reserves before their introduction into the battle.

According to NATO leadership estimates, in order to fulfill the demands of the AirLand-Battle and FOFA plans, many problems must be solved. Above all, the establishment of new weapons systems must be settled, and the troops must be equipped with them. At least five years are necessary for this. In addition, it is necessary to establish and achieve a mission limit for aircraft that is enough for the simultaneous realization of both plans, the improvement of cooperation between the land forces with the air force as well as the raising of combat and, especially, reconnaissance potential of the army corps of the Western European forces to the level of the American armed forces.

The U.S. and NATO leadership have big expectations for the materialization of these plans in order to achieve military superiority over the Warsaw Pact. This means that on our side, it is necessary to pay significant attention to the enemy's steps with respect to their technical and operational support and the commitment to corresponding countermeasures.

The analysis in this report of the steps the U.S. and NATO have taken towards the development of armed forces placements in the Western and Southwestern theaters shows that the enemy is persistently forcing the pace of material war preparations. He is striving not only to preempt us in the technical armament of the armed forces, but also in the completion of effective methods for carrying out operations in war as a whole. At the beginning of the 1990s, the possibilities for the U.S. and NATO to suddenly wage a nuclear war or a conventional war will increase significantly. The likelihood and danger of an aggression on the side of the U.S. and NATO under cover of a large exercise, as well as the danger of a surprise attack from the [peace time] positions of the armed forces will also increase.

[Source: VA-01/32871, BA-MA. Translated by Catherine Nielsen.]

Document No. 106: Speech by Gorbachev at the Warsaw Treaty Summit in Moscow, April 26, 1985

The April 1985 Warsaw Pact summit was the first since January 1983, and Mikhail Gorbachev's first in his position as general secretary of the CPSU. The intervening period was one of disarray within the Soviet leadership, which Gorbachev hoped to bring to an end. Among the views he expresses here is that the Warsaw Pact's attainment of strategic military equilibrium with NATO was a historic accomplishment, yet it had so far produced no visible improvement in international relations. Instead, the West continued its struggle for superiority, including in the area of conventional arms, which would allow it to destroy Warsaw Pact forces in depth (a reference to the concept of AirLand Battle). He also repeats the previous Soviet position that the United States initiated the production of offensive weapons and that if the "Star Wars" concept of President Reagan's Strategic Defense Initiative were to be pursued, the Soviet Union would have to respond by deploying weapons in outer space.

[...]

We have met to extend the validity of the Treaty on friendship, co-operation and mutual assistance. To extend it using the same wording, as it was concluded 30 years ago right here in Warsaw. Thus our tested political and defense bond is born for a second time.

[...]

Above all, through unity of action, as the spirit and letter of the Treaty entail, have we upset the imperialists' efforts to subvert or "disintegrate" the socialist constitution in any of the fraternal countries. Even the current "crusade" against socialism, as it was designed by the imperialist reactionaries, has, so to speak, clashed against our uniform, firm will.

[...]

In response to the military challenge imposed upon us, we have by our joint efforts accomplished a task of historic importance: we have achieved a state of military and strategic balance with NATO. It was far from easy.

After all, the imperialist powers enjoyed a strategic predominance in nuclear weapons. And in all these years they have continued to strengthen their military power. The more distinct achievement is that of our countries, of our bond. A military and strategic balance is an essential prerequisite for the security of the socialist countries. Naturally, securing a military balance calls for—and will call for, if the situation does not improve—a great many resources and efforts.

[...]

The Warsaw Treaty has existed for a third of a century and for all this time, peace has persisted in Europe. Surely it is not a mere coincidence. Our bond has multiplied the possibilities for an active fight against a military threat. It is a drive of constructive ideas, focused at relaxing and limiting the arms race, at developing all-European cooperation and peaceful relations.

[...]

An apparent shift for the better in the international situation has not yet occurred. The very re-election of [Ronald] Reagan shows that in U.S. political life, reactionary and aggressive circles still prevail. The right wing sets the pace in other NATO countries and Japan, too. It follows that in the coming years, we will still have to deal with those who were blinded by anticommunism and who naively bank on power in world politics.

When it comes to military and strategic aspects, the danger lies in the fact that the U.S. and NATO have been trying to regain superiority, counting on a breakthrough in science and technology. This is the goal of the programs aimed at creating the potential for a disarming first-strike nuclear capability, which would be based on high-precision modern weaponry, short flight time to targets and the ability to reach them surreptitiously. Increasing the non-nuclear potential, approaching in destructive power that of the nuclear potential, would allow [Warsaw] Treaty forces to be struck to the deepest extent of their configuration.

Why is the Pentagon pushing into space? Because the nuclear arms race unleashed by the USA has given it no advantage. One after another strategic offensive weapons system has been integrated into the U.S. arsenal. Not a single one adds to a feeling of invincibility, though. We have been answering in kind. The hopes of the USA and NATO to win a nuclear war are losing their meaning because of the inevitability of a nuclear retaliation.

Under these circumstances, the United States has chosen space as the area where it wants to achieve a military advantage over the socialist countries. It gambles on the chance of outrunning the Soviet Union by devising space-based offensive weapons. The goal is, on the one hand, covering U.S. territory with a multi-level anti-missile defense [shield] that would deny the USSR the capability to deliver a retaliatory strike, and, on the other hand, developing new, space-based, strategic forces, designed to destroy targets on the ground, on the sea, in the air and in outer space. This is the substance of Reagan's "Star Wars" plan. Such is the real danger.

[...]

Yes, indeed, even in the Soviet Union scientific research of a military nature is being conducted in the space. It is, however, related to the improvement of space systems for early warning and intelligence, communications, navigation and the modernization of permissible components of the anti-missile defense of the Moscow area. We are not developing any offensive weapons and are not building another anti-missile defense system. Therefore, the claim that the same kind of work that is being done in the USA is being conducted in the Soviet Union is just another deceit. We are adhering to the valid treaty of 1972 without any time limitations.[40]

If, however, the United States continues its preparations for "Star Wars" and drags the other NATO member-states and Japan further along with it, we will be forced to adopt counter-measures. For the sake of a military and strategic balance

---

[40] The ABM Treaty on the Limitation of Anti-Ballistic Missiles Systems of May 26, 1972.

and to reliably secure the safety of our countries we will have to develop appropriate space weapons and improve our strategic nuclear forces.

[...]

If the USA agreed to negotiate a total prohibition of offensive space weapons, the road to radical reductions in the number of strategic assault weapons would be opened. This reduction would apply to both the total number of nuclear warheads for all strategic delivery vehicles and the total number of vehicles. The question of NATO or Soviet intermediate-range nuclear missiles could be dealt with in a constructive way, i.e. by decreasing their numbers to a given level or, better yet, to reciprocally rid Europe of both intermediate-range and tactical nuclear weapons altogether.

We have informed you of the content of the particular proposals, which we submitted in Geneva. I can only add that in the first round of talks the American party failed to express any interest in negotiating seriously on the issue of space demilitarization, and concerning nuclear weapons, it obstinately insisted on its old, unacceptable proposals. The United States is indeed trying to step back from the subjects and objectives laid down in January in Geneva, which may bring these talks to a dead end.

The first round of talks does not really raise any optimism. It is difficult to say how the negotiations will advance. For its part, the Soviet Union will continue to act for the sake of their success. Expressing good will, we come with a new initiative. The deployment on the territory of the GDR and ČSSR of the SS-20 missiles as well as of the tactical-operational missiles of enhanced range has been unilaterally suspended until November 1985.

[...]

Maintenance of the principles of parity and noninterference in the internal affairs of states remains an essential prerequisite for the improvement of Soviet–American relations and a test of U.S. readiness for a serious dialogue with us.

In March, when he was in Moscow, [Vice President George] Bush delivered [Ronald] Reagan's message to me, suggesting I visit Washington. Of course, Reagan has his intentions. He is especially interested in the very fact of a meeting, which he could refer to and thus appease both Americans and America's allies.

[...]

Having considered all this thoroughly, we declared in our message to the U.S. president that we were in favor of a Soviet–American meeting at the highest level, and left the question of a place and time open for the time being. We believe, comrades, that such an attitude regarding relations with the USA will be met by understanding and support on your part.

Within the scope of the Warsaw Treaty, we also pay unwavering attention to mutual cooperation on European matters. Great attention is paid to the efforts of every single fraternal country, which makes the ruling circles of Western Europe adopt a more realistic attitude and act for the sake of improving the situation.

[...]

When talking about the primary goals of our foreign policy, it is necessary to say that the Warsaw treaty members are now conducting a more active political offensive. Each country naturally makes use of its opportunities and contacts. What is most important, however, is to advance in a coordinated way, in a unified line and

509

to proceed from a single common objective—to strengthen the position of socialism and to secure peace.

[...]

What do we believe is necessary in this situation? Above all, a maximum level of confidence in the relationships between the leaderships of our parties and countries. We suggest that we inform each other thoroughly of all basic matters and coordinate our activities better. We favor open discussion of and a common approach to any differences of opinion that may arise. We favor the timely disposal of any mutual reservations and the resolution of any misunderstandings that may arise, so that misapprehensions or feelings of injustice do not accumulate between us.

It is obvious that each country independently sets its own policy and answers for it to its people. In addition, experience affirms that national objectives are solved more quickly and efficiently if the tasks and goals of the entire community are taken into account and if they are supported by our common potential. Despite the peculiarities of each of our countries, their different economic level, size and historical or national traditions, we have one thing in common—our class concerns.

When we met recently in Moscow, a common view was expressed that it is necessary to improve our political cooperation. Meetings of the general secretaries and deputies of Central Committees were regarded as useful. The Soviet leadership fully agrees with the idea of similar meetings, where actual problems could be evaluated and solved, without the expense of an unnecessary protocol. It is possible to consider in the future that the general secretaries of Central Committees from other countries within our socialist community could participate at these meetings, depending on the problems discussed. This would in no way replace the meetings of the Political Consultative Committee of the Warsaw Treaty member-states.

[*Source: 8696/24, AÚV KSČ, SÚA. Translated by Stan Mareš.*]

Document No. 107: Warsaw Pact Information concerning Improvements in NATO Military Technology, November 11, 1985

This East German document, prepared for a session of that country's National Defense Council, provides information on the latest improvements in NATO's military technology. It argues that NATO is aiming to achieve superiority in that area, and then, interestingly, specifies the equipment and new conventional weapons systems the Warsaw Pact considers critical. At the time, the Western alliance was stepping up the introduction of so-called "smart" munitions and technically superior tracking systems, such as AWACS reconnaissance aircraft.

Achieving technical superiority is regarded by the U.S. and NATO as the best way to alter the present strategic balance of forces, in order to attain military superiority over the USSR and other states of the Warsaw Treaty.

[...]

The new combat technology that is being introduced in all parts of the armed forces will be followed in the coming years by new types of ammunition and modern command, targeting, reconnaissance and interference technology.

These improvements will qualitatively increase the effectiveness of the new combat technology in action.

The introduction of modern command technology and the improvement of automated command and information systems will increase the resilience and flexibility of commanding troops, even in complicated situations, and shorten the command processes to a half or a quarter of the time presently needed. The connections of the command process will at the same time be linked to automated data analysis and presentation systems, and to locating systems capable in some cases of identifying targets down to the lowest level.

The new reconnaissance and locating systems are designed to work reliably under all weather conditions and permit reconnaissance deep within the territory of the Warsaw Treaty states without having to actually penetrate it. For instance, they make it possible to carry out multiple surveillance of the lines of communication and airspace of the GDR. In connection with automated recording and targeting methods, they make it possible to locate, follow and identify hundreds of targets, including moveable land targets in the future, and to guide far-reaching weapons systems.

In the USA and the UK work is now underway to combine combat technology with command, targeting and reconnaissance systems to form new reconnaissance-strike weapons with enormous destructive power. These combined systems are due to be completed within the 1980s. The first completed system is to be put at the disposal of the NATO air force in central Europe in 1986, to fight the radar and automatic command systems of the air defense of the Unified Armed Forces of the Warsaw Treaty.

A further reconnaissance-strike system will be delivered to the U.S. Armed Forces in the FRG, probably at the end of the 1980s, to fight tank formations deep within enemy territory.

Used together with the new types of ammunition, these systems will allow NATO forces to conduct effective surprise attacks and to direct their fire at a great number of very distant point and area targets, practically without a time delay.

The new types of ammunition make it possible to attack command locations, tanks, armored vehicles, aircraft under cover, airport take-off and landing strips, radar stations, ships, bridges and other point targets easily and with high precision.

[...]

All reconnaissance and other evidence indicates that the NATO armed forces are striving for superiority over the armed forces of the states of the Warsaw Treaty not only in the areas of outer space and nuclear armaments but also in the technology of conventional warfare. In compliance with U.S. strategy, the intention is to rely on superior technology to ensure superiority in the waging of a conventional war.

The potential consequences of this development in the case of war are very dangerous, especially for Europe. Due to high population density and large urban industrial areas, the massive deployment of the new conventional weapons would be devastating.

[*Source: DVW1/39532, pp. 61–69, BA-MA. Translated by Ursula Froese.*]

Document No. 108: Speech by Marshal Kulikov at the Committee of Ministers of Defense Meeting in Strausberg, December 2–5, 1985

In this speech, Kulikov declares in shrill tones the warning that the United States is essentially preparing the ground for an attack against the Warsaw Pact, and forcing the rest of NATO to go along with it. It is interesting to compare his viewpoint with that of East German leader Erich Honecker, by no means soft on the West, who is much more at ease during this period (see Document No. 109). The timing of Kulikov's speech is also of interest, coming one week after the Geneva summit between Reagan and Gorbachev, which while initiating a process of dialogue between the superpowers yielded no concrete aggreement, particularly on SDI, which was not reassuring for the Soviet side.

The U.S. is accelerating its development of first-strike weapons and new types of strategic carriers—the intercontinental "MX" ballistic missiles, the submarine-based "Trident-2" missiles, and the B-1B heavy bomber. The stationing of long-range cruise missiles of various types is being stepped up. Especially in Europe, nuclear capability is being reinforced.

Parallel to these preparations for nuclear war, preparations for conventional warfare are also underway. The main emphasis is on preemptive attacks by army groups and naval formations already existing in times of peace, and the simultaneous firing of long-range precision weapons practically to the total depth of the build-up of our armed forces in the western and southwestern theaters of war. In this connection, NATO has officially adopted the concept of "the fight against the second echelon" [Follow-On Forces Attack (FOFA)] and the U.S. has adopted the term "AirLand Battle."

The other NATO countries are becoming increasingly drawn into the U.S. administration's adventurous war plans.

The most active partners of the U.S. are the Federal Republic of Germany and Great Britain. There is a strong contingent of NATO armed forces on Federal Republic of Germany territory. West Germany is becoming a major supplier of the most modern weapons. The thrust and attack potential of the Federal German Armed Forces is constantly being increased.

The policies of Great Britain, Italy and Turkey are displaying increasingly militaristic tendencies. The national armed forces are being strengthened and equipped with modern war technology, and U.S. air force and naval bases are being established in these countries. Furthermore, nuclear missiles are being stationed on UK and Italian territory.

An all-encompassing plan for perfecting the process of putting NATO forces into a state of readiness for combat and mobilization has been worked out and is now in the implementation stage. Our probable enemy is doing everything it can, both strategically and operationally, to be ready for attack.

[Source: DVW 1/71044, BA-MA. Translated by Ursula Froese.]   513

Document No. 109: East German Intelligence Assessment of NATO's Intelligence on the Warsaw Pact, December 16, 1985

This Stasi document shows that the East had an accurate indication of how NATO evaluated the Warsaw Pact. The authors judge that NATO's knowledge is "mostly accurate and reliable," and that the west has concluded that Warsaw Pact military strength and war preparations are constantly on the rise. Intelligence information, such as that compiled in this kind of document, usually came from various sources, mainly West German, thus showing that East German spies and their informants had an extensive run of the FRG Defense Ministry as well as of NATO headquarters.

Assessment of Adversary's Intelligence
on Development of Warsaw Treaty Forces,
1983–1985

PREFACE

The Intelligence services and military intelligence of the NATO countries relentlessly pursue their activities aimed at a comprehensive exploration and assessment of the Warsaw Treaty's military policy and doctrine, armed forces and armaments Treaty.
[…]
For these purposes, they continuously use all sources of information (human intelligence, technical intelligence, official channels). Intelligence collection is realized through a comprehensive and intensive evaluation increasingly based on the use of electronic data. NATO countries conduct this business on a national level and synchronize the results through an intensive informational exchange within NATO structures. These data are constantly being updated at NATO's operational headquarters. […] These assessments also serve as justification for NATO force requirements and as guidelines for developing weapons technology.

The main actors in intelligence activities, in qualitative as well as quantitative terms, are always the United States, Great Britain and the FRG. France is also very active in this respect and integrated into joint NATO actions through informational exchanges.

Other NATO countries make their contributions according to an agreed division of labor (e.g. the Netherlands against Poland) and their specific potential. Intelligence information also comes from other capitalist countries. Cooperation between the U.S. and the FRG concerning intelligence services and military intelligence has been increased. Besides [providing] mutual support to complete the actual state of knowledge on a worldwide scale, they [NATO] primarily undertake efforts to clarify unresolved questions. […] It is evident that not all the intelligence obtained flows into NATO channels.

All in all, the adversary is believed to possess an appropriate, and in the details mostly accurate and reliable, state of knowledge about the Warsaw Treaty. Two major conclusions have been drawn from this intelligence:

1. The Warsaw Treaty is constantly increasing its military potential, especially in quantitative terms. Concerning the technological state of armaments, the Warsaw Treaty does not lag behind NATO in most areas (with the exception of electronics). This tendency will continue.

2. The Warsaw Treaty's war preparations have reached a high level and will be pushed further.

The adversary is going public with its knowledge in a targeted and planned manner. That activity is cleared within NATO as well. There are limits, however. In particular in the U.S. they are restrictive with certain kinds of intelligence. For instance, this results in the publication of drawings instead of pictorial documentation that has been obtained, as the 1985 issue of *Soviet Military Power*[41] demonstrated. Demands by NATO's supreme commander, U.S. General [Bernard W.] Rogers, "not to protect the enemy's secrets" were not accepted. The U.S. in particular goes to some lengths to prevent the Warsaw Treaty from obtaining clues about the real internal state of NATO's knowledge. In general the other NATO countries follow the same principle. Thus a contradiction exists between increasing requirements for classifying information, and the intention to influence their own people and the public around the world with the "Warsaw Treaty Threat" by means of outwardly correct facts.

[*Source: Die Bundesbeauftragte für die Unterlagen des Staatssicherheitsdienstes (BStU), Zentralarchiv, HVA, 39, pp. 62–147. Translated by Bernd Schaefer.*]

---

[41] The U.S. Defense Department began to produce this annual publication under the Reagan administration in the early 1980s.

Document No. 110: Scenario for the "Granit-86" Exercise, December 23, 1985

The Warsaw Pact's "Granit 86" exercise aimed at creating a permanently functioning air defense system in both peace time and war time. As was often the case, the alliance presumed for purposes of the exercise that a NATO attack would take place under cover of maneuvers, and that it would lead to substantial Warsaw Pact casualties. Unlike many earlier exercises, this one assumed that no nuclear weapons would be used. In this respect, it seems the Warsaw Pact was taking account of the West's AirLand Battle concept—an innovation during the Reagan presidency, which involved the coordination of air and ground forces with attacks on advancing Warsaw Pact troops deep to the rear. The Soviets interpreted the new concept rightly as representing an increased offensive capacity on the part of NATO forces. Soviet Army and Warsaw Pact Chief of Staff General Anatolii Gribkov remarks below that the capabilities of new systems, such as the use of helicopters firing uranium-tipped bullets against Warsaw Pact tanks, are becoming nearly as destructive as unconventional weapons.

THEME OF THE EXERCISE

"The organization and implementation of air defense to repulse enemy aggression in the Western theater of operations."

[...]

The aim of the "Western troops" calls for completing the deployment of allied armed forces of the [NATO] bloc in Europe and the eastern Atlantic and, beginning the morning of April 4 (operational time: April 6), unleashing war against the Warsaw Pact countries, all under the guise of preparing and carrying out strategic exercises. Military action in the Western Theater is planned to begin with air attacks involving wide use of guided missiles, guided Pershing-2s, tactical air strikes by Allied 2nd and 4th Tactical Air Commands (Baltic Straits area), aircraft carriers and strategic aircraft, along with the use of precision weapons, with the goal of achieving nuclear superiority and air superiority within the theater.

At the same time, using attacks by ground troops of the Army Central Group and Northern Group heading toward Berlin, Leipzig and Prague, along with cooperation from the Allied air and naval forces, they intend to destroy the basic forces of the "Eastern" troops in East Germany, the ČSSR and Baltic Straits area, and after 10–12 days of fighting take control of the line Bratislava, Wrocław, Poznań, Kołobrzeg.

Further, the plan includes increasing the forces of the first operational echelon by commissioning the second echelons and reserves, then defeating "Eastern" troops advancing from Soviet territory and, after 20–25 days of operation, reaching borders of the Soviet Union.

The Allied naval forces, in conjunction with tactical air support from the Baltic Straits and using active naval missiles, naval air forces, submarines, and wide application of mines, are projected to provide seaborne support for the attack by ground troops, to inflict defeat on the main groups of the "Eastern" unified fleet, and to block its forces in the Baltic Sea.

The air attack operation in the theater is projected to be carried out over the course of three days with four large-scale attacks on nuclear weapons sites, enemy air troops, anti-aircraft targets, enemy administrative posts, storage facilities, and bases.

[...]

The plans of the "Eastern" forces call for carrying out a possible invasion of the "Western" forces by using defensive operations with forces on two fronts. Under their cover, the "Eastern" forces are to carry out a strategic deployment of alignments; with supplemental supplies, to prepare to head into a decisive attack on northern German and southern German strategic areas with the goal of destroying troops and the enemy fleet, and then forcing the Western forces' NATO countries located in the western theater out of the war.

From the beginning of the military action, there are plans to carry out anti-aircraft maneuvers with the goal of disrupting the enemy's air operations and creating conditions for switching to active combat.

[...]

Over the course of three days of battle, while under attack from superior enemy forces, the troops of the "Eastern" forces suffered great losses, and in individual areas they retreated some 60–80 km to the interior regions of their territory. However, while getting reinforcements from the interior and using sweeping counter-attacks, they forced the "Western" forces to decrease the rate of attacks and, in certain areas, change to defensive maneuvers.

[...]

[*Source: VS, OS, 1987, č.j. 75 186/3, VÚA. Translated by Paul Spitzer for the National Security Archive.*]

Document No. 111: Summary of the Meeting of Ministers of Foreign Affairs in Warsaw, March 19–20, 1986

Eduard Shevardnadze's presentation at this foreign ministers' meeting aimed at demonstrating to the other Warsaw Pact members that Gorbachev was serious about encouraging input from the allies in negotiations on common security policy toward the West. After providing background to the Soviet leader's recent proclamation on eliminating nuclear weapons, Shevardnadze made recommendations for expanding cooperation within the alliance. The following remarks by other ministers are rather wide-ranging and free-flowing, ending with detailed proposals on disarmament by the Romanian representative.

[...] The meeting was based on documents drafted by Poland in cooperation with the Soviet Union. The discussion was tough, primarily because of the attitude and position of the Romanian delegation, which disagreed with the structure of the draft and furnished a number of comments about its contents. Until the very last moment, Romania refused to mention new initiatives resulting from the XXVIIth Congress of the Communist Party of the Soviet Union, including a proposal to build up a comprehensive international security system, and to support them. Romania disagreed with a proclamation supporting the Soviet approach to the Geneva negotiations with the United States[42], and refused to condemn plans to build up a "European Defense Initiative,"[43] and to point out the responsibility of both those who had initiated the introduction of arms into space and those who intend to join in it. The non-class-based approach of the Romanian delegation was manifested in its assessments of the international situation.

[...] Romania proposed deferring the decision to the subsequent meeting of the Committee of Foreign Ministers in Bucharest, the agenda of which will be prepared by an ad hoc team of experts.

The meeting proper of the Committee of Foreign Ministers took place on March 19, 1986.

The first to speak and deliver a lengthy address was [Soviet Foreign Minister] E.A. Shevardnadze.

He dealt with the proclamation of M.S. Gorbachev of January 15, 1986, (liquidation of nuclear weapons) and the creation of a comprehensive international security system. He emphasized that the belief in the viability of the no-nuclear-weapons

---

[42] Negotiations on limitations of intermediate-range nuclear forces in Europe (INF).

[43] In 1985, the U.S. government invited European companies to take part in the Strategic Defense Initiative, a project which seemed to threaten European technological independence. In response, 18 European nations at French initiative inaugurated in April 1985 the European Research Agency (later known as EUREKA) to promote European high-technology industries. The agency, with a secretariat in Brussels, was formally established in 1986.

plan was based on military and strategic parity, which could be maintained no matter which way the situation developed. He mentioned that the concept of Gorbachev's proclamation had been born as a result of a comradely dialogue between the Soviet leadership and the leaders of fraternal parties, and pointed out the increasing importance of political cooperation between Warsaw Treaty members, which was aimed at improving its forms and methods.

[...] He noted that European issues were a matter of prime interest for the Soviet Union. Referring to Gorbachev's proclamation, he emphasized that it was necessary to proceed from the initial phase of détente to a more mature and permanent one, followed by a reliable security system based on the Helsinki process and a dramatic downsizing of stockpiles of nuclear and conventional weapons. For the first time ever, Europe may realistically perceive a future without nuclear weapons. [...]

He recommended establishing the practice of a regular exchange of opinions at the working level on issues relating to Western Europe, e.g. during preparations of the subsequent meeting of the Committee of Foreign Ministers.

[...] Toward the end of his speech, he voiced satisfaction at the strengthening of political cooperation among Warsaw Treaty countries (he also mentioned the joint initiative of the German Democratic Republic and the Czechoslovak Socialist Republic vis-à-vis the Federal Republic of Germany). He noted that the coordination of actions through Foreign Ministries had been improving and becoming more flexible, although there were still some reservations.

In their respective addresses, the foreign ministers of the Czechoslovak Socialist Republic, the People's Republic of Bulgaria, the People's Republic of Hungary, the German Democratic Republic and the Polish People's Republic voiced their full agreement with the analysis of international developments and conclusions presented by Comrade Shevardnadze.

[Czechoslovak Foreign Minister Bohumil] Chňoupek informed that Czechoslovakia had been considering the possibility of presenting at the subsequent meeting of the Conference for Security and Cooperation in Europe in Vienna an initiative aimed at convening an "Economic Forum" in Czechoslovakia. [...]

He noted that environmental issues were becoming increasingly important and were often reflected at the political level. In this respect, he informed the audience about the start of CzCP–SPD negotiations on these issues.[44]

He proceeded to provide information on a trilateral exchange of opinions involving the Czechoslovak Socialist Republic, German Democratic Republic and Federal Republic of Germany on a possible chemical weapons-free zone in Central Europe. He pointed out that the proposal continued to be a very topical issue, supporting his view by [referencing], inter alia, information that came to light during his talks with SPD representative E[gon] Bahr.

He advocated establishing a multilateral group for the exchange of current information, which would be situated in Moscow and comprise special representatives.

---

[44] Negotiations between the Communist Party of Czechoslovakia and the West German Social Democratic Party.

He proposed a meeting of a working group of experts in Prague, which would discuss related issues.

[*Bulgarian Foreign Minister Petar*] *Mladenov* advocated concerted political and propaganda efforts aimed at proposals, such as the ban on nuclear explosions and intermediate-range missiles in Europe, which have already become popular to some extent in the West, and with respect to which the U.S. position is obviously untenable and without any solid ground.

He opined that it would be advisable, at the subsequent meeting of the Conference for Security and Cooperation in Europe to be held in Vienna, to submit a proposal to convene a meeting of experts on economic and social rights.

[*Hungarian Foreign Minister Péter*] *Várkonyi* emphasized that, insofar as the step-by-step liquidation of intermediate-range nuclear weapons in Europe was concerned, it would be advisable to intensify the joint pressure on political elements in France and the United Kingdom by countries that *do not possess* nuclear weapons or *have them* on their territory. [...]

Referring to the meeting of experts on contacts among people in Bern[45], he emphasized that Warsaw Treaty countries should espouse ideas of enhanced socialist democracy and increased humanitarian contacts, and strive for a matter-of-fact assessment of various issues.[...]

[*East German Foreign Minister Oskar*] *Fischer* advocated more active and coordinated relations with the European Economic Community and its institutions. He emphasized that the increased importance of issues related to EEC bodies, such as the European Parliament, EEC Commissions and possibly also the Political Secretariat, could have been envisaged a long time ago. He suggested that these issues be assessed on a de facto basis, i.e. even if we do not recognize them.[...]

[*Polish Foreign Minister Marian*] *Orzechowski* condemned attempts to question political realities in Europe; he emphasized that, together with the Yalta and Potsdam Accords, these political realities continued to be the basis of peace in Europe. The Polish comrades had been conveying this message to their Western partners, clearly stating that a firm and irreversible return to détente and stabilization in Europe not involving or even aimed at Poland was unthinkable.

He pointed out the fact that the first symptoms of a healthier international situation did not automatically lead to positive changes in the West's policy toward Poland. He emphasized that the U.S. policy of differentiating among socialist countries had to be met by a united front.

He briefed the audience on Poland's activities, the purpose of which was to implement the proposal submitted by W[ojciech] Jaruzelski at the 40th U.N. General Assembly, namely to prepare, under the auspices of the U.N. Secretary General, a report on the potential consequences of the militarization of space.

As to the Helsinki process, he mentioned that there should be efforts aimed at creating a better balance, in particular with respect to Basket II. At the subsequent meeting of the Conference for Security and Cooperation in Europe to be held in

[45] CSCE Meeting of Experts on Human Contacts in Bern, April 15–May 27, 1986.

Vienna, Poland intends to propose an initiative to convene a meeting of experts on issues of scientific and technical cooperation.

Compared to his predecessors, [*Romanian Foreign Minister Ilie*] *Vaduva* did not emphasize the importance of the XXVIIth Congress of the Communist Party of the Soviet Union for the joint foreign policy efforts and activities of Warsaw Treaty countries.

Apart from a proposal to prepare a document for the Warsaw Treaty countries on the issue of backwardness and the establishment of a new economic order (the Socialist Republic of Romania had already presented it at the meeting of the Political Consultative Committee in Sofia), he also advocated a specific program of actions in support of developing countries. The program should be approved at a meeting of supreme representatives of socialist countries—members of Comecon, and other socialist countries could accede to it.

Based on a decision by the Political Executive Committee of the Central Committee of the Communist Party of Romania, he presented the following supplementary proposals regarding the nuclear disarmament program that had been tabled by the Soviet Union (he otherwise voiced his support for the program):

I. The first stage should consist of the liquidation of Soviet intermediate-range missiles, not only in Europe but also elsewhere (in Asia and Far East), or at least to reduce their numbers.

II. In addition to the program to liquidate nuclear weapons, a comprehensive disarmament program should be drafted, which would comprise:

1. A reduction of conventional armaments in the first stage—by 20 to 30 percent by 1990, and by an additional 50 percent by 2000;

2. An annual reduction of troops—by 30 percent by 1990, and by an additional 50 percent by 2000;

3. An annual reduction of military appropriations—by 30 percent by 1990, and by an additional 50 percent by 2000;

4. The closing down of all military bases abroad and withdrawal of troops from territories of foreign countries;

5. The comprehensive disarmament program should also address the issue of liquidation of military blocs. In this respect, meetings of representatives of the Warsaw Treaty and NATO on ways and means of disarmament, including proposals that would help achieve accords at the Soviet–U.S. negotiations in Geneva, would be very important.

The simultaneous dissolution of the Warsaw Treaty and NATO should take place by the year 2000.

[*Source: Č.j. 011.638/86, Archives of the Ministry of Foreign Affairs, Prague. Translated by Marian J. Kratochvíl.*]

Document No. 112: East German Intelligence Assessments of an FRG Appraisal of the National People's Army, April 28 and May 27, 1986

Providing more evidence of the depth of the spy-versus-spy operations that took place between the two Germanys (see Documents Nos. 80, 97 and 109), the following two reports document East Germany's acquisition and assessment of a secret West German evaluation of the GDR's army. The first report was prepared for Chief of Staff Fritz Streletz to solicit his evaluation of the accuracy of the FRG's information. In the second document, he concludes that it was mostly on the mark, although he offers some corrections. Streletz provides his views to Erich Mielke, Minister of State Security, responsible for the Stasi security service. Aside from what such materials reveal about the espionage activities of both sides, this kind of assessment also indicates how each side viewed its opponent's capabilities, and by comparison its own. Western observers were sometimes swayed by the GDR's impressive modern equipment and level of organization. But since the end of the Cold War, some East German generals have acknowledged that in the event of a major war they believed their forces would not have stood a realistic chance of victory. One of the key uncertainties concerned the reliability of their troops in fighting other German soldiers.

---

a) East German Intelligence Summary,
   April 28, 1986

[...]

The government of the Federal Republic of Germany has evaluated the military significance of the GDR within the Warsaw Treaty. As a result of military–strategic classification, it is figured that the GDR has neither a nationally based military doctrine nor an independent military strategy. Its military projects are determined by the Soviet military doctrine and strategy, as valid for the Warsaw Treaty. The GDR places its entire military potential, its territory, and its forces at the disposal of the Soviet Union by way of the Warsaw Treaty organization. Leadership, structure, equipment, training, safeguarding, and also the concept of combat of the NVA [National People's Army] are much more closely oriented towards Soviet demands and instructions than is the case in other Warsaw Treaty countries. [...]

From Soviet military doctrine, it is inferred that a definite victory in a clash with the main adversary (the United States and the U.S.-dominated NATO) can only be achieved by offensive action. Therefore a strategic offensive action is expected in the European theater of war in the case of a war against NATO. Leadership principles as developed by Soviet military strategy as well as strength, structure and training of the forces of the Warsaw Treaty are characterized as offensive. The territory of the GDR with its geographical reach far into the West provides favorable conditions for such offensive deployments. [...] Resulting from this outstanding strategic role of the GDR in the center of the Central European and West European theaters of war directly opposite the main forces of NATO in the central area, the GDR keeps those forces deemed to be necessary for conducting such initial operation, as well as the means for the conduct and maintenance, already on alert during times of peace. [...] The Group of Soviet Forces in Germany with its more than 430,000 men is considered as the strongest strategic operational group of forces of the Soviet Army with respect to quantity and quality. This means that approximately 20 percent of the Soviet army, and more than 10 percent of the tactical forces, are stationed in the GDR.

The NVA is more closely tied to the organization of the Treaty and intertwined with the Soviet forces than other armies of the Warsaw Treaty member-states are. The almost complete subordination under the Warsaw Treaty is regarded as a special feature detrimental to the GDR. Besides political and military considerations, the main reason for that is seen in certain security interests of individual member-states. At the same time, the NVA maintains an established position in relationship to other Warsaw Treaty constituent armies due to its modern structure and armament, increasing effectiveness, and the high level of combat readiness. The NVA is acknowledged as equal in rank to the others during military exercises. With respect to its equipment, training and military strength, it is seen as the number one among the non-Soviet forces of the Warsaw Treaty. With reserves of 1.8 million men, it can be assumed with certainty that the peacetime personnel of 185,000 men (without the 49,000 men in the border troops) can be increased in war time by as much as one third by mobilization and reinforcement.

[...]

The evaluation of the *internal situation* of the NVA assumes that the different political and psychological patterns and trends within GDR society will be necessarily infused by the approximately 95,000 annually drafted soldiers into a conscript army consisting of approximately 55 percent of military draftees. Still, a negative impact on the discipline and the internal situation of the NVA has been an exception so far. The NVA is much more subject to political and ideological diversion than are the other armies of the Warsaw Treaty. Counteraction by the political apparatus is considered to be mostly futile. Especially among the younger soldiers, indifference and a skeptical attitude with respect to the image of the enemy, as communicated by the political apparatus, are common. Despite these unresolved problems of delimitation [*Abgrenzung*] against the Federal Republic, and the overall low motivation of soldiers towards service, the Federal Republic does not doubt the functioning and reliability of the NVA. Besides the activity of intelligence units within the forces, loyalty and professional ambitions of the officers and non-commissioned officers are considered crucial in this respect. High performance expectations, fear of reprisals, and a usually opportunistic attitude result in accommodation. The Federal Republic of Germany is certain that the Soviet military leadership will grant the NVA a top position among the allied armies and considers it a politically reliable, well-equipped and trained and therefore powerful army, despite a continued mistrust of "the German". [...]

b) Gen. Streletz's Evaluation of
   the West German Appraisal,
   May 27, 1986

[...]
Dear Comrade Minister,

I carefully checked the "Information on Assessment of the Military Significance of the GDR within the Warsaw Treaty by the Federal Republic" which I had received from you.

Overall it can be stated that the adversary is obviously conducting ambitious intelligence activities and intensely evaluates data having become known.

Facts mentioned in the information partly correspond to the real situation or come very close. There are some larger differences with regard to numbers of personnel and technology.

[...]

Re. page 3:
- The potential of reservists of the National People's Army (age 18 to 50) is not 1.8 millions, but 3.4 million soldiers.
- The border troops of the GDR (without the 6th Coastal Border Brigade) comprise of 42,000 soldiers.
- The army within the National People's Army has about 110,000 people in times of peace.
- After mobilization, there would not be four, but five additional divisions available.
- In the case of mobilization, the National People's Army can calculate with 1.3 million previously drafted soldiers now serving as reservists.
- Nothing is stored on the territory of the GDR for the Polish army.

Re. page 4:
- The air force/air defense of the National People's Army does not have any tactical air division.
- The battle-helicopter squadrons mentioned are not subordinated to the air force/air defense, but to the army.
- The air force/air defense does not have 43,000, but approximately 37,000 soldiers available.
- The air force has not approximately 780, but 685 aircraft.
- The early warning and fighter system does not consist of approximately 30 positions close to the border of the Federal Republic of Germany and to the Baltic Sea coast. Depending on the assumed depth of the territory of the GDR, a maximum of 15 positions could be imagined.
- There are no intentions to modernize the stock of air craft of the bomber fighter squadron in the South of the GDR (base Drewitz).

Re. page 5
- The National People's Army has hangars for about 60 percent of the fighter aircraft.
- The air force/air defense has stocked fuel for approximately 20 days [and] ammunition for approximately 40 days.
- The People's Navy counts approximately 16,000 people.
- The People's Navy, including the Coastal Border Brigade, deploys 225 fighter and auxiliary boats, of which are 83 auxiliary boats of all kinds.

Re. page 7
- The National People's Army does not own 340 fighter and bomber-fighter aircraft, but only 291.
- No chemical weapons are produced in Kapen near Dessau. This is a factory for ammunition.

Re. page 8
- The National People's Army does not have any stocks of chemical weapons.
- Currently approximately 106,000 people are drafted annually, and the same number is discharged.
  [...]

[*Source: Die Bundesbeauftragte für die Unterlagen des Staatssicherheitsdienstes (BStU), Zentralarchiv, ZAIG, Information 7466, pp. 1–13. Translated by Karen Riechert.*]

Document No. 113: Bulgarian Memorandum on the Bulgarian–Romanian Proposal for a Chemical Weapons-Free Zone in the Balkans, March 21, 1986

This Bulgarian document refers to a proposal by Bulgaria and Romania to create a nuclear-free zone in the Balkans. It shows that by this time the Soviets came to regard such initiatives by their allies not only as acceptable but consistent with their own goals. This particular proposal met with a reserved response from Turkey and, not surprisingly, Albania. Greece, and especially Yugoslavia, were more positive in their reactions.

MEMORANDUM

At the initiative of the Bulgarian side, talks between the foreign ministers of the People's Republic of Bulgaria, Petar Mladenov, and of the Socialist Republic of Romania, Ilie Vaduva, were held on March 19, 1986, in Warsaw, where views were exchanged regarding the work accomplished on the Bulgarian–Romanian initiative to turn the Balkans into a chemical weapons-free zone.

The Romanian minister informed that, in compliance with the agreements between Comrade Todor Zhivkov and Comrade Nicolae Ceaușescu, the Romanian side has submitted a Declaration-Appeal to all Balkan states. The governments of Turkey, Yugoslavia and Albania have sent a written response. Greece has replied verbally on behalf of [Prime Minister Andreas] Papandreou to the Romanian ambassador in Athens. Vaduva expressed his personal opinion that the Greek side had intended to submit a written reply during Papandreou's delayed visit to Bucharest.

The replies received differ substantially. Turkey has some reservations about the proposal. So does Albania. However, Yugoslavia and Greece appreciate the initiative and would readily participate in taking the next steps. Turkey's reservations center on the point that problems like this can be resolved only on a global scale. Albania has declared that the country possesses no chemical weapons and has no intentions to produce or store any on its territory. Moreover, problems of this kind can be solved only within the framework of Europe. Yugoslavia has a similar position, connecting this idea with the progress of the Geneva talks.

Vaduva stated that the document has been submitted to Geneva, Stockholm and about 35 other states. Most of the countries have assessed the proposal in a positive way. They regard it as a contribution to the abolition of chemical weapons. Vaduva informed that Comrade Ceaușescu pays special attention to the responses coming from these countries. There is a common feature in that no Balkan country has in its possession, or would like to be the recipient of, chemical weapons. Upon receiving a written response from Greece, we could come to an agreement on the next steps.

After expressing thanks for the information, Cde. Petar Mladenov qualified the replies of the different states as an expression of their positive attitude towards this idea. Most of the governments, the public and other organizations support the proposal. It was unanimously supported here at the session of the Warsaw Pact Committee of Foreign Ministers. This initiative falls within the scope of our joint peace program.

Comrade Mladenov emphasized that he would personally inform Comrade Todor Zhivkov on the progress of the work, and asked Vaduva to tell Comrade Ceauşescu that Comrade Zhivkov is closely observing this matter in person.

Making a comment on the information available, Cde. Mladenov stressed that we had not expected an immediate positive solution to this issue. We have some experience from our work on establishing a nuclear-free zone in the Balkans. Turkey's position is not a surprise—this is NATO's position. This, however, should not be an obstacle that will delay our future activities. Albania has sent a reply. Greece was the first to respond positively. The dissemination of the document in the United Nations and through other channels is a good representation for us. It is obvious that we are not only making this idea popular, but we are also contributing to its clarification and realization.

What should we do next? We need to go on with the preparatory work. It is hardly necessary to discuss a high-level meeting at the moment; however, we are making a proposal to hold a meeting with government experts from the Balkan states. Those who wish will participate. If a country does not send experts, nothing serious has happened. We would like to make that clear. We do not imagine this zone without Turkey. The situation with Albania is different, though. To conduct a session to discuss the idea is something we can do and we should do, even if someone does not participate. It would be good if they join us later.

Where should the meeting be held? We would not mind having the first meeting in Bucharest, where the initiative started and the declaration was officially submitted. Besides, our relations with Turkey at the moment are not flourishing. In case the meeting is held in Bucharest, this circumstance will not be used as a pretext to refuse participation.

Comrade Mladenov suggested as well that the process should not be delayed for long. If the Romanian side agrees, we would not mind, he said, holding the meeting sometime in mid-June.

Comrade Vaduva accepted Comrade Mladenov's comments for his information. We do not reckon either, he said, that we should be very slow with this experts' meeting.

[*Source: TsDA, Fond 1-B, Record 68, File 394–86, p. 8–10. Translated by Greta Keremidchieva.*]

Document No. 114: East German Ideas concerning a Nuclear Weapons-Free Zone in Central Europe, May 21, 1986

The following two East German documents exemplify the range of proposals that emerged in the mid-1980s to reduce the confrontation along the East–West fault line. They also reflect the prominence of the GDR which, though the most conservative and anti-Western Warsaw Pact member-state, took the lead role in trying to demilitarize the confrontation in Central Europe. One proposal was to create there a zone free of tactical nuclear weapons. This was a variation of the Rapacki Plan[46] but under entirely new circumstances. Formally it was a proposal by the East German SED and the West German Social Democratic Party rather than the respective governments, thus emphasizing the ideological affinity of two parties that had previously considered each other wholly incompatible. Their joint draft proposal for a nuclear-free zone in Central Europe is interesting for its invocation of the late Swedish Prime Minister Olaf Palme, who had been assassinated in February 1986 and whom both parties regarded as an inspiration.

a) Memorandum on Negotiations with the
   West German Social Democratic Party, May 21, 1986

In preparation for the next meeting with the SPD[47] on May 29 and 30, 1986 in Bonn, a revised draft of the "Proposal for the Creation of a Central European Nuclear-Free Zone" [...] was presented.

This new draft takes account of the results of the third meeting with the SPD. It contains the following important new elements:

- the call for negotiations about the creation of a nuclear-free zone, i.e.
  tactical nuclear weapons
  intermediate-range nuclear weapons and
  strategic weapons.

This demand corresponds with the goal set in the Declaration by the Member-States of the Warsaw Treaty on October 23, 1985 in Sofia.

According to the Soviet plan, the creation of a nuclear-free zone would proceed in two stages:

- The first stage would be the creation of a zone measuring about 150 km on either side of the dividing line between the two military–political alliances in central Europe.
- In the second stage, the zone could be expanded to about 300 km on either side

---

[46] The Rapacki Plan of October 2, 1957, called for a nuclear-free zone in Central Europe, consisting of the two German states, Poland and Czechoslovakia, which was to be guaranteed by the superpowers.

[47] Sozialdemokratische Partei Deutschlands (Social Democratic Party of [West] Germany).

of the dividing line. This should take place about 5 years after the completion of the first stage.

Nuclear weapons would be defined to include all nuclear-capable delivery systems, as well as the nuclear ammunition itself. If a delivery system can fire both conventional and nuclear ammunition, then all weapons of this dual-use system would fall under the category of nuclear weapons.

This definition complies with the Soviet recommendations at the consultations held on November 25, 1985 in Moscow. However, those recommendations did not enumerate the individual weapons categories, to avoid burdening an essentially political document with additional technical problems.

On May 20, 1986, the SPD presented its "Proposal for a Nuclear-Free Zone in Central Europe." [...]

While reflecting the essential elements of the consultations to date, this proposal contains a number of totally unacceptable demands:

- the creation of a nuclear- free zone measuring only 150 km on either side of the dividing line
- the inclusion of all artillery systems (the suggestion of the SED[48] is that only dual-use artillery systems be included).
- the limitation of the commitment of the participating states to the withdrawal of nuclear weapons. (The SED suggests also prohibiting the possession, stationing, storage and production of nuclear weapons in the zone.)

Furthermore, the SPD has left all questions concerning the control of a future zone unaddressed. This leaves it with the option of making unacceptable demands in future negotiations, thereby jeopardizing all results achieved thus far.

[...]

The unacceptable demands of the SPD do not constitute a basis for negotiation, and should be rejected.

[...]

b) Proposal for Creation of a Nuclear-Free Zone,
   End of May 1986

1. The SED and the SPD consider that the continuation of the arms race on earth and the attempt to extend it to outer space is creating the risk of a nuclear inferno that would threaten the very existence of the peoples of Europe and the whole world. The European continent in particular, due to the high concentration of dangerous weapons of mass destruction, has become a powder keg that could explode anytime and thrust mankind into disaster. This fills the people of Europe with deep anxiety.

2. Therefore, the SED and the SPD have decided to act upon their conviction that the tension on the continent must be eased.

---

[48] Sozialistiche Einheitspartei Deutschlands (Socialist Unity Party, communist party of East Germany)

Following the legacy of the unforgotten Olaf Palme[49], they propose that a first stepbe made to remove or withdraw the most dangerous weapons, that is, all nuclear weapons, from the line dividing the two world systems and military political alliances. [...]

4. The SED and the SPD believe that the removal of nuclear weapons from central Europe along the dividing line between the two military–political alliances would be a decisive contribution towards creating a healthier situation on our continent, towards lowering the level of security maintained on both sides.

It would lessen both the nuclear and the conventional attack capability of the opposing armed forces groups and reduce the confrontation between NATO and the Warsaw Pact in Europe.

The SED and the SPD expect that in the negotiations between the USSR and the USA presently underway in Geneva over the whole complex of space-based and nuclear weapons, an agreement will soon be reached about the liquidation of American and Soviet intermediate-range missiles in Europe. Such an agreement would make it much easier to rid large parts of central Europe of all types of nuclear weapons, and would be a step towards the goal of gradually removing nuclear weapons from the life of mankind altogether.

Measures for creating a nuclear-free zone in central Europe would be in agreement with the Helsinki Final Act. They would be an expression of the special responsibility of the two German States, to ensure that war shall never again originate on German soil, that henceforth German soil shall breed peace. [...]

The SED and SPD are proposing the creation of a nuclear-free zone along the dividing line between the military political alliances in central Europe. They call upon the governments of the German Democratic Republic, the Czechoslovak Socialist Republic and the Federal Republic of Germany to begin negotiations at the state level on this matter as soon as possible. [...]

Nuclear weapons should, according to the SED and the SPD, include all nuclear-capable delivery systems, as well as the ammunition itself (including nuclear mines). If a delivery system can fire both conventional and nuclear warheads, then all weapons of this dual-use system would fall under the category of nuclear weapons.

Obligations: Both parties are of the conviction that an agreement to create a nuclear-free zone would have to be based on the principle of equality and equal security.

Controls: The extent and nature of controls would depend on the extent of the disarmament measures agreed upon. National controls have priority over international ones.

International controls would have to be implemented by a permanent international commission. All states committed to the nuclear-free zone have the right to become members of this commission. The participating states would have to commit themselves to working together with the permanent international commission to solve any problems that may arise in the fulfillment of the obligations agreed upon, and to support it in its work.

[*Source: VA-01/40372, BA-MA. Translated by Ursula Froese.*]

[49] Olaf Palme (1927–1986), a Social Democratic prime minister of Sweden, was an advocate of cooperative security. He was assassinated in Stockholm on February 28, by a vagrant.

Document No. 115: Minutes of the Political Consultative Committee Party Secretaries' Meeting in Budapest, June 11, 1986

This East German document records a revealing discussion among Warsaw Pact party secretaries on the question of disarmament. Taking place within weeks of the April 26 Chernobyl nuclear disaster, it shows how that accident influenced Soviet and East European perceptions of what a nuclear war in Europe might look like. As Polish leader Wojciech Jaruzelski put it, "No one should have the idea that in a nuclear war one could enjoy a cup of coffee in Paris five or six days later." The document also shows that the Soviet Union was pursuing across-the-board nuclear and conventional force reductions although the Warsaw Pact would remain better off than NATO. During this period, Gorbachev is still arguing for maintaining an advantage over the capitalist enemy with whom he sees no common interests other than in preventing war.

Comrade János Kádár opened the meeting. He welcomed the participants and expressed his satisfaction over the successful completion of the meeting of the PCC. The leading comrades of the fraternal parties had gathered to continue a practice already started in Sofia, namely to meet for comradely and casual discussion among leaders of delegations of the fraternal countries of the Warsaw Treaty. [...] These meetings proved to be a very useful form of collaboration. They will become an extremely important part of future concrete cooperation.

Meetings in this circle are rather recent, although they had occurred previously. [...] As had already been agreed in Sofia, each comrade can contribute the issues he is concerned about.

[...]

Comrade Mikhail Gorbachev expressed his deep satisfaction over the results of the meeting concerning the speech by Comrade Ceaușescu at the meeting of the PCC. [...] Comrade Gorbachev agreed with Comrades Ceaușescu and Kádár at the meeting of the PCC and highly valued the atmosphere at the meeting in the name of the Soviet delegation. [...] He also agreed that cooperation is going well.

[...]

Comrade Gorbachev stressed that the Soviet Union is currently witnessing serious problems.

[...]

Comrade Gorbachev informed extensively about the accident at the power plant in Chernobyl.

[...]

One should not pretend that nothing happened, that everything would be under control. Very serious problems are still to be faced, the majority of which are new to the Soviet Union.

[...] It was like war. People were evacuated, families were separated and only slowly found their way back to each other. All this was extraordinarily serious. The situation and its impact must not be played down in any way.

The tragedy of Chernobyl is closely related to the issue of disarmament. Medical experts all over the world clearly state that there would be no medical help in case of a nuclear war. Soviet and American physicians agree on this. [...]

Comrade Gorbachev provided information on the recent meeting at the Ministry of Foreign Affairs of the Soviet Union. Such a consultative meeting took place for the first time in the history of Soviet diplomacy. It was realized that stronger control by the party would be needed in this field. Above all, a more specific orientation was necessary and a stronger party spirit needed to be infused. He himself has given a two-and-a-half hour presentation. A thorough discussion took place in an open atmosphere. Many issues had been raised concerning all areas of Soviet foreign policy. The main problem was the existence of a lot of laziness and old thinking [and] that Soviet diplomacy did not sufficiently respond to the challenge of current dynamic developments. The work of the foreign policy apparatus was not up to date with regard to its approach, analysis, and reaction to many events. However, the comrades also criticized many aspects of the work being done at headquarters, which is also contributing to the situation. In short, it was decided to modernize this area as well, and to fully adjust to the challenge of internal and international developments. Comrade Gorbachev also stressed the issue of perfecting cooperation within the socialist community with respect to the realities of today's world. The focus of this segment was on concretely shaping the increasingly close cooperation of the socialist countries. According to him, there was a major need for common action, for more active contributions by the socialist countries towards the general line and tactics of foreign policy. Based on a coordinated policy this includes a certain division of labor. He had already discussed these questions with Comrade Kádár. Also, he tried to frame these needs in a more general way in his speech at the meeting of the PCC. It was certainly not necessary for all initiatives to originate from the Soviet Union. It is important that the fraternal countries have a common basis and a coordinated policy. Based on this, many possibilities would arise for initiatives by the respective socialist countries.

One problem was accentuated during the meeting: Declarations at the highest level by the fraternal countries should be translated into negotiations through concrete proposals in the shortest time possible. Currently there is a gap at this point. Useful political declarations had been made that were jointly coordinated. However, real negotiations often did not rise to that level because old methods and the old routine are still in use.

[...]

Also the functional parts of the Foreign Ministry had been changed. A new Department for Arms Control and Disarmament had been created. This was a fundamental issue, asking for experts with specialized knowledge. Furthermore, departments for the peaceful use of nuclear power, for space-related issues, for international economic relations, and for humanitarian issues had been created. The Department of Planning was transformed into a Department for Analysis and Prognostication.

[...]

Comrade Gorbachev stressed that he considered it necessary to bring up these issues since those were important problems. He assumed that foreign policy activities of the fraternal countries should be active and replete with initiatives. The point was to distribute capacities accordingly.

Comrade Kádár brought up the question of regular scheduled meetings of the general secretaries of the fraternal parties of the Warsaw Treaty member-states. If the comrades would agree, Comrade Gorbachev would invite them to Moscow for such a meeting in the fall in the name of the Soviet leadership. A suitable date for everyone still needs to be found. At this meeting everybody will be entitled to ask any questions he has in mind. It is important to find the major parts of the chain which need to be linked together. It is certainly good to find one of these major parts of the chain, a main subject for each of the meetings. At the meeting of the PCC, one important subject, the integration and serious promotion of economic cooperation, had been mentioned. Maybe it would be useful to choose this as subject for the next meeting. If the comrades agree, this will now be considered as arranged.

[...] Fidel Castro and other comrades should not feel ignored. Therefore it must be considered in which framework the meeting should take place, whether in the framework of the Warsaw Treaty or Comecon.

Comrade Erich Honecker remarked that the meeting should be held within the framework of the Warsaw Treaty. Comrade Todor Zhivkov expressed the opinion that fundamental questions should be discussed first within the common framework, and then the other members of Comecon might be included.

[...]

Furthermore, Mikhail Gorbachev informed on the situation of Soviet–American relations.

[...]

A couple of days before his departure to Budapest, Comrade Gorbachev had received another personal message from Reagan. It did not contain anything really new, however it was written in a smooth and communicative style. Again Reagan had invited him to a meeting. This was also typical. The Soviet side is still working on its response, but the basic idea will be the same: if something substantial is scheduled for discussion, Comrade Gorbachev would join a meeting.

With respect to policy regarding the FRG, Comrade Gorbachev explained the following: he believes that the socialist countries should conduct a workable policy of pressure towards the [Helmut] Kohl government. The government of the FRG has started to feel that. The Soviet Union has transmitted the following to the government of the FRG: if Bonn would have something new to say in comparison to Washington, the Soviet Union would consider inviting Kohl to discuss with him current issues of interest to the Europeans and the entire world.

Kohl was cursing about this: Gorbachev would meet with the demagogue [François] Mitterrand and with [Bettino] Craxi[50], but not with Kohl. The FRG would be in favor of continuing Ostpolitik and wants a dynamic relationship with the Soviet

---

[50] President of France and Prime Minister of Italy, respectively.

Union. He was told that one would [only] meet with him if he would show an independent political face as chancellor. He had responded that he would take notice of this attitude.

Comrade Gorbachev expressed the opinion that this would teach the government of the FRG a lesson.

[...]

Finally, Comrade Gorbachev said that he was delighted that the comrades had found the opportunity to meet within this circle. It was no less important than the meeting of the PCC itself that such a style [of meeting] was possible. This type of meeting would mean more mutual attention, more openness. He himself would be very much in favor of it. [...]

Comrade Nicolae Ceaușescu started by remarking that the meeting of the PCC had produced good results.

[...]

With respect to the information from Comrade Gorbachev on the activity of the Soviet Foreign Ministry, Comrade Nicolae Ceaușescu expressed the opinion that these would, of course, be internal issues for the Soviet Union. The Romanian Communist Party would not intend to discuss that type of issue in the near future. However, he would like to thank Comrade Gorbachev for this information; he had drawn conclusions for himself. Those would refer especially to Comrade Gorbachev's explanations of the more active participation of the Warsaw Treaty countries in drafting and implementation of various issues in international affairs. Concerning cooperation in this area, it would certainly be necessary to draw more fundamental conclusions. It is not about general declarations; the jointly adopted declarations are fine with respect to the ideas that have been formulated. However, it is a long way from those declarations to their realization.

He brought up two issues in this context during his speech at the meeting of the PCC. The first was the Stockholm conference to be concluded soon.[51] It is necessary to ensure that it will not end without result. The second issue is the Vienna negotiations, which have already lasted 12 years.[52] These could also be brought to an end in a couple of months. Maybe the fraternal countries should not only adopt general declarations, but undertake concrete steps towards their realization. Of course, one would assume that the parties are in charge of foreign policy [formulation] while the foreign ministries conduct executive policy. The parties should take a more active role by realizing [efforts at] cooperation. This should be a matter of thorough discussion within these circles.

[...]

Comrade Erich Honecker expressed his deep satisfaction over the course and the results of the PCC meeting in Budapest. It had been correctly stated that it took place just at the right moment for considering the issues on the agenda more thoroughly. However, this meeting was also extremely important for achieving a much higher level of socialist construction, and for fulfilling the peace initiative of the Soviet Union

---

[51] Conference on Confidence- and Security-Building Measures and Disarmament in Europe.
[52] Conference on Mutual and Balanced Force Reductions (MBFR).

and the fraternal countries. He would fully support a meeting of the general secretaries at the end of the year. [...] Since the most developed socialist countries are united in the Warsaw Treaty, he would deem it useful to meet first within the framework of the Warsaw Treaty, and expand this circle later.

The meeting in December could be approached in such a way that everybody would report his experiences. He himself would emphasize that cooperation has become more fertile and coordinated after the meetings in Sofia and Prague and after his talks with Comrade Gorbachev. This is true for the collective draft on common policy, as well as for actual operational cooperation.

Also, the recent conventions of the fraternal parties have taken place against the background of agreement on all fundamental questions of socialist construction and international politics. He would agree with Comrade Gorbachev, who remarked that all the fraternal countries would currently face strategic challenges and would have to decide on the methods which will determine whether they will achieve their goals.

[...]

It has also been said that currently it is most important on the level of international politics to develop a broad offensive approach. Hereby it must be taken into account that the public, and many governments, have given clear signs of agreeing to maintain the SALT II treaty and the ABM Treaty.[53] All governments of the NATO countries, except for the U.S., have come out in favor of retaining these treaties. They are in agreement with the majority of people on this issue. Even the representative of a government like the FRG, [Hans-Dietrich] Genscher[54], has made a positive statement in this regard. Notwithstanding the reasons, he has also supported the idea of sticking with SALT II. This was the headline in today's papers in the West: Genscher against the U.S.!

The ABM Treaty on missile defense systems from 1972 also enjoys wide support among many governments.

A third issue was the new proposal by the Soviet Union and the fraternal countries on reduction of forces and conventional arms in Europe between the Urals and the Atlantic. This proposal has already been made public, and it will be difficult to ignore, especially since it included the question of [arms] control.

[...]

Comrade Honecker pointed out that he had already discussed with Comrade Gorbachev how the building of the European House must not ignore the FRG. It plays an important role within the European Community and NATO. Such a policy could provoke the wrong type of solidarity. Of course, it would be highly important for elections in the FRG in January 1987 to result in a government led by the SPD.

Despite all the good work the fraternal parties have accomplished jointly, and the SED on an almost daily basis together with the Social Democrats, nobody could foresee the results of the federal parliamentary elections [in the FRG]. The bourgeoisie does have many opportunities for manipulation. [...]

---

[53] The U.S.–Soviet Interim Agreement on Limitation of Strategic Offensive Arms of June 1979, never ratified by the U.S., and the Anti-Ballistic Missile Treaty of May 1972.

[54] West German foreign minister.

(Comrade Ceaușescu remarked that in any event Kohl and his party will continue to play a major part in the FRG's public life.)

Comrade Erich Honecker agreed. There is even a question whether someone even worse could follow Kohl. He had talked twice very openly to [SPD candidate Johannes] Rau about how he himself would place his bets on the election. Here it became apparent, too, that the bourgeoisie is very well versed in manipulating public opinion. Sometimes public opinion is stirred up overnight.

The basic line for the SED would be clear: supporting progressive forces left of the CDU with whom good cooperation already exists.

[...]

Comrade [Wojciech] Jaruzelski welcomed the opportunity for a meeting of the general secretaries and of the first secretaries. This practice should be maintained. So far such meetings have taken place [only] in special cases. Now it had been proposed to meet in addition to discuss certain topics. One does not exclude the other.

[...]

Comrade Jaruzelski thanked Comrade Mikhail Gorbachev for the comprehensive information on the events at the nuclear power plant in Chernobyl and its impact.

[...]

However, it would be necessary to draw further conclusions. Among others, he had talked about that with the supreme commander of the Unified Forces of the Warsaw Treaty, Comrade [Viktor] Kulikov. The latter had demonstrated a deep sympathy for paying more attention to issues of civil defense. Another issue would be to examine all the plans and concepts, as well as all the military exercises of our alliance, and to approach them more realistically. For instance, no one should have the idea that in a nuclear war one could enjoy a cup of coffee in Paris five or six days later. This tragic event should be used to approach all these questions much more realistically.

With respect to the results of the meeting of the PCC, Comrade Jaruzelski remarked that a document had been adopted relevant to all European countries, but not only to them. At stake is not just the availability of nuclear weapons to certain countries only, but of arms being made available to all countries.

The fact that actually all countries are interested in these issues should be much more utilized by us. It would be important to prepare a scenario, and to come up with ideas already, for our potential reaction in case the counterpart tries to ignore our proposal.

Such a reaction by the adversary is already apparent, and we need to be prepared in order to be able to push the other side to the wall. The documents are written in a matter-of-fact way, but cannot elicit a major propaganda impact.

We have to present our proposals even more convincingly, and have to better coordinate the discussion of the adversary's arguments (e.g. on the superiority of the Warsaw Treaty in conventional [arms]). We have to find a common language, and must not remain too unspecific but provide concrete answers to the adversary's position.

Maybe it would be useful to set up a special team of representatives from the Foreign Ministry and the Unified Supreme Command in order to follow this process efficiently in Moscow or elsewhere, and to draft recommendations for our propaganda in order to fully seize the opportunity.

Comrade Gustáv Husák agreed with the evaluation of the meeting of the PCC and its results. He also valued highly the information provided by Comrade Gorbachev. Everybody would feel that Comrade Gorbachev has brought fresh élan to the meetings of the general secretaries and to the cooperation among the fraternal parties and the fraternal countries.

[...]

Comrade Todor Zhivkov supported the positive evaluation of the meeting of the PCC. He emphasized especially the comradely, friendly atmosphere.

[...]

Comrade Todor Zhivkov expressed his sympathy for the accident at Chernobyl. [...] It would be appropriate to look at this tragedy in the context of nuclear arms. One has to come back to this question again and again, since this incredible danger for mankind exists. If such a plant would explode, e.g. in the FRG, the FRG would be turned into a desert and the neighbors would also receive terrible fallout. How much worse would a real nuclear strike be?

(Comrade Gorbachev pointed out that acts of sabotage would also be possible against nuclear power plants. Nowadays, there would be many interested in doing such things.)

It would be enough, as Comrade Zhivkov further explained, just to fire an artillery salvo on a nuclear power plant. The question of all questions would be how to save mankind from extermination and to preserve civilization. This question has not yet been answered. We need a more offensive approach in order to demonstrate more effectively our sense of responsibility for all mankind. In his opinion, the great opportunities for mobilizing large forces for the fight for peace would have to be better used with regard to this question.

(Comrade Husák remarked that the enemy had been successful in fueling panic on this issue.)

Comrade Gorbachev considered this an important remark. It was illustrative that no new power plant had been built in the United States since 1979, the year of the big nuclear power plant accident.[55]

[...]

Comrade Nicolae Ceaușescu also asked for the opportunity to add something. In the report of the supreme commander of the Unified Forces he had noticed that expenses for military technology had risen from 40 to 60 percent. When economic questions are discussed at the general secretaries' meeting in fall, it would also be necessary to discuss the level of expenses for the military.

During the past five-year-period, the national economies of the fraternal countries had grown 12 to 16 percent on average. However, expenses for military equipment increased 50 to 60 percent. If this matter continues to be dealt with in the same

---

[55] The partial meltdown of a reactor core at the Three Mile Island nuclear plant in Pennsylvania on March 28, 1979, resulted in only minor off-site radioactive leakage and no immediate injuries but led to sweeping changes in the operation of U.S. nuclear power facilities.

manner, it will create development problems for the fraternal countries. He would suggest discussing this question at the fall meeting of the general secretaries. [...]

Comrade Mikhail Gorbachev pointed out that in the jointly adopted appeal, a reduction of forces, of conventional weapons, and of military expenses was proposed. As soon as this process would start, a reduction of military expenses would follow.

Comrade Ceaușescu remarked that he was concerned with a reduction of expenses beyond this proposal.

Comrade János Kádár suggested that Comrade Mikhail Gorbachev should summarize the results of the meeting in a concluding speech.

Comrade Gorbachev said that he did not see any need in doing so, and that Comrade Kádár should speak.

[...]

Comrade János Kádár welcomed the initiative by Comrade Gorbachev to organize a meeting of the general secretaries in Moscow in the fall. The previous three meetings in Sofia, Prague, and Budapest had been scheduled for specific reasons. They had been very well received by the Hungarian People's Republic. He valued in particular the open and comradely atmosphere of these meetings. Therefore, he suggested continuing along the lines begun in Sofia. There should be no formal meetings with a lot of paper on the table, and where formal resolutions would be adopted. If the general secretaries declare their agreement on certain issues, then this would weigh as heavily as the decision of some committee.

Meetings should continue to offer the opportunity for everybody to raise current issues of concern.

[...]

Comrade Kádár made his remark about the "papers" at meetings of the general secretaries more precisely. When he said that there should be no stacks of paper on the table, this did not mean that he is against any paper at all. Of course, Comrade Gorbachev could send a paper as background for discussion.

[...]

[*Source: DY/30/2353, SAPMO. Translated by Karen Riechert.*]

Document No. 116: Report to the Bulgarian Politburo on Romanian Arms Reduction Proposals, September 22, 1986

In this report to the Bulgarian Politburo, Foreign Minister Petar Mladenov describes the state of recent Romanian efforts to get the Warsaw Pact to initiate unilateral arms cuts. Despite Gorbachev's more open attitude on such questions, the rest of the alliance, including the Soviets, balk at the idea once more. Mladenov suggests that the issue be tabled temporarily.

Ministry of Foreign Affairs
01-05-10
To: Politburo of CC of BCP

Comrades,

In his statements at Warsaw Pact forums, RCP [Romanian Communist Party] General Secretary and President of Romania Nicolae Ceauşescu proposed several times that Warsaw Pact countries should unilaterally freeze and reduce their force levels and military expenditures.

At the PCC Sofia meeting (1985), the Romanian party laid out this proposal as a condition for signing the closing documents. As a result, at the Warsaw meeting (March 19–20, 1986) it was decided that the CMFA had to create an Expert Group for examining this possibility.

At the Third Congress of the Working People [trade unions] of Romania, held in the beginning of September 1986, Ceauşescu called on all European states to reduce their armaments by at least 5 percent. Following a referendum, the Congress adopted a decision to reduce Romanian armaments, forces and military expenses by 5 percent till the end of the year.

On September 11 and 12, 1986, the allied countries' Working Group held a meeting in Bucharest. The Warsaw Pact delegations succeeded in avoiding the discussion put forward by Romania regarding the reduction mentioned above. They stated that it was not possible to take unilateral actions because these would harm their security, having in mind the fragile equality existing between NATO and the Warsaw Pact. The Soviet Army General Staff representative proved on the basis of facts that U.S. and NATO military programs aim at achieving military superiority over the Warsaw Pact. The coordinated position for adhering strictly to the equality principle as the only possible basis for disarmament agreements was confirmed.

As a result of the efforts of the six allied countries, the Romanian proposal was neutralized to a great extent. That's why the Romanian representatives insisted on a second session of the Group before the CMFA meeting in Bucharest, set for October 16 and 17, 1986.

In this connection, I consider it expedient that the Bulgarian experts delegation, which will participate in the second session of the Working Group, express the official statement of PR [People's Republic] of Bulgaria. *At the present it is not in our country's interest to carry out the proposed unilateral 5 percent reduction of forces, armaments and military expenses.* Such a step would invalidate the Budapest proposal to NATO for simultaneous and substantial reductions of armed forces and conventional weapons in Europe.[56]

With friendly greetings,
[signed]
P. Mladenov

[*Source: Fond 1, Opis 11a, a.e. 353, pp. 33, Bulgarian State Security Archives, AMVR. Translated by Vania Petkova.*]

---

[56] Appeal of the Budapest meeting of the PCC, 11 June 1986. See also document no. 115.

Document No. 117: Czechoslovak Summary of the Committee of Ministers of Foreign Affairs Meeting in Bucharest, October 18, 1986

Following shortly after the Reykjavik summit between Mikhail Gorbachev and Ronald Reagan, this Warsaw Pact foreign ministers' meeting provided a forum for the Soviets to explain the content of the summit to the allies and to solicit their cooperation in taking follow-up action. In answer to the Soviet call to retain the initiative in international affairs, the ministers agree to wage a "broad offensive" not only in the ongoing Geneva talks but also at the CSCE. Each Warsaw Pact representative proceeds to advance proposals for how to accomplish this task.

A regular session of the Warsaw Pact Committee of Foreign Ministers took place in Bucharest on October 14–15, 1986, in accordance with the timetable of meetings of the Warsaw Pact's highest political institutions. This had been approved at the 1986 Budapest session of the Warsaw Pact Political Consultative Committee within the framework of strengthening the Warsaw Pact mechanism. Originally, the session had been planned for October 16–17, 1986; the change occurred because of the USSR leadership's initiative to inform the foreign ministers about the proceedings and results of the Gorbachev–Reagan Reykjavik meeting immediately after its conclusion. [...]

Before the session of the Committee of Foreign Ministers, *an informal private meeting of the ministers* took place [...], in which [Foreign Minister] Shevardnadze gave detailed information on the preparation, course and conclusions of the meeting between Gorbachev and Reagan in Reykjavik on October 11–12, 1986. [...]

The decision to meet at Reykjavik amounted to a psychological turning point for Reagan. [Secretary of State] G. Shultz played a constructive role in that. At the same time, influential forces had been opposing the meeting. The meeting has been a tactical success for the Soviet leadership. [...]

Reagan saw the aim of the meeting as probing the possibility of Gorbachev's visit to the United States. The USSR replied that the visit would take place when possibilities for reaching particular agreements were visible. A summit without any results would be a political scandal.

Seeing that he could not expect any initiative by Reagan, Gorbachev suggested opening specific negotiations on nuclear and space disarmament at the ministerial level.

In strategic affairs, the USSR introduced a new variant of the 50 percent reduction without including missiles in forward areas. The United States had not expected this approach. The USSR further declared that it would consider the United States' interest in a reduction of heavy inter-continental ballistic missiles, and proclaimed its expectation that the United States would understand the USSR's interest in a reduction of U.S. submarine-launched ballistic missiles.

As far the INF[57] is concerned, the USSR accepted the zero option in Europe. It even agreed to freeze vehicles with a range of up to 1,000 kilometers and start negotiating about them. It proposed freezing the numbers of missiles in Asia and beginning negotiations on their reduction so that only 100 nuclear warheads would remain in the Asian part of the USSR; the United States could keep the same number on its territory.

USSR further suggested strengthening the regime of the Anti-Ballistic Missile Treaty (ABM).[58] It accepted the method proposed by the United States, namely, setting up a period during which the treaty could not be renounced or the ensuing negotiations discontinued. [...]

Gorbachev stressed that he understood the SDI matter[59] is a prestigious one for the president who is bound with this program. Therefore he suggested agreeing with research under laboratory conditions. [...]

The USSR further suggested restoring negotiations on a complete nuclear test ban either with the participation of Great Britain or without it, considering that it would be possible to reach a compromise, provisional solution, for example reducing the number and yield of detonations.

The United States only raised its old proposals in Geneva, refurbished to look as if they amounted to a new position. Gorbachev responded that he had heard of these proposals from [U.S. chief negotiator] M[ax] Kampelman in Geneva. He handed the president a table with precise numbers of U.S. and USSR strategic forces. Reagan asked whether he could keep the document; Gorbachev replied that the document is secret, but that the USSR trusts the United States. A whole strategic weapons triad was included in the table. Reagan and Shultz were impressed by Gorbachev's approach. [...]

Gorbachev further asked whether the United States was willing to go for a zero option in Europe on the assumption that the means of enhanced range of delivery in Europe would be frozen pending negotiations and their numbers in Asia would be addressed. Reagan appeared indecisive, saying that the United States would agree on condition that an acceptable solution would be found in Asia. Gorbachev replied that he accepted the president's proposal and gave his consent.

The negotiations on adhering to the ABM Treaty were the hardest. It turned out that the United States was not ready to negotiate on this matter. It came to Reykjavik with a decision not to sign anything and not to take up anything serious. Therefore the delegation improvised.

The next day, Reagan accepted in principle the proposal for a 50 percent reduction of the strategic means of delivery. After a long discussion, the president agreed on the INF matter with the zero option for Europe. The USSR suggested keeping 100 nuclear warheads in Asia considering that the United States would keep the same number on its territory. [...]

---

[57] Intermediate-range Nuclear Forces.
[58] Treaty on the Limitation of Anti-Ballistic Missile Systems of May 26, 1972.
[59] Strategic Defense Initiative, announced by President Reagan on March 23, 1983.

Regarding nuclear testing, the United States refused to accept a complete ban. They were willing to promise to ratify the 1974 and 1976 agreements.[60] A compromise seemed possible regarding a limitation on the yield and number of explosions.

The main discrepancy appeared in the negotiations on the ABM. Gorbachev explained that the agreements achieved so far presumed a full liquidation of strategic means within 10 years. Shultz suggested a reduction of strategic means within five years and their complete liquidation within another five years. The USSR agreed immediately, considering that it was in line with its proposal of January 15. A shorter term is not feasible for technical reasons. The president did not conceal his allergy to the ABM. It was clear that the SDI was his baby, that he was tied to it and could not abandon it. Reagan showed clearly that they [the Americans] did not want an agreement on the ABM at the moment they were about to proceed toward the attainment of SDI outside the laboratory. The USSR warned that fulfilling this program would render any agreement on weapons limitations impossible.

Gorbachev expressed understanding of the necessity to maintain the [U.S.] president's prestige. Therefore, he repeated his approval of laboratory research. He said finally that Reagan had been offered an opportunity to take only one step in order to become a great president. The president was touched by this approach but it was obvious he could not act freely (a dependence on the military-industrial complex), and could not abandon the [SDI] program even if he understood the situation.

In evaluating the Reykjavik meeting, Shevardnadze said it could not be considered unproductive. It was a step forward on a road to the summit. [...]

In the end, Shevardnadze voiced thanks for allied support of the USSR's position. All the ministers welcomed this prompt and comprehensive information. [...]

In the *session of the committee of ministers* on October 14, Foreign Minister of the Romanian Socialist Republic [Ioan] Totu delivered the opening speech.

The first one with a substantial speech was Shevardnadze. He concentrated on the key matters of cooperation and coordination among the socialist countries. He stated that effective cooperation among them presupposed self-control, which called for correction if not successful. The more flexible we are adapting this mechanism to our needs, the more effective it would be. It should be clear when we are making mistakes and what has passed the test of time.

He mentioned his speech to the committee of ministers in Warsaw and the three main theoretical conclusions of the CPSU's XXVIIth Congress:
- The antagonism between socialism and capitalism could be resolved only through peaceful competition;
- the concept of an international security system was a practical way to strengthen peaceful coexistence;
- improving democratic institutions in our society is closely related to expanding democratization in interstate relations. [...]

The road from the Geneva summit[61] to Reykjavik provides evidence that social

---

[60] The Threshold Test Ban Treaty of July 3, 1974, and the PNE [Peaceful Nuclear Explosions] Treaty on Underground Nuclear Explosions for Peaceful Purposes of May 28, 1976.

[61] Reagan–Gorbachev summit of November 19–21, 1985.

ism is becoming more and more a synonym for peace in the awareness of the masses. Our ideas are today more popular due to qualitative changes within the socialist commonwealth as well as within every socialist country.

He mentioned Gorbachev's remark that Soviet troops would not stay in a number of countries forever. The Soviet leadership and the people wish for a quick return home for all their troops. [...]

Nowadays, the USSR's approach to the nuclear forces of France and Great Britain is quite different, in part for tactical reasons (reaching for yet a higher aim), and in part because the contacts with [Margaret] Thatcher and [François] Mitterrand have led to the assumption that in their nuclear rearmament, France and the Great Britain will not cross a certain limit agreeable to us. After Reykjavik, it will be difficult for them to avoid the process of medium-range missile removal from Europe.

The Soviet approach to nuclear testing and SDI proved successful. Reykjavik showed that the United States was prepared to sacrifice a lot to save it. Now, it is necessary to play up the notion that SDI is an obstacle on the road to a nuclear-free world. At the same time, two options must be weighed realistically:

1. Holding to one's stand and react by matching increases in armaments. This is possible, but not desirable from any point of view.

2. Proposing a compromise that would delay and limit research on SDI. This is realistic and productive.

The September contacts between the USSR and the United States in New York and Washington showed that the Americans could be confronted with a situation where they would have to react in a relatively realistic way, thus showing that only a dynamic policy would bring results.

He described the international situation as complicated, alarming and somewhat dangerous, even though there were new encouraging moments:

– the effect of a [nuclear] moratorium (propagandistic, but mainly as a symbol of the new thinking), which must be exploited,
– the particular steps that have destroyed the West's position on the matter of control, which had been misused against the socialist commonwealth,
– a qualitatively new level of cooperation among the Warsaw Pact countries, as demonstrated by the Budapest appeal for the reduction of conventional armaments.

He stressed that it was necessary to continue trying to keep the ball in NATO's court. Even the situation at the Stockholm conference did not prompt any optimism until all of us together pulled out the car that had gotten stuck in the swamp of negotiations.[62] Even if our consent to inspections might create certain problems, we won politically. The political climate in Europe had changed. Until then, NATO had not wanted to conduct negotiations on the reduction of military forces in Europe. Our position is stronger today, we have a real chance to fight for a Stockholm-2 and we can develop an aggressive [approach] in the CSCE. [...]

---

[62] Conference on Confidence- and Security-Building Measures in Europe from January 17, 1984, to September 10, 1986.

Stockholm paved the way to Vienna and Reykjavik marked it in a new way. The Vienna follow-up meeting would undoubtedly be taking place under the impact of a US–Soviet summit and Gorbachev's call for relieving our European house of nuclear weapons. [...]

With regard to improving foreign policy cooperation within the Warsaw Pact, [Shevardnadze] stated that even if the Warsaw Pact had come into existence as a military defense organization, and remained such, its political function had grown considerably, especially as a generator of peace initiatives. It was necessary to further stimulate the activity of the Committee of Foreign Ministers, to expand the range of topics of consultation by deputy foreign ministers and experts. The matter of creating an expert group for elaborating particular positions on international cooperation in the fight against terrorism had become ripe. With regard to the group for mutual exchange of information, he said that if a rotation were necessary we would agree to it. Moscow did not aspire to serving as the location of the group.

It was necessary to pay attention to the relations with European socialist countries that are not members of the Warsaw Pact—to cooperate with the Socialist Federal Republic of Yugoslavia more actively in the international area and to strive for normalization with Albania. [...]

[*Source: č.j. 014.617/86, Archives of the Ministry of Foreign Affairs, Prague. Translated by Karel Sieber.*]

Document No. 118: Summary of Statements at the Military Council Meeting in Bucharest, November 10–11, 1986

At this gathering of the Military Council, Marshal Kulikov continues his refrain of warning about the relentless growth of NATO's military potential. A large part of Kulikov's concern is over the prospective "perfection of strategic nuclear forces" although, in his view, Euromissiles also represent an increased danger of war. Even if an arms control agreement is eventually reached, he says, the imperialists will continue to pose the threat of war. While this is not a new position for Kulikov, it was in line with Gorbachev's own pessimistic attitude towards the prospects for arms control following the recent Reykjavik summit, where he had failed to convince Reagan to give up SDI. Not suprisingly, though, is the fact that Ceauşescu holds an entirely contradictory view. The Romanian leader declares emphatically that there is currently no danger of war, and urges further steps towards disarmament.

a) Statement by Marshal Viktor Kulikov

Following are remarks by the supreme commander of the unified armed forces on questions concerning the increase of fighting strength and combat readiness of the unified armed forces.

The United States and the other NATO countries continue to stir up the danger of war. The material foundation for all kinds of war have been expanded. A special danger lies in the perfection of strategic nuclear forces.

[…]

Considerable efforts have been undertaken to increase the fighting options of the general purpose forces concentrated in the European theater of war and the Atlantic. In Europe we face a group of NATO troops ready for battle, fully equipped and well trained.

[…]

The intensity and scope of the operational preparation of the NATO forces have assumed a dangerous character. The increased danger of war that all this implies requires us to take measures for further increasing the security of our countries and people and to increase the combat readiness of the forces of Warsaw Treaty member-states, beyond the continued struggle for peace.

Based on the conclusions from the meeting in Reykjavik, we have to consider the qualitatively new situation, which could be the result of a new policy orientation by the United States and the NATO bloc.

Two possible directions for the development of the military–political situation became apparent.

The *first and most dangerous* would be the refusal by the United States to sign any agreements on the reduction of nuclear armaments and their elimination. In this case, tensions in the world would increase even more, the arms race would be accelerated and reach into space. The danger of war would increase considerably.

The *second* direction of this development would result from certain agreements: Under these circumstances the nuclear arms race could be limited in a certain way. A certain re-evaluation of the types of arms could be expected.

Obviously, conventional weapons, especially precision weapons would be favored. The danger of war would remain, since the aggressive character of imperialism would not change.

Irrespective of the way international relations will develop, questions of security and the strengthening of the defensibility of the socialist countries as well as maintenance of a high battle readiness for the unified forces will remain of utmost importance. They should not be less challenged.

[...]

b) Statement by Nicolae Ceauşescu

After the presentation of the results of the 34th meeting of the Military Council of the unified forces by Marshal of the Soviet Union Kulikov, comrade Nicolae Ceauşescu expressed his thanks to the Supreme Commander of the Unified Forces and to the members of the military council for their work.

He had learned with satisfaction from the presentation by Marshal of the Soviet Union Kulikov, that the decisions on safeguarding peace and promoting disarmament by the party leadership [of the members] of the Warsaw Treaty were the focus of the deliberations of the military council.

[...]

The meeting between Mikhail Gorbachev and Ronald Reagan in Reykjavik has to be seen within this context as well. We support the proposals by the Soviet Union for the reduction and limitation of strategic armaments, of intermediate-range missiles in Europe and of conventional forces and armaments.

[...]

We have emphasized the importance we attach to the removal or reduction of intermediate-range missiles in Europe.

The Budapest appeal[63] for the reduction of conventional forces by 25 percent has to be carried out and the military balance kept on as low a level as possible.

[...]

Romania thinks that both blocs, the Warsaw treaty and NATO, should enter into direct contact and search for solutions acceptable to both sides.

[...]

The Romanian proposal for a reduction of military expenses by 5 percent is welcomed by many states in Europe and is of strong interest to many [other] countries.

---

[63] At its meeting in Budapest on June 11, 1986, the PCC issued an appeal calling for reductions of conventional forces by 25 percent and for the convocation of a Conference on Disarmament in Europe within the CSCE to replace MBFR. See also Document No. 115.

Also, many government leaders fully agree. The Romanian proposal is based on the Budapest appeal, which calls for a reduction by 25 percent.

The demobilized members of the forces have no reason to fear unemployment.

[...]

The Romanian economy needs many workers. Even tanks and other technical equipment will be used in the national economy.

Tanks, for example, have been really useful in agriculture for irrigation and reclamation. The Romanian army is in charge of irrigating and reclaiming approximately 500 ha. by 1990. It has been doing an outstanding job.

All countries urgently need the resources that are currently being spent on the armed forces for economic development

[...] I know that the supreme commander of the Unified Forces is opposed to such practices.

However, we are a democratic country acting according to the rules of socialist democracy. Besides, the unity between the people and the army will be further enforced by [the use of the army for agricultural work].

[...]

We assume that there is no imminent danger of war.

[Source: VA-01/32647, BA-MA. Translated by Karen Riechert.]

Document No. 119: Summary of Soviet Statement at the Committee of Ministers of Defense Meeting in Warsaw, December 1–3, 1986

In these remarks, Soviet Deputy Defense Minister Gen. J.F. Ivanovskii reveals some of the improvements the Warsaw Pact plans to make in its conventional forces in order to counter advancements on the NATO side. Not a political speech, the statement is a straight description of how the alliance plans to upgrade its forces. One innovation would be the addition of new airborne assault troops, which he says would "make offensive operations more dynamic." Another would be the introduction of marine amphibious units. There is little sense here that the Warsaw Pact is falling significantly behind NATO, which is a more typical theme in many official statements.

[...]

The ground forces of the allied armies are currently equipped with modern arms and combat technology which allow for striking in considerable depth behind the enemy lines. In order to take more advantage of these strikes it is currently expedient to increase the mobility of the army by creating air assault unit detachments within the fronts and armies.

The large-scale deployment of air assault troops will make offensive operations more dynamic. It will enable us to extend the effect on the enemy from the frontline deep into the hinterland, and will increase the speed of attack by our troops.

The kind of tasks to be solved by the air assault groupings and detachments will in many regards be determined by their combat possibilities, which in turn will depend on the quantity and quality of armaments and the organizational structure. According to our experience, the most efficient structure is the air assault brigade in the front and the air assault battalion in the army corps.

The air assault brigade is capable of capturing three to four objects within an area of 200 to 300 square kilometers, or of defending an area 10–15 km wide and deep, and can resist an attack by up to two mechanized enemy infantry brigades. In many cases, the brigade can conduct raids to a depth of up to 80 to 100 kilometers.

The air-strike battalion is capable of capturing and defending one to two objects within an area of 10 to 15 square kilometers. And with the support of the attacking troops it is capable of fighting superior enemy forces for some hours.

As calculations have demonstrated, it takes 240 to 260 helicopters, among them up to 60 Mi-26s, to land an air assault brigade. For an air assault battalion it takes 50 to 60 helicopters, among them 15 to 20 Mi-26s.

[...]

The necessity of having specialized troop detachments and groupings as part of our unified forces is dictated by the existence of major naval operation zones at the flanks of the area of responsibility of the Warsaw Treaty, and the specific conditions of warfare deriving from that situation.

[...]

The independent marine infantry brigade is the perfect organizational form for marine infantry, corresponding to all the major requirements of employment in combat. The brigade is capable of fighting as a tactical operational unit for amphibious landing and of capturing a bridgehead on the enemy's coast up to 10 kilometers wide, a naval base, a harbor, an island or a group of smaller islands. During amphibious operations together with ground forces, the brigade is capable of providing the first echelon of the landing troops, or else of making available two to three advance detachments, each consisting of one reinforced marine battalion.

[*Source: DVW 1/71046, BA-MA. Translated by Karen Riechert.*]

Document No. 120: Outline of a Czechoslovak Command Post Exercise, January 27–28, 1987

This command post exercise appears to mark a transitional phase in Warsaw Pact strategic planning. The scenario consists of an act of aggression by NATO, together with Austria, whose forces would advance 100 km into Czechoslovakia while Turkish and Greek troops would enter Bulgaria and Italian units would go into Hungary. French, Spanish and other NATO forces would also take part. The emphasis of this battle plan is to pursue the defense of Warsaw Pact territory only by conventional means. Even after 15 days of hostilities, the enemy is presumed to still be using conventional forces as it attempts to hold onto occupied territory while also moving toward the capture of Prague. For its part, once its counter-offensive begins, the Warsaw Pact is slated to use only tactical nuclear weapons to destroy NATO's nuclear bases in order to prevent their use. There is no provision for deep penetration into West Germany as there had been in the 1960s and 1970s. This maneuver takes place before the alliance's adoption of a new "nonoffensive defense" doctrine in May 1987, but as this document shows, a serious reconsideration of strategy was already underway.

The "West" has been conducting combat operations in the European theater for 15 days without using nuclear weapons. Even though the second echelons of field armies and army groups have been deployed, the "West" has achieved only partial successes along individual axes of advance, where its forces have penetrated to a depth of 100 to 150 kilometers. Its further advance has been slowed considerably.

The West's Order of Battle in the Central European theater comprises the Northern, Central and part of the Southern Army Groups, the 2nd and 4th Allied Tactical Air Force Central Europe and part of the 5th Allied Tactical Air Force Southern Europe, and the 1st French Tactical Air Force, altogether 73 divisions and 44 brigades in the first echelon and 2,100 combat aircraft, including 700 nuclear carriers.

Poised against Czechoslovakia are elements of the Central and Southern Army Groups, the 4th and 5th Allied Tactical Air Force Central Europe and the 1st French Tactical Air Force, altogether comprising 19 divisions, 12 brigades and 600 combat aircraft. Attacking along an axis of advance towards Prague are the 7th Field Army and 2nd Army Corps of Germany and the 1st and 2nd French Army Corps in the first echelon. Their reserve is the 66th Infantry Division. It is the 2nd French Army Corps that has achieved the greatest success, advancing to a depth of 120 kilometers along the Klatovy—Prague axis. The West has deployed the 9th Airborne Division east of Prague. Elements of the Southern Army Group, 5th German Army Corps and 1st and 2nd Austrian Army Corps are attacking toward Ostrava. The greatest success has been achieved by the 5th Army Corps, which has advanced to a depth of 80 kilometers. The force covering the gap between the Prague and Ostrava axes of advance comprises 15 mobilized regiments of the Austrian Army. [...]

1. Given the developments, the Supreme Command of the Unified Armed Forces has decided to continue defensive operations and to firmly hold the lines, the objective being not to allow further advance of the enemy and to inflict casualties on enemy units that have broken through.

2. To prepare and mount (subject to a special order) a strategic offensive operation to destroy the main forces of both enemy army groups.
[...]

1. The intention of the supreme commander of the Unified Armed Forces is to deploy second echelon forces in the battle and mount a counterattack, which will cut through and divide the Central and Southern Army Groups and crush their main forces. The main thrust will be mounted in the direction of Luxembourg.

The 2nd Front will mount a main thrust in the direction of Prague, Nuremberg and Stuttgart.

Right flank: The 4th Front will be deployed for battle from the area of Juterbog, Greditz and Cottbus in the direction of Leipzig, Frankfurt Am Main, Luxembourg. The boundary between the two fronts will be the Kraslice–Bamberg–Karlsruhe line.

Left flank: The 6th Front of the southwestern theater will mount a counterattack by its 48th Army in the direction of Papa, Vienna and Linz. The boundary between the two fronts will be the state frontier of the Czechoslovak Socialist Republic with Hungary and Austria, and the Austro-German frontier. Responsible for establishing and maintaining liaison between the two fronts shall be the commander of the 6th Front.

2. To mount an airborne operation the purpose of which will be to crush the opponent's nuclear missile, air and air defense forces. Taking part in the airborne operation will be Czechoslovak Air Defense forces and aviation, air assault, air defense, reconnaissance, electronic warfare and airmobile elements of the 2nd Front. Duration—4 to 5 days. Command of the airborne operation—together with the Supreme Command of the Allied Forces, Western Theater.
[...]

Conclusions resulting from the situation in the battlefield:
The 2nd Front will successfully complete its mission if:

1. It crushes the main strike concentration of the 7th Field Army in the area of Pilsen and regains control of routes and passages through border mountains and forests.

2. It crushes forces of the 5th Army Corps (German) at its left flank, and is able to release its forces there quickly in order to reinforce its units along the main axis of attack.
[...]

552

The ratio of forces (1:1.63 in our favor) confirms that both of the tasks outlined above can be fulfilled.

[...]

Insofar as the enemy thrust toward Prague is concerned, active defense operations of first-echelon divisions should prevent the opponent from consolidating its advance and reaching its airborne assault forces in the area of Český Brod. Elements of the 40th Motorized Rifle Division will be earmarked for the destruction of the enemy airborne assault forces referred to above. Air force, missile and artillery strikes will prevent the enemy from deploying his reserves arriving on the battlefield. A strike of the 14th Tank Division in the direction of Tábor and Pilsen, accompanied by a strike of the 29th Motorized Rifle Division in the direction of Horšovský Týn and Pilsen, should split the forces of the 2nd Army Corps (French), disturb its order of battle, and create prerequisites for the destruction of the 7th Field Army in the area of Pilsen.

At the same time, an offensive operation along the Prague–Nuremberg–Stuttgart axis should be prepared and mounted (subject to a special order) together with the 4th and 6th Fronts.

[...]

By deploying the 11th Army from the Nuremberg–Ingolstadt or Ansbach–Mannheim line in the direction of Nuremberg–Stuttgart–Freiburg, the attack will be developed in operational depth; enemy reserves arriving on the battlefield will be destroyed. By the 12th to 14th day of the operation, the front should reach the Rhine and the Swiss border, thus fulfilling another of its tasks.

[*Source: VS, OS, 1987, č.j. 74300/2 and 16, VÚA. Translated by Jiří Mareš.*]

Document No. 121: Report on the Committee of Ministers of Foreign Affairs Meeting in Moscow, March 24–25, 1987

At this Warsaw Pact foreign ministers' meeting in Moscow, the allies continue discussions on how to implement Gorbachev's new initiatives on arms control. They agree that the main goal is to support the Soviet Union in its attempts to reach an accord on the removal of intermediate-range missiles from Europe. Soviet Foreign Minister Eduard Shevardnadze says that the Pact should seek a compromise on SDI rather than expect the United States to abandon it. An arms race must be prevented at all costs, he says. He adds that the Warsaw Pact should formulate a common position on the CSCE so that due attention could be paid to negotiations on conventional forces. By this time, those talks have shifted venue to Vienna, where they were merged into the CSCE.

[...]

a) Providing comprehensive political, diplomatic and propaganda support for the Soviet initiative to conclude an agreement on the removal of intermediate-range missiles in Europe is regarded as the most important common task at present. All member-states are of the opinion that such an initial agreement would be of key significance for the whole nuclear disarmament process. In the estimation of comrade [Eduard] Shevardnadze, an agreement could possibly be reached before the beginning of the election campaign in the USA. [...]

A second task parallel to the efforts for an agreement on the removal of intermediate-range missiles is to broaden the political and propaganda front against the space-based weapons plan of the USA, thereby underpinning the Soviet position on this matter. Comrade Shevardnadze confirmed that the Soviet Union is steering towards a compromise on the question of SDI [Strategic Defense Initiative]. A new arms race must be avoided at all costs. [...]

b) All member-states consider it very important to exploit the new opportunities for political dialogue created by the most recent Soviet initiative in order to strengthen the process of intellectual reorientation and differentiation already underway in Western Europe, the USA and NATO itself. [...]

[...]

The ČSSR suggested that a serious effort be made to cultivate contacts between political and military representatives of the Warsaw Pact and NATO, thus creating a forum for multilateral dialogue.

c) The member-states agreed to take all the necessary steps to maintain an offensive position with regard to the Budapest Appeal.[64]

d) [...]

---

[64] Adopted at the June 11, 1986, PCC meeting in Budapest. See Document No. 15 and the footnote in Document No. 117.

The following was agreed upon as a basic position shared by all:
- Negotiations on conventional disarmament should be initiated within the framework of Stockholm-II.[65]
- The disarmament issue should not be treated in isolation from the general European process (future negotiations must remain the mandate of the Vienna meeting).
- The close connection between informal consultations with NATO and the CSCE meeting in Vienna should be maintained.
- Efforts in relation to neutral and non-aligned states, small NATO countries, and also France, should be increased.

The member-states agreed to proceed flexibly, in the interests of the imminent transition to concrete negotiations, so as not to provide NATO with any pretext for blocking negotiations while they are still at a stage of informal consultations. The People's Republic of Bulgaria, the Hungarian People's Republic, the Polish People's Republic and the GDR are in favor of actively exploiting the possibilities of informal consultations between the Warsaw Pact and NATO in Vienna.

[...]

The Socialist Republic of Romania, while expressing its general support for the Budapest Appeal, tried to make use of the meeting to gain the support of the other states for the separate suggestion it had put forward in Vienna—for convening a conference on conventional disarmament (new confidence-building measures: reduction in the armed forces, conventional armaments, and military expenditures of 50 percent by the year 2000).

e) All member-states agreed to try harder to find regional solutions both in the area of nuclear weapons and in the area of c[hemical] weapons, and to give such attempts the backing of the whole alliance. The USSR, the Hungarian People's Republic, the ČSSR, the Polish People's Republic and the People's Republic of Bulgaria expressed their support for the efforts and suggestions of the GDR. The GDR's ideas regarding further procedure were received positively, as was its proposal to examine suggestions for the disengagement of conventional forces in Europe.

[...]

f) With regard to the CSCE in Vienna, preparations need to be made within the alliance to promote the transition to negotiations. Suggestions from our side need to be specified and points of common interest with western suggestions identified, especially in the areas of economic, scientific and technical cooperation.

Generally speaking, member-states were urged to work more productively in the area of "Basket III".[66] The emphasis remains on the initiative of the USSR to convene a conference for humanitarian cooperation. Any other realistic suggestions for measures relating to individual humanitarian issues should not be rejected.

---

[65] Second round of the CSCE Conference on Confidence- and Security-Building Measures and Disarmament in Europe.

[66] The CSCE agenda concerned with human rights.

g) The member-states agreed to work out a proposal and an action plan for an all-encompassing security system in time for the next U.N. General Assembly, so that this common initiative could be further promoted. [...]

5. Regarding external political coordination, all foreign ministers confirmed an increase both in intensity and in scope of content. [...]

It was agreed:

a) that the deputy foreign ministers or representatives of the Foreign Ministries should meet regarding the following issues: the Vienna CSCE meeting (Warsaw), the reduction of armed forces and conventional armaments (Budapest), the initiative for the creation of an all-encompassing security system (Moscow), the Vienna negotiations (Prague).

b) to create a working group of experts on questions of nuclear disarmament, including the creation of nuclear-free zones (Moscow).

c) that the expert groups should continue their work on the following issues: the freeze on arms budgets (Bucharest); the work with the Budapest Appeal (Budapest); cooperation in the fight against terrorism (Moscow); creation of an encompassing system of peace and security (Moscow); active work on human rights (Sofia); elaboration of a document on overcoming underdevelopment (Bucharest).

Furthermore, the following were planned:

– an exchange of views on certain aspects of the role played by the FRG in the European balance of power (Warsaw).

– a workshop on the relations between Warsaw Pact states and Arab countries (Prague).

– a workshop on relations with Latin American states (Moscow).

– a meeting of military political experts to work out the complex questions of controls for all areas of disarmament and confidence building (suggestion by the USSR).

It was suggested that views on the improved functioning of the Committee of Foreign Ministers be exchanged before the next meeting, if possible at the margins of the meeting of the Political Consultative Committee in Berlin.

[...]

[Source: DC/20/I/3, 2453, p. 214–237, SAPMO. Translated by Ursula Froese.]

PART FIVE

Disintegration

Document No. 122: Soviet Explanation of the Warsaw Pact's New Military Doctrine at the Chiefs of Staff Meeting in Moscow, May 18–25, 1987

These two statements by Soviet marshals Sergei Sokolov and Sergei Akhromeev were intended to explain to their Warsaw Pact military colleagues the important impending shift in strategy by Gorbachev from offense to defense. The meetings they are addressing preceded by a few days the full PCC session at the end of May 1987, at which the new concept was adopted (see Document No. 123). While the two officers are constrained to follow the orders of their civilian leadership, Sokolov in particular betrays the military's reluctance to accept unilateral reductions in armaments or give up the capability to "definitively crush" the enemy.

On May 18, 1987, the Minister of Defense of the USSR, Comrade Marshal of the USSR [Vasilii] Sokolov, invited the chiefs of staff of the Warsaw Treaty member-states to a presentation of the draft "Military Doctrine of the member-states of the Warsaw Treaty" that is due to be considered by the Political Consultative Committee.

[…]

Even if every country has its own military doctrine, it is important at the present time to draw up a military doctrine for the Warsaw Treaty.

It is especially important to decide on the doctrine's political content, which will be binding for all member-states.

For 20 years, NATO has declared its own military doctrine to be a defensive doctrine and accused the Warsaw Treaty of having an aggressive military doctrine.

Although the Warsaw Treaty member-states have repeatedly stated their position on military issues, the military doctrine of the Warsaw Treaty has never been presented to the world community.

However, it is important to explain to the whole world:

– our relation to war and to the fight for peace, as well as
– our view of the likely nature of an aggressor and our planned counter-measures in case of an attack.

For this reason, it has been suggested that a unified military doctrine of the Warsaw Treaty be presented to the world community.

[…]

The military doctrine of the Warsaw Treaty States is decidedly defensive in nature. We will never be the first to begin a war.

[…]

Our defense doctrine requires that the army command and troops concentrate more than ever on defensive operations in their education and training.

This is an extremely difficult task.

At the same time, it must be taken into consideration that the only way to definitively crush an aggressor is by executing decisive attacks.

We must always be in a position to totally defeat the enemy.

Our defense must be prepared and carried out in such a way as to ensure that we do not lose or forfeit any territory.

Active defense must therefore begin at the border between NATO and the Warsaw Treaty.

We cannot first lose 100 or 200 km of territory before beginning our counterattack. Rather, every foot of ground of the Socialist states must be doggedly defended.

[...]

In every case we need to consider the real capabilities of the opponent. The measures we take to ensure military parity must preserve our capability to destroy the enemy in case of an attack.

Our political efforts in this regard are aimed at maintaining a near balance of military force at an ever decreasing level.

[...]

Under the present conditions, however, we must be prepared for nuclear war as well as a war with conventional weapons.

France and Great Britain are not prepared at the present time to participate in a reduction of nuclear weapons.

As long as these two states resist the reduction of their nuclear weapons, the Soviet Union cannot agree to a zero-solution in Europe, since this would give NATO a unilateral advantage.

It must be clearly understood that it is a question of reducing
- nuclear means of warfare,
- not only missiles. That is a big difference.

In general it can be observed that a widespread process of modernizing and introducing new fighting technology is underway in the NATO armies. For this reason, we cannot under any circumstances agree to unilateral reductions.

[...]

Marshal of the USSR [Sergei] Akhromeev began by pointing out that the political challenges we are presently facing require the elaboration of a basic military doctrine of the Warsaw Treaty member-states, in order to ensure that member-states present themselves in a unified manner.

Military doctrines are a system of principles and views on
- the nature and characteristics of a war
- preparations for a war and
- the methods of waging a war for the protection of socialist achievements.

[...]

It goes without saying that each member-state has its own independent military doctrine reflecting its concrete conditions, even if it belongs to an alliance like the Warsaw Treaty.

The likely opponent, NATO, officially adopted its military doctrine, the doctrine of flexible response, 20 years ago, and directs its actions accordingly.

[...]

Although the military doctrine has two sides, the political and the military, the draft concentrates on the political side of the doctrine.

[...]

Marshal of the USSR Akhromeev drew attention to the following particular features of the draft doctrine:

Because of the catastrophic consequences of a nuclear war and for practical reasons the military doctrine of the USSR includes the question of how to prevent any war whatsoever.

Given the fact that in the case of a nuclear war mankind would be threatened with extinction, the question of preventing a war has also been included in the draft Military Doctrine of the Warsaw Treaty.

It is important to highlight the defensive nature of the doctrine, since the opposing propaganda is constantly invoking the alleged military superiority of the Warsaw Treaty and its strategy of aggression.

On the other hand, the military superiority of NATO over the Warsaw Treaty cannot be tolerated.

The draft emphasizes that we are for military parity and do not strive to possess more forces and armaments than necessary.

This point of view has already been repeatedly emphasized by leading representatives.

The draft document summarizes concrete proposals of the Warsaw Treaty member-states expressing the defensive nature of the military doctrine.

Further evidence for the defensive nature of the doctrine is provided by the inclusion of a proposal to NATO for a meeting of experts from both sides to compare military doctrines.

The documents at hand refrain from elaborating on the technical aspect of the military doctrine. Certain military secrets exist and these are reflected in the concrete plans.

[...]

[*Source: VA-01/40373, 124–28 BA-MA. Translated by Ursula Froese.*]

Document No. 123: Records of the Political Consultative Committee Meeting in Berlin, May 27–29, 1987

This top-level PCC meeting took place shortly after the Soviet Union had adopted the American-proposed zero option on INF[1] (Intermediate-Range Nuclear Forces), a step which proved embarrassing to the Reagan administration because U.S. officials never expected Moscow to agree to it. The substance of this meeting was to approve a military doctrine that could supplement the Soviets' new peace campaign and make it more credible. The several speeches and stenographic record of the sessions excerpted below reflect a variety of viewpoints, including Gorbachev's, Kulikov's, the East Germans', and Romanians'. Of particular interest are Gorbachev's opening comments at the May 29 session in which he describes, with acute embarassment, the unauthorized landing in Moscow of a private plane by West German pilot Matthias Rust.

a) Letter by Heinz Kessler to Erich Honecker,
   May 27, 1987

[...]

As I already informed you the group of military experts of the PCC has continued its editorial work on the draft document on "the military doctrine of the member-states of the Warsaw treaty."

The editorial work continues to be complicated by the inflexible attitude of the Romanian representatives.

The representatives of the Socialist Republic of Romania insist on their positions as already communicated:

- that there is no common military doctrine of the member-states of the Warsaw Treaty but only doctrines of the individual countries and they have
- they repeatedly persisted in not using the phrase "allied countries."

By repeating the same statements several times they try to diminish the politico-military and military value of the document on military doctrine.

The Romanian representatives furthermore asked to add that "the existence of military blocs is a constant threat to the peace and security of mankind," which basically denies the peace-serving function and defensive character of the Warsaw Treaty and puts it on the same level with the NATO Pact.

During consultations of expert groups they have stated that everything that could "frighten" other countries and people has to be avoided.

They have also upheld their objections to the changes suggested by the GDR and added their own counterproposal with the following wording:

[1] President Reagan's proposal, announced on November 18, 1981, to forego the deployment of U.S. intermediate-range missiles in Europe in exchange for the dismantling of the Soviet INF missiles already deployed there.

"In the current strategic military situation, where the level of armaments and their destructive potential seriously endanger peace and the existence of mankind itself, even maintaining parity cannot guarantee the prevention of war. Stopping the arms race and disarmament becomes historically important in this situation. Only a complete abolition of nuclear weapons, of all weapons of mass destruction, and a significant reduction of conventional armaments can effectively guarantee the ultimate prevention of the danger of war."

Even after a one-hour discussion at the level of deputy ministers of foreign affairs of the GDR, the Soviet Union and the Socialist Republic of Romania, including consultation of military experts of those countries, the Romanian attitude did not basically change.

[...]

[Source: DC20/I/3/2477, SAPMO. Translated by Karen Riechert.]

b) Speech by Mikhail Gorbachev,
   May 28, 1987

[...]
I want to emphasize that at issue is not just a declaration of principles or confirmation of the strictly defensive character of the military policy of Socialism, but also a program for the development of our armed forces. We agreed to base this program on the principle of adequate defense. This means that the allied partners will keep their forces and armaments on a level where they would not be taken by surprise by an attack and would also not allow the aggressor to succeed. On the contrary, [the aggressor] would suffer unacceptable damage. Our military experts have to think about how to best integrate those basic positions into the military organization. The document on military doctrine is at the same time an open challenge to the West to exercise mutual military restraint. Since the character of NATO doctrine is offensive and anticipates first-use of nuclear weapons, a public comparison of those two doctrines will make the NATO Pact look bad. Public attention will again be drawn to the dangerous character of NATO military policy. Pressure to correct this doctrine will increase.

[Source: DC20/I/3/2477, SAPMO. Translated by Karen Riechert.]

c) Public statement on the Military Doctrine
   of the Warsaw Pact Member-States,
   May 28, 1987

In today's situation, there has been an increase in the importance of correctly understanding the goals and intentions of governments and military–political alliances in the military arena, as embodied in their military doctrines. Taking this into consideration and beginning with the necessity of ultimately banning war from human society; stopping the arms race; excluding the use of military force; strengthening peace and security; and realizing complete and general disarmament, the member-states of the Warsaw Treaty have decided to set forth the central positions of their military doctrine, which forms the basis for actions by the Warsaw Treaty and reflects the commonality of the defensive military–political goals of its member-states and their national military doctrines.

The military doctrine of the Warsaw Treaty—as well as that of each of its members—serves the goal of banning war, both nuclear and conventional. Owing to the very nature of the structure of socialist society, these governments have not attached and do not attach their futures to a military solution to international problems. They support the solution of all difficult international issues only by peaceful and political means.

In this nuclear-space age, the world has become too fragile for war and power politics. With the situation such that a huge number of the most lethal weapons has been amassed, humanity has come to confront the problem of survival. A world war—moreover, a nuclear war—would have catastrophic consequences not only for countries directly drawn into the conflict, but also for all life on Earth

The military doctrine of the Warsaw Treaty member-states is strictly defensive, and starts from the point of view that, under current conditions, the use of military force to solve any controversial issue is unacceptable. The essence of this approach is as follows:

The Warsaw Treaty member-states will never, under any circumstances, initiate military action against any government or alliance of governments whatsoever, unless they themselves become the targets of an armed attack.

They will never strike first with nuclear weapons.

They do not have any territorial ambitions toward any other government, either within Europe or outside Europe.

They do not regard any individual government or group of people as their enemy; on the contrary, they are prepared, without exception, to build relations with all countries around the world based on a mutual assessment of their interests in peace and mutual coexistence. The Warsaw Treaty member-states declare that their international relations are strongly based on a respect for the principles of independence and national sovereignty; ejection of the use of force or the threat of force; the inviolability of borders and territorial integrity; the resolution of conflicts by peaceful means; non-interference in internal affairs; equality; and the other principles and goals as covered in the United Nations Charter and the Helsinki Accords, as well as generally-accepted norms in international relations.

While supporting the implementation of measures for disarmament, the Warsaw Treaty member-states are forced to maintain their armed forces in such form and at such a level that would allow them to repel any attack from outside on any member-state of the Treaty.

The armed forces of the Treaty governments are maintained at a sufficient level of battle-readiness so as not to allow themselves to be taken by surprise. If they come under attack nonetheless, they will deal a crushing blow to the aggressor.

The Warsaw Treaty member-states have never attempted to possess armed forces or weapons above the level necessary for these purposes. Thus, they hold strongly to levels necessary for defense and for repelling possible aggression.

II.

The Warsaw Treaty member-states consider providing their peoples with reliable security as their primary task. The union of socialist governments has no ambitions to enjoy more security than other countries, but less security will not do. The current military–strategic parity remains the decisive factor in banning war. However, as experience shows, further increases in the level of parity will not bring greater security. For this reason they will continue to apply their efforts to maintaining a balance of military forces at an even lower level. Under these conditions, stopping the arms race and carrying out measures for real disarmament take on genuine historical significance. Governments in our time have no other way than to achieve agreement on a radical decrease in the level of military opposition.

The Warsaw Treaty member-states decisively support these positions. In complete accordance with the defensive approach of their military doctrine, they thus are attempting to achieve the following basic goals:

First. The most rapid, complete and general prohibition of nuclear tests as the most important step in halting the development, production, and improvement of nuclear armaments; their gradual reduction and complete liquidation; and a ban on the spread of the arms race into space.

Second. The prohibition and liquidation of chemical and other forms of weapons of mass destruction.

Third. In Europe, the reduction of armed forces and conventional weapons to such a level that neither one side nor the other, while providing for its own defense, has the means for a sudden attack on the other side nor for deploying offensive operations in general.

Fourth. Strict control over all measures of disarmament based on a combination of national technical means and international procedures, including creating appropriate international organs, exchanging military information, and carrying out on-site inspections.

Fifth. The creation of zones in Europe and other regions of the world which would be free of nuclear and chemical weapons, as well as zones of reduced concentrations of weapons and increased confidence. The implementation of military confidence-building measures by both sides in Europe and agreement on such measures in other regions of the world, as well as on the seas and oceans. The mutual rejection Treaty of the use of military force by both Warsaw Treaty member-states and NATO alliance members, and the acceptance of responsibility for supporting peaceful relations; the elimination of military bases on the territory of other countries; the relocation of troops to the limits of national borders; the mutual relocation of the most dangerous forms of offensive weapons from areas where both military alliances border each other, as well as a decrease in armed forces and weapons to a mutually-agreed upon minimal level in this zone.

Sixth. Considering the continuing split of Europe into opposing military blocs as abnormal, the Warsaw Treaty member-states support the simultaneous dissolution of the NATO alliance and the Warsaw Treaty and, as a first step, the elimination of their military organizations, and, ultimately, the creation of a comprehensive system of international security.

* * *

The Warsaw Treaty governments suggest to the NATO member-states holding consultations with the goal of comparing the military doctrines of both alliances, analyzing their content, and jointly reviewing the direction of their future evolution, with the aim of removing mutual distrust and suspicions accumulated over the years, achieving a better understanding of each other's intentions, and arranging it so that the military concepts and doctrines of these military blocs and their participants would be based on defense as the point of departure.

One topic in these consultations might also be the imbalances and asymmetries that have developed in individual types of weapons and armed forces and the search for ways to eliminate them based on a reduction by the party, which happens to possess more of them, with the understanding that such reductions will lead to the establishment of even lower levels.

The socialist governments in the Treaty also suggest holding consultations on authoritative, expert levels with military specialists from both sides participating. They are already prepared to hold such consultations in 1987. The consultations could be held in Warsaw or in Brussels, or alternate between each of these cities.

[...]

[*Source: VA-01/40373, BA-MA. Translated by Paul Spitzer.*]

d) Stenographic record of the
    meeting of party secretaries,
    May 29, 1987

[...]

Mikhail Gorbachev: First I'd like to inform you of a special incident. Yesterday the following happened: In the area of Tallinn, somewhat east of Tallinn, a sports plane coming from Helsinki entered our air space. It was detected by radar and six fighters took off. Two of those fighters noticed a violation of the border, one directly, the other by using his instruments. But everybody concluded that it could be a swarm of birds and they didn't believe their own eyes as to what they had seen. This happened at an altitude of 600 m. in the clouds, and clouds were everywhere. It [the aircraft] was flying at the speed of 160 to 180 km/h and landed on a bridge in Moscow. People say that it was on Red Square, but it wasn't. It was a small plane with a 10 m. wingspan and 8 m. length. It crossed the border after 2:00 p.m. and landed around 7:00 p.m. Therefore it was over Soviet territory for five hours. There is an investigation going on. The pilot is a citizen of the FRG and has already undertaken many flights with his sports plane.

The military have been trying to somehow explain the situation. I personally cannot be satisfied by any explanation. It is just impossible to allow a plane to land in Moscow after 800 km as the crow flies.

This is very embarrassing, you know. I think that this did not happen by accident. There have been all kinds of flights. This was all done in preparation for undertaking this flight later. There was the attempt in the past to spy on our air defenses in the Far East.[2] Measures were taken accordingly. But now, one tries to look for explanations. This cannot be explained! I will take this in hand myself upon my return. There have to be very severe consequences. How is this to be understood?

This is even worse than Chernobyl. This is a major embarrassment. When the information on the measures taken reaches you, you will already be pre-informed. Those measures will be very severe.

I had to start with this embarrassing incident, because the situation required it. Much is still open and unclear. Investigations have begun.

During the first interviews the pilot said that he had decided to fly to the Soviet Union in order to show the West that it must establish relations with the East. I say, of course this is nonsense. But it is not about him; it is about us who we have permitted such a thing [to happen].

Erich Honecker: It is a very serious matter, if it is possible to fly that far without being seen or stopped. From the point of view of the system on duty this is absolutely incredible! Indeed, this has to be taken very seriously.

János Kádár: You will certainly investigate the matter in the way you think appropriate. Such incidents happen in Hungary at the Austrian border. This has happened several times already. Sports planes are in the air, add unfavorable wind conditions, even trafficking in human beings has happened. Our radar stations were unable to detect them at that altitude. Our territory is very small and before our people understood what was the matter, everything had already been settled in a way that resulted in our air defense forces being given specialized planes.

Mikhail Gorbachev: I mean there had been information from radar and fighter planes took off. It is not understandable why this action was not followed through. Either they lost the object or a wrong decision was made. This might be possible as well. If this had happened in Italy or somewhere else—but in Moscow! I think that this is an extraordinary and unusual incident.

Nicolae Ceaușescu: It seems to me that the low flight altitude is not of importance. It is not about 100 km, but [that] this plane managed to reach Moscow. That means, questions remain about observation on one's own territory at low flight altitudes. In general, too much attention is paid to high-altitude flights. And maybe all countries underestimate the problem of low-altitude flights.

Mikhail Gorbachev: According to the strategy used in Vietnam and Afghanistan, we also control the lower flight altitudes. However the problem could have been the

---

[2] This is probably a reference to Korean Air Lines flight KAL-007, a passenger flight from Anchorage, Alaska, to Seoul, South Korea, which strayed into Soviet airspace near Sakhalin Island on September 1, 1983, and was shot down by at least one air-to-air missile fired by a Soviet fighter jet. All 269 passengers were killed. There is no evidence that KAL-007 was anything other than a commercial flight.

following: Everything is oriented towards military aircraft of particular shapes. But this small sports plane with a 10m wing span very much resembles a swarm of birds. This is also how it was seen. This has basically not been correctly recognized. This is a serious incident. You mention rightfully it wasn't for 50 or 100 km that the plane crossed the border but it flew to Moscow and landed there. This is impossible, this is a scandal, a provocation. The fast fighter planes, of course, are not as easy to maneuver as a sports plane. It was flying at low altitude, always in the clouds, in order to be able to see what would happen in case it was detected. This is a serious incident. As soon as we have investigated the matter, I'll inform you.

Gustáv Husák: This commonly happens at borders; in those cases they reach up to 20 to 30 km into the territory.

Todor Zhivkov: Obviously there are two issues. The first one, cde. Gorbachev, you mentioned: one has to look at the means to discover and pursue such objects, because cruise missiles also fly at low altitudes and have been deployed since March.

The second question is a political one: It all looks like a provocation. Both aspects have to be investigated, also the technological one. It is just impossible that one detects an object and then loses it again in the clouds. Clouds can always be there. Who lost the object again?

[…] The previous flights have been arranged so that blame could be put on Sweden. Or, maybe it was a provocation aimed at the meeting of the PCC here in Berlin since it isn't about the border but about the landing in Moscow.

Mikhail Gorbachev: […] I think, as far as air space is concerned we have to draw serious conclusions. As soon as a missile has been launched, we know about it. But now, something like this happens. After this plane had crossed the border, after it had disappeared, it was flying as a sports plane in the Soviet Union. Air defense should have followed it closely from the very beginning, as soon as the provocation started. This carelessness demands a very serious response. As I said, I will inform you afterwards about the result of the investigation. This is preliminary information. But, of course, this has been very embarrassing for us.

Wojciech Jaruzelski: Air defense is divided into different zones and depending where the flight takes place, this control is more or less tight. At the border it is especially tight. I believe that signals technology is able to discover everything up to 50 m. One should have been able to discover that at the border of the Soviet Union in order to follow the plane and force it to land to finish the matter. In the direction of Moscow there is a zone which is less tightly controlled, but the closer one gets to Moscow, about 100 km from Moscow, another defense zone begins where every object within 50 meters should be discovered. At that point there should not have been a question any more about whether it was a sports plane or not. If it has not declared [itself], if it is not legal, not notified, then this is a matter of a border violation. The second question is, how could it have happened so close to Moscow and not been apprehended there.

Mikhail Gorbachev: It was registered by signals intelligence. Six fighters took off. One pilot claims he saw the plane and then the operation was terminated. This is absolutely incomprehensible.

[…]

All this is very serious. Very often we have similar incidents with sporting planes at the border. Sometimes they land on our territory. This is a serious matter. But landing on a bridge in Moscow, that's a provocation. We have to get at the core of it.

Now I want to address our meeting. I want to express my satisfaction with the meeting of the PCC. I fully agree with what cde. Kádár had said about the results of our work. An important document has been adopted and the results of the meeting—it is with good reason we are talking about them—reflect the real process of our increased collaboration, an increase and deepening of collaboration in every respect.

[...]

I already said that there are certain problems, certain difficulties with regard to new issues in the restructuring [*perestroika*] of our relationships, in the perfection of our relationships, in the realization of the agreements of our workshop from last November. I think we can notice that all countries have started moving, that a search is going on. In one case we made progress, less in another. I repeat: this does not shock the Soviet leadership in any sense. There has been an opportunity to discuss these issues in a broader meeting. Progress has been made. We just talked about these issues with cde. Ceauşescu and have given out orders. The same with cdes. Kádár, Zhivkov and Husák. Just yesterday we spoke with the German friends; I personally talked to cde. Honecker.

[...]

Another international issue: The issue of conventional arms and reduction of forces will gain importance in our relationship with our partners in the West in any case. In the context of intermediate-range missiles and operational–tactical missiles it has become even more acute, if one might say so. Officially we had useful talks about that yesterday and drew up the forthcoming perspectives. I only want to address one question in the context of the overall issue. It is the question of the ratio of armaments in Central Europe. We probably all feel that right now. After we proposed the Budapest initiative,[3] the question of conventional arms and the balance of power between the Atlantic and the Urals, the West is now trying hard to stay within the "Vienna framework,"[4] the thing here in the center. They know as well as we do that we have more in terms of numbers. According to our information the situation is the following: Looking at Europe as a whole, from the Atlantic to the Urals, the Warsaw Treaty has 3,300,000 and NATO 3,370,000 [men], therefore almost an equal number. NATO has superiority of over 1,000 aircraft in raiding planes and fighter planes, and three times as many helicopters, tanks and naval forces. The Warsaw Treaty has seven times greater superiority than NATO in the area of operational–tactical and tactical missiles, and a 1.7 superiority in tanks. This allows us to talk about certain asymmetries, if things are left like that. We have made a good suggestion for solving this, not by increasing numbers, but by reducing [them] and making this system symmetrical. Well, the West picked up the problem and said: Give up the asymmetry in the heart

---

[3] At its meeting in Budapest on June 11, 1986, the PCC issued an appeal calling for reductions of conventional forces by 25 percent and for the convocation of a Conference on Disarmament in Europe within the CSCE to replace MBFR. See also Document No. 115.

[4] The framework of the Vienna negotiations of the Conference on Security and Cooperation in Europe.

of Europe and reduce the forces of the Warsaw Treaty in Central Europe. This is an important politico-military question. The difference here, as I said, is 170,000 [*sic*].

I think it is time that we give up pretending we don't see that and won't acknowledge the difference in Central Europe. We do see it. But today, with the Budapest initiative, when looking at the confrontation between the two groups, we see the overall context. This should make us think. Thus as we see the quantitative strength in tanks and other means, we should think about how we could somehow even out the asymmetry. This means we should raise this problem to a higher level with respect to the confrontation in Europe from the Atlantic to the Urals. We should be committed to this kind of scope for a future conference. This is real and realistic in my opinion. In this sense we don't have to be ashamed before the West. This is an honest position.

I mention this now in order that we consider it, since we have many contacts. Those questions will now be asked more frequently and more intensely. I think it is important to have agreed on a position. We recognize indeed that there are differences and asymmetries, but we are in favor of reducing them and leveling the asymmetries. Here we have the Budapest proposal. We are waiting for your suggestions in order to achieve a reduction within the global process.

I think if we pose the question this way: If there is superiority in troops in Central Europe, then we will reduce those in the GDR and the ČSSR. But, I think, first of all this would undermine the Budapest initiative, which is the basis for these negotiations, and second I don't know what message we would be sending to the enemy by this; if he would still be interested in negotiations on the overall European situation or would only restrict negotiations to Central Europe to avoid others. Third: What message would this send to our people?! Nothing would happen in the West and we would draw back once more to the hardest and hottest line of confrontation. I think that would provoke a lot of questions among people. However, if it were in the overall context of negotiations on the whole Europe, the whole thing would just look normal. This is the position I wanted to outline so we may agree on it.

[*Source: DY30/2354, SAPMO. Translated by Karen Riechert.*]

e) Speech by Nicolae Ceauşescu,
    May 29, 1987

I also positively assess the proceedings of the Political Consultative Committee. I told Cde. Gorbachev as well that we should, however, think about improving its activity from a military point of view. The practice of listening to a report about military activity at the end of a conference and making a decision that goes against the general orientation is not the best one. For example, it was said in the Report that we would have to double military expenditures and armaments by 1990. We, however, discussed an entirely different orientation. In practice, each country has a different orientation.

Frankly speaking, this time I added my signature to the document despite the fact that I did not want to sign it. Nevertheless, I did so in order to avoid discussions on this subject, but this decision does not correspond to our general orientation. We will also have to decide what we will do with regard to the development of armaments, from both a qualitative and a quantitative point of view because this issue should not remain strictly a military one.

In fact, we do not have such a plan. We have decided to maintain expenditures at the current level; we approved the five-year plan and will not develop armaments further. Consequently, we signed a decision which we know right from the outset we will not be able to fulfill.

[...]

I take the view that perhaps it would be better to consider a certain improvement in our activity with regard to the meetings of general or first secretaries. As a rule, we meet more on military and international issues having in mind the proper mandate of the Political Consultative Committee as well. But in my opinion it would be better to hold a general meeting focused on issues of socialist development and general political, economic, as well as military collaboration. It is within this framework, therefore, that we must consider certain military aspects, allowing the relevant authorities to take action. I think that the problem of development, of our general activity, is much more important; the economic issues are much more important. Consequently, it is these issues that we should be concerned with, not just military and international issues, as we are now.

[*Source: CC CPR Chancellery, 1345, 14.VII.1987, Romanian National Archives. Translated by Viorel Nicolae Buta for the PHP.*]

Document No. 124: Summary of a Consultation
of Chiefs of Staff in Moscow, October 14, 1987

At this meeting of Warsaw Pact chiefs of staff, an array of top Soviet military offici-als–Pavlov,[5] Kulikov, Akhromeev, Gareev[6]–took turns informing their colleagues of the changes in military doctrine agreed to by the recent PCC meeting (see previous document). While they dutifully present the official Gorbachev position, it is clear they disagree with important parts of it, especially such concepts as yielding territory to NATO in case of war.

[...]
The military doctrine of the Warsaw Treaty member-states:

[...]
All measures have to ensure strategic military parity and a reliable defense.

The main method of defense against aggression will be countermeasures and retaliatory strikes (meeting engagements).

The role of defense is increasing. Its character is changing to the effect that in strategic terms it is no longer an enforced, but an intended manner type of combat.

To a certain extent the adversary will have the strategic initiative by unleashing a war. Therefore, we have to thwart his aggressive goals, achieve a reversal in combat within short time, and take over the strategic initiative.

Thus forces and equipment corresponding to the aggressive capabilities of the adversary must be available constantly.

In order to lose as little territory as possible, a steadfast defense has to be organized. Therefore the main line of defense must not be at a distance of 20–40 kilometers from the state border, as it used to be, but only 5–10 kilometers, or else directly at the border.

[...]
Comrade Marshal of the Soviet Union, [Viktor] Kulikov [...] stressed that the Unified Forces' renunciation of preemptive action would result in certain military–strategic advantages for the aggressor, since he can choose the time to unleash a war, and get his forces and equipment fully ready.

[...]
The principle of defensive sufficiency of forces and equipment does not only include the ability to thwart aggression, but also the ability to destroy the adversary through resolute acts of aggression.

Sufficiency therefore means in no way a reduction of our military potential, as some comrades have wrongfully assumed.

---

[5] Aleksandr G. Pavlov, chief of military intelligence.
[6] Makhmut A. Gareev, deputy chief of general staff.

The extent of sufficiency does not primarily depend on us, but on NATO. Its forces and armaments obviously exceed the capacity needed for defense only.

Everything has to be done so that our forces will not fall behind the adversary. More attention than before must be paid to quality. Primarily those forces that would enter combat first are what need to be developed. If necessary, structural changes and a redistribution of forces and equipment must be undertaken.

The effort to equip the armies of the Warsaw Treaty member-states with modern technology still has its weak spots. This refers especially to tanks and anti-tank artillery. Forty-nine percent of our aircraft and 19 percent of our ships are outdated. Solving these problems requires us not to reduce military expenses.

[...]

The question of the enemy breaking through to our own territory during the opening period of a war still remains unresolved. In principle, we have to assume that such a possibility exists. Therefore, we have to train the leadership and the troops to destroy the invading enemy forces by counterattacks.

[...]

[*Source: AZN 32659, 65–71, BA-MA. Translated by Karen Riechert.*]

Document No. 125: Speech by General Iazov at the Ministers of Defense Meeting in Bucharest, November 26, 1987

At this Bucharest meeting of Warsaw Pact ministers of defense, Soviet Gen. (soon to be Marshal) Dmitrii Iazov argues against the notion that the Warsaw Pact armies are too large and should be cut back. Instead, he insists NATO's forces are larger and that the East needs to catch up both in terms of size and in terms of technical capabilities. He therefore opposes making any change in the kinds of data on Warsaw Pact military strength to be provided to the West, and urges the allies to increase their financial and other contributions to the alliance.

[...]

After the adoption of the Warsaw Treaty member-states' military doctrine, with its defensive character, at the Berlin meeting of the PCC, the doctrine was much discussed among civilians as well as in the military.

Opinions were heard, such as that times had changed due to the doctrine and that our armies are too large. This means that pacifism has caught on with a certain part of our population.

This opinion is wrong, since the purpose of the armed forces is to guarantee the protection of the state's interests.

With regard to questions of combat training, opinions had been voiced that a future war would be a people's war.[7] [...]

If this is the case, then the state has to do everything to enable the army to prepare the male population for a war.

What is the population of the two blocs [...]?
- Warsaw Treaty: ca. 330 million
- NATO: ca. 649 million

Thus, at the beginning of a war, NATO is therefore in a position to draw on forces not smaller, but much larger than those of the Warsaw Treaty.

In preparation for a potential war—though it is important to avoid [war]—we need trained forces.

There cannot be any reduction of our military. We would not be able to manage maintaining those armies in peace time with small armies, and without public funds. This is the first question we would have to talk about.

Second, we constantly have to observe how the adversary is equipped; comparable equipment should be available to us as well. The modern adversary has everything at his disposal that science offers:
- explosives of five to six times higher potency
- munitions amounting to precision weapons
- high-power fuel with new chemical characteristics

[7] Army General Iazov is referring to the statements by the Romanian comrades. [Footnote in the original.]

More and more guided munitions, bombs, and mines are produced. These weapons are expensive and cannot be built by a single state. We have to cooperate.

The NATO states have a higher national income than the countries of the Warsaw Treaty. They increase their spending for armaments annually. They understand that weapons cannot be produced without necessary funds.

We will build our entire argument on how to disarm. We are not in favor of maintaining a huge army. However, it must be equipped with the most modern technology.

The proportion of the army to the population is as follows:

- Soviet Army   1.5 percent
- Bulgarian People's Army   1.4 percent
- Hungarian People's Army   1.2 percent
- National People's Army   0.9 percent
- Polish Army   1.2 percent
- Army of the SRR [Romania]   0.8 percent
- Czechoslovak People's Army   1.5 percent

The countries of the NATO bloc have 1 percent of their population under arms, and the United States 1.4 percent. It is not the number of people in an army that matters but the armaments at the army's disposal. [...]

We talk a lot about parity, but nothing can be achieved by mere wishful thinking. This requires major efforts by the people. The countries of the Warsaw Treaty have to make their contribution to this parity. By evaluating the NATO countries, efforts towards collective defense, and, where possible, individual defense, can be assessed.

To this end, the United States stationed cruise missiles in other countries.

They are contributing to collective as well as to individual power, as long as they serve the interests of their countries.

Parity depends on the productive capacity of each country.

Conditions have to be prepared in such a way that people can be armed, reserves can be set up, or production capacities used, in order to produce the weapons to equip the army.

In a possible war, we assume a defensive posture. During the "Soiuz-87" exercise, we spoke to Comrade [Erich] Honecker about organizing the defense at the state border. Comrades [Gustáv] Husák and [Wojciech] Jaruzelski share this opinion. The line of main defense has to be chosen where the area is most convenient, where the adversary can be misled or ambushed.

The security zone can obviously not be 40 to 50 kilometers deep. However, it has to guarantee that the adversary is forced to spread out, and that his troops are exposed to our strikes. In this way they could suffer high losses.

Maybe it is possible to organize the line of defense along the state border. In this case the adversary's artillery should have no chance of targeting our troops. Considering the stage of development of [our] armaments, the defense has to remain active. It must enable us to fight the guided weapons of the adversary, and to withstand, in terms of damage and reconstruction to the area, the impact of the adversary's precision weapons.

We believe that these problems are not yet solved. We have to continue working on them during 1988, and tests have to take place during troop exercises.

With respect to the current and future technological stage of weapons for warfare, one has to be prepared for a general war with conventional weapons as well as with nuclear weapons.

The United States talks about the beginning of a war with conventional weapons, although selected deployment of nuclear weapons in the course of a war is possible.

Such selected strikes, though, [would] provoke a full-power and maximum-range counterstrike.

We should not get confused by such opinions. They only aim at soothing us.

At the meeting of the Committee of Ministers of Defense, under the topic of our countries' air defense it was discussed that the adversary has the ability to carry out massive strikes with cruise missiles. These cruise missiles, carrying major-impact conventional warheads (up to 500 kilograms of explosives), can be directed at the target within a range of 10–20 meters by the adversary. Possible targets are dams, power facilities, chemical facilities, nuclear power plants, and others.

The consequences cannot yet be determined. We can see this in the case of the nuclear power plant at Chernobyl where major areas are still contaminated, and the end is not yet in sight.

In Europe, however, there are between 100 and 150 nuclear power plants. What would happen if they were destroyed? Would that not be the same as a nuclear war? This has to be thought about and appropriate steps must be taken.

[…] No army can constantly remain in combat readiness. Also a sudden alert does not work everywhere. Therefore we regard directives for the covert transition of troops and navy forces from peace into war mode as the principal method. So it is possible to create in time the appropriate groups in the endangered area and the transit into defense.

[…] There is no such thing as a passive defense. The enemy would destroy it.

The active part of defense consists in steadfastly holding the designated areas of defense and conducting counterattacks and strikes.

The transition from defense to counterattack is subject to the directives of superiors. It is based on commonly known previous parameters.

In any case, the counterattack rolls on with the participation of allied armies.

[…] Under the conditions of a defensive military doctrine, combat cover has gained in importance.

One of its most important varieties is electronic warfare.

Whether during the Suez Crisis, in Vietnam or in Lebanon, U.S. forces have applied electronic warfare everywhere on a broad scale.

Also, in potential conflicts they will conduct electronic warfare.

However, we do not have the respective means. We have to think about that.

Likewise, the protection of our troops from the adversary's weapons of mass destruction has to be reviewed.

Not least important is the coverage of rear [areas]. If anybody thinks this could only be organized at the beginning of a war, that person is wrong.

[*Source: AZN 32651, BA-MA. Translated by Karen Riechert.*]

Document No. 126: Proposal to Establish a Warsaw Pact Information and Propaganda Department, March 11, 1988

Reflecting growing Soviet awareness of the need to enhance the Warsaw Pact's image, as well as both to propagate its goals and policies abroad, and justify them to its members Army Gen. Anatolii Gribkov informs East German Chief of Staff Gen. Fritz Streletz about a proposal to establish an information department for the Pact. (NATO had always had one.)

An Information and Propaganda Department, as the information and propaganda organ of the supreme commander of the Unified Forces of the Warsaw Treaty member-states should be established in order to promote understanding abroad of the military policy, life and activities of the armed forces of the Warsaw Treaty member-states, to neutralize anti-socialist and anti-Soviet attitudes, to eliminate "enemy images" of the USSR and the other socialist countries as well as their armed forces, and to exchange the fraternal armies' experiences on the promotion of foreign policy and counter-propaganda.

The Information and Propaganda Department may be assigned the following tasks:

- exert influence on members from the armed forces of the U.S. and other NATO countries by explaining the peace-loving domestic and foreign policy of the communist and workers parties, resolutions of the Political Consultative Committee, the defense-oriented military doctrine of the Warsaw Treaty member-states, and by unmasking the aggressive nature of imperialism and reactionary forces;
- study and analyze the ideological, political and military situation in the U.S. and other NATO states, as well as the political and moral condition of members of their armed forces; prepare theses and arguments for informational and propagandistic work as well as for counter-propaganda; synchronize the efforts by the fraternal armies with regard to these questions;
- organize a mutual exchange of information about the living conditions and activities of the national armies in the Warsaw Treaty with the intention of fortifying their brotherhood-in-arms, unity, and internationalist education of army members;
- organize information exchange among the fraternal armies on questions of conducting propaganda in foreign countries via military channels; analyze the

effectiveness of such propaganda; perfect its content, and that of the forms and methods of informational and propaganda work as well as of counter-propaganda.

[...]

It would make sense to create with the Information and Propaganda Department a joint editorial staff for the publication of "The Warsaw Treaty," a quarterly journal in the languages of the Warsaw Treaty and NATO countries. [...]

[Source: VA-01/40409, BA-MA. Translated by Bernd Schaefer.]

Document No. 127: Memorandum of Akhromeev–Kessler Conversation, March 19, 1988

One-on-one conversations between Soviet bloc officials are often very informative for outside observers because they sometimes take place in an informal setting where the parties are more likely to reveal personal points of view. Here, Soviet Chief of Staff Sergei Akhromeev expands openly on various problems the Soviet Union is facing— economic, administrative and morale-related—to East German Defense Minister Heinz Kessler. Akhromeev evidently supports Gorbachev's reform program, which many of his senior military colleagues vehemently opposed. Yet he also hastens to add that perestroika is not for everyone, and that each socialist country has to find its own way. Akhromeev goes on to explain other recent Soviet actions, such as commitment to unilateral weapons cuts in order to get the arms control process with Washington moving. But he also makes a point of reassuring Kessler that the Soviet leadership is "keeping this process firmly in their hands, and that 'Perestroika' does not constitute a threat to socialism."

Marshal of the Soviet Union [Sergei F.] Akhromeev used his introduction to talk about some problems of the situation in the Soviet Union:

[…]

- One might say that in the Soviet Union a decisive turn of events has occurred. For objective reasons, not because of subjective personal wishes, a series of especially economic measures must be introduced and implemented. […]
- This is particularly important to eliminate many shortcomings permitted over the last years.
- Many [otherwise] loyal party cadres have not been following certain methods of administrative work. There is a lack of interest among people in their work and its results. Working methods practiced thus far are not effective enough. There has always been much wishful thinking, but little of it has been realized.
- […]
- Obviously, 'Perestroika' in the USSR is not the universal way to follow for all socialist states. […]
- Each socialist country has to find its own way in these matters. […]
- Obviously this comes with many problems, and our true friends in the socialist countries are concerned about certain phenomena in the Soviet Union. From the vantage point of these comrades, this concern is certainly justified. But he [Akhromeev] wants to emphasize that the Central Committee and Politburo of the CC of the CPSU are keeping this process firmly in their hands, and that 'Perestroika' does not constitute a threat to socialism.

[…]

In further remarks, Marshal of the Soviet Union Akhromeev outlined current aspects of the USSR's foreign policy:

- The Soviet Union's foreign policy is most closely related to military policy.
- In connection with the conclusion of the agreement of December 8, 1987, between the USSR and the U.S. on the elimination of their intermediate- and short-range missiles, the foreign and defense ministries have acquired extensive experience.
- Extensive experience has been acquired by the Foreign Ministry, as well as by the Defense Ministry, during the conclusion of the agreement of December 8, 1987 between the USSR and the U.S. on the elimination of their intermediate- and short-range missiles.
- Many Soviet people ask with justification why we will dismantle more missiles than the U.S. But this first step was necessary politically, though not easy for us military to cope with, since we constantly have to take into account the actual balance of forces.
- Comrade Gorbachev has had a lot of patience with us military, and has listened to our reservations concerning individual problems over and over again.
- The main problem was that the U.S. has not been in a position to include the nuclear weapons of Great Britain and France in the reductions talks. […] Finally the decision was made to introduce this first phase in such a manner that we would destroy more missiles than the U.S. This was necessary in order to achieve a first step towards disarmament, otherwise there would have been no disarmament results.

  […]
- Concerning the future pattern of relations with the U.S., Marshal of the Soviet Union Akhromeev called it major progress that the foreign ministers of the USSR and the U.S. are going to meet for an exchange of opinions once a month.

[…]
- As of now, however, no figures certified by NATO's leading bodies have been made available about the strength of the NATO forces. […]
- The Soviet side has these thoughts about such issues:
  - It would be helpful if, at a certain point, the Warsaw Treaty would publicly announce data about the armed forces and main classes of armaments of the Warsaw Treaty member-states, as well as on the armed forces of NATO member countries. Then NATO should publish figures about the strength of its armed forces as well as its estimates of the Warsaw Treaty [forces].
  - However, these publications must include data on the armed forces and military potential of France and Spain. But this is an issue which the NATO states permanently refuse to deal with. On this subject, we have to go more on the offensive to force the adversary to show its colors.
  - [Only] then could one negotiate about the strength of the armed forces and make comparisons between them.
  - Currently there is work being done on this proposal by the Foreign Ministry and the Ministry of Defense of the USSR. It will be forwarded to the fra-

ternal countries within the coming days. Consultation on these matters with the Warsaw Treaty member countries will certainly turn out to be necessary over the coming days.

— Starting from the assumption that an approximate strategic military balance does exist, it would be advisable from the Soviet perspective to enforce comprehensively the principle of "sufficiency" between the Warsaw Treaty and NATO. This may be done in three stages:

— through the elimination of asymmetries, according to the principle that whoever is ahead must reduce

— after the elimination of asymmetries, the general reduction of forces on both sides

— then the building on both sides of such small armed forces that no longer have the capability to attack.

[*Source: AZN 32660, 113–19, BA-MA. Translated by Karen Reichert.*]

Document No. 128: Speeches at the Foreign Ministers'
Meeting in Sofia, March 29–30, 1988

Two speeches from this meeting of the Committee of Foreign Ministers in Sofia are excerpted below. Both deal, from different perspectives, with the broader implications of disarmament for the Warsaw Pact. Eduard Shevardnadze's speech makes the point that the Warsaw Pact must prevent NATO from trying to compensate for the removal of missiles under the INF treaty by modernizing its conventional forces. He proposes that the East set an example by reducing Warsaw Pact military expenditures without fear of political consequences. East German Foreign Minister Oskar Fischer is skeptical, implying that such a move would be very risky.

a) Speech by Eduard Shevardnadze

As we have already pointed out numerous times before, the dominant theme of our times is the unavoidable and highly developed process of the form of a unified, all-encompassing world marked by changing relationships.

The four fundamental dimensions of this policy—military–political, economic, humanitarian, and ecological—demand a truly global scale.

[…]

The concept of priorities in national development is changing. Seen from the perspective of policy, examining the question of the potential level of defense spending is probably of greatest interest. Perhaps only now, for the first time since World War II, is it possible for us to talk about the creation of a relatively clear tendency toward limiting military spending in most of the countries and at least toward stabilizing them.

[…]

If it is correct to conclude that the demands in the life of a nation set tight limits on military spending, and we genuinely enter a phase in which armament efforts are decreased, this can have extremely significant consequences for policies.

Completely different conditions develop from this for the struggle to end the arms race, the elimination of nuclear and chemical weapons, and the persistent development of a cooperation zone among nations.

[…]

The NATO Council session in Brussels offered the opposite picture: nevertheless, it clearly showed that, in the western world, they have begun an intensive search for answers to the new realities and the new policies of the socialist countries as well as answers to the changing social consciousness.

Central to the policies for the NATO countries are the questions of conventional arms and weapons and the problem of trust and openness in military matters. It is well known that they have special groups for preparing programs which they intend to place in opposition to our general initiatives in the area of European security.

582

At the present time our alliance has at its disposal a thorough conceptual basis and an attractive foundation for practical activities.

[...]

Those are the proposals of the BDR and the Czechoslovak Socialist Republic as well as those of Romania and Bulgaria on the creation of nuclear weapon-free zones in individual regions of the continent and the same for chemical weapons.

That is the "Jaruzelski Plan," which envisions a set of measures to limit armaments and for increasing trust in Europe.

That is the idea of our Czechoslovak friends to create a zone of trust, cooperation, and good-neighbor relations along the line which borders both military alliances.

That is the call of Comrade Honecker to Chancellor Kohl with the proposal to carry out first-rate measures to ensure security on the European continent and to create an atmosphere of mutual trust.

That is the initiative of the three parties—the Hungarian Socialist Workers' Party, the Finnish Social Democratic Party, and the Italian Socialist Party—on cooperation among countries which do not have nuclear weapons for the sake of disarmament in Europe.

We also have a common program for reducing weapons and armaments which was accepted at the session of the Budapest session of the Political Consultative Committee.

It would certainly be wrong if one were to say that this program were as effective today as it was at the time it first appeared. In politics, attention is quickly given to new proposals. Thus, we must consider that from now on, in the minds of many, the image will prevail that the Brussels Declaration is a working concept for today and, in fact, for the simple reason that the Declaration came after the Agreement on intermediate-range and shorter-range missiles was completed.

[...]

Under today's conditions, the question regarding the work with European public opinion has become considerably more critical. It has become so because the process of re-thinking the previously-existing concepts has accelerated. Likewise, our representatives must go where, to a significant degree, the new views on the order of things are being formulated—in the European Council, in the West European Union, in the North Atlantic Council and the European Parliament.

For many years, these organizations were our active opponents. Now, thanks to the internal renewal in our countries, a more favorable situation has developed for constructive work with these organizations.

Something has already been done in this direction. Our Bulgarian friends have adopted an initiative on holding a meeting of members of parliament of European countries on the questions of nuclear weapon-free zones in the Balkans and in other regions of Europe.

Our Polish comrades are planning to set up a meeting in Warsaw for the Parliament Presidents of the participating countries of the CSCE. We support the contacts with the European Parliament.

Along these same lines, it would be worth it to rapidly work out the question of creating an inter-parliamentary organ of the socialist countries.

[...]

Compliance with the conclusion from the Berlin session of the Political Consultative Committee has given clear outline to the working mechanism of our common foreign policy. The work of the new institutions—the multilateral group for operational information exchange and the special commission on the question of disarmament—as a whole do not provoke any particular comments. The most critical part of their work is manifestations of formalism. Until now, there haven't been any at all. Our representatives should probably inquire, after some time, how the efficacy of their work could be increased to the same degree that the group and the commission gather practical experience.

[...]

The creation of two new institutions does not solve the problem of completing the political infrastructure of our alliance. Perhaps in the interim we should consider creating a permanent functioning political institution which could discuss foreign policy questions which arise and one that could strategically prepare recommendations to the leadership. Let me now once again turn from the questions of day-to-day work to a general statement. In keeping with this genre, it will be thinking out loud, which I believe, is in direct relation to the content and form of our Committee's work.

The new dimension which has developed in international relations after the Agreement on Intermediate-range and Short-range Missiles was concluded allows for an even greater depth in intellectual considerations of the balance of power. We need a prognosis of the development of the situation both within as well as outside our alliance.

[...]

I would stress the word "constant" here. The constancy of the enormous changes around us and in us disperses the givens of previous goal-setting and stimulates the perpetual search for an option. The whole question boils down to how far along we are prepared for it.

[...]

Our common opponent is at work and mobilized in his activities against us. He will not forgive us even one mistake and attempts to punish us at every favorable opportunity that comes to him. It would nonetheless be a gross methodological and practical mistake to ignore other tendencies as well, not to take note and not to observe. In the minds of a growing number of politicians, national and social officials—people of scientific and creative intelligence—and in the minds of representatives of Western social circles, the disastrous idea of instability of earlier methods suffices and the knowledge of the realities of the nuclear-cosmic age increases. More and more intellectuals begin to understand that policies toward us must be built on other foundations, that relations with us will have to be formulated so that people will be led by new political thought.

[...]

The re-evaluation of traditional views for many leads unavoidably to the view that the eternal antagonism of class interests should take a back seat to the priority of general human interests.

This is an objective necessity. However, even this necessity gives us no reason to let up in our endeavors nor to celebrate euphorically.

[...]

It is impossible to hold a conversation with the West on the same level when one finds oneself on the periphery of the technological world. Economic solvency is a political factor. Modernization of the economic system will be determined by security considerations, both ours and those of our friends. However, this process, as we have convinced ourselves, is narrowly connected to the constant development and the completion of the political structures of our countries.

[...]

As I ponder these things aloud, I come to the conclusion that it is necessary to see the functions and forms of the work of our committee in a new way. After the emergence of its working institutions which function on a permanent foundation, one can demand maximum efficiency and setting our meeting times free for direct and less formal dealings. Let this be a direct exchange of views on our mutual strategy for the community of nations in the international arena, or the collective understanding of developing realities, an open and bold posing of pointed questions which the worry the public in our countries, questions which are not usually discussed in diplomatic circles.

Let this be, ultimately, a discussion among comrades of how we need to live and behave in tomorrow's world in order to respond to the demands of the times or to the mistakes.

It can also be done another way, however. Our ministries have departments concerned with analyzing, planning and forecasting policies—why shouldn't we give them the task of preparing a thorough study of the tendencies in today's world, of the prospects for development in our countries? It would be good if this were to result in a forecast full of possibilities, with conclusions for our mutual policies.

We still have no experience in this matter. However, it seems that, until the next meeting of the Foreign Ministers Committees, we could consider maintaining a suitable report. It is clearly better to begin our mutual work with a meeting of the leaders of our "Brain Trusts." They themselves could determine how to organize the work.

This proposal is open to criticism. Less than ever before do we want to promote our views and opinions as absolutes.

[...]

b) Speech by Oskar Fischer

With its Brussels summit, the NATO leaders attempted to bring together and mobilize all those forces which continue to be used for military superiority and "nuclear deterrence". Their main thrust is to replace some of the potential they lost through the elimination of intermediate-range missiles with a new build-up and modernization, and above all, to exclude disarmament from other regions.

[...]

A key question is to begin negotiations on conventional disarmament in Europe. NATO wants to do this from a position of strength and to begin with demands for unilateral reductions on the part of the Warsaw Pact nations, as the latest Brussels Declaration shows.

[...]

All our experiences show that our side—steeped in the principles of equality and equal security—meets [the Western side] best when we go to the negotiating table thoroughly *united* and *coordinated*. Thus I especially welcome the fact that those of us on the Disarmament Commission—having started at the beginning of February—are concentrating on the rapid development of this negotiating concept.

At this time it is essential to work out negotiating fundamentals on these questions.

We support the suggestion of our Soviet comrades to quickly and thoroughly work up data on the weapons and armaments of our alliance and to publish that information.

In this way, we will simultaneously and effectively counter the flood of false information disseminated by western media and politicians. We should purposefully work with military experts on: the concept of asymmetries and the possibilities of eliminating them; on a definition of defensive capabilities; and also on proposals for controls. The same holds true for the set of measures to build trust and security, above all for bilateral limits on military activities.

It seems important to us not to limit it to observations of maneuvers and inspections. The core of our concept of confidence-building measures in which we participated in Stockholm—and which are valid for Stockholm II—consists of attaining genuinely drastic limitation measures. In the same way, the Disarmament Commission also has to work out propositions to extend negotiations on measures for building trust and security.

[...]

5. It is the view of the GDR that, as before, tactical nuclear weapons are still of particular concern. It hardly seems possible that a special negotiating level could be reached for them in the near future, or that they could be expressly included in the mandate for conventional weapons disarmament in Europe.

[...]

In this sense, we are continuing to work alongside and in coordination with the Czechoslovak Socialist Republic toward a nuclear-free corridor. After the Agreement on intermediate-range missiles, this topic is worthy of our attention, as it would provide a more practical opening for nuclear weapons with a range of up to 500 km. All the more so, if the proposed "corridor" were expanded to a central European zone.

[...]

In order to contribute as best we can and not to allow for any break in the flow of disarmament talks, we are preparing an "International Meeting for Nuclear-Free Zones" in Berlin for June 20–22, 1988. Interest in, and approval for, the meeting have been extensive, from western nations and developing countries as well.

[...]

6. In view of the start of production of binary weapons by the USA and the recent difficulties at the Geneva negotiations in conjunction with that fact, the GDR sup-

ports strengthening the efforts toward a general and complete prohibition and destruction of chemical weapons.

[…]

The GDR actively supports the initiatives of the fraternal countries; the Jaruzelski Plan; the initiative of Comrade Miloš Jakeš; the proposal submitted by our Hungarian Comrades along with the Social Democratic Party of Finland and the Italian Socialists; and the proposals of our Romanian and Bulgarian comrades. They are all united to improve the climate on our continent, to create more security, and thereby contribute to the more rapid construction of a collective house of Europe.[8]

[…]

With the Murmansk speech[9] of Comrade Gorbachev, the Warsaw Pact countries are provided with a concept for peace and security in northern Europe.

[…]

At the meeting of foreign ministers of the Balkan countries in Belgrade, the Bulgarian and Romanian comrades provided an important contribution to the shift in peace strategies of the Warsaw Pact for this sensitive region. With this action, perspectives for growing cooperation and confidence-building measures emerge for the southern flanks of our alliance as well. At the same time, possibilities increase for constructing a nuclear-free zone from northern and central Europe to southern Europe.

8. In our opinion the integration processes in Western Europe demand greater attention. These processes are taking place whether we like it or not. In assessing them, it is essential whether they fit in into a common house of Europe according to our harmonious collective image or not. In this process it certainly concerns the European Community, the European Parliament, and others.

[…]

The negotiating situation previously achieved in Vienna does not correspond to the significance of the CSCE meeting, nor to the prerequisites. NATO, in an especially extortionary move, is attempting to pressure us in the areas of human rights and humanitarian issues. This otherwise already complicated situation in Vienna is made more difficult by the fact that the situation in this area differs in each individual socialist country and is also handled differently. A show of unity is of critical significance in Vienna and for the protection of our common interests.

The GDR supports, as a matter of principle as well as for the sake of flexibility, working toward *substantive* results that are acceptable for both sides in *all* areas of the final agreement. However, relenting will not help, but will only encourage the other side.

It is essential to clearly demarcate the limits of our willingness to compromise in a united way. In our opinion, these limits lie at the point where human rights and

---

[8] The references are to various plans for the reduction of conventional forces, nuclear- and chemical weapons-free zones. For further details, see "Chronology of events" in this volume.

[9] Gorbachev's speech in Murmansk on October 1, 1987, proposed a variety of cooperative undertakings with countries in the far north of the globe, including the Arctic; first on the list was the idea for a nuclear-free zone across northern Europe.

humanitarian issues are removed from national sovereignty and, through the creation of a multilateral control mechanism, a "Right to Interfere" with the "Right to Complain" against the country should be set up within the framework of the CSCE.

In view of the massive efforts in imperialist circles—above all with help from their mass media—but also those by certain church authorities in socialist countries to build an "internal opposition", to create possibilities for being effective internally as well as [promote] legitimacy and publicity externally, these question are of a particularly sensitive political nature. Decisions—I now repeat something which has been stated for a long time—decisions cannot be handled by our delegation in Vienna, they must be handled by the leadership.

On all these issues, prompt and universal response as well as process coordination among the leadership leaves much to be desired.

[*Source: DC/20/I/3-2640, pp. 64–81, SAPMO. Translated by Paul Spitzer for the National Security Archive.*]

Document No. 129: Draft of a Revised Statute of the Unified Command in War Time, March 30–31, 1988

This is from the draft excerpt of a revised 1980 war time statute, which had been so unpopular with the Soviet allies (see Document No. 86). Although Moscow felt the need to loosen up the degree of control by the supreme commander, the revisions ended up being rather insignificant. For a detailed critical analysis of the revised statute by the Romanians, see Document No. 131.

In order to centralize the leadership of the Unified Armed Forces of the Warsaw Treaty in war time, the Unified Command is established in the following composition:

The supreme commander of the Unified Armed Forces of the Warsaw Treaty is the supreme commander of the Armed Forces of the Union of Soviet Socialist Republics.

The supreme commanders of the Armed Forces in the People's Republic of Bulgaria, the Hungarian People's Republic, the German Democratic Republic, the People's Republic of Poland, the Socialist Republic of Romania and the Czechoslovak Socialist Republic. Their deputies on the Unified Command are the ministers of defense of the respective countries. The First Deputy of the supreme commander of the Unified Armed Forces is the minister of defense of the Union of Soviet Socialist Republics.

The deputy of the supreme commander for the Armies of the Warsaw Treaty states is the main commander of the Unified Armed Forces of the Warsaw Treaty.

The Unified Command and its leadership bodies are responsible for the leadership, strategic planning and military actions of the Unified Armed Forces of the Warsaw Treaty as well as the employment of the national armed forces and the resources of countries allied with the Warsaw Treaty Organization for a particular period.

The first deputy of the supreme commander of the Unified Armed Forces carries out his work on the basis of decisions by the supreme commander of the Unified Armed Forces.

The representative of the supreme commander for the armies of the Warsaw Treaty states ensures cooperation with the military–political leadership of the allied countries in fulfilling decisions by the supreme commander of the Unified Armed Forces on the preparation and employment of forces and resources from the allied countries in the interests of the Unified Armed Forces.

The executive body of the Unified Command is the General Staff of the armed forces of the USSR, which coordinates the functions of all executive bodies in fulfilling the assignments of the Unified Command of the Unified Armed Forces.

In war time, the Staff, the Committee on Technology and the other executive bodies of the Unified Command of the Unified Armed Forces of the Warsaw Treaty will change to wartime structure and strength to fulfill the assignments of the deputy of the supreme commander for the Warsaw Treaty forces.

The Staff, the Committee on Technology and the other executive bodies of the Unified Command of the Unified Armed Forces of the Warsaw Treaty carry out their duties in cooperation with the ministers of defense from the member-states to ensure that decisions by the Unified Command on the preparation and employment of member-states' national armed forces and resources are fulfilled in the interests of the Unified Command with respect to the following:

- transfer to war footing;
- deployment and subordination to the main commands of the Unified Armed Forces on the battlefields;
- mobilization of reserves;
- increase in the capacity of facilities in the rear areas and preparation of lines of communication;
- use of weapons stockpiles, supplies of materiel and locally available resources;
- expansion of production and repair capacity;
- transformation of industry to production based on the B-Plans[10]
- ensuring the delivery and establishment of production of new military technology;
- assistance to the territorial and civil defense organizations;
- jurisdiction over the members of the Unified Armed Forces;
- fulfillment of the assignments of an auxiliary (reserve) executive bodies of the Unified Command of the Unified Armed Forces in the European theater.

The direction and implementation of combat activities is the responsibility of the Unified Command directly and through the unified and national executive bodies in charge of troops and fleets (General Staff, Staff of the Unified Forces, Main Commands of the Unified Forces in the western and southwestern theaters, national army leaderships, Commands of the Unified Baltic Fleet and the Black Sea Fleet, air defense commanders of the member-states of the Warsaw Treaty, etc.)

In the preparations for and carrying out of an armed struggle, the national military–political leaderships of the respective member-states follow the decisions of the Warsaw Treaty member-states and the Unified Command.

[...]

During war, the leading representatives of the Unified Command of the Unified Forces of the Warsaw Treaty in the allied armies serve as representatives of the Unified Command of the Unified Forces to the ministry of defense in the respective country. The supreme commander for the Armies of the Warsaw Treaty oversees the functions of the representative of the Unified Command.

In order to ensure cooperation and increase efficacy in the managements of troops and fleets, the Unified Command of the Unified Armed Forces at the front and the command of the unified naval forces will develop operational groups under the command of the allied armies and the fleet. Their number, composition, working

---

[10] Plans for production in war time.

methods and provisioning will be determined in peace time by the Staff of the armed forces in the western and southwestern theaters.

Deployment of the operational groups is decided by the Main Commands of the Unified Armed Forces on the battlefields.

[...]

The military–political leadership of the Warsaw Treaty member-states appoints the generals, admirals and officers of the Staff, the Committee on Technology and other agencies of the Unified Command as well as the executive bodies of the Unified Command in war time with respect to their organizational and personnel structure.

The appointment and transfer of the commanders of the national units and their deputies as well as of the leading cadres of the executive bodies of the Unified Armed Forces in war time are made by the national military–political leadership in coordination with the Unified Command. All other questions related to cadres in the allied forces with respect to the Unified Armed Forces in war time are the responsibility of the national military leadership.

Jurisdiction with respect to members to the Unified Armed Forces is to be carried out on the basis of intergovernmental agreements.

[Source: VA-01/40409, BA-MA, pp. 30–52, 129–31. Translated by Catherine Nielsen.]

Document No. 130: Summary of Statement by Marshal Akhromeev on Exchange of Data between NATO and the Warsaw Pact, May 17, 1988

Ever since the beginning of the MBFR negotiations in 1973, NATO and the Warsaw Pact had been unable to agree on data about each other's military strength. This meeting, held at the invitation of the Soviet General Staff and Foreign Ministry, shows how the Pact prepared for the exchange of data and what difficulties and problems this posed for the Soviet military. Marshal Sergei Akhromeev provides some of the background, noting that the Americans had opposed swapping data with the Soviet Union, having insisted instead on an exchange between the two alliances, which would compare their overall strength. Although this was the kind of collaboration both sides agreed was needed in order to build mutual trust, this document and others show how the Warsaw Pact tried repeatedly to avoid revealing accurate and relevant data. The fact that the Soviet Foreign Ministry was a co-organizer of this meeting indicates that pressure for compliance was coming from political quarters.

[...] In March 1988, the Soviet side made a proposal for the exchange of data about the armed forces and conventional armaments of NATO and Warsaw Treaty in Europe.

Currently the U.S. is rejecting bilateral talks on the exchange of data between the USSR and the U.S. It only considers them possible after negotiations within the framework of alliances.

Based on agreements between the Soviet Union and [other] Warsaw Treaty member-states in 1986, the Soviet comrades are now prepared for a possible exchange of data between NATO and Warsaw Treaty.

Accordingly, Marshal of the Soviet Union [Sergei] Akhromeev proposed a "Zone of Reduction of Forces and Conventional Armaments" that would permit an assessment of the two military alliances [...] as a whole, according to regions (Northern Europe, Central Europe and Southern Europe), as well as according to individual countries.

[...]

For the prospective negotiations, the following initial figures on the most important categories of armed forces and conventional armaments of NATO and Warsaw Treaty in Europe were provided:

1. Taking into account the components proposed for reductions, the personnel numbers of land forces and air force (tactical air force) are:
   - in NATO   – 2.4 million men
   - in the Warsaw Treaty   – 2.3 million men

2. The number of units (divisions, brigades, and equivalents of divisions) is approximately the same, i.e.
- in NATO — 171 divisions
- in the Warsaw Treaty — 175 divisions

3. Most important armament types:
- Superiority of NATO
  - tactical air force — 1.2 fold
  - among them fighters — 1.6 fold
  - combat helicopters — 1.5 fold
  - anti-tank missile systems — 1.5 fold
- of Warsaw Treaty
  - launching pads for tactical missiles — 7.6 fold
  - tanks — 2.0 fold
  - mine launchers, cannons, and mortars — 1.2 fold
  - armored personnel carriers — 1.3 fold

[...]

Marshal of the Soviet Union Akhromeev emphasized in this context how there will be a number of problems in general negotiations, since overall 23 states have to be brought "under one hat."

From the USSR's perspective, the following negotiating stages between the Warsaw Treaty and NATO might be considered:

1st Stage

Exchange of data on armed forces and conventional armaments, and elimination of asymmetries

2nd Stage

Reduction of forces on both sides by the same percentage

3rd Stage

Creation of an inability to attack on both sides (so far there are no clear ideas concerning this 3rd stage)

Marshal of the Soviet Union Akhromeev envisaged organizing the preparation of the respective figures, if possible, as follows:
- at the end of May/beginning of June 1988 bilateral consultations between the General Staff of the USSR forces and the respective General Staffs (the Main Staff) [of the Warsaw Treaty member-states] and
- between 20 June and 25 June 1988 conclude work on these problems, including a joint consultation in Moscow, and prepare the required figures for the Political Consultative Committee

The Political Consultative Committee would have to decide whether a reciprocal publication of figures is envisaged, or whether, in case of a rejection by NATO, a different decision will have to be made.

Proposals tabled by the Soviet side met in principle with the consent of the delegation leaders of fraternal armies.

[*Source: VA-01/32661, BA-MA. Translated by Bernd Schaefer.*]

Document No. 131: Transcript of Romanian
Party Politburo Meeting, June 17, 1988

At this Romanian Politburo meeting, Nicolae Ceauşescu and his colleagues discuss the draft revision of the 1980 war time statue (see Document No. 129), and find little difference from the original. Having refused to sign the 1980 document, the Romanians conclude there is no reason to sign the revised one either. There follows a discussion of the kinds of data Romania will provide on the state of its armed forces. Ceauşescu insists that it go directly to the Warsaw Pact, not to the Soviet Union.

Report regarding the statute of the Unified Armed Forces
of the Warsaw Treaty member-states:

[...]
Cde. Vasile Milea: The Unified Command sent us a draft of a new "Statute of the Unified Armed Forces of the States Participating in the Warsaw Treaty and of the Leading Command Organs of These Forces for War Time." This document comprises a number of modifications in comparison with the statute adopted in 1980 by the other states—without our country['s vote]—and does not solve the essential issues with which the Romanian side did not agree at that time.

I also want to report that the statute has been discussed time and again for eight years, and now they have brought it here again for us to finalize. In fact, it is, by and large, the old statute but with a number of additions.

[...]
I report that after the signing, as I said before, of the statute in 1980 by the leaders of the other countries, the Ministry of National Defense, with your approval, also held discussions with the Unified Command relating to this document up to 1983, without reaching any agreement.

At the discussions to be resumed at the request of the Unified Command, the Ministry of National Defense proposes to use the following viewpoint, drawn up in compliance with your specifications, as a guideline:

"The Political Consultative Committee is to be the supreme organ empowered to decide on the state of war and on defense issues of the socialist states participating in the Warsaw Treaty; the working organ of the Political Consultative Committee should not be the General Staff of the Soviet Army, but the current Command of the Unified Armed Forces."

Cde. Nicolae Ceauşescu: First of all, the principle provided for in the Warsaw Pact is the rotation principle. There are commanders from each country, and each year there are [different] presidents. They cannot decide whether or not we go to war.

I think, however, that the Political Consultative Committee should decide on that score. But let us assume that the decision to take part in a war or not is made by the

594

supreme organs of each state. Actually, the Political Consultative Committee should be the Supreme Court, but it can only act after the supreme party and state organs of the Warsaw Treaty member-states have decided on that score. We have to write this point in this form into the statute.

Cde. Vasile Milea: The commander of the theater of operations should be appointed from the national army which provides most of the forces, and the chief of the General Staff should not be from the same army. The commander of the theater of operations should have representatives from the national army as his first deputies, and the other functions of leadership and responsibility should be filled with cadres belonging to the same armies.

Cde. Elena Ceauşescu: This point is not clear.

Cde. Nicolae Ceauşescu: There is a theater of operations in the south. There will be Romanian, Soviet, and Bulgarian troops there.

Cde. Elena Ceauşescu: And it is the Soviets who have the majority of troops.

Cde. Vasile Milea: It is not they who have the most troops.

Cde. Elena Ceauşescu: We recognize that. We do not say with "the most forces"!

Cde. Nicolae Ceauşescu: The manner of rotation. The theater of operations had different commanders.

Cde. Vasile Milea: This remark is correct because there were both Bulgarians and Poles in the western theater.

Cde. Elena Ceauşescu: Consequently, not depending on size but on rotation. This way is correct.

Cde. Vasile Milea: And with the governments in agreement.

The large units and the units composing the Unified Armed Forces should remain subordinated to the national commands, which will appoint their commanders, and combat missions are to be delegated to the first deputies of the commander of the theater of operations appointed from the national armies.

Cde. Nicolae Ceauşescu: The fact that each army acts in collaboration with a national command is something different. But for example, the Romanians act under Romanian command, the Bulgarians under their command, and so do the Soviets. There is a coordinating command, a supreme command, but each army has its own command.

Cde. Vasile Milea: Purely temporarily.

Cde. Nicolae Ceauşescu: [The national commands are not subordinated to the supreme command.] However, there must be coordination.

Cde. Elena Ceauşescu: But each commands its own army.

Cde. Nicolae Ceauşescu: And the commanders of these large front units. And the supreme command is created and together they decide on the actions and on what they have to do, and periodically one of them coordinates; that is to say, he is chairman.

Cde. Vasile Milea: Of this Council.

Cde. Elena Ceauşescu: And each has its own army.

Cde. Nicolae Ceauşescu: The army cannot act at random! It must be coordinated. For example, if in the case of this issue everybody does as he likes, where do we get? For example, the three [armies] in the south have their commanders.

Cde. Vasile Milea: Of the national army.

Cde. Nicolae Ceaușescu: And they lead the troops and make decisions and from these three the commander of the theater of operations is appointed; by rotation, for a year or every six months, this commander is also the head of this command.

Cde. Vasile Milea: Understood.

Cde. Nicolae Ceaușescu: The situation will arise where a decision will be made concerning nuclear weapons, and then it will be something quite different.

Cde. Elena Ceaușescu: Is this statute of any use then?

Cde. Nicolae Ceaușescu: Until we do away with nuclear weapons and military blocs. This is its use!

Cde. Vasile Milea: Military actions by allied forces on the territory of a state taking part in the Warsaw Treaty should be carried out only at the request of the constitutional organs of the respective state and with the agreement of the state providing the troops, under conditions to be established by bilateral governmental conventions concluded in peace time.

Cde. Nicolae Ceaușescu: This point is a good one.

Cde. Elena Ceaușescu: This point is clear.

[...]

Cde. Nicolae Ceaușescu: Naturally, these would be the main issues, the remaining ones are minor. That is why I wanted to discuss them in the Political Consultative Committee, and I think it is good to do so.

At the relevant time we discussed them, but it has been eight years. The issues have been forgotten to some extent and now they want to raise them again since a "restructuring" is going to take place.

Do you agree?

(All of the comrades agree.)

Point 4: Data to be transmitted by the Ministry of National Defense in connection with the negotiations on conventional arms reductions.

Cde. Vasile Milea: The Ministry of National Defense and the Ministry of Foreign Affairs have analyzed the content of the documents sent by the General Staff of the Armed Forces of the Soviet Union, to which data concerning the effective military technical means and armaments are to be added by the Romanian side, so that a decision may be taken on the manner of their use at the negotiations with the member-states of NATO on the issue of conventional disarmament in Europe.

Cde. Nicolae Ceaușescu: First of all, we must say: the data should be centralized by the Warsaw Pact command; nobody else can meddle with it. Afterwards, the data will be sent to the unified command; it is to this command that we will send the data, not to the Soviet Union; what [the Soviet Union] does with the data is its business because it is also a part of this command. More precisely, according to the same principles.

Cde. Elena Ceaușescu: Of equality. They are well known.

Cde. Vasile Milea: Understood.

Cde. Nicolae Ceaușescu: And, comrades, there is still the question of communicating the respective data, as I said at the outset.

Cde. Vasile Milea: I report that these are the issues resulting from the meeting in Warsaw, and that is why the representatives [of the Ministry of National Defense] along with the representatives of the Ministry of Foreign Affairs agreed to hold talks with the NATO bloc.

Cde. Nicolae Ceauşescu: The discussions are between the Warsaw Pact and the NATO pact, not the Soviet Union. And these should be the data. Let us say it in a crystal-clear manner. These issues were not clear to us either.

Cde. Vasile Milea: In relation to the data, it is proposed that we communicate the effective levels that we have.

Cde. Nicolae Ceauşescu: In peace time.

Cde. Vasile Milea: How many ground troops—the number of divisions—how many of them are in a state of combat readiness?

Cde. Nicolae Ceauşescu: We are going to communicate that the effective level of our army is 210,000 troops.

Cde. Elena Ceauşescu: I thought there were 220,000 troops.

Cde. Vasile Milea: We have reduced their number somewhat.

Cde. Nicolae Ceauşescu: 15,000 in the air force, from what we have. The number 210,000 troops does not include effective levels of the navy.

Cde. Elena Ceauşescu: And must the effective levels of the navy be added?

Cde. Vasile Milea: The issue of the navy has not been discussed.

Cde. Nicolae Ceauşescu: We should have 18 large units, of which 14 divisions. Some of the divisions are to be full-fledged, others will have reduced effective levels—so it is said here in the material. At combat readiness—6 divisions; at reduced effective levels—8 divisions and 4 brigades. Eighteen large units all told.

Aircraft—450; helicopters—380; launch pads for tactical missiles—85; tanks—4,500; artillery pieces and antitank missile installations ("bazookas")—6,500; combat vehicles for infantry, armored troop carriers—5,500. Further: response systems for salvo firing ("Katyusha" launchers)—8,100; antiaircraft artillery and missiles—2,500.

These are, by and large, our data. Our armament is not complete because we do our equipping in compliance with a program. These are in an organizational stage. And we must take measures to have the necessary capacity in case the situation worsens, [and to have relevant equipment] operational.

And on this basis to enter discussions, but we will have to add one more thing: the reduction presupposes NATO, and the respective Western countries, will make a reduction of, not automatically 10 percent, but so that an equitable ratio between the Armed Forces, between [kinds of] armaments, can be insured. A certain ratio must be established.

Cde. Manea Mănescu: This first of all since not all have the same effective levels.

Cde. Nicolae Ceauşescu: Otherwise we will take into account what they have now—3 million—and the Soviets should reduce 10 percent of it, but 2.6 million will still remain.

That is why we have to see, to propose and, when the issue is raised, to call attention to it. We must insist on this issue but in our turn we have to understand the matter very well.

[…]

[*Source: CC RCP, Chancellery, File 66/1988, Romanian National Archives. Translated by Viorel Nicolae Buta for the PHP.*]

Document No. 132: Memorandum of Kulikov–Honecker Conversation, June 27, 1988

Mikhail Gorbachev's decision to change Warsaw Pact strategy met continued resistance from elements of the Soviet military. Here, almost a year later, Marshal Viktor Kulikov describes to GDR leader Erich Honecker the continuing problem of how to stop a potential NATO attack. Notwithstanding the new defensive orientation of Warsaw Pact strategy, he declares that the only possible way is to launch a counter-offensive.

USSR Marshal Kulikov began by stating that the purpose of his trip was to inform the General Secretaries of the sister Parties about the content of his report to the Political Consultative Committee of the Warsaw Pact States and of the associated Draft Resolution. He wished to show them the results of the fine-tuning of the documents by the military leaders of the Bulgarian Peoples' Republic, the Romanian Socialist Republic, the Hungarian People's Republic and the ČSSR.

He stated that his main concern was to get approval for the Report of the Supreme Commander of the Unified Armed Forces to the Political Consultative Committee. A discussion is planned on the report during the meeting in Warsaw, but the corresponding Resolution is to be signed by all the General Secretaries of the sister states.

[...]

At the present time the Unified Armed Forces is undergoing a process of reorientation, away from the one-sided focus on attack towards the organization and command of a strong and active defense at the onset of a war.

Much work still needs to be done before the common military doctrine is put into practice on all sides. Readjusting training and service regulations to the problematic of defense is a major undertaking.

Thereby the guiding principle is that the only possibility for destroying the enemy in to case of aggression is by decisive attacks in the form of a counter-offensive.

[...]

At the same time, Comrade USSR Marshal Kulikov emphasized that the military dangers associated with the nature of Imperialism itself must not be forgotten.

[...]

It remains important to keep sight of the enemy, to follow all developments and activities attentively and from all angles and draw the appropriate conclusions in time in order to avoid any surprises.

[...]

In conclusion, USSR Marshal Kulikov emphasized that all member-states of the Warsaw Pact are carrying out their obligations with the greatest precision and punctuality, except the Hungarian Peoples' Republic, which has major problems.

[...]

The production and reciprocal delivery of weapons is a serious problem at present. This affects above all the USSR, the ČSSR and the Hungarian People's Republic.

[...]

Comrade Erich Honecker thanked the Supreme Commander of the Unified Armed Forces, USSR Marshal Kulikov, for his presentation and expressed his full agreement.

[...]

Comrade Honecker also warned of the illusionary statements to be found in several Soviet newspapers according to which the USA wants peace, whereas the opposite is the case.

The USA is doing everything it can to strengthen its offensive position and to prepare for dealing a first strike with nuclear weapons.

[*Source: VA-01/40374, 66–73, BA-MA. Translated by Ursula Froese.*]

Document No. 133: Romanian Proposal for
Reform of the Warsaw Pact, July 4–8, 1988

Despite Romania's history of carping at the Soviets over the organization and structure of the Warsaw Pact, Bucharest eventually produced a serious proposal for improving the alliance, described in the letter below to the party central committees of the member-states. Along with promoting "democratization" through such steps as separating the PCC from the alliance's other institutions and establishing a rotating presidency that would include non-Soviet representatives, the Romanians wanted to make membership open to any European communist country. This was an attempt to keep the door open to new members, such as Yugoslavia and Albania, who could all be expected to back up Romania's position within the alliance. The Soviets, as indicated in the second document below, did not reject the proposal out of hand. For reasons of their own—namely, the belief that the Warsaw Pact indeed needed an overhaul—they regarded it as a basis for discussion. The proposal nevertheless made no progress for more than a year, until Bulgaria presented a counter-proposal (see Document No. 144).

a) Letter by the Romanian Party Central Committee
  to Central Committees of the Warsaw Pact Member-States,
  July 4, 1988

Esteemed Comrades!

The Central Committee of the Romanian Communist Party puts before you a few suggestions for improving the organization, and for democratizing the work of the executive body of the Warsaw Treaty.

These recommendations take into consideration current global changes and the special attention that socialist countries give to the questions of disarmament, and the easing of tensions and cooperation in Europe and the entire world, including the establishment of conditions for achieving the simultaneous dissolution of NATO and the Warsaw Pact as quickly as possible.

We believe it is important during the upcoming meeting of the Political Consultative Committee to discuss and decide on a series of measures concerning the reorganization and improvement of the leadership of the Warsaw Treaty Organization.

The Central Committee of the Romanian Communist Party believes that the current function of the Political Consultative Committee of the Warsaw Treaty member-states is too focused on military questions, which gives the impression that the party and national leadership are primarily concerned with these questions and have a military character.

Therefore, the Central Committee of the Romanian Communist Party would like to consult with you regarding the following suggestions that it intends to put before the upcoming meeting in Warsaw:

1. Reorganization of the Political Consultative Committee of the Warsaw Pact for the purpose of moving away from its current focus on military questions and achieving a Political Consultative Committee for the socialist states of Europe that is not connected with the Warsaw Pact, which is pursuing military goals. It must be a committee that ensures general cooperation between our parties and states in the political and economic arena.

In this regard, the Political Consultative Committee should concentrate its work on investigating and discussing the fundamental problems of building up socialism in our countries, cooperating for the well-being of social–economic development, raising the cultural level and standard of living of our people, strengthening social democracy, strengthening the power of socialism and peace as a whole and—in this context—guaranteeing the ability of socialist states to defend themselves.

This Committee—whose term would remain unchanged—would at the same time be open to any European socialist state that would want to participate.

2. The creation of a military defense committee—as the military organ of the Treaty—with a minister of defense from each member-state who is accountable to the government and the supreme commander of each country.

3. In order to strengthen its democratic character, we suggest that the work of the Political Consultative Committee of the socialist states in Europe be based on the principle of an annual rotation of the chairmanship. Additionally, we recommend that the chairmanship of the military defense committee also be based on the principle of an annual rotation, whereby each participating state is guaranteed the opportunity to serve as chair.

4. In connection with the current agreement, according to which the supreme commander serves for 4–5 years, we believe it is important that, in future, senior officers from member-states hold this function for 2 years at a time on a rotating basis, or even for 1 year.

In this connection, appointing a supreme commander from representatives or other officers selected for this function by their governments could be considered.

As before, the chief of staff should be chosen for an interval of 4–6 years.

Soviet officers could serve the function of chief of staff for multiple terms, provided that the governments of the other states are also in agreement.

Additionally, it is important to improve the organization and function of other military organs.

The Central Committee of the Romanian Communist Party believes that the adoption of these suggestions will further strengthen general cooperation among our parties and countries in achieving national plans and programs for socio-economic development and in increasing the strength of and respect for socialism worldwide, as well as in the struggle for disarmament, security and peace.

Central Committee of
the Romanian Communist Party

Bucharest, July 4, 1988

[*Source: DY/30/2355, SAPMO. Translated by Catherine Nielsen.*]

b) Information from the CPSU CC to
  the Central Committees of the Warsaw Pact
  Member-States,
  July 8, 1988

As agreed with the Soviet leadership, we are forwarding to you the following strict-ly confidential information.

On July 4 [1988] the Romanian leadership addressed a request to us for bilateral consultations to discuss the proposal "On the democratization and improvement of the organization and functioning of the Warsaw Treaty organs." The content of this proposal was not made public.

Although we consider all questions regarding the functioning of the Warsaw Treaty organs an issue of concern to all member-states, the CPSU CC approved consulta-tions, bearing in mind their strictly preliminary status. The consultations took place in Moscow on July 7–8 [1988]. On the Soviet side, Cdes. E[duard] Shevardnadze and V[adim] Medvedev[11] took part, and on the Romanian side, Political Executive Committee member and Secretary of the CC of the RCP I. Coman, who acted as a special representative of the secretary general of the RCP.

Coman forwarded [to the Soviet representatives] letters from Cde. N[icolae] Ceaușescu to Cde. M[ikhail] Gorbachev and the CC of the CPSU, which contained Romanian proposals for improvement of the functioning of the Warsaw Treaty. Coman announced that, on Ceaușescu's initiative, these proposals were considered and approved by the Political Executive Committee of the CC of the RCP. (According to mass media reports regarding the Political Executive Committee of the CC of the RCP session on the July 1 [1988], the intent was to present these proposals at the forthcoming session of the Political Consultative Committee in Warsaw.)

The Romanian proposals suggest:

1. Taking the PCC out of the Warsaw Treaty [structure] and transforming it into a Political Consultative Committee of the European Socialist States, which should be open to any European socialist state. This new body would deal primarily with questions of mutual cooperation between the parties and the member-states in the political and economic fields. It should not be connected to the Warsaw Treaty.

2. Creating a military committee on defense, which would become the military organ of the Warsaw Treaty. It should unite ministers of defense from the allied states, who would report on this organ's activities to the governments and the com-manders-in-chief of their respective states.

3. Introducing the annual rotation principle for the chair of the "Political Cons-ultative Committee of the European Socialist States," as well as for the military com-mittee on defense.

4. Introducing the principle of rotation—every 1–2 years—for the supreme com-mander of the Unified Armed Forces instead of the current practice of appointing him for a term of 4–6 years. The supreme commander should be a high-ranking officer from one of the member-states.

---

[11] Vadim Medvedev was a CC secretary and adviser to Gorbachev on East European affairs.

5. Once the governments of the member-states agree, having the chief of staff of the Unified Armed Forces be, as he is now, a Soviet officer appointed for a 4–6 year term.

In the course of the consultations Coman said that the essence of the Romanian proposals is the intention to bolster the substantive agenda of the PCC, considering the crucial changes that have taken place in the international situation. In the circumstances of the incipient process of arms reduction, the Warsaw Treaty is still a predominantly military alliance, whereas the RCP promotes PCC activities focused on the economic, political and social issues of the future while not denying [the importance] of military issues. According to Romanian opinion, the PCC should not be directly connected to the Warsaw Treaty, which should nevertheless be preserved as well.

In the reorganized PCC, according to the view of the Romanian comrades, no defense ministers from the member-states will participate. Nevertheless, Coman could not explain what would actually be changed in the way the PCC is organized, since discussions of military issues will still take place there.

He said that while working on the proposals regarding the military structure of the Warsaw Treaty, they [the Romanians] were considering the efficacy of the work of the military organs with a view toward ensuring substantive discussion of matters of the highest priority.

The Soviet side stated that the Romanian proposals would be studied. At the same time, it was reiterated that the USSR seeks to improve of the work of the PCC, broaden the range of issues discussed, and improve the organizational structure of the alliance by creating a permanent working organ connected with the PCC.

Attention was paid to the fact that the activities of the Warsaw Treaty and its highest organ, the PCC, have never been limited to discussion of military problems. Lately, the range of non-military issues discussed by the PCC has considerably increased. For example, at the Berlin PCC session, at the initiative of the Romanian comrades, a document on overcoming under-development was accepted. During the forthcoming session in Warsaw, we plan to discuss problems of ecology. As for military issues, we mostly discuss arms reduction. Consequently, nothing prevents the PCC from being instrumental in developing cooperation among the fraternal parties and states in the political, economic and social fields.

It was said that since the Romanian proposals need to be considered carefully and on a collective basis, it would hardly be possible to discuss them and make respective decisions at the forthcoming PCC session.

We reiterated that we see improvement of the efficacy of Warsaw Treaty activities as a common objective for the allied states. We also reiterated that the style of the meetings within the framework of the Warsaw Treaty has significantly changed within the past years; global questions of European and world security have been raised, the allied states have presented initiatives to the U.N., and presentations to other international forums are being considered.

There are various options available with regard to improving the efficacy of the Warsaw Treaty. Nevertheless, we should avoid radical decisions. We should consider any structural changes very carefully, so as not to undermine our position in negotiations [with the West].

Once again we have drawn the attention [of the Romanians] to the fact that creating a permanent working organ connected with the PCC could be quite useful. This new working organ would, along with other functions, control the functioning of the Warsaw Treaty mechanism, as well as the initiative of the Romanian comrades and other possible proposals from other allied socialist states.

Existing institutions of the Warsaw Treaty are starting to work more actively; the mechanism of the allied states for making common decisions on important international issues is working as well.

We paid special attention to the fact that improvement of both the military and the political mechanisms of the Warsaw Treaty is a strictly confidential, internal matter for our alliance. It is important that discussion on these questions stay within the framework of the alliance. We expressed our hope that the Romanian proposals would not become a subject of public discussion. Coman said to that that the Romanian side understands that questions of the functioning of the Warsaw Treaty are internal and should not arise outside the [alliance's] framework.

An analysis of the Romanian proposals, as well as of Coman's remarks during the consultation, allows us to make the following preliminary conclusions about the nature of Ceauşescu's proposals.

It is obvious that there an intent to reorganize the Warsaw Treaty by separating political functions from the military ones, and taking the PCC out of the Warsaw Treaty framework and converting it into a consultative body of European socialist states on matters of political and economic cooperation. As a result, the Warsaw Treaty would acquire a solely military character, which means that the result that the Romanian side is now formally opposing would be accomplished.

The proposed reorganization of the Warsaw Treaty Committee of the Ministers of Defense into a military defense committee aims at changing the existing order by providing for collective decisions on military development and the common use of armed forces in war time.

Proposals concerning the rotation of the chairmanship of the military defense committee and the post of the supreme commander aim at weakening the existing system of the alliance's military organization.

We do not exclude the possibility that Ceauşescu will want to present his proposals during the forthcoming PCC summit in Warsaw. In this case we are considering the possibility of suggesting that the Committees of the Ministers of Defense and of the Ministers of Foreign affairs consider the Romanian proposals at a joint session and report on the results to the PCC.

In his letter to Gorbachev, Ceauşescu expressed a wish to present his proposals together with the Soviet side. However, Coman did not raise this question during the consultation. For our part, we did not mention it either.

[*Source: Fond 1b, opis 35, a.e. pp. 88–108, TsDA. Translated by Anya Jouravel.*]

Document No. 134: Summary of Gorbachev's Speech at the Committee of Ministers of Defense Meeting in Moscow, July 7, 1988

Gorbachev's previously unpublished speeches at Warsaw Pact meetings, such as this one before a gathering of defense ministers, offer an enlightening glimpse of the behind-the-scenes context in which events during this period were taking place, and provide new evidence on Soviet leadership thinking. In this address, Gorbachev outlines his vision of a Warsaw Pact with significant differences from what the organization was before. One of the key new features he foresees is that each member-state will be "independently active." In effect, he is allowing other members to follow their own policies. But, contrary to the belief held by many in the West in later years that he was actively encouraging reform, he was not. As this speech and other documents demonstrate, he was largely indifferent about it. His main interest was to disengage the Soviet Union from excessively burdensome obligations in Eastern Europe.

Cde. Gorbachev [...] emphasized that the work of the committee testifies to the increased activity of the Warsaw Treaty. After the Committee of the Ministers of Foreign Affairs, the Committee of the Ministers of Defense is now also proving how the alliance has entered a stage of quite some dynamics. This is good, and it is all right that the alliance has agreed to become more active in all directions. This has proved successful since it guarantees the best option for our decision-making.

[...]

Each party is responsible for its own affairs and fulfills its tasks on its own. There will be no toleration of attempts not to respect each other, or to interfere with the domestic matters of others.

We now have a new situation. During the last three years we faced many problems, which we can only solve by way of exchanging opinions.

Our parties inform each other about their most important projects. Altogether we can testify that a new level of cooperation has been reached.

[...]

I received documents from the United States proving that the United States is not afraid of weapons. They know that we can mutually destroy each other. However, they are afraid that the Soviet Union could achieve a new quality by means of a restructuring [*perestroika*] of society. Therefore they will do everything to continue the arms race.

In Toronto, Reagan and Kohl have expressed the opinion that the old means of fighting socialism will no longer be appropriate in the future. Cde. Kessler knows this very well since the GDR is following this development very closely.

Now they try to discredit us by discussing environmental problems. The adversary wants to divide our society in order to thwart *perestroika*.

[...]

He [Reagan] behaved preposterously and shamelessly in Moscow. For instance, he met with former supporters of the fascists. Since the mass media report everything back to the United States, he soon had to correct himself. He also had to change his opinion about the "evil empire." The people of the United States, for the first time, saw Russians live on their TV screens. This had an impact on the whole of public opinion in the United States.

Still we have to be concerned about our defense, and should not give in to illusions. We have to strengthen defense even when people all over the world campaign for a political solution to problems.

The adversary seeks to gain influence on people through the mass media. The GDR, e.g., continuously feels this pressure. Therefore we have to discuss whether it would make sense to create a political institution at the Unified Command. I would like to ask you to consult with the general secretaries on this issue. We should not defend ourselves only politically and through propaganda, but should also move onto the attack on a political–ideological level. Though we sometimes do attack, we do not carry it out professionally enough.

We have made great progress in our policy.

With regard to the negotiations between the Soviet Union and the United States, I want to announce that Reagan would be ready for a fifth meeting. However, both the candidates for president, [George] Bush and [Michael] Dukakis, have written to me, indicating I should not finalize an agreement with Reagan.

We have suggested publishing the numbers of forces. The Americans and the NATO states, however, reject this although they talk about our superiority. We are looking for compromises based on equality in order to enable military–political comparisons.

Military cooperation between our armies depends on the level of cooperation between our parties and states. Certain circles introduce into the discussion [the question of] withdrawing Soviet troops from certain countries.

Confidentially, I want to tell you that currently it is certainly not the right moment to discuss the withdrawal of Soviet troops here and there.

Sometimes unpleasant things happen in Hungary, sometimes in the GDR. The question of a pull-out should therefore not be raised.

The adversary knows that the Group of Soviet Forces [in Germany] is a stabilizing force. Our troops have the closest relationship with the people in the GDR. However, they are on the ideological front line since they are exposed almost daily to ideological attacks by the adversary's mass media. [...]

In this way, we have to consider that we [Warsaw Pact member-states] share a common fate.

[*Source: DVW 1/71049, BA-MA. Translated by Karen Riechert.*]

Document No. 135: Speech by Gorbachev at the Political Consultative Committee Meeting in Warsaw, July 15, 1988

Speaking to the PCC, Gorbachev by this time has begun to develop more fully some of his ideas about reducing world tensions, armament levels, and especially mutual hostility between the two major military groupings. His remarks represent something of a dress rehearsal, or perhaps an internal justification, for his famous speech at the United Nations on December 7.[12] Among the many interesting comments he makes are references to the growing power of the European Community, which he says the Soviet Union had made a mistake in underestimating, to the necessity of building bridges with the new American administration after the difficult Reagan years, and to the paramount need to reduce not only nuclear but also conventional weapons—the only "usable" ones in a conflict.

[...]

[Recent developments] allow Socialism to be included more broadly and actively in the formulation of world politics, and to influence it more effectively and in a multi-faceted way, stimulating positive changes throughout the world.

Above all, the new face of Socialism now taking shape will undermine the traditional pretenses of the Western right-wing circles in exerting their dominating influence in the world, an influence which they have maintained with the help of an image of the enemy as a "Communist totalitarian monster." The conservative front that emerged in the West during the 1980s and was openly hostile toward Socialism, has begun to erode.

Being realists, we cannot wait—as if for manna from heaven—for new administrations to take over the helm in the West, with new partners and more democratic alternatives; but, in fact, we can facilitate the possibility that such alternatives will appear.

There is, for example, something of a paradox in the fact that, although several leading West European government figures maintain, shall we say, an even more reserved position in relation to the Socialist countries than does the United States, the business community of Western Europe, on the other hand, is beginning to come to us as if over the heads of the politicians.

[...]

A great deal will be determined by how and where the process of West European integration acquires its power. For the foreseeable future, it is apparently a steady and pivotal direction of development for this part of the continent.

[...]

We must openly admit that we were slow to determine the power and effectiveness of Western integration. We were lulled by the gentle sounds of [our] skeptical

---

[12] For the text of the speech, see *Vital Speeches of the Day* 55, no. 9 (February 1, 1989).

pronouncements about the difficulties and hypocrisies in the European Economic Community.

[...]

In the meantime, 1992 is not far off, when the formation of a single market for goods, services, and capital will give birth—judging by all appearances—to a qualitatively new structure of Western Europe, one that is not only economic, but also political and possibly military in nature.

To the west of our Pact's border, there is a new giant developing, one with a population of 350 million people, which surpasses us in its level and rate of economic, scientific, and technical growth.

We could hardly say that we are indifferent to the political direction this process is taking, or to the forces which will predominate there—right-wing, conservative or moderate—or to its military tendencies and how strong they turn out to be.

Under these conditions, we feel the demand for our own "European" action plan. It should be a goal of the internal development of our country, and at the same time, it would be a realistic and attractive one for the broad social forces of all of Europe.

The concept of a "common European house" would seem to be the answer.

[...]

The construction of a "European house" might include, for example, a pan-Balkan cooperative community, where Bulgaria and Romania would actively participate. Similar arenas of cooperation might be the Baltic states as well as central Europe.

Finally, an important element in this concept is the building of bridges between the Warsaw Pact states and NATO, the gradual transformation of the relationship between them from a source of tension to one of fundamental stability in Europe.

This is essentially because a fear is being expressed in the West: behind the idea of a "European house": isn't there a hidden attempt to break up NATO, to "excommunicate" the U.S. from Europe? We take the position that Europe today is an inseparable part of the integral world, connected to the other continents by thousands of threads. This is reality.

But reality is something else, too: the special position of Europe, where a unique structure is being erected, one of interaction between two social systems. One is not swallowed up by the other, there is no fusion of the two—would be utopia—but precisely an interaction, a cooperation, the fabric of which would become stronger and stronger.

In this connection, we repudiate any argument about "overcoming the legacy of Yalta." We call for respect for national sovereignty in the European community, of combined territorial–political realities created by the people in their choice of social structure.

The concept of a "common European house" it seems, requires not only theoretical comprehension but also a practical revamping of the program for constructing all the "walls" of this house—military, political, economic and humanitarian.

Now, in the first stage of European—in fact, global—politics, the problem of reducing armaments and armed forces has arisen. Without a solution to this problem, it will be impossible to diminish the level of military opposition in Europe and to move forward toward a world without nuclear weapons. However, any steps in this direc-

608

tion are being blocked by the West by making reference to our superiority in conventional armaments.

Moreover, it is precisely in this area that those who adhere to power politics count on imposing an arms race based on modern technology, hoping to wear us down and thereby provide themselves with the advantage.

In negotiations with Reagan in Moscow, we attempted to arrive at a detailed conversation with NATO on European disarmament through the US administration, to accelerate the coordination of a mandate for negotiations.

While developing our general principles worked out in Budapest and Berlin,[13] we presented the Americans with a three-step plan for reducing weapons and armed forces in Europe. You already know about this plan. These suggestions might become the key to solving the problem.

Our general staffs have made an accounting of the number of troops in the Warsaw Pact states and in the NATO member-states, and the relationship between them in Europe. Included in the accounting are naval forces active in European waters and areas of the ocean adjoining the continent.

What does the gist of this information tell us? The number of personnel in our armed forces in Europe is approximately equal, with each side having 3.6 million people.

The Warsaw Pact countries have a greater number in Central Europe and NATO has a greater number in Southern Europe. As for tanks, we have a distinct advantage, 2:1. But when it comes to tactical air force strikes, the ratio is 1:1.8 in favor of NATO. So the configuration of forces is complex.

The West regularly publishes its figures on NATO and on Warsaw Pact countries and uses these in their propaganda. It is obvious that we should also promulgate our evaluation. It will show the actual ratio of forces.

In addition, the data for the upcoming round of negotiations have been prepared, according to the mandate being worked out in Vienna. We have these data already. As you know, we are the ones who suggested to NATO to exchange such data now, before the negotiations, but they didn't take us up on the idea.

It is possible to do that later. After all, in the final analysis, it is important to provide for constructive interaction during the negotiations themselves, to achieve a compromise and solution to one of the central military–political questions of our time.

And now about the negotiations themselves with the NATO countries. I think there is the possibility of structuring our approach in a detailed, step-by-step fashion, taking into account changes and variations in the positions taken by our western partners.

We recently gained unique experiences in fruitful dialogue in the area of security. I include here the actual document, Agreement on intermediate-range and long-range missiles,[14] and the genuine progress on strategic weapons, as well as Stock-

---

[13] See documents nos. 115 and 123.

[14] The INF Treaty between the United States of America and the Union of Soviet Socialist Republics on the Elimination of Their Intermediate-Range and Shorter-Range Missiles, signed in Washington on December 8, 1987.

holm-I.[15] Some of these lessons can be used in the discussions on conventional weapons as well.

This means establishing, early on, final ceilings for weapons and forces for both sides and determining concrete time limits for the corresponding mutual reductions.

Later, this will also mean a minimum of various "links", maintaining a good negotiating pace and establishing priorities. In particular, it might be possible to propose to NATO members separating the most troublesome imbalances of both sides and occupying oneself with eliminating them in a rather short period of time, say, within a year or two.

Finally, it is worth taking a close look at the positions held by our western partners, to analyze them without prejudice.

It makes sense for all of us to confer with each other about actions in cases of delays in the negotiations by the West. What could be their hesitancy in taking the initial steps? They are needed, moreover, to carry out the data inspections we suggested in the huge expanse from the Atlantic to the Urals—a rather complex task.

And this approach could be used by those who would like to drag their feet. In no way can we afford to make the mistake of the fourteen fruitless polemics about Central Europe.[16] Time is of the essence today. Are we in a position to somehow forestall, to avoid an undesirable turn of events? It is possible.

The proposal to create a Center for Military Threat Reduction in Europe is aimed at exactly this issue. We could say that this idea has been bandied about already. In essence it would be a first step, working hand in hand with the West toward the creation of a mutual structure of security and trust, aimed at averting surprise attacks on the European continent, that would—and this is important—transcend both blocs. We see the possibility of attracting the participation not only of the NATO and Warsaw Pact countries, but also of neutral and non-aligned European governments. The joint Center would serve to avoid and eliminate emergency situations. Within the framework of this Center it would be possible to agree on and then publish data on the armed forces of both sides as well as organize a system to check these data.

Along these same lines is our proposal to reduce our air forces located in the Warsaw Pact countries, if Washington agrees not to relocate F-16s[17] from Spain to Italy.

Of course, it is preferable to have mutually agreed upon, balanced reductions in arms and armed forces; but we should not, apparently, also reject the possibility of taking preventive steps—it goes without saying to the extent that they do not threaten our general security and at the same time yield a tangible political gain.

What exactly are we talking about? During the next two to three years, we are proposing to examine the question of changes in the organizational structure of the armed forces in the Warsaw Pact countries, moving them more in the direction of defense, certainly. And in Central Europe as well, in a word, [the question is] about reducing them in full agreement with the military defense doctrine, which we have

[15] The CSCE Conference on Confidence- and Security-Building Measures and Disarmament in Europe, concluded on September 19, 1986.

[16] The reference is to the inconclusive MBFR negotiations on mutual and balanced reductions of conventional forces in Europe.

[17] The F-16 Fighting Falcon fighter aircraft.

worked out together. From our point of view, the security of the Warsaw Pact countries will not suffer. But there will be a certain political gain.

We invite the West to have a dialogue with us on one of the key questions of European stability, that of the change in operational structure of the first echelons of the Warsaw Pact counties and NATO.

We propose the transformation of their structure and removal strictly in accordance with the requirements of defense, i.e. to limit the functions of Warsaw Pact and NATO troops, each group on its own territory.

In our view, it is expedient to plan out the possibility of decreasing the number of forces and basic types of weaponry of the Warsaw Pact member-states in Central Europe.

As our military personnel see it, at this stage, the conversation might turn to the reformulation of units and formations of approximately 70,000 troops with corresponding weapons and military technology, including tanks and artillery.

Exactly which troops would undergo reformulation based on their relocation and nationality is yet to be determined—jointly, of course. It follows that this question would be worked out in coordination with corresponding steps from NATO.

The concrete proposals of Poland, East Germany, Czechoslovakia and Hungary, aimed at avoiding a surprise attack; reducing troop concentrations in Central Europe; strengthening trust; and developing good-neighborly relationships and cooperation are a good basis for the conversation under consideration.

Close coordination of our complementary efforts is the guarantee of their successful results. Moreover, now the conversation is about troops and weapons of our entire union, of each member of the Pact. And here we must carefully weigh the communication for the measures we have suggested, to jointly work through not only their political aspect but also their military–technical aspect.

In order to study the whole set of questions connected with implementing the measures proposed earlier and with a study of possible steps for the future, I imagine that it would be useful to hold a joint session of committees with the ministers of foreign affairs and ministers of defense, if possible, in autumn this year. Before that, experts could work on it in earnest.

As you know, based on our experience of negotiating with Americans, we presented a proposal in the Polish Parliament for a kind of "European Reykjavik"—a call for a meeting of all the European countries on the highest level, with the U.S. and Canada participating, of course, in order to discuss the question of reducing conventional troops and weapons in Europe.

I think that this suggestion itself—and moreover the call for this proposed meeting as well as all the steps we have undertaken for the future as a whole—would make sense not only in the military–strategic area but also in the greater, general political arena.

There would be a rise in the level of trust toward the line taken by the Warsaw Pact governments in international matters; the image of the enemy as cultivated in the West would be undermined; and we would clearly see "who's who" when it comes to arms reduction. The two sides' positions would become obvious for the community as a whole and would not be hidden behind the curtains of the negotiations nor drown in a labyrinth of details.

Genuine support would come from those forces—political, societal—which strive to strengthen cooperation with us and which search for various ways to create systems of "non-offensive defense."

The practical steps for lowering the level of military opposition may be more successful when non-military components for international cooperation and security are expanded more actively.

And the first order of business here is the development of a broad political dialogue on constructive and stable political relationships among the governments of both parts of Europe.

This could be facilitated by giving regularity within the all-European process to the meetings of foreign ministers, who have thus far been meeting more or less "accidentally." The proposal of our Hungarian comrades takes us in that direction.

The all-European process would be stimulated by implementing the program worked out by the Socialist Unity Party of [East] Germany and the Social Democratic Party of [West] Germany, a program which they took to the participants in the Helsinki process[18] in order to create a trust and security zone in Central Europe.

[...]

Thus it would be worthwhile weighing, for example, the expediency of putting forth a large-scale idea to convert at least part of the military industry of the Warsaw Pact and NATO countries into producing equipment, machinery, and materials intended to preserve and renew the environment, and to maintain the health and lives of millions of people. This would be something worthy of the humanistic tradition of Europe. And it would be appropriate for Socialism to take the position of an initiator and leader.

The development of relations with the governments of the West presumes the development of humanitarian contacts as well. On this topic, our western partners have long seen a weak spot in us. This in itself has been facilitated by our avoiding serious conversation about human rights and, at times—we must be honest here— our dogmatic position, as if Socialism had not already achieved its goals, and had limits in the area of civil rights and freedoms.

The development of the democratization process, the rise in the political and overall culture of the masses; and the achievement of socialist relations within societies change matters in a fundamental way. We have the opportunity to demonstrate more convincingly the unjustifiable pretension on the part of the NATO governments to their role as mentor when it comes to human rights, the opportunity to carry on a dialogue about humanitarian problems, not using confrontation, but through realistic cooperation.

It is also important that these questions not become obstacles to the successful conclusion of the Vienna meeting, that they not provide NATO members with a way to block the beginning of negotiations on conventional weapons.

Of course, we have not allowed anyone to preach at us, nor to meddle in our internal affairs. But we approach the matter with the understanding that humanitarian

[18] The CSCE.

problems, human rights—these are subjects of legal concern to the entire world community.

[...]

And to conclude. The development of cooperation in the framework of the Warsaw Pact and the new questions confronting us make it necessary to substantially increase collective political thought and, possibly, to have our countries create a kind of research "think tank" for international issues.

We would consider it useful to adjust the process for holding qualified discussions on issues in world politics; and to conduct concrete, systematic analysis of the interaction of general human and social class interests and contradictions applicable to the tasks facing our Pact group.

We are for organizing shared information in international affairs. It would be useful, say, to have multi-faceted research done on the changes in the balance of European and world powers, and on the outlook for European integration, its military aspects and its probable consequences for the Warsaw Pact, as well as the possible steps on our part. We hope that scientists and experts in our countries can work together—of course, those who want to participate.

And, on the same subject, a wider variety of research institutes has appeared in the NATO countries, analyzing the prospects for development in Europe and the world. Even with all the conditions of their prognoses, they contain useful reference points.

It seems sensible to us for our internationalists to confidently make contact with them, to present initiatives based on joint research, and to discuss vital world and regional problems of our time

Our Polish comrades have presented an initiative for creating a parliamentary group, uniting representatives from the upper legislative bodies of our governments. It seems this initiative is worth supporting: with the growth of political activity in the Warsaw Pact governments, there will also be a growth in the significance of the work elucidating the essential direction of that work and of individual initiatives by Pact governments on the parliamentary level.

[...]

And lastly, the sooner we can confirm that providing security will be transferred more and more often from the area of correlating military potentials to the area of politics, the sooner the accompanying development will need the infrastructure of our Pact. It is, after all, a living political entity.

The consistency we have achieved in the work of the Political Consultative Committee and in that of the committee of foreign ministers and defense ministers; the active work on other levels, including the information group and the commission on the disarmament question—all of this allows us to influence conditions in Europe and the world more effectively. It is obvious that we must continue to move further in this direction.

While not giving up the Pact's rather broad and flexible positions, of course, in general it seems, the time has come to somehow "take inventory" of the workings of the Pact—both political and military—to see what would be worth changing here, or correcting or revising in accordance with the new realities found in Europe and the

613

world, using the expediency of fuller and more active participation by all the Pact's member-states.

Taking into consideration the importance of the matter, it might be possible to charge the committees of the foreign ministers and defense ministers with reviewing these questions at a joint session in autumn of this year, and to present the results to the Political Consultative Committee.

Qualitative changes in our mutually agreed-upon activities within the framework of the Pact reflect positive movement in the development of Socialism. Remaining like a shield guarding the peaceful work of our peoples, our Pact, it can be said, has become politicized, and is gaining momentum across a broad spectrum in the safeguarding of security.

[*Source: f. 1-B, op. 35, a.e. 88–111, TsDA. Translated by Paul Spitzer for the National Security Archive.*]

Document No. 136: Summary of Discussion among Defense Ministers at the Political Consultative Committee Meeting in Warsaw, July 15, 1988

As part of this discussion among Warsaw Pact defense ministers, the issue of sharing military data with NATO receives further attention. By this time, the internal debate has changed significantly (see Document No. 130, for example). Soviet Defense Minister Iazov specifically declares that the East must be truthful in its reporting because the enemy knows the real figures, down to the order of tens of thousands of men and thousands of tanks. If less or more were published, he argues, the Warsaw Pact would be open to accusations of lying before all humankind. One cannot keep anything secret anymore, he opines. He also admits that the Soviet Union maintained 2 percent of its population under arms, whereas other countries had only 1 percent. On the subject of existing international military structures, he reminds his colleagues that they date back to the 1950s on the Warsaw Pact side. This prompts a debate between various allied representatives present over the proper pace of changing those structures.

[...]

The first speaker, Comrade Minister [Dmitrii] Iazov, explained that the forces of NATO and the Warsaw Pact are more or less evenly balanced. The number of persons is approximately equal. The Warsaw Pact has about 30,000 more tanks, but the NATO tanks are of better quality. The Warsaw Pact has more launch pads for non-nuclear tactical missiles. Also, as regards artillery, the relation is about 1.2:1. But the USA has more aircraft. Their superiority in helicopters and anti-tank weapons balances out our superiority in tanks and artillery. However, the Americans put quantity first.

Neither side is in a position to begin an attack without major regrouping.

The USA claims, however, that our formations are attack formations. They point to the equipment of our pioneer troops with bridges and our superiority in tanks and artillery as proof.

They demand a unilateral correction of the asymmetries in land forces.

They are unwilling to negotiate the inequalities in attack aircraft, helicopters and naval fleets.

[...]

An inadequately prepared publication of the figures would be considered by the West Germans and Americans as a victory for their side. For this reason, it must be thoroughly prepared politically, so that we do not suffer a loss in prestige.

[...]

The publicized data must be objective, since the opponent knows our figures down to the level of c. 10,000 men and 1,000 tanks.

If we publicize less, their intelligence will notice it and accuse us of lying before the entire world.

Similarly, if we publicize more than we have, in order to minimize what we are lacking, the figures will be checked on the spot and our deception will be exposed before the eyes of the world. We can no longer hide anything.

[...]

Again: the figures must be exact. If you agree, then we can decide what to put into storage.

We should prepare the data in the months of August and September and come to an agreement about publication of the total figures in October.

The following speaker was Comrade Minister [Heinz] Kessler. He expressed his agreement in principle with the explanation of Comrade Minister Iazov. He pointed out that, once the figures submitted by the Warsaw Pact had been gone over once again, it was up to the Committee of the Ministers of Defense to decide about their publication. At the same time, he emphasized that the assignment of groups to theaters of war must not be changed and that this is not the time to discuss the withdrawal of the Soviet army groups.

Comrade Minister [Milan] Václavík voiced his agreement and called for charging the Army generals with the task of going over the data. Structural changes should not be undertaken hastily, but rather be realized gradually, taking into account the direction of the operations of the individual armies as well as of the opposing army. Divisions are needed that are in a position to act independently, without the assignment of different units for cover.

A reduction of the armed forces must not harm the Warsaw Pact in any way. In estimating the individual types of weapon the principle of sufficiency must be applied, in cooperation with the staff of the Unified Armed Forces.

[...]

Comrade Minister [Ferenc] Kárpáti pointed out that in view of a new rethinking of the division of the European theaters of war, thorough preparation of the data was very important. Comrade [Károly] Grósz, he said, had already raised this question before the Political Consultative Committee.

In working out the structures, the strength of the opposing groups must be taken into consideration. The Hungarian People's Army has begun reorganizing its units and has changed to the brigade system, which, however, is not yet regarded as the final solution.

[...]

Comrade Minister [Vasile] Milea observed that the solution of these questions is very important for all countries. He suggested that commissions on the question of publicizing the data should be formed in the armies. For the development and equipment of individual armies and decisions about structures, the geographic conditions of each country must be taken into account.

[...]

Army General [Anatolii] Gribkov pointed out once again that the data to be publicized are total figures and not information according to theaters of war and countries.

The operational plans must be reworked on the basis of the commitments made in connection with the Military Doctrine of the member-states of the Warsaw Pact,

616

on the agreed-upon dates. A change in organizational structures should only be undertaken gradually.

In conclusion, Comrade Minister [Florian] Siwicki summarized the meeting by saying that all participants were of the opinion that the data on the Warsaw Pact should only be publicized after the Committee of the Ministers of Defense has checked the figures and confirmed them.

The leading role should be played by the USSR, since it assesses these questions on a global scale. But each country must make its contribution.

The propaganda machine must be prepared for the publication, to prevent the opponent from exploiting our figures for a new round of the arms race.

The question of the technical equipment of the allied armies is a problem of quality. Therefore, parity must be reached in the area of the quality of military technology.

One should take account of the fact that NATO can translate research and development into production more quickly than the Warsaw Pact.

[*Source: VA-01/40374, BA-MA. Translated by Ursula Froese.*]

Document No. 137: Summary of Discussion at the Committee of Ministers of Defense Meeting in Prague, October 17–18, 1988

The main topic of discussion at this defense ministers' meeting was the Romanian proposal for reform of the Warsaw Pact (see Document No. 133). Most of the ideas proposed in it failed to generate support from the other member-states. For example, there was little interest in abolishing collective decision-making at a time when most of them believed that unilateral arms reductions required even greater coordination within the alliance. During the discussion, according to other records, Soviet Defense Minister Dmitrii Iazov nevertheless conceded, among other points, that the supreme commander did not have to be a Soviet citizen. The prevailing view was that the organization needed improvements in quality and effectiveness, not a new structure altogether.

During the meeting of the Committee of the Ministers of Defense, there was an exchange of views on the suggestions made by the Central Committee of the Romanian Communist Party for "Improvement of the Organization and Democratization of the Work of the Political Bodies of the Warsaw Pact."

The ministers of defense and the supreme commander together with the chiefs of staff of the Unified Armed Forces of the Warsaw Pact member-states expressed agreement on the following points:

In the present military and political situation, it is important that the handling of political and military questions be closely linked.

With regard to improving the work of the Political Consultative Committee, there was unanimous accord (with the exception of the Romanian colleague) that the separation of military and political tasks is not an option.

Political decisions are the basis for any cooperation in military operations or military technology in our alliance.

Only the Political Consultative Committee of the member-states of the Warsaw Pact possesses the necessary competence for the unified performance of political and military functions.

Therefore, it is deemed absolutely necessary to continue the proven practice of handling political and military questions at the meetings of the Political Consultative Committee of the member-states of the Warsaw Pact, and having the supreme commander of the Unified Armed Forces report on them.

[...]

The effectiveness of the Committee of the Ministers of Defense in solving a wide range of problems in connection with improving the defensive capability of the Warsaw Pact states has been confirmed by almost 20 years of experience.

The proposal for reorganizing the Committee of the Minister of Defense to create a "Military Defense Committee" is not considered practical or necessary in the present military and political situation, since it would go against the tried and true principle of collective decision-making in building up the Unified Armed Forces.

[...]

The practice of appointing the supreme commander and the chief of staff of the Unified Armed Forces from the ranks of the Soviet Army has proven practical and useful, and should be continued as far as possible.

The functioning of the Military Council of the Unified Armed Forces as a forum for consultations and recommendations among colleagues has proven advantageous.

[...]

On the other hand, it seems practical and absolutely necessary to expand the functions of the Technical Committee of the Unified Armed Forces to cover all needs of the allied armies as well as the development and production of qualitatively new military technology and weapons.

Our common defense doctrine and also the possibility of arms reductions in some areas (tanks, artillery) make it necessary to pay special attention to this question.

Even now, individual important arms factories are operating at less than their full capacity. One of the contributing factors is the constant rise in prices, which makes the purchase of technology more difficult.

If these arms factories can no longer be used to their full capacity, they should be converted to the production of consumer goods, so that no morale or material damage occurs.

[...]

All in all, the ministers of defense are of the opinion that priority should be given not to creating new organizational structures but rather to improving the quality and effectiveness of the work of the leading bodies of the Unified Armed Forces on the basis of comradeship and equality.

On behalf of the Central Committee of the Romanian Communist Party, Comrade Colonel General [Vasile] Milea, minister of defense of the Socialist Republic of Romania, presented once again the proposal for the "Improvement of the Organization and Democratization of the Work of the Political Bodies of the Warsaw Pact," which had already been brought before the Central Committees of the allied parties.

He particularly underlined the suggestions:

- to reorganize the Political Consultative Committee of the Warsaw Pact states to form a committee, open to "all socialist states of Europe," for the coordination of the political and economic problems facing the socialist states.
- to create a "Military Defense Committee," to which only the ministers of defense should belong
- to shorten the term of office of the supreme commander of the Unified Armed Forces of the Warsaw Pact states to 1–2 years, and to fill it according to the principle of rotation among all member-states of the Warsaw Pact.

Concerning the further improvement of the work of the staff and the leading bodies of the Warsaw Pact, he pointed out that the drafts of the "Defense Guidelines for the Unified Armed Forces of the Member-States of the Warsaw Pact and their Leading Bodies" were unacceptable because:

- they do not take sufficient account of the national rights of member-states to command their own armed forces and prepare their country for self-defense.
- they do not adequately describe the role of the supreme commander of the national armed forces.
- they do not entirely guarantee the sovereignty of the member-states (foreign troops should only be able to operate on foreign territory upon the bilateral agreement of the respective state leaders).

In conclusion, Comrade Minister Milea pointed out that the Central Committee of the Romanian Communist Party was still waiting for an answer to its written communication to the Central Committee of the member parties.

[...]

[Source: DVW 1/71050, BA-MA. Translated by Ursula Froese.]

Document No. 138: East German Evaluation of NATO's
1988 Exercises, November 15, 1988

This report of various Western maneuvers continues in the vein of previous assessments of the threat of a surprise attack. Throughout the 1980s, these fears persisted, encouraged by NATO's growing ability to stop advancing enemy forces by swift air attacks to their rear, and by events such as NATO's "Able Archer 83" exercise which was meant to simulate the release of nuclear weapons, but because of its use of encrypted codes could have been misread as an indication that a surprise attack might be forthcoming. During the Gorbachev period, the Warsaw Pact continued to upgrade, including maritime operations forces such as would have been needed to counter "Team Work 88," analyzed below. Within a month, however, Gorbachev would address the United Nations with a radical plan to reduce troop strength in Europe.

[...]

1. Our estimate has been confirmed that NATO aims to achieve a favorable relationship between the intended surprise and the strong offensive forces necessary for a successful conventional war in Central Europe.

On the one hand, under the cover of exercises across almost the entire front, approximately 40 percent of combat-ready units were deployed within 24 hours.

On the other hand, 41,000 troops stationed in the Netherlands and Belgium were transferred to the FRG; and the NATO armed forces in Central Europe and the Baltic region were, within a period of 5 to 8 days, reinforced with 70,000 mobilized troops and strategic reserves.

As a result, NATO has proven its increased capability to make available relatively covertly within 10 days enough military force for its main theater of war during a conventional war.

The air force has proven that, as a part of NATO's forces, it could begin a war within 12 to 24 hours with a massive surprise attack.

The navy exercise "Team Work 88" demonstrated that NATO is in a position to bring the bulk of its fleet into position in 5 days and intervene in a land battle.

2. During the fall exercises, a stronger shift towards conventional warfare was clearly noticeable.

In all exercises, the offensive forces predominated.

[...]

3. The close connection between strategic forces during the exercises as well as the goals and results clearly demonstrate that the strategic operations of NATO's forces in Central Europe are increasingly characterized by land-air warfare.

[...]

The air force was responsible for offensive operations into the depth of Warsaw Pact territory.

[...]

NATO counts on rendering the Warsaw Pact's operational airfields useless for 6 to 8 hours and destroying on the ground the aircraft that have been diverted to secondary and less well defended airfields.

[...]

4. The naval exercises were coordinated even more closely [than before] with the land and air exercises and, particularly in the Baltic and Norwegian Seas, fully integrated with them.

The sea operations were characterized by the "maritime forward strategy." The essence of this strategy is the rapid achievement of naval supremacy in the Atlantic and its adjacent seas by cutting off and destroying the Warsaw Pact navies at their bases.

[...]

5. Training in the use of nuclear weapons during the NATO's Supreme Headquarters Allied Forces Europe exercise "Able Archer 88"[19] was limited to a selective first and second strike. With a selective first and second strike, the NATO states would use the threat of nuclear war to force the Warsaw Pact to surrender. NATO hopes that a cease-fire with one of the socialist states would have the long-term effect of breaking up the community of socialist states.

Chemical weapons would also be used in conventional warfare for tactical and operational reasons.

[...]

Conclusions

– NATO continues to practice each fall the deployment of massive military forces in exercise areas near the border, thereby producing an acute military threat that violates the spirit of the Stockholm Accord.[20]

   At the same time, NATO is shifting towards exercise methods that allow for possible broader confidence-building measures, or achieve approximately the same goals with fewer participants.

– The growing complexity of the exercises, their growing mutual coordination, the training of the staff and troops at the army group level and the more effective incorporation of territorial forces, civilian officials and organizations in the fall exercises allow NATO to test its offensive plans in a more realistic fashion and make their implementation more effective.

[...]

[Source: VA-01/39538, BA-MA. Translated by Catherine Nielsen.]

---

[19] For details of the exercise, which by simulating the release of nuclear weapons led to Soviet belief that NATO's surprise attack might be forthcoming, see "NATO's 'Able Archer 83' Exercise and the 1983 Soviet War Scare," on the PHP website, http://www.isn.ethz.ch/php/collections/coll_17.htm.

[20] The "Document of the Stockholm Conference on Confidence- and Security-Building Measures and Disarmament in Europe," of September 19, 1986, provided for compulsory notification of large movements of troops, among other provisions.

Document No. 139: Record of Conversation between Erich Honecker and the East German Defense Minister December 4, 1988

Three days before Mikhail Gorbachev's United Nations speech (see Document no. 135), GDR leader Erich Honecker describes for his defense minister, Heinz Kessler, a conversation he has just had with Soviet Ambassador Viacheslav Kochemasov about the new directions of Soviet policy. The Soviet leadership has concluded that arms cutbacks based on reciprocity with the West are not feasible, therefore the Warsaw Pact must make unilateral reductions, as long as they do not affect defense readiness. Furthermore, the Soviets imply these cuts should take place before the next round of conventional force reduction talks (CFE) in Vienna, otherwise those talks will lead nowhere. The Soviet ambassador pointed out that even after reductions that have already been made, there are still 170,000 more Warsaw Pact than NATO troops in Central Europe. He then informs Honecker that unless there are objections the Soviets plan to withdraw four army regiments, plus a number of tanks and other units not needed for the GDR's defense. Honecker agrees, although he has reason to be worried.

On behalf of the general secretary of the CPSU CC and chairman of the Presidium of the Supreme Soviet, Cde. Mikhail Gorbachev, the extraordinary and plenipotentiary ambassador of the Soviet Union in the GDR, Cde. [Viacheslav] Kochemasov, informed the general secretary of the Central Committee of the SED and chairman of the National Defense Council, Cde. Erich Honecker, on Sunday, December 4, 1988 about a resolution by the party and state leadership of the Soviet Union applying the results of the meeting of the PCC of the Warsaw Treaty member-states from August 5–6, 1988 in Warsaw.

Cde. Ambassador Kochemasov laid out in detail:

– It is the goal of the resolution to give a more defensive character to Soviet forces through a developmental process in limited time. At the same time, it has been decided to reduce the Soviet army and navy by 1 million men altogether (500,000 men [each]).

– According to Soviet opinion, this decision corresponds with the agreement of the PCC meeting in Warsaw concerning the guarantee of a sufficient defense.

– Having done so, the Soviet side has taken into account the regulations agreed by the PCC in August 1988, namely undertaking all measures for a reduction according to the principle of reciprocity.

So far the West has not paid attention to the proposed reciprocity with respect to the drafting of disarmament measures.

We want to communicate some ideas to the other side in this context, in which we:

– will consider the military situation, and will at the same time
– draw specific conclusions for the future

Since the Warsaw Treaty has some superiority in the conventional area, the other side expects us to start reducing. It is well known that this is what our adversaries mean when talking about reciprocity in disarmament measures.

What is the most important content of the planned measures, in which we take into account the considerations of our friends and allies?

– The Soviet party and state leadership has once again been confirmed in analyzing the joint resolutions of the PCC's Warsaw meeting, according to which the course of reducing the forces and weapons of NATO and the Warsaw Pact, as drafted in Warsaw, and based on reciprocity, cannot be realized in that way.

– Since the mandate on future negotiations to be drafted in Vienna is about to be completed, the Soviet leadership has once again thoroughly analyzed the military situation and the balance of military forces, especially in Central Europe.

As a result, it concluded that the Soviet Union and the states of the Warsaw Treaty could agree to unilateral measures

   – without this having an impact on forces needed for defense, and
   – without waiting for upcoming negotiations on conventional disarmament and related problems.

– After considering the current situation, and carefully analyzing all related questions, the Soviet party and state leadership assumes that the Warsaw Treaty should remain strong in military terms within Europe.

– Our military forces in this region should remain to the extent that any attempt by the United States or NATO to exert military pressure on us will have no effect, and will remain hopeless.

– I want to report in this context that the party and state leadership of the Soviet Union has recently decided to realize certain measures within the Soviet forces during 1989 and 1990, which will attribute to them a strongly defensive character.

In the course of this, we found options to reduce manpower as well as some types of weapons, including tanks, within the timeframe mentioned.

Between 1989 and 1990, we plan to withdraw some divisions of the Group of Soviet Forces in Central Europe from the GDR and the ČSSR to the Soviet Union and dissolve them.

According to our estimate, in this area the Warsaw Treaty has 170,000 soldiers more than NATO.

   – If you, dear Cde. Honecker, have no objections, we will
   – withdraw four tank divisions from our forces in the GDR
   – transform some independent tank regiments into motorized rifle regiments
   – withdraw other units and facilities, among them training facilities and
   – units without substantive importance for the defense of the GDR and fighting capability of our forces.

   [...]

– As a result of this measure we are promising [to implement], and about which we would like your opinion, the numerical strength of the forces in the GDR will be reduced by 50,000. This will make things easier in the Central European area.

– We will also withdraw 5,000 tanks from the Group of Soviet Forces in the GDR. At the same time, the number of defensive weapons will increase.

624

[...]
- By realizing these projects we will
  - actually increase the defensive character of our military coalition, and
  - give a new (and, we hope, a strong) impetus to the process of reducing the military-strategic balance in Europe, and to the
  - improvement of relations between East and West, and of the process of disarmament.
- These measures will in no way weaken our position during the upcoming negotiations on the reduction of forces and arms.
- By communicating our considerations to our friends, we will provide them with the opportunity to prepare for respective measures within their forces as well.
- The measures are intended to enhance the defensive character of our forces. In the course of this, we hope that the role, and the place, of the forces of our countries within the collective defense of our alliance, and within the framework of the Unified Forces of the Warsaw Treaty, will be discussed collectively.
- If you agree, we could begin with a detailed analysis of the questions during the first half of December and place our ministers of defense in charge of it.

[...]

If there is agreement in principle, Cde. Mikhail Gorbachev, in accordance with the agreed interests of the countries of the Warsaw Treaty, will deal with these questions in his speech before the United Nations General Assembly on December 7, 1988.

* * *

Following this information by Cde. Ambassador Kochemasov, Cde. Erich Honecker replied as follows:
- Cde. Honecker thanked him for the information and consented to the proposals transmitted.

He expressed the opinion that such an approach would further the process of disarmament and thwart all efforts by those desiring to obstruct it.

[*Source: VA–01/32663, BA–MA. Translated by Karen Riechert.*]

Document No. 140: Minutes of the Sofia Meeting of the Committee of Ministers of Defense, December 17, 1988

At this Warsaw Pact defense ministers' meeting 10 days after Mikhail Gorbachev's U.N. speech (see Document no. 135), Iazov and Kulikov explain the Soviet rationale for making unilateral arms cuts. Although they do not say so below, they were themselves deeply worried about the consequenses of such a move, as were many of their colleagues. Not coincidentally, more than 100 Soviet officers, including Kulikov, were fired within weeks of this meeting.

General Iazov: [...] During its meeting in July 1988, the Political Consultative Committee of the member-states of the Warsaw Pact passed a resolution on the development of recommendations to improve the organizational structure of the Unified Armed Forces of the Warsaw Pact in order to give them a distinctly defensive character as well to achieve the possible reduction of military forces and armaments in Europe.

Commensurate with this resolution, the political and military leadership of the Soviet Union has been working to bring the organizational structure of the Soviet military into line with the defensive military doctrine of the Warsaw Pact. [...]

After a complex assessment of the military–political situation and the power ratio, in particular in Central Europe, the Soviet leadership has concluded that the Soviet Union and Warsaw Pact could undertake several measures without waiting for a concrete agreement at the upcoming negotiations on mutual force reductions.

[...]

The grouping of our land forces in Europe as well as a significant portion of our weaponry have been moved forward to face the NATO forces on the FRG border with the GDR and Czechoslovakia. This came about in the wake of World War II. However, at the same time, it was also a conscious decision on our part in response to the continuous buildup of NATO forces in Europe and other actions by the U.S.

A significant reduction in tensions in Europe in recent years is noticeable. The current situation does not completely correspond to the Warsaw Pact's new military doctrine and will be used by the West to insinuate that we intend to attack.

Considering the West's (publicly) expressed uneasiness over the number of divisions and tanks in the Soviet armed forces, we have decided, in coordination with the leadership of all Warsaw Pact member-states, to withdraw six tank divisions (Group of Soviet Forces in Germany—4, Central Group—1, Southern Group—1) as well as an independent anti-aircraft missile contingent (Northern Group) from our military forces and to dissolve these divisions.

In addition, the aerial attack squadrons, the army's aerial attack battalions, as well as several transport units, all training and attack divisions and equipment will be withdrawn and transferred to the Soviet Union.

All remaining mobile defense and tank divisions in the GDR and ČSSR will be transferred to a new organizational structure, whereby the number of tanks will be reduced as follows:
- from 260 to 155 in the mobile defense division
- from 320 to 250 in the tank division

[...]

These measures will result in a reduction in the number of military personnel in the Soviet armed forces by 50,000 and the number of tanks by 5,000, thereby partially rectifying the imbalance in the number of personnel and tanks in Central Europe.

[...]

In this connection, the divisions in the GDR and ČSSR will have increased defensive capabilities, and their offensive capabilities will be proportionately decreased.

[...]

Altogether, in this region and in the territory of our European allies, the number of tanks will be reduced by 10,000, the number of artillery systems by 8,500 and the number of fighter jets by over 800. [...]

These measures will in no way weaken our position in the upcoming negotiations on the reduction of military forces and weapons in Europe.

We are of the view that information on the planned organizational changes in the Soviet forces will give the ministries of defense in the member-states the opportunity to prepare for corresponding steps to give their national forces a distinctly defensive character within the next two to three years.

In completing these measures, we should assume that it is possible to carry out a reduction of the larger armed forces and principal armaments of the member-states in an agreed manner, taking into consideration their position and duties in the collective defense as well as their part in the Unified Forces of the Warsaw Pact.

At the same time, the evolving military political and strategic situation in Europe and in each of the regions needs to be assessed from all angles. Therefore, a clear approach to completing and realizing these organizational measures is necessary.

We believe that after December 14, 1988 consultations in Moscow and during the current meeting of the Committee of the Ministers of Defense there was a collective decision for the ministers of defense in each member-state to develop concrete suggestions for organizational changes in their armed forces in order to be able to submit these to their governments for approval. [...]

Marshal Kulikov: [...] The Soviet minister of defense, General Dimitrii Timofeevich Iazov, has comprehensively informed us of the structural changes planned for the Soviet military. They allow for a reduction in the imbalance of military personnel and weaponry in Europe, areas where we possess supremacy over NATO, particularly in Central Europe.

During consultations by the heads of the General Staffs and the chief of staff, the discussion of this issue stemmed from the premise of a profound and general analysis of the enemy's situation, his military forces and their organizational structure, as well as his objectives. Based on this premise, we must fulfill all Political Consultative Committee resolutions that obligate us to consider the question of force reductions.

I fully approve of each comrade who put forward their suggestions and expressed their concerns regarding the complicated and extensive work we have to achieve.

It is with great satisfaction that I state that the Romanian army has carried out such measures—this is good; however, the Unified Command should have been informed of what had been done. It was just stated here, that such work must be realized together with the Unified Command and the General Staff of the Armed Forces in the USSR on the basis of a profound and general analysis of the enemy, the character of his actions and his place in the operative steps towards the end of hostilities.

As you know, the chief of the General Staff of the Armed Forces in the USSR[21] spoke about the organizational structure of the mobile defensive and tank divisions. He clearly stated that with the development of a defensive character, military personnel will not be reduced, but rather increased, that there would possibilities for new mobilized defensive forces, that the enemy's actions are confronted and at the same time that the active leadership of military action can be converted to defense.

[...]

The talk of considerably reducing the available financial means is not completely compatible with the high priority we place on the qualitative improvement of our armed forces, their reduction and their readiness; at the same time, it does not provide what is necessary to support the Political Consultative Committee.

What is reasonably and reliably adequate will be determined by the circumstances under which we actually live.

As a result of analyses by the Staff of the Unified Armed Forces and the General Staff of the USSR armed forces, we consider it important to have personnel up to 60–70 percent of their wartime strength permanently available in the divisions. [...]

With respect to military personnel, comrade Defense Minister, I must state that if a reduction of 500,000 were announced, this would mean a total reduction of 100,000 for Europe. Of this, 50,000 [would be] on the territory of the USSR and another 50,000 outside of Soviet territory. Therefore, when we speak of a reduction, it should not simply be a mathematic calculation. Such a reduction must be ascertained from the role and the place, the operative decision corresponding to the operative plan that we drew up together and presented to the heads of government for approval.

That is why I would like to state that, in discussing force reductions, it would be good to make use of those successful, traditional methods that have served us until now. That is the profound and general treatment of all issues. Undoubtedly, each allied army has the last word, the government decides, but a joint examination that also considers the experiences of other armed forces is the best solution for the task that has been put before us by the communist and workers' parties. [...]

[*Source: AZN 32877, 16–50, BA-MA. Translated by Catherine Nielsen.*]

---

[21] Marshal Sergei F. Akhromeev.

Document No. 141: Report by the Bulgarian Foreign Minister at the Unofficial Meeting of Foreign Ministers at Niederschönhausen near Berlin, April 10, 1989

In a fascinating reversal of past practice, the foreign ministers of the Warsaw Pact met—without their Soviet counterpart—to discuss subjects of mutual interest. Meeting at a government castle outside Berlin, the so-called "closed circle" focused on the implications of Gorbachev's reforms, including his unilateral force reductions. Not only did the meeting, described here by Bulgarian Foreign Minister Petar Mladenov, show that they recognized their interests did not always coincide with Moscow's, but it placed the foremost supporters of the Warsaw Pact, the East Germans, uncharacteristically in agreement with the Pact's main detractors, the Romanians. Of course, those two reactionary regimes had a vital stake in preserving the status quo in Eastern Europe. In sharp contrast to previous bloc crises in 1956, 1968 and 1980–81, fears that reform tendencies might spill over to other countries no longer originated with the policies of runaway satellites but with those of the Soviet Union itself.

[...]

We are under pressure, [GDR Foreign Minister Oskar] Fischer pointed out, because we are rejecting the "import" of imperialist views concerning human values. The other side is not content with cosmetic changes only; it wants us to operate on and to amputate socialism as such. This has been expressed unambiguously by [Zbigniew] Brzezinski, [Henry A.] Kissinger, and NATO Secretary General [Manfred] Wörner. Following Vienna,[22] the other side is undertaking an offensive in Europe to export bourgeois values.

We are required, pointed out the GDR foreign minister, to pull down the [Berlin] Wall, to dismantle socialism. They are stating that they do not want to change the border. Actually, they are aiming at a revision of the state borders in Europe, in violation of Helsinki. They are talking about human rights, but they mean disrupting production relations.

They want more markets and less Marx.[23]

[...]

Romanian Minister of Foreign Affairs Ioan Totu thanked O. Fischer for "the most serious issues" raised by him. At that moment it was difficult to give a direct answer to each question and to draw conclusions. The Romanian delegation, however, highly evaluates Cde. Fischer's statement, which touched the most significant issues. Totu agreed both with the assessments and the principled approach of the GDR delegation leader.

---

[22] CSCE review meeting from November 4, 1986, to January 19, 1989.
[23] Pun in German: "Mehr Markt, dazu aber weniger Marx."

Further on, the Romanian minister presented his detailed views on "the ratio of capitalist and socialist forces" and particularly on the "situation after Vienna." According to him, there are no changes in the Western strategy. Capitalism is fighting against us and this has been explicitly declared by Western politicians like Reagan, Thatcher, Nixon, Kissinger and others. It was possible that they had changed their tactics; Helsinki, the common European process documents, the three components of the agreements, were evidence for this. However, according to Cde. Totu, the real outcome was discouraging. Little has been achieved on the first item; nothing on the second; on the third item they had played the game the way they liked. They did not want to hear about real human rights—right to work, education, housing—although there was much to be done both by them and by us.

Owing to their tactics, stated Totu, they have gained a number of advantages. They applied the linkage approach. Their ideological and political advance has gained speed. They do not account for their intentions but their future plans are clear. The differentiated approach towards our countries is central.

The Romanian position was clear; it had been displayed in Vienna for two years and they were not going to retreat from it.

In his answer to Fischer's question "what should we do next?" Totu repeated that everyone was free to act in a sovereign and independent manner. They [the Romanians] were against any external intervention. The reputation of socialism was questioned, though. In order to advance against capitalism, in addition to the actions of an individual country, it was necessary to unite the revolutionary forces whose numbers around the world were large enough to exert resistance against bourgeois claims.

According to Totu's opinion, developing countries were a great reserve in this respect. "We have common interests. One of them is free development without external prerequisites. If we ally with those countries, we could solve a number of problems falling under item 2." This was a difficult task because apart from the differences among us, even more serious differences existed among themselves. In any case, a strategy was needed for joint actions with the developing countries that have a large potential to fight capitalism.

An important issue was also to activate the international communist movement and to achieve unity of action with socialist countries. Naturally, this unity of action was different compared to the past. Totu believed that if we did not realize those two components, we could not successfully counteract the West.

Having in mind all views shared and the general atmosphere, the following preliminary conclusions could be drawn:

This was the first time in such a forum that one of the countries—the GDR in particular, the host country—presented such a profound assessment of the international and European situation, asserting and reserving to itself a specific approach to the issues discussed. The GDR position was immediately supported by Romania and it could be undoubtedly assumed that the two countries had agreed in advance on their action. This act gives reason to believe that the intention was to probe the views and reactions of other states in advance of the Warsaw Pact Political Consultative Council meeting two months from now.

E[duard] Shevardnadze's absence reflected on the way the discussion was conducted and on the meeting as a whole. The Soviet representative carefully avoided commenting on Oskar Fischer's views, [but] addressed them in effect in his statement the following day. He expressed [Soviet] willingness not to form a second "closed circle" for taking a firm position on different delicate issues of principle or a specific character. Evidently, the absence of the Soviet minister absolved his Polish counterpart from expressing any views at all.

It should be noted that [Hungarian Foreign Minister] Cde. [Péter] Várkonyi is about to leave his position, which explains his passive behavior.

[Source: Fond 1b, Opis 35, a.e. 71–89 Page(s): 1–15, TsDA. Translated by Greta Keremidchieva.]

Document No. 142: Summary of Statement by the Soviet Defense Minister to Warsaw Pact Chiefs of Staff, April 28, 1989

Speaking to his alliance colleagues not long after Gorbachev's purge of hard-line military officers, Marshal Dmitrii Iazov defends Moscow's policy of going ahead with unilateral military reductions. He advocates opening the East's military secrets to Western scrutiny and inviting closer ties to the capitalist states—all based on a revised conception of the international situation that no longer foresees the prospect of war. (Two years later, Iazov would take a dramatically different stand by playing a leading role in the August 1991 coup attempt to restore hard-line communists to power in the Soviet Union.)

[…]

The state of the Vienna talks[24] is generally known. We have the initiative there and must keep it. It is also a matter of using this opportunity to mobilize world opinion for our politics of peace.

For the past 20 years, when we asked the question whether it could come to war, the answer was "yes." Today the situation is different. Today we can say that "tomorrow there will be no war."

[…]

Earlier, it was stated: We need defense and bread. Today, it is stated: We need bread; that means the economy.

A portion of the defense industry should be converted to civil production. Until now, the USSR produced 3,500 tanks yearly. T-72 tanks were also produced in the ČSSR and Poland. As a result of our defense doctrine, the production of tanks to this extent is no longer necessary.

[…]

Regarding the withdrawal of Soviet troops from member-states, Comrade [Defense] Minister Dmitrii Iazov explained that the withdrawal from Hungary was being well organized through the press, radio and Hungarian television, as well as through the population. It is correct that western mass media were also admitted on this occasion so that they could report on this within the NATO states. Thereby, we have documented that, in contrast to NATO, we are in keeping with word and deed. It was understood that western reporters could photograph everything and report on everything. They should have also received access to individual objects and facilities. We have nothing to fear from this.

[…]

As a whole, we must be open and not seek to keep everything secret.

Comrade Minister Iazov emphasized that the Warsaw Pact member-states should strengthen their contact with the capitalist states, including in the area of the military.

---

24 The parallel Negotiations on Confidence- and Security-Building Measures (CSBM) and on Conventional Forces in Europe (CFE), both started on March 9, 1989.

Next time, the Soviet Union intends to invite the ministers of defense from Spain, Great Britain, Venezuela, and a series of other capitalist states. [...]

Such measures will further strengthen trust and peace. For example, Swiss Minister of Defense Kaspar Villiger visited the Soviet Union one month ago.

After his visit, he appeared as a political agitator for Soviet peace politics. The French Minister of Defense[25] also publicly expressed his positive impressions in the USSR.

In this connection, it would be a good idea for the ministers of defense from the Warsaw Pact member-states to meet together more often to collectively discuss pending questions.

The Soviet Union would also welcome an exchange of soldiers and junior officers of the fraternal armies.

The mutual visits could last from a few days to a few weeks.

In future, there should be meetings not only with high-level military personnel and diplomats but also with soldiers.

This will substantially contribute to the further strengthening of friendship and military comradeship between our people and the military.

[...]

[Source: VA-01/40365, 144–47, BA–MA. Translated by Catherine Nielsen.]

---

[25] Jean-Pierre Chevenement.

Document No. 143: Czechoslovak Description of "Vltava-89" Exercise, May 23, 1989

The 1989 "Vltava" exercise in Czechoslovakia differed significantly from previous such maneuvers. It showed that the Warsaw Pact had already begun to implement the transformation from an offensive to a defensive strategy introduced by Gorbachev. It exposed a number of practical implications that resulted from this important change. For example, there were difficulties in timing the retaliatory measures that were anticipated in the event of a NATO attack. Exercise directors also found it hard to simulate the release of nuclear weapons because their staffs no longer knew how to do so—one of several signs at the time that the Warsaw Pact's elaborate planning had been slipping.

In connection with the plan for joint measures to prepare the Unified Armed Forces in the 1988–1989 training year, from May 22–26, 1989, a joint frontal command-staff exercise of the Czechoslovak People's Army and the Central Group of Forces "Vltava-89" was carried out. Its theme was "The preparation of a defensive operation with the front of the coalition. Driving back aggression by the adversary in the face of incomplete mobilization and deployment of forces. Conduct of combat operations to keep [control of] the tactical defense zone, and execution of a counter-strike by the front."

The exercise was based on the requirements of the military doctrine of the member-states of the Warsaw Pact as a defensive doctrine, on the decisions of the meeting of the Political Consultative Council and of the sessions of the Committee of Defense Ministers and the Military Council of the Unified Armed Forces. What was new in the exercise was [...] that the Czechoslovak People's Army and the Central Group of Forces were integrated within a new organizational [...] structure. Austria retained her neutrality.

[...]

At the first stage, the participants noted difficulties in organizing and supplying the counter-engagement operations, especially those by the air forces, and those of the illumination support on the battlefield. The exercise confirmed our lagging behind the NATO armies in terms of air force equipment with means enabling combat operations at night, and also showed that such equipment in other branches of the armed forces required further perfection.

[...]

The experience of "Vltava-89" revealed the difficulties the participants in the exercise had in choosing the time period for carrying out counter-engagements in conformity with the principles of our defensive military doctrine.

[...]

At the second stage, in the course of 2 days and 4 hours (after an operational leap to D-7), the participants practiced the destruction of enemy forces that had penetrated into [our] defenses with the use of nuclear weapons. They made decisions on the restoration of the fighting capabilities of the troops, the development of combat operations, and the elimination of the effects of nuclear strikes by the enemy. Headquarters of the territorial military districts throughout the exercise solved problems connected with the protection and defense of territory, the evacuation of the population, the elimination of the consequences of the destruction of the nuclear power stations, and the formation of reserves and compensation for troop losses of the front.

[...]

The shift to nuclear weapons by both sides at the second stage of the exercise allowed the commanders and staff to resurrect somewhat lost practical skills in solving tasks [related to] directing the delivery of nuclear strikes and restoring the fighting capacity of the troops.

[*Source: VS, KaMO, 1989, č.j. 60060/29, VÚA. Translated by Malcolm Byrne for the National Security Archive.*]

Document No. 144: Bulgarian Proposal for Reform of the Warsaw Treaty, June 14, 1989

The Bulgarians, after consulting with Moscow, made this counter-proposal in response to the 1988 Romanian proposal for Warsaw Pact reform (see Document No. 133). The Bulgarians proposed retaining the PCC but expanding its agenda, and providing for informal meetings at various levels, among other points. For the first time, the Soviets supported the idea of creating a unified secretariat with a rotating secretary general slot, similar to NATO. The bottom line, however, was that both the Bulgarians and Soviets wanted to maintain the Warsaw Pact—incorporating reforms as they deemed necessary—in hopes this would help strengthen the present regimes in power.

---

1. Intensification and improvement of the activities of the PCC, CMFA and CMD of member-states of the Warsaw Treaty

Political Consultative Committee (PCC)
Keep the Political Consultative Committee within the framework of the Warsaw Treaty. Deepen the practice of carrying out its meetings in the spirit of principled comradely discussion, and free exchange of opinions. Widen the range of topics discussed, above all by [bringing in] questions of multilateral political and economic cooperation, and socialist construction in the allied states.

Inform each other ahead of time about new initiatives and ideas, which this or that side intends to put forward at a meeting of the PCC.

Strengthen the practice of conducting, in the course of PCC consultations, restricted meetings of the leaders of delegations and ministers of foreign affairs. Inform them in a timely way about the approximate topic without prejudice to the possibility of raising, at the same time, any questions during the meetings.

Conduct multilateral informal meetings of heads of governments, secretaries of the CC and ministers of defense with the participation of the supreme commander and chief of staff of the UAF.

Track the results of restricted meetings. The representatives of the organizing country [should] summarize at the closing session the essence of agreements [reached] at the restricted meetings.

Create a mechanism for accounting for and controlling the implementation of agreements, proposals and thoughts contained in the statements at the PCC. The secretary general of the Warsaw Treaty [should] systemize and table them for discussion in practical terms at deputy foreign ministers' meetings [called to discuss] the results of the PCC meetings.

In keeping with the existing practice of having defense ministers, the supreme commander and chief of staff of the UAF participate in meetings of the PCC, periodically hear reports of the supreme commander, as a rule, when reviewing the implementation of decisions of the PCC regarding improvement of the UAF and setting tasks for the subsequent time period. In addition to oral reports, present written reports to the meetings of the PCC.

Committee of Ministers of Foreign Affairs (CMFA)

Widen the practice of principled comradely discussion and free exchange of opinions, as well as the range of questions discussed at the CMFA meetings. Inform each other ahead of time about new initiatives and ideas which this or that side intends to put forward at the sessions. Improve the practice of conducting ministers' meetings in a narrow circle, for example informing about their approximate topics, without prejudice to the possibility of raising any questions at the meetings. Abandon the practice of composing extended communiqués, if this is not caused by special circumstances. Orient oneself towards the adoption of concise and interesting documents.

Provide mandates with clear instructions for actual work to the special commission on disarmament questions, the special organ on problems of the all-European process, the multilateral group of current mutual information and other meetings of experts, and hear reports on work they have carried out.

Committee of Ministers of Defense (CMD)

Look into the possibility of renaming the CMD the Military Committee of Defense, keeping its membership, place, functions and working order in the form determined by the decision of the PCC dated March 17, 1969. Continue efforts to improve the work style of this organ, increase its role in the qualitative implementation of decisions, in connection with the strengthening of the defense capacity of the allied countries. Broaden the control functions of the CMD with regard to the implementation of decisions of the PCC on military questions. At sessions of this organ, raise more frequently questions of disarmament, cutbacks in military forces and armaments, implementation of the Stockholm document, military–industrial activities of the allied countries, and conversion. Invite to the meetings of the Committee of Ministers of Defense, as necessary, the deputies of the chief of staff of the UAF from allied armies. Create a permanent unified secretariat of the CMD and the Military Council of the UAF under the supreme commander of the UAF by drawing on the existing cadres of the administrative organs of the UAF. Invite the secretary general of the Warsaw Treaty to sessions of the CMD.

2. Creation of a permanent political working organ of the member-states of the Warsaw Treaty (PPWO)

Create a permanent political working organ a unified secretariat, which would have the following basic tasks:
- operational discussion and exchange of information on international questions, on questions of socio-economic development and on multilateral cooperation of allied countries;

– operational analysis of the international situation and the elaboration of estimates and prognoses of its development, the preparation of recommendations and thoughts, the elaboration of joint positions and the co-ordination of actions at the working level;

– co-ordination of the preparation and conduct of meetings of the PCC and sessions of the CMFA, the elaboration of initial drafts of their documents, as well as of other documents upon instruction of the political organs of the alliance, or on the initiative of individual countries;

– taking stock of the implementation of decisions of the PCC and the CMFA, moving forward joint and individual initiatives and proposals, including their informational and propaganda support;

– synchronization of work of the Special Commission on Disarmament Questions (SCD), the special organ on the problems of the all-European process, the Multilateral Group on Current Mutual Information (MGCMI), and expert groups; the elaboration of proposals for further improvement of the mechanism of cooperation within the framework of the Warsaw Treaty.

3. Widening the range of powers of the secretary general of the PCC

Raise the status of the secretary general of the PCC, who would become the secretary general of the Warsaw Treaty. Assign him the role of coordinator of joint working activities within the framework of the alliance, including preparation of meetings of the PCC and sessions of the CMFA. When appointing the secretary general, observe the principle of rotation; he would work on the basis of the decisions of the PCC and the CMFA, and make reports at their meetings and sessions about the work of organs of the Warsaw Treaty. The secretary general of the Warsaw Treaty would carry out general oversight of the activities of the permanent political working organ (PPWO), prepare reports for the PCC and CMFA about the work of organs of the Warsaw Treaty, convene meetings of deputy ministers of foreign affairs for consultations and the elaboration of decisions. The secretary general could make contacts with international organizations and alliances, above all with NATO (when necessary, together with the supreme commander of the UAF), and take diplomatic initiatives.

4. The practice of working meetings of deputy ministers of foreign affairs

Strengthen the practice of conducting working meetings of deputy ministers of foreign affairs, conduct them ahead of meetings of the PCC and sessions of the CMFA in order to reach agreement on drafts of the final documents, as well as after these forums in order to agree on the order and dates of the work on ideas and proposals put forward at the meetings, including meetings within the restricted circle. Decisions could be made and recommendations agreed upon at meetings of the deputy ministers.

5. Improvement of the work of the SCD, MGCMI and working groups of experts

Special Commission on Disarmament Questions (SCD)

Intensify the activity of the SCD in the main directions of the disarmament initiatives, increase its role in the preparation of decisions of the CMFA and CMD, and in the formulation of positions approved by the PCC. Increase its efficacy. Subordinate the groups of experts working on disarmament questions to the SCD, which would report to each meeting of the PCC on the work they have carried out.

Multilateral Group on Current Mutual Information (MGCMI)

Widen the functions of the MGCMI, increase its effectiveness by supplying it with clear mandates from the PCC and the CMFA with subsequent reporting to these organs; subordinate certain expert groups to the MGCMI. Improve the content of the MGCMI materials by directing them towards making appraisals, conclusions and proposals. Bring in experts to exchange opinions according to an agreed agenda. Widen the powers of the group by giving it an opportunity to work out joint positions and recommendations for the organs of the W[arsaw] T[reaty].

Working groups of experts

Carry out an inspection of the existing working groups of experts with the aim of deciding on the expediency of keeping them, transforming them or transferring their problems to other organs of the Warsaw Treaty.

6. Concerning a special organ for the problems of the all-European process

Create a special organ for the problems of the all-European process to exchange information and opinions, work out joint positions and coordinate actions of the allied states at the working level concerning problems of further development of the Helsinki process and the development and advancement of ideas for the "all-European home."

7. Improvement of mechanisms for military cooperation and democratization of activities of military organs of member-states of the Warsaw Treaty

The Unified Command of the UAF

Continue to appoint senior officers from the ranks of the M[ilitary] F[orces] of the USSR to the positions of supreme commander of the UAF, chief of staff of the UAF and A[ir] F[orce] and N[avy] deputy heads of the UAF for a period of 4–6 years with the possible re-appointment of the chief of staff of the UAF with the agreement of all allied states. See to the introduction of positions of 1–2 deputies to the supreme commander from allied armies stationed in Moscow and rotating after 2 years.

Military Council of the UAF

Improve the style and methods of work of the Military Council of the UAF, while retaining its membership and functions. Include supreme commanders of the Western and the Southwestern fronts in the membership of the Military Council of the UAF or invite them to its meetings.

Staff of the Unified Armed Forces

Increase the effectiveness of the activities of the staff of the UAF as a working organ of the CMD, taking into consideration a possible cutback in its personnel. Provide for more even representation by the ministries of defense of all allied countries in the Staff and other administrative organs under the UAF supreme commander at the level of heads of directorates and departments. The chief of staff of the UAF together with the deputies from the allied armies [should] specify to which concrete positions one could appoint officers from the allied armies on a rotating basis. Widen the participation of representatives of all allied armies in the Staff of the UAF when the supreme commander inspects forces provided [by member-states] to the UAF.

Committee on Technology of the UAF

Widen the functions of the Committee on Technology of the UAF, related to the elaboration of recommendations on the questions of technical support, specialization of research and development, and arms production. Detail the membership and functions of the Military Scientific–Technical Council of the UAF, include deputy ministers of defense (deputy heads of the general (main) staffs of the allied armies) or heads of armament and technical support [sections] into its membership.

Creation of an organ for information and propaganda

Continue working to create an organ for information and propaganda of the UAF and specify the main principles of its activities, structure, tasks and staffing methods.

Main documents regulating the activities of the UAF and
administrative organs in times of war and peace

Continue work to specify the basic documents regulating the activities of the UAF and their administrative organs in times of war and peace. Introduce along with this necessary correction to Statute of the UAF for peace and war time, without changing the principal points.

Status of the representatives of the Supreme Command

Work out the legal status of the representatives of the Supreme Command of the UAF under the ministers of defense of the allied countries in time of war.

Agreement on jurisdiction in time of war

Continue joint work on the draft agreement on jurisdiction with respect to UAF servicemen in time of war.

Contributions of individual countries to the budget
of the UAF in time of peace

Consider it inexpedient currently to review the shares of contributions by individual member-states of the Warsaw Treaty to the budget of the UAF. Keep contributions [at the level] mentioned in appendix 2 of the Statute of the Unified Armed Forces and Unified Command of the member-states of the Warsaw Treaty in time of peace, approved by decision of the meeting of the PCC dated March 17, 1969.

8. Interaction of political and military organs of the Warsaw Treaty

Representatives of the ministries of foreign affairs [should] participate in the preparation and work of the meetings of the CMD and Military Council; representatives of ministries of defense and Unified Command [should participate] in the preparation and work of the sessions of the CMFA.

Conduct joint sessions of the CMFA and CMD on important questions of security and on questions of improving cooperation within the framework of the Warsaw Treaty.

9. Procedural questions

Work out relevant procedural rules, which would create preconditions for non-stop work by all sections of the Warsaw Treaty. To this end, create a working group of experts.

10. Creation of a joint scientific-research center of the member-states of the Warsaw Treaty

Create a joint scientific-research center of member-states of the Warsaw Treaty for research in the field of international relations.

[*Source: Opis 60n, a.e. 161, pp. 54–63. Diplomatic Archive, Sofia. Translated by Sergey Radchenko.*]

Document No. 145: Letter from the Bulgarian CC to the Romanian CC, June 21, 1989

In this letter to the Romanian Central Committee, the Bulgarian CC argues its case for a different approach to reforming the Warsaw Treaty (see Document Nos. 133 and 144). It particularly regards the Warsaw Pact as a "key factor for security and stability in Europe."

Dear Comrades,

The CC of the BCP has carefully examined your proposals of July 4, 1988, regarding the organization, improvement, and democratization of the Warsaw Treaty bodies and activities.

We share your opinion about the necessity of further improving the Warsaw Treaty's political and military cooperation mechanism, which at present is especially topical. At the PCC Warsaw meeting in July 1988, this question was put before our parties and states as a primary task.

We also believe that positive changes in international relations, arms reduction, confidence building, and European and world cooperation will create the necessary prerequisites for military–political groupings to simultaneously disband their military organizations. In the future, we will work toward achieving this aim. At the same time, realism requires admitting that conditions are not yet mature, as can be seen from the lack of any change in NATO's negative position in this respect.

In the present circumstances, the Warsaw Treaty provides a unique basis for cooperation among our socialist countries, an inseparable element and key factor for security and stability in Europe whose vitality and effectiveness have once again been confirmed with its renewal in 1985. Its unilateral demise would destroy this stability.

We have no doubt about the necessity of preserving the PCC as the main unit in the structure of political and military cooperation within the Warsaw Treaty. Removing it from this structure would lead to disorganization of the mechanisms of cooperation.

We share the opinion that it is necessary to direct the PCC's activity towards a broader discussion among our countries in the spheres of the construction of socialism and multilateral cooperation. We should exchange experiences in the socio-economic and ideological development of our people to foster the development of socialist democracy. This would fully conform to current trends in international relations, including the increasing role of non-military factors in international security. We do not see legal or organizational difficulties in integrating these issues into the PCC's normal activities in accordance with our mutually expressed desire.

Dissolving the PCC would be contrary to our views regarding the most effective way toward the simultaneous disbanding of the military–political alliances in Europe by further strengthening the political element of their activities and establishing non-confrontational relations. Depriving the Warsaw Treaty of its main political organ would strengthen its military aspect and undermine our efforts in that direction. The idea of creating a political body for multilateral cooperation among the European socialist countries could become topical in the future, once the international situation allows for the disbanding of the military–political groupings.

As you know, we have made several proposals for strengthening the political functions of these groupings and for their increasing cooperation, while enhancing their democracy as well as their effectiveness. In our opinion, the creation of a permanent working group would contribute to this process as well as to the promotion of the coordinating functions of the PCC general secretary, and improvement of the activities of the PCC and other working groups.

According to us, this practice has proven the vitality of the Committee of the Ministers of Defense as well as its structure, role, place and function, as defined in the PCC's decision of March 17, 1969. At the same time, we share the opinion that it is necessary to further democratize the military cooperation mechanism within the network of the Treaty, as well as the working style of the CMD, and to ensure closer cooperation between the political and military structures.

In conclusion, we would like to express our hope that the exchange of opinion between our parties on the questions you posed will play a positive role in our joint efforts toward the further improvement of political and military cooperation within the Warsaw Treaty, and will give them an additional impulse.

We are convinced that by using a constructive approach and mutual respect, our parties and states will find mutually acceptable solutions to political questions. Holding a joint meeting of the Committees of Ministers of Foreign Affairs and Ministers of Defense in the near future would be an important step in carrying out our decision of July 1988. We are ready to make the necessary effort to constructively contribute to the successful resolution of these questions at the upcoming PCC meeting in Bucharest.

[*Source: Fond 1b, Opis 35, a.e. 120–189, pp. 1–4, TsDA. Translated by Vania Petkova.*]

Document No. 146: Records of the Political Consultative Committee Meeting in Bucharest, July 7–8, 1989

Although the substance of this PCC session was recognized at the time from its public statements,[26] the speeches delivered there by the main participants behind closed doors have never been published before. Together they provide a unique, multi-dimensional view into the deliberations of the Warsaw Pact at a key moment late in its existence. Among the conclusions that can be drawn is that Gorbachev is virtually alone in predicting the imminent end of the Cold War. Despite the generally positive tone of the other speeches, the recollections of Heinz Kessler, below, reveal that they glossed over serious issues and concerns facing each member of the Pact.

a) Speech by Mikhail Gorbachev

[…]
I think everybody will agree that in the last two or three years the military danger has moved away, [and] the atmosphere in the world has cleared up substantially. The first real steps have been made on the path of nuclear disarmament. The winding down of regional conflicts has begun. Capital in the form of trust is being created in relations between East and West.

Maybe the most obvious demonstration of the scale of the changes is the fact that not only the theorists, but many political figures also, M[argaret] Thatcher and G[eorge] Bush among them, speak today about the end of the "Cold War."

If that is so—and in this case we have no grounds not to agree with the Western leaders—then we are talking about the end of a period that has lasted over forty years, about the beginning of a transition to a new international order.

[…]
I believe that today we have a right to say that the processes unfolding on the international stage are to a substantial degree a result of our common work. It is not a secret—this is what they think everywhere in the world—that the current turn in world affairs became possible first of all because of the course of *perestroika*, the reform and perfection of certain elements of the socialist governing system, which have commenced in the recent years in the Soviet Union, [and] which are being implemented with varying degrees of intensity and are taking account of national conditions in practically all the fraternal countries.

By changing ourselves, we are thus inspiring the rest of the world to change. The initiatives introduced by us on all the key problems of international life could find a

[26] See the documents on the PHP website, http://www.isn.ethz.ch/php/documents/collection_3/PCC_meetings/coll_3_PCC_1989.htm.

[positive] response only in the favorable political atmosphere that was created by the process of the renewal of socialism.

And this is a characteristic feature. In the present situation, the gradual realization of not only our most recent proposals, but even of those that had been introduced earlier but remained unanswered, and had practically no chance of implementation, is now becoming possible. In particular, I have in mind many important initiatives proposed by us during the previous PCC sessions, including here in Bucharest.

[...]

First of all [let me talk] about the reductions of armed forces in Europe.

In the recent past, we undertook many efforts to move this process away from a dead end. The realization of a new military doctrine, the transition to a new model of defensive sufficiency became confirmation of the peace-loving nature of the Warsaw Treaty.

The restructuring of the composition and the structure of the armed forces, which began in connection with [the new military doctrine], allowed us to cut troops and armaments substantially in a unilateral fashion without any harm to our security.

Today, the task of reducing conventional weapons has moved to the forefront. The prospects for the solution [to this task] became more defined after the Brussels session of NATO. As they say, it is our move now.

There are points in NATO's position, which are clearly calculated to take over the initiative on issues of disarmament, for propaganda effect. It is also easy to discern in that position the intention to push aside the thorny issue of tactical nuclear weapons. However, in general one has to admit, a step has been taken in the direction of the proposals of the Warsaw Treaty.

[....]

We all are very aware of the fact that the first significant reduction of troops by the USA and the USSR, from both military alliances, will have a strong and multi-faceted impact on the entire political situation in Europe, and will become one more sign of the end of the period of confrontation. Of course it will find a reflection in the situation in the socialist countries. It is a serious question, and we would like to know your opinion.

[...]

Naturally, the significant changes taking place in the world arena presuppose changes in the character of the activity of our alliance itself. While remaining the guarantor of security of the member-states, it should obviously transform [itself] more and more from a military–political alliance into a politico-military one.

[...]

Therefore, we share the opinion of the Romanian comrades and of the representatives of other allied countries that the need is ripe, if one may say so, to make our cooperation more political. And now the next step would be to translate this formula into functioning mechanisms.

During the PCC session in Warsaw, [we] gave instructions to [our] diplomats and military to develop recommendations for the improvement of treaty mechanisms, for its democratization. However, they have not succeeded in preparing such recommendations so far.

Obviously, the novelty of the situation is making itself felt, as well as the complexity of the task, and the organizational weaknesses of our coordination.

Our delegation is introducing a proposal to entrust it to the ministers of foreign affairs to undertake an in-depth exchange of opinions on these issues, and to supply concrete and coordinated proposals to the next session of the PCC.

The Warsaw Treaty is our collective property. In the past, the alliance helped us all to survive in conditions of confrontation. I am convinced that it will serve the security interests of all our states in the present stage as well.

[Source: VA-01/40375, BA-MA. Translated by Svetlana Savranskaya for the National Security Archive.]

b) Speech by Erich Honecker

[...]

Looking at the state of international affairs, we cannot say that there has been a fundamental change for the better. Fearing that disarmament could become irreversible, NATO is dragging its feet in all negotiations and trying to win time to rearm and confront us with a fait accompli. Their goal remains to tip the international balance of power in their favor, to attain military superiority and to get ever more one-sided concessions from us. Banking on the exploitation of revolutionary scientific and technical advances, NATO still wants to force Socialism into an intensified arms race. That is shown by the resolutions of the NATO summit meeting held in May of this year and of the subsequent meeting of ministers of defense. NATO's general plan for arms control and disarmament is to maintain the strategy of deterrence and, as is stated literally, to "continue the modernization of conventional and nuclear weapons."

This stance on disarmament is openly coupled with the goal of overcoming the division of Europe on the basis of Western values. The opinion that chances are better than ever to transform our social system according to ideas of the West, to imbue it with Western "values" and lifestyles, is clearly dominant in Western leadership circles, and not only in internal discussions. Catch phrases such as "the inexorable demise of Socialism" or "the post-communist era" are ever more frequent in the statements and comments of leading NATO politicians.

Although the various imperialist powers employ different methods, they are all working more and more openly and unabashedly towards the destabilization of Socialism. Their goal is to change the political, and eventually the territorial, status quo in Europe in favor of imperialism. Obviously, the realization of such plans is not and will not be tolerated.

[Source: DC20/I/3/2840, SAPMO. Translated by Ursula Froese.]

c) Speech by Wojciech Jaruzelski

[…]
Since the last meeting of the PCC, there has been significant progress in disarmament. I am referring first and foremost to the liquidation of Soviet and American mid- and short-range missiles, the one-sided reduction in armed forces by the USSR and other Warsaw Pact states, and the positive developments in the reconvened Vienna negotiations.

The proposals by the Warsaw Pact Organization demonstrate to our partners that we are ready to take major steps in disarmament based on reciprocity and equal security. Thanks to our attitude, the decision on so-called modernization has been postponed. The negotiation offer made by the Warsaw Pact member-states has been accepted, albeit with hesitation and resistance.

Precisely because of these positive developments, it remains necessary, not only to be vigilant and ready to defend ourselves, but also to act decisively to turn the Warsaw Pact's proposals for disarmament into reality.

This meeting of the PCC will doubtlessly be a very important step in that direction.

The summit meeting in Brussels appears to us to be the first serious attempt at a response to the Soviet proposals. Of course, we register the continued presence of remnants and clichés of the "Cold War." On the other hand, we also register the accentuation of the political and non-military role of NATO, which means in our opinion that chances for a reduction in the military component of international relations are becoming visible on the horizon. International controls, confidence-building measures and the cultivation of various contacts all serve to support this change.

In the past years, two important factors of the CSCE process have shown marked progress: the military and the humanitarian factor. Cooperation in the areas of commerce and technology (the so-called 2nd basket) is still very unsatisfactory. Certain Socialist countries continue to be the victims of discriminatory practices.

[…]

[*Source: DC20/I/3/2840, SAPMO. Translated by Ursula Froese.*]

d) Speech by Rezső Nyers

[…]
We are of the opinion that the Warsaw Pact, besides carrying out its usual functions, needs to take steps to ensure that it can continue to play a role in these rapidly changing times. Besides maintaining the balance of power, our alliance should work actively to help create new guarantees for European security and make its contribution to the construction of the common European dwelling.

[…]
In view of developments in Europe as a whole, we need to develop democracy and cooperation within the Warsaw Pact Organization. We consider it desirable that the following issues be addressed:

We propose that meetings on all levels take on more the character of working groups with a free exchange of opinion. It would be desirable to increase transparency and reduce formalities. We suggest that the length and as far as possible also the number of published documents be limited. On the other hand, more internal recommendations are needed to guide leaders of member-states on important international issues.

We suggest that the bodies of political and military cooperation become more democratic and flexible. Rules of procedure should be worked out, including rules for how differences of opinion are to be reflected in internal documents and referred to in material meant for publication.

It is desirable to expand the General Secretary's sphere of activity in the areas of coordination and organization, and to provide him with opportunities to represent our common position to third countries or organizations.

In view of the large and constantly growing importance of humanitarian and human rights issues, we propose the creation of a special commission, on the level of deputy ministers, that would regularly discuss all aspects of these matters. To confirm a similar proposal already put forward by our specialists, I would like to repeat: Hungary is prepared to take on the task of coordinating activities in this area.

It is desirable that the special commission on disarmament work more regularly. Expanding participation in the commission to include chiefs of staff in addition to the Deputy Ministers of Foreign Affairs would heighten its level of responsibility.

It is also necessary to improve the cooperation of political and military bodies.

The democratization of the work of the military bodies is an urgent task. We welcome the readiness of the Soviet side to look for creative solutions in this area. The Hungarian side considers that the present situation already permits the transfer of the tasks of the Military Council to the Committee of the Ministers of Defense and the Officers of the Unified Armed Forces. The leading representatives of the allied armies to the Unified Armed Forces could also become more active in the areas of cooperation and the cultivation of contacts.

In view of the above, the guidelines for the Unified Armed Forces in peace- and war time need to be reformulated to express the new political thinking and the new doctrine of defense, and to better realize the interests of the member-states together with common interests.

The specialists that have been tasked with improving cooperation should properly be given the task of elaborating a draft document on the part of the member-states containing suggestions for changes, and presenting it at a joint meeting of the Ministers of Foreign Affairs and the Ministers of Defense. The latter would then prepare a proposal for recommended changes in time for the next meeting of the PCC in Moscow.

[*Source: DC20/I/3/2840, SAPMO. Translated by Ursula Froese.*]

e) Speech by Nicolae Ceaușescu

[...]

Deep political, social, economic and military changes have taken place in international life, which have also brought significant changes to the global correlation of forces.

The development of events, and realities demonstrate that relative equality in the correlation of forces has been achieved and maintained, which has allowed us to overcome a series of difficult moments and to preserve peace on earth over the course of almost 45 years. [...]

It is well known that the NATO countries have not attained the necessary appreciation for the repudiation of old policies of force, war, and "nuclear deterrence." On the contrary, they proclaimed [the old policies] anew at the recent NATO anniversary session. They advocate a transition toward modernizing short-range and tactical nuclear weapons, which will significantly increase their destructive force and danger to the very life of the people of Europe and the entire world.

[...]

This is why in these circumstances the fundamental question in international relations is, above all, the question of repudiating the modernization of nuclear weapons.

[...]

In this context I would mention that in 1966, during a similar period, and in this very building, the socialist countries were the first to elaborate a proposal for the Conference on Security and Cooperation in Europe in pursuit of disarmament and peace. Therefore the socialist countries must also act in the future, in the spirit of the documents signed in Helsinki, and not allow the distortion of, or deviation from, these documents in the name of so-called human rights.

We have no reason to reproach ourselves over the resolution of tasks concerning the increase in well-being, freedoms, right to work, life, and culture in the socialist countries. Our achievements in this respect are evident proof of these realities. I cannot fail to mention that after the Vienna meeting of a year ago, the socialist countries did not act in unison, precisely on this very important question and, in our opinion, certain demands of the capitalist countries were adopted, which opened the way for interference in our internal affairs, and for injuries to socialism, and that have nothing to do with genuine human rights. We raised this question at the appropriate time and we did not want to assume certain obligations in Vienna. We in the leadership of our party discussed this for a long time and reached the conclusion that we would have been acting against the interests of our people and of socialism if we had agreed to some of the proposals in the Vienna documents, which, by the way, [...] want mankind to return to the Middle Ages, and have nothing to do with the era in which we live, or with the prospects for peace and cooperation based on principles of full equality and non-interference in internal affairs.

[...]

We want a unified Europe, but if you will, a Europe of independent houses, in which each organizes his life and evolves as he considers best, but under conditions of effective cooperation in all areas with all other states and peoples.

Therefore we have put forward our thesis, which somehow repeats de Gaulle's thesis with respect to a unified Europe of free and independent nations.[27]

[...]

It would be very good if we could achieve the simultaneous dissolution of NATO and the Warsaw Pact. However we are not in favor of the unilateral dissolution of the Warsaw Pact. That would be a big mistake, and it would not serve the interests of our countries. I would like to point out that even after the dissolution of the Warsaw Pact we consider that the socialist countries should preserve cooperation and joint action among ourselves, including from the military point of view.

[...]

I do not completely share certain opinions expressed here that we supposedly have fallen behind in the area of science and technology. No, comrades. The socialist countries have achieved very important successes in this area as well. I am not just speaking about the Soviet Union. I think that the comrades themselves can speak about this. Romania itself, the GDR, Czechoslovakia, each of our countries has important achievements in this area and the Romanian delegation and the delegations of other countries have passed competitions with honor, and in many countries their goods are preferred to those from capitalist countries. [...]

I am in favor of broad criticism and self-criticism, but I am not for throwing out and negating everything our people are doing, or everything they have done over the long era of the construction of socialism. We have reason to be proud. While criticizing everything that is negative, we must take everything that is good, we must combine our forces in order to go forward both in the national and international arenas. The unity of revolutionary forces in each country is a requirement for a united people, but on the basis of a revolutionary program. The unity of the socialist countries is a historical necessity. [...]

We must perfect the workers' democracy. This is our perpetual task. On what basis? Bourgeois parliamentarianism is not a model for the workers' revolutionary socialist democracy. [...]

Bourgeois democracy under conditions of capitalist society has its role and meaning. Under conditions of socialism, it becomes an obstacle and can lead to the liquidation of the power of the working class.

There are many problems, which must be analyzed and discussed in the spirit of high communist responsibility. Therefore I once again turn to the participants of this conference with a call to strengthen our cooperation in resolving all of these problems. We must perfect the work of the Warsaw Pact. [...] It is necessary for our PCC, beginning with this conference, to pose the tasks before us more broadly, and to analyze the problems of socio-economic development in their entirety, so that they become priority problems when it becomes necessary also to analyze military questions. [...]

[*Source: DC20/I/3/2840, SAPMO. Translated by Malcolm Byrne for the National Security Archive.*]

---

[27] The reference is to French president Charles de Gaulle's vision of a "Europe from the Atlantic to the Urals."

f) East German Summary of the PCC Meeting,
July 11, 1989

[...]

In its assessment of the general tendencies of international development, the conference agreed that the turn from confrontation to détente can be reinforced; the situation, however, remains complicated and contradictory. One cannot talk of a decisive breakthrough.

Comrade Gorbachev gave a positive assessment of the changes that have taken place. He stated that in Europe the East–West relationship has achieved a new quality, providing enormous possibilities for the politics of peace.

However, the shift in thinking ruling circles in the West has not yet led to stability in their policy or actions. This period will take longer.

Comrade [Rezső] Nyers stated that the Vienna final document[28] has led to a new stage in the CSCE process and has raised all-European cooperation to a qualitatively higher level.

The USSR, GDR and the SRR [Socialist Republic of Romania] had a different view of the situation and drew attention to the increasing activities of forces hostile to détente. They [the three countries], as well as the PPR [Polish People's Republic], spoke in favor of pointing out in the conference document the danger of increased neo-Nazi activities in Western Europe. The HPR [Hungarian People's Republic] indicated that such a statement was incompatible with the "new thinking."

Only after a persistent discussion on the foreign ministers' level, were the reservations regarding the appropriate formulation of the declaration dropped.

The PPR, HPR and ČSSR predominantly assessed the decision of the NATO Council meeting positively.[29] [...]

Regarding the Vienna negotiations on conventional disarmament, there was agreement that the detailed negotiation methods of the Warsaw Pact were a good basis for achieving an aggressive negotiating stance. The Bush Initiative[30] was judged as approaching the Warsaw Pact position. [...]

The conference participants underlined the importance of being more aggressive in exerting influence over all areas of the structure of the CSCE process and developing appropriate conceptual ideas and effective initiatives.

– The participants were in favor of a policy of constructive dialogue and cooperation in the area of human rights and humanitarian cooperation. However, there were considerable differences over concrete approaches. The USSR as well as the GDR and SRR emphasized the importance of representing sever

---

[28] Adopted on January 17, 1989. For full text, see *CSCE: A Framework for Europe's Future*, (Washington: US Information Agency, 1989).

[29] The North Atlantic Council meeting in Brussels on May 29–30, 1989, expressed satisfaction with the progress of arms control negotiations. See http://www.nato.int/docu/basictxt/b890529b.htm.

[30] At the a NATO summit meeting on May 29, 1989, President Bush proposed a four-part plan that included cutting troop levels on both sides to 275,000, incorporating ceilings on certain combat and transport aircraft, and calling for an agreement within 6–12 months, among other elements.

al value systems and demanding from the Western states recognition of the obligations they had undertaken.

- On the other hand, the Soviet Union was assuming that "international standards" in the humanitarian area must be accepted in the socialist states regardless of the difficulties. The position was supported by the HPR in particular.
- The GDR, ČSSR, SRR and BPR [Bulgarian People's Republic] spoke in favor of a cohesive stance against every Western attempt to interfere in the internal affairs of the socialist states. [...]

During an exchange of opinions on the internal developments of the member-states the majority of participants spoke of the necessity of bringing about substantial socio-political changes. There were considerable differences in the approach. The USSR, ČSSR and BPR emphasized that these must be based on socialist principles. The HPR presented its concept of "democratic socialism." This is based on a market economy, different forms of property while maintaining the dominant role of the collective farms as well as pluralism and self-government. Linking political and economic reforms in the HPR could supposedly prevent extremist tendencies. Comrade Nyers was obviously trying to gain support of the Soviet Union and other member-states for this course.

- Comrade [Wojciech] Jaruzelski gave an assessment of the actual situation in the PPR. The Polish United Workers' Party sees the dangers of changes to the political system, but hopes that by integrating those opposed to maintaining the decisive influence of the party in the solution of internal issues, confrontation can be prevented.
- The PPR was anxious to avoid emphasizing in the conference document the socialist character of social developments in member-states.
- The participants were unanimous in favoring deepened interaction among the fraternal states. Despite diversification in the socialist countries, the majority was in support of strengthening efforts to bolster their unity and resisting imperialist attempts at differentiation among them. The HPR supported moving away from the "monolithic" notion of the unity of socialist countries and basing their relations on the norms of international law and the CSCE process. [...]

The importance of effectively creating mechanisms for political and military cooperation in the framework of the Warsaw Pact was unanimously stressed. All member-states (except the SRR) spoke in particular for the creation of a standing political working body. The SRR did not repeat its ideas contained in the letter from the RCP to the fellow parties on reorganizing the Warsaw Pact. Due to the SRR's stance, it was not possible to come to a concrete agreement at the joint conference of the committees of foreign and defense ministers the eve of the PCC meeting. The committees were instructed to submit concrete steps for improving the decision-making mechanism. A corresponding mandate was given to the expert group. [...]

[*Source: DC20/I/3/2840, SAPMO. Translated by Catherine Nielsen.*]

g) Recollections of East German Defense Minister Heinz Kessler

[...]

For someone who, like me, had taken part in the consultations of this Committee very often—as foreign minister but also previously as chief of staff of the NVA and chief of the Administrative Head Office—this conference was different from before, impenetrably, frighteningly different. It wasn't the speeches that were given and officially recorded. They were as they always had been and barely made mention of major problems. They invoked friendship and cooperation and kept to the line already dictated by Gorbachev: each Party is responsible for itself and its own country. They concentrated on a few very general estimations of the state of things thus far and future challenges facing the alliance. The speakers kept silent about current or imminent crises in their own countries and made it clear that no-one from the other members-states would or should feel called upon to comment on developments in the countries of their friends and brothers.

Here too, there was no serious joint taking of stock and, so, no really thorough political discussions. The final declaration of the conference, an appeal to the peoples and governments of the world that had been prepared in advance, did not contain one word about the inner problems of the Warsaw Pact.[31] Its basic thought, already expressed in the title, no doubt had the agreement of all the participants: "For a Stable and Safe Europe, Free of Nuclear and Chemical Weapons, for a Major Reduction of Armed Forces, Armaments and Military Expenditures." Except that the expectations in the member countries and in the world went much farther. Other than this "Declaration," a "Communiqué" (essentially a listing of many names and a few dry words about the good atmosphere in the conference room) and the two dinner speeches by Gorbachev and Ceauşescu, nothing appeared in the press about this conference. No speeches by the heads of delegation, not a single mention of conflict. Only a short report about a concluding press conference was published, in which one single short passage deviated from this rule, but actually hid more than it revealed.

[...]

No one had spoken about what we considered to be Hungary's obvious "fiddling" with border security regulations. No one had asked for detailed explanations about the results of the elections that had taken place shortly before the conference in Poland: it was known that the list of the opposition [group] "Solidarity" had won almost all the seats in the Sejm and that a storm was brewing in Poland. Nor had anyone asked Mikhail Gorbachev about the meaning of his most recent statements, saying that what was at stake now was no longer primarily Socialism as a system but rather the higher principles of liberalism and humanity.

Was the atmosphere at the conference perhaps better, more hearty, because of this reticence and mutual consideration? On the contrary, for me there was something schizophrenic about this conference; it was like an assembly of ghosts.

---

[31] For the declaration and communiqué, see http://www.isn.ethz.ch/php/documents/collection_3/PCC_docs/1989/1989_8_I.pdf, and 9_I.pdf.

On the sidelines, however, during the breaks, at meals, in the corridor and after the closing of the sessions, there were lively discussions, there was whispering, heads were put together. Despite the maintenance of the necessary politeness of all towards all, there were obvious partnerships: Honecker, Zhivkov and Ceauşescu were particularly often seen together and they often spoke heatedly—even though just a short while earlier, relations with Romania had been severely compromised due to its over-pronounced nationalist position within the alliance. Gorbachev spoke particularly often and intensely with the Hungarians and the Poles.

On the day after the official meeting of the Political Consultative Committee, the general secretaries of the represented parties traditionally met for consultations. This intimate gathering usually provided an occasion to discuss differences or urgent doubts about the correctness of this or that decision.

[…]

This session also took its course without any thorough debate on shared, very complicated problems. It was short and ended abruptly. In contrast with the usual practice, the delegations departed quickly, even hastily. The reason: urgent tasks in the individual countries were calling. Also a break with tradition: the Soviet delegation was the first to depart.

[…]

[*Source: Heinz Kessler,* Zur Sache und zur Person: Erinnerungen *(Berlin: Edition Ost, 1996), pp. 244–47. Translated by Ursula Froese.*]

Document No. 147: Records of the Foreign Ministers's Meeting in Warsaw, October 26–27, 1989

This late October 1989 foreign ministers' meeting in Warsaw was an attempt to find joint solutions to a number of difficult problems that the PCC had been unable to resolve before. The speeches cover a range of topics which help to understand the differing perspectives of the member-states just days before the fall of the Berlin Wall. While differing in their particulars, most members shared the view that the Warsaw Pact's role should evolve in the light of recent global developments toward new priorities, from promoting all-European integration to fighting the war on drugs.

---

a) Speech by Soviet Foreign Minister Eduard Shevardnadze

[...]

Dear Mr. Chairman, dear colleagues, friends,

We have met in Warsaw at what is a turning point for the Warsaw Treaty.

The changes taking place in our respective countries cannot help but affect our alliance as well.

We have to ask ourselves a question about the purpose and mission of our alliance, and find an answer. If we fail to do that, we will run the risk of losing our sense of purpose and finding ourselves in the dangerous position of contradicting reality.

We are convinced that the foundation of our alliance is the common national interests of its member-states and the need to ensure national security in view of the historical experience of two world wars and the realities of post-war Europe.

If all of us agree on the motivation of our alliance as outlined above, we can find solutions to our alliance's problems, rebuild it in accordance with current requirements and needs, and find a new balance of national and collective interests.

[...]

The phase we are going through now requires mutual trust, understanding and even generosity, more than ever before. We have been living in an artificial political atmosphere for too long. Now we have walked out to breathe some fresh air. However, such a change may bring about a feeling of drunkenness or sickness. There is nothing terrible about that.

What matters most—and I must apologize for my rather naturalistic metaphor—is not to become an alcoholicand not to lose faith in the possibility of healing and recuperation.

If we allow the former to happen, history and our respective nations will judge us very harshly.

[...]

Now I will proceed to some general issues concerning the work of our alliance. In today's difficult and dynamically evolving situation, the practical actions of the Warsaw Treaty continue actively to assist the process of real disarmament, help create a vision of a secure and peaceful Europe—a continent of trust and cooperation—and contribute to the rebuilding of the entire concept of international relations in the spirit of new political thinking. This is one of the most important missions of our alliance, one of a long-term nature and a high priority rating. This mission is purely political and reflects our comprehensive approach to the notion of security.

Obviously, the changing situation referred to above cannot but influence our alliance and its evolution, which anticipates a transformation of the Warsaw Treaty from a military–political alliance to a political–military one. The very term "political alliance" has become all-encompassing and multi-faceted. This is why the term "political–military organization" is too conventional in this respect. We all are witnessing a process whereby external "non-political" or "low-political" issues invariably find their way into the political sphere.

The expansion of the issues being dealt with, combined with an increased emphasis on purely peaceful areas of cooperation, strengthens the authority of the Warsaw Treaty and helps gain trust on the part of the European and world public in the policy of our countries.

In our opinion, it is necessary to give impetus to the group of experts from the allied nations, whose work is based on the conclusions of the Warsaw and Bucharest meetings of the Political Consultative Committee, to focus on drafting proposals and ideas to improve mechanisms of cooperation within the Warsaw Treaty. It would be advisable to agree on practical recommendations for a joint meeting of the Committees of Foreign Ministers and Defense Ministers.

We assign a great deal of importance to the establishment of a permanent political working body; Poland has submitted an extensive proposal to this effect. We need a mechanism for permanent, continuous, flexible cooperation at the working level as much as we need air. The current setup is too clumsy and immobile. There is no need to be afraid that such a permanent body would reduce national sovereignty and become a supranational tool. This will not happen, as we ourselves can decide that it will employ the most democratic standards and rules. Work on improving this mechanism [of cooperation] should start as soon as possible.

[...]

[*Source: 8957/25, AÚV KSČ, SÚA. Translated by Jiři Mareš.*]

b) Speech by Hungarian Foreign Minister Gyula Horn

[...] Only two weeks have passed since the last Workers Party Congress where an epoch in our land came to an end—the dramatic shakeup of the Stalinist model for the building of Socialism. The Hungarian Socialist Party, which was established at the Party Congress, announced its goal to develop democratic socialism, which has as its basis equality of opportunity, a constitutional state, the legitimization of political and economic pluralism and the will of the people. [...]

The Hungarian government confirmed our foreign policy course, the international sovereignty of states, membership in the Warsaw Pact.

[...]

Today, international relations have a positive influence on the reshaping of our countries through helpful political, social and economic reforms. Our experiences prove that the West positively assesses the changes in our countries. Their behavior is not characterized by a hostile stance, but, rather, it is characterized by a great sense of responsibility and a willingness to cooperate.

This is a result of developments throughout Europe.

It is our opinion that it is also possible to further strengthen these positive steps in international relations if we follow our primary course and dynamically promote dialogue and cooperation between East and West. This is dictated by the interests of our people and the people of Europe and the world. Neither the West nor the East can move away from this course without serious consequences.

[...]

We believe that the Warsaw Pact, as a military–political alliance, is not the appropriate forum for discussing general developments in the economic relationship between our countries. I want to stress that, just as the absence of our own integration system or its underdevelopment did not present any obstacles for talks with western integration models, so, and here I am certain, the cooperation with their capable and effective models will not impede cooperation between the Comecon member-states, but rather, will accelerate it.

In relations between the blocs, it is increasingly recognized that attention to human rights and humanitarian cooperation is not only an essential component of international security and relationships between states, but also directly influences the building of relationships between states. The Vienna agreement likewise reflects this new obligation of member-states.

The recognition of the universality of human rights naturally gives no state, group of states or social order the grounds to expropriate this. Disagreements can only be settled if its fulfillment is always fully guaranteed. The practice of bringing domestic norms in line with the norms of international law is expanding gradually, and it is becoming clearer that it is the inalienable right and obligation of the community of nations to monitor how states adhere to their commitments in the area of human rights and humanitarian issues, and to hold them accountable. We are witnesses to the broader acceptance of the strengthening of international control mechanisms that supports this. This practice proves the viability of the human dimension.

As far as Basket III and the human dimension are concerned, we must devote special attention to an important aspect of this issue—the situation of ethnic and national minorities. This will be dictated primarily by the international aspect and by the immediate domestic experiences of the Warsaw Pact member-states and their relationship with each other. National tensions are increasingly a source of conflict and have become a sensitive area of international security. The recognition of this fact and the measures derived therefrom have already been placed on the agenda of a number of states.

International forums, such as the meeting on the human dimension in Paris, testify to the fact that when individual states bring their domestic legal norms and practices in line with their international obligations it serves as a basis for substantive dialogue on human rights and humanitarian issues and for a situation whereby disputes can be resolved through objective dialogue. This leads to broad support for the creation of a European legal zone and the building of a general understanding of the elements of the rule of law. This should in future also be a factor in the shaping of relationships between member-states.

[...]

In our organization as well, the demand has been emerging that the generally acknowledged principles governing intercourse among states, cooperation between them, and their proper relationships ought be made organic to relations between [our] allied states. At the same time, it is especially important that we remove the ideological element from relations between member-states, jointly observe the principle of non-interference in domestic issues, and fulfill the obligations [set out] in European and other treaties. I agree with Comrade Shevardnadze that the Warsaw Pact does not find itself in a crisis situation, but, rather, has made the necessary changes in the domestic and foreign policies of its member-states, and has modernized. Genuine alliance relations, reflecting mutually agreed interests, can only be based on comprehensive application of these norms. And it is especially at a tumultuous time of change that [external] relations built on such a firm basis guarantee stable and predictable internal relations. With the increasing easing of tensions, the development of the pan-European process and the removal of the concrete threat level, as well as developments on both sides, a reassessment of the role, duty and function of the Warsaw Pact has taken place. Our alliance system must become an organization decisively committed to European cooperation and to moving forward and supporting that process. [...]

[Source: DC 20 I/3-2863, SAPMO. Translated by Catherine Nielsen.]

c) Speech by Polish Foreign Minister Krzysztof Skubiszewski

[...]

The member-states of the Warsaw Treaty are co-initiators of profound changes taking place in Europe. It seems we are strengthening the policy aimed at stability and détente in relations between East and West, a united Europe and democratization of international relations based on international law. International law and its essential principles also determine our own relations, i.e. mutual relations between the member-states of the Warsaw Treaty.

The Polish delegation notes with satisfaction that joint documents drafted at our meeting are in line with the objectives and assumptions outlined above. [...]

While noting the changes for the better, we feel that some of the positive processes are not stable enough, and lack reliable economic support, while there are also instances of violations of international law.

This is why we believe there is no military threat to our alliance at the moment.

However, our alliance cannot ignore the emphasis given to the German question, as manifested in attempts to reopen discussions on borders in Central Europe. The issue involves elements of potential destabilization, not just for European cooperation, but also with respect to the future of Europe. [...]

In today's situation, the principal reason for the existence of the Warsaw Treaty is to help advance stabilization in Europe and to maintain a balance between East and West as the levels of military potential are being reduced. [...]

Allow me now to proceed to the last topic—the issue of our alliance.

In this respect, Poland's position was explained in a speech by Prime Minister Tadeusz Mazowiecki to the Sejm. He emphasized that "it is important that all military treaties and alliances be concerned solely with the external security of member-states, and not with their internal economic and political arrangements." [...]

The essence of any alliance, and cooperation within it, consists in setting a common goal for all parties concerned, and promoting and implementing that goal. In doing so, common security interests must be taken into account. However, such a union cannot, and does not, restrict the freedom of any member-state to choose its own path of development, based on its own experience, circumstances and needs. The application of single patterns and universal models of internal arrangements is not permissible. [...]

We are convinced that the changes taking place in member countries give credibility to the the nature and missions of the Warsaw Treaty, especially insofar as the processes assisting and improving European security are concerned.

Poland tries to actively participate in efforts aimed at the further democratization of relations within the alliance based on the Warsaw Treaty. We will continue to support changes in the structure and functions of the Warsaw Treaty organization, so that the latter reflect and are consistent with the nature of the changes taking place in the member countries and their respective foreign policies, as well as with changes in relations between East and West.

Having in mind these changes, I will revisit the ideas outlined earlier, namely that a permanent secretariat or an auxiliary consultative body should be established, if possible. This would improve coordination in the area of the alliance's missions concerning the external security of its members, and also facilitate establishing relations with the North Atlantic Alliance.

[...]

[*Source: 8957/25, AÚV KSČ, SÚA. Translated by Jiří Mareš.*]

d) Czechoslovak Summary of the Meeting

The session of the Committee of Foreign Ministers took place at a time of increasing international dynamism and serious changes in East–West relations, as well as within the Warsaw Pact member-states.

The session was notable for certain specific features. It was organized in a country, in which a government was established that is led by a Solidarity supporter, and whose new foreign minister, K[rzysztof] Skubiszewski, is also a [Solidarity] follower. For the first time, ministers responsible for foreign economic relations attended the negotiation, too.

The general session took place in a [more] matter-of-fact, and from the political standpoint more constructive, atmosphere than expected. The change in government in the Polish People's Republic did not influence the negotiation in any substantial way. The Polish representation stressed continuity with its participation in the Warsaw Pact.

[...]

The hosts prepared drafts of three documents: a memorandum, an internal protocol and a declaration on all-European economic cooperation. Upon completion, the first two documents were approved at the level of ministers. Despite all the efforts of the majority of the delegations, however, the declaration on economic affairs was not finalized.

The negotiation on the memorandum and protocol was straightforward, with an effort to find compromise solutions.

[...]

The memorandum includes several new or more precise proposals, such as for establishing contacts between the Warsaw Pact and NATO in various areas; for accelerating the Vienna talks[32] and signing preliminary agreements on conventional disarmament with heads of state in attendance in the second half of 1990; for creating an "open sky" regime; for opening talks on naval forces; for concluding a convention for a complete ban on and liquidation of chemical weapons in 1990; and for conducting international consultations on military conversion.

[...]

Besides routine information on the course of the session, the protocol includes a paragraph on extending the mandate of expert working groups including the group on ecological security, which is directed by the ČSSR. Approval was granted to hold a deputy foreign ministers' consultation on the non-aligned movement in Sofia before the next session of the Committee. An experts' meeting on preparations for the Copenhagen session on the CSCE human dimension will take place in Moscow, in Berlin there will be an expert meeting on the Bonn conference on economic cooperation. The Bulgarian People's Republic suggested forming a working group on the European integration processes, but the Romanian Socialist Republic opposed it. In the protocol, due note was taken of Hungary's intention to hold a second session of the international conference on the "open sky" regime in Budapest.

A particular declaration was to be elaborated for the previously discussed all-European economic cooperation.

[...]

The negotiation about the declaration was characterized by considerable substantive and procedural problems. At first, the Romanian Socialist Republic delegation did not have the necessary mandate [from their leadership] to assess the pro

---

[32] Talks on limitations of conventional forces in Europe (CFE) and on confidence- and security-building measures (CBM).

posal. Later it refused to accept the Polish proposal as a basis for negotiation. [...] It rejected a realistic evaluation of integration processes and even use of the term integration. [...]

The Hungarian delegation did not have great interest in adopting the declaration either, and in the final phase did not prove to be prepared for compromises.

[...]

The speeches of the ministers confirmed the member-states' accord on essential matters. All the participants stressed strengthening cooperation within the Warsaw Pact in the interests of disarmament, security and confidence-building, democratization of inter-state relations and the development of cooperation. The delegations paid great attention to the necessity of unconditional respect for the inviolability of state borders, territorial integrity, and the independence and sovereignty of states. The effort to give impetus to the acceleration of the Vienna talks on conventional armed forces as well as on confidence and security building measures in Europe was also a collective one. [...]

E. A. Shevardnadze said in his speech that [...] there are problems in relations among the WP states, but not a crisis. [He said] the Soviet leadership would initiate a maximum effort to surmount these difficulties and would do everything to prevent a crisis.

[...]

The Vienna talks on conventional forces are becoming increasingly prominent. For the USSR, the greatest problem is naval forces. A reduction of conventional armaments is not possible until it is certain that a shift will occur in the navy as well. The current situation is disadvantageous for USSR and the Warsaw Pact. Despite that, there is always hope for reaching an agreement on conventional forces.

[...]

Regarding all-European economic cooperation, there are favorable conditions for a new level of multilateral partnership. This cannot be discussed without [noting] the connection to European integration. It is important that the integration processes in the East and West should not be isolated and should help form a united European economic zone.

[...]

[Bulgarian Foreign Minister] P. Mladenov was substituted for by his deputy, I. Ganev. [...] Of special importance, he pointed toward elaborating a strategy of accelerating the Vienna talks. He suggested assessing the positive and negative qualities of the minimum nuclear deterrence concept and working out approved positions to the "open sky" regime, military doctrines and chemical weapons.

He spoke in favor of working out a common Warsaw Pact document on cooperation in the anti-drug campaign. He stood up against attempts to destabilize the situation in some socialist commonwealth countries. He made clear the stance of the Bulgarian People's Republic on the dispute with Turkey. He stressed that Warsaw Pact unity is receiving new content under conditions of a plurality of opinions and patterns of socialist development. The Bulgarian People's Republic ascribed special importance to the creation of a permanent Warsaw Pact institution. He highlighted the Polish initiative for creating a joint parliamentary institution of the Warsaw Pact states.

Hungarian [Foreign] Minister Gy. Horn stressed the positive tendencies that are creating good conditions for political, economic and social reforms in the socialist countries. According to his words, the West had reacted to this development in a favorable way, thus displaying a high level of responsibility. A potential revision in the current course of developing a dialogue and cooperation with the West would have serious consequences for the socialist countries.

In the interests of accelerating the Vienna disarmament talks, he found closer cooperation among the Warsaw Pact foreign ministries and generals staffs was necessary. [...]

GDR Foreign Minister O. Fischer pointed out the continuing armament of the NATO countries, coordinated intervention in the internal affairs of the socialist countries, the danger of a rise of neo-Nazism in the FRG, and the proclamation of slogans about the need to overcome the results of World War II. He spoke in favor of accelerating the ongoing disarmament negotiations. [...]

Polish [Foreign] Minister K. Skubiszewski stated that the reforms [*perestroika*] in the USSR and other countries had contributed to building confidence between East and West. He enunciated the view that NATO and the United States had not used the changes in the Central and East European states to exert pressure on these countries. In Western Europe, the trend toward building a unified continent had become stronger, which the Polish People's Republic welcomed.

[...]

In view of the CSCE's position outside blocs and the diversification of policies among the coalition countries, the Polish People's Republic has concluded that it is not always necessary to speak [at the CSCE] with a single voice. It is necessary to evaluate the perspectives of the all-European process that is gradually exhausting its existing possibilities. A need had arisen to give it new content. [Skubiszewski] stated the necessity of intensifying the dialogue with NATO and making it more precise with the aim of strengthening the territorial status quo on the continent, and of reducing the level of military confrontation.

He spoke out in favor of a substantial implementation of the Vienna agreement on the CSCE's human dimension.

[...]

He criticized the existence, much less further creation, of new administrative obstacles impeding contacts among both individuals and organizations within the Warsaw Pact, which were at odds with the acknowledged principles and standards of international relations. [...]

The Romanian Socialist Republic Foreign Minister I. Totu pointed out the inconsistency of international developments with an accent on negative phenomena. There had been no radical changes in the international situation. He assessed the results of the Vienna talks with restraint. He paid substantial attention to the all-European process. He criticized Western attempts to destabilize internal developments in the socialist countries and to force them to adopt a certain way of life. [...]

[Czechoslovak Foreign] Minister J. Johanes [...] pointed out the attempts of the West to influence the internal situation in our countries, to take advantage of our economic difficulties and to misuse the matter of human rights. [...]

He acquainted the participants with the progress of the Czechoslovak initiative for creating a zone of confidence, cooperation and good neighborly relations along the line where the Warsaw Pact and NATO meet and with the initiative for environmental protection in Central Europe. [...]

As one of the essential priorities of Czechoslovak foreign policy, he pointed to cooperation within the Warsaw Pact. He fully supported the effort to strengthen the political character of our covenant. [...]

Differing approaches and evaluations of the current state of all-European cooperation and its prospects were evident in the presentations made by the ministers responsible for foreign economic relations at the plenary session. [...]
Hungary and the Polish People's Republic accentuated the necessity of further economic de-monopolization and deregulation, including in foreign economic relations, in connection with the overall reconstruction of economic mechanisms and political structures. They consider cooperation with the West a key factor in the necessarily radical modernization of their national economies. [...] In emphasizing the specifics of each situation, the USSR's attitude to the reconstruction of foreign economic relations was close to the Hungarian and Polish bloc points of view. The Bulgarian minister's speech traditionally stressed the importance of cooperation in environmental protection. The speeches by the Romanian and GDR representatives did not demand the reconstruction of cooperation mechanisms and socialist economic integration. They dwell on improving the forms and principles of existing cooperation. The Romanian Socialist Republic, as well as in part the GDR, considers the reluctance of the developed capitalist countries to remove obstacles as a major cause of the stagnation of trade and of economic, scientific and technical cooperation between East and West. [...]

[*Source: 8957/25, AÚV KSČ, SÚA. Translated by Karel Sieber.*]

Document No. 148: East German Statement at the Committee of Ministers of Defense Meeting in Budapest, November 27–29, 1989

The statement below, delivered by East Germany's Defense Minister Adm. Theodor Hoffmann to his fellow Warsaw Pact defense ministers shortly after the fall of the Berlin Wall, shows that the East German army had become paralyzed by events and was in danger of disintegrating. His call for reform in order to draw the army closer to the people and confirm its loyalty to the Pact alludes to the delicacy of the situation, but he clearly still believes that the GDR and the alliance can and should be preserved. Gorbachev, too, held to this view at the time.

[...]

As you know, my appointment as minister of national defense occurred in a difficult situation for our country and our armed forces. It is the result of a deep crisis of our party and is linked to the renewal of our whole society.

[...]

We are currently designing a thorough military reform. Its main goal is to better emphasize the character of the National People's Army as an army of the entire people, and to address the new defense adjustment to the new conditions.

In the course of all this, many general problems are still under discussion.

However, it is absolutely clear that we will remain loyal to our duties to the alliance, and that we will further develop close cooperation with the Soviet army and the other armies of the Warsaw Treaty member-states.

[...]

We also agree [with Army General Petr G. Lushev, supreme commander of the Unified Forces] that the political initiatives and practical measures by the member-states of the Warsaw Treaty have succeeded in improving the dialogue between the Warsaw Treaty and NATO, and the international atmosphere, to a certain extent.

However, it cannot be ignored that the ongoing process of military détente in Europe is not yet irreversible and remains complicated.

[...]

Also, NATO continues to realize its programs for expanding forces and equipment with highly modern technology and armaments, although it had indicated a certain readiness for disarmament in Vienna.

We have to take this contradictory attitude into account in preparing the concept of the development of our forces from 1991 to 1995, and on to the year 2000.

[...]

[*Source: DVW 1/71052, BA-MA. Translated by Karen Riechert.*]

Document No. 149: Memorandum of Conversation between Soviet Deputy Foreign Minister Aboimov and the Romanian Ambassador to the USSR, December 21, 1989

The violence that led to Nicolae Ceauşescu's overthrow in Romania was sparked ini-tially by a protest on December 16 in the Transylvanian city of Timişoara after gov-ernment officials tried to deport a local priest. That protest grew exponentially despite, and indeed in the wake of, bloody reprisals by the Securitate secret police. Ceauşescu's own reactions grew increasingly extreme as his security forces proved unable to stop the unrest from spreading to the capital. Typically, when Soviet bloc leaders faced significant domestic opposition, for instance in 1953, 1956, 1968 and 1980–81, they pro-fessed to see the causes in imaginary foreign conspiracies from the West. But here Ceauşescu actually blames Moscow and its allies for allegedly provoking the "events" in Timişoara. From the memorandum, excerpted here, as well as from other sources,[33] it seems clear Moscow had no connection with the turmoil in Romania, for which years of Ceauşescu's misrule was more than sufficient explanation.

[...]

I told the ambassador that during N. Ceauşescu's meeting with the Soviet chargé d'affaires in the SRR on December 20, [Ceauşescu] expressed surprise that Soviet representatives had issued declarations on the events in Timişoara. Besides, during the meeting [Ceauşescu] asserted that the Romanian side possessed information that the action in Timişoara had allegedly been prepared and organized with the consent of member-states of the Warsaw Treaty Organization. Moreover, the actions against Romania were allegedly plotted within the framework of the Warsaw Treaty Organization.

According to our information, officials in Bucharest in conversation with ambas-sadors from allied socialist states expressed an idea about some kind of interfering action in the internal affairs of the SRR that was allegedly under preparation in the Soviet Union.

I must declare on behalf of our side that such assertions can only puzzle us, that they have no foundation and do not correspond with reality.

[...]

[*Source:* Diplomaticheskii vestnik, *no. 21/22, November 1994, pp. 74–79. Translated by Vladislav Zubok.*]

---

[33] See Thomas Blanton, "When Did the Cold War End?," CWIHP *Bulletin* 10, (1998) pp. 184–191.

Document No. 150: Czechoslovak Report on a Meeting at the Soviet General Staff, January 29, 1990

After their transition to non-communist rule, some Warsaw Pact member-states imme-diately sought talks with Moscow about withdrawing Soviet troops from their terri-tory. At this January 1990 meeting, Soviet officials lay out their plans for keeping 275,000 troops in Central Europe, specifically in the GDR and Poland. Mikhail Gor-bachev had already accepted Hungarian and Czechoslovak demands for a swift pull-out, but at this meeting, the Polish delegate confirms that Warsaw has made no simi-lar request. The Poles were worried about obtaining final recognition of their Western border from united Germany and believed—wrongly—that they might need leverage.

[...]

The meeting dealt with preparations for a new initiative at the Vienna negotia-tions.

[...]

Since Soviet estimates and calculations indicate that North Atlantic alliance forces already enjoy superiority over those of the Warsaw Treaty (2.956 million vs. 1.965 million) and, as far as Central Europe is concerned, the United States and Soviet Union propose that NATO and the Warsaw Treaty should have 982.000 and 570.000 troops, respectively, in the Central European theater, the Soviet side believes that the reduction referred to above, where there is no agreement to downsize both blocs' forces in Europe to 1.350 million, is unilaterally disadvantageous for the Warsaw Treaty, and submits the following proposal:

The issue of overall levels of NATO and Warsaw Treaty armed forces in Europe (1.350 million) should be dealt with in the next round of negotiations (to accommo-date the U.S. requirement.)

Troop levels in the armed forces of the United States and Soviet Union on the territories of their respective allies in Central Europe should be set at 275,000 in both cases (or even lower); to accede to the U.S. requirement (the USSR had proposed a ceiling of 300,000 troops).

As far as Central Europe is concerned, the ceiling should be somewhere between 600,000 and 750,000 troops (the North Atlantic Alliance's current proposal is 982,000—which means no reduction; the Warsaw Treaty proposes 570,000).

[...]

All participants at the meeting, including our delegation, concluded that there had not been enough time for preparations, supporting documents had been incomplete, and they thus did not have the appropriate mandate. Consequently, the meeting was of an informative nature only.

Judging from the speeches by heads of delegations, it can be expected that there will be a consensus regarding Items 1 and 2 above.

[...]

During the discussion, both Colonel-General Omelichev and the chief of the General Staff of the Soviet Armed Forces made statements to the effect that they planned to station the proposed 275,000 troops on the territory of the German Democratic Republic and Poland. The Polish delegate confirmed that Poland did not demand the departure of Soviet troops.

[*Source: VS, KaMO, 1990, č.j. 211, VÚA. Translated by Jiří Mareš.*]

Document No. 151: East German Summary of the Ottawa Meeting of NATO and Warsaw Pact Foreign Ministers, February 12–13, 1990

The Ottawa meeting of NATO and Warsaw Pact foreign ministers, originally convened to discuss President Bush's May 1989 "Open Skies" proposal for greater transparency of the two alliances, was a landmark event in the process of diminishing mutual hostility between them. It may be surprising, given their historical antagonisms, that high-level officials on both sides were willing to go to such considerable lengths to preserve the two organizations, but by this time East and West generally saw them as contributing to international stability. Among the important particulars discussed in Ottawa was the status of Germany, one of the core issues of the Cold War since its inception. By mid-1989, most of the East European representatives agreed unification was inevitable, a stance in notable contrast to the views of Soviet Foreign Minister Eduard Shevardnadze.

[...]

1. In their opening remarks, all the foreign ministers welcomed this first opportunity for a meeting of states from both alliances to discuss the decisive changes in Europe.

[...]

There was no consistent view on the developments in Europe in the assessments of the Warsaw Pact member-states. This illustrated an approach solely and directly oriented toward national interests. However, there was still some common interest in important issues such as:
- joint efforts towards the breakdown of the bloc structure and the use of an effective CSCE framework to establish a new European security structure,
- the convening of a CSCE summit in 1990 to sign an initial agreement on conventional disarmament in Europe,
- including a solution to the German question in the CSCE process, and
- the continuation of the CSCE process.

[...]

Almost all the NATO states saw the changes in Eastern Europe as a victory and as justification for NATO's policy for the past 40 years. It is very important that NATO continue to exist, allowing, however, for the possibility of modifications to the future activities of the Pact.

2. All of the speakers dealt with the *German question*. It was generally acknowledged that, based on the right to self-determination, both German states have the right to unify. At the same time, it was pointed out in numerous speeches and in bilateral talks between the foreign ministers of NATO and the Warsaw Pact that German

unification must be a process that does not threaten its European neighbors and does not hinder the unity of the continent. States such as Poland, the Netherlands and Italy called for the right to directly participate in discussions on the external aspects of German unification. In virtually all talks, concern was expressed regarding the rapidity of the unification efforts, for which nobody in Europe was prepared; and the wish for the stable development of the GDR as an important partner in the unification process was stated.

There was far-reaching uncertainty over the future military status of a unified Germany. While, on the one hand, the NATO states saw full membership of a unified Germany in NATO as essential, on the other hand, there was also agreement by the NATO states that the balance of power in Europe could not be unilaterally changed to the disadvantage of the Soviet Union.

[...]

6. *Open Skies*

The foreign ministers spoke in support of an "Open Skies" treaty. This would build trust and support the disarmament process. It was stated that the achievement of an "Open Skies" regime could also contribute to greater openness in other areas.

[...]

[Source: DC/20, I/3/2917, pp. 168–90, SAPMO. Translated by Catherine Nielsen.]

Document No. 152: Memorandum of Eppelmann–Iazov Conversation, April 29, 1990

One of many striking signs of how much had changed in Eastern Europe by early 1990 was the fact that the first non-communist defense minister to be appointed in the GDR, Rainer Eppelmann, was a Protestant minister and a pacifist. Here he discusses the future of East Germany's army with his staunchly communist Soviet counterpart, Dmitrii Iazov. Eppelmann hopes that Germany can serve as a bridge between the two alliances, and expects, among other things, that Soviet forces will remain in the GDR, with West Germany taking over their financial support. Iazov remarks that maintaining two German armies in one Germany is unrealistic, and opposes Eduard Shevardnadze's idea that a united Germany should be a member of both NATO and the Warsaw Pact. He also assumes, as did many observers, that German unification would take at least five years. In fact it was accomplished just seven months after this meeting.

[...]

At the beginning, Minister [for Disarmament and Defense Rainer] Eppelmann expressed his opinion that it was the courageous and far-sighted policy of the Soviet Union, especially by General Secretary Gorbachev, which facilitated the current developments in the GDR and in Germany as a whole. The unification process of the two countries is currently occurring faster than the establishment of a collective security structure. However, this process cannot be stopped anymore without millions of citizens leaving the country [GDR]. Therefore immediate solutions acceptable to the Soviet Union, the United States, the other countries, and the Germans are needed. This is why we currently consider a policy of integrating a unified Germany into NATO as realistic. But we demand that there be no extension of NATO beyond the Elbe river, that no NATO troops be stationed on GDR territory, and that there be no unification according to Article 23 [of the German Basic Law] unless the structure and strategies of NATO have previously been revised.

The NVA [East German National People's Army] will be heavily reduced after Vienna I,[34] but maintain its independent leadership. And the NVA is not supposed to receive NATO weaponry. As long as NATO and the Warsaw Treaty exist, there will also be two German armies. The GDR abides by the treaties it has entered into.

However, the situation demands a change in economic and military relations. All these issues have to be dealt with by agreement. Security encompassing both alliances must be achieved. The unification process in Germany has to take into account the legitimate security interests of all European countries, especially the Soviet Union.

---

[34] The conclusion of the first stage of the CFE negotiations on reductions of conventional forces.

A unified Germany must be a step towards a unified Europe. This means there should be no German *Sonderweg*.[35] European development amounts to having a common security develop from the CSCE process. Preconditions could be:

- Regular meetings of the foreign ministers of the CSCE countries and the United States (twice annually).
- Also regular meetings of the ministers for defense of these countries.
- Establishment of joint commissions.
- Creation of arbitration commissions.
- Conclusion of a security treaty following the Two-plus-Four Negotiations.

Minister Iazov replied by saying, "Those who want to dance have to pay the piper." He wanted to know who would pay for the NVA, and who would determine what it would be permitted to do, or not. The Soviet Union will consistently favor a policy avoiding destabilization. However, this prospect will not offer his country any guarantee. The existence of two armies in one country is not realistic. Peace in the world depends on stability in Europe. A strengthening of NATO would automatically have the effect of weakening the Warsaw Treaty, and would inevitably lead to destabilization. The German people have a right to unification. The Soviet Union recognizes this right, however, according to the principle of equal security for both sides. The results of World War II must be legally certified. Current negotiations in Vienna are not balanced. The Soviet Union started from certain figures on troop strength. It would agree to the stationing of 195,000 Soviet troops within the GDR, and the same number for the United States within the FRG. This, however, does not take into account the other contingents of troops stationed within the FRG.

Perestroika encouraged the readiness for disarmament within the countries of the Warsaw Treaty and resulted in unilateral troop reductions. The Western side has not taken any appropriate steps so far. However, NATO's predominance increases the danger of war.

With respect to the situation in Germany, Marshal Iazov tends toward the opinion that not all Germans will rejoice in reunification. Furthermore, he does not believe that the entire population would try to flee to the West. The development of the GDR is closely linked to the Soviet Union. Both countries started out together at zero hour after the war. Now the GDR has become the tenth strongest economic power in the world. All this was only to be achieved through the close link with the Soviet Union. It is unimaginable, and economically unacceptable, to destroy these common ties. However, recently public opinion has changed. In particular the relationship with the Western Group of Soviet Forces has deteriorated. The population has been turned against the Western Group, friendly contacts are severed. In Leipzig a directive has been issued by Minister of the Interior [Peter-Michael] Diestel forbidding citizens from having contact with Soviet units. Soviet forces will be prohibited to fly, to shoot, to hold maneuvers, and much more. We ask you to be understanding about our duties.

---

[35] Separate road.

Unification of the two German states will not be as fast as many might believe. According to the Soviet leadership, it will take at least five years. Many things could happen before then, for example the withdrawal of all foreign troops from Germany. [...]

Minister Eppelmann emphasized the opinion of the GDR government that the Western Group of Soviet Forces should remain on GDR territory, as long as NATO troops are stationed in the Federal Republic. The GDR is interested in a good relationship with the Western Group. The information on a directive by Minister of the Interior Diestel regarding ties to the Western Group is dubious. With respect to the deterioration of relations between the population and the Western Group, it can be said that the NVA is confronted with the same problems. There is currently a broad rejection of anything military among the GDR population. [...]

Minister Eppelmann elaborated with respect to the wish for unification by the German people that the [Lothar] de Maizière government feels in sync with about 80 percent of the people, according to election results. Germany is supposed to, and will, assume a bridge function between NATO and the Warsaw Treaty. In the course of further negotiations it is assumed that the costs to the Western Group of stationing Soviet Forces will be borne by the FRG. Overall, the GDR is in favor of the further development of economic cooperation with the Soviet Union.

The GDR government is aware that the NVA has to stay loyal to the Warsaw Treaty.

This means:
- maintaining the security interests of the member-states of the Warsaw Treaty
- supporting the transformation of the blocs into a single security system
- not allowing any NATO troops on our territory
- assuming a bridge function between NATO and the Warsaw Treaty

Issues are:
- improvement of the conditions for stationing the Western Group
- the safeguarding of the early warning [system]
- secrecy of operational planning
- protection of technological secrets
- information on all military activity on the territory of the GDR
[...]

Minister Eppelmann has been authorized by the FRG to offer help for solving the housing problems of discharged Soviet army personnel. The FRG would be willing to build apartments comparable to the aid for victims of earthquakes. It relates this support to the expectation that the withdrawal of Soviet troops will not cause ecological problems similar to the ones encountered in the ČSFR.[36]

Minister Iazov rejected such assertions but expressed his gratitude for any help offered.

[36] Czechoslovak Federal Republic.

Upon inquiry by Minister Eppelmann, Minister Iazov explained that he himself did not support the idea of dual membership of a unified Germany in NATO and the Warsaw Treaty, as had been raised for discussion by [Soviet] Foreign Minister [Eduard] Shevardnadze. He considers this suggestion unrealistic. If at all, it would only be achieved by a serious reduction of armies in both German states. He emphasized Gorbachev's argument that a unified Germany as a member of NATO is unacceptable to the Soviet Union.

[*Source: DVW 1/44501, BA-MA. Translated by Karen Riechert.*]

Document No. 153: Records of the Political Consultative Committee Meeting in Moscow, June 7, 1990

The materials presented below record the last formal meeting of the PCC. That historic session produced a public declaration asserting that the ideological enemy image in both East and West has been overcome and conditions have been created for peaceful cooperation. Internal discussions at the meeting, however, show that differences among the members remained over how the Pact could or should be reformed. Czechoslovakia went the farthest in favoring elimination of its military structures and eventually played an influential role in steering the group toward dissolving the alliance. But for the time being, the members were prepared to see the Pact continue to exist, at least for a transitional period.

---

a) East German report on the meeting

[...]

The conference took place under completely new conditions. For the first time legitimate representatives chosen thorough free and democratic elections in all member-states took part.

2. As a result of the far-reaching democratic changes in Eastern Europe, the meeting was faced with the complicated task of overcoming the Warsaw Pact's crisis of existence and legitimacy and achieving, through a fundamental reshaping of the character, function and the activities of the Warsaw Pact, conditions whereby it can contribute during the transition period to the building of a pan-European security system. The participating states agreed to begin this radical renewal immediately.

Opinions about the reorganization of the alliance, especially in the military area, were considerably divided.

The most extensive demands were raised by the ČSFR[37] and Hungary. The ČSFR was particularly focused on dismantling the military structures (dissolution of the Unified Armed Forces, placing the armed forces under national command only, defense of national territory as the only alliance obligation, transformation of the Staff of the Unified Armed Forces into a Coordinating Group).

Hungary stressed that under the present conditions, the military organization of the Pact has lost its right to exist and is no longer important. Based on the Hungarian view, it could possibly be liquidated by the end of 1991. [...]

With a view to protecting its security interests, Poland is currently not prepared to go along with such a far-reaching position. The USSR agreed with the need for balance and stability in reshaping the Warsaw Pact. Bulgaria supported this position.

---

[37] Czechoslovak Federal Republic.

The GDR's position, and also partially Romania's, of carefully and democratically testing all of the political and military aspects of this and coming to goal-oriented decisions, had a conciliatory effect.

As a result of lengthy discussions, it was decided for the short-term to establish a commission of authorized government representatives that will begin work no later than July 15, 1990 and submit suggestions for reform to the member-states by the end of October of this year. An extraordinary conference of the Political Consultative Committee in Budapest in November of this year will make the corresponding decisions, which should come into effect as of January 1, 1991.[38] General doubt about the ability to reform the Warsaw Pact was expressed.

The ČSFR and Hungary clearly stated that, without radical renewal of the Warsaw Pact, they would pull out in 1991/1992.

[...]

5. The participants were critical of the status of the Vienna negotiations.[39] The Soviet Union, GDR, Poland and Hungary reinforced the importance of accelerating this work so that the agreement would be ready to sign by the CSCE conference. [Mikhail] Gorbachev suggested a meeting of civilian and military representatives to advise on the draft for the further proceedings in Vienna and to eventually correct the current draft. In this connection, he asked for closer cooperation between Warsaw Pact member-states and a stronger consideration of Soviet interests.

6. Based on the opinions of all the participants, the solution of the external aspects of German unification must:
  – guarantee security and stability in Europe and be based on recognition of the current borders,
  – be linked to concrete disarmament steps and
  – guarantee their [all the participants'] own security interests.

The USSR again objected to NATO membership [for reunited Germany]. It was for the association of the future German state with both blocs, as long as these continued [to exist] as forerunners of an all-European security structure. The future Germany should accordingly belong to a modified version of both alliances. This position means that the USSR would, for the first time, accept a NATO-association for a unified Germany for a transitional period under certain conditions: simultaneous association with the Warsaw Pact; fulfillment of the obligations of the GDR and FRG; placing the armed forces of the GDR under the command of the government of the new Germany along with continued subordination of the Bundeswehr to NATO; additional stationing of Soviet troops on the territory of the current GDR; reduction of the number of foreign troops in Germany and an agreement on a ceiling for a German army. All of this should be regulated by a special agreement between the Warsaw Pact and NATO.

In this connection, the USSR warned against neglecting its security interests. This would complicate European developments and, in particular, the disarmament process.

---

[38] The conference never took place.

[39] The reference is to negotiations on the reduction of conventional forces in Europe conducted within the framework of the Conference on Security and Cooperation in Europe (CSCE).

In his statement, Gorbachev did not touch on the question of decoupling the external aspects from the internal ones.

The USSR, however, will not abuse the right of the victor.

From the side of the GDR it was confirmed that it would accept temporary membership of a unified Germany in a reformed NATO with corresponding commitments with respect to the status of the territory of the former GDR. Germany could perform the function of a bridge between both blocs and aid the building of European peace.

7. Based on the fact that the results of his meetings with President [George H.W.] Bush have been mostly made public, Gorbachev stressed the responsibility of both superpowers in overcoming the negative consequences of earlier SU/USA relations. According to his estimate, this would have a positive effect on the improvement of the international climate, on the disarmament process, in particular on the opinion of the other nuclear powers, and on the settling of global and regional problems.

Gorbachev expressed understanding for the security interests of the USA and for the U.S. presence in Europe. He underlined a new type of relationship with the USA. The USSR hopes that the other Warsaw Pact member-states understand that this cooperation is an indispensable factor for stability.

Conclusions

1. A conference of the commission for the examination of the character, function and activity of the Warsaw Pact in Prague is to be organized.
   – State Secretary in the Ministry of Foreign Affairs Dr. H. Domke was named as the representative of the GDR government on the commission.
   The Ministry of Foreign Affairs and the Ministry of Defense are to name experts.
   – The suggestions of the Ministry of Foreign Affairs and the Ministry of Defense on the renewal of the Warsaw Pact contain concepts to be developed.

2. The ambassadors of the GDR in the Warsaw Pact member-states will give information on the report and the speeches of the representatives in the respective states where they are posted.

3. The embassies of the GDR in the remaining states are to receive information on the conference. They will be instructed to inform the governments of the countries they are in of the results of the conference and to report to the Ministry of Foreign Affairs on the reactions.

[...]

b) Declaration

I.

The current developments in Europe fulfill the conditions for overcoming the security model based on bloc politics and the division of the continent. These developments will be irreversible. They are in agreement with the desire of the people to live without artificial barriers and ideological divisions. The participants in the conference were for a new, all-European security system and a unified Europe of peace and cooperation.

The states that participated in the conference are taking an active part in this process. They see examining the character and function of the Warsaw Pact as important. They are certain that only when this is done can the Warsaw Pact fulfill the current new tasks in the transition period that are connected with disarmament and the building of a pan-European security system.

The participating states agree that the ideological enemy images have been overcome through the obliging efforts of both the East and West and that the purely geographical meaning of East and West has been reacquired. [...] The confrontational elements that were contained in the Warsaw Pact and North Atlantic Alliance documents in recent years no longer reflect the spirit of the times.

[...]

[Source: DC/20/I/3/3000, SAPMO. Translated by Catherine Nielsen.]

Document No. 154: Recollections of Czechoslovak Foreign Ministry Adviser Jaroslav Šedivý, 1990–1991

Jaroslav Šedivý, an adviser to the first post-communist Czechoslovak foreign minister, Jiří Dienstbier, was involved in negotiations with the Soviets over the withdrawal of their troops from Czechoslovakia. He also attended the last meeting of the PCC. His memoir provides an excellent account of how the withdrawal was accomplished— essentially by pressing the Soviets when they were most susceptible (see also Document No. 150).

[...] As if fascinated by the success in the media of his foreign policy, Václav Havel turned to the Central European area this time. He invited Polish President [Lech] Wałęsa and [Árpád] Göncz, his Hungarian counterpart, to a conference in Bratislava on Monday, April 9, 1990. He intended to discuss jointly the role of Central Europe in opening up European politics, the eventual coordination of Central European policies with the Soviet Union, including the institutions that ensured the hegemony of that power in Central and East Europe, as well as approaches towards West European structures. An excellent idea, indeed; however, the preparation of the meeting was thoroughly amateurish, if not inadequate.

[...]

These three presidents were well-known, distinguished disputants. Perhaps it would not be necessary to undertake any preparations at all with regard to the original concept of the meeting; the entire original scenario got somewhat out of our hands, however. The Hungarians announced that Prime Minister [József] Antall intended to accompany his president: he would not leave his president unaccompanied in major talks. That implied the participation of our Prime Minister [Marián] Čalfa in the Bratislava delegation. But then, the foreign minister must be present, too! The invitation was subsequently extended to prime ministers, foreign ministers, plus some ten other VIPs; finally, the foreign ministers of Yugoslavia, Italy and Austria were invited as observers.

[...] We at the Foreign Ministry were not too pleased that the foreign ministers had also been invited. There was barely any time left to prepare the conference. All our efforts concentrated on organizational backup, and on elaborating a draft final presidential communiqué. This draft was beyond the capacity of ministry officials. They produced the text with an age-old routine. [...] One of its paragraphs attested to how difficult it was for some of them, as late as the end of April 1990, to get rid of the concept that the Warsaw Treaty should carry on in some way or the other. The idea of there being a chance of reforming the Treaty was still firmly rooted among some ministry officials. The draft final communiqué reads that the Presidents agreed that, "within the context of overcoming the partition of Europe into blocs" the Pact had undergone "radical changes, including the abolition of the privileged position of one of the Treaty signatories and the consistent introduction of the principle that military bodies were subordinated to political ones." And so forth. [...]

The central issue at the meeting, which was also included in the communiqué, was the common desire to convene regular consultations with the intention of coordinating the efforts of these three Central European states toward the gradual institutionalization of the Helsinki process. All of the participants also assessed what the unification of Germany would mean for Europe.

The Bratislava meeting was not too successful. The embarrassment could be sensed everywhere. The next meeting, at Visegrád a year later, was much better organized and provided for the eventual future cooperation of these three countries, which were later called "the Visegrád group."[40]

Bratislava demonstrated embarrassment again about what to do with the whole system of security agreements around the 1955 Warsaw Treaty. In principle, it was clear that Czechoslovakia would not stay in that alliance; nevertheless, we were getting signals from different sides that we should not rush its dismantling. In the early months of spring 1990, it was especially the Americans, but also the British, who were telling us this. We ourselves told each other that no radical measures should be taken before most of the Soviet troops have been withdrawn from our territory, but also that we should not participate in any attempts to substantially reform the alliance.

The Political Consultative Committee of the Warsaw Treaty member-states was to be convened in Moscow in the early days of June 1990 at the level of heads of state. The main agenda was an exchange of opinions on democratization, or the improvement of cooperation within the Pact. Gorbachev was in favor, but so were the Romanians, Bulgarians, and even the Poles to a certain extent, not to mention the East Germans, who foresaw possibilities for preserving their position during the process of German unification. At a preliminary session of experts, our people pushed through as the first point on the agenda "the prospects for an all-European process, the formation of new security structures and the consolidation of European stability." The road to our maneuver had been opened by our proposal in March of that year for the establishment of a European Security Commission.

[...]

I did not leave for Moscow with the delegation headed by President Havel on June 7, 1990. At that time, I was already getting ready to leave for France. But I was asked to comment on the draft of the final protocol of the meeting, which was not supposed to be open to the public, and on the draft final communiqué. At the preliminary session of experts, Czechoslovakia was commissioned to prepare these documents. The reason was perhaps that—along with the Hungarians—our opinions on the further existence of the Pact were the most coherent; at the same time, we were taking over the presidency of the Pact as of June. The draft protocol corresponded therefore with different opinions on the further existence of the Pact, as manifested during preliminary discussions. Alternative wording was suggested on key questions

[40] The February 15, 1991, meeting of the heads of state of Poland, Czechoslovakia, and Hungary in the northern Hungarian town of Visegrád.

and the delegation heads were supposed to decide [on it] towards the end of the Moscow talks. For instance, the Soviets, joined by the Germans and even by the Bulgarians, were pushing for "gradual deactivation of the organs of military cooperation," whereas we supported "the formation of all-European structures of security and cooperation". The Soviets, again joined by some others, even proposed a resolution stating that "the statute of the Unified Armed Forces, including their staff, shall be reconsidered," an attempt once again to brush up the proposal to develop within the Warsaw Treaty some structures analogous to those in NATO. We had already rejected this idea in Budapest earlier that year, at the end of February. Therefore, we amended the previous phrase on the Staff with: "as well as the question of its transformation to a body of a different character." The Hungarians wanted to dissolve the Warsaw Treaty immediately, at least so they said; however, they did not submit a particular proposal. In view of the Vienna talks on disarmament, a disarmament commission was constituted within the Warsaw Pact whose practical purpose consisted in its being intended to assign arms limitations quotas applicable to the respective member-states, provided a general agreement had been reached in Vienna on reduction of forces and armaments within both the Warsaw Treaty and NATO. Each of the alliances was to decide internally the extent of the reductions of troops and armaments by each signatory state. During this meeting in Moscow, we successfully buried the work of the commission of experts that had been constituted in 1988 to improve cooperation within the Warsaw Treaty.

[...]

While stressing "the temporary justification of the Warsaw Treaty" we rejected any "gradual deactivation" of military cooperation. We wanted to disband the military structures of the Pact as soon as possible. Upon his return from Moscow, our president said that we had managed to reject the subordination of armies of Treaty states to Soviet command, and reached an accord to transform the alliance into a political body serving the processes of disarmament, integration and stabilization in Europe.

[...]

Proposals for transforming the Warsaw Treaty were due to be submitted by the end of October 1990. The PCC was supposed to assess them in November during its Budapest session. Moscow, however, boycotted all efforts to convene this consultative committee. By the, of course, events were taking another course. Instead of starting to implement reform measures within the Warsaw Treaty as of January 1, 1991, things were moving in the opposite direction. The dissolution of the Warsaw Treaty became topical following the massacre instigated by Russian Interior Ministry troops in Lithuania. That corresponded to our concepts and tactics; at the same time, the whole process was accelerated by the domestic changes in the member, especially the disorderly and chaotic development in the Soviet Union.

The foreign ministers of Czechoslovakia and Poland [Jiří] Dienstbier and [Krzysztof] Skubiszewski met with their Hungarian colleague [Géza] Jeszenszky in Budapest on January 21, 1991. Referring to the explosive situation in the Baltic states caused by Moscow's politics of force, they stated that the Warsaw Treaty had to be disbanded by the end of 1991. Should Moscow avoid negotiations, these three states would simply abandon it.

They gave Gorbachev the deadline of the end of February, by which time PCC meeting postponed since November was to be convened.

A great power does not like to be pushed against the wall. In the middle of February, Soviet ambassador to Prague [Boris D.] Pankin came up to Dienstbier to notify him that Gorbachev had sent a letter to President Havel proposing disbanding the Warsaw Treaty's military structures as early as April 1, 1991, rather than in the second half of the year. The PCC gave its consent at the end of February in Budapest, just ten days after the Visegrád meeting of the three presidents.

At the meeting of the same Political Consultative Committee of the Warsaw Treaty on July 1, 1991, in Prague, the alliance was simply dissolved.[41]

[*Source: Jaroslav Šedivý, Černínský palác v roce nula (Prague: Železný, 1997), pp. 124–130. Translated by Marian J. Kratochvíl.*]

---

[41] The meetings were, strictly speaking, not those of the PCC because the member-states were not represented at the highest level.

Document No. 155: Agreement on the Cessation of the Military Provisions of the Warsaw Pact, February 25, 1991

This historic document provided for an end to the military provisions of the Warsaw Pact, a key step in the eventual dissolution of the alliance. It was prepared at a meeting of foreign ministers of the treaty's member-states. Unfortunately, this was also the meeting where members agreed to withhold all important Pact documents from third parties unless the signatories unanimously consented to their release. Not only did they neglect to formulate any declassification procedures, but they failed to anticipate the very disappearance of some of the signatory states themselves—the Soviet Union and Czechoslovakia.

[...]
1. As of 31 March 1991, the following documents will cease to be in force:
   - Protocol on the creation of a Unified Command for the Armed Forces of the member-states of the treaty of friendship, cooperation, and mutual assistance from 14 May 1955
   - Statute of the Committee of Ministers of Defense of the member-states of the Warsaw Pact in peace time from 17 March 1969
   - Statute of the Unified Armed Forces and Unified Command of the member-states of the Warsaw Treaty in peace time from 17 March 1969
   - Statute of the Military Council of the Unified Armed Forces of the member-states of the Warsaw Treaty in peace time from 17 March 1969
   - Statute of a common anti-aircraft defense system for the member-states of the Warsaw Treaty in peace time from 17 March 1969
   - Statute of the Unified Armed Forces of the member-states of the Warsaw Treaty and their leadership organs in war time from 18 March 1980

As well as all other documents adopted in connection with the above-mentioned acts, as implemented, altered, or amended.

In accordance with the foregoing, as of 31 March 1991 all military organs and structures created within the framework of the Warsaw Treaty—the Committee of Ministers of Defense, the Unified Command of the Unified Armed Forces, the Military Council of the UAF, the Staff and Committee on Technology of the UAF, the Military Scientific and Technical Council of the UAF, the Unified Air Defense System of the member-states of the Warsaw Treaty—are abolished. In addition, all military activity conducted within the framework of the Warsaw Treaty is terminated.

2. In accordance with point 1, as of 31 March 1991 the activity of military personnel of national armies in the administrative organs of the Unified Armed Forces and in the apparatus of the agencies of the supreme commander of the Unified Armed Forces in the national ministries of defense is terminated, as is the payment of financial dues to the Unified Command.

682

3. The further handling of documents received by the ministries of defense of the member-states of the Unified Command of the Unified Armed Forces, as well as those received by the Unified Command from the ministries of defense, is to be determined by agreement between the Unified Command and the ministries of defense of the member-states. These documents are not to be transferred to third countries and are not to be divulged.

4. This protocol enters into force upon its signature.

[…]

[*Source: Anatolii I. Gribkov,* Судьба Варшавского Догорова: Воспоминания, документы, факты [The Fate of the Warsaw Treaty: Recollections, Documents, and Facts] *(Moscow: Russkaia Kniga, 1998), pp. 198–200. Translated by Malcolm Byrne for the National Security Archive.*]

Main Actors

*Leading Officials of the Warsaw Treaty Organization and
its Member-States, 1955–1991*

WARSAW TREATY ORGANIZATION

Supreme Commanders of the Unified Armed Forces:
- Ivan S. Konev (1955–1960)
- Andrei A. Grechko (1960–1967)
- Ivan I. Iakubovskii (1968–1976)
- Viktor G. Kulikov (1977–1989)
- Petr G. Lushev (1989–1991)

Chiefs of Staff of the Unified Armed Forces:
- Aleksei I. Antonov (1955–1962)
- Pavel I. Batov (1962–1965)
- Mikhail I. Kazakov (1965–1968)
- Sergei M. Shtemenko (1969–1976)
- Anatolii I. Gribkov (1976–1989)
- Vladimir N. Lobov (1989–1991)

ALBANIA

First Secretaries of the Communist Party:
- Enver Hoxha (1941–1985)
- Ramiz Alia (1985–1991)

Chairmen of the Presidium of the People's Assembly (or President):
- Haxhi Lleshi (1953–1982)
- Ramiz Alia (1982–1992)

Chairmen of the Council of Ministers:
- Mehmet Shehu (1954–1981)
- Adil Çarçani (1981–1991)

Prime Ministers:
- Fatos Nano (1991)
- Ylli Bufi (1991)

Ministers of Defense:
- Beqir Balluku (1953–1974)
- Mehmet Shehu (1974–1980)
- Kadri Hazbiu (1980–1982)
- Prokop Murra (1982–1990)
- Kico Mustaqi (1990–1991)
- Ndricim Karakaci (1991)

Ministers of Foreign Affairs:
- Behar Shtylla (1953–1970)
- Nesti Nase (1970–1982)
- Reiz Malile (1982–1991)
- Muhamet Kapllani (1991)

BULGARIA

First Secretaries of the Bulgarian Communist Party:
- Todor Zhivkov (1954–1989)
- Petar Mladenov (1989–1990)

Chairmen of the Bulgarian Socialist Party (after April 3, 1990):
- Aleksander Lilov (1990–1991)
- Zhan Videnov (1991–1996)

Chairmen of the Council of Ministers:
- Vŭlko Chervenkov (1950–1956)
- Anton Yugov (1956–1962)
- Todor Zhivkov (1962–1971)
- Stanko Georgiev (1971–1981)
- Grisha Filipov (1981–1986)
- Georgi Atanasov (1986–1990)
- Andrei Lukanov (1990)
- Dimitŭr Popov (1990–1991)
- Filip Dimitrov (1991–1992)

Presidents:
- Todor Zhivkov (1971–1989)
- Petar Mladenov (1989–1990)
- Zhelyu Zhelev (1990–1997)

Ministers of Defense:
- Petar Panchevski (1950–1958)
- Ivan Popov (1958–1962)
- Dobri Dzhurov (1962–1990)
- Yordan Mutafchiev (1990–1991)
- Dimitŭr Ludzhev (1991–1992)

Ministers of Foreign Affairs:
- Mincho Neychev (1950–1956)
- Karlo Lukanov (1956–1962)
- Ivan Bashev (1962–1971)
- Petar Mladenov (1971–1989)
- Boiko Dimitrov (1989–1990)
- Lyuben Gotsev (1990)
- Viktor Valkov (1990–1991)
- Stoyan Ganev (1991–1993)

CZECHOSLOVAKIA

First Secretaries (or Chairmen) of the Communist Party:
- Antonín Novotný (1953–1968)
- Alexander Dubček (1968–1969)
- Gustav Husák (1969–1987)
- Miloš Jakeš (1987–1989

Presidents:
- Antonín Zápotocký (1953–1957)
- Antonín Novotný (1957–1968)
- Ludvík Svoboda (1968–1975)
- Gustáv Husák (1975–1989)
- Václav Havel (1989–1992)

Chairmen of the Council of Ministers:
- Viliam Široký (1953–1963)
- Jozef Lenárt (1963–1968)
- Oldřich Černík (1968–1970)
- Lubomír Štrougal (1970–1988)
- Ladislav Adamec (1988–1989)
- Marián Čalfa (1989–1992)

Premiers of the Czech Republic:
- Stanislav Rázl (1969)
- Josef Kempný (1969–1970)
- Josef Korčák (1970–1987)
- Ladislav Adamec (1987–1988)
- František Pitra (1988–1990)
- Petr Piťhart (1990–1992)

Premiers of the Slovak Republic:
- Štefan Sádovský (1969)
- Peter Colotka (1969–1988)
- Ivan Knotek (1988–1989)
- Pavol Hrivnák (1989)
- Milan Čič (1989–1990)
- Vladimír Mečiar (1990–1998)

Ministers of Defense:
- Bohumír Lomský (1956–1968)
- Martin Dzúr (1968–1985)
- Milan Václavík (1985–1989)
- Miroslav Vacek (1989–1990)
- Luboš Dobrovský (1990–1992)

Ministers of Foreign Affairs:
- Václav David (1953–1968)
- Jiří Hájek (1968–1968)
- Oldřich Černík (1968)
- Václav Pleskot (1968)

- Ján Marko (1969–1971)
- Bohuslav Chňoupek (1971–1988)
- Jaromír Johanes (1988–1989)
- Jiří Dienstbier (1989–1992)

EAST GERMANY

General Secretaries (or Chairmen) of the Socialist Unity Party:
- Otto Grotewohl and Wilhelm Pieck (1946–1950)
    [of the SPD and KPD, respectively]
- Walter Ulbricht (1950–1971)
- Erich Honecker (1971–1989)
- Egon Krenz (1989)
- Gregor Gysi (1989–1990)

State Presidents:
- Johannes Dieckmann (1949, acting)
- Wilhelm Pieck (1949–1960)
- Johannes Dieckmann (1960, acting)

Chairmen of the Council of State:
- Walter Ulbricht (1960–1973)
- Friedrich Ebert (1973, acting)
- Willi Stoph (1973–1976)
- Erich Honecker (1976–1989)
- Egon Krenz (1989)
- Manfred Gerlach (1989–1990, acting)
- Sabine Bergmann-Pohl (1990)

Chairmen of the Council of Ministers:
- Otto Grotewohl (1949–1964)
- Willi Stoph (1964–1973)
- Horst Sindermann (1973–1976)
- Willi Stoph (1976–1989)
- Hans Modrow (1989–1990)
- Lothar de Maizière (1990)

Ministers of Defense:
- Willi Stoph (1956–1960)
- Heinz Hoffmann (1960–1985)
- Heinz Kessler (1985–1989)
- Theodor Hoffmann (1989–1990)
- Rainer Eppelmann (1990)

Ministers of Foreign Affairs:
- Lothar Bolz (1953–1965)
- Otto Winzer (1965–1975)
- Oskar Fischer (1975–1990)
- Markus Meckel (1990)

HUNGARY

First Secretaries of the Hungarian Workers' Party (until October 31, 1956):
- Mátyás Rákosi (1945–1956)
- Ernő Gerő (1956)

First Secretaries of the Hungarian Socialist Workers' Party (from October 31, 1956):
- János Kádár (1956–1988)
- Károly Grósz (1988–1989)

President of the Hungarian Socialist Party (from October 7, 1989):
- Rezső Nyers (1989–1990)
- Gyula Horn (1990–1998)

Chairmen of the Council of Ministers:
- András Hegedűs (1955–1956)
- Imre Nagy (1956)
- János Kádár (1956–1958)
- Ferenc Münnich (1958–1961)
- János Kádár (1961–1965)
- Gyula Kállai (1965–1967)
- Jenő Fock (1967–1975)
- György Lázár (1975–1987)
- Károly Grósz (1987–1988)
- Miklós Németh (1988–1990)
- József Antall (1990–1993)

Presidents:
- István Dobi (1952–1967)
- Pál Losonczi (1967–1987)
- Károly Németh (1987–1988)
- Brunó Ferenc Straub (1988–1989)
- Mátyás Szűrös (1989–1990)
- Árpád Göncz (1990–2000)

Ministers of Defense:
- István Bata (1953–1956)
- Janza Károly (1956)
- Pál Maléter (1956)
- Ferenc Münnich (1956–1957)
- Géza Révész (1957–1960)
- Lajos Czinege (1960–1984)
- István Oláh (1984–1985)
- Ferenc Kárpáti (1985–1990)
- Lajos Für (1990–1994)

Ministers of Foreign Affairs:
- János Boldóczki (1953–1956)
- Imre Horváth (1956)
- Imre Nagy (1956)
- Imre Horváth (1956–1958)

- Endre Sík (1958–1961)
- János Péter (1961–1973)
- Frigyes Puja (1973–1983)
- Péter Várkonyi (1983–1989)
- Gyula Horn (1989–1990)
- Géza Jeszenszky (1990–1994)

POLAND

First Secretaries of the Communist Party:
- Bolesław Bierut (1954–1956)
- Edward Ochab (1956)
- Władysław Gomułka (1956–1970)
- Edward Gierek (1970–1980)
- Stanisław Kania (1980–1981)
- Wojciech Jaruzelski (1981–1989)
- Mieczysław F. Rakowski (1989–1990)

Presidents of the People's State Council:
- Aleksander Zawadzki (1952–1964)
- Edward Ochab (1964–1968)
- Marian Spychalski (1968–1970)
- Józef Cyrankiewicz (1970–1972)
- Henryk Jabłoński (1972–1985)
- Wojciech Jaruzelski (1985–1989)

Chairmen of the Council of Ministers:
- Józef Cyrankiewicz (1954–1970)
- Piotr Jaroszewicz (1970–1980)
- Edward Babiuch (1980)
- Józef Pińkowski (1980–1981)
- Wojciech Jaruzelski (1981–1985)
- Zbigniew Messner (1985–1988)
- Mieczysław F. Rakowski (1988–1989)
- Czesław Kiszczak (1989)

Ministers of Defense:
- Konstanty Rokossowski (1949–1956)
- Marian Spychalski (1956–1968)
- Wojciech Jaruzelski (1968–1983)
- Florian Siwicki (1983–1990)
- Piotr Kołodziejczyk (1990–1991)

Ministers of Foreign Affairs:
- Stanisław Skrzeszewski (1950–1956)
- Adam Rapacki (1956–1968)
- Stefan Jędrychowski (1968–1971)
- Stefan Olszowski (1971–1976)
- Emil Wojtaszek (1976–1980)
- Józef Czyrek (1980–1982)
- Stefan Olszowski (1982–1985)

- Marian Orzechowski (1985–1988)
- Tadeusz Olechowski (1988–1989)
- Krzysztof Skubiszewski (1989–1993)

Presidents of the Republic:
- Wojciech Jaruzelski (1989–1990)
- Lech Wałęsa (1990–1995)

ROMANIA

General (and First) Secretaries of the Communist Party:
- Gheorghe Apostol (1954–1955)
- Gheorghe Gheorghiu-Dej (1955–1965)
- Nicolae Ceaușescu (1965–1989)

Chairmen of the Council of State (Presidents):
- Gheorghe Gheorghiu-Dej (1961–1965)
- Chivu Stoica (1965–1967)
- Nicolae Ceaușescu (1967–1974)

Presidents of the Republic:
- Nicolae Ceaușescu (1974–1989)
- Ion Iliescu (1989–1996)

Chairmen of the Council of Ministers:
- Gheorghe Gheorghiu-Dej (1952–1955)
- Chivu Stoica (1955–1961)
- Ion Gheorghe Maurer (1961–1974)
- Manea Mănescu (1974–1979)
- Ilie Verdeț (1979–1982)
- Constantin Dăscălescu (1982–1989)

Prime Ministers:
- Petre Roman (1989–1991)
- Theodor Stolojan (1991–1992)

Ministers of Defense:
- Emil Bodnăraş (1950–1955)
- Leontin Sălăjan (1955–1966)
- Ion Ioniță (1966–1976)
- Ion Coman (1976–1980)
- Constantin Olteanu (1980–1985)
- Vasile Milea (1985–1989)
- Nicolae Militaru (1990)
- Victor Stănculescu (1990–1991)
- Niculae Spiroiu (1991–1994)

Ministers of Foreign Affairs:
- Simion Bughici (1952–1955)
- Grigore Preoteasa (1955–1957)
- Ion Gheorghe Maurer (1957–1958)

- Avram Bunaciu (1958–1961)
- Corneliu Mănescu (1961–1972)
- George Macovescu (1972–1978)
- Ștefan Andrei (1978–1985)
- Ilie Văduva (1985–1986)
- Ioan Totu (1986–1989)
- Ion Stoian (1989)
- Sergiu Celac (1989–1990)
- Adrian Năstase (1990–1992)

SOVIET UNION

General (and First) Secretaries of the Communist Party:
- Nikita S. Khrushchev (1953–1964)
- Leonid I. Brezhnev (1964–1982)
- Iurii V. Andropov (1982–1984)
- Konstantin U. Chernenko (1984–1985)
- Mikhail S. Gorbachev (1985–1991)

Chairmen of the Council of Ministers:
- Georgii M. Malenkov (1953–1955)
- Nikolai A. Bulganin (1955–1958)
- Nikita S. Khrushchev (1958–1964)
- Aleksei N. Kosygin (1964–1980)
- Nikolai A. Tikhonov (1980–1985)
- Nikolai I. Ryzhkov (1985–1991)

Presidents:
- Andrei A. Gromyko (1985–1988)
- Mikhail S. Gorbachev (1988–1991)

Ministers of Defense:
- Nikolai A. Bulganin (1953–1955)
- Georgii K. Zhukov (1955–1957)
- Rodion Ia. Malinovskii (1957–1967)
- Andrei A. Grechko (1967–1976)
- Dmitrii F. Ustinov (1976–1984)
- Sergei L. Sokolov (1984–1987)
- Dmitrii T. Iazov (1987–1991)
- Mikhail A. Moiseev (1991)
- Evgenii I. Shaposhnikov (1991)

Ministers of Foreign Affairs:
- Viacheslav M. Molotov (1953–1956)
- Dmitrii T. Shepilov (1956–1957)
- Andrei A. Gromyko (1957–1985)
- Eduard A. Shevardnadze (1985–1990)
- Aleksandr A. Bessmertnykh (1991)
- Boris D. Pankin (1991)
- Eduard A. Shevardnadze (1991)

Selected Bibliography on the Warsaw Pact

Compiled by Vojtech Mastny

PRINTED OFFICIAL DOCUMENTS

Jain, Jagdish P., ed., *Documentary Study of the Warsaw Pact* (Bombay: Asia Publishing House, 1973).

Maltsev, V.F., ed., *Организация Варшавского Договора 1955–1985: Документы и материалы* [The Warsaw Treaty Organization, 1955–1985: Documents and Materials] (Moscow: Politizdat, 1986).

Die NVA in der sozialistischen Verteidigungskoalition: Auswahl von Dokumenten und Materialien 1955/56 bis 1981 (Berlin: Militärverlag der DDR, 1982).

Reiman, Michal and Petr Luňák, eds., *Studená válka 1954–1964: Sovětské dokumenty v českých archivech* [The Cold War 1954–1964: Soviet Documents in Czech Archives] (Brno: Doplněk-Ústav pro soudobé dějiny AV ČR, 2000).

Tratatul de la Varşovia, 1955–1980: Culegere de documente [The Warsaw Treaty, 1955–1980: A Collection of Documents] (Bucharest: Politica, 1981).

MEMOIRS

Akhromeev, Sergei F., and Georgii M. Kornienko, *Глазами маршала и дипломата* [Through the Eyes of a Marshal and a Diplomat] (Moscow: Mezhdunarodnye otnosheniia, 1992).

Aleksandrov-Agentov, Andrei M., *От Коллонтай до Горбачева* [From Kollonai to Gorbachev] (Moscow: Mezhdunarodnye otnosheniia, 1994).

Betea, Lavinia, *Alexandru Bârlădeanu despre Dej, Ceauşescu şi Iliescu: Convorbiri* [Alexandru Bârlădeanu about Dej, Ceauşescu, and Iliescu: Conversations] (Bucharest: Editura Evenimentul Românesc, 1998).

Betea, Lavinia, *Maurer şi lumea de ieri: Mărturii despre Stalinism* [Maurer and the World of Yesterday: The Witnesses of Stalinism] (Cluj-Napoca: Dacia, 2001).

Brucan, Silviu, *Generaţia irosită: Memorii* [The Wasted Generation: Memoirs] (Bucharest: Univers şi C. Hogas, 1992).

Corneliu Mănescu în dialog cu Lavinia Betea: Convorbiri neterminate [Dialog between Corneliu Mănescu and Lavinia Betea: Unfinished Conversations] (Iaşi: Polirom, 2001).

Gaston Marin, Gheorghe, *În serviciul României lui Gheorghiu Dej. Însemnări din viată* [In the Service of Gheorghiu Dej's Romania: Signposts of Life] (Bucharest: Editura Evenimentul Românesc, 2000).

Gribkow, Anatoli I., *Im Dienste der Sowjetunion: Erinnerungen eines Armeegenerals* (Berlin: Edition Q, 1992).

Gribkow, Anatoli I., *Der Warschauer Pakt: Geschichte und Hintergründe des östlichen Militärbündnisses* (Berlin: Edition Q, 1995).

Gribkov, Anatolii I., *Судьба Варшавского Договора: Воспоминания, документы, факты* [The Fate of the Warsaw Treaty: Memories, Documents, and Facts] (Moscow: Russkaia kniga, 1998).

Grinevskij, Oleg, *Tauwetter: Entspannung, Krisen und neue Eiszeit* (Berlin: Siedler, 1996).

Hoffmann, Heinz, *Mannheim – Madrid – Moskau: Erlebtes aus drei Jahrzehnten* (Berlin: Militärverlag der DDR, 1981).

Hoffmann, Heinz, *Moskau – Berlin: Erinnerungen an Freunde, Kampfgenossen und Zeitumstände* (Berlin: Militärverlag der DDR, 1989).

Hoffmann, Theodor, *Das letzte Kommando* (Berlin: Mittler, 1993).

Horn, Gyula, *Freiheit, die ich meine* (Hamburg 1991).

Jaruzelski, Wojciech, *Mein Leben für Polen: Erinnerungen*. (Munich: Piper, 1993).

Kessler, Heinz, *Zur Sache und zur Person: Erinnerungen* (Berlin: Edition Ost, 1996).

Kwizinskij, Julij, *Vor dem Sturm: Erinnerungen eines Diplomaten* (Berlin: Siedler, 1993).

Löffler, Hans-Georg, *Soldat im Kalten Krieg. Erinnerungen 1955–1990* (Bissendorf: Biblio-Verlag, 2002).

Mladenov, Petar, *Животът: Плюсове и минуси* [Life: Its Pluses and Minuses] (Sofia: Peteks, 1992).

Niculescu-Mizil, Paul, *O istorie trăită* [History Experienced] (Bucharest: Editura Enciclopedică, 1997).

Olteanu, Constantin, *România—o voce distinctă în Tratatul de la Varşovia: Memorii, 1980-1985 (Dialog cu Dumitru Avram)* [Romania—A Dissenting Voice within the Warsaw Pact] (Bucharest: Aldo, 1999).

Pióro, Tadeusz, *Armia ze skazą: W Wojsku Polskim 1945–1968 (wspomnienia i refleksje)* [The Defective Army: In the Polish Army, 1945–1968 (Memories and Reflections)] (Warsaw: Czytelnik, 1994).

Pożegnanie z armią: Z gen. Zdzisławem Ostrowskim, pełnomocnikiem rządu do spraw pobytu w Polsce wojsk byłego ZSRR, rozmawia Mieczysław Szczepański [Farewell to the Army: Mieczysław Szczepański Speaks with Gen. Zdzisław Ostrowski, Government Plenipotentiary on the Stationing in Poland of the Troops of the former USSR] (Warsaw: Czytelnik, 1992).

Semerdzhiev, Atanas, *Преживаното не подлежи на обжалване* [No Appeal for the Years Survived] (Sofia: Trud, 2004) .

Vacek, Miroslav, *Generál studené války* [A Cold War General] (Prague: Erika, 2004).

Vacek, Miroslav, *Proč bych měl mlčet* [Why Should I Keep Silent] (Prague: Nadas, 1991).

Vacek, Miroslav, *Na rovinu* [Speaking Frankly] (Prague: Periskop, 1994).

Wolf, Markus, *Spionagechef im geheimen Krieg: Erinnerungen* (Munich: Econ & List, 1998).

LITERATURE AND ARCHIVES

Ehlert, Hans, and Hans-Joachim Beth, *Die Militär- und Sicherheitspolitik der SBZ/DDR: Eine Bibliographie (1945–1995)* (Munich: Militärgeschichtliches Forschungsamt, 1996)

Epley, William W., ed., *International Cold War Military Records and History: Proceedings of the International Conference on Cold War Military Records and History Held in Washington, D.C., 21–26 March 1994* (Washington: Office of the Secretary of Defense, 1996).

Mastny, Vojtech, "The New History of Cold War Alliances," *Journal of Cold War Studies* 4, no. 2 (2002): 55–84; also at http://www.isn.ethz.ch/php/research/NewLiterature/JCWS4_-2_02_Mastny.pdf

GENERAL

Clawson, Robert W., and Lawrence S. Kaplan, eds., *The Warsaw Pact: Political Purpose and Military Means* (Wilmington: Scholarly Resources, 1982).

Holden, Gerard, *The Warsaw Pact: The WTO and Soviet Security Policy* (Oxford: Blackwell, 1989).

Holloway, David, and Jane M.O. Sharp, eds., *The Warsaw Pact: Alliance in Transition?* (London: Macmillan, 1984).

Johnson, A. Ross, "The Warsaw Pact: Soviet Military Policy in Eastern Europe," in *Soviet*

Policy in Eastern Europe, ed. Sarah Meiklejohn Terry (New Haven: Yale University Press, 1984), pp. 255–83.

Johnson, A. Ross, Robert W. Dean, and Alexander Alexiev, *East European Military Establishments: The Warsaw Pact Northern Tier* (Santa Monica: RAND, 1980).

Mastny, Vojtech, "Did NATO Win the Cold War? Looking over the Wall," *Foreign Affairs* 78, no. 3 (May/June 1999): 176–89.

Steury, Donald P., ed., *Estimates of Soviet Military Power 1954 to 1984: A Selection* (Washington: Central Intelligence Agency, 1994).

Umbach, Frank, *Das rote Bündnis: Entwicklung und Zerfall des Warschauer Paktes 1955–1991* (Berlin: Links, 2005).

Wolfe, Thomas W., *Soviet Power and Europe, 1945–1970* (Baltimore: Johns Hopkins Press, 1970).

INSTITUTIONS

Fodor, Neil, *The Warsaw Treaty Organization: A Political and Organizational Analysis* (New York: St. Martin's Press, 1990).

Harms, Karl, "Im Oberkommando der Vereinten Streitkräfte," in *NVA, ein Rückblick für die Zukunft: Zeitzeugen berichten über ein Stück deutscher Militärgeschichte*, ed. Manfred Backerra (Cologne: Markus, 1992), pp. 338 sq.

Locher, Anna, "Shaping the Policies of the Alliance: The Committee of Ministers of Foreign Affairs of the Warsaw Pact, 1976–1990," http://www.isn.ethz.ch/php/documents/collection_3/CMFA_texts/CMFA_intro.htm

Mastny, Vojtech, "Learning from the Enemy: NATO as a Model for the Warsaw Pact," in *A History of NATO—The First Fifty Years*, ed. Gustav Schmidt, vol. 2 (New York: Palgrave, 2001), pp. 157–77, 393–401; also at http://www.isn.ethz.ch/php/research/MutualPerceptions/ZU58_Mastny.pdf

Nünlist, Christian, "Cold War Generals: The Warsaw Pact Committee of Defense Ministers, 1969–90," http://www.isn.ethz.ch/php/documents/collection_3/CMD_texts/introduction.htm

Sadykiewicz, Michael, *The Warsaw Pact Command Structure in Peace and War*, R-3558-RC (Santa Monica: RAND, 1988).

Simon, Jeffrey, *Warsaw Pact Forces: Problems of Command and Control* (Boulder: Westview Press, 1985).

Streletz, Fritz, "Der Nationale Verteidigungsrat und das Vereinte Kommando des Warschauer Vertrages," in *Rührt euch! Zur Geschichte der Nationalen Volksarmee der DDR*, ed. Wolfgang Wünsche (Berlin: Edition Ost, 1998), pp. 130–73.

Truta, Florian, "La Statul Major al Fortelor Armate Unite ale Tratatului de la Varşovia" [The General Staff of the Unified Armed Forces of the Warsaw Treaty], *Dosarele Istoriei*, 2001, no. 6.

THREAT PERCEPTIONS AND INTELLIGENCE

Brühl, Reinhard, "Bedrohungswahrnehmungen der DDR," in *Kalter Krieg auf deutschem Boden*, ed. Hans Modrow (Berlin 1994).

Mastny, Vojtech, *NATO in the Beholder's Eye: Soviet Perceptions and Policies, 1949-56*, Cold War International History Project Working Paper no. 35 (Washington: Woodrow Wilson International Center for Scholars, 2002), also at http://www.isn.ethz.ch/php/research/MutualPerceptions/WP35_Mastny.pdf

Schäfer, Bernd, "The Warsaw Pact's Intelligence on NATO: East German Military Espionage Against the West," (http://www.isn.ethz.ch/php/documents/collection_17/texts/schaefer.htm)

Schäfer, Bernd, "Stasi Files and GDR Espionage against the West". *IFS Info* [Oslo] 2 (2002): 1–13, also at http://www.isn.ethz.ch/php/research/MutualPerceptions/ifs2_02_schaefer.pdf

Schunke, Joachim, "Zur Bedrohungsanalyse der militärischen Führung der DDR," in *Landesverteidigung und/oder Militarisierung der Gesellschaft der DDR?*, ed. Günther Glaser and Werner Knoll (Berlin: Trafo, 1995), pp. 34–48.

Weiser, Benjamin, *A Secret Life: The Polish Officer* [Ryszard Kukliński]: *His Covert Mission, and the Price He Paid to Save His Country* (New York: Public Affairs, 2004).

DOCTRINES

Deim, Hans Werner, "Militärische Konzeption der UdSSR und des Warschauer Vertrages im Wandel," *Jahrbuch für Wehrpolitik und Militärwesen* 2 (1996): 148–77.

Heuser, Beatrice, "Warsaw Pact Military Doctrines in the 1970s and 1980s: Findings in the East German Archives," *Comparative Strategy* 12, No. 4 (1993): 437–57.

MccGwire, Michael, *Military Objectives in Soviet Foreign Policy* (Washington, DC: Brookings Institution, 1987).

Rühl, Lothar, "Offensive Defence in the Warsaw Pact," *Survival* 33 (1991): 442–50.

Tsymburskii, Vadim L., *Военная доктрина СССР и России: Осмысления понятий «угрозы» и «победы» во второй половине XX века* [The Military Doctrine of the USSR and Russia: Understanding the Notions of "Threat" and "Victory" in the Second Half of the Twentieth Century] (Moscow: Rossiiskii Nauchnyi Fond, 1994).

WAR PLANS

Bautzmann, Georg, "Zu den Kriegsplanungen des Warschauer Paktes in den achtziger Jahren: Darstellung unter Berücksichtigung der Quellenlage nach Ende der DDR," in *Österreichisches Jahrbuch für internationale Sicherheitspolitik 1997*, ed. Erich Reiter (Graz: Styria, 1997), pp. 279–99.

Gemzell, Carl-Axel, "Warszawapakten, DDR och Denmark: kampen för en maritim operationsplan" [The Warsaw Pact, GDR, and Denmark: The Struggle for a Naval Operational Plan] *Historisk tidskrift* 96 (1996): 32–84.

Gemzell, Carl-Axel, "Die DDR, der Warschauer Pakt und Dänemark im Kalten Krieg," in *Deutsch-skandinavische Beziehungen nach 1945*, ed. Robert Bohn, Jürgen Elvert, and Karl Christian Lammers (Stuttgart: Steiner, 2000), pp. 44–56.

Heuser, Beatrice, "Victory in a Nuclear War? A Comparison of NATO and WTO War Aims and Strategies," *Contemporary European History* 7 (1998): 311–27.

Johnson, A. Ross, *East European Armed Forces and Soviet Military Planning: Factors of Change*, N-2856-AF (Santa Monica: RAND, 1989), declassified 2003.

Kramer, Mark, "The Official (West) German Report: Warsaw Pact Military Planning in Central Europe: Revelations from East German Archives," *Cold War International History Project Bulletin* 2 (1992): 1, 13–19.

Luňák, Petr, "Planning for Nuclear War: The Czechoslovak War Plan of 1964," *Cold War International History Project Bulletin* 12/13 (2001): 289–298.

Luňák, Petr, "War Plans under Stalin and Khrushchev: The Czechoslovak Pivot," paper presented at the conference, "NATO, the Warsaw Pact and the European non-aligned 1949–1979: Threat assessments, doctrines and war plans," Longyearbyen, 12–16 June 2003.

Mastny, Vojtech, "Imagining War in Europe: Soviet Strategic Planning," paper presented at the conference, "NATO, the Warsaw Pact and the European non-aligned 1949–1979: Threat assessments, doctrines and war plans," Longyearbyen, 12–16 June 2003.

Okváth, Imre, "A Magyar Néphadsereg háborús haditervei a Varsói Szerződésben, 1955–1965" [War Plans of the Hungarian People's Army in the Warsaw Pact, 1955–1965]. *Ármádia* 5 (2002): 38–39.

Piotrowski, Paweł, "Desant na Danię" [The Landing Operation in Denmark], *Wprost* [Warsaw], 25 June 2002; English translation, in "A Landing Operation in Denmark," http://www.isn.ethz.ch/php/documents/collection_12/texts/piotrowski.htm

INTRA-ALLIANCE RELATIONS

Anderson, Sheldon, *A Cold War in the Soviet Bloc: Polish-East German Relations, 1945–1962* (Boulder: Westview Press, 2000).

Gati, Charles, "Hegemony and Repression in the Eastern Alliance," in *Origins of the Cold War: An International History*, ed. Melvyn P. Leffler and David S. Painter (New York, 1994).

Hutchings, Robert L., *Foreign and Security Policy Co-ordination in the Warsaw Pact* (Cologne: Bundesinstitut für Ostwissenschaftliche und Internationale Studien, 1985).

Ihme-Tuchel, Beate, *Das "nördliche Dreieck": Die Beziehungen zwischen der DDR, der Tschechoslowakei und Polen in den Jahren 1954 bis 1962* (Cologne: Wissenschaft und Politik, 1994).

Nelson, Daniel N., *Alliance Behavior in the Warsaw Pact* (Boulder: Westview Press, 1986).

Johnson, A. Ross, and Alexander R. *Alexiev, East European Military Reliability; An Emigré-Based* Assessment, R-3480 (Santa Monica: RAND, 1986).

Mioara, Anton, "1965–1967: Moscova-Bucureşti: Disensiuni întro alianţă a 'egalilor'" [1965–1967: Moscow-Bucharest: Divergences within an Alliance of "Equals"], *Revista de Istorie Militară*, 2003, no. 1–2: 21–26.

Nelson, Daniel N., ed., *Soviet Allies: The Warsaw Pact and the Issue of Reliability* (Boulder: Westview Press, 1984).

Oşca, Alexandru, "Poziţia României faţă de sistemul de gestionare a crizelor din interiorul Tratatului de la Varşovia" [Romania's Position on the System of Crisis Management within the Warsaw Treaty), *Revista de Istorie Militară*, 2002, no. 5–6.

Ouimet, Matthew, *The Rise and Fall of the Brezhnev Doctrine in Soviet Foreign Policy* (Chapel Hill: University of North Carolina Press, 2003).

Rakowska-Harmstone, Teresa, et al., *Warsaw Pact: The Question of Cohesion*, 3 vols. (Ottawa: Operational Research and Analysis Establishment, 1984–86).

Retegan, Mihai, *Război politic in blocul comunist: Relaţii româno-sovietice în anii '60* [The Political Struggle in the Communist Bloc: Romanian-Soviet Relations in the 1960s] (Bucharest: RAO, 2002).

Sadykiewicz, Michael, Organizing for Coalition Warfare: The Role of East European Warsaw Pact Forces in Soviet Military Planning, R-3559-RC (Santa Monica: RAND, 1988).

Selvage, Douglas E., "Poland, the German Democratic Republic and the German Question, 1955–1967" (unpublished doctoral dissertation, Yale University, 1998).

ORIGINS AND EARLY DEVELOPMENT (1955–64)

Baev, Iordan, "България и създаването на воената организация на Варшавския договор" [Bulgaria and the Establishment of the Military Organization of the Warsaw Treaty], *Voennoistoricheski sbornik* [Sofia] 64, no. 4 (1995): 39–61.

Baev, Iordan, "Изграждане на воената структура на организация на Варшавския договор 1955–1969" [The Building of the Military Structure of the Warsaw Treaty Organization], *Voennoistoricheski sbornik* 66, no. 5 (1997): 56–77.

Békés, Csaba, "Titkos válságkezeléstől a politikai koordinációig. Politikai egyeztetési mecha-nizmus a Varsói Szerződésben, 1954–1967" [From Secret Crisis Management to Political Coordination: Political Coordinating Mechanism in the Warsaw Pact, 1954–1967] in *Múlt századi hétköznapok. Tanulmányok a Kádár rendszer kialakulásának időszakáról* [Every-days in the past century: Essays on the period of the emergence of the Kádár regime], ed. János M. Rainer, (Budapest: 1956-os Intézet, 2003), pp. 9–54.

Bílek, Jiří and Vladimír *Pilát*, "Bezprostřední reakce československých politických a vojen-ských orgánů na povstání v Maďarsku" [Czechoslovak Political and Military Authorities' Reaction to the Uprising in Hungary], *Soudobé dějiny* [Prague], 1996/4, pp. 500–511.

Mastny, Vojtech, "'We Are in a Bind': Polish and Czechoslovak Attempts at Reforming the Warsaw Pact, 1956-1969," *Cold War International History Project Bulletin* 11 (1998): 230–50.

Mastny, Vojtech, "The Soviet Union and the Origins of the Warsaw Pact in 1955," in *Mecha-nisms of Power in the Soviet Union*, ed. Niels Erik Rosenfeldt, Bent Jensen, and Erik Kulavig (New York: St. Martin's Press, 2000), pp. 241–66.

Okváth, Imre, "In the Shadow of the Kremlin: Hungarian Military Policy in the Early Period of the Cold War, 1945–1956," in William W. Epley, ed., *International Cold War Military Records and History: Proceedings of the International Conference on Cold War Military Records and History Held in Washington, D.C., 21–26 March 1994* (Washington: Office of the Secretary of Defense, 1996), pp. 457–69.

Okváth, Imre, "A Varsói Szerződés és a magyar forradalom" [The Warsaw Pact and the Hungarian Revolution], in *Tizenhárom nap, amely... Tanulmányok az 56-os magyar for-radalom és szabadságharc történetéből* [Thirteen days that... Studies on the History of the 56' Hungarian Revolution and the Fight for Freedom], ed. Miklós Horváth (Budapest: Hadtörténelmi Intézet és Múzeum, 2003), pp. 61–74.

Poksiński, Jerzy, "Memorandum sztabu generalnego WP w sprawie Układu Warszawskiego oraz planu rozwoju sił zbrojnych PRL na lata 1955–1965" [Memorandum by the General Staff of the Polish Army Concerning the Warsaw Treaty and the Plan for the Development of Poland's Armed Forces in 1955–1956], *Przegląd historyczno-wojskowy* 1, no. 1 (2000): 81–96.

Scurtu, Ioan, ed., *România—Retragerea trupelor sovietice, 1958* [The Withdrawal of Soviet Troops from Romania in 1958] (Bucharest: Editura Didactică și Pedagogică, 1996).

Vartic, Gheorghe, "Retragerea trupelor sovietice din România. O victorie a Bucureștilor sau o decizie a Moscovei?" [The Withdrawal of the Soviet Troops from Romania. A Bucha-rest Victory or a Moscow Decision?], *Revista de Istorie Militară* 3 (2003): 1–6.

THE BERLIN AND CUBAN CRISES

Bonwetsch, Bernd, and Alexei *Filitow*, "Chruschtschow und der Mauerbau: Die Gipfelkonf-erenz der Warschauer-Pakt-Staaten vom 3–5. August 1961," *Vierteljahrshefte für Zeitge-schichte* 48, no. 1 (2000): 155–98.

Harrison, Hope M., *Driving the Soviets up the Wall: Soviet-East German Relations, 1953–1961* (Princeton: Princeton University Press, 2003).

Kramer, Mark, "The 'Lessons' of the Cuban Missile Crisis for Warsaw Pact Nuclear Oper-ations," *Cold War International History Project Bulletin* 5 (1995): 59, 110–15, 160.

Lemke, Michael, *Die Berlinkrise 1958 bis 1963: Interessen und Handlungsspielräume der SED im Ost-West-Konflikt* (Berlin: Akademie, 1995).

Luňák, Petr, "Khrushchev and the Berlin Crisis: Soviet Brinkmanship Seen from Inside," *Cold War History* 3, no. 2 (2003): 53–82.

Menning, Bruce W., "The Berlin Crisis from the Perspective of the Soviet General Staff," in William W. Epley, ed., *International Cold War Military Records and History: Proceedings* of the *International Conference on Cold War Military Records and History Held in Washington, D.C., 21–26 March 1994* (Washington: Office of the Secretary of Defense, 1996), pp. 49–62.

Pernes, Jiří, "Československo a berlínská krize v roce 1961" [Czechoslovakia and the Berlin Crisis in 1961], *Soudobé dějiny* [Prague], 2002, no. 2: 215–229.

Uhl, Matthias, "Storming on to Paris: The 1961 'Buria' Exercise and the Planned Solution of the Berlin Crisis," paper presented at the conference, "NATO, the Warsaw Pact and the European non-aligned 1949–1979: Threat assessments, doctrines and war plans," Longyearbyen, 12–16 June 2003.

Uhl, Matthias, and Armin *Wagner, Ulbricht, Chruschtschow und die Mauer: Eine Dokumentation* (Munich: Oldenbourg, 2003).

1964–68

Baev, Jordan, "A Prelude to Détente: the Strange Case of a Regional Inter-Blocs Cooperation and Intra-Blocs Confrontation in the Balkans: 1964–1974," paper presented at the conference, "NATO, the Warsaw Pact, and the Rise of Détente, 1965–1972," Dobbiaco," 26–28 September 2002.

Betea, Lavinia, "Gheorghe Gheorghiu-Dej—Strategii de putere şi influenţă în relaţiile din interiorul Tratatului de la Varşovia" [Gheorghe Gheorghiu-Dej's Strategies of Power and Influence within the Warsaw Treaty), *Revista de Istorie Militară*, 2003, no. 1–2: 1–8.

Ermarth, Fritz, *Internationalism, Security, and Legitimacy: The Challenge to Soviet Interests in East Europe, 1964–1968* (Santa Monica: RAND, 1969).

Garthoff, Raymond L., "When and Why Romania Distanced Itself from the Warsaw Pact," *Cold War International History Project Bulletin* 5 (1995): 111.

Ionescu, Mihail E., "Rumunsko a vojenská reforma Varšavské smlouvy (1964–1968)" [Romania and the Military Reform of the Warsaw Treaty], *Historie a vojenství* [Prague], 2003, no. 3–4: 699–705.

Madry, Jindřich, "Sovětské zájmy v pojetí obrany Československa (1965–1970)" [Soviet Interests in the Concept of the Defense of Czechoslovakia], *Historie a vojenství*, 1992, no. 5: 126–40.

Navrátil, Jaromír, "K otázce výstavby Československé armády před rokem 1968" [The Building of the Czechoslovak Army before 1968], *Historie a vojenství*, 1992, no. 5: 101–25.

Opriş, Petre, "Relaţiile militare româno-bulgaro-sovietice la mijlocul anilor '60" [Military Relations between Romania, Bulgaria and the USSR in the mid-1960s] *Revista de Istorie Militară*, 2001, no. 3–4: 14–20.

Otu, Petre, "Dispute referitoare la crearea Comisiei de Politică Externa a Tratatului de la Varşovia" [Divergences Concerning the Creation of a Foreign Policy Commission within the Warsaw Treaty), *Revista de Istorie Militară*, 2002, no. 5–6: 43–47.

Otu, Petre, "Războiul de Şase Zile, o nouă problemă pentru Tratatul de la Varşovia" [The Six-Day War: A New Challenge for the Warsaw Pact], *Revista de Istorie Militară*, 2002, no. 3: 3–7.

Selvage, Douglas, *"The Warsaw Pact and Nuclear Proliferation, 1963–65,"* Cold War International History Project Working Paper, no. 32 (Washington: Woodrow Wilson International Center for Scholars, 2001), also at http://www.isn.ethz.ch/php/research/RelationsWithAllies/Wp32_Selvage.pdf

Selvage, Douglas, "The Warsaw Pact is Collapsing: Poland, the GDR and Bonn's Ostpolitik, 1966–69," paper presented at the conference, "NATO, the Warsaw Pact, and the Rise of Détente, 1965–1972," Dobbiaco," 26–28 September 2002.

Wolfe, Thomas W., *Soviet Power and Europe, 1945–1970* (Baltimore: The Johns Hopkins Press, 1970).

THE CZECHOSLOVAK CRISIS

Benčík, Antonín, *Operace „Dunaj": Vojáci a Pražské jaro 1968: Studie a dokumenty* [Operation "Danube": The Military and the Prague Spring: Studies and Documents] (Prague: Ústav pro soudobé dějiny AV ČR, 1994).

Benčík, Antonín, Jaromír Navrátil, and Jan Paulík, eds., *Vojenské otázky československé reformy, 1967–1970: Vojenská varianta řešení čs. krize (1967–1968)* [Military Issues in the Czechoslovak Reform, 1967–1970: The Military Option in the Solution of the Czechoslovak Crisis] (Brno: Doplněk, 1996).

Dvořák, Jaroslav, "Vojenské důvody invaze do Československa v roce 1968" [Military Reasons for the Invasion to Czechoslovakia in 1968], *Soudobé dějiny* [Prague], 1994/4–5, pp. 591–97.

Gheorghe, Ion, and Corneliu Soare, *Doctrina militară românească 1968–1969* [The Romanian Military Doctrine] (Bucharest: Militară, 1999).

Kramer, Mark, "The Czechoslovak Crisis and the Brezhnev Doctrine," in *1968: The World Transformed*, ed. Carole Fink, Philipp Gassert, and Detlev Junker (Cambridge: Cambridge University Press, 1998), pp. 111–71.

Kramer, Mark, "Soviet-Romanian Relations and the Warsaw Pact: Repercussions from the Czechoslovak Crisis," paper presented at the conference, "NATO, the Warsaw Pact, and the Rise of Détente, 1965–1972," Dobbiaco," 26–28 September 2002.

Madry, Jindřich, *Sovětská okupace Československa, jeho normalizace v letech 1969–1970 a role ozbrojených sil* [Soviet Occupation of Czechoslovakia, Its Normalization in 1969–1970 and the Role of the Armed Forces] (Prague: Institute for Contemporary History, 1994).

Mastny, Vojtech, "Was 1968 a Strategic Watershed of the Cold War?" *Diplomatic History* 29, no. 1 (2005): 149–77.

Pajórek, Leszek, *Polska a "praska wiosna": Udział Wojska Polskiego w interwencji w Czechosłowacji w 1968 r.* [Poland and the "Prague Spring": The Participation of the Polish Army in the 1968 Intervention in Czechoslovakia] (Warsaw: Wojskowy Instytut Historyczny AON, 1998).

Pikhoia, Rudolf G., "Чехословакия, 1968 год: Взгляд из Москвы: По документам ЦК КПСС" [Czechoslovakia 1968 As Seen from Moscow: From the Documents of the CPSU Central Committee], *Novaia i noveishaia istoriia* 1994, no. 6: 3–20, and 1995, no. 1: 34–47.

Retegan, Mihai, *In the Shadow of the Prague Spring: Romanian Foreign Policy and the Crisis in Czechoslovakia, 1968* (Iaşi: Center for Romanian Studies, 2000).

Wenzke, Rüdiger, *Die NVA und der Prager Frühling 1968: Die Rolle Ulbrichts und der DDR-Streitkräfte bei der Niederschlagung der tschechoslowakischen Reformbewegung* (Berlin: Links, 1995).

DÉTENTE

Baev, Jordan, "The 'Crimean Meetings' of the Warsaw Pact Countries' Leaders," http://www.isn.ethz.ch/php/documents/collection_16/texts/intro_baev.htm

Hutchings, Robert L., *Soviet-East European Relations: Consolidation and Conflict, 1968–1980* (Madison: University of Wisconsin Press, 1983).

Kaiser, Monika, *Machtwechsel von Ulbricht zu Honecker: Funktionsmechanismen der SED-Diktatur in Konfliktsituationen 1962 bis 1972* (Berlin: Akademie, 1997).

"Magyarország és az európai biztonsági konferencia előkészítése, 1965–1970" [Hungary and the making of the CSCE process, 1965–1969], in *Évkönyv 2004* (Budapest: 1956-os Intézet, 2004).

Mastny, Vojtech, "The Soviet Union, Détente, and Military Rivalry," paper presented at the conference, "NATO, the Warsaw Pact, and the Rise of Détente, 1965–1972," Dobbiaco," 26–28 September 2002.

Sarotte, M.E., *Dealing with the Devil: East Germany, Détente, and Ostpolitik* (2001).

Tiedtke, Stephan, *Die Warschauer Vertragsorganisation: Zum Verhältnis von Militär- und Entspannungspolitik in Osteuropa* (Munich: Oldenbourg, 1978).

THE POLISH CRISIS, 1980–81

Gribkov, Anatolii I., "Доктрина Брежнева и польский кризис начала 80-х годов" [The Brezhnev Doctrine and the Polish Crisis of the Early 1980s], *Voennoistoricheskii zhurnal*, 1992, no. 9.

Gutsche, Reinhard, "Nur ein Erfüllungsgehilfe? Die SED-Führung und die militärische Option zur Niederschlagung der Opposition in Polen in den Jahren 1980/81," in *Geschichte und Transformation des SED-Staates: Beiträge und Analysen,* ed. Klaus Schröder (Berlin: Akademie, 1994), pp. 166–79.

Jaruzelski, Wojciech, *Stan wojenny—dlaczego* [Why Martial Law] (Warsaw: BGW, 1993).

Kramer, Mark, "The Warsaw Pact and the Polish Crisis of 1980-1981: Honecker's Call for Military Intervention," *Cold War International History Project Bulletin* 5 (1995): 124.

Kramer, Mark, "The Anoshkin Notebook on the Polish Crisis, December 1981," *Cold War International History Project Bulletin* 11 (1998): 14–31.

Kubina, Michael, and Manfred Wilke, "Das 'Mosaiksteinchen' Polen 1980/81: Verantwortungsgemeinschaften in Deutschland," in *Geschichte und Transformation des SED-Staates: Beiträge und Analysen,* ed. Klaus Schröder (Berlin: Akademie, 1994), pp. 149–65.

Kubina, Michael, and Manfred Wilke, eds., *"Hart und kompromißlos durchgreifen!": Die SED contra Polen 1980/81, Geheimakten der SED-Führung über die Unterdrückung der polnischen Demokratiebewegung* (Berlin: Akademie, 1994).

Kukliński, Ryszard J., "Wojna z narodem widziana od środka" [War Against the Nation As Seen from the Center] *Kultura* [Paris] 475, no. 4 (April 1987): 3–57.

Mastny, Vojtech, "The Soviet Non-Invasion of Poland in 1980–1981 and the End of the Cold War," *Europe–Asia Studies* 51, no. 2 (1999): 189–211.

Olteanu, Constantin, "Furtună in Tratatul de la Varşovia" [Storm Inside the Warsaw Treaty], *Dosarele Istoriei*, 2001, no. 2.

Paczkowski, Andrzej, *Droga do "mniejszego zła": Strategia i taktyka obozu władzy, lipiec 1980-styczeń 1982* [The Road to "Lesser Evil": The Strategy and Tactics of the Ruling Establishment, July 1980–January 1982] (Cracow: Wydawnictwo literackie, 2002).

Serediuc, Mircea, "Criza poloneză din anii 1980–1981 şi poziţia României" [The Polish Crisis of 1980–1981 and the Position of Romania], *Revista de Istorie Militară*, 2002, no. 3: 29–36.

Wejdą nie wejdą—Polska 1980–1982: wewnętrzny kryzys, międzynarodowe uwarunkowania [They Will Enter and They Will Not—Poland 1980–1982: The Internal Crisis and Its International Ramifications] (London: Aneks, 1999).

THE "SECOND COLD WAR"

Asmus, Ronald, *East Berlin and Moscow: The Documentation of a Dispute* (Munich: Radio Free Europe, 1985).

Fesefeldt, Joachim D. C., *Der Warschauer Pakt auf dem Madrider KSZE Folgetreffen und auf der KVAE (ohne Rumänien)* (Cologne: Bundesinstitut für Ostwissenschaftliche und Internationale Studien, 1984).

NATO and the Warsaw Pact: Force Comparisons (Brussels: NATO Information Service, 1984).

Ploetz, Michael, "NATO and the Warsaw Treaty Organisation at the Time of the Euromissile Crisis, 1975 to 1985," in *A History of NATO—The First Fifty Years*, vol. 2, ed. Gustav Schmidt (London: Palgrave, 2001), pp. 209–224.

Wettig, Gerhard, *The Smaller Warsaw Pact States in East–West Relations* (Cologne: Bundesinstitut für Ostwissenschaftliche und Internationale Studien, 1985).

DISINTEGRATION

Baev, Jordan, "The End of the Warsaw Pact, 1985-1991: Viewed from the Bulgarian Archives," http://www.isn.ethz.ch/php/documents/collection_2/texts/introduction.htm

Barany, Zoltán D., "East European Armed Forces in Transitions and Beyond," *East European Quarterly* 26, no. 1 (March 1992).

Békés, Csaba, "Back to Europe: The International Context of the Political Transition in Hungary, 1988–1990," in *The Roundtable Talks of 1989: The Genesis of Hungarian Democracy*, ed. András Bozóki (Budapest and New York: Central European University Press, 2002), pp. 237–272.

Leebaert, Derek, and Timothy Dickinson, eds., *Soviet Strategy and New Military Thinking* (New York: Cambridge University Press, 1992).

Lévesque, Jacques, *The Enigma of 1989: The USSR and the Liberation of Eastern Europe* (Berkeley: University of California Press, 1997).

Mastny, Vojtech, "Did Gorbachev Liberate Eastern Europe?" in *The Last Decade of the Cold War: From Conflict Escalation to Conflict Transformation*, ed. Olav Njølstad (London: Cass, 2004), pp. 402–23.

Odom, William E., *The Collapse of the Soviet Military* (New Haven: Yale University Press, 1998).

Pecka, Jindřich, *Odsun sovětských vojsk z Československa, 1989–1991* [The Withdrawal of Soviet Troops from Czechoslovakia] (Prague: Ústav pro soudobé dějiny AV ČR, 1996).

Philipps, R. Hyland, and Jeffrey I. Sands, "Reasonable Sufficiency and Soviet Conventional Defense," *International Security* 13, no. 2 (Fall 1988): 164–78.

Snyder, Jack L., "Limiting Offensive Conventional Forces: Soviet Proposals and Western Options," *International Security* 12, no. 4 (Spring 1988): 48–77.

Strzelczyk, Joanna, *Ucieczka ze wschodu: Rosja w polskiej polityce 1989–1993* [Escape from the East: Russia in Polish Politics, 1989–1993] (Warsaw: Rytm, 2002).

Taylor, Brian D., "The Soviet Military and the Disintegration of the USSR," *Journal of Cold War Studies* 5, no. 1 (Winter 2002): 17–66.

POLAND

Babula, Julian, *Wojsko Polskie 1945–1989: Próba analizy operacyjnej* [The Polish Army, 1945–1989: An Attempt at Operational Analysis] (Warsaw: Bellona, 1998).

Kowalski, Lech, *Komitet obrony kraju w systemie obronnym PRL w latach 1959–1989 (studium historyczno-wojskowe)* [The Committee of Homeland Defense in Poland's Defense System in 1959–1989: A Study in Military History] (Warsaw: Wojskowy Instytut Historyczny, 1995).

Piotrowski, Paweł, "Front Polski—próba wyjaśnienia zagadnienia" [The Polish Front: An Attempt to Clarify the Issue], in *Wrocławskie Studia z Historii Najnowszej* [Wrocław Studies in Contemporary History], ed. Wojciech Wrzesiński, vol. 6 (Wrocław 1998), pp. 221–233.

Wandycz, Piotr, "Adam Rapacki and the Search for European Security," in *The Diplomats, 1939–1979*, ed. Gordon A. Craig and Francis L. Loewenheim (Princeton: Princeton University Press, 1994), pp. 289–317.

"Warsaw Pact Generals in Polish Uniforms: Oral History Interviews," http://www.isn.ethz.ch/-php/collections/coll_9.htm

EAST GERMANY

Ehlert, Hans, and Hans-Joachim Beth, eds., *Armee ohne Zukunft: Das Ende der NVA und die deutsche Einheit: Zeitzeugenberichte und Dokumente* (Berlin: Links, 2002).

Ehlert, Hans, and Armin Wagner, eds., *Genosse General! Die Militärelite der DDR in biografischen Skizzen* (Berlin: Links, 2003).

Forster, Thomas M., *The East German Army: The Second Power in the Warsaw Pact* (London: Allen & Unwin, 1980).

Herspring, Dale R., *Requiem for an Army: The Demise of the East German Military* (Lanham: Rowman & Littlefield, 1998).

Naumann, Klaus, ed., *NVA: Anspruch und Wirklichkeit nach ausgewählten Dokumenten* (Berlin: Mittler, 1996).

Nielsen, Harald, ed., *Die DDR und die Kernwaffen: Die nukleare Rolle der Nationalen Volksarmee im Warschauer Pakt* (Baden-Baden: Nomos, 1998).

Prüfert, Andreas, ed., *Die Nationale Volksarmee im Kalten Krieg: Militärisches Denken und Handeln an Schnittpunkten des Kalten Krieges: Zur Rolle der NVA in internationalen Krisen- und Konfliktsituationen* (Bonn 1995).

Schunke, Joachim, "Militärpolitische und -strategische Vorstellungen der Führung der NVA in der Zeit der Block-Konfrontation," in *Nationale Volksarmee—Armee für den Frieden: Beiträge zum Selbstverständnis und Geschichte des deutschen Militärs 1945-1990*, ed. Detlef Bald, Reinhard Brühl, and Andreas Prüfert (Baden-Baden: Nomos 1995).

Wagner, Armin, *Walter Ulbricht und die geheime Sicherheitspolitik der SED: Der Nationale Verteidigungsrat der DDR und seine Vorgeschichte(1953–1971)* (Berlin: Links, 2002).

Wenzel, Otto, *Kriegsbereit: Der Nationale Verteidigungsrat der DDR, 1960 bis 1989* (Cologne: Wissenschaft und Politik, 1995).

Wenzke, Rüdiger, "Die Nationale Volksarmee (1956–1990)," in *Im Dienste der Partei: Handbuch der bewaffneten Organe der DDR*, ed. Torsten Diedrich, Hans Ehlert, and Rüdiger Wenzke (Berlin: Links, 1998), pp. 422–535.

CZECHOSLOVAKIA

Müller, Adolf, *Die Tschechoslowakei auf der Suche nach Sicherheit* (Berlin: Berlin Verlag, 1977).

Pecka, Jindřich, et al., ed., *Sovětská armáda v Československu 1968–1991: Chronologický přehled* [Soviet Army in Czechoslovakia 1968–1991: A Chronological Overview] (Prague: Ústav pro soudobé dějiny AV ČR, 1996).

Rice, Condoleezza, *The Soviet Union and the Czechoslovak Army, 1948–1983: Uncertain Allegiance* (Princeton: Princeton University Press, 1984).

HUNGARY

Békés, Csaba, "Hungary and the Warsaw Pact, 1954–1989: Documents on the Impact of a Small State within the Eastern Bloc," http://www.isn.ethz.ch/php/documents/collection_13/-texts/intro.htm

Dunay, Pál, *Hungary's Security Policy* (Hamburg: Institut für Friedensforschung und Sicherheitspolitik, 1987).

ROMANIA

Deletant, Dennis, and Mihail E. Ionescu, *Romania and Warsaw Pact, 1955–1989: Selected Documents* (Bucharest: Paideia, 2004).

Dumitru, Mircea C., "Aspecte ale relaţiilor dintre conducerea armatei române şi structurile militare ale Tratatului de la Varşovia" [Relations between the Romanian Army Leadership and the Military Structures of the Warsaw Pact], *Dosarele Istoriei* 2001, no.8.

Duţu, Alesandru, "Tratatul de la Varşovia: Divergenţe româno-sovietice în adoptarea statutelor" [The Warsaw Pact: Romanian-Soviet Disagreements Concerning the Adoption of Statutes], *Document*, 2002, no. 1.

Ionescu, Mihail E., "Romania and the Warsaw Pact, 1955–1989: Introduction," working paper no. 43, Cold War International History Project, http://wwics.si.edu/topics/pubs/ACF368.pdf

Miroiu, Andrei, "Controverse privind rolul României în cadrul Tratatului de la Varşovia: Perspective militare şi diplomatice" [Controversies on Romania's Role within the Warsaw Pact: Military and Diplomatic Perspectives], *Revista de Istorie Militară*, 2002, no. 5–6: 48–55.

Munteanu, Mircea, ed., *Romania and the Warsaw Pact, 1955–1989*, 2 vols. (Washington: Woodrow Wilson International Center for Scholars, 2002).

Şuţa, Ion, "Acţiuni distincte ale militarilor români in cadrul Tratatului de la Varsovia" [The Activities of the Romanian Military within the Warsaw Pact], *Dosarele Istoriei*, 2001, no. 1: 23–27.

BULGARIA

Baev, Iordan, *Военнополитическите конфликти след втората световна война и България* [Military–Political Conflicts since World War II and Bulgaria] (Sofia: Izdatelstvo na Ministerstvoto na Otbranata "Sv. Georgi Pobedonosets," 1995).

България във Варшавския Договор [Bulgaria in the Warsaw Treaty] (Sofia: Izdatelska K'shcha BM, 2000), CD-ROM.

Eyal, Jonathan, ed., *The Warsaw Pact and the Balkans: Moscow's Southern Flank* (New York: St. Martin's Press, 1989).

ALBANIA

Griffith, William E., *Albania and the Sino-Soviet Rift* (Cambridge, MA: MIT Press, 1963).

RELATIONS WITH CHINA

"China and the Warsaw Pact under Mao and Khrushchev," http://www.isn.ethz.ch/php/collections/coll_11.htm

Liu, Xiaoyuan and Vojtech Mastny, eds., *China and Eastern Europe, 1960s–1980s: Proceedings of the International Symposium, Beijing, 24–26 March 2004* (Zurich: Center for Security Studies, 2004).

Lüthi, Lorenz M., "The Sino-Soviet Split" (unpublished Ph.D. dissertation, Yale University, 2003).

Rijnoveanu, Carmen, "Politica de autonomie a României în contextul conflictului chino-sovietic: 1960–1968" [Romania's Autonomous Policy within the Context of the Sino-Soviet Conflict: 1960–1968], *Revista de Istorie Militară* 3 2003, no. 3: 7–11.

Selvage, Douglas, "Poland and the Sino-Soviet Rift, 1963–1965," http://wwics.si.edu/index.cfm?topic_id=1409&fuseaction=topics.publications&doc_id=43898&group_id=13349

FOR FURTHER REFERENCE SEE:

Collections Overview on the Parallel History Project website, www.isn.ethz.ch/php:

Warsaw Pact Records

PARTY LEADERS

Records of the Political Consultative Committee, 1955-1990

DEFENSE MINISTERS

Records of the Committee of the Ministers of Defense, 1969-1990

FOREIGN MINISTERS

Records of the Committee of the Ministers of Foreign Affairs, 1976-1990

CRIMEA MEETINGS

Records on the Informal Meetings of Warsaw Pact Leaders, 1970s

SECRET GDR JOURNAL MILITÄRWESEN

Tables of content and sample articles from the formerly secret East German equivalent to Voennaya mysl'

GERMAN MILITARY ARCHIVES

Warsaw Pact Records in the German Military Archives: Finding Aids

Intelligence

STASI INTELLIGENCE ON NATO

Stasi Intelligence on NATO, 1969-89: East German Military Espionage Against the West

NATO's SECRET ARMIES

Secret Warfare: Operation Gladio and NATO's Stay-Behind Armies

ZHUKOV'S 1957 SPEECH

Superpower under Pressure: The Secret Speech of Minister of Defence Marshal Zhukov in East Berlin, March 1957

Crises

1961 BERLIN CRISIS

The 1961 Berlin Crisis and Soviet Preparations for War in Europe

LIBYA 1986

A Confidential Soviet Account from the Stasi Archives on the U.S. Air Raid on Libya in April 1986

Warsaw Pact War Plans

1964 WAR PLAN

The 1964 Warsaw Pact Plan for Nuclear War in Europe and Related Documents

1965 WAR GAME

The 1965 Warsaw Pact War Game Related Documents from Hungarian Archives, 1965-1971

Warsaw Pact Generals

POLISH GENERALS

Warsaw Pact Generals in Polish Uniforms: Oral History Interviews

CZECHOSLOVAK GENERALS

Oral History Interviews on Czechoslovakia's Security Relations During the Cold War

National Perspectives

BULGARIA IN THE WARSAW PACT

Documents on the Irresistible Collapse of the Warsaw Pact from Bulgarian Archives, 1985-1991

ROMANIA AND THE WARSAW PACT, 1955-89

Documents Highlighting Romania's Gradual Emancipation from the Warsaw Pact, 1956-1981

HUNGARY AND THE WARSAW PACT

Documents on the Impact of a Small State within the Eastern Bloc 1954-1989

WAR ON TITO'S YUGOSLAVIA

The Hungarian Army in the Early Cold War

POLISH EXERCISES

A Landing Operation in Denmark: New Evidence from Polish Archives

CHINA AND THE WARSAW PACT

Documents on Sino-Soviet Cooperation under Mao and Khrushchev

CHINA AND EASTERN EUROPE, 1960s-1980s

International Conference, Beijing, 24-26 March 2004

NATO Records

NATO MILITARY PLANNING

Declassified U.S. and British Documents on NATO Military Planning and Threat Assessments of the Warsaw Pact

THE FUTURE TASKS OF THE ALLIANCE

The NATO Archives' Subject Files on the Harmel Report, 1966-67

Records of the Warsaw Pact on the PHP website:

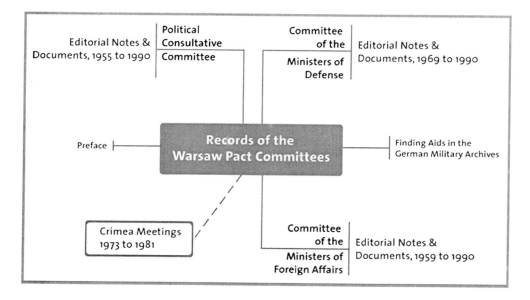

Index

consultations in 5, 17, 20, 27, 42–43, 58, 60–61, 66, 78, 187–188, 208–209, 210–211, 358, 424, 510, 518–519, 531–538, 633, 658
crisis of
  in 1956 7–8, 296
  in 1965–1968 28–34
and CSCE principles 67
data exchange with NATO (see Data, exchange)
Defense Ministers' meetings May 1966 31–32, 217–219
deployment of forces on members' territories 8–9, 323, 350–353
and dialogue with NATO 554, 566
discord within 26, 28, 32, 34, 84–86, 219, 223, 226–228, 253–254, 257, 286–293, 393, 486
dissolution of 65–72, 395–396
  inevitability of 68
  not sought by West 69
  sought together with NATO's 4–5, 7, 12, 13, 27, 31, 95, 521
dispensability of 4
dissent in Warsaw Pact countries 44
diversity of views among members 35, 180, 200, 258–260, 302–304, 332–338, 358–364, 655–663
effect of changes in Eastern Europe on 655, 657, 674
and the environment 391, 582, 603, 663
Eppelmann concept 70–71
estimates of NATO plans and capabilities 105–107, 161, 170–173, 242–244, 343, 357, 404–405, 406, 451–452, 469–471, 505–506, 514–515, 516–517, 522–525, 615
expectations of war 122, 170
and expected NATO use of nuclear weapons 93–94, 105–107, 131–132, 140, 141, 173, 480, 189, 242–243, 342, 516
as extended arm of Soviet general staff 39
as factor for stability 642
financial contributions by members 31
force development 17

formation of 1–3, 77–79
Fronts
  Central 37, 56, 59, 150, 402–403
  Czechoslovak 22, 147, 161–163, 166, 167
  Maritime 149, 150, 151
  Polish 10, 147
  Southwestern 60, 189–190, 640
  Soviet 147
  Western 60, 98, 157, 162–164, 167, 206, 346, 481, 640, 655, 658
functions of
  as agent of change 58
  as "cardboard castle" 1, 4, 39, 73
  difficulty in determining 5
  as diplomatic tool 15, 19, 28, 39, 55, 74
  as "empty shell" 5
  as framework for "Finlandization" 65
  as framework for foreign policy coordination 33, 39, 42, 44, 55
  as framework for new European security system 4–5
  as framework for pursuing CSCE 40
  as framework for troop and arms reductions 65, 69, 78
  as instrument of alliance management 2, 11, 15, 28, 35, 72, 93, 347
  as instrument of economic cooperation 65
  as instrument of intervention 67
  – in Czechoslovakia 36–39, 294–301
  – in Poland 50–55, 66
  – in Romania
  – internal 67–68
  as means for consulting allies 78, 140, 510, 518–519
  as means for fighting war on drugs 655
  as means for protecting the environment 391, 582, 603, 663
  as means of weakening NATO 95
  as mechanism for retaining Soviet power 68

as military tool 15, 19, 28, 39, 44, 65, 70–74, 294–301
as "mutual rescue association" 65–67
as obstacle to German unification 68
as organization for political cooperation 70–72
as pretext for stationing troops in GDR 13
separation of 65–66
and German unification 68–69
Information Office 62
institutionalization of 28, 32, 38–39, 77–79, 80–82, 84–86, 220–224, 249, 317–319, 323–329
internal criticisms of 9, 31–32, 35, 84–86, 87–90, 91–92, 208–209, 223
joint elaboration of plans 140, 146–147, 208–209
and Khrushchev's successors 26
military balance in favor of 173, 345, 357, 549, 570
Military Council 203–204
  Bulgarian reform proposal 640
  compared with NATO's Military Committee 29, 39, 195, 249
  as conceived by Czechoslovakia 29, 279, 281
  as conceived by Romania 29, 211, 218, 249–251, 253, 257, 265, 267–268
  considered useful for consultations 619
  established 39
  in November 1986 546–548
  proposed by Soviet Union 28, 261–263, 264
  Soviet representatives at 59
  statute of 323, 328
Military Defense Committee, proposed by Romania 601, 604, 618, 619
and military parity with NATO 474, 507
military preparedness of 19, 33, 35–37, 48, 100, 124, 173, 195, 196, 204, 211, 245–248, 277, 280, 281, 344–345, 395–396, 413–414, 560, 576